Encyclopedia of
AMERICAN RELIGIOUS HISTORY

Revised Edition

VOLUME I   A–L

Edward L. Queen II,
Stephen R. Prothero,
and
Gardiner H. Shattuck, Jr.

Foreword by Martin E. Marty, Editorial Adviser

Book Producer: Marie A. Cantlon, Proseworks, Boston

Facts On File, Inc.

Encyclopedia of American Religious History, Revised Edition

Facts On File, Inc.
132 West 31st Street
New York NY 10001

Library of Congress Cataloging-in-Publication Data
Queen, Edward L.
 The encyclopedia of American religious history / Edward L. Queen II,
  Stephen R. Prothero, and Gardiner H. Shattuck, Jr.; foreword by Martin
  E. Marty, editorial advisor.—Rev. ed.
 p. cm.
 Includes bibliographical references and indexes.
  ISBN 0-8160-4335-3
  1. United States—Religion—Encyclopedias. 2. Religious biography—United States—Encyclopedias. I. Prothero, Stephen R. II. Shattuck, Gardiner H. III. Title.

BL2525.Q44 2001
200'.973'03—dc21   00-069512

Facts On File books are available at special discounts when purchased in bulk quantities for businesses, associations, institutions or sales promotions. Please call our Special Sales Department in New York at (212) 967-8800 or (800) 322-8755.

You can find Facts On File on the World Wide Web at http://www.factsonfile.com

Text design and layout by by Rachel L. Berlin
Cover design by Cathy Rincon. Cover illustration by Smart Graphics.

Printed in the United States of America

VB FOF 10 9 8 7 6 5 4 3 2 1

This book is printed on acid-free paper.

Authors and Contributors

Principal authors

EDWARD L. QUEEN II is Director, Islamic Society of North American Fellowships in Nonprofit Management and Governance, and Senior Researcher, Project on Religion and Welfare Reform, Indiana University—Purdue University, Indianapolis.

STEPHEN R. PROTHERO is an Associate Professor in the Department of Religion at Boston University in Boston, Massachusetts.

GARDINER H. SHATTUCK, JR., is a Lecturer in the History of Christianity at Andover Newton Theological School in Newton Centre, Massachusetts.

Contributors

TONY FELS is an Associate Professor of History at the University of San Francisco in San Francisco, California.

MATTHEW GLASS teaches in the Religion and Culture Department at Wilfrid Laurier University in Waterloo, Ontario, Canada.

LAURIE F. MAFFLY-KIPP is an Associate Professor of Religious Studies at the University of North Carolina at Chapel Hill, North Carolina.

TINA PIPPIN is an Associate Professor in the Department of Religious Studies at Agnes Scott College in Decatur, Georgia.

RICHARD H. SEAGER is an Associate Professor in the Department of Religion at Hamilton College in Clinton, New York.

ROBERT H. STOCKMAN is the Coordinator of the Institute for Bahá'í Studies in Wilmette, Illinois.

BRON R. TAYLOR is the Oshkosh Foundation Professor of Religion and Social Ethics and Director of Environmental Studies at the University of Wisconsin, Oshkosh.

ANDREW WALSH is Associate Director of the Leonard C. Greenberg Center for the Study of Religion in Public Life at Trinity College in Hartford, Connecticut.

CONTENTS

FOREWORD

One of the coeditors of this encyclopedia used to hear me urge graduate students to pay attention to an observation by Eugen Rosenstock-Huessy. That European scholar observed that one book is about one thing, at least the good ones are. We were to carry that observation over to course papers, articles for learned journals, dissertations that were to become books, and, of course, books themselves.

Well and good, one would hear from time to time in response: that works for short papers or books with narrow themes. Write on "Roofing Technology Among Folk Architects in Southwest Virginia, 1878–1881" and there will be no mistaking the "one book, one thing," theme. What about comprehensive works that include disparate materials? What about, for instance, the *Sears, Roebuck* catalog, the register of students in their dormitories or, of course, the phone book? Easy: mention them; think about them; it is simple to grasp what is the "one thing" that these "many-thinged" inclusive works were about.

What is complex about such works for anyone who wants to remain clear about the plot of each is their pattern of organization. This encyclopedia, like most others, is alphabetically ordered. What does that pattern do to reality? I had a colleague who was more at home with what that year was being considered representative of the postmodern. He thought that I, who found the postmodern a less congenial concept, was resisting it. That concept, as he would explain it, rendered everything arbitrary,

disconnected, remote from reality as a person using common sense would grasp it.

One day I mentioned having dealt with the yellow pages of the Chicago phone book. Now, "religion" and "religious institutions" are a significant part of the reality that surrounds us. How does religion make its presence felt? First of all, it appeared in that case in a book called *Chicago Consumer Yellow Pages.* Not all religious people like to think of their commitment as representing "consumption." (Let it be said that some schools of thought do think that all religious participation represents "rational choice" among faiths as market options, but that is a different topic for a different day.)

Next, a section called "Churches" follows "Chiropractors" and antecedes "Cigars." That ought to suggest something arbitrary and disconnected. Continuing along that line, we note that "Churches—Islamic" has to be a less-than-congenial category for Muslims, who see "Churches" to be a specifically Christian classification. And, I had finally noted, alphabetization formed and forced strange company. Think of what gets clustered under the letter "U":

Ukrainian Catholic
Ukrainian Orthodox
Unitarian Universalist
United Church of Christ
United Holy Church of America
United Methodist
United Pentecostal
United Protestant
Unity School of Christianity

Universal Fellowship of
    Metropolitan Community Churches
Universal Life
Unification Church

This sequence led to the observation that here were mainly black, mainly white, liberal and conservative, straight and gay (MCC), Christian and non-Christian, held together by nothing except names that begin with the letter 'U'. "Gotcha, Marty," pounced the colleague; "we catch you here in a postmodern moment!"

Agreed. Ways of organizing reality do seem arbitrary, unconnected. One could as well learn about the religion of a city by driving along its avenues and noting the names on church signs in front of edifices. Or by knocking on doors and asking about the religious choice of consumers beyond them. Or by turning on tape recorders and listening to what people have to say about their faiths or non-faiths. Little of what they say might match what the signs in front of church buildings say. Still, the alphabet helps one make sense of the sets of realities that confront observers. On such terms, *Encyclopedia of American Religious History* has a secure and helpful place. "Consumers" who buy or borrow and use it will not have access to all the ways of learning about American religion, but they will be better off by far than those who have no way of satisfying curiosity or gaining access to information they need.

The yellow pages, however, deal only with present-day representations of religious realities. How did they come to their present-day situations? Historian R. H. Tawney provided an autobiographical explanation of what motivated his life work: he found the world to be so odd, and wanted to know how it got that way. All those different ways of looking at this world and, perhaps, worlds beyond it, ways typed in one illustration by organizations that begin naming with a "U," look odd to those who belong to other organizations. They may even look odd to those affiliated with them today. Why do Unitarian Universalists think of "God" and "Jesus" so differently than do United Pentecostals? Answer: because they have different pasts, different histories. That's it: the curious, the information seekers, whether they think of themselves as historically minded or not, need and welcome historical information of the sort this book provides.

Having pointed to the obvious in two of its forms, there remains a third kind of obviousness that needs pointing out, one that this encyclopedia so well exemplifies. The code name for that is not "alphabet" or "history" but "pluralism." This revised edition of *Encyclopedia of American Religious History* is in its own way a celebration of an ever-richer pluralism. The publishers and editors, having asked me to reread many of the updated articles to serve as one more checker of accuracies or blocker of inaccuracies, also included dozens of entirely new entries to appraise. Some of them represented catch-up work. All revising editors revisit the original material to see what they might have slighted or missed completely in an earlier edition. But in the present case they also included phenomena or personalities who had not been on the scene, had not yet made a name for themselves, had not roused curiosity way back in 1996, the time of the first edition.

Some day there may be a third edition, and my successor or I will have to note that there is more of everything going on in religion, and that this expansion will also call for expansion of the number of entries in the new edition. There is never going to be a moment in dynamic America when everything is in place, settled, historically located, completely comprehended. There will always be more, but each generation can only reckon with what is presently before it.

To say that such an encyclopedia as this suggests ever-expanding pluralism is not to exhaust what goes on between these covers. It is, after all, not very interesting to talk about "mere" pluralism. Let an encyclopedist say that there are 1,200 or 1,500 organized, visible denominations and new religious movements in the United States and you have not served the hearers well. Will they be more impressed if they hear that there are 12,000 or 15,000? Once a chronicler or encyclopedist gets past a dozen or a score, the sight of what we are calling "mere" pluralism would overwhelm.

What citizens do about the welter of religious movements is what is interesting and worthy of remarking and referencing. How are they searching for and holding to truth among these options? How are they keeping from engaging in holy wars of the sort many religious societies pursue? What inspires measures of tolerance, civility, cooperation, ecumenism, and interfaith dialogue in our culture? The reader cannot get answers to all that by reading a single entry. But the more one consults this work, the more she or he will learn about the shapers and dissenters, the healers and the wounders, the dominators and the victims, who have contributed in positive and negative ways to the shaping of today's pluralism.

One way to test this observation (call it a thesis) is to start sampling. Turn to any letter of the alphabet and read five articles in a row. You will have been launched on a pilgrimage that will help explain the oddness of "religious America" in a time that was supposed by many to have been "merely" secular, nonreligious, profane. And you will have met characters from the past or movements shaped long ago, and found reference points and landmarks that will help you make sense of the odd reality around you, be it organized on classic or modern or postmodern lines. You will find yourself more informed as you make connections between them or make more sense of the disconnections. In either case, welcome to the endlessly fascinating American religious scene, approached on these pages in accurate and lively ways.

—Martin E. Marty

INTRODUCTION

The United States has always been religiously diverse. In colonial times, Catholics ruled
New Spain and New France, while Protestants
dominated New England. New England itself
was home not only to Puritans but also to
Quakers, Baptists, and deists. The Puritans were
divided into two factions: those who wanted
to separate from the Church of England and
those who did not. Outside the settlements of
these Europeans, Native Americans practiced
an astonishingly wide array of indigenous religions. Nonetheless, at the time the United
States was born, pluralism was largely an intra-
Protestant affair. During the 18th and 19th centuries, to speak of American religious diversity
was to invoke the differences between Congregationalists and Anglicans, Baptists and Presbyterians. In the wake of the great immigration
waves of the 19th century, Catholics and Jews
contested this Protestant dominance, and by
the 1950s it made sense to speak of the United States as a Judeo-Christian country. After
World War II, to speak of American religious
diversity was to invoke the differences between
Christians and Jews, Catholics and Protestants.

Today the American religious landscape
remains to a great extent the province of churches and synagogues. More than nine out of every
10 Americans believe in God, and 85 percent
describe themselves as Christians. But since
1965 and the passage of landmark legislation
that opened the country's doors to widespread
immigration, America's religious landscape has
changed dramatically. Islam is now by most
accounts the country's fastest-growing religion,
and increasingly citizens speak of the United
States as a "Judeo-Christian-Islamic" nation in
which churches, synagogues, and mosques all
struggle to meet spiritual needs and social challenges. But even "Judeo-Christian-Islamic" is
inadequate, since Asian religious traditions such
as Buddhism and Hinduism are also growing
rapidly. Today the United States is neither a
Judeo-Christian nor a Judeo-Christian-Islamic
country. It has become, as U.S. Supreme Court
Justice William Douglas observed in 1965, "a
nation of Buddhists, Confucianists, and Taoists,
as well as Christians."

These new realities present a huge challenge to American church history, which during the past quarter-century has taken on the
more cosmopolitan moniker of American *religious* history and, with it, a host of previously
ignored topics. While scholars still analyze the
influence of the Bible on American life, they
now also explore the influence of the Book of
Mormon and of the Qur'an. When they study
congregations, they examine Methodist and
Pentecostal churches, but they also investigate
Sikh *gurdwaras* and Buddhist temples.

Encyclopedia of American Religious History
attempts to describe and interpret this diversity, both past and present, in a readily
accessible format. We authors tell not one
story but many stories of America's myriad
religions, and our narratives range from colonial to contemporary times. Ironically, our
attempts at inclusivity have forced us to leave

out much. But we are comforted by the knowledge that encyclopedias are by nature peculiar beasts. While aiming at breadth, all must submit in the end to the ancient strictures of the book: There are only so many pages in a volume, and those pages can be filled with only so many words.

As our title indicates, *Encyclopedia of American Religious History* is neither an encyclopedia of American church history nor an encyclopedia of contemporary American religions. It attends not only to Christianity but also to Judaism, Islam, Hinduism, Buddhism, and many new religious movements. It examines all these traditions—their beliefs and practices, people and places—from a historical perspective. As a result, it ignores topics covered in more narrowly focused works. Many of the important Christian groups included in Daniel G. Reid's *Dictionary of Christianity in America* (1990), for example, do not make an appearance here. The same is true of individuals included in Henry Warner Bowden's *Dictionary of American Religious Biography* (1993), J. Gordon Melton's *Biographical Dictionary of Cult and Sect Leaders* (1986), June Melby Benowitz's *Encyclopedia of American Women and Religion* (1998), Samuel S. Hill's *Encyclopedia of Religion in the South* (1984), and John J. Delaney's *Dictionary of American Catholic Biography* (1984). Moreover, some of the current topics included in Wade Clark Roof's *Contemporary American Religions* (2000) simply cannot be included here because of our mandate to cover the past as well as the present.

A word may be in order about the space we have allotted to various topics. Certainly most of the subjects in this encyclopedia are given the space their significance warrants. Our entry on the Baptists, the largest denomination in the United States today, is quite long. Our entry on the much smaller and less significant American Humanist Association is, by contrast, quite short. In some cases, however, we have allotted many words to organizations that have not been particularly important or

influential. We have also slighted some key subjects by giving them fewer words than they would seem to deserve. In making these decisions we have been guided by fairly practical criteria. The purpose of an encyclopedia, in our view, is clear: to provide curious readers with the information they want. If, in our judgment, information about a given topic is easily obtainable elsewhere, we reduced our coverage of that subject. This approach allowed us extra space for topics that have been comparatively neglected.

Consider, for example, our articles on Thomas Jefferson and Louis Farrakhan. The contributions of Jefferson to American religious history are at least as significant as his contributions to American history in general. While scholars may debate how much credit he should be given for crafting the Declaration of Independence, there is little doubt about the key role he played in constructing what he referred to as "the wall of separation" between church and state. In pushing for First Amendment protections for freedom of religion, Jefferson irrevocably altered the course of American religion, setting the country on a path to becoming what is arguably the most religiously diverse nation on earth. Most readers, however, are quite familiar with Jefferson, and information about his life is readily available elsewhere, so we have allotted him only modest space. Accurate information about the controversial Nation of Islam leader Louis Farrakhan, on the other hand, is difficult to come by, and many readers will be less familiar with his life and work. Although Farrakhan has clearly influenced American religious life far less than Jefferson has, he merits in our judgment a slightly longer entry.

Our decision to emphasize previously neglected topics and underemphasize more time-honored subjects has resulted in a tilt toward entries in newer areas of inquiry such as Native American religions, African-American religions, and Asian religions. Students of Native American religions, for example, may be surprised that their favorite figure is missing from our volume, but there are entries here on five different Native American culture areas. And the inclusion of Indians such as Handsome Lake and Wovoka has caused us to excise entries on better-known figures in the Christian tradition.

In its focus on the diversity of American religion, this encyclopedia reflects the state of the art in the writing of American religious history. For most of the 20th century, a Protestant paradigm reigned among historians of American religion. Scholars not only focused on Protestantism, they tended to equate the story of American religion with the story of American Protestantism. Over the last quarter-century or so, that old Protestant paradigm has given way to a new pluralist paradigm, which sees the United States not as a Christian nation but as a nation of religions. Sydney Ahlstrom's *A Religious History of the American People* (1972) is a key text in that historiographic shift from Protestantism to pluralism. This massive work of more than 1,000 pages was mainly a Protestant history. But while Ahlstrom directed the Protestants to center stage in his drama, he managed to find supporting roles for Catholics and Jews, Mormons and Theosophists, Rosicrucians and Vedantists. Ahlstrom also devoted considerable attention to the black church. His project is best seen, therefore, as a bridge between the Protestant and pluralist paradigms—a work that served as a capstone to the old Protestant historiography while gesturing toward the pluralistic scholarship to come.

Today that pluralistic scholarship has arrived. There are now a handful of good books on Santería, on Sikhism, and on snake handling. Scholarship in African-American religion has exploded, and there are experts in that field who focus on Black Muslims and even Black Jews. Today scholarship in American religion is as vast and vibrant as American religion itself. All this work has been to us both a boon and a challenge. New books and articles come out daily, and the proliferation of

scholarship makes simple syntheses difficult, if not impossible.

This encyclopedia does not presume to push the field of American religion to higher ground. Cutting-edge interpretations are not our goal, neither are they appropriate to this genre. We authors make no attempt to solve the controversies that currently bedevil scholars in the field. In fact, in many cases we do not even discuss those controversies. For many events (the Great Awakening, for example) this work sticks close to received wisdom. We are certainly aware of new scholarship that questions whether the Great Awakening occurred at all. But we have decided to craft essays that are historical rather than historiographic in nature, focusing as much as possible on the subjects themselves rather than on academic controversies about them. So while we have made use of the best new materials available, our goal throughout has been to present general readers with the information they need. Few readers coming to an entry on the Great Awakening want to be told that the Great Awakening never happened. Readers who want to learn more, of course, can delve into the books we recommend at the end of each article. There they will encounter the many controversies that consume the day-to-day energies of historians.

Finally, it should be admitted that an encyclopedia by its nature cannot provide one overarching interpretation of its general subject. What readers encounter on the pages that follow are articles on key movements, themes, individuals, and groups in American religious history. They will not encounter a consistent narrative of American religious life. Happily, readers desiring a narrative approach to this subject have a host of general studies to consult, many of which substantially informed the entries that appear here. Those general studies are legion and growing rapidly. Some of the most influential are: Catherine L. Albanese, *America: Religion and Religions* (1998); Edwin Scott Gaustad, *A Religious History of America*

(1990); George M. Marsden, *Religion and American Culture* (1990); Martin E. Marty, *Pilgrims in Their Own Land: Five Hundred Years of Religion in America* (1984); and R. Laurence Moore, *Religious Outsiders and the Making of Americans* (1986).

If this book reflects the recent pluralist turn in the writing of American religious history, it also reflects the transitional nature of that scholarship. The old verities have plainly passed away; new ones are not yet clearly in focus. Historians continue to struggle to create relatively coherent narratives out of a plethora of new information and an array of competing interpretations. Some now object in principle to the project of constructing a comprehensive interpretation of American religious life, preferring limited studies of particular groups to grand narratives of American religion. Others have almost entirely jettisoned Christian figures and themes as ancient relics of a bygone era. We have not chosen that route. Today in the United States, two out of every three adults say that they have made "a personal commitment to Jesus Christ." In the halls of power in the U.S. Congress, Christian affiliations also predominate. Of the 535 members of the 107th Congress seated in 2001, 150 were Roman Catholics, 72 were Baptists, and 65 were Methodists. There were no Muslims, Buddhists, or Hindus in either the Senate or the House. In our view, you cannot make sense of American religion today without talking about Roman Catholicism and mainline and evangelical Protestantism. And you certainly cannot understand the course of American religious history without considering influential Protestant movements such as revivalism, Pentecostalism, and fundamentalism.

Since this encyclopedia first appeared in 1996, thousands of new books on American religion have been published. Many new religious groups have appeared, and others have vanished. In preparing this new edition, we have revisited all the entries that appeared in the first edition, taking into account both new scholarship and new developments. Some of our subjects died in the late 1990s. In one grisly case from 2001, the remains of atheist Madalyn Murray O'Hair (assumed murdered in the late 1990s) were discovered. Some religious organizations changed names, and others were radically reorganized through mergers or schisms.

In addition to revising old entries, we have added new ones. The Dalai Lama emerged as a powerful presence in the United States in the late 1990s. In fact, as the millennium turned he was arguably the most talked-about religious leader active in the United States. We have included a new entry on him. On a more ominous note, the Identity Movement also gained visibility, in part because of the diffusion of the Internet, where these nativistic Christians are active. The Identity Movement merited in our view a separate entry. So did the Branch Davidians and Heaven's Gate, new religious movements whose unorthodox beliefs and practices led to tragedies in the 1990s, and Jesse Jackson and Pat Robertson, Christian clergymen with divergent political bents who emerged as important religious figures as the century came to a close. Given the increasing significance in American religious life of Islam, Buddhism, and Hinduism, we also included a variety of new entries in these areas—on topics ranging from the Hsi Lai Temple and the Islamic Society of North America to Krishnamurti and Bruce Lee. There are also new entries on previously neglected Asian religions, including Taoism and Jainism. Finally, because tremendous amounts of information have migrated in recent years to the Internet, we have done more than merely update the lists of suggested reading that conclude each entry. We have in many cases added websites to consult.

It may or may not take a village to raise a child, but it certainly takes a lot of people to make a book—and even more to make an encyclopedia. This project was originally conceived by Facts On File editor James Warren, now of Columbia University Press, who commissioned it about a decade ago and adroitly shepherded it to publication. The revision has been ably edited by Owen Lancer at Facts On File, who first suggested that the success of the original edition merited a revised edition. Professor Martin E. Marty graciously agreed to serve as our editorial adviser and produced much-appreciated forewords for both editions. Once revered as a "dean" of American religion scholarship, Marty has clearly ascended to sainthood if not divinity, and we are grateful to have him aboard. Marie Cantlon of Proseworks produced both editions. Throughout the many storms that struck during the conceptualization and creation of both versions of this encyclopedia, she has kept a steady hand at the helm. She carefully edited all our work and did a fabulous job with the illustrations. For her hard work throughout, we authors are deeply indebted.

Some of our scholarly debts are acknowledged in the bibliographies that appear at the end of each entry. Unfortunately our massive debts to many others can be acknowledged only generally. This encyclopedia, in fact all contemporary work on American religion, is indebted to a long tradition of scholarship in the field—a tradition that goes back to pioneering works like Robert Baird's *Religion in America* (1843) and Daniel Dorchester's *Christianity in the United States* (1887). While almost all scholarship has moved beyond the Protestant preoccupations of these authors (to say nothing of their triumphalist view of Americans as God's chosen people), we authors inherit their conviction that American religion is as fascinating as it is dynamic. The first colonial settlements in the New World may have been experiments in perfecting Protestantism, but they have spawned a radically pluralistic nation of religions.

Encyclopedia of
AMERICAN
RELIGIOUS
HISTORY

Revised Edition

A

Abbott, Lyman (1835–1922) Lyman Abbott was a Congregational clergyman and successor of Henry Ward BEECHER as minister at the fashionable Plymouth Church in Brooklyn, New York. Editor for many years of the *Outlook*, a weekly journal of modernist (see MODERNISM) theological opinion, Abbott was one of the foremost popularizers of Christian evolutionary (see EVOLUTION) thought in late 19th-century America.

Abbott was born in Roxbury, Massachusetts, on December 18, 1835. He graduated from New York University in 1853 and, after a short career as a lawyer, was ordained to the Congregational ministry at Farmington, Maine, in 1860. During the Civil War, Abbott served in a church in Terre Haute, Indiana. His concern for relating religion to questions of moral and social reform, however, led him to return east in 1865 to accept the executive secretary's position of the newly created American Freedmen's Union Commission (AFUC) in New York City. During the four years he held that position, the AFUC was an important voluntary agency overseeing educational work among former slaves in the South.

From 1869 to 1871, Abbott contributed articles to *Harper's Weekly* and the *Independent*. He edited the *Illustrated Christian Weekly* between 1871 and 1876 and, in 1876, assumed editorship of the *Christian Union* (renamed *Outlook* in 1893). Although Abbott replaced Beecher as pastor of the Plymouth Church in 1888, his talents were those of an editor and writer rather than of a preacher, and in 1899 he resigned his ministerial position to concentrate fully on journalism. Under Abbott's guidance, the *Outlook* was enormously successful. Its circulation soared from 15,000 to more than 100,000 subscribers by the end of the century.

During the 1890s, Abbott published a half-dozen books on evolution and on the Bible. In *The Evolution of Christianity* (1892) and *The Theology of an Evolutionist* (1897), for example, he applied principles of biological evolution to the development of the Christian faith. Celebrating the idea of humankind's inevitable upward ascent to God, these books displayed what biographer Ira Brown has called Abbott's greatest talent: the ability to bring together "the aristocracy of the mind and the thought of the masses." Thus, while Abbott was neither a sophisticated theologian nor a true scientist, he managed to touch a large audience of ordinary people interested in the relationship between SCIENCE AND RELIGION. And despite only modest sales for his publications, Abbott's frequent lectures and public addresses reached thousands of curious middle-class Americans.

Abbott continued to be active as the editor of the *Outlook* and as a liberal Protestant opinion-maker well into the 20th century. He died in New York City on October 22, 1922.

GHS, Jr.

Bibliography: Ira V. Brown, *Lyman Abbott: Christian Evolutionist* (Cambridge, Mass.: Harvard University Press, 1953).

Abernathy, Ralph (1926–1990)   One of the most important leaders of the CIVIL RIGHTS MOVEMENT of the 1950s and 1960s, Ralph Abernathy was born on March 11, 1926, in Hopewell, Alabama, the 10th child of Louivery and W. L. Abernathy. At his birth, his maternal grandmother, who was the community midwife, predicted that he would "be known throughout the world." Originally given the name David, he became Ralph only later when an older sister tagged him with it, after one of her teachers.

Abernathy's childhood differed from that of most African Americans growing up in rural Alabama and from the middle-class, urban childhood known by his colleague and friend Martin Luther KING, Jr. Abernathy's father, a moderately successful farmer, owned several hundred acres, and his attention to religion, duty, and family earned him the respect and admiration of his fellow blacks in Hopewell as well as most whites. Although Abernathy grew up in a segregated society, the grudging respect that whites granted his father, along with his family's hard-earned economic self-sufficiency, protected him from many of its humiliations.

Abernathy's parents were committed to religion and education, and David attended both the Hopewell Baptist Church and the segregated black elementary school. Later, he attended a private black high school organized by the county's black Baptist churches—the state of Alabama not having seen fit to provide a public one for its black citizens.

His plans to attend college were interrupted by World War II, and Abernathy enlisted in the army in 1944. After basic training, during which time he had been promoted to platoon sergeant, Abernathy was shipped to Europe as the war neared its close. A case of rheumatic fever prevented him from being shipped to the Pacific with the rest of his company and probably saved his life. The company was ambushed on an island in the Pacific and all but one man was killed.

After the war Abernathy gained his high school diploma and, using his G.I. benefits, enrolled at Alabama State University in Montgomery. Following his graduation he attended Atlanta University, doing graduate work in sociology for a year before returning to Alabama State as Dean of Men. During this time he began preaching in rural churches and eventually was called to the pastorate of First Baptist Church of Montgomery, Alabama, in spring 1952. This call presented a major challenge for the 26-year-old Abernathy, and he entered into the endeavor with much concern. Also during this time he married Juanita Odessa Jones.

Shortly after Abernathy became pastor of First Baptist, the other leading black Baptist church in Montgomery also called a new minister. This call, issued to Martin Luther King, Jr., would have momentous repercussions. The King and Abernathy couples became close friends, and King and Abernathy began to discuss when they could introduce issues of social and political justice into their work, which given their youth and recent arrival they felt had to be postponed for several years.

The arrest of Rosa Parks in 1955 for refusing to surrender her seat on a city bus to a white man shredded this timetable. King and Abernathy became the leaders of the Montgomery Improvement Association, designed to end unequal treatment on the city's buses. This eventually successful endeavor took a major toll on both pastors and their families. Their homes were bombed, and Abernathy's church, a historic building, was nearly destroyed by a bombing attack.

The work in Montgomery led to the formation of the SOUTHERN CHRISTIAN LEADERSHIP CONFERENCE (SCLC) with King and Abernathy as its primary leaders. By this time King had moved to Atlanta, where he had become an assistant to his father at Ebenezer Baptist Church. King worked to convince Abernathy to join him in Atlanta, and when Atlanta's West Hunter Baptist Church approached him he accepted its call, albeit with much hesitation and regret.

After moving to Atlanta in November 1962 Abernathy increasingly spent his time working for the SCLC. He and King directed the work in Albany, Georgia; Birmingham, Alabama; St. Augustine, Florida; and Selma, Alabama. Abernathy also was instrumental in organizing the 1963 March on Washington. More comfortable with rural and working-class people than was the city-bred King, Abernathy played a major role in communicating the SCLC's message to them. An able leader and administrator, Abernathy channeled into action the passions King engendered with his sermons.

Following King's assassination in 1968, Abernathy became head of the SCLC and led it for the next several years. During this time, changes in the country began to affect the organization's work, and many people increasingly challenged the idea of nonviolence. The war in Vietnam, campus unrest, and increasing militancy among many blacks presented severe challenges to the SCLC's message of nonviolent resistance. Additionally, the SCLC's increasing commitment to economic justice and its opposition to the war alienated and confused some of its earlier supporters.

Abernathy was a victim of these changes. Despite having led the organization through difficult times, in 1976 he found himself under pressure to resign as president of the SCLC. He did so, using his campaign for Andrew Young's recently vacated congressional seat as the reason. He came in third in a field of eight.

Abernathy's public life eased up somewhat after this period, and he devoted more time to his church work and to black economic development. These concerns led him to endorse Ronald Reagan for the presidency in 1980, but when the Republican Party's promises of economic assistance to black Americans failed to materialize, Abernathy returned to the Democratic Party, supporting Jesse Jackson in the 1984 and 1988 Democratic primaries.

Heart problems increasingly troubled Abernathy in the mid-1980s, and he suffered several strokes. Nonetheless, he continued his pastoral work until April 17, 1990, when he died of a heart attack.

EQ

Bibliography: Ralph David Abernathy, *And the Walls Came Tumbling Down* (New York: Harper & Row, 1989); Taylor Branch, *Parting the Waters: America in the King Years, 1954–1963* (New York: Simon & Schuster, 1988); David Garrow, *Bearing the Cross: Martin Luther King, Jr. and the Southern Christian Leadership Conference, 1955–1968* (New York: William Morrow, 1986); Thomas R. Peake, *Keeping the Dream Alive: A History of the Southern Christian Leadership Conference from King to the Nineteen-Eighties* (New York: Peter Lang, 1987); Catherine Reef, *Ralph David Abernathy* (Parsippany, N.J.: Dillon Press, 1995).

abolitionism   The American movement to abolish SLAVERY was one of many reforming (see SOCIAL GOSPEL) efforts that arose in American religious circles in the 1820s and 1830s. The antislavery impulse was rooted first in the confidence nurtured by 17th-century Puritanism that the world could (and should) be reformed in accordance with God's law. The revivalism of the SECOND GREAT AWAKENING intensified this view and helped produce a vision of America as an ideal Christian republic. The revolutionary era's belief in natural rights, the enlightened rationalism of leaders like Thomas Jefferson, and the emphasis on human perfectibility in Unitarianism further bolstered the abolitionist movement in the early 19th century.

Although Quakers and Methodists had taken antislavery positions in the late 18th century, the expansion of slavery (especially after the Missouri Compromise of 1820) and the South's increasing dependence on the slave system muted opposition to the institution in the early days of the republic. The founding of the American Colonization Society in 1817, organized to raise funds to remunerate slave owners and repatriate ex-slaves to Africa, actually diverted antislavery opinion. Accepting the notion of black inferiority, this movement sought to rid the country altogether of a freed black population. But beginning in 1831 with the publication of William Lloyd Garrison's radical newspaper, *The Liberator*, which advocated immediate emancipation, abolitionist voices in the North became progressively more militant.

Several prominent northern Protestants were in the forefront of the antislavery movement. The publication of revivalist Theodore Dwight WELD's anonymous tracts, *The Bible Against Slavery* (1837) and *American Slavery as It Is* (1839), widely influenced religious opinion against slavery. Presbyterian clergyman Elijah P. Lovejoy argued that slaves were human beings who possessed natural and inalienable rights given them by God, who was the sole true master of human beings. Calling slavery a moral evil for its usurpation of those rights, Lovejoy so inflamed his fellow citizens in Alton, Illinois, that in November 1837 he was murdered for his views.

Garrison and other abolitionists, however, accused the majority of Christian leaders of impeding, rather than aiding, the cause of freedom. Former slave Frederick Douglass, the most famous African-American spokesman of his day, declared in his 1845 autobiography that the slaveholding religion of the United States bore no relation to the faith of Jesus Christ and ought not be labeled *Christianity* at all. "Revivals of religion and revivals in the slave-trade," he said, always went "hand in hand together."

The antislavery movement occasioned the publication of perhaps the most influential American novel. Harriet Beecher STOWE, daughter of a well-known Congregational minister and wife of a seminary professor, probed the moral conscience of the nation in *Uncle Tom's Cabin* (1852), which vividly described the terrible cruelties of slave life in the South. Stowe's story electrified readers throughout the North.

The antislavery movement zealously spread the message of abolitionism through such publications as the *Anti-Slavery Almanac*. (*Billy Graham Center Museum*)

Stowe herself claimed that she was not the author of the novel but merely a medium recording God's words of condemnation against slavery.

In the decades preceding the coming of the CIVIL WAR, the three largest American denominations were disrupted by schisms relating to the issue of slavery. The effects of abolitionism on the institutional life of the churches was first evident in 1837, when the Presbyterians split into New School and Old School, a theological controversy exacerbated by the rise of the anti-slavery movement. While the New School Presbyterians tended to favor both revivalistic methods of evangelism and political reform, the Old School insisted on conservatism in matters of doctrine, worship, and politics. At the Methodist General Conference of 1844, moreover, the northern section of the church adopted an antislavery position, forcing the departure of southerners and the formation of the Methodist Episcopal Church, South in 1845. Between 1839 and 1842 isolated groups of Methodists in New England, New York, and Ohio also withdrew from the main church, organizing the Wesleyan Methodist Church in 1843 on a platform of Christian perfection that included abolition. Finally, a firm stand by northern Baptists against appointing slaveholders as missionaries aroused the anger of the South. The Virginia Baptist Foreign Mission Society issued a call for a consultative convention of southern members of the church, and in Augusta, Georgia, in May 1845 the Southern Baptist Convention was organized.

To the young American abolitionists who rose to prominence in the early 1830s, slavery was the greatest of all their nation's sins. Often more focused on the power of ideas than on actions or planning, the abolitionists focused on whether the United States could continue to accommodate itself to a social system of organized violence and abuse. What the times required, they believed, was the creation of a new moral perspective and an awakening of public opinion that would force politicians to work out the practical details of emancipation. By the mid-1840s, however, there was a distinct movement in the North away from mere rhetorical agitation toward the attainment of concrete goals. The birth of the Liberty Party in 1839, the formulation of the Free Soil platform in 1848, and the rise of the Republican Party in 1854 demonstrated that the older religious ideal, recast into a different mold, had entered the political mainstream.

Uncle Tom's Cabin concluded with the plea that North and South together repent of their slavery-related sins and thereby preserve the Union and spare themselves a visitation of God's wrath. American Christians proved unwilling to follow Stowe's advice. Religiously motivated arguments concerning the injustice of slavery were critical factors in leading the United States, first, into the political divisions of the 1840s and 1850s and, later, into the military struggle of 1861–1865.

(See also GRIMKÉ, ANGELINA EMILY AND SARAH MOORE; PENNINGTON, JAMES WILLIAM CHARLES; PROSLAVERY THOUGHT; TRUTH, SOJOURNER; TUBMAN, HARRIET; TURNER, NAT; VESEY, DENMARK.)

GHS, Jr.

Bibliography: C. C. Goen, *Broken Churches, Broken Nation: Denominational Schisms and the Coming of the American Civil War* (Macon, Ga.: Mercer University Press, 1985); John R. McKivigan, ed., *Abolitionism and American Religion* (New York: Garland, 1999); Timothy L. Smith, *Revivalism and Social Reform: American Protestantism on the Eve of the Civil War* (Baltimore: Johns Hopkins University Press, 1980).

abortion   See SEXUALITY.

Act of Toleration   See MARYLAND (COLONY).

Adler, Cyrus (1863–1940)   Perhaps no individual did as much to ensure the success of CONSERVATIVE JUDAISM as did Cyrus Adler. His organizational and administrative abilities helped create or sustain the institutions designed to preserve traditional Jewish learning in the United States. This is all the more significant when one considers that Adler was not a rabbi and lacked the religious authority that position would have given him.

Although born in Van Buren, Arkansas, on September 13, 1863, Adler led a life centered primarily in Philadelphia. There, in an uncle's home, he absorbed the Jewish faith and traditions, as well as a penchant for learning. After graduating from the University of Pennsylvania

Cyrus Adler, educator and professor of Semitic languages, founded the Jewish Publication Society (1888) and the Jewish Historical Society (1892).

in 1883, he attended Johns Hopkins University, from which in 1887 he received the first Ph.D. in Semitics granted in the United States. After six years of teaching, he joined the Smithsonian Institution as librarian, later rising to assistant secretary. He left the Smithsonian in 1908 to become president of Dropsie College in Philadelphia, which he built into one of the most significant Semitic language schools in the country. He served as president of Dropsie, and after 1924 as president of Jewish Theological Seminary as well, until his death on April 7, 1940.

Such a brief outline tells little about Adler's true accomplishments in American JUDAISM. An early member of the so-called Historical School, Adler was concerned with main-

taining traditional Judaism, while simultaneously making it responsive to new intellectual and social developments. He deplored the radical alterations in Judaism (see REFORM JUDAISM) undertaken by such men as Isaac Mayer WISE and David EINHORN but equally had little patience for what he saw as parochial Orthodoxy of Yiddish-speaking eastern European Jews (see ORTHODOX JUDAISM).

Adler's leadership qualities emerged early. At the age of 23 he helped create Jewish Theological Seminary in New York and the Jewish Publication Society in Philadelphia. His expertise in Semitic languages served him well as he supervised the translation of the Tanakh, the Hebrew Bible (known to Christians as the Old Testament), into English between 1892 and 1917. Adler also was instrumental in founding the American Jewish Historical Society in 1892.

Although involved in the formation of the Union of Orthodox Jewish Congregations (1898), Adler, along with the other members of the Historical School, left to found the United Synagogue of America in 1913. This organization, of which Adler served numerous terms as vice president, became the institutional center of Conservative Judaism in the United States.

Adler's greatest accomplishment, however, lay in "saving" Jewish Theological Seminary. Following the death of its first president in 1897, Jewish Theological Seminary entered a period of decline and by 1901 was in danger of closing. Adler managed a successful fundraising campaign that put the school on a sound financial footing. He then convinced the noted rabbinical scholar Solomon SCHECHTER to come from England to assume its presidency. Following Schechter's death in 1915, Adler became acting president of the seminary, a position he held until 1924, when—despite his lack of rabbinical credentials—he was appointed president. During those years, Adler's leadership helped solidify the position of Conservative Judaism in the

United States and provide it with the institutional base upon which it would build itself into a powerful branch of American Judaism.

EQ

Bibliography: Cyrus Adler, *I Have Considered the Days* (Philadelphia: Jewish Publication Society, 1941); ———, *Lectures, Selected Papers, Addresses* (Philadelphia: privately printed, 1933); ———, *Selected Letters* (Philadelphia: Jewish Publication Society; New York: Jewish Theological Seminary, 1985); Murray Friedman, *When Philadelphia Was the Capital of Jewish America* (Philadelphia: Balch Institute Press, 1993); Abraham A. Neuman, *Cyrus Adler: A Biographical Sketch* (New York: American Jewish Committee, 1942).

Adler, Felix (1851–1933)

Founder of the ETHICAL CULTURE SOCIETY, Felix Adler can be said to have taken REFORM JUDAISM to its most radical conclusion. Adler believed that religious particularism slowed spiritual development, and that it was necessary to distill religion down to its true core, a core comprised of ethical action and inner purity. For Adler, this "ethical culture" was to be realized in philanthropic and educational activities designed to extend and deepen the relations between the individual and the wider society.

Born in Alzey, Germany, on August 13, 1851, Adler came to the United States when his father accepted the position as rabbi of Temple Emanuel in New York City. Groomed to succeed his father, Adler was educated at Columbia University and the University of Heidelberg. His studies in biblical criticism at Heidelberg fused with the extreme rationalism of Reform Judaism and caused a crisis of conscience. Adler questioned whether he could in good conscience recite the traditional prayers or read from the Torah believing that the statements were untrue. As Adler described it in his autobiography, "Was I to act a lie in order to teach the truth? . . . Was I to repeat these words? It was impossible. It was certain they would stick in my throat. On these grounds the separation was decided by me." After one

year as rabbi at Temple Emanuel (1873–1874), Adler left to become a professor of Hebrew literature at Cornell University.

In 1876 Adler founded the Ethical Culture Society, which became the central activity of his life. The entire thrust of Ethical Culture was to strip away the religious particularities that separated people and to concentrate on the moral good within human nature. This moral good, or ethical reality, took on an almost supernatural cast for Adler. Individuals were to mold their lives and behaviors to this reality. Adler believed that through moral actions one brought one's life into accord with this ethical reality.

As a result Adler involved himself and the Ethical Culture Society in numerous political and social activities. These included support for the rights of labor, medical care for the poor, child welfare legislation, and political reform. Adler was extremely interested in education and instituted free kindergartens and teacher training schools. His ethical theories and involvement in social reform led to his appointment as professor of political and social ethics at Columbia University in 1902, a position he held until his death on April 24, 1933.

Although Ethical Culture never became a mass movement, Adler's ideas touched many. He attempted to maintain the spiritual impulse of religion while avoiding any particular confession, or even an appeal to a supernatural deity. He envisioned a shared ethical ideal designed to bring people together while they attempted to realize their moral nature through doing good.

EQ

Bibliography: Felix Adler, *An Ethical Philosophy of Life Presented in its Main Outlines* (Hicksville, N.Y.: Regina Press, 1975); ———, *The Religion of Duty* (New York: McClure, Phillips & Co., 1903); Horace Leland Friess, *Felix Adler and Ethical Culture: Memories and Studies* (New York: Columbia University Press, 1981); Benny Kraut, *From Reform Judaism to Ethical Culture: The Religious Evolution of Felix Adler* (Cincinnati: Hebrew Union College Press, 1979).

Adventism   See MILLER, WILLIAM; SEVENTH-DAY ADVENTIST CHURCH; WHITE, ELLEN GOULD (HARMON).

African-American religion   The religions of African Americans have had a powerful impact upon the religious life of the United States. African Americans' adoption and adaptation of Christianity to their own distinctive circumstances and as a bulwark against racism and oppression have strengthened American Christianity, just as the development of indigenous religious forms and the spread of Islam have deepened the country's religious texture.

The earliest Africans to arrive in the Americas were in the service of the Spanish invaders, as commanders, soldiers, interpreters, and slaves. They were Catholic as the laws of the kingdoms of Aragon and Castile demanded, although as Spain began to import large numbers of African slaves into their colonies this Catholicism became nominal at best. Spanish and Portuguese priests would baptize hundreds of enslaved Africans as they passed into the holds of ships bound for the Americas (see NEW SPAIN).

The first blacks to arrive in British North America came under different circumstances. They arrived at the Jamestown, VIRGINIA, colony in 1619 aboard a Dutch ship. Accepted into the colony as indentured servants, they originally were no different from most English arrivals who were expected to work for several years to pay their passage and board, after which time they would be freed and allowed to go on their way.

These Africans arrived in a region with a fluid economic and social situation. The need for labor was high, and the colonists attempted many ways of guaranteeing a constant labor supply. Indians were enslaved. Paupers, rogues, and ne'er-do-wells from England and Ireland were brought over as indentured servants. Neither of these groups provided a sufficiently stable labor force. Africans seemed to offer a suitable alternative. Though highly resistant to enslavement, they were thousands of miles from home, without family or friends to succor them. They did not blend in with the white population and they were not Christian. As a result they seemed to be perfect candidates for enslavement. Christianization was a problem, however. It was generally understood that British law forbade the enslavement of Christians, so the possibility of being forced to free slaves if they became Christians was a concern.

This issue became moot in 1667. In that year the Virginia House of Burgesses passed a law declaring that "the conferring of baptisme doth not alter the condition of the person as to his bondage or freedom." With this law, the codification of black slavery begun in the 1620s became complete, and the importation of Africans into the British colonies increased dramatically. By 1776 there were 50,000 Africans in the 13 colonies. This number would grow to 4 million by the time of the Civil War.

The religious lives of these slaves were varied. Torn from their roots, separated from family and society, many found it impossible to retain their traditional religions. This was all the more true given that slave owners, to aid in "breaking" and controlling the slaves, attempted to eliminate all African traditions. Ironically, in those regions where the labor was most difficult and mortality the highest—the rice and indigo plantations of South Carolina and the sugar plantations of Louisiana— African traditions remained strongest. The high mortality rate required constant resupply of newly imported blacks who brought African beliefs and practices with them. In these regions blacks had less contact with whites and were, therefore, less affected by white institutions and beliefs. While African religiosity rarely survived intact in the United States, cultural elements from Africa did remain and shaped how slaves interpreted and presented the Christian message.

The conversion of Africans to Christianity proceeded slowly in the 17th and 18th centuries. In the early decades both Africans and whites resisted it. Africans struggling to retain their cultural identities rejected the alien religion. Slave owners feared that Christianity would ruin their slaves, making them impudent and assertive. Christianity made blacks too much like whites and raised troubling questions of conscience.

Some were not satisfied with these answers, and in 1701 the Society for the Propagation of the Gospel in Foreign Parts (SPG) was organized in England to provide for missionary work in the English colonies. Part of this work was to be among the slaves, especially in the Southern colonies where there was an Anglican establishment (see SOUTH; EPISCOPAL CHURCH). The missionaries needed to convince slave owners to allow slaves to receive religious instruction. While the missionaries were compelled to tell slave owners that it was a duty to provide religious instruction, the argument that Christianity would make slaves better workers was more successful. If slaves understood Christianity aright, they would do their masters' bidding out of a sense of duty rather than compulsion, or so the missionaries argued. In this regard the epistles of Paul were particularly useful, for example, Ephesians 6.5. "Servants be obedient to them that are your masters."

Convincing the slave owners was only part of the problem. Insufficient numbers of missionaries, slave resistance, and the labored catechetical process of the Church of England also hampered the society's work. African-born slaves were written off completely as the few missionaries concentrated on those born in America.

Not until the SECOND GREAT AWAKENING (1797–1820) would blacks convert to Christianity in significant numbers. BAPTISTS and METHODISTS proved most successful at converting slaves and freed blacks to Christianity since their requirements for both the ministry and conversion were simpler than those of the Anglicans. The Baptist ministry was open to any man who had a call to preach. The Methodist system of circuit riders provided a method for allowing one minister to cover vast distances. Baptists and Methodists converted the slaves because these groups were there, and because conversion depended not on what one knew but only on the experience of God's grace.

Cultural attitudes also played a major role in African acceptance of Baptist and Methodist forms of Christianity. The more emotional worship that produced dramatic physical responses had correlations in African traditional religion. To Africans, Christianity in its Baptist and Methodist forms looked like religion, in a way that Anglicanism and PRESBYTERIANISM did not.

Theologically Baptists and Methodists had a greater appreciation for the equality of all believers under God's rule. Chafing under Anglican domination in the South and Puritan control in New England, these denominations preached against those in power who oppressed the weak and the poor. Such seeds did not fall on stony soil when sown among the slaves and freed blacks. This vision of the equality of all believers had practical effects as well, especially in Baptist churches where slaves met whites on close-to-equal terms.

Even within these denominations, however, blacks suffered as whites failed to accept them as equals. Blacks often left white churches and formed their own congregations. At St. George's Methodist Episcopal Church in Philadelphia, an attempt to force black members to sit in the gallery led to an exodus and the formation of the first black Methodist congregation in the United States, Bethel, in 1794. (See ALLEN, RICHARD; AFRICAN METHODIST EPISCOPAL CHURCH). It also led to the formation in 1794 of the first black Episcopal congregation, St. Thomas, under Absalom JONES. Conflicts among Presbyterians in Philadelphia also led to a schism and the formation of a black Presbyterian congregation (1807).

In the South, slaves under watchful eyes found their actions more constrained. Even there, black congregations, such as the First African Baptist Church of Charleston, flourished. Founded in 1788, First African Baptist had grown to more than 2,400 members by 1830. Although these African congregations were rare (most blacks attended churches with whites until after the Civil War), they did provide a social space absent of direct white control and oversight.

Such absence was difficult to achieve. While missionaries argued that Christianity would produce a more docile and obedient slave, this was not necessarily the case. Whites preached, "Servants be obedient to your masters"; slaves heard, "Let my people go." Realizing that white preachers and authorities emphasized only part of the story, slaves slipped away to worship on their own. Throughout the South, blacks gathered to sing, dance, and pray far from the prying eyes of white overseers, masters, and mistresses. In this setting the cultural traditions from Africa became the medium for expressing a new religion in a new world. Here story and song brought the age-old messages of redemption from sin and freedom from slavery to a poor, oppressed, and illiterate people.

Christianity figured prominently in many of the more than 200 slave rebellions in the United States. The most famous of these was the Nat TURNER rebellion of August 1831. Turner understood himself to be chosen by God to "fight against the Serpent, for the time was fast approaching when the first should be last and the last should be first." The rebellion struck terror into the whites of Virginia and North Carolina before it was suppressed with the slaughter of many innocent blacks.

The thwarted Charleston, South Carolina, rebellion of 1822 led by Denmark VESEY combined Christian and African religious motifs, as well as appeals to the rights of men. Other, lesser uprisings had their motivating force in the vision of God freeing the Hebrew children from Egyptian slavery and destroying Pharaoh and his army.

Slave revolts and abolitionist (see ABOLITIONISM) attacks on slavery as an immoral and un-Christian institution prompted a white Southern response. Some of these responses were legislated—increased limits on black mobility, prohibition of unsupervised black meetings, and laws against black literacy. Another response was increased religious teaching among the slaves. The so-called "mission to the slaves" was designed to insure that blacks did not continue to interpret the biblical stories "erroneously" and to prove to the abolitionists that slavery was good because it led to the Christianization of these "heathens." While the mission did not stop the slaves from interpreting and manifesting Christianity in their own way, it did bring larger numbers of blacks into contact with Christianity.

The Civil War ended the system of slavery that had been the social norm of the antebellum South. During Reconstruction, with its relative social and political equality, blacks moved from integrated, white-dominated churches to black churches. Although the white denominations struggled to keep them, primarily as part of their struggle to re-create the system of inequality and control that had marked the period before the war, the freed slaves—aided by northern missionaries, both black and white—formed their own congregations and denominations. This led to rapid growth of both the African Methodist Episcopal Church and AFRICAN METHODIST EPISCOPAL CHURCH, ZION, and to the formation of the Colored Methodist Episcopal Church (see CHRISTIAN METHODIST EPISCOPAL CHURCH). Other separate black denominations included the Colored Primitive Baptists and the Colored Cumberland Presbyterian Church.

The biggest growth, however, occurred among the Baptist churches that soon dominated the black religious landscape. Not until 1895 did they combine into an organized denomination, the National Baptist Convention (see NATIONAL BAPTIST CONVENTION, U.S.A., INC.). Although rent by conflicts over politics, theology, and personalities into three separate organizations, it remains one of the largest black denominations in the country.

With the collapse of Reconstruction and the smothering of black hopes for freedom and political rights, the black church in the Southern United States became a locus for black self-determination. In the churches blacks could maintain their dignity and independence. There, generations of black leaders would be reared and blacks would try to make sense of the oppression they suffered.

While the church may have provided blacks with solace from the racism experienced in their daily lives, and may even have provided a theological understanding of it, it rarely advocated acceptance. The dawning of the 20th century saw several responses to this racism and oppression couched in religious language.

Although not identified with religion, W.E.B. DUBOIS articulated the significance of black religion most eloquently in his book *The Souls of Black Folks.* DuBois, a founder of the National Association for the Advancement of Colored People (NAACP), argued vigorously for black political and legal rights. Recognizing that the problem of the 20th century would be the "problem of the color line," he saw within black religion a reflection of the power and dignity of African Americans. He also saw there the possibility of transforming America by demonstrating the true power of Christianity.

This idea of black dignity was reflected in the views of several black leaders. Many were ministers who saw within the black religious experience the possibility for the realization of true Christianity. The darker races were to show the Europeans and Americans a Christianity freed of racism, hatred, and violence. Others saw a need for a return to Africa as the only escape from American racism. While such voices were a minority, they touched responsive chords in the lives of many blacks.

The onset of World War I saw wide-scale black migration from the rural South to northern and western urban centers. In those unfamiliar environs religion provided blacks with security and familiarity, just as it did for millions of European immigrants who flocked to America's shores. Many urban black churches were no more than storefronts holding a couple of dozen people. Others, such as Olivet Baptist in Chicago, were major institutions providing not only religious activities, but also housing and employment assistance, day care services, and educational opportunities.

The most distinctive response to this urban environment was the emergence of the so-called black cults. These varied tremendously in their goals and methods, from the Peace Mission Movement of Father DIVINE to the racially separatist NATION OF ISLAM (NOI). What these movements shared was the presence of a charismatic and powerful individual leader, a black man or woman unafraid of existing power structures both white and black, who articulated a message of individual, social, and economic improvement that appealed to poorer blacks.

Many, such as the Peace Mission Movement, the United House of Prayer for all People (see GRACE, DADDY), and Ida Robinson's Mt. Sinai Holy Church, emerged out of the HOLINESS MOVEMENT or PENTECOSTALISM. All demanded strict moral behavior, often determining most aspects of members' lives, including where they lived and whom they married. Their emphasis on healing and personal transformation gave members a sense of identity, self-worth, and pride in the face of poverty and racism.

Radically different in their intent were the black nationalist movements. These movements preached a message of African-American pride, independence, and self-reliance. Although some were more secular, like the Universal Negro Improvement Association (UNIA) of Marcus GARVEY, others, such as the Nation of Islam and the BLACK JEWS, were expressly religious. Significantly, few were Christian, which was identified as the religion of the oppressors. Most adapted a different religious tradition to create not only a message of black self-worth but of black (moral) superiority. In doing so they spurned

Religion has been a primary source of independence for African Americans, producing such dynamic leaders as Mary McLeod Bethune, shown attending Sunday chapel service at Bethune–Cookman College. *(Library of Congress)*

the color-blindness of Father Divine, affirming black distinctiveness and separatism.

The most significant of these movements was the NOI. Garvey's UNIA numbered its members in the tens of thousands at its height in 1925, but it collapsed following Garvey's conviction for fraud in connection with his Black Star shipping lines. The NOI has been much longer lived and, despite its insularity, played a role greater than its size would suggest.

Begun in Detroit in 1931 by W.D. FARD, who preached black superiority, a rejection of Christianity, and a system of rigid moral and individual discipline, the NOI made slow but steady inroads among the black underclass of that city. Following Fard's disappearance in 1934, a power struggle broke out that resulted in the removal of numerous members to Chicago. There, under the leadership of Elijah MUHAMMAD, the NOI (Black Muslims) emerged as a significant force in the African-American community, and eventually American society.

The Black Muslims were proud, self-disciplined, self-sufficient, and determined. They had no qualms about using any means necessary to defend themselves. The Black Muslims completely rejected white society.

They did not want a place at the American banquet table—they wanted their own table and were determined to get it. Achieving a high degree of visibility through the work of its national representative, MALCOLM X, the Nation of Islam articulated a radical vision of black independence, going so far as to demand that white America should give blacks several states in reparations for the wealth that they believed whites had stolen from them.

In this respect the NOI differed greatly from the CIVIL RIGHTS MOVEMENT of the 1950s and 1960s. If anything attests to the vitality and strength of African-American life and religion it is "the Movement." Although the roots of the civil rights struggles of the third quarter of the 20th century lay with men of a secular bent, such as Du Bois, A. Philip Randolph, and Roy Wilkins, as a movement infused with a religious drive and fervor it transformed a nation. The civil rights movement drew its strength from the African-American church. The reasons for this are historical, sociological, and theological.

Historically and sociologically the black church was the primary location of black independence and leadership. From the 18th century on it had been active in fighting against the discrimination suffered by Africans in North America. Free of white control and involvement, the black church was the only place where African Americans could attain positions of power and influence without competing with or risking humiliation from whites.

In some cities the ministers of leading black churches functioned as political leaders of the black community. Not only were black ministers a black elite, they were also the only members of the black elite with regular contact with the black masses. Therefore it was through the churches that the movement for black civil rights became a mass movement.

Although a movement of many paths and individuals, one person came to symbolize it. This was Martin Luther KING, Jr. The son and grandson of ministers whose father led one of the largest and most prestigious churches in Atlanta, King grew up immersed in the black church, which was the source of his vision and his moral power. He saw in African Americans the last true hope for America. Only through their willingness to suffer as innocents could the United States be transformed. Their refusal to accept the evil of racism could remove it from the soul of America. Opposition to racism became part of a process of national salvation, whereby the sins of a country would be washed away by the blood of innocents.

This religious dimension affected many whites as they heard King's speeches steeped in the language of the Bible. The sight of black demonstrators and onlookers attacked by police dogs in Birmingham in 1963 and clubbed by mounted state troopers at Selma in 1965 did much to garner white support for black demands for civil rights.

Some blacks disagreed with King's emphasis on nonviolence, feeling that it further served to demean black America. Frederick Douglass's dictum that "He who is beaten easiest is beaten oftenest" rang in their ears. This opposition came earliest from secular or non-Christian sources. The most vocal and articulate of these opponents was Malcolm X.

As white America proved increasingly intransigent, the voices against nonviolence increased, especially after King's assassination in 1968. Movements within black religion mirrored these developments. Amid growing demands for "Black Power" and black pride many black church leaders within predominantly white denominations began organizing black caucuses. This movement became most visible to whites when, in 1968, James Forman strode into Riverside Church in New York City and on behalf of all African Americans demanded $500 million in reparations for past white abuses. Many whites derided Forman and the Conference of Black Churchmen, which had formulated the demands in the "Black Manifesto." Others, morally challenged by Forman's call, agonized over their response. Dr. Joseph

H. Jackson, the leading black Baptist, berated both Forman for the demands and the NATION-AL COUNCIL OF CHURCHES for organizing a black development corporation in response to them.

While solving little, and in many ways exacerbating existing tensions, the "Black Manifesto" raised to bold relief the increasing polarization of white and black America. Such polarization emerged out of the radically different experiences of the two communities, and despite the universal elements they shared, overcoming these different experiences would not and could not be easy, especially given the disparity of power between the two communities.

During this period there also emerged a self-consciously African-American theology. Although African-American religious reflection had always been different from that of whites, the black theology that emerged in the late 1960s and early 1970s was new in its awareness of that distinctiveness and its intentional reflection on it. Religious thinkers such as James Cone also brought about more serious attention to traditional forms of African-American religiosity. The church music, preaching, and prayer once derided by intellectuals and theologians as crude were now viewed as vivid expressions of a people's experience, expressions that could not be judged by criteria external to that experience but had to be analyzed in light of it.

Despite assaults by poverty, despair, secularization, and racism, African-American religion remains a powerful force. Nearly 18 million blacks belong to one of the leading black Baptist, Methodist, or Holiness/Pentecostal denominations alone. This is not counting smaller denominations and non-Christian religions and is a phenomenal number out of a total African-American population of 28 million. Religious leadership remains the training ground for black political leaders, from Jesse JACKSON to Louis FARRAKHAN.

Surveys conducted in the 1990s suggest that black churches exert a much more powerful force on their members than do white churches. This is especially true for teenagers and young adults, who look to the churches for their moral values and codes of behavior.

Religion remains central to the black community in America. It does so by being preeminently theirs—true to their experiences, needs, and aspirations. It has been, and remains, the source of moral authority within the community, its gathering place, and its refuge. The centrality of black religion to the black community was summed up best by the African-American theologian Kelly Miller Smith. "The line of demarcation between the black secular community and the black religious community, or the church, is at times invisible."

(See also CHURCH OF GOD IN CHRIST.)

EQ

Bibliography: Randall K. Burkett, *Garveyism as a Religious Movement: The Institutionalization of Black Civil Religion* (Metuchen. N.J.: Scarecrow Press, 1978); James Cone, *Black Theology and Black Power* (New York: Seabury Press, 1969); ———, *The Spirituals and the Blues: An Interpretation* (New York: Seabury, 1972); ———, *Black Theology: A Documentary History, 1966–1979* (Maryknoll, N.Y.: Orbis, 1979); Arthur H. Fauset, *Black Gods of the Metropolis: Negro Religious Cults of the Urban North* (1944; New York: Octagon Books, 1970); E. Franklin Frazier, *The Negro Church in America* (New York: Schocken, 1969); Eugene Genovese, *Roll, Jordan, Roll: The World the Slaves Made* (New York: Pantheon Books, 1974); Vincent Harding, *There Is a River: The Black Struggle for Freedom in America* (New York: Vintage Books, 1983); C. Eric Lincoln, and Lawrence Mamiya, *The Black Church in the African American Experience* (Durham, N.C.: Duke University Press, 1990); Albert J. Raboteau, *Slave Religion: The Invisible Institution in the Antebellum South* (New York: Oxford University Press, 1978); ———, *African American Religion* (New York: Oxford University Press, 1999); Milton C. Sernett, *African American Religious History: A Documentary Witness* (Durham, N.C.: Duke University Press, 1999); ———, *Bound for the Promised Land: African American Religion and the Great Migration* (Durham, N.C.: Duke University Press, 1997); Carter G. Woodson, *The History of the Negro Church* (Washington, D.C.: The Associated Publishers, 1945).

African Methodist Episcopal Church

The oldest African-American denomination (see AFRICAN-AMERICAN RELIGION) in the United States, the African Methodist Episcopal (A.M.E.) Church has its roots in the white refusal to grant blacks equality in worship. Although not organized as a denomination until nearly three decades later, the A.M.E. church traces its beginnings to 1787.

In that year, Richard ALLEN, Absalom JONES, and two other black worshippers were assaulted by white ushers at St. George's Methodist Church in Philadelphia who forced them from their seats. Outraged by this treatment, they led a secession from the church, organizing the Free African Society. Dismayed by the society's increasingly Quaker orientation, Allen and Jones left to form another black church, St. Thomas's. Still smarting at the affront offered them by the Methodists of St. George's, a majority of St. Thomas's members voted to affiliate the new church with the EPISCOPAL CHURCH in the United States. When the office of minister was offered to Allen, who along with Absalom Jones had voted for Methodist affiliation, he refused, telling them that he was a Methodist and "indebted to the Methodists for what little religion" he had.

Allen then organized Bethel Church along Methodist lines. Bethel grew steadily and by 1794 had completed its own church building, consecrated by the United States's first Methodist bishop, Francis ASBURY. Growing increasingly restive under white control, Allen called a meeting in 1816 of leading black Methodists from churches in Pennsylvania, New Jersey, Delaware, and Maryland to discuss the formation of an African Methodist denomination. The suggestion met with general approval, and the representatives voted to organize the African Methodist Episcopal Church. Allen was chosen as the first bishop and over a period of several days was ordained an elder and consecrated as bishop. Under Allen's leadership the A.M.E. experienced a period of strong growth and activity. It spread throughout the Northeast and Midwest, and even made some inroads in the South. There, however, its position as an independent black denomination and Allen's outspoken opposition to slavery aroused suspicion and legal difficulties.

Feeling a kinship with their ancestral homeland and with fellow blacks, the A.M.E. early began a program of foreign missions, sending its first missionary, Scipio Bean, to Haiti in 1827. Other missions followed to Liberia, southern Africa, and the Caribbean. Africa remained a center of A.M.E. work, and in 2000 four of the A.M.E.'s 19 districts were located there.

The Civil War provided a significant impetus to growth of the A.M.E. Missionaries went to the South to aid the freed blacks. Although the staid church services of the A.M.E. alienated many Southern blacks, others were impressed by its organization and independence. For these the A.M.E. provided an alternative to the white-dominated Methodist churches.

The A.M.E. has been active in black education and social improvement from its earliest times. Its book publishing concern was the first owned by blacks in America, and *The Christian Recorder* and *The A.M.E. Review* are the oldest black newspaper and magazine in the world, begun in 1841 and 1883, respectively. A.M.E. founded its first college, now Wilberforce University, in 1856 and now runs several colleges and seminaries, many founded by Daniel Payne, one of the A.M.E.'s leading missionaries to the South. The Reverend Vashti McKenzie was elected as the A.M.E.'s first woman bishop on July 11, 2000. In 2000 the African Methodist Episcopal Church claimed a membership of 2.25 million in more than 6,000 churches, making it the third-largest historically black denomination in the United States.

Bibliography: Richard Allen, *The Life, Experience and Gospel Labors of the Rt. Rev. Richard Allen, Written by Himself* (Nashville: Abingdon, 1983); Carol V. R. George, *Segregated Sabbaths: Richard Allen and the Emergence of Independent Black Churches* (New

York: Oxford University Press, 1973); Lawrence S. Little, *Disciples of Liberty: The African Methodist Episcopal Church in the Age of Imperialism, 1884–1916* (Knoxville: University of Tennessee Press, 2000); Daniel A. Payne, *History of the African Methodist Episcopal Church* (Nashville: A.M.E. Sunday School Union, 1891); Charles H. Wesley, *Richard Allen: Apostle of Freedom* (Washington, D.C.: Associated Publishers, 1969); www.amecnet.org (African Methodist Episcopal Church).

African Methodist Episcopal Zion Church

Like the AFRICAN METHODIST EPISCOPAL CHURCH, the African Methodist Episcopal Zion Church has its origins in the failure of white American Methodists to treat their black coreligionists as equals. It dates back to 1796, when several black members of the John Street Church in New York met together in order to worship free from racism. Services conducted by black lay ministers were held in the shop of a black cabinetmaker. These services were so successful that the participants soon built their own chapel. It was completed in 1801 and incorporated as the "African Methodist Episcopal Church [called Zion] of the City of New York."

The ordained minister of the church continued to be white until 1820, when Zion Church and the Asbury African Methodist Episcopal Church, also in New York, merged to form a separate denomination. Organized in October of that year as the African Methodist Episcopal Church, the new denomination quickly became embroiled in conflict with the older A.M.E. Church from Philadelphia under the leadership of Richard ALLEN. This conflict continued for decades, easing slightly with the addition of Zion to the denomination's name in 1848.

The church always has been politically active. From its earliest days, it boasted leading black abolitionists among its members, including Harriet TUBMAN, Sojourner TRUTH, and Frederick Douglass. This commitment to justice has continued up to the present with the A.M.E. Zion Church being the first Methodist denomination (white or black) to ordain women.

Although growing slowly during its early years, the church experienced rapid growth after the Civil War and again in the early part of the 20th century. By 2000 the African Methodist Episcopal Zion Church claimed a U.S. membership of more than 1.25 million members in slightly fewer than 3,000 congregations.

(See also AFRICAN-AMERICAN RELIGION.)

EQ

Bibliography: James Clinton Hoggard, *African Methodist Episcopal Zion Church, 1972–1996: A Bicentennial Commemorative History* (Charlotte, N.C.: A.M.E. Zion Publishing House, 1998); Wardell J. Payne, *Directory of African American Religious Bodies: A Compendium by the Howard University School of Divinity* (Washington, D.C.: Howard University Press, 1991); William J. Walls, *African Methodist Episcopal Zion Church: The Reality of the Black Church* (Charlotte, N.C.: A.M.E. Zion Publishing House, 1974).

Albright, Jacob   See UNITED METHODIST CHURCH.

Alcott, Amos Bronson (1799–1888)

An influential educational, religious, and social reformer in 19th-century New England, Amos Bronson Alcott was at once brilliant and erratic. Best known for his attempts to combine antislavery activism with progressive and utopian social experiments, Alcott is also notable for the mystical bent of his commitment to TRANSCENDENTALISM.

The youngest of eight children, Alcott was born on a farm in Wolcott, Connecticut, and reared an Episcopalian. After traveling in Virginia and the Carolinas as a salesman in his youth, Bronson returned to New England and began his career as an educator. In 1830 he married Abigail May, by whom he had four children (among them the noted author Louisa May Alcott). That same year he published his first educational treatise, *Observations on the Principles and Methods of Infant Instruction.*

Alcott based his educational theories on his experiences as a teacher in Boston and Germantown, Pennsylvania, in the 1820s and 1830s, and later as the superintendent of public schools in Concord, Massachusetts, in the 1850s. In 1836 he published *Record of Conversations on the Gospels*, in which he summarized discussions among his students on moral and religious themes. His pedagogy, as outlined in this work and in his other educational treatises, proved controversial, particularly his frank discussions of sexuality with a "mixed" class of children.

At the same time, Alcott was also influenced by a mystical and Neoplatonic strain of transcendentalism, and he surrounded himself with fellow members of the Transcendentalist Club. Never able to attain financial stability through his work, Alcott periodically relied on financial assistance from Ralph Waldo EMERSON, and later from the royalties his daughter Louisa garnered from the success of *Little Women*. Emerson paid for a trip to Europe in 1832, where Alcott met Charles Lane, a fellow reformer who was to become his partner in the establishment of Fruitlands, a transcendentalist communal experiment in Harvard, Massachusetts. In 1834, Lane and Alcott organized the community, consisting of Alcott's family, Lane and his son, and a few other friends. Although the experiment lasted only seven months, it demonstrated the practical social commitments of some transcendentalists.

At Fruitlands, Alcott insisted upon a strict and somewhat idiosyncratic physical and social regimen: He banned the consumption of meat, alcohol, tea, coffee, milk, and even carrots (because they developed away from the sun). In keeping with his advocacy of the antislavery cause, he forbade the wearing of cotton as a protest of the slave system, and even prohibited the use of wool clothing because it represented the enslavement of sheep. He required his followers to take cold water baths for their health. Finally, Charles Lane tried to institute a standard of celibacy. But that regulation, along with the general agricultural and financial failure of the enterprise, spelled the end of the social experiment at Fruitlands.

Although neither his utopian dreams nor his educational philosophies captured the public imagination, Alcott's ideas and his example were influential among his circle of New England acquaintances and fellow philosophical idealists. He left a rich written record of his many interests, including *The Doctrine and Discipline of Human Culture* (1836), *Concord Days* (1872), and *Ralph Waldo Emerson: An Estimate of His Character and Genius* (1882).

LMK

Bibliography: Frederick C. Dahlstrand, *Amos Bronson Alcott: An Intellectual Biography* (London: Associated University Presses, 1982); Odell Shepard, *Pedlar's Progress: The Life of Bronson Alcott* (New York: Greenwood Press, 1968).

Allen, Richard (1760–1831)

The man who organized the first black denomination in the United States, Richard Allen was born a slave on February 14, 1760, in Philadelphia. With his parents and siblings, Allen was sold in 1867 and taken to Dover, Delaware. There he was converted by a Methodist (see METHODISM) minister and soon began preaching the Gospel. Among those he turned to the Methodist path was his owner, who allowed Allen and his brother to purchase their freedom around 1781.

Allen returned to Philadelphia, where he became a businessman and lay preacher. Attending the first General Conference of the Methodist Episcopal Church in the United States in Baltimore, 1784, he was accepted as a "minister of promise." At the conference, the United States's first Methodist bishop, Francis ASBURY, reportedly asked Allen to accompany him on his preaching trips to the South, on the condition that Allen not associate with slaves. Allen refused and returned to Philadelphia, where he worked as a Methodist teacher among freed blacks.

Richard Allen, the first bishop of the African Methodist Episcopal Church, founded in Philadelphia in 1816.

Despite his position as a respected member of the congregation of St. George's Methodist Episcopal Church, Allen, along with the other black members, experienced much discrimination at the hands of his white coreligionists. The breaking point was reached one day in 1787 when Allen, Absalom JONES and William White were assaulted by a church usher while praying. Angered by such treatment, they withdrew from the church and founded the Free African Society on April 12, 1787.

The society grew away from its founders, however, and displeased with its increasing Quaker (see FRIENDS, THE RELIGIOUS SOCIETY OF [QUAKERS]) orientation, Allen and Jones left to found a new church, St. Thomas. When this congregation affiliated with the new Episcopal church, Allen organized a black Methodist church, Bethel, in 1794. The church and

Allen's influence grew steadily. In 1799 Bishop Asbury himself ordained Allen as a deacon.

At a meeting of 16 black Methodist congregations at Bethel on April 9, 1816, an agreement was reached for these churches to join together to form the AFRICAN METHODIST EPISCOPAL CHURCH. Two days later Allen was consecrated as its bishop.

Allen was committed to the moral, educational, and political development of America's blacks, and to their spiritual development. Bethel organized a day school in 1795, and in 1804 Allen founded the Society of Free People of Colour for Promoting the Instruction and School Education of Children of African Descent. An active abolitionist, he led petition drives demanding the abolition of slavery in Pennsylvania (1799, 1800) and in the United States (1800). He vociferously opposed the American Colonization Society, fearing—as did many free blacks—that its emphasis on returning blacks to Africa would result in forced colonization. Allen also organized the "colored conventions," whose purpose was to organize blacks politically to oppose the injustices they suffered.

Allen's drive and personality often led him into conflicts with his colleagues, many of whom felt that he was more interested in consolidating his own power than in aiding black Methodism. As a result, several black Methodist churches split from the A.M.E. or refused to join.

Despite these conflicts, Allen created the basis for independent black churches and independent black political organization. The A.M.E. grew dramatically under his leadership until by the time of Allen's death on March 26, 1831, it had more than 7,000 members in the United States and missions in Canada, Haiti, and West Africa.

(See also AFRICAN-AMERICAN RELIGION; AFRICAN METHODIST EPISCOPAL ZION CHURCH.)

EQ

Bibliography: Richard Allen, *The Life, Experience and Gospel Labors of the Rt. Rev. Richard Allen, Written*

by Himself (1793; Nashville: Abingdon, 1983); Carol V. R. George, *Segregated Sabbaths: Richard Allen and the Emergence of Independent Black Churches* (New York: Oxford University Press, 1973); Charles Spencer Smith, *History of the African Methodist Episcopal Church, 1856–1922* (Philadelphia: Book Concern of the A.M.E. Church, 1922; New York: Johnson Reprint Corp., 1968); Charles H. Wesley, *Richard Allen: Apostle of Freedom* (Washington, D.C.: Associated Publishers, 1969).

American Baptist Association   See BAPTISTS.

American Baptist Churches in the U.S.A.

The American Baptist Churches in the U.S.A. is the fourth-largest denomination of BAPTISTS in the United States today. The most theologically liberal of the Baptist denominations, it is a federated body of churches that share two principal beliefs: the BAPTISM of adult believers by immersion and the independence of the local congregation (see CONGREGATIONALISM).

Baptists originally appeared on the radical fringes of the English Puritan movement in the 1630s. Although they agreed with orthodox Puritans that church membership should be limited to those who could testify to an experience of divine grace, Baptists contended that no one, including the children of church members, ought to be baptized until that person had made a personal confession of faith. Baptists were also opposed to religious establishments in all forms and believed that the church should maintain itself solely by voluntary (see VOLUNTARYISM), not by state-supported, means. When they arrived in America during the "Great Migration" of Puritans from England to Massachusetts between 1620 and 1640, their theological principles quickly brought them into conflict with the colony's leadership. Roger WILLIAMS, a Puritan minister banished from Massachusetts in 1635 for advocating the separation of church and state, founded the first Baptist church in America at Providence, Rhode Island.

Baptists found a more favorable atmosphere in the middle colonies of New Jersey,

Pennsylvania, and Delaware, where they enjoyed religious toleration. In 1707 five congregations in those colonies united to form the Philadelphia Association, the first Baptist organization in America. Each local congregation was said to receive its authority directly from Jesus Christ, so the association could hold no binding power over the individual churches. Nonetheless, it facilitated interaction among them, especially in channeling their efforts in evangelism. The association also adopted a common confessional statement that provided some theological unity among the congregations.

The GREAT AWAKENING of the mid-18th century represented a critical turning point for the Baptist movement in America. The revivals of the Awakening inspired many to separate from the denominations in which they had been raised. In New England, many revival-oriented New Light (see NEW LIGHTS/OLD LIGHTS) Congregationalists challenged the parish system in Massachusetts and Connecticut and became Separate Baptists. Chief among this group was Isaac BACKUS, who organized a Baptist church in Middleborough, Massachusetts, in 1756. Baptists generally adapted well to the changing religious climate in America, for their institutions embodied the most significant features of the Awakening: lay leadership, local autonomy, and the ready acceptance of a voluntary system of church support. These emphases fit the country's democratic mood in the second half of the 18th century, and Baptist congregations increased dramatically in that period.

As the 19th century began, the renewed religious excitement brought by the SECOND GREAT AWAKENING further aided Baptist growth. Beginning in 1802, New England Baptists organized a series of benevolent societies to advance their denominational interests. These societies allowed congregations to maintain their nominal independence while combining resources for evangelistic, missionary, publishing, and educational endeavors. The General Missionary Convention (later called the Triennial Convention, because it met every three years) became the first national Baptist body. It was founded in 1814 to support the work of Baptist missionaries Adoniram JUDSON and Luther Rice.

Although the Triennial Convention intended at first to promote all sorts of benevolent activity, it later decided to limit its role to foreign missions. Other societies were soon formed to meet the convention's original aims. The Baptist General Tract Society was organized in 1824 and the American Baptist Home Mission Society came into being in 1832.

As their denomination grew, Baptists also saw the need for educational institutions that would train church leaders. The earliest Baptist college, Rhode Island College (now Brown University), had been organized in 1764. In the early 19th century, the Baptists founded many other colleges that hold national stature today. These schools include Colby College and Bates College in Maine, and Hamilton College, Colgate College, and the University of Rochester in New York.

The movement to abolish slavery and the coming of the Civil War permanently divided Baptists in the North from their fellow church members in the South. During the 1830s it became increasingly clear that the Triennial Convention and the Home Missionary Society reflected the interests of the northerners who ran them. A firm stand against appointing slaveholders as missionaries soon aroused Baptists in the South to action. A call was issued for a consultative convention to meet in May 1845, and the SOUTHERN BAPTIST CONVENTION was officially organized, distinct from the churches in the North. Although northern Baptists at first insisted that their southern brethren were not truly separated from them, the Civil War effectively sealed the division and Baptists in the South henceforth went their separate way.

After the war, northern Baptists formed new missionary and educational organizations to increase their influence throughout the nation. Women's home and foreign missionary societies were chartered in the 1870s, and separate church conferences for German, Swedish, Danish, and other ethnic groups were also started. Overlapping programs and fundraising drives, however, coupled with the jealous guarding of local church autonomy, threatened the financial stability of many church agencies. As a result, the various Baptist societies sought to coordinate their efforts by coming together in 1907 in a single, 1-million-member structure, the Northern Baptist Convention. The convention engaged ecumenically (see ECUMENICAL MOVEMENT) with other denominations and in 1911 became a charter member of the Federal Council of Churches. The majority of Free Will Baptists in the North, moreover, remnants of an 18th-century schism over the question of the freedom of the human will to choose salvation, also merged with the convention in 1911.

During the late 19th and early 20th century, northern Baptists established themselves as participants in the great theological debates of the day. Some of the premier American intellectual figures of the time taught at Baptist seminaries: William Newton Clarke at Colgate, Augustus Hopkins Strong at Rochester, and William Rainey Harper and Shailer Mathews at Chicago. Most influential of all was theologian and seminary professor Walter RAUSCHENBUSCH. Rauschenbusch's SOCIAL GOSPEL theology confronted Baptists and other Christians with the challenge of integrating their religious faith with a practical commitment to working for the establishment of God's kingdom on earth.

By the 1920s, the Northern Baptist Convention, like some other Protestant evangelical denominations in the North, found itself embroiled in internal controversies between fundamentalists (see FUNDAMENTALISM) and modernists (see MODERNISM) over the proper interpretation of the Bible. Baptist clergyman Harry Emerson FOSDICK, who served a church in New York City, protested sharply in his 1922 sermon "Shall the Fundamentalists Win?" against the growing spirit of exclusivity among conservatives. He pled for mutual forbearance between the contending parties not only within his denomination, but also within Protestantism generally. But Fosdick's advice went unheeded. Conservative congregations left the convention and formed two new denominations: the General Association of Regular Baptist Churches and the Conservative Baptist Association. The northern Baptists as a whole adopted a moderate position about the role of Scripture in the church's life. The convention affirmed that the New Testament was simply the "all sufficient ground" of Christian belief and practice.

The main northern Baptist denomination has changed its name twice since WORLD WAR II. It renamed itself the American Baptist Convention in 1950 in order to stress its national character in the heady period of postwar church growth. An open invitation was then extended to other Baptist bodies to unite with the convention. While many congregations in the African-American Baptist tradition entered into dual membership with the American Baptists and with one of the black Baptist conventions, no full-scale, organic union of denominations took place. In 1972, a second major revision occurred and a more connectional, less centralized polity was formalized in the renamed American Baptist Churches in the U.S.A. In the new denominational structure, a greater share of authority—true to long-standing Baptist tradition—was given to local churches and regional bodies.

The membership figures of the American Baptists have remained fairly stable since 1925. Although the 1950s was a period of general growth within churches in the United States, the American Baptists have lost almost as many members as they have gained over the past 50 years. For example, various European ethnic groups, among whom Baptists once concentrated their missionary work, formed their own independent denominations. And the espousal of social and theological stances that some conservative congregations deemed too liberal caused a loss of membership as well. In 2000, the American Baptist Churches reported approximately 1,500,000 members in 5,800 congregations.

GHS, Jr.

Bibliography: William H. Brackney, *The Baptists* (Westport, Conn.: Greenwood Press, 1988); Howard R. Stewart, *American Baptists and the Church* (Lanham, Md.: University Press of America, 1997); Robert G. Torbet, *A History of the Baptists,* rev. ed. (Valley Forge, Pa.: Judson Press, 1973); www.abc-usa.org (American Baptist Churches USA).

American Bible Society   See BIBLE SOCIETIES.

American Board of Commissioners for Foreign Missions   See MISSIONS, FOREIGN.

American Humanist Association   This organization, which has survived for more than 60 years, provides humanists with literature and a community in a cultural climate often hostile to their commitment to reason and their suspicion of organized religion.

Founded in 1941, the American Humanist Association emerged out of a long tradition of religious and philosophical rationalism in the United States dating back to the ENLIGHTENMENT, but noticeable particularly in the rise of humanist organizations like the Society for Ethical Culture and the Free Religious Association in the late 19th century (see ETHICAL CULTURE; UNITARIAN UNIVERSALIST ASSOCIATION).

In the late 1920s a variety of small, local humanist associations had been founded around the country. Humanists were often at odds with each other as much as with the religious establishment they rejected. In particular, some humanists wanted to maintain connections with the liberal religious effort to fill ordinary life with aesthetic and moral value. Others thought humanism required a radical rejection and critique of religion in any form. A third group, mostly literary scholars, were seen by other humanists as representing an elitist view of culture.

In 1941 John H. Dietrich, a Unitarian minister, brought together some of the fledgling groups to form the American Humanist Association. The organization underwrote the publishing of a journal, originally entitled *The New Humanist* but renamed *The Humanist* to differentiate the more political version of humanism from that of literary critics such as Irving Babbit. Members of the new organization actively pressed issues of religious and intellectual freedom. Philosopher Corliss Lamont became involved in several civil liberties cases, including one leading to a 1963 Supreme Court ruling that prohibited government monitoring of mail. While many notable intellectuals, including psychologist Abraham Maslow and biologist Edward O. Wilson, have been members of the AHA, membership levels have remained low. In 2000, the group claimed 74 local chapters in the United States.

Attacked repeatedly during the 1980s and 1990s by religious conservatives who claimed humanists were conspiring to promote a new religion of "SECULAR HUMANISM," association members continued at the century's end to press civil liberties issues, organize an annual Humanist Institute, and publish the magazines *Free Inquiry* and *The Humanist*. Those venues give voice to both secular and religious humanism.

Bibliography: *The Humanist: 50th Anniversary Issue* 51.1 (January 1991); Paul Kurtz, *Embracing the Power of Humanism* (Lanham, Md.: Rowman & Littlefield, 2000); ———, *Challenges to the Enlightenment: In Defense of Reason and Science* (Buffalo, N.Y.: Prometheus Books, 1994); http://www.humanist.net (American Humanist Association).

American Indian Religious Freedom Act (AIRFA)

Native Americans have endured a long history of persecution against their traditional religions, running from colonial times into the 21st century. But the story of Native–white religious interaction entered a new phase with the passage of AIRFA by Congress in 1978. During the 1980s a number of cases testing AIRFA appeared in the nation's courts, in which native groups argued against various government policies on FIRST AMENDMENT grounds. However, in most instances the courts ruled that AIRFA did not provide cause for government agencies to seriously alter their practices affecting Native Americans, leading native groups and activists back to Washington. Their lobbying efforts resulted in significant legislative victories, with both Congress and President Clinton eventually supporting enactment of new laws.

Christopher COLUMBUS suspected that the Arawak islanders he encountered had no religion, a mistake stemming from his equation of religious life with Christianity. In subsequent centuries European colonists and their American descendants were often troubled by the religious beliefs and practices, or apparent lack thereof, among America's indigenous peoples. Endeavoring to make up for this deficiency, colonizers sought to spread the Gospel among the Indians (see MISSIONS, FOREIGN) in conjunction with incorporating Indian fur trade networks or lands into the realm of the European mercantile economy (see NEW FRANCE; NEW SPAIN), often asserting a "right of discovery" to claim native land.

Apart from a number of French Jesuits who established missions to the Hurons and other tribes along Quebec's St. Lawrence River in the 1630s and 1640s, many missionaries assumed that native religious practices were demonic. Thus John ELIOT's "Praying Indians" among the Massachusetts were encouraged to abandon most aspects of their culture in order to become regenerated Protestants, and Franciscans ministering to the Pueblos prior to 1680 (see NATIVE AMERICAN RELIGIONS: SOUTHWEST) repeatedly raided and destroyed kivas, village ceremonial centers.

Colonial missions remained largely unsuccessful, perhaps because, as one Huron noted in the 1630s: "Death and the faith walk hand in hand." But in the early 19th century, as Congress gave monies set aside in its "civilization fund" to various denominational mission enterprises, Christians seeking to implant the Gospel were increasingly able to prohibit would-be Indian converts from practicing traditional ceremonies as they established mission schools among Cherokees, Muskogees (Creeks), and other tribes in the Southeast.

The ideology of "civilization," equating Protestant Christian faith with Americanism, became particularly powerful in the years after the CIVIL WAR, when the country turned full attention to western expansion and pacification of intransigent western tribes. In 1882 Secretary of the Interior Henry M. Teller ordered an end to "heathenish dances," which he claimed were a "great hindrance to civilization." Government regulation increased with the subsequent establishment of a Court of Indian Offenses on numerous reservations in 1883, which prosecuted Indians found in violation of increasingly strict codes of behavior. Men were ordered to cut their braids. Ceremonies for public mourning such as the "give away," the Sun Dance, polygamy, and any religious practice that an agent might deem uncivilized were outlawed, violators being jailed and fined. In 1888 the agent in charge of the Kiowa, Comanche, and Wichita agency in Oklahoma issued regulations prohibiting the ingestion of peyote, a sacred hallucinogenic plant (see NATIVE AMERICAN CHURCH).

President Franklin Roosevelt's New Deal restructuring of the federal government finally curtailed legal means of religious persecution. John M. Collier, appointed commissioner on Indian Affairs in 1932, reorganized tribal government and, being attracted to native art and religious mysticism, ordered the end of prohibitions against Indian religious practices. At the same time, prosecution of peyotists continued. The general impetus of the "termination" policy of the Eisenhower era, which relocated Indians to urban areas and abolished federal responsibility for several smaller tribes,

such as the Klamaths and Menominees, served to advance the cause of assimilation into the dominant society (see ASSIMILATION AND RESISTANCE, NATIVE AMERICAN).

In the 1960s, spurred on in part by the example of the CIVIL RIGHTS MOVEMENT and increasing public dissent, Indian people undertook a variety of campaigns to secure control over their lands and lives. Encouraged by President Nixon's approval of the return of Blue Lake to the Taos Pueblo in 1971, Indian activists began pushing western congressional leaders and others for legislation granting free exercise of religion to native people. Other victories, including a modification of the 1940 Bald and Golden Eagle Protection Act allowing Indians to capture eagles for ceremonial use, led in 1977 to Senator James Abourezk of South Dakota introducing the AIRFA bill that passed through both houses with a minimum of debate, apart from the assurance by one cosponsor, Rep. Morris Udall of Arizona, that the bill "had no teeth."

AIRFA contained an extensive prologue noting the disparity practiced by the government in relation to native religions, and the general failure of the First Amendment to cover infringements on Indian practices. The act resolved that "henceforth it shall be the policy of the United States to protect and preserve for American Indians their inherent right of freedom to believe, express and practice the traditional religions." A final clause also called upon all federal agencies to evaluate the need for change in the implementation of any government policy that might affect Native Americans.

The act succeeded in addressing some complaints in the years after its passage. Some of many thousands of human remains disinterred and stored at the Smithsonian Institution and other museums were repatriated to tribes such as the Pawnees in Oklahoma, along with ceremonial pipes and other equipment taken during the Plains Wars of the 19th century. Indian prisoners were granted some of the same freedom to worship shared by other convicts.

But impediments to free religious exercise remain, particularly when Indian religious practices are based on locale, as many are. Many western tribes regard particular lands as sacred, often places of the peoples' origin (Blue Lake—Taos Pueblo), the home of supernatural beings (San Francisco Peaks—Navajos and Hopis), or places of revelation and inspiration (Bear Butte—Cheyennes and Lakotas). Native access to such sites, or preservation of their unsullied character, is difficult in view of the federal role in administering vast amounts of land in western states through agencies such as the Bureau of Land Management, the National Park Service, the National Forest Service, and the Department of Defense. Powerful economic interests dependent upon public lands—ranching, timber, mining, and the federal bureaucracies themselves—have been adamantly opposed to arguments for greater access or special use by native peoples. Thus controversies over sacred sites took on some of the same zeal associated with the Indian wars of the last century.

Serious impediments to free religious exercise remained following AIRFA's passage, however. Conflict was frequent in the 1980s and 1990s between native groups advancing claims over sacred sites and government agencies. In addition, representatives of the economic interests dependent upon western public lands expressed suspicion of native intentions. Former Utah governor Scott M. Matheson declared before Congress in 1993 that accommodating native religious needs would violate the First Amendment's establishment clause. South Dakota governor William Janklow remarked publicly in 1995 that he feared a conspiracy by the Lakota Sioux to take back the Black Hills.

Landmark Supreme Court rulings in *Lyng v. Northwest Cemetery Protective Association* (1988) and *Employment Division v. Smith* (1990) revealed that AIRFA was nearly as powerless as Senator Udall had claimed. In those rulings the Court held that the government had no obligation to modify its policies in order to protect Indian religious practices. In *Lyng* the court reviewed an appeal favoring Forest Service plans to construct a marginally useful logging road in northern California through a sacred area that Yurok, Hoopa, and Tolowa tribal members showed was crucial to their cultural survival. In the majority opinion Justice Sandra Day O'Connor maintained that even though the road would shatter the tribes' religions, the Forest Service could build the road where it desired since the government is free to administer its own internal affairs as it sees fit.

In *Smith* Justice Antonin Scalia reversed a long-established First Amendment interpretation and upheld the state of Oregon's denial of unemployment compensation to two NATIVE AMERICAN CHURCH members fired without pay for sacramentally ingesting peyote. Scalia argued that state laws intended for the public good were to be generally applicable, and that this outweighed any individual desire for exemption. The government has no obligation to shield minority religious practices from legitimate laws, he added, since the effort to accommodate diverse religious minorities "is a luxury that a democratic society cannot afford."

In the aftermath of these opinions many nonnatives feared that the Court's reading of the First Amendment threatened the religious liberty of all Americans. In 1994, accordingly, Congress passed the Religious Freedom Restoration Act (RFRA) (see CHURCH AND STATE). Indian religious practitioners sought redress in separate legislation, resulting in passage of the American Indian Religious Freedom Act Amendments of 1994. In this act Congress finally closed the loopholes that had allowed 22 states to criminalize Indian sacramental peyote use in spite of an exemption in federal drug law dating from 1965.

In addition, in May 1996 President Clinton issued Executive Order 13007, which required federal land management agencies to "accommodate access to and ceremonial use of Indian sacred sites by Indian religious practitioners" and to "avoid adversely affecting the physical integrity of such sacred sites." At the same time, however, the order stated that it created no "right, benefit, or trust responsibility" that might be enforceable against the federal government.

Although guarantees of American Indian religious freedom seemed stronger by the end of the 20th century than they had been at the beginning, much remained insecure. As recent laws indicate, there is still ambiguity in the status of native people's rights. Western economic interests are still inclined to view government protection of native religious practices as a threat. In 1999 a Wyoming lumber company took the National Forest Service to court over its efforts to accommodate native access to the Big Horn Medicine Wheel. In 1997 the Supreme Court ruled in *Boerne v. Flores* that RFRA, the act heralded by religious groups of all sorts, was unconstitutional. Native Americans seemed assured of a continued struggle to protect their religions in spite of recent victories.

MG

Bibliography: John R. Wunder, ed., *Native American Cultural and Religious Freedoms* (New York: Garland Publishing, 1999); http://www.narf.org (Native American Rights Fund).

American Lutheran Church   See EVANGEL-
ICAL LUTHERAN CHURCH IN AMERICA.

American Missionary Association   The
American Missionary Association (AMA) was the most prominent of the northern religious agencies that worked among African Americans following the CIVIL WAR. Formed in 1846 to protest the alleged complicity of the American Home Missionary Society with southern slaveholders, the AMA advocated abolitionist (see ABOLITIONISM) ideas and enabled New England Protestants to use the Christian gospel as a weapon against slavery.

As the Civil War came to an end and the defeat of the Confederacy appeared inevitable, many northern Christians viewed the South as a vast missionary (see MISSIONS, HOME) field, where the religious and political ideals they cherished might be planted for the first time. The leadership of the AMA believed that the legal emancipation of blacks should be merely a prelude to their social and educational emancipation. By 1865, more than 250 teachers and preachers employed by the AMA were at work throughout the southern states. They participated in the "ecclesiastical and Christian reconstruction" of the South—an action parallel to political Reconstruction. Hampton Normal and Agricultural Institute in Virginia, where the African-American leader Booker T. WASHINGTON studied, was one of several black colleges staffed and funded by the AMA during Reconstruction. Other prominent schools opened by the AMA for African Americans included Atlanta University (1865), Fisk University in Nashville (1865), and Howard University in Washington, D.C. (1867).

After the abandonment of missionary work in the South when the Reconstruction era ended, the AMA turned its attention principally to home missions work with Native Americans. It published a monthly journal, *American Missionary,* and employed agents not only in the United States and Canada but also overseas. In the 20th century, the AMA lost its separate identity and was subsumed into the home missions department of what is now the UNITED CHURCH OF CHRIST.

GHS, Jr.

Bibliography: Clara Merritt De Boer, *His Truth is Marching On: African Americans Who Taught the Freedmen for the American Missionary Association, 1861–1877* (New York: Garland, 1995); Joe M. Richardson, *Christian Reconstruction: The American Missionary Association and Southern Blacks, 1861–1890* (Athens: University of Georgia Press, 1986).

American Muslim Mission   See NATION OF
ISLAM (BLACK MUSLIMS).

American Revolution/Revolutionary War

Americans drew upon religion to serve a number of tasks during the Revolutionary War (1775–1783). In the process, they established a pattern for interpreting military conflict prominent throughout much of American history. Religion shaped the yearning for revolution and the language by which revolutionary hopes were expressed. In addition, church pulpits provided a ready forum for articulating revolutionary support or opposition. Many Americans also understood the Revolution itself, which drew upon the powerful themes of new birth and freedom from bondage, as a form of religious experience. Finally, the Revolution greatly influenced the development of American CIVIL RELIGION, as continuing generations have looked to their revolutionary birth as a source of national identity and purpose.

The yearning for revolution emerged out of two mainstreams of thought regarding social and political order: PURITANISM and the ENLIGHTENMENT views of liberals like John Locke and radical Whigs, who often combined Protestant dissent with republican political theory. Colonial Americans had come to think right political order was ordained by God, which allowed for the formation of critical views of political power: Power could be unjust. In the Calvinist (see CALVINISM) tradition prominent in 17th-century England, humans were not obligated to suffer unjust authority, but rather were capable of modifying existing institutions to make them accord more with the divine will.

The years prior to the Revolution were marked by dramatic events that many Americans regarded as signs of the imminent end of the world. The widespread religious revivals of the GREAT AWAKENING, a series of portentous earthquakes shaking the country in 1755, and the dramatic French and Indian Wars ending in 1763 all encouraged Americans to draw upon millennial language in order to understand their times and political conditions. While Puritans had often seen the Church of England (see ANGLICANISM) as the Antichrist depicted in the Bible, such language became explicitly political in 1774, when news of the Quebec Act, granting toleration to Catholicism in Canada, persuaded many colonists that the English crown itself was an agent of Satan. Increasingly preachers and popular writers spoke of bondage to the devilish English "tyrant" as damnation, and political liberty itself as salvation.

With the outbreak of armed resistance in 1775, American revolutionists continued to rely upon the Great Awakening (which helped to create a distinctive national consciousness among colonists) as a pattern for understanding their experience, speaking of the spreading revolutionary fervor in the same ways colonists had referred to the religious zeal of the 1730s and 1740s. A number of public rituals helped maintain the revivalistic climate. Some, such as the unruly processions marking Pope's Day, a traditional anti-Catholic holiday (see ANTICATHOLICISM) that provided the model for massive demonstrations against the Stamp Act, carried over from earlier years. In ordering regular days of public fasting and thanksgiving, the Continental Congress continued the old Puritan tradition of viewing the public welfare as attendant upon the repentance of sin. FREEMASONRY, the Enlightenment fraternity of many revolutionary leaders, contributed its own ritual forms, heightening the leaders' bonds of brotherhood through initiation ceremonies. Other rituals emerged out of the revolutionary process itself: civic funeral processions to eulogize the death of Liberty, hanging King George in effigy from the "Liberty Tree," the public reading of Thomas JEFFERSON's Declaration of Independence, and the 1778 establishment of July 4th to commemorate the nation's birth of freedom.

Churches, providing colonial Americans with an important gathering place, also mobilized opinion. Denominations naturally differed in their support for the revolt, and as many as one-third of the colonists opposed the war. Loyalists, supporters of the British crown, were often Anglican, though southern Anglicans, such as George Washington, frequently favored the revolution, and METHODISTS. Presbyterians (see PRESBYTERIANISM), Congregationalists (see CONGREGATIONALISM), and BAPTISTS held the Loyalist position. Such Loyalist Anglican clergy as Samuel SEABURY argued that the revolt was bound to substitute mob rule for a divinely sanctioned monarchical system that provided great benefits to colonists. Many Anglicans were forced to flee the country.

Opposition to the war also stemmed from pacifist grounds (see PEACE REFORM). MENNONITES, MORAVIANS, and especially Quakers (see FRIENDS, THE RELIGIOUS SOCIETY OF), who abjured violence as contrary to the Christian faith, were likely to resist paying war taxes and foreswear loyalty oaths, for which a number were imprisoned. Some pacifists, such as Quaker Anthony Benezet, spoke publicly against the war and urged other reforms, in particular the abolition of SLAVERY. Neutrality, rather than strict pacifism, gained a public voice from Lutheran leader Henry Melchior MUHLENBERG.

But if significant numbers of Americans found religious justification to oppose the war, the larger emphasis was on support, which also spread among particular denominations. As one Loyalist wrote, the revolution was led by "Congregationalists, Presbyterians and Smugglers." And in truth, the inheritors of English Calvinism contributed the most vocal religious support to the war. Countless clergy, including such luminaries as college presidents John Witherspoon and Ezra Stiles, were influential in spreading patriotic fervor from the pulpit. Perhaps even more important than the support of religious elites, however, was the fact that the basic millennial thrust of the struggle, the forces of God against those of Satan, encouraged a religious populism. This populism continued to affect public life during the SECOND GREAT AWAKENING, even while the political institutions created in the aftermath of revolution

The Boston Massacre in 1770 was the first battle in the armed war against England, which was fueled in part by Enlightenment ideals. *(Engraving by Paul Revere. Boston Public Library)*

sought to erect barriers between the religious and the political.

The millennial hopes that inspired the Revolution have retained a significant power throughout American history, providing subsequent generations with the means for patterning public life and criticizing the failures of American society to uphold its ideals, even when shorn from their traditional Christian roots. In addition, the confluence of revolution and revival had a dramatic impact on the country's development during the Second Great Awakening, by elevating popular over elite control of religious institutions.

MG

Bibliography: Catharine L. Albanese, *Sons of the Fathers: The Civil Religion of the American Revolution* (Philadelphia: Temple University Press, 1976); Ruth Bloch, *Visionary Republic: Millennial Themes in American Thought, 1756–1800* (New York: Cambridge University Press, 1985); Mark Noll, *Christians in the American Revolution* (Grand Rapids, Mich.: Eerdmans, 1977); Kevin P. Phillips, *The Cousins' Wars: Religion, Politics, and the Triumph of Anglo-America* (New York: Basic Books, 1999).

American Unitarian Association   See
UNITARIAN UNIVERSALIST ASSOCIATION.

Americanism   During the late nineteenth
century, the conflict over "Americanism" within the Roman Catholic Church (see ROMAN
CATHOLICISM) in the United States, often
referred to as the "Americanist Crisis," resulted from numerous threads woven into the tap-
estry of U.S. Catholic history. Personal,
theological, and practical differences within
the American church hierarchy became heresy
when viewed from the perspective of Rome,
although never was heresy so ambiguously
defined or heretics so difficult to locate.

The source of the conflict was the church's
relationship to American society and was occasioned by its ethnic mix. The United States during the 19th century presented a peculiar
reality for the Roman Catholic Church in the
West. Its commingling of numerous ethnic
groups—each with its own spirituality, language, and customs—presented problems
unknown in France, Germany, or Ireland.

The conflict surfaced over how the needs
of these various groups should be met. One
segment of the hierarchy, led by Archbishop
John IRELAND and supported by Cardinal James
GIBBONS, felt that all Catholics in the United
States should conform to a single Catholic culture, a culture open to the possibilities and
promises of the United States. This group,
known as Americanists, believed that the failure to create such a culture threatened episcopal authority, endangered morals, and
embarrassed the church within the wider society. This singular culture would be both American and Catholic. It would create a unified
church, no longer foreign and alien, to be a
beacon to America, its strength highlighting
the weaknesses of divided Protestantism.

The opponents, primarily Bishops Michael
Corrigan and Bernard McQuaid, believed that
any concession to the wider culture threatened
Catholics and Catholicism. The world was hostile to everything Roman Catholics believed

and the greater the contact with it, the greater
the threat of apostasy.

During the early years of the pontificate of
Leo XIII (1878–1903), the Americanists' star
rose. Leo's cautious openings to the modern
world, exhibited in his encyclical *Rerum
Novarum* (1891) and his call for French
Catholics to support the third republic coincided with the Americanists' attitude toward
the modern world. The Americanists welcomed Leo's 1889 appointment of Archbishop Francesco Satolli as apostolic delegate to
the United States and attempted to win him
to their cause. At first all seemed to go well.
Accompanied by Archbishop Ireland, Satolli
urged those attending the 1893 Catholic Congress in Chicago to carry in one hand "the
book of Christian truth and in the other the
Constitution of the United States."

He responded less favorably to Catholic
participation in the WORLD'S PARLIAMENT OF RELI-
GIONS held that same year, a criticism underscored by a papal letter condemning Catholic
participation in interdenominational congresses. European events also endangered the Americanists' position. Catholic support for the
French republic collapsed amid its anticlericalism and the machinations of conservative
French Catholics and monarchists. Intellectually, new ideas—evolution, biblical criticism—
appeared to threaten Catholic dogma. The
modern world seemed increasingly inhos-
pitable to Catholic truth.

These events signaled the weakening of the
Americanists, demonstrated unmistakably by
the papal encyclical LONGINQUA OCEANI (January 6, 1895). Ostensibly a letter praising the
strength and growth of the American church,
its language unnerved the Americanists and
provided ammunition for anti-Catholics for
the next half-century: "It would be very erroneous to draw the conclusion that in America
is to be found the type of the most desirable
status of the Church, or that it would be law-
ful or expedient for State and Church to be, as
in America dissevered and divorced." Acknowl-

edging that the Church had done well under this system, it continued, "but she would bring forth more abundant fruits, if, in addition to liberty, she enjoyed the favor of the laws and the patronage of public authority." For Rome, obviously, the United States was not the model for nations or the Church to follow.

The final blow came from European rather than American events. Two talks by Americans at the International Catholic Congress in Fribourg in 1897 drew European attention. One, given by Denis O'Connell, who recently had been forced to resign as rector of the American College in Rome, argued in favor of the American system, which emphasized inalienable individual rights, in contrast to the Roman Empire, in which the arbitrary will of the emperor was law. While not recommending it universally, he claimed it was at odds neither with faith nor with morals.

The second, on evolution, by Father John Zahm, C.S.C., a professor of biology at the University of Notre Dame, also antagonized the conservatives. For many Europeans these talks proved that the American church was overrun with heresy and infidelity.

This was solidified with the appearance of the French edition of Walter Elliott's biography of Isaac HECKER. Hecker's belief in democracy was too much for those French Catholics who equated Catholicism with monarchy, and the book's preface by the liberal abbé Felix Klein did much to tar it with the brush of European progressivism.

America's rapid defeat of Catholic Spain in the Spanish-American War, along with the near-universal support for the American cause by the Catholic hierarchy—Bishop John SPALDING being the lone exception—conclusively demonstrated to the conservatives ascendant in Rome that "Americanism" was a danger to the Roman Catholic Church.

The Vatican's response to this danger was the encyclical *Testem Benevolentiae* (January 22, 1899), which explicitly condemned "Americanism" by name. Stating that the pope had heard that there were those in the American church who believed that the Roman Church should alter its essentials in order to adapt to the modern world and incorporate greater democracy in its structure, the letter condemned these doctrines and warned the bishops against them.

Responding for the bishops, Cardinal Gibbons assured the pope that no one among them held such views and affirmed the orthodoxy of all the bishops. The resulting fear that any new ideas would be labeled heretical led to a half-century of cultural and intellectual isolation in the American church.

EQ

Bibliography: Scott Appleby, *Church and Age United: The Modernist Impulse in American Catholicism* (Notre Dame: University of Notre Dame Press, 1991); R. D. Cross, *The Emergence of Liberal Catholicism* (Cambridge, Mass.: Harvard University Press, 1958); Gerald P. Fogarty, *The Vatican and the Americanist Crisis: Denis J. O'Connell, American Agent in Rome, 1885–1903* (Rome: University Gregoriana, 1974); Thomas Timothy McAvoy, *The Americanist Heresy in Roman Catholicism, 1895–1900* (Notre Dame: University of Notre Dame Press, 1963).

Ames, Edward Scribner (1870–1955)

One of the leading Christian Modernists (see MODERNISM) and an influential philosopher of religion, Edward Scribner Ames played a major role in both the academic study of religion and its popular understanding.

Born April 21, 1870, in Eau Claire, Wisconsin, where his father was a Disciples of Christ (see CHRISTIAN CHURCH [DISCIPLES OF CHRIST]) minister, Ames attended Drake University and Yale Divinity School. In 1895 he received the first Ph.D. in philosophy granted by the newly founded University of Chicago. With the exception of three years as professor of philosophy at Butler College, Ames would be associated with the University of Chicago until his death on June 29, 1955.

Ames rejected claims that one could know God as an objective reality. Knowledge of

God's presence, he believed, emerges from the positive elements of human existence. The realization that health, beauty, knowledge, justice, friendship, and hope exist demonstrates the reality of God. Religion is the human act of striving for improvement or advancement. Salvation, rather than being a supernatural act of God, is the struggle of human beings to realize the soul's natural powers, to actualize the ideal human achievement as seen in Christ. Heaven was the result, on this earth, of participation in that ideal, hell the failure to achieve that ideal. Ames's views left little room for such traditional doctrines as the virgin birth, the Trinity, life after death, or the reality of miracles.

Despite the apparent radicalness of these views, Ames maintained that they were consistent with the tradition of his denomination, the Disciples of Christ. Ames understood his reinterpretation of Christianity in light of science and modern thought as nothing more than a continuation of the traditional Disciples struggles against sectarianism and creedalism.

Along with his colleague Shailer MATHEWS, Ames was one of the most important modernists in American Protestantism. This was due both to the quality of his thought and to the positions he held. He was a popular philosophical writer, and his widely read books contributed to the spread of liberal theology in the United States. As professor of philosophy at the University of Chicago for 35 years (1900–1935), Ames influenced innumerable philosophers and theologians.

Ames's significance was greatest, however, within his denomination. As dean of Disciples Divinity House for 18 years (1927–1945), Ames played a major role in the training of future ministers. His positions as minister at Hyde Park (now University) Church (1900–1940) and editor of the denominational newspaper *The Scroll* (1925–1951) enabled Ames to introduce modernist views within the mainstream of Disciples of Christ thought.

EQ

Bibliography: Edward Scribner Ames, *Beyond Theology: The Autobiography of Edward Scribner Ames* (Chicago: University of Chicago Press, 1959); ————, *The New Orthodoxy* (Chicago: University of Chicago Press, 1918); ————, *The Psychology of Religious Experience* (Boston: Houghton Mifflin, 1910); Creighton Peden, *The Chicago School: Voices in Liberal Religious Thought* (Bristol, Ind.: Wyndham Hall Press, 1987).

Amish, the   Offshoots of the Mennonite tradition, the Amish are undoubtedly modern America's best-known antimoderns. They live in rural areas rather than cities, farm with horses rather than tractors, dress in simple clothing rather than up-to-date fashions, use biblical High German rather than English in their worship services, and opt for mutual aid for the elderly rather than Social Security. Their Old World style has made them a major attraction for nostalgia-starved Americans touring Amish strongholds such as Lancaster County, Pennsylvania.

Like the MENNONITES and the HUTTERITES, the Amish are products of the Anabaptist movement of the Radical Reformation in 16th-century Europe. But they did not emerge as a distinct Protestant sect until the last decade of the 17th century. In 1693, a Swiss Mennonite preacher from Berne named Jakob Ammann began to criticize fellow Mennonites for compromising their collective vow to withdraw from the corrupt world into a pure community of visible Christian saints. He called upon his followers to live in accordance with the primitive patterns of the early church instead of the modern examples of European society, urging them to practice foot-washing during the communion service and to simplify even more than the Mennonites their habits of dress and grooming. His most controversial innovation, however, was the practice of shunning. This practice dictated that community members who had deviated from the group's *Ordnung* ("order") be ostracized by other members, including family members and spouses of offenders.

Ammann attracted Mennonite followers in Switzerland, Holland, Alsace, south Germany, and Russia. In the 1720s, the first Amish immigrated to the United States. Like other German-speaking Anabaptist sectarians, they came largely to escape religious persecution, and they arrived for the most part in Pennsylvania. About 500 Amish immigrated to the United States in the 18th century. Some 3,000 more came by the end of the next century. Despite these meager numbers and their refusal to proselytize, Amish communities prospered. Thanks to high birthrates, low infant mortality, and high retention, there are now roughly 75,000 Amish living in the United States. The vast majority reside in Ohio, Pennsylvania, and Indiana.

The Amish are typically more antiworldly than their Mennonite kin. They eschew buttons as overly decorous, do not use electricity, and do not own telephones or cars. They often meet for worship services in homes rather than meetinghouses, and they have not founded ecclesiastical organizations or institutions of higher learning. Despite their refusal to use modern farming machines such as tractors, the hardworking Amish maintain highly productive farms.

The Amish typically do not vote or enlist in the military, but they do pay taxes. Women are not permitted to work outside the home or to use birth control. The Amish rarely marry outside the faith, and divorce is not allowed. They frown on higher education that is devoid of practical applications. In 1972 they earned the right not to send their children to public schools beyond the elementary level in a landmark Supreme Court case called *Wisconsin v. Yoder.*

Like other American sects of German origin, the Amish have experienced schisms between ultraconservative and moderate factions. The most conservative group, the Old Order Amish Mennonite Church, is also the largest. It reported 68,700 members in 2000. More moderate groups such as the Beachy Amish Mennonite Churches (named after their founder, Moses Beachy), claimed 7,255 members (a total that includes congregants in other countries). These groups have found a place in their congregational order for modern niceties such as automobiles, tractors, electricity, and trimmed beards. And, unlike their more conservative Amish kin, they maintain church buildings, run Sunday schools, and reach out to nonmembers through missions.

SRP

Bibliography: Sue Bender, *Plain and Simple: A Journey to the Amish* (New York: HarperCollins, 1989); J. A. Hostetler, *Amish Society,* 4th ed. (Baltimore: Johns Hopkins, 1993); Donald Kraybill and Marc Oshan, eds., *The Amish Struggle with Modernity* (Hanover, N.H.: University Press of New England, 1994).

Anabaptists   See AMISH, THE; BAPTISM; BAPTISTS; CHURCH OF THE BRETHREN (DUNKERS); HUTTERITES; MENNONITES.

Anglicanism   Anglicanism is the religious tradition that arose out of the REFORMATION of the church in England during the 16th century. The term itself derives from the Latin word *Anglicanus,* meaning "English," and its use was first popularized in John Jewel's *Apology for the Anglican Church,* published in 1562. Although the Church of England retained the episcopal (see EPISCOPACY) polity and many of the theological beliefs and customs of medieval Christianity, it became independent of Roman Catholicism in 1534 when Henry VIII repudiated papal control over his kingdom. The EPISCOPAL CHURCH is the chief heir of the Anglican heritage in the United States today.

Unlike Martin Luther, John Calvin, and other early leaders of the Reformation, Henry VIII split with Roman Catholicism more for personal and political than theological reasons. When Pope Clement VII refused to grant him a divorce from his first wife, Catherine of Aragon, Henry directed Parliament to declare that he, not the pope, was the head of the church in England. Henry's Act of Supremacy of 1534, however, represented only a constitutional action, and the Church of England continued to affirm Catholic doctrines and worship practices. Only with the accession of Henry's daughter, Elizabeth I, as queen in 1558 did Anglicanism begin to emerge in its present distinct form. In opposition both to Puritans (see PURITANISM), who desired the Church of England to be more fully Protestant, and to Catholic loyalists, who desired a return to papal supremacy, Anglicans sought what they called a *via media*, or "middle way." They emphasized the liturgical uniformity that *The Book of Common Prayer* (the first edition appeared in 1549) provided, while relying on the interaction of biblical teaching, religious tradition, and human reason for a highly flexible approach to theological authority.

The English settlers who came to Virginia in 1607 brought Anglicanism to America. Throughout the colonial period in American history, the Church of England was established by law as the official state church in Virginia, Maryland, North and South Carolina, Georgia, and the counties around New York City. Missionaries of the SOCIETY FOR THE PROPAGATION OF THE GOSPEL IN FOREIGN PARTS also helped found Anglican churches amid the hostile religious environment of Puritan New England in the mid-18th century. Because the War for Independence forced many Anglicans to flee the country and eventually led to the abolition of the church's privileged position in the South, Anglicanism barely survived the AMERICAN REVOLUTION. However, with the organization of the Episcopal Church in 1789, an American denomination was created that was loyal to the Anglican theological tradition and free of British control.

GHS, Jr.

Bibliography: Stephen Neill, *Anglicanism*, 4th ed. (New York: Oxford University Press, 1978); Nancy L. Rhoden, *Revolutionary Anglicanism: The Colonial Church of England Clergy During the American Revolution* (New York: New York University Press, 1999).

Anglo-Catholicism   Anglo-Catholics are adherents of the high-church party (those most oriented toward the practices and beliefs of Roman Catholicism) within ANGLICANISM. Anglo-Catholicism traces its roots to the Oxford Movement that arose in the Church of England in the 1830s. The Oxford Movement asserted the independence of the church from the English state and insisted on the importance of the apostolic succession of bishops from Jesus Christ to the present day. The emphasis of the Oxford Movement on piety and holiness of life led, moreover, to liturgical experimentation and to renewed interest in monasticism. By the end of the 19th century, forms of medieval ritualism also began to characterize high-church Anglicanism.

In the American EPISCOPAL CHURCH, interest in the Oxford Movement first appeared in the late 1830s in strongholds of the old high-church tradition, notably in the diocese of New York, where John Henry HOBART had earlier been bishop. The emergence of Anglo-Catholicism increased the already simmering rivalry between high-church and low-church Episcopalians, as those most comfortable with the dominant Protestant ethos (the low-church party) repeatedly challenged their Catholic-oriented colleagues. This high-church/low-church polarization had a number of ramifications, among them the harassment of three high-church bishops (Benjamin Tredwell Onderdonk of New York; his brother, Henry Ustick Onderdonk of Pennsylvania; and George Washington Doane of New Jersey) on morals charges. No less sensational was the conversion of Levi Silliman Ives, the Episcopal bishop of North Carolina, to Roman Catholicism in 1852.

Despite gaining grudging acceptance in the Episcopal Church over the course of the 19th century, Anglo-Catholicism has never been far from controversy. Because of the interest of high-church Anglicans in seeking organic unity with the Roman Catholic Church, the ordination of women to the Episcopal priesthood in the 1970s (an action officially unacceptable to Roman Catholicism) again strained relationships between Episcopalians. A significant number of Anglo-Catholics formed an organization known as the Episcopal Synod of America in 1989. The synod sought to preserve the tradition of an all-male ministry by continuing opposition to the ordination of women as priests and bishops.

Although it remains a minority position within the Episcopal Church, Anglo-Catholicism, through the richness of its rituals in worship and its commitment to ancient understandings of Christian belief, still influences American church life today. Its geographic strength lies principally in the upper Midwest, as well as in many urban areas and academic communities.

GHS, Jr.

Bibliography: Owen Chadwick, ed., *The Mind of the Oxford Movement* (London: A. & C. Black, 1960); Clarence A. Walworth, *The Oxford Movement in America* (New York: United States Catholic Historical Society, 1974).

anti-Catholicism   Anti-Catholicism arrived in North America with the first British settlers. They brought with them the anti-Catholicism that was part of the political and social environment in England and enacted into colonial law the anti-Catholic statutes of their homeland. Part of the British colonial project was the creation of a Protestant bulwark against French and Spanish Catholics on the continent. In the course of America's history anti-Catholicism would ebb and flow until 1960, when the election of John F. Kennedy as president brought an end to socially acceptable and overt anti-Catholicism.

Among no group of colonists was anti-Catholic sentiment more complete than the group of Puritans (see PURITANISM) who founded the MASSACHUSETTS BAY COLONY. For them anti-Catholicism was a mission. Their goal was to purify the Church of England of its remaining "Popish" elements. In Massachusetts Bay

This cartoon of Pope Pius IX crumbling the Constitution captured the fears of American Protestants at the height of Irish immigration in the mid-19th century. *(Library of Congress)*

public performance of the Mass was outlawed. Priests and Jesuits found in the colony were to be banished. For those who dared return the penalty was death. Most other colonies placed similar limits on Catholics, denying them the right to vote and to hold public office. New Jersey limited Catholics' right to any state office until 1844, New Hampshire until 1876.

During the American Revolution, anti-Catholicism weakened somewhat due to

American Catholic support for the revolution and the military and economic assistance of Catholic France. This tolerance continued into the postwar period. The Constitution of the new United States prohibited any religious test for national political office. Despite this newfound tolerance, suspicions of Catholicism based on political and social reasons did not disappear. Few feared American-born Catholics, whose spiritual leader, Bishop John CARROLL, was as committed to the republic as to his faith. The fear was of Catholic immigrants who, raised among princes and prelates, came to the new country with no knowledge of republican government or independent thought. Many argued that such immigration must be ended to avoid the destruction of the republic.

The immigrants to whom the anti-Catholics of the 1830s objected were the Irish (see NATIVISM). By that decade the development of what has been called the "Protestant Empire" in America had begun. Into this land of "pure" religion and republican virtue poured a seemingly vulgar, superstitious "horde" from Ireland. To counter this influx, many popular newspapers and journals appeared whose purpose was "to inculcate Gospel doctrines against Romish corruptions. . . ." Among these were the mildly named *Protestant* and the more explicit *Anti-Romanist, Priestcraft Unmasked,* and *Priestcraft Exposed.* Public lectures and meetings on such topics as "Is Popery Compatible with Civil Liberty?" drew large and enthusiastic crowds.

The anti-Catholicism of the 1830s was strengthened by three key events. The first was the publication of Lyman BEECHER's *Plea for the West.* In this pamphlet he called for an organized attempt to convert the Mississippi Valley region to Protestantism to prevent a Papal conspiracy designed to conquer the region for the Catholic Church. The second event was the burning of the Ursuline convent in Charlestown, Massachusetts. A mob, spurred by rumors of immoral convent activities and inflammatory sermons by Protestant ministers, including the visiting Lyman Beecher, attacked the town's Irish quarter, sacking and burning the Ursuline convent and its girls' school.

The 1830s also saw the beginning of an indigenous anticonvent literature; previous examples had been brought from England or the Continent. The 1835 publication of Rebecca Reed's rather tame *Six Months in a Convent* was followed by the salacious *Awful Disclosures of Maria Monk* in 1836. The latter, a repetition of every centuries-old rumor of sex, sadism, and murdered babies behind convent walls, provided fuel for nativist fires and fanned the flames dampened by the shock at the destruction of the Ursuline convent.

Despite the virulence of the anti-Catholicism of the 1830s, the movement did not receive an organized form until the 1841 founding of the American Republican Party on an anti-Catholic, anti-immigrant basis. Although dead as a political organization by 1846, it had a major impact in the intervening five years. In Philadelphia, a series of marches by the party in May and July 1844 resulted in pitched battles between "native Americans" and Irish Catholics. Churches and homes were burned. More than 30 people were killed and hundreds were wounded. Gunfire and artillery duels rocked the city, and martial law was imposed. In New York City similar anti-Catholic agitation by the party brought the threat from Archbishop John Hughes that, "If a single Catholic Church is burned [here]," the entire city will be torched.

The famine in Ireland between 1845 and 1851 and the resulting increase in immigration gave birth to the next major wave of anti-Catholicism. The influx of immigrants generated anti-Catholic and anti-immigrant feelings. Charles B. Allen founded the Organization of the Star Spangled Banner in 1849 to address such concerns. Reorganized by James W. Barker in 1852, the organization became the leading nativist and anti-Catholic organization in the country. All members pledged never to vote for a foreign-born or Catholic candidate. Wealthier and more powerful members of a community worked for the removal of aliens and Catholics from positions of authority and to deny them jobs and public office.

Dedicated to secrecy, the organization was dubbed the Know-Nothings. By 1854 the political branch of the movement, the American Party, dominated state politics in Massachusetts and New York. But the chaos of American politics during the antebellum period attracted voters as much as opposition to foreigners and Catholics. Following the 1856 presidential election, the American Party, unable to deal with the issues of slavery and union, found anti-Catholicism an insufficient unifying issue and disbanded.

While the Civil War gave Americans more immediate concerns than fear of a Catholic takeover, it provided other reasons for anti-Catholicism. Traditional Irish Catholic support for the Democratic Party, Pope Pius IX's rumored support for the Confederacy, and the silence of the bishops on slavery made Catholicism suspect to the Republicans. The Democratic Party was tarred as the party of Rum, Romanism, and Rebellion. While this slogan cost Republicans the presidency in 1886, it served them well as a vote-getting appeal until 1932.

Increasing immigration after the Civil War—with attendant poverty, urban corruption, and rising crime—gave birth to a renewed assault on immigrants in general and Catholics in particular. Attempts to clean up urban politics included attacks on Catholics whose religious views were believed to make them susceptible to manipulation and corruption. The American Protective Association, formed by Henry Bowers in Clinton, Iowa, in 1887 to work for clean city government, exemplifies this movement. Members pledged never to vote for, hire, or strike with a Catholic. In 1893 William J. H. Traynor replaced Bowers as president and, by blaming the depression of 1893 on the Catholics, he turned the A.P.A. into a mass movement. The A.P.A. was moderately successful and found a niche within the Republican Party. But in 1896, divided over William McKinley's presidential candidacy and weakened by the arrest of the national paper's editor for selling salacious literature (the convent literature again), the A.P.A. collapsed like its predecessors.

The collapse of the A.P.A. did not end either anti-Catholicism or nativism. The waves of immigrants arriving in the United States, the fear of political radicalism following World War I, and the rise of "scientific racism"—the notion that certain races were biologically superior to others—only strengthened the movement.

These elements became fused in a revived KU KLUX KLAN. Reorganized in 1915, the Klan grew slowly until the 1920s, when it burgeoned. By 1923 its membership was nearly 3 million. The new Klan opposed radicals, immigrants, Jews, and Catholics. In 1924 its opposition helped deny the Democratic presidential nomination to Al Smith, a Catholic. The eventual nominee, John W. Davis, repudiated the Klan but the election was a foregone conclusion as Calvin Coolidge swept to a landslide victory. By 1928 the Klan was a shell of its former self, destroyed by the convictions of many leaders for murder, fraud, and corruption.

In 1928 Al Smith became the first Roman Catholic nominated for the nation's highest political office by a major party. Smith entered the campaign with much against him. That he was from New York and opposed Prohibition were as significant in his defeat as was his Catholicism. His religion, however, did play a part. During the campaign the liberal *Christian Century* claimed that Smith represented an "alien culture," "an undemocratic hierarchy," and a "foreign potentate." Smith went down in defeat. Although he carried fewer states than Davis had in 1924, his popular vote was greater and, despite his Catholicism, he maintained the Democratic hold on the deep South.

The defeat of Al Smith was the last gasp for organized anti-Catholicism in the United

States. While organizations such as Protestants and Other Americans United for Separation of Church and State continued to look suspiciously at the Catholic Church over issues of church-state separation, anti-Catholicism decreased from the 1930s on. Among other factors, this was due to assimilation of the earlier immigrants, World War II, and the Roman Catholic Church's outspoken anti-Communism. In 1955 Will Herberg could write *Protestant, Catholic, Jew* arguing that these were America's three faiths, and that to the populace at large it did not matter which of the three one believed, just that one did.

The election of John F. Kennedy as president in 1960 finally ended anti-Catholicism as a movement with any respectability. While his religion was an issue and did cost him votes, Kennedy met the religious issue straightforwardly. He opposed federal aid to parochial schools and proclaimed his commitment to the separation of church and state. Kennedy's presidency eased suspicions of Catholicism among average Protestants. These fears were further reduced by the radical transformations in the Roman Catholic Church following VATICAN COUNCIL II. By 1990 Catholicism had become part of mainstream American life and religion. The magnitude of this transformation is illustrated by the fact that between 1964 and 1988 five vice presidential nominees were Roman Catholic. At no time was the issue of religion raised against their candidacies. By 2000 the merest hint of anti-Catholicism could prove politically damaging. When George W. Bush, the leading Republican presidential candidate, spoke at Bob Jones University, he came under a storm of criticism since the school views Catholicism as a dangerous cult. The controversy contributed to his defeat in the Michigan primary the following week and forced him to issue a public apology, acknowledging that he should have used his speech as an opportunity to condemn religious hostility and division.

On the other, hand there remains some truth to Father Andrew Greeley's quip that "anti-Catholicism is the anti-Semitism of the educated class." Opposition to the Catholic Church's policies on abortion, homosexuality, and women's ordination has manifested itself in forms bordering on the anti-Catholicism of the 19th century with disruption of services and disparagement of the Church and its leaders. This, however, has remained a fringe movement among small activist groups, and widespread manifestations of anti-Catholicism in the United States had become almost nonexistent by the end of the 20th century.

EQ

Bibliography: Ray A. Billington, *The Protestant Crusade, 1800–1860: A Study of the Origins of American Nativism* (Gloucester, Mass.: Peter Smith, 1963); John Higham, *Strangers in the Land: Patterns of American Nativism, 1860–1925* (New York: Atheneum, 1963); Allan J. Lichtman, *Prejudice and the Old Politics: The Presidential Election of 1928* (Chapel Hill: University of North Carolina Press, 1979); Jody M. Roy, *Rhetorical Campaigns of the 19th Century Anti-Catholics and Catholics in America* (Lewiston, N.Y.: Edwin Mellen Press, 2000).

anti-Communism   See COMMUNISM.

anticult movement   The term *anticult movement* refers to the organized opposition to a number of NEW RELIGIOUS MOVEMENTS active during recent decades.

America's long history of religious ferment has given rise to a wide variety of movements. Whether indigenous (such as Mormonism [see CHURCH OF JESUS CHRIST OF LATTER-DAY SAINTS]) or imported (see ROMAN CATHOLICISM), the spread of non-Protestant religions often challenged the existing social order. Such challenges in turn generated considerable hostility from those within the social mainstream. Consequently, a long history of religious persecution accompanied the growth of new American religions (see NATIVISM). Well into the 20th century Mormons and JEHOVAH'S WITNESSES were subjected to the legislative harassment, barrages of inflammatory propaganda, and violence that originally greeted Catholic immigrants (see ANTI-CATHOLICISM). While religious PLURALISM has become a more accepted feature of the American cultural landscape during recent decades, voices echoing the themes of Protestant nativism have continued to see America's health threatened by the spread of new religious movements.

During the most recent spurt of religious creativity, growing out of the religious idealism of the COUNTERCULTURE, a number of groups emerged outside the lines of more traditional denominations. Many of these new movements, such as the INTERNATIONAL SOCIETY OF KRISHNA CONSCIOUSNESS or TRANSCENDENTAL MEDITATION, drew upon some form of Asian mysticism. Others, such as SCIENTOLOGY, reinterpreted popular psychology. Many, including the JESUS MOVEMENT, were indigenous; but some, such as the UNIFICATION CHURCH, migrated from abroad, particularly Asia.

Social scientists disagree about the features constituting "cults," as well as the nature of their impact on society. Some refuse to use the term, claiming it is irredeemably polemic. Sociologists, anthropologists, and historians of religion often stressed commonalities between cults and more socially acceptable religious groups. By contrast, a number of psychologists viewed cult members as mentally unhealthy. Responding to the social turmoil of the 1960s (see VIETNAM WAR, CIVIL RIGHTS MOVEMENT), many Americans greeted the proliferation of new religions with fear and anxiety, particularly family members of the mostly young people who joined the movements and assorted churches. These two groups of opponents developed distinct approaches to dealing with cults.

Families of cult members began organizing local and regional groups in the early 1970s to provide each other with information and support as they dealt with the dissonance of values created by their children's participation in unconventional religious movements. By the late 1970s these groups had coalesced into national organizations, such as the Massachusetts-based American Family Foundation, Inc., which were capable of exerting political pressure in a number of states to secure official investigations of cults and legislation to control the spread of "pseudo-religious" movements. Family groups were sometimes aided by "deprogrammers," such as Ted Patrick, coauthor of *Let Our Children Go!* (1976), who used blatantly illegal means, including kidnapping and prolonged restraint, to remove individuals from religious groups, claiming that the religious groups were "brainwashing" their converts. The deprogrammers contended that the only possible explanation for the conversion of largely upper-middle-class youths to new ascetic movements lay in the coercive "mind-control" techniques developed by charismatic leaders. By invoking the supposed success of brainwashing practiced by North Koreans on American prisoners during the Korean War, deprogrammers and mental health professionals gave scientific, medical legitimacy to the fears of parents.

By contrast, more socially accepted denominations, particularly Protestant evangelicals (see EVANGELICALISM) and various Jewish groups, sought to combat the influence of new religions on a theological level. A large literature, produced both by evangelical and Jewish groups concerned over membership loss and by independents such as the Berkeley-based Spiritual Counterfeits Project, emphasized the threats cults posed to orthodox Christian or Jewish belief. The success of new religious groups was said to stem from the breakdown of social and family values, from the work of Satan, and especially from the failure of the churches themselves to spiritually undergird the American public.

The family groups, the deprogrammers, and the churches often worked separately to foster the public's anticult sentiment and were not ultimately successful in their legislative goals. Nevertheless, they were able to create, particularly in the wake of the Jonestown massacre in 1978 (see JONES, JAMES WARREN), a national climate of suspicion regarding new religious movements. As a result, they served to repress religious groups with messages of social transformation and to shore up a culture threatened by religious change.

Popular concerns about "cults" intensified when a seven-week standoff between residents of the heavily armed compound of the Branch Davidians near WACO, Texas, and officials of the Bureau of Alcohol, Tobacco and Firearms ended on April 19, 1993, in an inferno that killed self-styled messiah David Koresh and scores of his followers. While critics of Koresh denounced the Branch Davidian leader as a child molester and religious fanatic who, like Jim Jones, engineered a mass suicide among his followers in order to fulfill prophesies of an apocalyptic clash between good and evil, critics of the federal agents, who first launched a failed attack on the compound and later battered it with armored vehicles and tear gas, charged that the tragedy, which left dozens of children dead, could have been averted had cooler heads prevailed. More specifically, the latter group of critics claimed that the perception of Koresh's Seventh-Day Adventism–influenced group as a dangerous "cult" fueled the fire that resulted in the conflagration.

MG

Bibliography: Anson D. Shupe, Jr., and David G. Bromley, eds., *Anti-Cult Movements in Cross-Cultural Perspective* (New York: Garland, 1994); James Tabor and Eugene Gallagher, *Why Waco?: Cults and the Battle for Religious Freedom in America* (Berkeley: University of California Press, 1995).

Antimission Baptists   See BAPTISTS.

Antinomian Controversy   The Antinomian Controversy experienced by the MASSACHUSETTS BAY COLONY between 1636 and 1637 severely threatened the colony's stability. The controversy stemmed from disagreements over the implications of theological issues involving salvation, human freedom, and human action. These came to the fore due to the activities of Anne HUTCHINSON and the perception by several of the colony's leaders that she and her followers believed that salvation freed one from obligations to follow the moral and civil law.

Hutchinson had a gifted theological mind and held religious discussions in her home. Originally small, these gatherings soon grew to 60 or 70 people, including both men and women. Like all Puritans, she believed human activity was unable to effect individual salvation. Unlike many of her contemporaries, however, Hutchinson rejected the claim that personal behavior was a clue to the presence of grace within a person, the doctrine of preparation. Hutchinson also had a strong sense of the Holy Spirit acting within the saved person. This was so strong that she seemed to imply that such an individual had an immediate knowledge of the will of God. This view threatened the Puritan belief in the Bible as the ultimate source of religious knowledge.

These ideas, or more precisely the application of these ideas, endangered the colony. To a great extent the ideas themselves were within the acceptable range of Puritan theology. But the "antinomians" added the claim that they could recognize who was under the "covenant of grace" and attacked most of the colony's ministers. This challenged the ordered society the Puritans were attempting to create.

The conflicts were not limited to the theological and political. Hutchinson's position as a woman undermined the accepted idea of male dominance and power. The conflict also pitted Boston, where Hutchinson lived, against the rest of the colony. The antinomians' strength, while limited to Boston, was great there and included the colony's governor, Henry Vane, and seemingly the influential minister John COTTON.

The existence of the conflict was obvious as early as October 1636, when some members of the Boston church recommended calling Hutchinson's brother-in-law, John

Wheelwright, as a third minister. John WINTHROP—already suspicious of the individuals involved—was able to prevent this, although it took the greater part of his skill and prestige. In consolation, Wheelwright was placed in charge of a new church in Wollaston, 10 miles outside of Boston. This compromise did not end the conflict, and tensions increased through the winter. A ministerial interrogation of Hutchinson in December accomplished nothing except to divide the parties further. By January 1637 hostilities had reached such proportions that the General Court ordered a day of fasting and prayer to mourn the division.

John Wheelwright took advantage of his fast-day sermon to attack his opponents. He criticized those who argued that sanctification (godly behavior) was proof of justification and claimed that the righteous would have to strike them down: "kill them with the word of the lord." Despite its figurative nature this language smacked of rebellion, and in March the General Court convicted him of sedition, postponing sentencing until its next meeting, which also was to be the occasion for elections to the court.

Many objected to Wheelwright's conviction and petitioned the General Court for a reversal. When the court met on May 17, Governor Henry Vane raised the issue of the petition; others insisted that the election be held first. This created a tumult, and violence was narrowly averted. The election was held and the antinomians saw their supporters defeated, including Henry Vane, who was replaced as governor by John Winthrop.

The petition was dismissed, Wheelwright's sentencing was again postponed, and the court passed a law forbidding the colony's inhabitants to entertain newcomers for longer than three weeks without permission. This was directed at the antinomians, since rumor had it that many attracted to Hutchinson's views were coming from England.

The antinomians were not the only problem facing the new government. The king, hearing rumors of conflict in the colony, sent commissioners to investigate, hoping to find some reason to repeal the colony's charter. The entire colony united against this outside threat, claiming unity and peace. The outbreak of an Indian war (the Pequot War) also distracted the government. This time, however, the response was anything but unified. The Boston church supplied neither money nor men for the war, further antagonizing the outlying towns.

Not until November 1637 was the situation sufficiently settled for the government to turn its attention to Anne Hutchinson and her supporters. In that month the General Court moved against those who had signed the petition supporting Wheelwright. Nearly all were disfranchised and disarmed. Hutchinson was banished. This broke the back of the movement, ending this threat to the colony's peace.

The restoration of internal peace led to magnanimity toward the vanquished. The desire to maintain order and unity had forced the colony's government to act. This same desire allowed the granting of reprieves, as early as 1637, to those who acknowledged their errors and asked forgiveness. In 1639 this was followed by a general amnesty for all "remaining among us, carrying themselves peacefully." As a result no lingering hostilities remained within the colony and social harmony was reestablished.

EQ

Bibliography: Emery John Battis, *Saints and Sectaries: Anne Hutchinson and the Antinomian Controversy in the Massachusetts Bay Colony* (Chapel Hill: University of North Carolina Press, 1962); David D. Hall, *The Antinomian Controversy, 1636–1638: A Documentary History,* 2nd ed. (Durham, N.C.: Duke University Press, 1990).

anti-Semitism Anti-Semitism, hostility toward or hatred of Jews, arrived in the New World with the Europeans. Christopher COLUMBUS's first voyage to America coincided with the expulsion of the Jews from Spain by King Ferdinand I and Queen Isabella. Columbus, in fact, was forced to depart from a minor Spanish port because Cadiz was overflowing with ships transporting the expelled Jews. Christians lived in tension with the Jews, whom they held responsible for Jesus' crucifixion. Spain's expulsion of the Jews was not unique. England had expelled its Jews in 1290, and France in 1306 and again in 1394.

The Europeans brought these anti-Semitic attitudes to the New World. The Inquisition in NEW SPAIN was as active in hunting down Protestants and Jews as in old Spain. French Louisiana (see NEW FRANCE) forbade the practice of any religion other than Catholicism and specifically disallowed the immigration of Jews. By 1758, however, Jews had settled permanently in New Orleans with the knowledge of the French governor.

The colonies of British North America also enforced religious uniformity. Although the English colonists were preeminently concerned with outlawing Catholicism, all dissenting religions suffered. Maryland (see MARYLAND [COLONY]), designed as a refuge for Catholics, limited civil rights to those who did not deny the Trinity, effectively excluding Jews, Muslims, and Unitarians. Rhode Island, the most tolerant colony, allowed freedom of conscience but denied the vote to Catholics and Jews. Colonies that officially denied civil rights to Jews often bent or ignored the rules. South Carolina bestowed citizenship on Joseph Tobias in 1741, allowing him to delete all references to Christianity when taking the oath of citizenship. In 1658 Maryland tried one Jacob Lumbrozo for blasphemy (the only Jew ever tried for that crime in the United States). The case ended with a hung jury, and a few years later Lumbrozo served as a juror in violation of Maryland law limiting such service to Christians.

The ratification of the United States CONSTITUTION in 1788 abolished religious tests for national office. The ratification of the FIRST AMENDMENT in 1791 guaranteed the national government's neutrality in religion. Barriers to equal treatment remained at the state level,

however. While most states acted to remove religious tests, some did so slowly. Laws in Maryland and Rhode Island limited the ability of Jews to hold state office until 1826 and 1842, respectively. The North Carolina Constitution barred nontrinitarians from state office until 1868, although at least one Jew served as a state legislator in violation of the law. No state admitted after the original 13 ever instituted a religious test for political office.

Unlike ANTI-CATHOLICISM, organized anti-Semitism in the United States as a mass movement has been rare and has never achieved the political acceptability anti-Catholicism occasionally did. This, however, is not to deny its vicious reality. Anti-Semitism in the United States has been a constant cultural phenomenon that on occasions has burst into violence.

No act of anti-Semitism has attained the notoriety attendant upon the 1915 lynching in Georgia of Leo Frank. Frank, accused of raping and murdering a young factory worker in Atlanta, was convicted in an atmosphere of anti-Semitic hostility and intimidation. Following the commutation of his sentence, a mob dragged him from the state prison farm and hanged him on August 17, 1915. Although class and regional conflicts played a role in the lynching, Frank's Jewishness provided a convenient target for the hostility. Tom Watson, former Populist senator from Georgia, led the chorus against Frank. In his newspaper, *Jeffersonian*, Watson called for an example to be made of Frank and actively encouraged his murder. This event served as a precursor for the growth of anti-Semitism that emerged in the 1920s, including a resurgence of the KU KLUX KLAN. (See NATIVISM.)

More discreet, and less violent, was the so-called genteel anti-Semitism that developed in the late 1800s and early 1900s. This anti-Semitism led to quotas on Jewish admissions to colleges and universities, halving the Jewish enrollment at Columbia and Harvard. As a result many hotels, restaurants, and clubs refused service to Jews, and some employers refused to hire Jews, especially for management positions.

A series of anti-Semitic articles published by Henry Ford's newspaper, the *Dearborn Independent*, strengthened this anti-Semitism. These articles, drawn from *The Protocols of the Elders of Zion*, a spurious document alleging a Jewish conspiracy to dominate the world, claimed that the Jews used both capitalism and Communism to subvert Christian civilization. Among the many evils allegedly perpetrated by these "elders" was the fixing of the 1919 World Series.

The late 1960s and early 1970s saw growing anti-Semitism among American blacks. Jews and blacks, once political allies against discrimination, began to draw apart due to differing interests over many issues. The Six-Day War of 1967 made many Jewish Americans fear for the state of Israel and strengthened their interest in it. At the same time many African Americans identified their struggle for civil rights as part of a wider movement against European hegemony within the developing world. They, therefore, tended increasingly to support the Palestinians and the Arab states in their conflicts with Israel.

Tensions between Jews and blacks were not eased by presidential candidate Jesse JACKSON's 1984 reference to New York City as a "Hymietown," nor his association with Louis FARRAKHAN, the leader of the NATION OF ISLAM, who once referred to Judaism as a "gutter religion" and maintained contacts with the more extreme Arab leaders including Muammar Qaddafi, the president of Libya. These conflicts were heightened by differences over the role of quotas in affirmative action placement and the diplomatic-military relationship between Israel and South Africa. In fact, survey research shows that, among blacks, unlike the populace at large, anti-Semitism increases with the level of education. Additionally, in certain segments of American liberalism, support for the Arabs in their conflict with Israel occasionally borders on anti-Semitism.

Among most segments of society, anti-Semitism as an active hostility toward Jews has decreased since World War II. The horror created by the Nazi destruction of the European Jews caused much reflection about anti-Semitism and moved active anti-Semitism into the fringes, where it remained a constant among the small, but occasionally violent, Ku Klux Klan, neo-Nazis, and the IDENTITY MOVEMENT. Suspicion on religious grounds remains, as does a level of cultural anti-Semitism. The English language itself carries this. People often speak of being "jewed down" in a continuation of the traditional anti-Semitic view of the Jews as sharp traders. Hypocrisy and self-righteousness are referred to as "pharisaical," from Jesus' traditional opponents. Despite these vestiges, however, anti-Semitism has lessened, and the social and political structures of the United States have served to provide a safer haven for Jews than anywhere except Israel.

EQ

Bibliography: Morton Borden, *Jews, Turks, and Infidels* (Chapel Hill: University of North Carolina Press, 1984); Frederic Cople Jaher, *A Scapegoat in a New Wilderness: The Origins and Rise of Anti-semitism in America* (Cambridge, Mass.: Harvard University Press, 1994); Leonard Dinnerstein, *Antisemitism in America* (New York: Oxford University Press, 1994); ———, *The Leo Frank Case* (New York: Columbia University Press, 1968); David A. Gerber, ed., *Anti-semitism in American History* (Urbana: University of Illinois Press, 1986); Jeffrey S. Gurock, *Anti-semitism in America* (New York: Routledge, 1998); John Higham, *Send These to Me: Jews and Other Immigrants in Urban America* (Baltimore, Md.: Johns Hopkins, 1984); ———, *Strangers in the Land: Patterns of American Nativism, 1860–1925* (New York: Atheneum, 1963).

antislavery   See ABOLITIONISM.

apocalypticism   See ESCHATOLOGY.

Arminianism   Arminianism is named for Jacobus Arminius, a Dutch theologian of the early 17th century, who modified the teachings of John Calvin (see CALVINISM) in order to affirm that human beings were actively involved in the process of attaining salvation. Unlike Calvinism, which taught that God's elect (see ELECTION) are saved without regard to their own actions, Arminian theology stressed that salvation is a matter of choice. Arminianism appealed to the American desire for self-determination and became critical in the development of Protestant thought in the United States, especially within the revival-oriented WESLEYAN TRADITION.

James Harmens (in Latin, Jacobus Arminius) was born in Holland in 1560 and received part of his theological education in Calvin's Geneva. Although still a convinced Calvinist when he was called to minister in Amsterdam in 1587, Arminius gradually came to doubt the "high" Calvinist view on predestination: the belief that, from eternity, God has arbitrarily chosen to save some human beings and damn others. Arminius was formally charged with heresy but acquitted in 1603.

Controversy arose again, however, after Arminius's death, when a group of Dutch clergy became advocates of his views, setting forth their doctrines in the *Remonstrance* of 1610. Reacting against the deterministic logic of Calvinism, the Remonstrants argued that God foreknew, but did not foreordain, who would be saved and who would be damned. God, they said, gives all people the grace to accept eternal salvation. Orthodox Calvinists vigorously reacted against the Remonstrants' position and upheld God's absolute sovereignty over the fate of men and women. Assembled at the Synod of Dort in April 1619, the Dutch Reformed Church officially condemned Arminianism and asserted that human beings are wholly sinful and entirely incapable of saving themselves.

After Dort, many Arminians were banished from Holland, and Arminianism was not granted toleration there until 1795. In England, however, where those beliefs found acceptance as a liberalized version of Calvinist theology, Arminianism continued to be influential throughout the 17th century. While the distinguishing mark of strict Calvinists was their emphasis on divine, not human, initiative in spiritual matters, Arminians stressed the need for piety and moral effort in living a Christian life.

By the mid-18th century in America, Arminianism became the principal theological force impelling two new religious movements that diverged from Calvinist orthodoxy. In its more liberal form, Arminianism influenced the development of Unitarianism (see UNITARIAN CONTROVERSY) out of the Congregational churches of New England. Congregational clergy Charles CHAUNCY and Jonathan MAYHEW of Boston, for example, insisted that God was benevolent and had given Christians the ability to improve themselves morally and spiritually. A theologically conservative version of Arminianism also inspired the heartfelt piety of Methodist founder John Wesley. Wesley taught that Christians should strive for personal conversion and seek to lead lives of visible holiness.

As Arminianism found expression within Protestant EVANGELICALISM in the 19th century, its impact upon American religion proved to be tremendous. The Methodists quickly became the largest Protestant denomination in the United States. Arminianism, moreover, dominated the revivals of the SECOND GREAT AWAKENING, in which Methodist, Baptist, and even Presbyterian evangelists exhorted sinners to abandon evil and come to God. Consistent with the self-reliant spirit of the early republic, revival leaders assumed that individuals had the innate ability to reform themselves and attain moral perfection (see PERFECTIONISM) in the present life.

GHS, Jr.

Bibliography: Carl Bangs, *Arminius: A Study in the Dutch Reformation*, 2nd ed. (Grand Rapids, Mich.: F. Asbury, 1985).

Armstrong, Herbert W. See WORLDWIDE CHURCH OF GOD.

Asbury, Francis (1745–1816)   Francis Asbury was the one of the first two superintendents of the Methodist Episcopal Church and the patriarch of American Methodism. He was an aggressive evangelist who traveled almost incessantly preaching the Gospel and building up his denomination. He became a model for the many intrepid circuit riders who later helped spread Methodism across the American FRONTIER.

Asbury was born at Hamstead Bridge (near Birmingham) in England on August 20, 1745. He received little formal education and was apprenticed to a blacksmith when he was 16 years old. Although raised an Anglican, Asbury experienced a religious conversion around 1763 and became a Methodist lay preacher. He served as an itinerant preacher in England until 1771, when he responded to John Wesley's (see WESLEYAN TRADITION, THE) call for workers to aid the Methodist movement in America. Asbury arrived in Philadelphia in the fall of 1771 and continued his itinerancy in the New World.

Asbury stayed in America during the War for Independence, the only missionary appointed by Wesley to remain there throughout that critical period. Since Wesley himself opposed the American Revolution, Methodists were often suspected of Tory sympathies. Still, Asbury refused to return to England. When the war ended, he emerged as the acknowledged leader of the American movement and, with Thomas Coke, was appointed by Wesley as a superintendent of the Methodists in the newly independent United States.

In 1784 Coke, who had been ordained by Wesley in violation of Anglican practice, arrived from England with authority to ordain Asbury. Asbury insisted, however, that a gathering be held to discuss the implications of such an action. Now known as the "Christmas Conference," the meeting called by Asbury was convened in Baltimore on December 24, 1784. At that conference, the Methodist Episcopal Church was officially formed, separate from the Episcopal Church, which at the same

Francis Asbury, the first bishop of the Methodist Episcopal Church. Asbury's support of circuit riders and camp meetings enabled Methodism to spread quickly into frontier country.

time was organizing itself apart from the Church of England. Asbury and Coke were unanimously elected superintendents, a title Asbury later changed to "bishop" contrary to Wesley's wishes. Coke and two other English Methodist ministers, in succession, ordained Asbury as deacon, elder, and superintendent.

Asbury used his position to foster church growth and build Methodism into the most vigorous American denomination of the early 19th century. He proved to be an indefatigable leader, crossing the Appalachian Mountains more than 60 times and helping establish Methodism in the upper South. Asbury recognized the value of "circulation," prodding Methodist clergy to reach out for converts in even the most remote locations. He was also an early advocate of camp meetings, which became the most important institution of Methodist outreach on the frontier. He supported these open-air revivals at which participants camped for several days on the site where religious exercises were held. Both circuit riding and camp meetings became keys to the Methodists' phenomenal success.

Asbury is estimated to have traveled 300,000 miles in the course of his ministerial career, delivering 16,500 sermons, ordaining 4,000 preachers, and presiding over more than 200 annual conferences. Although he accepted William McKendree to be his associate bishop in 1808, he remained active until the end of his life. Still functioning as a missionary, Asbury died at Spotsylvania, Virginia, on March 31, 1816.

GHS, Jr.

Bibliography: Frank Baker, *From Wesley to Asbury: Studies in Early American Methodism* (Durham, N.C.: Duke University Press, 1976); L. C. Rudolph, *Francis Asbury* (Nashville: Abingdon Press, 1966).

Assemblies of God   The Assemblies of God is the largest Pentecostal (see PENTECOSTALISM) denomination in the world and one of the fastest growing churches in the United States. It was organized in April 1914 when 300 leaders gathered in Hot Springs, Arkansas, and formed the General Council, which became the denomination's governing board. The Assemblies of God has traditionally asserted that speaking in tongues is evidence of a person's having been baptized by the Holy Spirit. The church also affirms the premillennial (see PRE-MILLENNIALISM) coming of Jesus Christ, a distinctive belief of modern American EVANGELICALISM.

The Pentecostal movement emerged out of American Protestantism in the early 20th century. The AZUSA STREET REVIVAL, a period of intense spiritual excitement at a storefront church in Los Angeles, sparked the growth of Pentecostalism after 1906. Pentecostals united around one central conviction: Genuine conversion is represented by a miraculous experience known as the baptism of the Holy Spirit.

The ability to speak in tongues, that is, uttering ecstatic languages claimed to be intelligible only to God (also called *glossolalia*), was generally considered evidence that a person had received Spirit baptism.

The Assemblies of God blended together members of several Pentecostal groups in the American Midwest and Southwest. The largest contingent came from followers of Charles F. Parham's Apostolic Faith movement in Texas. The tongues phenomenon had first appeared in 1901 at the Bible institute Parham founded in Topeka, Kansas. The Apostolic Faith missions spread, and several thousand people eventually espoused Parham's type of Pentecostalism. In 1905 he opened a school in Houston, Texas. That institution not only served as the center of Parham's movement in southeast Texas, it also trained William J. Seymour, the preacher who led the great revival in Los Angeles.

William Durham was the most significant figure in the shaping of the Assemblies of God. Durham had attended the Azusa revival, where in March 1907 he experienced Spirit baptism. He was responsible for bringing a distinctly non-Wesleyan view of SANCTIFICATION into the Pentecostal movement. His beliefs were far closer to Reformed theology, which understood holiness as a lifelong process that was not completed before death, than to the Wesleyan tradition, which emphasized the attainment of spiritual perfection in the present life. Durham was afraid that overemphasis on the Holy Spirit would overshadow Christ's redemption of the world on the cross, and he rejected the idea, common among Pentecostals, that human sin was eradicated when a believer experienced sanctification through Spirit baptism. Although Durham died in the summer of 1912, he helped articulate many key theological differences between the Assemblies of God and other Pentecostal denominations.

Those who founded the Assemblies of God initially disliked the idea of becoming an established denomination and preferred simply to remain a religious movement. They desired only a voluntary confederation of churches and rejected the idea of promulgating a common creed. They eventually realized, however, that an organization could provide needed discipline, guard against the growth of unorthodox theological views, and prevent Pentecostalism from falling prey to charlatans and fanatics. As a consequence, a Statement of Fundamental Truths was adopted in 1916, and the process of creating a formal structure was completed in 1927, when a constitution was ratified.

An early schism occurred after a dispute about baptism. Members of the church debated whether believers should be baptized in the name of the Trinity (Father, Son, and Holy Spirit), as the New Testament Gospel of Matthew prescribed, or only in the name of Jesus, as the New Testament Book of Acts suggested. Eventually, some denied belief in the traditional Christian doctrine of the threefold nature of God. They argued instead that there is but one person in the Godhead—Jesus Christ. This "Jesus only" faction (also known as the "Oneness Pentecostals") was expelled from the Assemblies of God in 1916. Many years later, that group organized themselves as the United Pentecostal Church, International.

The Assemblies of God expanded rapidly over the middle decades of the 20th century, and the denomination gradually entered the mainstream of American religious life. The church began with a membership of 6,000 in 1914. It numbered just under 50,000 in 1926 and nearly 300,000 at the end of World War II. This growth, and the accompanying upward social mobility of the denomination's membership, challenged the assumptions of an earlier era when Pentecostalism was considered an exclusively antiestablishment faith. Shortly before World War II, the Assemblies of God also affiliated with the NATIONAL ASSOCIATION OF EVANGELICALS, an action that symbolized the denomination's thorough acculturation and identification with conservative American Protestantism. Moreover, the defrocking of scandalous televangelists Jim Bakker and Jimmy Swaggart in the 1980s reveals how much the Assemblies of God now wished to project a more moderate, less flamboyant public image.

That effort is being frustrated, however, by the success of one member church in Pensacola, Florida. Since the summer of 1995 the Brownsville Assembly of God Church has been the site of the controversial Brownsville Revival and a mecca of sorts for world Pentecostalism. Led by evangelist Steve Hill and Pastor John Kilpatrick, the Brownsville Revival draws thousands of attendees daily, many from overseas. According to church officials, millions of visitors have attended the church and hundreds of thousands have responded to altar calls by accepting Jesus Christ as their savior. Those numbers may be inflated, but the outpouring is nonetheless one of America's most powerful revivals since the events on Azusa Street in 1906. Still, the Brownsville Revival has drawn criticisms from many quarters for the unusual manifestations that take place there. Those manifestations, which include uncontrollable shaking in addition to more standard Pentecostal fare such as speaking in tongues, are defended by Brownsville Revival partisans as manifestations of the return of "Pentecost" to modern-day Pentecostalism.

Like the Brownsville Revival, the Assemblies of God has seen tremendous recent growth. The denomination has benefited not only from support among its traditional constituency of European Americans but also from new Hispanic and Asian-American congregations. In 2000 the Assemblies of God reported just under 2.5 million American members and approximately 30 million worldwide. Its weekly newspaper, *The Pentecostal Evangelical*, had a circulation of 268,000.

GHS, Jr.

Bibliography: Edith L. Blumhofer, *Restoring the Faith: The Assemblies of God, Pentecostalism, and American Culture* (Champaign: University of Illinois Press, 1993); Margaret M. Poloma, *The Assemblies of God at the Crossroads: Charisma and*

Institutional Dilemmas (Knoxville: University of Tennessee Press, 1989); Steve Robey, *Revival in Brownsville: Pensacola, Pentecostalism, and the Power of American Revivalism* (Nashville, Tenn.: Thomas Nelson, 1999) http://www.ag.org (Assemblies of God); http://www.brownsville-revival.org (Brownsville Revival).

assimilation and resistance, Native American

Native people faced what often seemed like two separate options in dealing with the Europeans and Americans: either adopt the ways of the newcomers or resist. Given the fluidity of culture, in practice these options frequently overlap. Thus the long history of assimilation is also one of creative adaptation, as is the equally long history of resistance.

In the terms set by the myth of MANIFEST DESTINY, native peoples in the United States were expected to "pass away," as one 19th-century poet put it: "Like the fleeting years and days/Like all things that soon decay." This viewpoint shaped American perceptions of the Indians' only two options: either abandoning their cultures and learning the ways of the newcomers or dissolving in the ruins of disease, warfare, and degeneracy. American leaders often accepted the underlying assumption of both, that native people were passive beings, incapable of directing their own destinies. Thus the frequent portrayals of Indian defeat in American culture excited either justification or melancholy.

However, this viewpoint, shaping numerous portrayals of native life both past and present, obscures the creative strategies Native Americans have relied upon to cope with the changes stemming from the European colonial movement into the Americas and makes the steady advance of colonial power seem far more inevitable in hindsight than it actually was. It also leaves inexplicable the dramatic population recovery and cultural/political resurgence achieved in the 20th century. From an all-time low of 250,000 in 1890, the 1990 census indicated nearly 2 million Native Amer-

icans, one-quarter still on reservations. But even in modern urban centers, native people have often exerted considerable energy on retaining or revamping tradition.

Assimilation refers to the various ways in which members of a subordinate group come to adopt the practices and views of a more dominant group. In American history the campaign for assimilation rested on the assumption that "savages" would become "civilized" (see MISSIONS, FOREIGN). While rejecting the racism inherent in this idea, social scientists and historians have been concerned to understand the ways in which native people have adopted the ways of the dominant order. *Resistance*, conveying the image of "hostile" or "renegade" warriors, carries some of the same problems but also indicates ways in which subordinate groups might reject the values or modes of life held by the dominant culture. Distinct in theory, the two can be closely related in practice. Given that cultural and religious identity is always a fluid thing, the strong polarity suggested by the terms *assimilation* and *resistance* might be questioned.

Native people were encouraged, and sometimes forced, to accept various features of the European-American world. Through missions, it was hoped Indians would abandon tribal religions in favor of Christianity. But Christianity also went hand in hand with other parts of a colonizing culture. Eastern tribes, such as the Hurons in the 1640s, received the gospel message along with the lure of the European fur market, which they often accepted in conjunction, even if French Jesuits themselves chose to distinguish between the fruits of faith and those of wealth. Campaigning for the souls of individual Indians, missionaries often drove a wedge into native kinship networks. Quakers (see FRIENDS, RELIGIOUS SOCIETY OF) instructing the Senecas in European agriculture in the 1790s sought to replace Seneca family structure with their own.

In the years following the CIVIL WAR, the concerted effort to assimilate Indians relied heavily upon education. By 1889 every reservation in the country had a boarding school, often patterned on the Carlisle Industrial Training School, founded by retired Captain Richard Pratt in 1879. While many Indian children graduated from these schools, some to choose such prosperous careers as doctors, lawyers, and actors, many more returned home, "going back to the blanket," as Pratt called it, or were forced to accept menial work. The schools had a severe impact on children and on communal life. Support for a mission and a federal school at Oraibi by Hopi leaders in the early 1880s resulted in a split between the Bear and the Spider clans and the eventual breakup of the community as a whole.

While attendance at boarding school or acceptance of the new religion suggests the obliteration of older values and practices, certainly the frequently stated goal of educators and missionaries, this did not often happen in total. Students employed the powers of the weak to resist their teachers. Christianity rarely proved capable of erasing older religious worldviews. Rather, native members of a mission church took up the new faith selectively, quietly ignoring those ideas that made little sense, or reinterpreting them in light of traditional religious knowledge. Many significant popular movements, such as that begun by HANDSOME LAKE, or the more recent NATIVE AMERICAN CHURCH, combined Christian themes and traditional practices into new religions. In the PLURALISM of the 20th century, native Christians frequently demonstrated the power to influence Christian symbols, rituals, and institutions.

Some scholars distinguish movements like peyote religion, which often focus on individual redemption within the new social order of reservation life or urban America, from those that seek social transformation. The most extreme forms of resistance to Euro-American culture are the transformative movements leading to war and revolt. Revolts often emerged after a generation or two of contact

had put the new colonial system in place. Forging pan-Indian alliances in the period immediately preceding the AMERICAN REVOLUTION and lasting into the 1820s, prophetic leaders among eastern tribes (see NATIVE AMERICAN RELIGIONS: EASTERN WOODLANDS) like the Seminole Osceola, the Delaware Neolin, the Shawnee Tenskwatawa, the Winnebago Wabokieshiek, and a group of Muskogees rallied large numbers of their people in armed opposition to colonial policies, land cessions, and the influence of white culture. Undergirding many of these movements were religious visions of a future in which Indian prosperity would be restored as a result of common participation in these inspired revolts.

The Plains Wars (see NATIVE AMERICAN RELIGIONS: PLAINS), during which members of numerous western tribes sought to halt western expansion in the post–Civil War years, are often portrayed as the last gasp of Native American resistance. However, throughout the 20th century, individuals, tribes, and increasing numbers of supratribal voluntary associations have worked both to resist the influence of the dominant society and to gain control of the resources necessary for tribes to exercise autonomy. Such efforts are visible at a number of levels in the years since WORLD WAR II. Newer organizations such as the National Indian Youth Council, the Native American Rights Fund, and the older National Congress of American Indians (established in 1944), drew upon growing pools of native people trained in law, the social sciences, or public administration, taking on the role of pursuing tribal needs directly in Congress, often bypassing the United States government's Bureau of Indian Affairs.

In the years after John Collier lifted the official bans on native religion (see AMERICAN INDIAN RELIGIOUS FREEDOM ACT), traditional religious leaders reemerged from the relative seclusion into which they had been forced by assimilative administrators. These traditional leaders came to develop alliances with younger activists, seeking to avoid the bureaucratic entanglements of their seniors. Members of the American Indian Movement, formed in 1962 in Minneapolis, Minnesota, took a nationally prominent role in promoting an Indian form of activism, somewhat analogous to the CIVIL RIGHTS MOVEMENT. Undergirded by a pan-Indian spirituality derived in part from the influence of Lakota and Anishenabeg (Chippewa) members, AIM worked in cities to extract Indians from the confines of urban poverty and on reservations to restore tribal sovereignty. With a militant rhetoric derived from the Plains Wars, AIM forced a number of confrontations with authorities between 1968 and 1975, such as the long siege at Wounded Knee in 1973. AIM's dramatic flair insured it substantial media coverage, but also created lasting tensions among Native Americans of various ideological viewpoints, at times alienating the very traditionalists it claimed to represent.

In many ways, assimilation and resistance work together. Indian leaders have developed increased abilities to make use of dominant political institutions in order to achieve the goals of tribal autonomy and cultural resurgence advocated by AIM and others in the 1960s. Recent decades have also seen a renewed commitment among many Indians to preserve or rekindle important elements of traditional religious life while also promoting economic development and education.

MG

Bibliography: Stephen Cornell, *The Return of the Native: American Indian Political Resurgence* (New York: Oxford University Press, 1988); Gregory Evans Dowd, *A Spirited Resistance: The North American Indian Struggle for Unity, 1745–1815* (Baltimore: Johns Hopkins University Press, 1992); Frederick E. Hoxie, *A Final Promise: The Campaign to Assimilate the Indian, 1880–1920* (Lincoln: University of Nebraska Press, 1984); Paul Chaat Smith and Robert Warrior, *Like a Hurricane: The Indian Movement from Alcatraz to Wounded Knee* (New York: New Press, 1996).

atheism   Atheism, literally the absence of belief in God, has always been a minority viewpoint in American culture. Nevertheless, its influence can be seen throughout American life. Free thinkers helped shape the Constitution's general silence in regard to religious belief, insuring that religious groups would avoid contributing to conflict over the basic structure of American government. In the years after the CIVIL WAR free thinkers were active in a number of social reform movements, and during the 20th and 21st centuries their organizations often pressured the courts to protect religious liberty and prevent the surreptitious growth of a religious establishment.

Atheism may well be possible in all times and places. But in Western culture, public acknowledgment of unbelief was quite rare until the ENLIGHTENMENT. Its growing acceptability in the ensuing centuries was due in part to the great cultural shifts that formed the basis of modern society: the Protestant Reformation and the rise of capitalism and modern science. The numerous reformers, scientists, revolutionaries, and entrepreneurs who gradually loosened the hold of the Catholic Church over the totality of European culture were certainly not themselves given to unbelief. Nevertheless, in seeking to make the public standards of political order, scientific truth, and even faith itself independent from the authority of a particular religion, they created the possibility of doubting the existence of God.

In America, unbelief took a different course than in Europe, where it was fueled by popular resentment over the Catholic Church, particularly, as in revolutionary France, over the Church's support of the *ancien régime*. The emergence of religious freedom in the United States (see ESTABLISHMENT, RELIGIOUS), while gradual, has meant that those who choose not to believe are free to live without religious interference. Consequently, unbelievers have been under no obligation to engage in religion, nor have they been compelled to organize their own institutions, rituals, or public forms of expression in order to counter religion.

Nevertheless, American free thinkers, a phrase that gained currency in the early 18th century among English dissenters and which was adopted by American deists, often found a need to create societies of their own. Some notable leaders in the postrevolutionary era, such as Thomas JEFFERSON, Benjamin Franklin, and George Washington (see AMERICAN REVOLUTION), while intensely critical of religious orthodoxy, maintained nominal relations with various Protestant churches. Others, however, such as radical Tom PAINE and ex-Baptist Elihu Palmer, sought to organize fellow rationalists. Palmer, for instance, sought to form a "Druid" group and in the end drew limited support from a small number of ex-Masons (see FREEMASONRY). While free thought made little headway as a movement, revolutionary leaders drew upon the rationalistic, Enlightenment worldview itself in framing the Constitution, which avoided any reference to God as a founder of the new republic.

During the years prior to the Civil War, critiques of religious orthodoxy often came from movements that were themselves religious, such as TRANSCENDENTALISM, or alternative communitarian movements such as the SHAKERS and the Mormons (see CHURCH OF JESUS CHRIST OF LATTER-DAY SAINTS; COMMUNITARIANISM). One such community, New Harmony, founded by socialist Robert Dale OWEN, explicitly opposed religion. Owen traveled widely, debating religious leaders, and in the process established a pattern of mutual dependence that characterized the continuing relations between the voices of belief and unbelief. Religious leaders debated free thinkers in public forums, each attracting attention to themselves by portraying the other as the enemy of civilization. As a consequence, while free thought produced little direct impact on public consciousness, many were made aware of the intellectual possibility of atheism by the churches themselves.

American culture took a secular turn following the Civil War (see SECULARISM). With the creation of research universities such as Johns Hopkins, the growth of knowledge proceeded with little reference to the traditional religious outlooks undergirding the previously dominant church-supported colleges. Academic professionals saw their new careers as based on the unbiased search for truth, and in the post-Darwinian climate, science seemingly became the enemy of religion (see CREATIONISM; EVOLUTION; SCIENCE AND RELIGION). By the end of the century universities, both state-supported and private, had secured organizational autonomy from religious bodies, and in the ensuing decades many on their faculties have retained a suspicion of religion.

In addition to the secular atmosphere of the university, Americans were exposed to free thought through a variety of public figures, such as Samuel Clemens (Mark Twain). Robert Green INGERSOLL and H. L. MENCKEN gained notoriety espousing the cause of free thought, debunking what they saw as the stifling, antiquated religious atmosphere of their times.

Free thinkers also began to organize somewhat more effectively in the late 19th century. Most enduring has been the ETHICAL CULTURE movement, organized by Felix ADLER, a secular-leaning Reform rabbi, in 1876. Immigrants from Europe, themselves inheritors of the antireligious, socialist impulse that swept Europe in the 1840s, often established their own centers for free thought. Thus Czechs, Germans, and Finns all created lodges in which free thought, radical social criticism, and ethnic culture could flourish in the new land. But the anticlericalism that sustained these groups in Europe had little power in America's climate of religious disestablishment. In addition, the growing American labor movement, to which many immigrants were attracted, did not depend on hostility toward religion, and the groups evaporated over time.

For the most part, the secularism of American institutions, though undergirded by what has become known as CIVIL RELIGION, and the wide-ranging PLURALISM that characterizes American religious life in the 21st century, has meant that free thought has little to push against, little institutional resistance to confront. While groups such as the AMERICAN HUMANIST ASSOCIATION, the American Association for the Advancement of Atheism (founded in 1925), and American Atheists (see O'HAIR, MADALYN MURRAY) have held on over the decades, they draw few members, likely numbering less than 10,000. By contrast, surveys indicate that the overwhelming majority of the American population continues to retain some kind of belief in a deity.

While atheism has perhaps remained most noticeable through its adherents' willingness to engage in public debate with religious figures, or as a foil for those religious groups seeking to reform the society, free thought has exerted enormous influence on American culture. The continued secularism of universities in a knowledge-dependent society insures that those educated in public settings gain exposure to critical assumptions about the world inherited from the rationalist tradition espoused by free thinkers. It has frequently been the free thinker, such as the lawyer Clarence Darrow (see SCOPES TRIAL), who has fought to preserve religious liberty and prevent the de facto establishment of religion. In addition, numerous free thinkers, from Jefferson on down, have offered powerful arguments that the preservation of freedom and dignity in America is not dependent upon organized religion, which has a checkered record in that regard.

MG

Bibliography: Stow Persons, *Free Religion: An American Faith* (New Haven: Yale University Press, 1947); James Turner, *Without God, Without Creed: The Origins of Unbelief in America* (Baltimore: Johns Hopkins University Press, 1985); www.atheists.org (American Atheists, Inc.).

Azusa Street revival   The Azusa Street revival, which began in April 1906 under the leadership of Holiness minister William J. SEYMOUR, signaled the emergence of PENTECOSTALISM as an important force in American religion.

The revival lasted three years and drew worshippers to a poor section of Los Angeles where thousands were engulfed by a new form of religious enthusiasm.

Seymour, the son of freed slaves, was an itinerant preacher who espoused the doctrine of entire SANCTIFICATION, the belief that Christians could be set free from the power of sin and attain holiness in the present life. He attended Charles F. Parham's Bible institute in Houston, Texas, in 1905 and adopted Parham's Pentecostal views. Seymour accepted speaking in tongues as the definitive evidence that a person had been sanctified. He traveled to Los Angeles in January 1906. Three months later the group he led experienced its first outbreak of glossolalia, the ecstatic, incoherent speech that characterized the phenomenon of "tongues." When the private home where religious services were held proved too small for the crowds flocking to the revival, Seymour moved the meetings to an old building at 312 Azusa Street, now considered the birthplace of the Pentecostal movement.

At the height of the revival excitement, worship at the Azusa Street Mission was held three times a day, beginning at midmorning and continuing past midnight. Miraculous healings and a general spiritual delirium marked the worship. The revival was also noted for its interracial makeup, a feature some observers saw as a special sign of divine favor.

Opinions about the revival were mixed, however, even among Pentecostals. Charles Parham, for example, described the meetings as "Holy Ghost Bedlam," in which worshippers "pulled all of the stunts common in old camp meetings among colored folks." On the other hand, Jennie Moore, the first woman to speak in tongues and later Seymour's wife, gave a positive report: "The power of God fell and I was baptized in the Holy Ghost and fire. It seemed as if a vessel broke within me and water surged through my being, which when it reached my mouth came out in a torrent of speech."

The revival on Azusa Street continued unabated for three years, before fervor began to wane and Seymour himself lost influence. Seymour died in 1922, and although services took place at the mission until 1929, by that time the church's congregation had become exclusively black. The city of Los Angeles eventually condemned the building, and it was torn down in 1931.

GHS, Jr.

Bibliography: Robert Mapes Anderson, *Vision of the Disinherited: The Making of American Pentecostalism* (New York: Oxford University Press, 1979); Fred T. Corum, ed., *Like as of Fire: A Reprint of the Azusa Street Documents* (Springfield, Mo.: Gospel Publishing House, 1981); Robert R. Owens, *Speak to the Rock: The Azusa Street Revival, Its Roots and Its Message* (Lanham, Md.: University Press of America, 1998).

—B—

Backus, Isaac (1724–1806) Isaac Backus was a Baptist (see BAPTISTS) minister and champion of the separation of church and state in the late 18th century. Converted during the GREAT AWAKENING, he concluded that his experience of divine grace required him to separate from the Congregational church to which he belonged. Backus was eventually rebaptized and formed a new Baptist congregation in Middleborough, Massachusetts. He spent the rest of his life trying to win freedom for his church from the legal constraints of the Massachusetts religious establishment.

Backus was born on a farm in Norwich, Connecticut, on January 9, 1724. He received no formal education. Although raised conventionally as a Congregationalist, Backus said that his dramatic conversion at age 17 enabled him to see clearly for the first time "the riches of God's grace." This experience soon brought him into conflict with his church. Since the passage of the HALF-WAY COVENANT of 1662, it had been the custom in New England to accept morally upright adults who had never undergone a conversion experience as partial members of congregations. They were allowed to come to worship and bring their children for baptism, but they did not receive communion or enjoy voting privileges until they could testify that God had spiritually regenerated them. Backus became convinced that this practice was wrong and that only adults who had experienced the "divine light" could really be considered Christians.

As a consequence of their vocal opposition to the Half-way Covenant, Backus and others emerged as a party of "Separates." Backus became an itinerant evangelist and formed a church of like-minded believers in Middleborough, Massachusetts, where he was ordained to the ministry in 1748. His study of the Bible and his beliefs about church membership, however, led him further outside the bounds of Congregationalism. Concluding that only the baptism of consenting adults by immersion could be considered a valid Christian rite, Backus openly adopted Baptist principles. In 1756, a small remnant of his congregation withdrew and organized a Baptist church in Middleborough.

Baptists had no legal place within the New England church establishment. At this time, town governments in Massachusetts assessed all taxpayers for support of a minister and maintenance of a church building. Not only were the separate Congregationalist and Baptist congregations unsupported by their town governments, their members were often forced to support financially churches they had repudiated. As the principal Baptist spokesman, Backus argued in various tracts and petitions that state-supported churches corrupted true Christianity. In his most famous work, *An Appeal to the Public for Religious Liberty Against the Oppression of the Present Day* (1773), Backus asked for the full separation of church and state. This idea became a reality on the national level in the adoption of the FIRST AMENDMENT to the United States Constitution in 1791.

Since the state religious establishment in Massachusetts did not officially end until 1833, Backus continued to lobby indefatigably against the civil control of religion long after the American Revolution. He also served for 50 years as minister of the First Baptist Church in Middleborough. At the time of his death, Backus was recognized as one of the greatest advocates of American religious freedom. He died at Middleborough on November 20, 1806.

GHS, Jr.

Bibliography: William G. McLoughlin, *Isaac Backus and the American Pietistic Tradition* (Boston: Little, Brown, 1967).

Baconianism   See SCOTTISH COMMON SENSE REALISM.

Bahá'í faith   The Bahá'í faith is a world religion founded in 1863 that teaches the oneness of God, the oneness of the world's major religions, and the oneness of humanity. It claims a new divine revelation that will provide the foundation for a world civilization. The Bahá'í religion was started by an Iranian named Mírzá Husayn 'Alí Bahá'u'lláh (1817–1892), who claimed he was a messenger of God. This claim—blasphemy to most Muslims—led to his exile and imprisonment by the Ottoman Turkish government for 29 years. He wrote extensively; more than 15,000 of his works, primarily letters (though some are of book length), are extant. Together they constitute the central body of Bahá'í scripture.

Bahá'u'lláh's writings contain a detailed theology that describes the nature of God, messengers of God, humanity, the human soul, and the nature of the spiritual quest. An important aspect of his theology is the idea that God progressively reveals truth to humanity through a series of messengers, and that the existing world religions were all founded by divine messengers. Bahá'u'lláh's writings include numerous prayers for Bahá'ís to say for their spiritual growth, for physical healing, for the development of their families, and for the improvement of society. They also describe basic Bahá'í religious practices similar to the five pillars of Islam, such as obligatory prayer, an annual period of fasting, pilgrimage, and contribution of a percentage of one's surplus income to the faith. The scriptures outline basic institutions for organizing the Bahá'í religion after Bahá'u'lláh's death. They specify an elaborate set of social reform teachings based on the principle of the oneness of humanity, such as racial and ethnic equality and integration, equality of the sexes, universal compulsory education, and creation of international political, economic, and legal systems that would prevent war and gradually eliminate the extremes of wealth and poverty.

After Bahá'u'lláh's death his son 'Abdu'l Bahá (1844–1921), whom he appointed to be his successor, elaborated on Bahá'u'lláh's teachings and offered authorized interpretations. 'Abdu'l-Bahá is not considered a messenger or prophet by Bahá'ís, but his writings (which are almost twice as extensive as Bahá'u'lláh's) are also considered a part of Bahá'í scripture. 'Abdu'l-Bahá appointed a successor, Shoghi Effendi (1897–1957), whose writings are also considered binding and authoritative. In 1963 the Universal House of Justice was first elected, as called for by Bahá'u'lláh. As head of the Bahá'í faith, the House of Justice is empowered to legislate on matters not covered by the Bahá'í scriptures. The body's nine members, who reside in Haifa, Israel, are elected every five years by the members of the national spiritual assemblies (the national Bahá'í governing bodies).

Under Bahá'u'lláh, the Bahá'í religion spread beyond Shi'ite Islam, from which it arose, to include Sunni Muslims, Jews, Zoroastrians, Christians, and Buddhists. As a result of the migration of a Bahá'í of Lebanese Christian background to Chicago, the first Americans became converts in 1894; by 1899 Chicago had more than 700 Bahá'ís. From Chicago the Bahá'í religion spread to 24 states by 1900. Chicago has remained the center of Bahá'í activity in North America, where a House of

The Bahá'í House of Worship in Wilmette, Illinois, is a national landmark. *(Courtesy of the National Spiritual Assembly of the Bahá'ís of the United States)*

Worship, begun in 1903 and completed in 1953, was built in the suburb of Wilmette. The headquarters of the Bahá'í faith in the United States is also located in Wilmette.

Bahá'í growth in the United States has gone through several distinct phases. From 1894 to 1905, Bahá'í efforts to teach their religion to the public focused on the fulfillment of prophecy, because Bahá'ís venerate the Bible and view its prophecies as referring to the coming of Bahá'u'lláh. 'Abdu'l-Bahá's nine-month visit to the United States in 1912 shifted the emphasis to Bahá'u'lláh's social reform principles. The initial biblically centered message attracted disillusioned white evangelical Protestants to the religion; the latter approach brought in more Catholics, Jews, and black Protestants. Lack of organization, however, limited membership in the United States to about 1,500.

In 1922, Shoghi Effendi began his leadership of the Bahá'í faith by inaugurating a new emphasis on local and national organization, an effort that in 10 years saw a doubling of the American Bahá'í community. Shoghi Effendi replaced the poor and occasionally confusing English translations of Bahá'í scriptures with new, improved translations and wrote numerous epistles clarifying basic Bahá'í teachings. He launched a series of international growth plans, for which the United States Bahá'í com-

munity was given the lion's share of the goals. By 1963 the United States had 10,000 Bahá'ís.

The late 1960s and early 1970s saw two important developments in the American Bahá'í community: outreach to America's youth counterculture and door-to-door teaching of the faith in the rural South. The former caused Bahá'í membership rolls to swell in the years 1969 to 1974. The latter brought 10,000 African Americans into the Bahá'í faith in South Carolina in two years. Probably another 5,000 blacks became Bahá'ís in other parts of the South. By 1974, the American Bahá'í community had 60,000 members.

The rest of the 1970s saw much slower growth and loss of some of the converts; by 1979, membership stood at 75,000. The 1980s saw relatively slow attraction of the middle class to the Bahá'í faith in the United States, although Native Americans on reservations continued to become Bahá'ís, Hispanics were attracted in larger numbers, and rural blacks continued to join. Further diversifying the American Bahá'í community was the arrival of about 10,000 Iranian Bahá'í refugees, who fled persecution in their native land. Vietnamese, Cambodians, and Laotians who were Bahá'ís in their home country or converted in refugee camps also came to the United States by the thousands.

Since 1920, converts from the middle classes have come more from the secular-minded who are concerned about social issues, although seekers of various religious backgrounds remain significant. American Bahá'ís have been very active in efforts to heal racism since the turn of the century, and in this area they have had a modest impact on American society. A smaller but growing focus of Bahá'í attention has been the peace movement.

There are more than 5 million Bahá'ís worldwide; the Bahá'í faith may be the most geographically widespread religion in the world after Christianity. In the United States, there were 137,000 Bahá'ís in 2000.

RHS

Bibliography: William S. Hatcher and J. Douglass Martin, *The Bahá'í faith: The Emerging Global Religion*, rev. ed. (Wilmette, Ill.: Bahá'í Publishing Trust, 1998); Moojan Momen, ed., *Studies in Bábí and Bahá'í History, Volume One* (Los Angeles: Kalimát Press, 1982); Robert Stockman, *The Bahá'í faith in America: Origins, 1892–1900*, Vol. 1 (Wilmette, Ill.: Bahá'í Publishing Trust, 1985); www.bahai.org (The Bahá'í World).

Ballou, Hosea (1771–1852)   One of the most prominent early leaders and ministers of UNIVERSALISM in New England, Hosea Ballou helped to popularize and systematize Universalist ideas in the late 18th and early 19th century. The youngest son of a Baptist farmer and preacher who espoused strict Calvinist beliefs, Ballou was born in Richmond, New Hampshire, in 1771 and studied briefly at local Quaker academies. Shortly after experiencing a conversion at age 19, he came under the influence of itinerant preachers of Universalism as well as the writings of Ethan Allen. Ballou began to preach Universalist principles in 1790 in Rhode Island, Massachusetts, and later in Vermont.

In 1805 he wrote one of the early declarations of liberal Protestantism and his most important work, *A Treatise on Atonement*. In that study, which formalized and popularized many Universalist tenets, Ballou emphasized the importance of reason in religious faith; he rejected the concept of the Trinity; he stressed the benevolence of God and the innate goodness of humanity; and, most significantly, he reasoned that a loving and omnipotent God intended that all humanity would be saved from damnation. The publication of the book marked Ballou's emergence as a leader of the Universalist movement and a central promulgator of religious liberalism.

Ballou continued writing and preaching in Massachusetts from 1815 until his death. After several years in Salem, he assumed the pulpit of the Second Universalist Society in Boston, a post he held for 35 years. From there,

he helped to organize both the theological and institutional foundations of the Universalist movement. In 1819 he became the first editor of the weekly *Universalist Magazine*, a publication that became the leading denominational newspaper. In 1830 he and his great-nephew, Hosea Ballou 2nd, founded the scholarly *Universalist Expositor*. His second major theological treatise, *An Examination of the Doctrine of Future Retribution*, appeared in 1834. His organizational abilities, keen intellect, and popular preaching style led him to be widely considered as the most creative thinker and the greatest theologian of Universalism.

LMK

Bibliography: Anne Lee Bressler, *The Universalist Movement in America, 1770–1880*. (New York: Oxford University Press, 2000); Ernest Cassara, *Universalism in America* (Boston: Beacon Press, 1971); Russell E. Miller, *The Larger Hope* (Boston: Unitarian Universalist Association, 1979); George Huntston Williams, "American Universalism: A Bicentennial Historical Essay," *Journal of the Universalist Historical Society* 9 (1971).

Baltimore Catechism   What is generally referred to as the Baltimore Catechism was really a series of catechisms used in the Roman Catholic Church in the United States. Recognizing the need for an English-language catechism directed to the American context, the American bishops meeting in the first Plenary Council of Baltimore (see BALTIMORE, COUNCILS OF) in 1852 authorized the *General Catechism of the Christian Doctrine*. This was followed in 1884 with the third Plenary Council's *A Catechism of Christian Doctrine*. With some revisions these documents were the major source of catechetical training for U.S. Catholics until the 1960s.

Both followed the traditional purpose and form of catechesis, the teaching of doctrines of the faith, directed primarily at children and the newly evangelized. The Baltimore catechisms used a simple question-and-answer format. Designed for use by those who were not yet spiritually mature, they emphasized memorization rather than explanation and understanding. The Church's transformation following VATICAN COUNCIL II necessitated radical revisions, and the Baltimore Catechisms were replaced by those more attuned to the changing times. The most significant of these was *Sharing the Light of Faith: National Catechetical Directory for Catholics of the United States,* issued by the American bishops in 1979. The development of a single catechism for the entire Roman Catholic Church and the publication of its American edition in 1994 moved the Church into a new period of catechetical instruction. The depth and detail of this catechism moved away from the earlier question-and-answer format, seeking more for understanding rather than memorization. Although the source of much controversy prior to its introduction, with numerous conflicts over gender-specific language and questioning about the extent to which it was consistent with the spirit of Vatican II, the catechism undoubtedly will have a major impact on Roman Catholic instruction in the United States.

EQ

Bibliography: Rudolph George Bandas, *Catechetical Methods: Standard Methods of Teaching Religion for Use in Seminaries, Novitiates, Normal Schools and by All Teachers of Religion* (New York: J. F. Wagner, 1929); C. J. Carmody, "The Roman Catholic Catechesis in the United States, 1784–1930: A Study of its Theory, Development and Materials" (Ph.D. dissertation, Loyola University, Chicago, 1975); *Catechism of the Catholic Church* (Chicago: Loyola University Press, 1994).

Baltimore, Councils of   Until the 20th century the archdiocese of Baltimore was the center of Roman Catholic episcopal power in the United States, with the archbishop of Baltimore functioning as the primate of the American Church. From this position of authority several of the archbishops convened councils to deal with pressing church matters. The first two were convoked by Bishop John CARROLL himself, the first (1791) consisting of all American clergy and the second (1810) a meeting between Carroll and his several suffragan bishops.

The expansion of the United States Church led to a change in the nature of these councils. Originally synods under Carroll, they soon expanded into provincial meetings as all the bishops in the province of Baltimore—which stretched from Vermont to Louisiana—convened on seven occasions between 1829 and 1849. During these meetings the bishops were forced to respond to several vexing issues. Among the more important of these were conflicts over lay control of Church property (see TRUSTEEISM), clergy discipline and training, and education.

With the division of the United States Church into several provinces the occasional meetings of the bishops became plenary councils and took on even greater importance. The first Plenary Council of Baltimore was convened in 1852, and although it passed no significant legislation it did reaffirm episcopal control of Church property and urged the establishment of parochial schools in all dioceses.

The second Plenary Council, held in 1866, was a much more active and significant affair. Presided over by Archbishop Martin John SPALDING, it was attended by 45 bishops and archbishops and two abbots representing nearly 4 million Roman Catholic citizens, and its closing session was attended by President Andrew Johnson. Its decisions also suggested a maturing Church. This council not only reaffirmed earlier teachings about discipline and practice, it took up doctrinal matters as well. The council issued statements on the Trinity, Marian devotion, and the authority of the Church, as well as the doctrines of creation and redemption. Although these statements closely followed contemporary pronouncements by Pope Pius IX, they steadfastly avoided his most notorious document, the "Syllabus of Errors," with its condemnation of freedom of the press, religion, and speech. Even more significantly, the American bishops affirmed the collegiality and shared responsibility of all bishops, while acknowledging the primacy of the pope. This view was to be undone in the coming years with the growing centralization of power in the papacy and the affirmation of papal infallibility at VATICAN COUNCIL I.

The third Plenary Council, held in 1884, was most significant in that its decrees so regularized the functioning of the American Roman Catholic Church that no general Church council needed to be held for 30 years, when one was occasioned by the necessities of World War I. The third council again urged that parochial schools be established in every diocese, a plea that had become nearly formulaic, but this time truly began to take hold. The long-term crowning achievement of the third council was its authorization of the establishment of a Catholic university in America. Although the history of this school was marked by controversy and suspicion, the eventual establishment of the Catholic University of America in 1887 signified the growing institutional strength and maturity of Roman Catholicism in the United States.

The third Plenary Council of Baltimore would be the last such meeting for the American Church. The establishment of the NATIONAL CATHOLIC WELFARE CONFERENCE and later the NATIONAL CONFERENCE OF CATHOLIC BISHOPS would regularize episcopal meetings to an extent that such extraordinary meetings became unnecessary.

(See also ROMAN CATHOLICISM.)

EQ

Bibliography: Peter Guilday, *A History of the Councils of Baltimore* (New York: Arno Press, 1969).

baptism   Baptism (from the Greek *baptizo*, meaning to "wash" or "dip") is the Christian rite of initiation in which participants are either immersed in water or have water poured upon their heads. It is believed to symbolize not only admission into full participation in the church, but also the forgiveness of sins and the spiritual regeneration of the believer.

The practice of baptizing converts began in the period of the early church. It was instituted to commemorate Jesus' baptism in the Jordan River by John the Baptist, an event to which all four New Testament Gospels refer. According to Jesus' admonition at the conclusion of the Gospel According to Matthew, Christians are to "make disciples of all nations, baptizing them in the name of the Father and of the Son and of the Holy Spirit" (28:19). Although baptism of infants with the sprinkling of water over the forehead was introduced in the second century, adult baptism with complete immersion in a pool of water was the usual custom until the Middle Ages. Infant baptism eventually became normative, however, as Christian theologians emphasized the need to wash away "original sin" from the souls of newborn children. The Protestant reformers of the 16th century continued to baptize infants. They adamantly condemned the radical Anabaptists, who, demanding the baptism of adults only, sought to rebaptize those already baptized as children.

Baptism has been a subject of significant controversy on a number of occasions in American religious history. The first involved Puritan minister Roger WILLIAMS, who emigrated to Massachusetts from England in 1631. Williams concluded that the Puritan idea about church membership, namely that true Christians should be able to testify to an experience of conversion, implied that only the baptism of adult believers was a valid sacramental rite. Most New England Puritans disagreed with Williams, however, and for this and other dissenting viewpoints he was eventually banished from the Massachusetts colony. Williams is credited with founding the first Baptist church in America, establishing it at Providence, Rhode Island, in 1639.

Another controversy over baptism arose in the 1650s. According to Puritan custom, only church members were allowed to have their

Creek Baptism on Sunday in 1974 in Eastern Tennessee by Rev. "Pappy" Beaver. *(Eleanor Dickinson)*

children baptized. Yet as time passed, increasing numbers of those who had been baptized as infants, but failed to become full church members themselves, desired to have their children baptized. Although they attended church regularly, they had not undergone the transforming spiritual experience that qualified them to formally join the church. Puritan leaders were faced with a dilemma for, while they wished the church to be composed of genuine believers, they did not want to alienate morally upright, albeit technically unconverted, people. The problem was resolved in 1662 through the passage of what was known as the HALF-WAY COVENANT. The decision stipulated that even if they had not undergone a conversion experience, otherwise faithful churchgoers were accepted as "half-way" members of congregations and allowed to bring their children for baptism.

During the GREAT AWAKENING of the mid-18th century, the meaning of baptism again became central to debates within the American churches. Religious life was so radically altered by the revivalism of the Awakening that many churchgoers felt it necessary to separate from the denominations in which they had been raised and form new churches based upon Baptist principles. Chief among the "Separates" was New England Congregationalist Isaac BACKUS, who reaffirmed the old Puritan view that only adults who had undergone an experience of spiritual regeneration could be considered Christian. He eventually concluded as well that only baptism by immersion was a valid rite of Christian initiation. In 1756 he organized a Baptist church in Middleborough, Massachusetts, one of more than 100 new Baptist churches formed in New England during the Awakening.

The SECOND GREAT AWAKENING of the early 19th century helped arouse further disputes over baptismal practices. Presbyterian minister Barton Stone, for example, had organized the spectacular, but controversial, revival at Cane Ridge, Kentucky, in 1801. In response to growing opposition within their denomination, Stone and his followers chose to abandon Presbyterianism and in 1804 began calling themselves simply "Christians." Attempting to restore (see RESTORATION MOVEMENT) the purity of New Testament times to American church life, they eschewed all creeds except the Bible and practiced adult baptism by immersion.

A related movement was led at the same time by Presbyterian Alexander Campbell, a minister noted for his detailed expositions of the structures and practices of primitive Christianity. Campbell maintained that Christians should attempt in all ways to reconstruct the first-century church. As a result, he became convinced in 1813 that believer's baptism was the only genuinely scriptural initiation rite. Appealing mainly to those who were already Baptists, Campbell formed groups called the "Disciples of Christ," a movement that emerged as one of the fastest-growing American religious organizations of the period.

The final historical controversy over baptism that divided American Christians was the so-called Landmark movement within the SOUTHERN BAPTIST CONVENTION in the mid-19th century. In 1848, James R. GRAVES, pastor of a church in Nashville, Tennessee, began to publish articles defending what he regarded as the distinctive tenets of the Baptist faith. Although the term *landmark* was actually coined by another minister, Graves popularized its use among Southern Baptists: the belief that the baptism of adults by immersion was one of the indispensable trademarks of Christianity. There had been an unbroken line of Baptist churches observing this practice since apostolic times, Graves declared, and any deviation from it nullified a church's claim to being a "true church." Landmarkism became a highly potent force in the Southern Baptist Convention. It stimulated a heightened denominational self-consciousness and generally negated attempts at rapprochement with other southern Protestants throughout the rest of the century.

Since World War II, the heightened interest in ecumenism has led many American Christians to stress the similarities, rather than the differences, among their denominations. As a result, most Christians recognize that baptism contains both divine and human elements. Denominations that baptize infants (e.g., Roman Catholics and the Eastern Orthodox) have traditionally underscored the divine action (reception of the Holy Spirit and forgiveness of sins) that takes place in baptism. Churches that baptize older children and adults (e.g., Baptists), on the other hand, highlight the faithful human response to God's prior offer of grace.

(See also CHURCH OF THE BRETHREN [DUNKERS].)

GHS, Jr.

Bibliography: William H. Brackney, *The Baptists* (Westport, Conn.: Greenwood Press, 1988); G. R. Beasley-Murray, *Baptism in the New Testament* (Grand Rapids, Mich.: Eerdmans, 1981).

baptism in the Spirit   See PENTECOSTALISM.

Baptist General Conference   See BAPTISTS.

Baptists   Baptists are the largest Protestant denominational group in the United States today. Although no official church structure or creed unites all Baptists, they do share two distinctive beliefs: the BAPTISM (from which their name derives) of adult believers by immersion, and the independence of each local congregation (see CONGREGATIONALISM). The first Baptists were found on the radical fringes of English PURITANISM among those who believed it was necessary to withdraw from the Church of England in order to preserve true Christianity. A group under the leadership of John Smyth emigrated from England to Holland, where they came into contact with the Anabaptists (that is, rebaptizers), who rejected the validity of infant baptism. Smyth baptized himself and several others in 1609, thereby forming the first English Baptist church.

Baptists appeared again in England during the tumultuous Puritan interregnum of the mid-17th century. Baptists and orthodox Puritans both agreed that church membership should be limited to those who could testify to an experience of divine grace. Baptists, however, contended that no one, including the children of church members, ought to be baptized until that person had made a personal confession of faith. Baptists also opposed religious establishments in all forms. They believed that government, like the church, had been divinely instituted, but God intended the church to maintain itself by voluntary, not state-supported, means.

Baptists began to arrive in America as part of the Puritan migration from England to Massachusetts between 1620 and 1640. The Baptists' rejection of infant baptism, insistence on freedom from civil control, and emphasis on spiritual liberty quickly brought them into conflict with colonial leaders. Roger WILLIAMS, a Puritan minister who was banished from Massachusetts for advocating the separation of church and state, founded the first Baptist church in America at Providence, Rhode Island, in 1639. A few years later, John Clarke, another Puritan dissenter, founded the second Baptist church at Newport, Rhode Island. William's colony, which obtained a royal charter in 1663, became a refuge for Baptists and others fleeing the Puritan establishments in Massachusetts and Connecticut. By 1671, a Seventh-day Baptist Church had also been established in Newport. Seventh-day Baptists celebrated Saturday (the "seventh day") rather than Sunday as their day of Sabbath rest.

Baptists found a more favorable atmosphere in the middle colonies of New Jersey, Pennsylvania, and Delaware. There they enjoyed religious toleration and freedom from taxation in support of an established church. In 1707 five congregations united to form the Philadelphia Association, the first Baptist organization in America. While the association held no binding power over the individual churches, it facilitated interaction among them, especially their evangelistic efforts. The association also adopted a confessional statement, based on the Calvinist Westminster Confession of 1646, that provided some internal theological unity among the congregations.

The GREAT AWAKENING of the mid-18th century represented a critical turning point for the Baptist movement. During that period, Baptists were transformed from a collection of scattered churches into a major American religious force. The revivals of the Awakening inspired many to separate from the denominations in which they had been raised and become Baptists. Chief among these "Separates" was Isaac BACKUS. Backus came to the conclusion, first, that only adults who had undergone a conversion experience could be considered Christian and, later, that only baptism by immersion was a valid rite of Christian initiation. In 1756 he organized a Baptist church in Middleborough, Massachussetts, one of more than 100 new Separate Baptist churches formed by disaffected Congregationalists in New England during the Great Awakening.

Baptists adapted well to the post-Awakening religious climate in America, for their institutions embodied the most significant features of the Awakening: lay leadership, local autonomy, and the ready acceptance of a voluntary system of church support. These emphases fit the country's democratic mood in the second half of the 18th century, and Baptist congregations increased dramatically from slightly fewer than 500 in 1775 to more than 1,100 by 1797.

As the 19th century began, moreover, the new wave of revivals in the SECOND GREAT AWAKENING further aided Baptist expansion. The Second Awakening is best remembered for the emotionalism of the western camp meetings, protracted religious assemblies at which thousands of Baptists, Presbyterians, and Methodists gathered to hear preaching. Less spectacular than the revivals but just as important for Baptist growth was the formation of mission-oriented societies. These societies allowed congregations to maintain their nominal independence yet combine resources to aid the task of evangelism.

The General Missionary Convention (later called the Triennial Convention because it met every three years) was the first national body of Baptists. It was founded in 1814 to support the work of missionaries Adoniram Judson and Luther Rice. Although Judson and Rice had been sent to India as missionaries of the Congregational American Board of Commissioners for Foreign Missions (see MISSIONS, FOREIGN), hey decided en route that only adult believers should be baptized. After their arrival in India, they resigned from the Congregational Board and gained the support of the Baptists instead. Although the Triennial Convention intended at first to promote all kinds of missionary, educational, and publishing activities, it decided in 1826 to limit its role to foreign missions. Other societies were formed to meet the convention's original publishing and home missionary aims: the Baptist General Tract Society in 1824 and the American Baptist Home Mission Society in 1832.

As their numbers grew, Baptists saw the need for educational institutions that would train the church's leaders. Their earliest college, Rhode Island College (now Brown University), was organized in Portsmouth, Rhode Island, in 1764. Under the leadership of James Manning, that school strengthened the intellectual life of the Baptists in the period before the Revolution. Francis Wayland, who served as the fourth president of Brown University from 1827 to 1855, reorganized the college curriculum and published works that became the standard college textbooks of his day. In the early 19th century, many other Baptist colleges were founded that hold national stature today: Colby College and Bates College in Maine; Hamilton College in New York; Furman University and Wake Forest University in North Carolina; Mercer University in Georgia; and Bucknell University in Pennsylvania.

While eastern Baptists centralized their educational and missionary activities, Baptists on the southern and western frontier reacted against this concern for greater organizational unity. A Primitive, or Antimission, Baptist movement arose in opposition to the missionary societies and reform agencies. Primitive Baptists argued that Baptist missionary efforts not only threatened the autonomy of local churches, but also undermined the traditional Calvinist emphasis on divine election, implying that persons could, if they wished, choose whether to accept or reject God's eternal decrees. The doctrinal strictness of the Primitive Baptists gave rise to the "hard shell" label that still describes a small, ultraconservative segment of the Baptist population in the South.

A far more serious challenge to Baptist unity occurred in 1845, when the slavery controversy permanently divided Baptists in the South from their fellow church members in the North. During the 1830s it became increasingly clear that the Triennial Convention and the American Baptist Home Missionary Society reflected the interests of the northerners who ran them. Thus, southern leaders complained that that the Home Missionary Society concentrated its work in areas of the West where antislavery Baptists from the North were settling. A firm stand by northerners against appointing slaveholders as missionaries soon aroused Baptists in the South to action. A call was issued for a consultative convention to meet at Augusta, Georgia, in May 1845. There the SOUTHERN BAPTIST CONVENTION (SBC) was officially organized. Although Baptists in the North at first insisted that their southern brethren were not truly separated from them, the bloody Civil War effectively sealed the division 20 years later.

In the era after the Civil War, the SBC became one of the major institutional expressions of the South's cultural identity. Despite its regional base, the SBC also emerged as the largest Protestant denomination in the reunited nation. At the same time, a major separation took place within the church's ranks that, while limiting the size of an already extensive denomination, demonstrated the overall strength of the Baptist religious ethos throughout the southern United States.

Within a few years after the Civil War ended, nearly 1 million black Baptists in the South had left the white-dominated churches and formed their own congregations. The absence of formalism and the democratic spirit and polity of Baptist churches had always appealed to African-American Christians. Slave churches appeared on southern plantations as early as the mid-18th century. The first black Baptist church was organized near Augusta, Georgia, in 1773, and in 1821 members of the Richmond African Baptist Missionary Society became the first American missionaries to Africa. Nat TURNER, the leader of the great slave revolt of 1831, was also renowned as a Baptist preacher. It is hardly surprising, therefore, that freed slaves began to exit the white churches in large numbers following the Emancipation Proclamation in 1863.

The first African-American Baptist denomination, now known as the NATIONAL BAPTIST CONVENTION, U.S.A., INC. and still among the largest black denominations in the United States, was organized in 1895. This body divided in 1915 after a dispute over the control of property and ownership of its publishing board. Although its basic beliefs were identical to the parent denomination, a new church, calling itself the NATIONAL BAPTIST CONVENTION OF AMERICA, INC. was formed. Then, in 1961, a debate over the election of officers in the National Baptist Convention of the U.S.A., Inc. led to a further schism and the formation of the PROGRESSIVE NATIONAL BAPTIST CONVENTION, INC. Again, the concerns that separated the two groups were bureaucratic rather than doctrinal. During the civil rights movement of the 1950s and 1960s, several African-American Baptist clergy from the South, most notably Martin Luther KING, Jr., and Jesse JACKSON, rose to national political and religious leadership.

Baptist life became further diversified in the mid-19th century with the arrival of immigrants from northern Europe who adopted a Baptist polity in the churches they formed in America. Some immigrants were already Baptists and either joined existing Baptist institutions or founded their own ethnic congregations. The Baptist General Conference, for instance, had originated within Swedish Pietism, a movement that emphasized simple biblical faith and rejected religious formalism. The first Swedish Baptist congregation in America was founded in Rock Island, Illinois, in 1852, and the term *Swedish* was dropped from the Baptist General Conference's name in 1945. The Baptist General Conference, whose present-day conservatism still reflects its roots in Pietism, now contains about 135,000 members.

Native-born Baptists also directed their home missionary efforts at these immigrants from northern Europe and brought many who were unchurched or seeking another faith into Baptist churches. The North American Baptist Conference, a small denomination of German

ethnic origins, is an example of the fruits of such missionary outreach. A general conference was organized in 1865 to unite German-speaking Baptist congregations scattered throughout the East and Midwest. August Rauschenbusch, father of the famed SOCIAL GOSPEL advocate Walter RAUSCHENBUSCH and a member of the faculty at Rochester Theological Seminary, was a prominent member of this denomination. The conference has outgrown its once exclusive German heritage and claims approximately 61,000 members today.

After the Civil War, northern Baptists reluctantly gave up their claims on their brethren in the South and instead formed mission and education societies to increase their influence in urban areas and in the West. By 1907, various Baptist societies in the North united and formed the Northern Baptist Convention, later known as the American Baptist Convention and now called the AMERICAN BAPTIST CHURCHES IN THE U.S.A. The majority of Free Will Baptists in the North, remnants of an 18th-century schism over the question of the freedom of the human will to choose salvation, also joined the merger in 1911. The American Baptists have consistently identified with MAINLINE PROTESTANTISM and engaged in ecumenical relations with other denominations, including participation in both the Federal Council of Churches and its successor, the NATIONAL COUNCIL OF CHURCHES.

In the early 20th century, Baptists in the North, like all the liberal Protestant denominations, found themselves embroiled in internal controversies between fundamentalists and modernists over the proper interpretation of the Bible. Baptist clergyman Harry Emerson FOSDICK, who served a church in New York City, protested in his 1922 sermon "Shall the Fundamentalists Win?" against a growing spirit of exclusivity among conservatives. He pleaded for mutual forbearance between contending parties within an already divided Protestantism. Fosdick's advice went unheeded, however, and two new conservative Baptist denominations were born out of the struggle among Northern

Baptists: the General Association of Regular Baptist Churches and the Conservative Baptist Association, which today have about 1,400 and 1,100 U.S. churches, respectively.

Despite its numerical strength and doctrinal conservatism, even the Southern Baptist Convention witnessed the schism of a doctrinally rigorist movement from its ranks early in the 20th century. James Robinson GRAVES, a Tennessee preacher who died in 1893, argued that the true church of Jesus Christ had, in unbroken succession from apostolic times, upheld the "old landmarks," namely the baptism of adult believers and congregational polity. Graves feared that the purity of the Baptist faith would be violated if Southern Baptists sought to work with churches that did not practice adult baptism. Although most Southern Baptists were not strictly opposed to Graves's position, his theological emphases stimulated controversy. When the SBC attempted to carry out mission work through its own centralized bureaucracy rather than through the local churches, an "anticonvention" force was born. This resulted in the formation of the separate American Baptist Association in 1905, a "Landmark" denomination that today contains approximately 250,000 members.

Despite the Landmark schism, the SBC has maintained both a distinctive conservative identity and a pattern of membership growth over the past 100 years. The church's organizational structure is complex, balancing the principle of local autonomy with cooperation on a denominational level. The SBC gained national exposure in the 1970s through the activities of its two most prominent members: the election of lay leader Jimmy Carter as president of the United States, and the founding of the conservative MORAL MAJORITY by Lynchburg, Virginia, minister Jerry FALWELL. In recent years, fundamentalists have gained control of the denomination and asserted that the Bible must be interpreted literally. This dispute over the scriptures has led to a small schism in the church's ranks, as some theological moderates chose to withdraw from the SBC.

There are now approximately 35 million Baptists who belong to more than 50 separate denominations in the United States. Nearly half belong to the Southern Baptist Convention, the largest Protestant denomination in the United States, which contains 15 million members. Other leading Baptist denominations include the National Baptist Convention, U.S.A., Inc.; the National Baptist Convention of America, Inc.; the Progressive National Baptist Convention, Inc.; and the American Baptist Churches in the U.S.A.

GHS, Jr.

Bibliography: William H. Brackney, *The Baptists* (Westport, Conn.: Greenwood Press, 1994); John Lee Eighmy, *Churches in Cultural Captivity: A History of the Social Attitudes of Southern Baptists* (Knoxville: University of Tennessee Press, 1987); Leroy Fitts, *A History of Black Baptists* (Nashville: Broadman Press, 1985); William G. McLoughlin, *Soul Liberty: The Baptists' Struggle in New England, 1630–1833* (Hanover, N.H.: University Press of New England, 1991).

Beat movement   Though the Beat poets and novelists of the post–World War II era are typically revered (or reviled) for their contributions to American literature, they also contributed significantly to American religion. By struggling to find a place in the American imagination for Asian religious traditions such as BUDDHISM, the Beats both anticipated and prompted the celebrated eastward turn of the 1960s and beyond.

The Beat movement constituted a revolt against postwar norms in literature, culture, and religion. That revolt, however, was also a protest *for* something. According to Jack Kerouac, the Catholic-born author of *On the Road* (1957) and other Beat novels and poems, "Beat" stood not for "beat down" but for "beatific." "I want to speak *for* things," he explained. "For the crucifix I speak out, for the Star of Israel I speak out, for the divinest man who ever lived who was German (Bach) I speak out, for sweet Mohammed I speak out, for Buddha I speak out, for Lao-tse and Chuang-tse I speak out." Echoing Kerouac, the Jewish-born Beat poet Allen Ginsberg described his signature poem "Howl" (1956) not as the revolt against civilization that many critics discerned but as a "pro-attestation, that is testimony in favor of Value." Like Kerouac he used religious language to describe his protest. "'Howl' is an 'Affirmation' by individual experience of God, sex, drugs, absurdity. . . . The poems are religious and I meant them to be."

Kerouac, Ginsberg, and other Beats were arguing not simply for new literary forms but also for new types of spiritual experience. They frequently found that experience not in the church or synagogue but on the road. From the perspective of comparative religions, therefore, the peripatetic beats shared much with pilgrims making their way to sacred shrines. Like pilgrims to Mecca or Jerusalem, the Beats were liminal, or border-zone, figures who expressed their social marginality by living spontaneously, sharing their property, dressing like hoboes (or not dressing at all), celebrating sexuality, seeking mystical awareness through drugs and meditation, acting like "Zen lunatics," and stressing the sacred interrelatedness of all human beings. What distinguished the Beats from other pilgrims, however, was their failure (or refusal) to arrive at some fixed sacred center. The Beats lived, in short, not to arrive but to travel. In their lives and their literature they appear not simply as pilgrims but as heroes of quest tales, wandering monks on a spiritual quest.

The Beats diverged from other seekers of their time in their interest in Asian religious traditions. While other Americans took solace in the Jewish and Christian texts such as Rabbi Joshua Liebman's *Peace of Mind* (1946), Monsignor Fulton J. Sheen's *Peace of Soul* (1949), and the Reverend Billy Graham's *Peace with God* (1953), the Beats were discovering ZEN koans and Mahayana Buddhist sutras. They

were also forging a far more radical ecumenism than the Judeo-Christian alliances other Americans were building in the postwar period. They incorporated into their worldviews not only the Catholic background of Kerouac and the Jewish background of Ginsberg but also the insights of Gnosticism, mysticism, Native American folklore, Aztec and Mayan mythology, Buddhism, and HINDUISM.

Of all these traditions, however, the Beats were drawn most strongly to Buddhism. The Beats' Buddhist interests are evident, for example, in Kerouac's *Dharma Bums* (1958). In that novel, Ray Smith (who stands in for Kerouac himself), encounters Japhy Ryder (a thinly veiled version of poet Gary Snyder), who initiates him into, among other things, the vexing practice of solving Zen koans, or word puzzles.

Like the heroes of TRANSCENDENTALISM who inspired them, the Beats championed individual spiritual experience over what Ralph Waldo EMERSON denounced as "corpse-cold" orthodoxies and worked to weave the truths of Asian religious traditions into their lives as well as their literature. They stand alongside the transcendentalists as important culture brokers who facilitated the encounter of modern Americans with the ancient religions of the East. Although Kerouac and Ginsberg have passed away, the Beat tradition continues in poets like Snyder, whose work reflects both the insights of formal Zen training in Japan and a commitment to the environment forged during hikes in the American Northwest.

SRP

Bibliography: John Lardas, *The Bop Apocalypse: The Religious Visions of Kerouac, Ginsberg, and Burroughs* (Urbana: University of Illinois Press, 2000); Carole Tonkinson, ed., *Big Sky Mind: Buddhism and the Beat Generation* (New York: Riverhead, 1995).

Beecher, Henry Ward (1813–1887)   Congregational minister and spokesman for liberal Protestantism, Henry Ward Beecher was one of the most popular preachers of his day. Called in 1847 to be pastor of the newly formed Plymouth Church in the fashionable Brooklyn Heights section of Brooklyn, New York, Beecher believed above all else that religious thought should be adapted to the culture and times in which Christians lived. Christianity, he said, was essentially "a natural experience, . . . something to be enjoyed."

Son of the great church leader Lyman BEECHER, Henry Ward Beecher was born in Litchfield, Connecticut, on June 24, 1813. He was also the younger brother of novelist and abolitionist Harriet Beecher STOWE. After graduating from Amherst College in 1834 and from Lane Seminary in Cincinnati in 1837, Beecher was ordained and served as minister of Presbyterian churches in Indiana, at Lawrenceburg (1837–1839) and at Indianapolis (1839–1847), before coming to the Plymouth Church.

Beecher preached openly in favor of social reform in the years before the Civil War, supporting rights for women and an end to slavery. During the 1850s controversy over the admission of the Kansas territory to the Union, he raised money from his pulpit to provide rifles (called "Beecher's Bibles") for the protection of antislavery northern settlers moving into Kansas. Throughout the Civil War he was an outspoken supporter of the northern war effort, and in February 1865 he delivered an address at the flag-raising in Fort Sumter in Charleston, South Carolina, that signaled the restoration of federal control over the rebellious South.

Beecher was a prolific writer, public speaker, and religious editor. From 1861 to 1863, he ran the prestigious interdenominational weekly the *Independent,* and from 1870 until 1881 he edited the *Christian Union.* Successive volumes of his Plymouth Church sermons reached a nationwide audience. He not only compiled *The Plymouth Collection of Hymns and Tunes* (1855), but he also composed a novel (*Norwood,* 1867) that examined changing social and religious mores in post–Civil War America.

Beecher's natural charm and deemphasis of doctrinal questions helped attract a large,

Henry Ward Beecher, the brother of Harriet Beecher Stowe and popular 19th-century liberal preacher at Pilgrim Church in Brooklyn Heights. *(Engraving by George E. Perkins)*

affluent congregation to the Plymouth Church. Typical of the emerging Protestant MODERNISM of the day, Beecher only asked the members of his church to pledge personal loyalty to the spirit of Jesus. His acceptance of evolutionary thought and rejection of many of the key theological points of Calvinism eventually led Beecher and his church to leave the Congregational denomination altogether. As he warned students at Yale Divinity School in 1872, God's providence was always rolling forward, and ministers could not afford to become apostles of "the dead past" or allow new truths to pass them by.

Beecher provoked another type of public attention when a sexual scandal erupted around him in the early 1870s. Theodore

Tilton, a member of the Plymouth Church, accused Beecher of seducing his wife, Josephine. The ensuing controversy was discussed on 105 occasions in the *New York Times* in 1874, 17 times on the newspaper's front page. When *Tilton v. Beecher* went to court, newspapers throughout the country openly took sides between the litigants, and for a period liberal American Protestantism itself seemed to be on trial. After a six-month trial and eight days of deliberation, the jury in the case was unable either to convict or to acquit Beecher, a decision satisfactory to no one.

Following the trial, most of Beecher's congregation continued to support their pastor. Sullied but unrepentant, he remained their minister for over a decade more. Certainly one factor in Beecher's ongoing popularity was his ability to combine theological liberalism with social conservatism, thus mirroring attitudes prevalent within white middle-class Protestant circles at the end of the 19th century. Beecher's life and thought were in many ways the quintessential religious expression of the Gilded Age era. He served as minister of the Plymouth Church for 40 years, and his death in Brooklyn on March 8, 1887, occasioned a huge outpouring of grief both in New York City and across the nation.

GHS, Jr.

Bibliography: Richard Wightman Fox, *Trials of Intimacy: Love and Loss in the Beecher-Tilton Scandal* (Chicago: University of Chicago Press, 1999); William G. McLoughlin, *The Meaning of Henry Ward Beecher: An Essay on the Shifting Values of Mid-Victorian America, 1840–1870* (New York: Knopf, 1970).

Beecher, Lyman (1775–1863)

A minister of both the Congregational and Presbyterian denominations and arguably the most influential clergyman of his day, Lyman Beecher's life illustrates many crucial forces at work within American Protestantism during the first half of the 19th century.

Beecher was born in New Haven, Connecticut, on October 12, 1775. He entered Yale College in 1793, and while there was converted during a revival led by Timothy Dwight, the president of the college. After graduation in 1797, Beecher became pastor at the Presbyterian church in East Hampton, New York. He won a reputation as a social reformer, and following Aaron Burr's fatal wounding of Alexander Hamilton, he undertook a crusade against dueling. Next, Beecher accepted a call to the Congregational church in Litchfield, Connecticut, where he served between 1810 and 1826. During the Litchfield years, the temperance movement elicited his special attention, and he published his *Six Sermons on Intemperance* in 1826.

Beecher initially viewed the 1818 disestablishment of Congregationalism in Connecticut as a grave "injury" to the cause of Christ and reported being thoroughly depressed for a long time afterward. In many ways, disestablishment in Connecticut symbolized the end of New England Puritan culture and its replacement by the new ethos of Protestant EVANGELICALISM. Thus, when Beecher later reflected on the religious revolution that had occurred, he realized that Christianity actually gained more than it lost. Cut loose from state support and thrown entirely upon their own resources, the churches had learned to exert new forms of influence through voluntary societies and revivals rather than through the "queues and shoebuckles, and cocked hats, and gold-headed canes" of the old order.

Beecher moved to the Hanover Street Congregational Church in Boston in 1826, and there he launched campaigns against two novel (and opposite) theological adversaries: Unitarianism emerging out of the Congregational churches of eastern Massachusetts, and the "new measures" of revivalism adopted by Presbyterian minister Charles Grandison FINNEY. Both movements, he believed, compromised the traditional Calvinist emphases on divine sovereignty and human sinfulness.

Beecher's struggle against Finney's activistic style and unconventional revivalistic methods was particularly dramatic. Meeting in New Lebanon, New York, in July 1827, Beecher and Finney sought to work out a compromise concerning their differences, but the conference only increased the animosity. Beecher allegedly said to Finney: "You mean to come into Connecticut, and carry a streak of fire to Boston. But if you attempt it . . . I'll meet you at the State line, and call out all the artillerymen, and fight every inch of the way to Boston." Still, despite his hostility toward Finney, Beecher eventually repented of his remarks and welcomed Finney to Boston to lead a revival.

In 1832, Beecher attained further prominence by accepting a call to become president of Lane Theological Seminary, a Presbyterian school recently founded in Cincinnati. Beecher believed that the West had tremendous importance for the future growth of the United States, and as he wrote in *Plea for the West* (1835), it has to be saved from Roman Catholicism. Originally an address to raise funds for Lane, his *Plea* exemplified some of the worst aspects of anti-Catholic (see ANTI-CATHOLICISM) and nativist sentiment that had begun to swell in the late 1820s. Beecher's *Plea* opened with a hymn of praise to the future destiny of the United States. Beecher discussed Jonathan Edwards's millennial beliefs, how the thousand-year reign of Christ was to be established through the reforming efforts of Protestants in America. Beecher then continued with lurid descriptions of attempts by the pope, reactionary kings of Europe, and immigrants to seize the Mississippi Valley. Protestants had to be on guard, he warned, lest Catholics thwart their efforts to build a truly Christian nation.

In Cincinnati, Beecher also served as pastor of the Second Presbyterian Church, where his ideas about the doctrine of sin underwent profound changes. Influenced by both the revivalism and voluntaryism then so prevalent in American Protestantism, Beecher came to believe more and more in the possibility of human progress. As a result, charges of heresy were brought against him in 1835 for allegedly abandoning traditional Presbyterian standards of orthodoxy. Although Beecher was acquitted, his heresy trial was among the first of many similar affairs that disrupted American Presbyterian life in the 19th century. It foreshadowed as well the impending division between the reform-minded New School Presbyterian faction and the doctrinally conservative Old School Presbyterian party that occurred two years later (see NEW SCHOOL/OLD SCHOOL).

Beecher retired from church work in 1843 and from the presidency of Lane in 1850. He spent the last years of his life lecturing and writing. His three-volume *Works* were published in 1852–1853, and a two-volume autobiography was compiled and published by his children following his death. He was married three times and had 11 children, several of whom—Catherine, Edward, Henry Ward (see BEECHER, HENRY WARD), and Harriet (see STOWE, HARRIET BEECHER)—were also important figures in American religious history. After 1856, Beecher lived at Henry Ward's home in Brooklyn, New York, where, after gradually slipping into senility, he died on January 10, 1863.

GHS, Jr.

Bibliography: Marie Caskey, *Chariot of Fire: Religion and the Beecher Family* (New Haven: Yale University Press, 1978); Barbara M. Cross, ed., *The Autobiography of Lyman Beecher*, 2 vols. (1864, Cambridge, Mass.: Belknap Press, 1961).

Beissel, Johann Conrad   See EPHRATA COMMUNITY.

Belavin, Tikhon (1865–1925)   Tikhon Belavin, Russian Orthodox archbishop of the Aleutians and North America from 1898 to 1907, envisioned and almost succeeded in creating a multiethnic Orthodox Church in North America. He was elected patriarch of Moscow in 1917. His steadfast leadership during the first years of Soviet persecution was recognized in 1988, when he was canonized as St. Tikhon the Confessor.

The son of a priest, Basil Belavin was born near Pskov in 1865 and educated at the Pskov Seminary and the St. Petersburg Theological Academy. Ordained after taking the monastic name Tikhon, he taught in seminaries and was consecrated as a bishop at the age of 32. In 1898 he was sent to lead the Russian mission in America, then called the Diocese of the Aleutians and Alaska.

As the only Orthodox bishop on the continent, Tikhon sought to organize the thousands of Orthodox and Eastern Rite Catholic immigrants pouring into North America. He shifted the mission's focus away from the Pacific Coast and attempted to cultivate a pan-Orthodox community with an American identity.

Taking the first step in 1899, Tikhon won permission to rename his jurisdiction the Diocese of the Aleutians and North America. In 1903, he won the approval of the Russian Holy Synod for a sweeping reorganization of the diocese, and requested more priests to help him attract Eastern Rite Catholics into Orthodoxy.

His goal was a cosmopolitan and autonomous "Orthodox Church in America," a single, unified church with a flexible and representative structure that would attract believers from many ethnic groups. His plan called for a single church in the United States and Canada to be led by a Russian archbishop. A number of auxiliary bishops would supervise ethnic subjurisdictions, or vicariates. This, Tikhon argued, would permit each ethnic group to perpetuate its own language, traditions, and communal identity, while maintaining fundamental Orthodox unity.

After gaining the approval of the Russian church, Tikhon moved his seat from San Francisco to New York and assigned a new auxiliary bishop to Alaska and the West Coast. He extended the Russian synod's offer to consecrate a Syrian Orthodox priest, Raphael Hawaweeny of Brooklyn, who then took charge of a vicariate for Syrian Orthodoxy.

Tikhon organized a Serbian vicariate in 1905 and then attempted, with very little success, to persuade Greek immigrants to join the Russian-sponsored archdiocese. He also founded several key institutions, including St. Tikhon's Monastery in South Canaan, Pennsylvania, and a seminary in Minneapolis.

Among the first modern Orthodox bishops to emphasize a style of leadership that involved consultation of the laity and the clergy, Tikhon summoned the first representative council held by an Orthodox body in America to Mayfield, Pennsylvania, in 1907. It approved the incorporation of the archdiocese as the "Russian Orthodox Greek Catholic Church of America."

Recalled to Russia in 1907, he was later enthroned as metropolitan of Moscow. Elected patriarch of Moscow by the famous "Sobor," or reforming council, in 1917, Tikhon's resistance to Communist terror made him a revered figure. Hundreds of thousands followed his cortege through the streets of Moscow in 1925.

The structure he fashioned for North American Orthodoxy did not survive the upheavals of World War I and the Russian Revolution. Separate ethnic jurisdictions emerged during the 1920s, and Orthodox union in America remains an unresolved issue.

AHW

Bibliography: John H. Erickson, *Orthodox Christians in America* (New York: Oxford University Press, 1999); Dimitry Pospielovsky, *The Russian Church Under the Soviet Regime, 1917–1982* (Crestwood, N.Y.: St. Vladimir's Seminary Press, 1984); Constance J. Tarasar, ed., *Orthodox America, 1794–1976: The Development of the Orthodox Church in America* (Syosset, N.Y.: Orthodox Church in America, Department of History and Archives, 1975).

Bellamy, Joseph (1719–1790) Joseph Bellamy was a Congregational minister, disciple of Jonathan EDWARDS, and early leader of the NEW DIVINITY movement of the mid-18th century. Along with other New Divinity theologians, Bellamy helped adapt Calvinist teachings about sin to the rationalist intellectual trends of his day.

Bellamy was born in Cheshire, Connecticut, on February 20, 1719. He graduated from Yale College in 1735 and, as was customary for the time, trained for the ministry as part of Jonathan Edwards's household. Bellamy was ordained at Bethlehem, Connecticut, in 1738, and he remained as pastor of that church for the rest of his life. When a revival began in Bethlehem, Bellamy not only enthusiastically supported it, but also became known as an active New Light (see NEW LIGHTS/OLD LIGHTS) minister and defender of the GREAT AWAKENING generally. He sought to be a conscientious advocate of both the traditional CALVINISM and the experiential religious faith that Edwards himself so eloquently championed.

Despite his insistent orthodoxy, Bellamy introduced elements that moved away from Edwards's theological positions. These changes significantly influenced future developments in American Protestant thought. Seeking, for example, to justify the ways of God to philosophers and theologians shaped by the ENLIGHTENMENT, Bellamy exonerated the divine role in allowing sin. He emphasized instead how God's permission of evil became the means of achieving the greatest possible good for humankind. Most notable of all was Bellamy's reinterpretation of the doctrine of atonement. He represented the sacrifice of Christ not as a legal "satisfaction" for human wrongdoing or the appeasement of an angry deity (the traditional views) but as a working out of God's abundant love for the world.

Bellamy published two major theological works: *True Religion Delineated* (1750), a lengthy treatise in which genuine Christianity was defended against the extremes of both theological formalism and spiritual enthusiasm; and *The Wisdom of God in the Permission of Sins* (1758), which discussed the problem of evil. Bellamy died at Bethlehem on March 6, 1790.

GHS, Jr.

Bibliography: Mark Valeri, *Law and Providence in Joseph Bellamy's New England: The Origins of the New Divinity in Revolutionary America* (New York: Oxford University Press, 1994).

Benevolent Empire   See EVANGELICAL UNITED FRONT.

Besant, Annie Wood   See THEOSOPHY.

Bible schools   Bible schools were institutions founded by conservative Protestants in the late 19th and early 20th century to prepare men and women to be pastors, missionaries, and Sunday school teachers. The schools offered courses primarily in the interpretation of the Bible, religious pedagogy, and techniques of Christian evangelism (see EVANGELICALISM). As religious historian Ernest R. Sandeen once asserted, Bible schools served as the "headquarters" of American FUNDAMENTALISM.

At the end of the 19th century, several Protestant leaders turned their attention to forming schools for lay people. The earliest Bible school was the Baptist Missionary Training School for women, established in Chicago in 1881. The creation of similar institutions followed in rapid succession. A. B. Simpson, founder of the Christian and Missionary Alliance, opened the Missionary Training Institute in New York in 1882. Popular urban revivalist Dwight Lyman MOODY raised $250,000 in 1887 to develop the Chicago Evangelization Society. A formal, year-round school emerged out of that effort two years later, and it was named Moody Bible Institute in 1900 in memory of its founder. And Baptist minister A. J. Gordon, who hoped to recruit a dedicated band of overseas missionaries, formed the Boston Missionary Training School in his church in 1889.

The Moody Bible Institute soon became the standard against which all other Bible schools were measured. Often called the "West Point of Fundamentalism," it was the largest and richest institution in the movement. Located in downtown Chicago, the Moody Bible Institute began as a three-story building, but by 1927 it owned 34 buildings and several city blocks, valued at $4.5 million. The area around the school was filled with students day and night. By the late 1920s, between 30 and 40 faculty members ran a two-year program that enrolled more than 1,000 students each term. Filled with knowledge of the Scriptures they gained at Moody, students were sent out together to convert Chicagoans to the Christian faith.

Most of the men and women who studied at the early Bible schools were relatively mature, usually in their mid-20s or older. Many had never pursued a formal education but had worked in blue- and white-collar jobs. Since at first there were no sleeping or eating accommodations for students, they commuted to school from their homes. These schools usually were oriented to educating laity, not clergy. As a consequence, women usually accounted for a larger portion of the student body. Uninhibited by usual educational conventions, the Bible schools attracted many people, especially women, who had not received access to formal theological instruction before.

The chief textbook of the institutes was, of course, the Bible. While Bible study in these schools was designed for conservative theological purposes, instructors often considered themselves reformers in scriptural analysis. Many teachers believed in mastering the original Hebrew and Greek texts of the Old and New Testaments to foster understanding of the Bible's true meaning. Like most American fundamentalists, Bible school teachers assumed that ordinary human beings were capable of gaining knowledge of the world through the use of their senses. Thus, students were taught to study the Scriptures through the "inductive method," that is, reading the Bible with a commitment to uncovering the "facts" it contained.

Focused on the Bible, an entire course of study took either one or two years and emphasized the practical application of the learning gained in the classroom. As Moody stated in his institute's first prospectus, "study and work go hand in hand." A. B. Simpson, moreover, criticized the methods the mainline churches had used to educate their clergy. He argued that Christianity needed "practical men, men that

are in touch with their fellowmen, . . . men that have been taught to go down into the depths and, hand to hand and heart to heart, pluck sinners as brands from the burning."

The heyday of the Bible schools ran, roughly, from 1885 to 1945. In that period, more than 100 schools were established in the United States. After the early 1940s, however, leaders in the older institutions became more concerned with academic standing than with providing the popular, practical education they once championed. This concern for academic respectability meant that the Bible schools generally moved away from their former distinctive status and closer to the American educational mainstream. A number of the largest Bible schools now subscribe to their own accrediting agency, the American Association of Bible Colleges. With their raised educational standards and increased liberal arts offerings, many of these institutions, for example, Gordon College in Wenham, Massachusetts, and Trinity College in Bannockburn, Illinois, today are indistinguishable from other Christian colleges and seminaries.

GHS, Jr.

Bibliography: Virginia Lieson Brereton, *Training God's Army: The American Bible School, 1880–1940* (Bloomington: Indiana University Press, 1990).

Bible societies   Bible societies are religious organizations formed to publish and distribute copies of the Bible. Although the Bible is certainly not just a Protestant book, the Protestant reformers of the 16th century stressed that, as the word of God, the Bible was an accurate, self-interpreting book that even the simplest Christian could comprehend. As a consequence of that belief, the wide dissemination of the scriptures has always been an important concern of Protestants. The first major Bible publisher in the United States was the American Bible Society (ABS), founded in 1816, while the Gideons International, famed for the Bibles it places in hotel rooms, is the most widely known Bible society today.

In the mid-17th century, Puritan minister John Eliot learned the Massachuset language and translated the Bible in order to aid in evangelizing Native Americans. The earliest Bible published in America in a European language was an edition of Martin Luther's German Bible, released in 1743. Prior to the American Revolution, the right to distribute the "authorized" English translation of the Old and New Testaments (the King James Version of 1611) belonged solely to the university presses of Oxford and Cambridge. When the War for Independence cut off communications between England and America, Robert Aitken of Philadelphia printed the first American editions of the King James Version: the New Testament in 1777, and the entire Bible in 1782. When the conflict ended, however, the American market was again opened to the British publishers, leaving Aitken with a large, unsold stock of books.

The Society for the Promotion of Christian Knowledge, established by the Church of England in 1698 to supply reading matter for clergy in British colonies, was a forerunner of the later Bible societies. The British and Foreign Bible Society, formed in London in 1804, provided the modern prototype, for in the first two decades of the 19th century, more than 100 Bible societies based upon the English model were founded in America. Beginning in 1808 with the Philadelphia Bible Society, these were all part of the grand Protestant missionary effort, often called the EVANGELICAL UNITED FRONT, that was inspired by the SECOND GREAT AWAKENING. Although some organizations were tiny operations that dispensed only a few hundred Bibles each year, together their reach extended throughout the young nation.

The most formidable organization was the American Bible Society. Formed originally in 1809 as the New York Bible Society, it was the strongest of the many local and state groups. In 1816, a convention of delegates representing various regional societies assembled in New York City and renamed the society, giving it a national scope. Although this idea was first opposed by some local societies, especially by the Philadelphia Bible Society, the organization was completed and Presbyterian layman Elias Boudinot (the first president of the United States Congress) was chosen as chairman of the ABS board. Led principally by Protestant laymen, the ABS adopted the policy of the British and Foreign Bible Society, namely, to publish the Scriptures "without note or comment."

Within a year of the founding of the ABS, 41 other societies aligned themselves with it as auxiliaries. By 1818 it had begun to appoint agents to travel within the United States seeking donations and subscriptions. The early accomplishments of the ABS were astounding. It distributed nearly 100,000 Bibles in the first four years of operation. Between 1829 and 1831 the ABS printed and distributed more than 1 million copies of the Scriptures, at a time when the total population of the United States was only around 13 million. Still strong today, the ABS reported that by the 1990s it had distributed nearly 300 million Bibles and portions of the Scriptures yearly.

Another 19th-century Bible society emerged out of a controversy over the translation of a portion of the biblical text. A schism occurred in the ranks of the ABS in 1835, when Baptists protested that the Greek verb *baptizein*, translated as "baptize" in the King James Version, should read "immerse" instead. Since this dispute concerned the Baptist practice of baptizing candidates by full immersion, ABS members who were not Baptists refused to yield and alter the traditional English wording. As a result, Baptists withdrew and formed their own organization, the American and Foreign Bible Society, in 1836. Further quarrels among the Baptists led to the creation of the American Bible Union, organized in 1850 with the financial backing of philanthropist William Colgate, for whom Colgate University is now named. However, following the Civil War, the rift between the ABS and American Bible Union was healed, and the Baptists rejoined the larger organization.

Certainly the most visible Bible society in the present day is the Gideons International. Founded in 1899 as the Christian Commercial Travellers Association of America, the society contained a group of business and professional people who were committed to lay evangelism. The Gideons took its name from the Book of Judges, in which the victory of the Israelite leader Gideon over his pagan enemies is described. In 1908 the Gideons began their now-familiar task of distributing Bibles (mostly the King James Version in the United States) in hotels, hospitals, prisons, and schools. More than 118,000 members belong to the organization worldwide today, and Gideons workers distribute more than 56 million Bibles in 175 countries annually.

GHS, Jr.

Bibliography: Nathan O. Hatch and Mark A. Noll, eds., *The Bible in American Culture: Essays in Cultural History* (New York: Oxford University Press, 1982); www.gideons.org (The Gideons International).

biblical interpretation   The Bible (Hebrew Old Testament and Greek New Testament) has been regarded by most American Christians throughout the centuries as the principal source of religious authority. Since the Reformation of the 16th century, Protestants have stressed that the Bible is both normative for faith and practice and accessible to the average reader. The remark made in 1809 by Thomas Campbell, one of the founders of the Disciples of Christ, has certainly been typical of much American religious belief: "Where the Scriptures speak, we speak; where the Scriptures are silent, we are silent."

The serious study and interpretation of the Bible in America began with the Puritan settlement of New England in the 17th century. Harvard College, founded in 1636, was named for the young Puritan minister who died in 1638 and left his library to the new school. Of the more than 300 volumes that John Harvard owned, more than half were biblical commen-

taries and similar works. Scriptural analysis, of course, was not an end in itself, but part of the process by which Christians gained an understanding of God's dealings with humankind. In the Bible, Puritans found teachings that applied not simply to the redemption of individuals but to the well-being of society as well.

Concern for the Bible remained strong during the 18th and early 19th century. In the GREAT AWAKENING, the period of intense spiritual excitement that swept through the colonies in the 1740s, Americans believed that the Scriptures contained the key to sin and salvation. In the War for Independence, Americans again looked closely at their Bibles, this time to find religious justification, usually in millennial (see POSTMILLENIALISM) themes, for their revolt from Great Britain. And after the Revolution, Protestant leaders considered the possibility of placing a copy of the Scriptures in the hands of every American citizen. During the SECOND GREAT AWAKENING in the early 19th century, moreover, more than 100 BIBLE SOCIETIES were formed to meet the challenge of publishing and distributing the Scriptures. Those Bible societies were part of a grand, interdenominational missionary effort often called "the Benevolent Empire."

So strong was the belief in the importance of reading the Bible that Protestant leaders pressed it forcibly upon many who did not wish to receive it. As a system of public schools began to develop, for example, spokesmen for that movement envisioned the Bible, especially the King James Version (the authorized translation for English-speaking Protestants), as an essential part of the standard curriculum. The growth of the Roman Catholic population of the United States in the mid-19th century, however, brought almost inevitable conflict over this issue. Many Catholics either did not speak English or used an English version of the Bible different from the King James; they rejected the Protestant standard. When Francis Patrick Kenrick, Roman Catholic bishop of Philadelphia, petitioned city officials to allow

Catholic children to hear readings from the Catholic Douay translation instead of the King James Version, an outcry ensued. Protestant mobs, believing they were defending the Bible, formed anti-Catholic organizations and rioted outside Catholic churches in Philadelphia.

Rival interpretations of the Bible also provided a crucial focus for the controversy over slavery before the Civil War. For most defenders of the institution, the acceptance of slavery in biblical times seemed sufficient proof that God justified holding human beings in bondage. Relying on a literal reading of the Scriptures, proslavery advocates in the South noted how the patriarchs of the Old Testament had owned slaves. They also cited the apostle Paul's return of a runaway slave to his master Philemon. White southern Christians argued that slavery represented a God-given opportunity to present the Bible and teach the faith to unconverted Africans, thereby saving the souls of their fellow human beings and—they hoped—keeping them docile.

African Americans (see AFRICAN-AMERICAN RELIGION), of course, had their own interpretations of the Gospel their masters preached to them. While whites might emphasize passages in the Bible that seemed to justify slavery, blacks focused upon biblical promises of liberation for God's chosen, but oppressed, people. Old Testament narratives were especially meaningful: Moses leading the enslaved Israelites from Egypt, Daniel in the lion's den, and the rescue of Shadrach, Meshach, and Abednego from the fiery furnace. In the New Testament, the promise of the Book of Revelation that the rulers of this world would be destroyed in an approaching age of cataclysm inspired African Americans to dream of future vindication. And Jesus the suffering servant heartened many like slave preacher Nat TURNER, who before his hanging asked his captors if they knew that Christ, too, had been executed.

Among abolitionists in the North, the liberating principles of the Bible also held great weight. Harriet Beecher Stowe's novel *Uncle Tom's Cabin*, for instance, presented a Christ-like black hero whose death was intended to redeem white Americans from the sin of slavery. Another antislavery leader, Presbyterian minister Albert Barnes of Philadelphia, declared that "the principles laid down by the Saviour and his Apostles are . . . opposed to Slavery, and if carried out would secure its universal abolition." And the title of abolitionist Theodore Dwight Weld's tract, *The Bible Against Slavery*, conveyed not only its author's belief that the Scriptures condemned human bondage, but also the convictions of a significant portion of the Protestant religious community in the North.

Despite disagreement about the Bible's teaching on slavery, most American Christians in the mid-19th century assumed that the Scriptures were infallible and divinely inspired. This trust in the essential veracity of the Bible depended upon a form of biblical interpretation based on SCOTTISH COMMON SENSE REALISM. A fundamentally optimistic philosophy, it allowed people to have great confidence in their own powers of reason. As a consequence of this emphasis on the certainty of human knowledge, Common Sense Realism led believers to assume that the words they read in the Bible were trustworthy. This philosophy provided the intellectual foundation for the doctrine of the INERRANCY of Scripture. As Charles HODGE, a professor at Princeton Seminary, asserted, the Bible was a "store-house of facts," truthful in every detail, whether scientific, historical, or doctrinal.

By the end of the 19th century, however, the "higher criticism" of the Bible began to appear in American academic circles. This approach, which originated in Germany, undermined commonly accepted beliefs about the Bible and called into question the concept of scriptural inerrancy. A host of questions about the authenticity and authorship of the Bible was raised, as the Bible's text was examined for the first time in a critical light. Did Moses really write the first five books of the

Old Testament? How could the story of creation that Genesis described be harmonized with the theory of EVOLUTION? How true were the stories of Noah and the flood or of Moses and the Red Sea?

The 1893 heresy trial of Presbyterian minister Charles Augustus BRIGGS of New York reveals the deep divisions within late 19th-century Protestantism over the Bible's proper interpretation. Throughout the 1880s, Briggs had written extensively about the higher-critical method of scriptural analysis. After the publication of his book *Whither?*, in which he asserted that divine revelation evolves over time, he came under intense criticism from his church's most conservative wing. In 1891, when Briggs contradicted orthodox Protestant belief and denied that every word of the Bible was inspired by God, he was brought to trial for heresy. Convicted for what was deemed false teaching, he eventually withdrew from the Presbyterian ministry.

Briggs's battle with Presbyterians over the Bible was one of the opening rounds of a protracted struggle between theological liberals and theological conservatives that continued into the next century. A series of pamphlets entitled *The Fundamentals* (from which the term FUNDAMENTALISM derives) encapsulated conservative teaching about the Bible's dependability. Composed of 12 volumes published between 1910 and 1915, *The Fundamentals* dealt with a number of topics, but the interpretation of Scripture was a central concern. Approximately one-third of the articles dealt with the Bible and defended it against liberals who questioned the validity of portions of its text. Although each author carefully nuanced his position, all believed that biblical teachings were not only scientifically verifiable but also errorless.

The Fundamentals themselves did not immediately have a strong impact either on the American churches or on American culture. A later controversy over the introduction of EVOLUTION into the curriculum of public schools,

however, symbolized how far apart American Christians had grown. In the 1920s, several southern states passed laws forbidding instructors from mentioning any theory that denied the divine creation of humanity as taught in the Bible. John T. Scopes, a biology teacher in Dayton, Tennessee, challenged the law in 1925. He was brought to trial and convicted, but the verdict was later overturned by a higher court.

The Scopes trial became a forum for the now-famous debate between the great Christian statesman William Jennings BRYAN and the agnostic trial lawyer Clarence Darrow. Their meeting was a study of contrasts: one side represented small-town America, poorly educated but militantly committed to the Bible; the other side saw itself as urbane and forward-looking in religious matters. When Bryan was called to testify on the veracity of the Bible, Darrow's cross-examination ridiculed his opponent's beliefs and made Bryan a laughingstock to the intellectually sophisticated. Although American Christians had earlier assumed that the Bible and the natural world fit harmoniously together, the Scopes trial revealed that the language of science and traditional religious language were no longer compatible in modern America.

Today the higher criticism of the Bible is generally accepted as the standard for interpretation in mainline Protestantism and in Roman Catholicism. This approach encourages a somewhat skeptical, but still reverent, approach to the scriptural text. Although liberal Protestants and Roman Catholics believe the Bible contains God's word, not every word in the Bible must be believed as literally true.

Among evangelical Protestants and other moderately conservative Christians, the primacy of the Bible as the medium of divine revelation is emphasized more strongly than it is among theological liberals. Nevertheless, many evangelicals accept modern scriptural criticism as a tool for better understanding the Bible.

Fundamentalists today continue to insist on the infallibility of the Bible. While they are willing to concede that current editions may contain textual impurities, they also believe that the Bible's original text is without error. In recent decades, the Lutheran Church—Missouri Synod and the Southern Baptist Convention have experienced divisions between fundamentalists and evangelical moderates over the proper interpretation of the Bible. Despite protests from moderates, the fundamentalist position has been accepted as normative by the leadership of both denominations.

(See also CREATIONISM; DISPENSATIONISM.)

GHS, Jr.

Bibliography: Jerry Wayne Brown, *The Rise of Biblical Criticism in America, 1800–1870: The New England Scholars* (Middletown, Conn.: Wesleyan University Press, 1969); Nathan O. Hatch and Mark A. Noll, eds., *The Bible in American Culture: Essays in Cultural History* (New York: Oxford University Press, 1982); Jack B. Rogers and Donald K. Mc Kim, *The Authority and Interpretation of the Bible: An Historical Approach* (San Francisco: Harper & Row, 1979).

black churches   See AFRICAN-AMERICAN RELIGION; AFRICAN METHODIST EPISCOPAL CHURCH; AFRICAN METHODIST EPISCOPAL ZION CHURCH; CHRISTIAN METHODIST EPISCOPAL CHURCH; CHURCH OF GOD IN CHRIST; NATIONAL BAPTIST CONVENTION OF AMERICA, INC.; NATIONAL BAPTIST CONVENTION U.S.A., INC.; PROGRESSIVE NATIONAL BAPTIST CONVENTION, INC.

Black Jews   The term *Black Jews*, or *Hebrews*, refers to several African-American religious movements that proclaim Judaism as the true religion of African Americans and claim a racial connection with the tribes of Israel through either descent from the Queen of Sheba and the Ethiopian Jews or the 10 lost tribes of Israel. The Judaism of these movements varies greatly, from the syncretistic mix of Christianity, Judaism, and black nationalism of the Church of God and Saints of Christ to the more orthodox Judaism of the Commandment Keepers Congregation of the Living God.

As early as the second decade of the 20th century there were itinerant black preachers traveling the South declaring that blacks were descendants of the Jews and that Judaism was their true religion. William Crowdy organized the Church of God and Saints of Christ in Lawrence, Kansas, in 1896, moving the headquarters to Philadelphia four years later. In 1917, following Crowdy's death, the headquarters were moved to Belleville, Virginia, soon becoming the largest of the Black Jewish sects. It is also the least Judaic in its religious forms. The church teaches that blacks are the descendants of the lost tribes of Israel (the reason for its inclusion among the Black Jews), and its doctrine is a syncretistic mix of black nationalism, Judaism, and Christianity. It demands a confession in Jesus Christ and has baptism by immersion, communion with water and unleavened bread, feet-washing, and the holy kiss as sacraments.

Prophet F. S. Cherry founded the Church of God (Black Jews) in Philadelphia. A seaman and railway worker for much of his life, Prophet Cherry was self-educated, picking up a good knowledge of both Yiddish and Hebrew. He claimed to have received a vision from God to return to America to preach the true religion to his people: that the blacks are the true Jews, that Judaism is their natural religion, and that the world will not be improved until the Black Jews get into positions of power.

Even closer to traditional Judaism is the Commandment Keepers Congregation of the Living God. Centered in Harlem and primarily composed of West Indian immigrants, the Commandment Keepers Congregation was organized in 1919 by Wentworth Arthur Matthew (1892–1973). Born in Lagos in modern-day Nigeria, he arrived in Harlem via St. Kitts in 1911. There he fell under the influence of Marcus GARVEY and A. J. Ford, music master of the Universal Negro Improvement Association (UNIA). Ford, occasionally confused by some with W. D. FARD, the founder of the NATION OF ISLAM, identified blacks with the

Jews of the Hebrew Bible and taught that blacks were the descendants of the ancient Israelites who would be freed by God from racism and oppression.

Failing to convince Garvey to adopt Judaism as the religion of the UNIA, Ford organized the Beth B'nai Abraham in Harlem in 1924. During the 1920s the rediscovery of the Falashas (the Ethiopian Jews) provided support for Ford's views. In 1930 Ford left the United States for Ethiopia, handing leadership of the Beth B'nai Abraham to Matthew, who merged it with the Commandment Keepers. Matthew moved progressively toward Orthodox Judaism and increasingly identified African Americans with the Falashas, arguing that blacks had to recover the nationality and religion that had been stolen by the whites who had enslaved them.

Perhaps the most familiar of all the Black Jews, due to the difficulties in which they have found themselves, is the Original Hebrew Israelite Nation. Claiming descent from the 10 lost tribes, the Black Israelites attempt to follow Orthodox Judaism and a form of black nationalism. Believing that Israel is their true homeland, a contingent left Chicago to settle there in 1971. Although most returned to the United States after the Israeli rabbinate refused to recognize their claim to be Jews by birth, a large number remained, eking out an existence in a settlement in the Negev. Since many of them had renounced their American citizenship and were refused Israeli citizenship, they lived as stateless persons for more than two decades. In the early 1990s the Israeli government agreed to grant them citizenship in return for formal conversions.

The various Black Hebrew movements had their strongest growth during the 1970s. At that time their beliefs, a mixture of black pride and black identity, found a ready hearing among urban blacks. With growth, however, came division and turmoil. By the end of the 1990s most groups had shrunk to only a few hundred members. Strongest in Chicago, they also could be found in Newark, New York, Philadelphia, and a few other major cities.

EQ

Bibliography: Howard M. Brotz, *The Black Jews of Harlem: Negro Nationalism and the Dilemmas of Negro Leadership* (New York: Schocken, 1970); Yvonne Patricia Chireau and Nathaniel Deutsch, *Black Zion: African-American Religious Encounters with Judaism* (New York: Oxford University Press, 2000); Arthur H. Fauset, *Black Gods of the Metropolis: Negro Religious Cults of the Urban North* (New York: Octagon Books, 1970).

Black Muslims   See NATION OF ISLAM.

Blavatsky, Helena Petrovna (1831–1891)
Helena Petrovna Blavatsky is renowned as a cofounder of the Theosophical Society (see THEOSOPHY) and one of America's most controversial mediums, yet relatively little is known about her life. After Blavatsky's death in London in 1891, Henry Steel OLCOTT, her closest friend and Theosophical collaborator, admitted that she remained even to him "an insoluble riddle." That admission undoubtedly would have pleased Blavatsky, who went to great lengths to shroud her life in secrecy.

Blavatsky was born to Russian nobles—her father was an army officer and her mother a novelist—in Ekaterinoslav in the Ukraine in 1831. While a teenager, she married Nikifor Blavatsky, a provincial governor of the czar. She left her husband soon thereafter, however, and fled to Constantinople and a life of adventure in 1849. Blavatsky claimed that she spent her next 25 years traveling the world as a pilgrim, sitting at the feet of gurus and undergoing initiations into ancient occult mysteries in, among other places, Tibet.

During her travels Blavatsky was introduced to SPIRITUALISM and became a medium. While in Cairo in 1871 and 1872, she attempted to launch a Spiritualist society, but she lacked the organizational skills to sustain the following her considerable charisma attracted, and her "Société Spirite" collapsed. In 1873 she moved to New York, where she earned a reputation as a rough-talking, chain-smoking bohemian who ate too much and slept too little. One year later, at a Spiritualist séance she teamed up with Olcott, a genteel reformer who would provide Blavatsky with the organizational skills she clearly lacked.

In 1875 Blavatsky and Olcott cofounded the Theosophical Society in New York. Inspired by Blavatsky's conviction that Spiritualist phenomena were caused not by mediums passively channeling disembodied spirits of the dead but by adepts whose initiation into ancient mysteries enabled them to actively manipulate occult forces in accordance with occult laws, the Theosophical Society aimed in its early years to investigate those Spiritualist phenomena and discover via experiments the occult laws undergirding them. This agenda, along with Blavatsky's first and most influential book, *Isis Unveiled* (1877), attracted elite New Yorkers to endless discussions in her fashionable salon. But the organization itself soon fizzled.

Hopeful that a change in venue would provide the Theosophical Society with new life, Blavatsky set sail with Olcott in 1878 for India, where she added to its mission two additional goals: promoting Asian religious traditions over missionary Christianity and constructing one "Universal Brotherhood of Humanity" out of the Babel of sectarian religions. In this work the Theosophists were inspired, according to Blavatsky, by a secret brotherhood of "Masters" who had been entrusted throughout the ages with conserving and propagating an ancient wisdom tradition that permeated the Hindu and Buddhist scriptures and all other truly Theosophical works.

While in Ceylon (now Sri Lanka) in 1880, Blavatsky officially converted to BUDDHISM by promising to take refuge in the Buddha, the Dharma (Buddhist teaching), and the Sangha (community of Buddhist monks). She was by her own admission, however, an "esoteric Buddhist" who saw Gautama Buddha as merely

Helena Petrovna Blavatsky, the charismatic spiritual teacher and cofounder of the Theosophical Society in 1875 in New York City. *(United Lodge of Theosophists)*

one Master among many and Buddhism as but one expression of the ancient wisdom.

The greatest crisis in the life of Blavatsky and her society occurred in 1884, when her former friend, Emma Coulomb, accused her of manufacturing through exceedingly ordinary means ostensibly extraordinary phenomena. After a lengthy investigation, Richard Hodgson of the London-based Society for Psychical Research issued in 1885 what came to be known as the "Hodgson Report." Hodgson claimed in that document that all the spiritual phenomena attributed to Blavatsky and her fellow Theosophists were produced either through fraud or hallucination. Blavatsky, he concluded, was "one of the most accomplished, ingenious, and interesting imposters in history."

After the report was issued, Olcott urged Blavatsky to leave the Theosophical Society's headquarters outside Madras, India. Reluctantly, she moved to London, where she continued to write and to attract followers. She published her most systematic Theosophical work, *The Secret Doctrine,* in 1888 and began her own magazine, *Lucifer,* as an alternative to the Olcott-controlled *Theosophist.*

After her death in 1891, Blavatsky's ashes were scattered in New York, London, and Adyar (near Madras). She left behind her an international organization with hundreds of branches on five continents. Today she is revered by Theosophists across the globe, who see her not as an imposter but as one of a handful of modern sages initiated into the ancient mysteries.

SRP

Bibliography: Bruce F. Campbell, *Ancient Wisdom Revived: A History of the Theosophical Movement* (Berkeley: University of California Press, 1980); Maria Carlson, *"No Religion Higher Than Truth": A History of the Theosophical Movement in Russia, 1875–1922* (Princeton N.J.: Princeton University Press, 1993); Sylvia Cranston, *HPB: The Extraordinary Life and Influence of Helena Blavatsky, Founder of the Modern Theosophical Movement* (New York: Tarcher/Putnam, 1994).

blue laws   See SABBATARIANISM.

Boardman, William Edwin   See HIGHER CHRISTIAN LIFE MOVEMENT.

Book of Mormon   The Book of Mormon is a scripture of the CHURCH OF JESUS CHRIST OF LATTER-DAY SAINTS and other Mormon churches. Published in 1830 by Joseph SMITH, Jr., the founder of the Mormon movement, the Book of Mormon is viewed by Mormons today as the word of God that fulfills even as it supplements the Bible.

The official title of the book that Mormons accept as "another testament of Jesus Christ" is *The Book of Mormon: An Account Written by the Hand of Mormon upon Plates Taken from the Plates of Nephi.* That account purports to be a translation of gold plates buried in pre-Columbian times on the Hill Cumorah in Manchester, New York. Mormons believe that Smith was first led to these gold tablets in 1823 by an angel named Moroni, who came to him in a vision. After taking possession of them in 1837, he began to translate the Egyptian-like hieroglyphics, which were supposedly inscribed on the plates.

More a work of history than of doctrine, the Book of Mormon tells the story of Near Eastern peoples who migrated to the "promised land" of America in the Old Testament period and of the appearance of Jesus in the New World following his crucifixion and resurrection. The book chronicles the story of the family of Lehi, a Hebrew prophet who fled Jerusalem shortly before that city was destroyed by the Babylonians in the sixth century B.C.

After crossing the Arabian desert, Lehi's family traversed the Atlantic Ocean by ship. Upon their arrival in the New World, Lehi's descendants tilled the earth, built cities, maintained temples, and followed the laws of Moses. But eventually Lehi's sons split into two antagonistic factions: the civilized Nephites and the barbarous Lamanites. These two groups were reconciled for 200 years after Jesus came to the New World to preach, perform miracles, ordain disciples, and found his church. In the third century, however, they resumed their internecine struggle. Although the Nephites emerged from the battle victorious, both groups were decimated. Some Lamanites survived and are known today as American Indians. The Nephites left behind only a lone prophet, Mormon (hence "Mormonism"), and his son Moroni. It was the sad chronicle of these last Nephites, inscribed on gold tablets in the fourth century, that Smith purportedly discovered in 1823. And it was Moroni himself, now in the form of an angel, who led Smith to his discovery.

When Smith's "translation" of the "golden bible" appeared in March of 1830, it created an immediate stir. Some of Smith's contemporaries accepted the claim that this new scripture contained "the fullness of the gospel of Jesus Christ." They saw in Smith the fulfillment of the Book of Mormon prophecy of a "choice seer" named Joseph who would come to restore Israel to its ancient glory. Others, however, denounced Smith as a fraud, his friends as coconspirators, and his followers as dupes and rubes.

Smith's enemies advanced a number of criticisms concerning the Book of Mormon, some of them contradictory. The book, some said, could not be a new divine revelation because large chunks of it were plagiarized from the Bible. Written in the style of the King James Version of the Bible and divided like the Bible into books, chapters, and verses, Smith's text borrowed copiously, they argued, from both the Hebrew Bible and the New Testament. Others argued, on the other hand, that the Book of Mormon should be rejected because it contradicted the Bible. They contended, moreover, that the book was riddled with grammatical errors.

Critics found it as difficult to agree about Smith's authorship as they had about the book's relationship to the Bible. Some argued that the largely unlettered Smith could not have written the book, while others claimed Smith's hand in the book's production was far more evident than the hand of God. One critic who found the text to be rife with "Smithisms" was Alexander CAMPBELL, the founder of the Disciples of Christ (see CHRISTIAN CHURCH [DISCIPLES OF CHRIST]). Why, Campbell asked, if the book was written so long ago, did it endeavor to "decide every question" asked by inquiring New Yorkers during the past 10 years? Why did it bear the mark of FREEMASONRY, republican political theory, and romantic nationalism? Why did it contain answers to virtually every theological controversy of the modern period: "infant baptism,

ordination, the trinity, regeneration, repentance, justification, the fall of man, the atonement, transubstantiation, fasting, penance, church government, religious experience, the call to the ministry, the general resurrection, eternal punishment," to say nothing of the origins of American Indians?

If Smith's and his followers' responses to these criticisms did not win over critics of Mormonism, they did satisfy early Mormons, who embraced this story of a God who continued to work throughout history to redeem his people from ancient apostasies and who promised to restore in the New World both ancient Israel and the primitive Christian church. Mormons today may disagree about how to interpret particularly knotty passages in the Book of Mormon, but they agree that God in all ages speaks to his chosen people in revelations given through prophets. In addition to the Bible ("so far as it is correctly translated") and the Book of Mormon, they recognize two collections of Smith's revelations and translations as divinely inspired scripture. Both those texts—*Doctrine and Covenants* (1835) and *The Pearl of Great Price* (1851)—address doctrinal and ecclesiastical matters on which the largely narrative Book of Mormon is either silent or ambiguous.

SRP

Bibliography: Philip L. Barlow, *Mormons and the Bible: The Place of the Latter-day Saints in American Religion* (New York: Oxford University Press, 1991); Richard L. Bushman, *Joseph Smith and the Beginnings of Mormonism* (Urbana: University of Illinois Press, 1984); http://scriptures.lds.org (Book of Mormon online).

Booth, William   See SALVATION ARMY.

Bradford, William (1590–1657)   Author of one of the classics of American literature and governor of Plymouth colony for 30 years, William Bradford is one of the best known PILGRIMS. The colony's survival, tenuous as it was, truly owes its existence to Bradford's wisdom and foresight.

Born in March 1590 in Austerfield, England, Bradford fell in with religious dissenters as a youth. At 16 he joined the separatist congregation at Scrooby and soon became a respected member. The congregation suffered increasing persecution from the civil authorities. In order to escape this persecution Bradford and others migrated to Holland in 1607.

While in Holland, Bradford, like most of his colleagues, worked in the textile industry. By 1619 he had become convinced that no future lay with the little group there. When the *Mayflower* left for America in 1620 he was among the 101 passengers aboard.

The first winter in America was a time of group and personal tragedy for Bradford. His wife fell overboard and drowned in December, and by March nearly half the colony at Plymouth had succumbed to illness and starvation. Among this number was the colony's governor, John Carpenter. Bradford was chosen to succeed him. He would hold this position for 30 years, between 1620 and 1657.

The choice of Bradford was a fortunate one. He developed a good working relationship with Massassoit, the leader of the neighboring Wampanoags, organized the distribution of land and supplies, and administered justice. If any criticism can be laid against him, it is of moderation and forbearance. His patience with troublemakers and toward the cheating and greedy stockholders back in England seems superhuman. Given to leniency, he seemed inclined to suffer others as long as they remained sufferable. Differences in religious and political opinions were less threatening to him than they were to the governor of the younger and larger MASSACHUSETTS BAY COLONY. Bradford could offer shelter and food to a Jesuit priest who was passing through, and voting at Plymouth was not limited to church members.

Beyond his service to the colony, which was instrumental to its survival, Bradford's importance is due to the tremendous number of writings he left behind at his death (May 9, 1657). His *History of Plymouth Plantation* is the best contemporary source of information about the colony. But Bradford also left journals, poems, and letters that provide a remarkable picture of the Pilgrims' struggle to build a new life in a new land.

EQ

Bibliography: William Bradford, *History of Plymouth Plantation, 1620–1647: The Complete Text, with Notes and an Introduction by Samuel Eliot Morison* (New York: Knopf, 1952); Kieran Doherty, *William Bradford: Rock of Plymouth* (Brookfield, Conn.: Twenty-First Century Books, 1999); George D. Langdon, Jr., *Pilgrim Colony: A History of New Plymouth, 1620–1691* (New Haven: Yale University Press, 1966).

Bradstreet, Anne   See ANTINOMIAN CONTROVERSY; LITERATURE AND CHRISTIANITY.

Bresee, Phineas Franklin   See CHURCH OF THE NAZARENE.

Briggs, Charles Augustus (1841–1913)
Charles Augustus Briggs was a biblical scholar, a Presbyterian minister, and, at the end of his career, a priest of the Episcopal Church. Briggs played a central role in theological battles that led to the fragmentation of mainline Protestantism into fundamentalist (see FUNDAMENTALISM) and modernist (see MODERNISM) camps in the late 19th and early 20th century. His 1893 heresy trial, perhaps the most famous in American religious history, reveals the bitter division between opposing definitions of theological and biblical orthodoxy.

Briggs was born in New York City on January 15, 1841. He was educated at the University of Virginia, where, in the midst of a college revival, he was converted to Christ and decided to enter the Presbyterian ministry. After graduating from Virginia in 1860, he studied privately for a brief time. He enlisted and served for three months in the Seventh New York Regiment early in the Civil War. Returning home in July 1861, Briggs enrolled at Union Theological Seminary in New York. He studied at

Union from 1861 to 1863 and abroad at the University of Berlin from 1866 to 1869. In the period between his studies, he managed his family's barrel-making business when ill health forced his father's withdrawal from work. Following his return from Berlin in 1869, Briggs was called as pastor of the First Presbyterian Church in Roselle, New Jersey. In 1874 Union Seminary in New York City appointed him professor of Hebrew. He served with distinction at Union for nearly four decades.

Although the Old and New School Presbyterian denominations in the North had mended their schism of 1837 and joined together again in 1870 as the Presbyterian Church, U.S.A., the reunited church did not at first possess a common theological journal. When the new *Presbyterian Review* was established in 1881, Briggs was nominated to serve as its coeditor with Archibald A. Hodge of Princeton Seminary. Princeton had long represented the doctrinally conservative Old School, and while Briggs himself had been an Old School Presbyterian, Union Seminary was a liberal New School institution.

The *Presbyterian Review*, rather than mollifying theological tensions within the denomination, actually exacerbated the differences between traditionalists and progressives. Briggs's own advanced views on scriptural interpretation soon came into conflict with the conservative approach to the Bible and to Presbyterian beliefs that the theologians from Princeton represented. Throughout this period Briggs published articles championing the higher-critical method of scriptural interpretation. Hodge and others, however, argued for the inerrancy of the Bible and the complete trustworthiness of the plain meaning of Scripture, positions that would eventually typify American fundamentalism. After the publication of Briggs's most famous scholarly work, *Whither?* (1889), in which he asserted that divine revelation evolves over time, he came under intense criticism from the denomination's conservative wing. Irreconcilable differ-

Charles Augustus Briggs, the foremost Old Testament scholar of his day, was excommunicated from the Presbyterian ministry after a much-publicized heresy trial in New York in the 1890s.

ences forced the demise of the *Presbyterian Review* by the end of 1889.

Briggs faced an even more formidable controversy in 1891. In his inaugural address on "The Authority of Holy Scripture," delivered when he assumed the chair of biblical studies at Union, Briggs denied both the verbal inspiration of the Bible and the doctrine of inerrancy, the linchpins of conservative teaching on Scripture. Briggs's address led the Presbyterian General Assembly, the highest decision-making body of the denomination, to veto his professorial appointment. He was subsequently tried for heresy and suspended from the ministry in 1893.

The decision against Briggs caused Union to renounce its affiliation with the Presbyterian

Church, U.S.A., and become an independent seminary. Briggs was thus able to retain his position at Union. The events of 1893, of course, also drastically altered Briggs's own denominational loyalties. He withdrew from the Presbyterian Church in 1898 and, attracted to the doctrinal broadness of Anglicanism, he was ordained to the Episcopal ministry in May 1899. Yet Briggs's progressive ideas aroused conflict even in the Episcopal Church. His growing concern for ecumenism, for example, led him to consider a future union of the Christian churches. The desire he stated in 1903 for "the recatholization" of Christianity was criticized by the low-church party within Episcopalianism. Many accused him of wishing to abandon Protestantism altogether for the Roman Catholic Church.

Briggs remained in the Protestant fold for the rest of his life. He wrote more than 20 books, including *Church Unity* (1909), his final contribution to the intellectual and cultural discussions that had occupied his mind since the 1860s. Together with Francis Brown and Samuel R. Driver, he also edited *A Hebrew and English Lexicon of the Old Testament* (1906), which remains in widespread use as a dictionary of biblical studies. Briggs also served as one of the original editors of the prestigious *International Critical Commentary* series.

Briggs retired from academic and ecclesiastical debates in 1910, for he had begun to suffer regular attacks of nervous exhaustion. He died quietly at his residence at Union Seminary on June 8, 1913.

GHS, Jr.

Bibliography: Mark Stephen Massa, *Charles Augustus Briggs and the Crisis of Historical Criticism* (Minneapolis: Fortress Press, 1990).

broadcasting, religious See ELECTRONIC CHURCH.

Brook Farm See TRANSCENDENTALISM.

Brooks, Phillips (1835–1893) Phillips Brooks was an Episcopal clergyman, author of the popular Christmas carol "O Little Town of Bethlehem," and one of the greatest preachers in late 19th-century America. Rector of Trinity Church in the fashionable Back Bay section of Boston, Brooks represented the "broad church" tradition in the Episcopal Church, a blend of theological liberalism and optimism about the human condition.

Brooks was born in Boston on December 13, 1835. He was graduated from Harvard College in 1855 and from the Virginia Theological Seminary in Alexandria in 1859. After his ordination in 1859, Brooks served in Philadelphia, first at the Church of the Advent between 1859 and 1862 and then at Holy Trinity Church from 1862 to 1869. In October 1869, Brooks began his lengthy career at Trinity Church. A few years later, after a terrible fire that destroyed large portions of downtown Boston in 1872, Trinity Church relocated to the newly developed Back Bay on land reclaimed from the Charles River marshes. There, Brooks oversaw the construction of a magnificent new building.

Brooks's broad churchmanship and conservative social views were well suited to his affluent parishioners. "The spirit of man is the candle of God," Brooks repeatedly told his congregation, and he believed in the goodness and nobility of humankind generally. His faith in progress also kept him untroubled by the inequalities of life in the post–Civil War Gilded Age. Although he believed that poverty and suffering among the urban masses were for the most part deserved, he also trusted that social inequalities were simply temporary problems that would one day be dispelled by the natural harmony of God's purposes.

Brooks published a number of volumes of sermons, as well as *Lectures on Preaching* (delivered at Yale in 1877) and a posthumous collection of *Essays and Addresses*. He wrote the words of "O Little Town of Bethlehem" for the Sunday school children at Holy Trinity Church, Philadelphia, in 1867. Although elected bishop of Massachusetts in 1891, he served in that capacity for only a few months and died after a short illness on January 23, 1893. Boston was so moved by his untimely passing that every pew in Trinity Church was filled for a memorial observance on the 10th anniversary of Brooks's death.

GHS, Jr.

Bibliography: Raymond W. Albright, *Focus on Infinity: A Life of Phillips Brooks* (New York: Macmillan, 1961); John Frederick Wolverton, *The Education of Phillips Brooks* (Urbana: University of Illinois Press, 1995).

Brownson, Orestes Augustus (1803–1876)

One of the most colorful figures in both American intellectual and Catholic history, Orestes Brownson was a religious and philosophical seeker who finally found a home in ROMAN CATHOLICISM. A controversialist by nature and a journalist by trade, Brownson's acerbic wit, independent mind, and willingness to follow his thoughts wherever they led made him enemies in all camps.

Born in Stockbridge, Vermont, on September 16, 1803, his father's early death interrupted his formal education. Brownson was, however, an avid reader with a particular interest in religious and political questions. Searching for spiritual stability, he joined the Presbyterian Church (see PRESBYTERIANISM) in 1822. Disgusted with the doctrines of election and eternal damnation, he left two years later, becoming a Universalist (see UNIVERSALISM.)

Although ordained a Universalist minister in 1827 and editor of the denomination's *Gospel Advocate,* the intellectual views that originally led him to reject Presbyterianism drove him ever further toward radical humanism. Breaking with organized religion, he became an itinerant preacher until contact with the English freethinker Fanny Wright turned him toward ATHEISM and radical politics. During this period Brownson joined an Owenite community in New York and edited the Owenite paper, *Free Enquirer* (see OWEN, ROBERT DALE).

He also served as an organizer of the Workingmen's Party and was a fervent socialist.

Beginning to doubt the wisdom of political action that set workers against capitalists, Brownson left the party. Estranged from organized religion intellectually and politically, Brownson embarked on another period as an independent preacher. As he did during all of his various passions, Brownson founded a newspaper, *The Philanthropist,* in whose pages he preached his religion of humanity.

During this time, Brownson fell under the influence of William Ellery CHANNING, viewing Channing's liberal Unitarianism and politics as consonant with his own views. Ordained a Unitarian minister, Brownson held pulpits in Walpole, New Hampshire (1832–1834), and Canton, Massachusetts (1834–1836), until he grew disillusioned with the cold rationality and materialism of Unitarianism.

At this time Brownson followed many other "post-Unitarians" into the transcendentalist movement (see TRANSCENDENTALISM). Although suspicious of transcendentalism's individualism and its tendency to identify God with nature, Brownson found a congenial home among those who viewed external authority with suspicion and affirmed the universal possession of what Brownson called spontaneous reason—an intuitive knowledge of God. Increasingly interested in community, Brownson was attracted to the socialism of the French thinker Henri de St. Simon and its demand for a cooperative society.

To spread these ideas he founded the *Boston Quarterly Review* (1838), in which he attacked inherited wealth, industrialism, wage labor, Christianity, and democracy and called for the abolition of all penal codes. The *Review* gained a wide audience for Brownson's views, and he quickly became a notorious figure. Following a merger of the *Review* with the *Democratic Review,* editorial disagreements with the new owners resulted in Brownson's resignation.

Brownson's concern with community and with locating the source of moral authority led

Orestes Augustus Brownson, famed 19th-century tran-scendentalist journalist who became a convert and leading spokesperson for American Catholicism. *(Engraving by Alexander L. Dick)*

him to look favorably upon the corporate model of the Roman Catholic Church as providing the most tangible means of divine communion and human community. Placing himself under the guidance of the co-adjutor bishop of Boston, John Bernard Fitzpatrick, Brownson undertook the instruction necessary to become a Roman Catholic, receiving communion on October 20, 1844. His period of religious questing was over, and Brownson would live the remainder of his days within the Church.

Although his religious searching ended, Brownson remained a controversial figure. His new journal, *Brownson's Quarterly Review,* took up the defense of Roman Catholicism and promptly lost readers throughout the country as he vigorously defended Roman Catholic orthodoxy and consigned all those outside the Church to hell, including his old comrades in arms. His spirited defense of Catholicism earned him official approbation from the U.S. Catholic bishops in 1849 and a letter of thanks from Pius IX in 1854. Brownson's erudition also led to an invitation from John Henry Newman to join the faculty of the new Catholic University of Dublin.

Brownson's orthodox views soon faded, and he became a strong advocate for a positive role for American culture in the Catholic Church. He advocated church-state separation and liberal democracy, while attacking parochial schools, Irish immigrants, Jesuits, and the temporal power of the popes. Such attacks cost him his Catholic audience and the support of the hierarchy. In 1865 he suspended publication of the *Review* due to ecclesiastical opposition. Although he revived the journal in 1872 with spirited defenses of papal infallibility and authority, Brownson was viewed with suspicion by his coreligionists who, like others before them, wondered about the stability of his mind. Bitter and disappointed, he died in Detroit on April 17, 1876. Seven years later he received the honors he undoubtedly deserved when his remains were reinterred in the Chapel of the Sacred Heart at the University of Notre Dame.

Although the meanderings of his mind and spirit led many to dismiss him as a crank, Brownson exerted a significant influence on 19th-century American life. Religiously he was among the first to argue publicly for the compatibility of American society with Roman Catholicism, and along with his fellow convert Isaac HECKER, he was influential in formulating an American Catholicism. Equally significant is the fact that *Brownson's Quarterly Review* was not only the center of Roman Catholic intellectual currents but a center for political and social thought beyond Catholic concerns.

EQ

Bibliography: Henry F. Brownson, *Life of Orestes Brownson*, 3 vols. (Detroit: H. F. Brownson, 1898–1900); Orestes A. Brownson, *Selected Writings.* (New York: Paulist Press, 1991); ———, *The Convert, or, Leaves from My Experience* (New York: D. & J. Sadler, 1886); Hugh Marshall, *Orestes Brownson and the American Republic* (Washington, D.C.: Catholic University of America Press, 1972); Arthur M. Schlesinger, Jr., *Orestes Brownson: A Pilgrim's Progress* (Boston: Little Brown, 1939).

Bryan, William Jennings (1860–1925)

William Jennings Bryan was the leading spokesman for American FUNDAMENTALISM in the early 20th century and a three-time candidate for the United States presidency. He is best known today for his militant opposition to the teaching of evolution in the public schools, the position he maintained at the famed Scopes Trial of 1925.

Bryan was born in Salem, Illinois, on March 19, 1860. He graduated from Illinois College in 1881. After his graduation from Union Law College in Chicago and admission to the bar in 1883, he practiced law in Illinois and Nebraska. A Democratic politician, Bryan held national office for the first time in 1891 when elected to serve as a congressman from Nebraska. Known as "the Great Commoner" because of his midwestern, agrarian roots, Bryan was nominated on three occasions (1896, 1900, and 1908) as the Democratic candidate for president. He lost all three times, however, and the election results revealed the limits of his national appeal. In 1896, he won 49 percent of the popular vote but did not carry a single state outside the South or east of the Mississippi River.

Bryan approached politics with the fervor of a moral reformer, and his greatest speeches had a decidedly religious, almost revivalistic, tone. His "cross of gold" speech at the 1896 Democratic convention, for example, won him tremendous support and soon became the most celebrated political oration since Lincoln's second inaugural address. "You shall not press down upon the brow of labor this crown of thorns," he shouted that day. "You shall not crucify mankind upon a cross of gold." Bryan spoke passionately on behalf of accepting silver as equal in value to gold as the basis of the national currency, a reform favored by the populist forces he represented but opposed by Republican bankers and businessmen in the East who advocated the gold standard.

In 1912, the American people finally turned to the Democratic Party for a president. Bryan's support was crucial to Woodrow Wilson's election that year. He was rewarded with appointment as Wilson's secretary of state. Yet because of his continuing commitment to the ideals of Christian pacifism, a position typical of his geographic and religious background, the advent of World War I in Europe quickly brought him into opposition to the policies of the Wilson administration. Troubled by protests over Germany's sinking of the *Lusitania* and fearing eventual American participation in the war, Bryan chose to resign his position in June 1915 rather than compromise his beliefs.

The final years of Bryan's life and career reveal similar conflict between the narrow conservatism of his religious views and the necessity for compromise characteristic of American politics. Always a temperance advocate, for instance, Bryan threw himself into the campaign for the prohibition of alcoholic beverages. Following the congressional elections of 1916, he played an important role in the eventual passage of the Eighteenth Amendment and the Volstead Act, which together outlawed the sale and manufacture of liquor after January 1920. In the same period, however, the center of the American population was shifting away from the Protestant rural and agrarian areas that favored prohibition and toward "wet" urban areas. The 1920 census showed that for the first time most Americans lived in cities—a death knell for the short-lived reform Bryan had championed.

In the early 1920s, Bryan attacked the growing modernist (see MODERNISM) emphasis within American churches and accused liberal Protestants of undermining both traditional morality and Christian civilization itself. He believed that the doctrine of EVOLUTION especially had weakened the trust men and women once placed in God. Championing theological views that soon bore the label "fundamentalist," Bryan campaigned against the teaching of that scientific theory in the nation's schools. Hoping to duplicate the success conservatives had enjoyed in passing prohibition laws, Bryan encouraged the movement in several southern state legislatures to ban instruction about biological evolution.

As a consequence of this antievolution crusade, Bryan headed the prosecution against John Scopes, a young biology teacher in Dayton, Tennessee, charged in 1925 with teaching evolution, thus violating a new state law. Scopes was defended by Clarence Darrow, a sophisticated lawyer and well-known religious agnostic, who made Bryan look like an ignorant fool. While Bryan believed it was better "to trust the Rock of Ages than to know the ages of rocks," Darrow forced his opponent to admit that no reputable modern scientist shared his views. Although Bryan actually won a conviction of Scopes on narrow legal grounds, the fundamentalist position became thoroughly discredited in the eyes of the national press who covered the trial.

Bryan himself not only was embarrassed by the trial but was also physically broken by the experience. He never left the trial site in Dayton and died on July 26, 1925, a few days after the announcement of the verdict.

GHS, Jr.

Bibliography: Robert W. Cherny, *A Righteous Cause: The Life of William Jennings Bryan* (Norman: University of Oklahoma Press, 1994); Edward J. Larson, *Summer for the Gods: The Scopes Trial and America's Continuing Debate over Science and Religion* (New York: Basic Books, 1997); Lawrence W. Levine, *Defender of the Faith: William Jennings Bryan, 1915–1925* (New York: Oxford University Press, 1965).

Buchman, Frank Nathan Daniel (1878–1961)

Frank Buchman was a Lutheran pastor and the founder of Moral Re-Armament, a movement created to prevent war through the promotion of a worldwide spiritual awakening. Buchman stressed the need of human beings to surrender their individual wills to the will of God. Using small gatherings, or "house parties," where influential people might be converted to his moral vision, Buchman hoped to lay the foundation of a new social order under God's rule.

Buchman was born in Pennsburg, Pennsylvania, on June 4, 1878. He graduated from Muhlenberg College in 1899 and studied at Mt. Airy Seminary from 1899 to 1902. He served as a Lutheran minister in Overbrook, Pennsylvania, between 1902 and 1905 and then directed the first Lutheran settlement house in Philadelphia from 1905 to 1909. Following a trip to Europe in 1908, Buchman became convinced that religious experience could actually change the way people behaved. Buchman felt called to become an evangelist of the nonsectarian gospel he discovered and to disseminate his spiritual and psychological insights as widely as possible.

Following service, first, as the secretary of the YMCA at Pennsylvania State College and, later, as a lecturer on evangelism at Hartford Seminary, Buchman arrived at Oxford University in 1921 and launched the movement to which he devoted the rest of his life. Known originally as the First Century Christian Fellowship or the Oxford Group Movement, Buchman's organization employed small, informal gatherings as a means of persuading participants to change their lives. At the house parties he arranged, Buchman used his "Five C's" (confidence, conviction, confession, conversion, and continuance) to bring people to a "God-guided" life under the "Four Absolutes" (honesty, purity, unselfishness, and love). The Oxford Group Movement attracted worldwide attention during the 1930s, when Queen Mary of Romania was numbered among its many notable patrons. Renamed Moral Re-Armament in 1938, the organization was dedicated to achieving personal, social, racial, national, and international change.

Moral Re-Armament soon lost much of its early spiritual vigor. Eager to attract intellectuals, the wealthy, and world leaders who could aid his goals, Buchman appeared to forget the original popular base on which his movement was built. His emphasis on international peace, moreover, fell into disrepute after war broke out in Europe in 1939. Adamantly opposed to Communism and sympathetic to fascism, Moral Re-Armament adopted a prewar policy of appeasement that later was viewed as controversial. Buchman revealed in 1936, for example, that he viewed the rise of Adolf Hitler as a heaven-sent opportunity to build "a front line of defense against the Anti-Christ of Communism." Only the many patriotic efforts of Moral Re-Armament members in assisting the war effort against Germany and Japan helped restore Buchman's group to favor in the public eye.

Buchman's health deteriorated in the 1950s, and he was unable to prevent his movement from again declining in influence. He died abroad at Freudenstadt, Germany, on August 7, 1961. Although Moral Re-Armament remains active today, it has never regained the prestige it possessed during its heyday in the 1920s and 1930s. Its popular "Up with People" program folded in 2001.

GHS, Jr.

Bibliography: Garth Lean, *On the Tail of a Comet: The Life of Frank Buchman* (Colorado Springs, Colo.: Helmers & Howard, 1988).

Buddhism Buddhism is one of the world's major religious traditions. It exists in three major forms. The Theravada ("Way of the Elders") tradition is the oldest and most traditional. It emphasizes monasticism and is widespread in Southeast Asia. The Mahayana ("Great Vehicle") form is dominant in East Asian countries such as China and Japan. It provides a more important role for the laity. The third major form is the Vajrayana ("Diamond Vehicle") path of Tibet. This tradition, which has been popularized in the West in recent years by the DALAI LAMA, integrates elements of the esoteric Tantric path of Hinduism into Buddhist practice.

In the United States, there are at least two distinct histories of the Buddhist tradition: the story of the Buddhism of Asian immigrants and their descendants and the story of the Buddhist interests of non-Asian-American sympathizers and adherents. The first story includes the transplantation to the United States of all three major forms of Buddhism by immigrants from Asia. The second story ranges from the interest in Buddhism demonstrated by Unitarians and transcendentalists in the mid-19th century to the more recent Buddhist explorations of the Beat Generation (see BEAT MOVEMENT) and the hip-hop group the Beastie Boys.

The first Asians in the United States came from China to the West Coast around the time of the gold rush of 1849. In 1853 the first Chinese temple in America was built in San Francisco's Chinatown. By the end of the 19th century there were 400 such shrines on the West Coast. These syncretistic temples enshrined a number of popular folk deities of China and made room not only for Buddhism but also for TAOISM and Confucianism. Chinese immigration declined precipitously after the Chinese Exclusion Act of 1882 and remained minute until the law's repeal in 1943. Many of the original temples closed for lack of patrons, and a number of less syncretistic Chinese Buddhist temples arose in their stead.

In the postwar period, new immigrants from China established Chinese Buddhist temples in major U.S. cities. Among the more influential are two in San Francisco: Buddha's Universal Church, established in 1963, which caters primarily to Chinese Americans, and the Sino-American Buddhist Association's Gold Mountain Dhyana Monastery, established in 1972, whose membership is primarily

Caucasian. The largest Buddhist monastery in the Western Hemisphere, HSI LAI TEMPLE in Hacienda Heights, California, outside Los Angeles, is also of Chinese origin.

Although Chinese Buddhist arrived in America first, Japanese Buddhists and their descendants have made the greatest mark on American Buddhism. The two largest Buddhist groups in Japan—Jodo Shinshu and Nichiren—are probably the two largest in the United States as well. Founded by the Japanese reformer Shinran (1173–1262), Jodo Shinshu, or "True Pure Land" Buddhism, emphasizes the recitation of the name of Amida, the Buddha of "Infinite Light." Faith in the saving grace of Amida Buddha is thought by Jodo Shinshu practitioners to assure one rebirth in a heavenly realm known as the "Pure Land." Nichiren Buddhism originated with a contemporary of Shinran named Nichiren (1222–1282). Nichiren Buddhists view the Lotus Sutra as the epitome of Buddhist teaching and emphasize their own recitation: "Hail to the Wonderful Truth of the Lotus Sutra." Nichiren Buddhists have traditionally distinguished themselves from most other Japanese Buddhists by their proselytizing zeal and their unusual intolerance toward other faiths, although both those characteristics are moderating in contemporary times.

The first Buddhist missionary to what was then the Republic of Hawaii was a Jodo Shinshu Buddhist from Japan. After landing in Honolulu in 1889, he founded Hawaii's first Buddhist temple. The earliest Buddhist missionaries to the continental United States were also Jodo Shinshu adherents from Japan. In 1898 in San Francisco, these men established the first Buddhist temple in the United States. They also founded, after the model of the YOUNG MEN'S CHRISTIAN ASSOCIATION, a Young Men's Buddhist Association. One year later Jodo Shinshu priests established the Buddhist Mission of North America (BMNA).

This organization, which would change its name to the BUDDHIST CHURCHES OF AMERICA (BCA) in 1944, is currently America's second-largest Buddhist organization, with 61 temples and roughly 17,000 members. Though the BCA consists almost entirely of Japanese Americans, it has nonetheless been considerably "Americanized" and "Protestantized." Worship services incorporate hymns, organs, and sermons. Temples are furnished with pews and pulpits as well as educational wings for Sunday schools.

The largest Buddhist organization in the United States is likely SOKA GAKKAI INTERNATIONAL-USA (SGI-USA). An outgrowth of the Soka Gakkai movement, a nationalistic lay organization within Nichiren Shoshu ("Pure Nichiren"), this organization came to the United States originally as the Nichiren Shoshu Academy, established in California in 1960. In 1991, however, longstanding tensions between priests and laypeople led to a split in the movement. Today SGI-USA runs approximately 70 community centers and claims 100,000 to 300,000 members. The priestly group, now called Nichiren Shoshu of America, controls six temples in the United States and its membership is considerably smaller. Like Nichiren Buddhists in Japan, members of both groups orient their spiritual lives around the Daimoku, a chant that invokes the name of their favored scripture, the Lotus Sutra. SGI-USA originally recruited mostly Japanese Americans but now is composed predominantly of non-Asian converts, with a high percentage of blacks and Hispanics.

European-American interest in Buddhism antedates the immigration of significant numbers of Asian Buddhists to the United States. American interest in Buddhism began, like American trade with India and China, in the late 18th century. While many traveler and missionary accounts presented "Orientals" and their religions as barbaric, books such as Hannah Adams's *An Alphabetical Compendium of the Various Sects* (1784) and Joseph Priestley's *A Comparison of the Institutions of Moses with Those of the Hindoos and Other Nations* (1799) represented Asian religions in a relatively sympathetic light. Both, however, seemed at a loss to distinguish Buddhism from Hinduism, and both in the end cast their vote for Christianity.

Thanks to the emergence of Buddhist studies in Europe and TRANSCENDENTALISM in New England, more cosmopolitan Americans began in the mid-19th century to distinguish between Buddhism and other "heathen" religions. In 1844 these two strands came together when the transcendentalist Henry David THOREAU published in the *Dial* an English translation of a French version of the Lotus Sutra by the pioneering Buddhologist Eugene Burnouf. Ralph Waldo EMERSON, another transcendentalist, also evinced a broad interest in the Orient, but he knew far more about Hinduism than Buddhism.

Despite the efforts of these authors, Buddhism remained largely unknown until the publication of Sir Edwin Arnold's poetic life of the Buddha, *Light of Asia* (1879), helped to touch off a Buddhist vogue in Gilded Age America. During this period American sympathizers and adherents actually traveled to Asia and reported on their experiences back home.

One influential group of American intellectuals took advantage of Commodore Perry's forced opening of Japan in 1853 by sailing for Japan to learn about Buddhism firsthand. This group included art historian Ernest Fenollosa, Harvard-trained medical doctor William Sturgis Bigelow, and journalist Lafcadio Hearn. Fenollosa and Bigelow officially converted to Buddhism in a Tendai Buddhist ceremony in 1885. Hearn, who took a Japanese name, Japanese citizenship, and a Japanese wife, never formally converted to Buddhism.

A second group that helped to popularize Buddhism in America in the Gilded Age were the Theosophists (see THEOSOPHY). In 1878, Henry Steel OLCOTT and Helena Petrovna BLAVATSKY, who together had cofounded the Theosophical Society in New York in 1875, moved themselves and their society to India. There they became harsh critics of missionary Christianity and equally spirited defenders of

Asian religious traditions. In 1880, during a trip to Ceylon (now Sri Lanka), Olcott and Blavatsky (Russian-born but a recently naturalized U.S. citizen) became the first non-Asian Americans formally and officially to convert to Buddhism overseas. Olcott subsequently published a *Buddhist Catechism* (1881) and became a major contributor to a revival of Sinhalese Buddhism on the island.

Although the Theosophists did much to popularize Buddhism in America, it was the arrival of Buddhist missionaries from Asia at the WORLD'S PARLIAMENT OF RELIGIONS that catalyzed 19th-century American interest in Buddhism. During the parliament, convened in conjunction with the World's Columbian Exposition in Chicago in 1893, Buddhists from Japan and Ceylon represented their own tradition for the first time to an American audience. Soyen Shaku, a ZEN master from Japan, outlined the principles and practices of the Rinzai Zen tradition, while Anagarika DHARMAPALA, a Theravada Buddhist and Theosophist from Ceylon, presented his own brand of Theosophical Buddhism. In the midst of the parliament, a Jewish man named C. T. Strauss became the first non-Asian American publicly to convert to Buddhism in the United States.

After the World's Parliament, a disciple of Soyen Shaku named D. T. SUZUKI moved to the United States in an effort to promote Zen. He lectured at American universities and translated books and articles for Paul Carus, the editor at Open Court Publishing Company. Under Suzuki's tutelage, Mrs. Alexander Russell became the first European American formally to study Zen.

Suzuki's efforts bore fruit in the 1950s when Beat authors like Jack Kerouac and Allen Ginsberg, inspired by Suzuki's lectures at Columbia University, began to champion Zen in bohemian circles in New York and San Francisco. Of all the Beats, however, the most serious student of Buddhism was undoubtedly the poet Gary Snyder, who like Fenollosa, Bigelow, and Hearn a century earlier, actually traveled to Japan, in his case to study Zen. Although Alan WATTS, another Zen popularizer, would eventually dismiss "beat Zen" as "phony Zen," the Beats contributed importantly to America's second Buddhist vogue, which occurred in the 1950s and 1960s.

During those two decades, Zen centers opened in cities from Los Angeles to Rochester, New York, as Americans of many faiths introduced themselves to Zen. Among the more serious students of Zen in this period was the Roman Catholic monk Thomas MERTON, who attempted to integrate Zen practices and insights into his spiritual life.

The newest form of Buddhism on the American scene is the Vajrayana ("Diamond Vehicle") Buddhism of Tibet. Vajrayana Buddhists distinguish themselves from practitioners of Theravada and Mahayana Buddhism by vowing to rely not only on the traditional "three refuges"—the Buddha, the Dharma (Buddhist teaching), and the Sangha (community of Buddhists)—but also on a fourth refuge, the guru. A guru is necessary in the Vajrayana tradition because the tantric practices employed as a means to enlightenment—chanting, prostrations, meditation, and so on—are said to be both difficult and dangerous. Tibetan Buddhists also look to a series of Dalai Lamas as their spiritual and political leaders. The 14th and most recent DALAI LAMA, His Holiness Tenzin Gyatso, has made frequent trips to the United States, and almost singlehandedly prompted a third Buddhist vogue. During the 1990s, Hollywood produced three feature films about Tibetan Buddhism (*Little Buddha*, *Seven Years in Tibet*, and *Kundun*) and celebrities such as Adam Yauch of the Beastie Boys embraced both Tibetan Buddhism and the campaign to free Tibet from Chinese rule. In 1997, *Time* magazine ran a cover story on "America's Fascination with Buddhism."

Tibetan Buddhists first came to the United States in the wake of China's invasion of Tibet in the 1950s. Since that time, all four major forms of Tibetan Buddhism have transplanted themselves into American soil. Of the Tibetan missionaries to the United States, the most important are Tarthang Tulku and Chogyam TRUNGPA.

A monk of the Nyingmapa sect, Tarthang Tulku was one of the first Tibetans to enter the United States. Shortly after his arrival in Berkeley, California, in 1969, he founded the Tibetan Nyingma Meditation Center, the first Tibetan Buddhist organization in the country. Chogyam Trungpa, a Kargyudpa monk, came to America in 1970. After settling in Boulder, Colorado, he established a series of Dharmadhatus, or meditation centers, in cities across America. In 1973, the year of the publication of his widely-read book, *Cutting Through Spiritual Materialism*, Trungpa gathered his Dharmadhatu centers into a national organization called Vajradhatu. Both Tarthang Tulku and Chogyam Trungpa also established educational institutions to complement their meditation centers. Tarthang's Nyingma Institute opened its doors in Berkeley in 1973, while Trungpa's Boulder-based Naropa Institute first offered courses in 1974.

Tibetan Buddhism is practiced not only by Tibetan refugees but also by European Americans. Among the most important non-Tibetan practitioners of Vajrayana Buddhism is Robert Thurman, the first American ordained as a Tibetan Buddhist monk. Thurman, who earned a Ph.D. in Buddhist studies from Harvard University and has taught at Columbia University, is one important representative of a new generation of Tibetan Buddhists in America who are also Buddhist scholars. In 1997, *Time* named him one of the 25 most influential Americans.

An interesting recent development in American Buddhism is the emergence of a generation of American-born Buddhist leaders beginning in the 1970s. While some of those leaders, like Thurman, devoted themselves primarily to teaching in secular universities, others established Buddhist institutes or meditation centers. Among those American-born innovators are Joseph Goldstein, Jack Kornfield, Jacqueline Schwartz, and Sharon Salzberg, who together established the Insight Meditation Society at a former Catholic seminary in Barre, Massachusetts, in 1975.

One of the most vexing problems facing all American Buddhists is whether and to what extent they should accommodate the Buddhist tradition to American circumstances. This problem is compounded by the fact that while some Americans seem to have been attracted to Buddhism by its commonalities with Christianity and American culture, others seem to have come to Buddhism through the COUNTERCULTURE.

Solutions by American Buddhists to the problem of acculturation and assimilation are varied and complex. On the one hand, Theravada monks from Sri Lanka who emigrated to the United States to run the Buddhist Vihara Society (established in 1966) in Washington, D.C., have insisted that Buddhism remain a tradition of monks who have withdrawn from the world in order to practice meditation and, ultimately, achieve nirvana. These monks have made few accommodations to American circumstances and have, as a result, attracted few members. An earlier attempt at a monastic order of celibates, the Followers of Buddha, was founded in 1934 by Dwight Goddard, a former missionary to China and the author of the widely read *Buddhist Bible*. But this experiment was also too anticultural for most Americans and quickly folded.

The list of American Buddhists who have self-consciously adapted their tradition to American soil is much longer. One leading advocate for "Americanizing" Buddhism is Philip Kapleau. Drawn to Zen by a D. T. Suzuki lecture in 1951, Kapleau moved to Japan in 1953 to study Zen. He returned to the United States in 1966 and established in Rochester, New York, the Zen Meditation Center. Noting that Zen was "Japanized" when it moved from China to Japan, Kapleau has worked eagerly and self-consciously to "Americanize" Zen by urging his students, for example, to chant Bud-

dhist sutras in English and to wear comfortable western clothes during sitting meditation.

Perhaps the most significant transformation that Buddhism has undergone in the United States is its "feminization." There is much truth to Gary Snyder's observation that "the single most revolutionary aspect of Buddhist practice in the United States is the fact that women are participating in it." In Theravada Buddhist countries in South Asia, Buddhism is almost exclusively an affair of celibate male monks. Even in Mahayana Buddhist countries, which carve out a place within the tradition for lay practitioners, women are typically seen as inferior beings who must be transformed magically into men before they can become bodhisattvas, or "enlightenment beings." In the United States, however, approximately half of Buddhist practitioners are women, and many Buddhist groups have female leaders.

Buddhism in America is now almost as diverse as Buddhism in Asia, so it is difficult to generalize about some generic American Buddhism. America's Buddhisms do seem, however, to be for the most part in continuity with a broader Mahayana trend away from a tradition of celibate male monks who have renounced the world and toward a tradition of male and female lay practitioners actively engaged in the public sphere.

Approximations of the total number of American Buddhists vary from about 1 million to 5 million. There is widespread consensus, however, that Buddhism is one of the country's fastest-growing religions. Scholars also agree that the vast majority of American Buddhists are Asian Americans. Of the 1,500 or so Buddhist centers in the United States, only about 2 percent were established before the new immigration boom began in 1965.

While Buddhism is clearly new to the United States, the country has already become an important Buddhist nation. Thanks to the old immigration from China and Japan and new immigration from Thailand, Kampuchea,

Laos, Vietnam, and Taiwan, the United States now offers a wider range of Buddhist beliefs and practices than any place in the world.

SRP

Bibliography: Rick Fields, *How the Swans Came to the Lake: A Narrative History of Buddhism in America*, 3rd ed. (Boston: Shambhala, 1992); Paul David Numrich, *Old Wisdom in the New World: Americanization in Two Immigrant Theravada Buddhist Temples* (Knoxville: University of Tennessee Press, 1996); Charles S. Prebish and Kenneth K. Tanaka, *The Faces of Buddhism in America* (Berkeley: University of California Press, 1998); Richard Hughes Seager, *Buddhism in America* (New York: Columbia University Press, 1999); Thomas A. Tweed, *The American Encounter with Buddhism, 1844–1912: Victorian Culture and the Limits of Dissent* (Bloomington: Indiana University Press, 1992).

Buddhist Churches of America   The Buddhist Churches of America (BCA), the nation's oldest Buddhist group, is a New World manifestation of Jodo Shinshu, or "True Pure Land" BUDDHISM. Jodo Shinshu traces its roots to the 13th-century Japanese Buddhist reformer Shinran and so is popularly known as Shin Buddhism. In the United States as in Japan, members of that school recite the name of Amida Buddha with the faith that the saving grace of this Buddha of "Infinite Light" will secure their rebirth in the "Pure Land."

Buddhists first came to America during the Japanese immigration boom at the end of the 19th century. In San Francisco in 1899, two True Pure Land missionaries sent by a Jodo Shinshu school known as Honpa Hongwanji founded what was then called the Buddhist Mission of North America (BMNA). As the organization spread across the West Coast, it attracted mostly Japanese Americans. However, in keeping with the westernization mandate of the Meiji Restoration in Japan, it pursued a policy of warding off anti-Japanese nativism by creatively adapting Buddhism to modern culture.

One BMNA member who facilitated this process was Julius Goldwater. The first European-American priest of Jodo Shinshu, Goldwater had converted to Buddhism after meeting Ernest HUNT, one of Hawaii's leading Jodo Shinshu Buddhists and himself an eager Americanizer of Buddhism. As a minister in the main BMNA temple in Los Angeles, Goldwater conducted English-language services, taught Sunday school, organized youth groups, and officiated at funerals and weddings.

During World War II roughly 120,000 Japanese Americans, including virtually all BMNA members and most of its priests, were forcibly relocated to internment camps. Goldwater worked hard to provide liturgical and devotional materials for Buddhists imprisoned in the camps. He founded an interdenominational publication and distribution society called the Buddhist Brotherhood of America, which published and distributed a liturgical manual for camp use. This liturgical manual incorporated Protestant liturgical and hymnodic forms into Buddhist services. Members affirmed Goldwater's anglicizations and Protestantizations of their tradition, at least semantically, when they renamed their organization the Buddhist Churches of America in 1944.

After World War II the organization continued to adapt itself to American culture. Fol-

Asian immigration to California has led to Buddhism's growth and distinctive places of worship, such as Shensin Temple, Los Angeles. *(Pluralism Project of Harvard University)*

lowing the example of the GIDEONS, the Buddhist Promoting Foundation (established in 1965) has placed more than 300,000 copies of *Teachings of Buddha* in hotel rooms across the country. The organization publishes periodicals in both Japanese (*Horin*) and English (*Wheel of Dharma*). The BCA also moved into higher education, establishing the Institute of Buddhist Studies (IBS) in Berkeley in 1966. The IBS is now affiliated with the Graduate Theological Union in Berkeley, California. During the 1980s and 1990s, the BCA began to make its presence known in the public sphere of politics, weighing in for multicultural education and against school prayer.

In 1999, the BCA claimed roughly 17,000 adult members in 61 temples across the continental United States. Now more than a century old, the BCA is struggling to keep its American-born generations in the fold, but it continues to provide its membership with a community that provides links to their ancestors' homeland of Japan even as it facilitates their descendants' full participation in American culture.

SRP

Bibliography: Buddhist Churches of America, *Buddhist Churches of America,* 2 vols. (Chicago: Nobart, 1974); Tetsuden Kashima, *Buddhism in America: The Social Organization of an Ethnic Religious Organization* (Westport, Conn.: Greenwood Press, 1977); Richard Hughes Seager, *Buddhism in America* (New York: Columbia University Press, 1999); Kenneth K. Tanaka, *Ocean. An Introduction to Jodo-Shinshu Buddhism in America* (Berkeley: Wisdom Ocean Publications, 1997).

Burned-Over District   A popular 19th-century designation for the region of upstate New York west of the Catskill Mountains and south of the Adirondacks, the term *burned-over* referred specifically to the effects of evangelical revivals (see REVIVALISM) on this area between 1800 and 1850. First used by the itinerant preacher Charles Grandison FINNEY (1792–1875) as a term of derision to describe the harmful effects of Methodist preaching on the local population, the phrase quickly came into wider use to indicate the analogy between the sweeping and recurrent effects of western forest fires and the burning "fires of the soul" that accompanied seasons of revival.

After 1790, increasing numbers of New Englanders seeking better soil and more land moved across the Appalachian Mountains into new settlements in the fertile valleys of the Genesee country. At the same time, a smaller migration moved northward up the Susquehanna River from Pennsylvania. In the 1820s, the construction of the Erie Canal lured more settlers, including significant numbers of foreign immigrants, to the area. Coinciding with this rapid movement were a series of evangelical revivals collectively known as the SECOND GREAT AWAKENING, events sponsored by traveling preachers with the support of local churches, in which large numbers of people were converted to Protestant evangelicalism. Although the Second Great Awakening affected settlers in other parts of the nation as well, its effects on the newly established settlements of western New York were perceived by contemporaries to be particularly intense, culminating in waves of revivals in 1799–1800, 1807–1808, and the late 1810s, reaching a peak in 1825–1837. During and after the depression of 1837, the seasons of revival reportedly subsided as swiftly as they had come.

The Burned-Over District has retained its importance because of several religious developments that had national impact but seemed to be more noticeably present or had their origins in this region. The first was the growth in evangelical organizational strength that resulted from the revivals. A good amount of "church-shopping" followed revivals, where religious "salesmen" tried to convince new converts to join their church rather than another, and denominations competed for members. Furthermore, as settlers moved into the area, Baptists, Methodists, Presbyterians, and Congregationalists all sent missionaries to the region in order to establish what they saw as "proper" Christian influence in new communities. The work of missionary societies in western New York thus established a pattern of domestic, or "home" missions (see MISSIONS, HOME) that governed denominational strategies throughout the antebellum era, as Euro-Americans continued to move westward across the Mississippi. Evangelical churches in the area, experiencing great numerical growth, also contributed financially to denominational efforts in other locales.

Revivals also led to religious and social innovations, many of which had their roots in the district. Charles G. Finney's famous preaching tours and revivals resulted not only in increased numbers of churchgoers, but in theological, revivalistic, and social changes that soon affected Protestants throughout the country. Rejecting key features of Calvinism that he felt interfered with the goal of conversion, Finney stressed the power of the individual to choose God's salvation. He also instituted a series of "new measures" in his revivals, including praying for people by name, calling them forward to an "anxious bench," and allowing women to pray in public, that laid the groundwork for the popular development of revivalism into the 20th century. Finally, he linked the advocacy of social transformation with conversion, compelling thousands of newly committed Christians to work for antislavery, temperance, and other reform movements of the day.

Other religious innovators also found fertile soil in western New York. Two indigenous American religions, the SHAKERS and the Mormons (see CHURCH OF JESUS CHRIST OF LATTER-DAY SAINTS), gained strength from revival participants who joined their movements after experiencing conversion. Communitarians and other utopians, including the Oneida community and Jemima WILKINSON's "New Jerusalem," moved to the area after experiencing persecution elsewhere. After the 1830s, one could find more religious and socialist utopian experiments in the Burned-Over District than any

other part of the country. The Millerites, an adventist group that attracted tens of thousands of Americans with the conviction that the world would end in the mid-1840s, were also centered in the region. When the world survived after their prophecies, the ensuing disillusionment, along with the nagging effects of prolonged economic depression, led to the slow decline of western New York as a thriving center for religious innovation.

LMK

Bibliography: Michael Barkun, *Crucible of the Millennium: The Burned-over District of New York in the 1840s* (Syracuse, N.Y.: Syracuse University Press, 1986); Whitney R. Cross, *The Burned-Over District* (Ithaca, N.Y.: Cornell University Press, 1950); Ronald L. Numbers and Jonathan M. Butler, eds., *The Disappointed: Millerism and Millenarianism in the Nineteenth Century* (Knoxville: University of Tennessee Press, 1993).

Bushnell, Horace (1802–1876)

Congregational minister Horace Bushnell, the greatest theologian of his generation and one of the most important thinkers in the history of American Protestantism, framed the intellectual system that eventually evolved into the movement known as theological MODERNISM.

Bushnell was born in the village of Bantam, Connecticut on April 14, 1802. After graduating from Yale College in 1827, he studied law for a time but, following a conversion experience during a revival in 1831, entered Yale Divinity School, from which he graduated in 1833. Although he studied under Nathaniel William TAYLOR there, Bushnell went beyond Taylor's liberalized version of Calvinism. He found greater inspiration in the religious romanticism of Samuel Taylor Coleridge and Friedrich Schleiermacher and their understanding of God's dwelling within the human soul and humanity's intuitive access to the divine.

After leaving Yale, Bushnell was called to the North Church in Hartford, Connecticut, where he served throughout his pastoral ministry. At the North Church, Bushnell sought to meet the religious challenges of the day not only by rejecting the harshness of traditional Calvinism and the excesses of revivalism, but also by projecting the optimistic spirit of American democracy into the theological sphere. Bushnell argued that nature and the supernatural constituted "the one system of God," faith and reason being part of a single continuum; religious truths, therefore, ought to correspond to actual human experiences.

In 1847 Bushnell published his important *Christian Nurture*, a work that dealt with the problem of original sin, provided a useful alternative to revivalism, and laid the foundation for future approaches to religious education. Accepting the insight of his teacher William Taylor that "sin is in the sinning," Bushnell denied the Calvinist notion that children were hopelessly lost in sin until they were converted. Instead, he hoped that children growing up would never know a time when they were not part of the Christian household. Bushnell's organic view of family and church helped him view Christian nurture as a means of drawing out the essential goodness in human nature. This opinion was sufficiently close to Unitarian theology, however, that it laid him open to charges by conservatives that he considered natural development, not conversion, the key to the Christian life.

Bushnell made another notable exposition of modernist religious thought in his *God in Christ* (1849) and *Christ in Theology* (1851). Both books suggested that verbal communication was essentially symbolic in nature and thus was never as precise as some orthodox theologians insisted. All religious language, including that of traditional Christian creeds, of doctrinal statements, and even of the Bible itself, Bushnell believed, was poetic rather than literal. Such assertions were anathema to many 19th-century believers. As a consequence of publishing them Bushnell was charged with heresy, but he retained his position at the North Church despite the uproar against him.

Bushnell also made important contributions to the development of American CIVIL RELIGION during the Civil War. In his sermon "Reverses Needed," delivered following the Northern defeat at Bull Run in July 1861, and in his postwar address to the Yale graduating class almost exactly four years later ("Our Obligations to the Dead"), Bushnell stressed the social nature of human existence and saw in the war a means by which his nation might realize its true, God-given unity. In the wartime period, moreover, Bushnell composed his treatise on the doctrine of the atonement, *The Vicarious Sacrifice*, which interpreted Christ's death at Calvary against the backdrop of young Americans suffering and dying in the Civil War. Bushnell thought the war was beneficial for

Horace Bushnell, the 19th-century Congregational theologian whose preaching at North Church in Hartford reshaped mainline Protestantism.

the United States in the same sense that the sorrows of Good Friday had been redemptive for the human race.

Bushnell's declining health led to his resignation from the North Church in 1859, although many years of travel and writing lay ahead of him. He lived long enough, in fact, to influence the emerging SOCIAL GOSPEL movement, which sought to relate religious beliefs and biblical insights to the need for social reform in the last decades of the century. Bushnell remained active in theological and church circles until shortly before his death in Hartford on February 17, 1876.

GHS, Jr.

Bibliography: Barbara M. Cross, *Horace Bushnell: Minister to a Changing America* (Chicago: University of Chicago Press, 1958); Robert Lansing Edwards, *Of Singular Genius, of Singular Grace: A Biography of Horace Bushnell* (Cleveland: Pilgrim Press, 1992).

Cabrini, Francesca Xavier (1850–1917)

The first U.S. citizen to be canonized and founder of the Missionary Sisters of the Sacred Heart, Francesca Cabrini was born in Lombardy, Italy, in 1850, the youngest child of a prosperous farmer. In 1870 she graduated with honors from an academy run by the Daughters of the Sacred Heart in Arluno. She desired to join the order, but a smallpox infection in 1872 left her so weak that she was refused for health reasons. Cabrini spent the next several years (1872–1874) as a schoolteacher and as the director of an orphanage (1874–1880). At the orphanage she attempted to form the staff into a religious order, taking vows herself on September 14, 1877. The closure of the orphanage led Cabrini to gather seven companions at an abandoned Franciscan monastery, where they organized the Missionary Sisters of the Sacred Heart on November 14, 1880, which received papal approval in March of 1888.

Although the sisters desired to undertake missionary work in China, they were directed to serve Italian immigrants in America, and one year later Cabrini and six compatriots arrived in the United States to begin that work. The poverty and need of the Italian immigrants threw the order into a flurry of activity, all under the careful administrative eye of "Mother Cabrini." She supervised the order's catechetical work with youth and prisoners and directed the establishment of numerous orphanages and schools as well as hospitals in New York, Chicago, and Seattle.

Cabrini was an indefatigable organizer. In the course of 35 years she made more than 30 trips across the Atlantic and organized 67 houses of her order throughout Europe, the United States, and South America—this

Francesca Cabrini founded an order of women religious who worked to alleviate the poverty of Italian immigrants. She became the United States's first citizen to be canonized by the Roman Catholic Church. *(Library of Congress Prints and Photographs Division)*

despite a physical weakness so marked that it would be noted in Pius XII's speech at her canonization. Suffering from malaria for much of her life, she succumbed to it in 1917, dying at her order's Columbus Hospital in Chicago on December 22, 1917.

The process leading to her canonization was begun by the archbishop of Chicago, Cardinal George Mundelein, in 1928. The list of her merits was approved by Pius XI in 1931, who pronounced her venerable in 1933, the first step toward canonization. Beatified in 1938, Mother Cabrini, who had become a naturalized U.S. citizen in 1909, officially became a saint in the Roman Catholic Church on July 7, 1946.

EQ

Bibliography: Pietro D. Donato, *Immigrant Saint: The Life of Mother Cabrini* (New York: St. Martin's Press, 1991); Kathleen Jones, *Women Saints: Lives of Faith and Courage* (Maryknoll, N.Y.: Orbis Books, 1999); Theodore Maynard, *Too Small a World: The Life of Francesca Cabrini* (London: J. Gifford, 1945).

Cahenslyism   Cahenslyism, a 19th-century movement in the U.S. Roman Catholic Church (see ROMAN CATHOLICISM) for the establishment of parishes organized along national and linguistic lines rather than geography, was named after Peter Paul Cahensly, a German parliamentarian who visited the United States in 1883. A member of the Germany Center Party and an official of the St. Raphael Society, founded in 1871 to aid German immigrants, Cahensly was shocked by Irish dominance of Roman Catholicism in the United States and appalled by the decline of the German language and traditions among the immigrants. Like many at the time, he blamed the indifference of the "hibernearchy"—the predominantly Irish bishops—for the loss of thousands of German Catholics from the faith.

His solution, and that of many others, was the establishment of Roman Catholic parishes based on culture and language. Such parishes would allow German-speaking Catholics to maintain German culture and the traditions of German Catholicism. Cahensly was instrumental in having a petition placed before Pope Leo XIII in 1890 that called for a radical restructuring of the American Church. Not only did it ask that parishes be organized along national lines but suggested that every parish should have priests of the same nationality as the parishioners, that parochial school instruction be in the students' mother tongue, and that there be representation of each nationality in the American hierarchy.

This petition infuriated most of the American bishops, who were committed to the creation of a unitary American Catholicism, and after a second petition on the subject was sent to Rome, Cardinal James GIBBONS formally protested the meddling in American affairs by "officious" European gentlemen. Although the pope rejected the idea of establishing national parishes, the letter from the papal secretary of state informing Gibbons of this rejection also urged the American bishops to pay greater attention to the needs of new immigrants.

(See also AMERICANISM.)

EQ

Bibliography: Colman James Barry. *The Catholic Church and German Americans* (Washington, D.C.: Catholic University of America Press, 1953); James Hennesey, S.J., *American Catholics: A History of the Roman Catholic Community in the United States* (New York: Oxford University Press, 1981).

California   See NATIVE AMERICAN RELIGIONS: INTERMONTANE/CALIFORNIA.

Calvert, Cecilius (1606–1675)   Born in London, England, in 1606, Cecilius Calvert was the eldest son and heir of George Calvert (1580–1632), the first Lord Baltimore. The Calverts were a Roman Catholic family who outwardly conformed to the rituals and practices of the Church of England until 1625, when Cecilius's father publicly announced his Roman Catholic faith (see ROMAN CATHOLICISM). Although legal proscriptions against Catholics forced him to resign several of his offices, George retained his position as a privy counselor to James I.

By this time the elder Calvert had turned most of his attention to aiding his fellow English Catholics, who suffered from social and legal liabilities in England. To accomplish this goal he devised various colonization schemes. Purchasing land in Newfoundland in 1620, Calvert established the settlement of Ferryland in 1623. A visit to the colony in 1628 forced him to realize that the climate was not conducive to easy colonization, and he persuaded Charles I to grant him the right to purchase land farther south in Virginia (see VIRGINIA, COLONY). The protests were so great that Charles rescinded the permission, granting him land north of the Potomac instead. George Calvert died (1632) before receiving the charter for this land, to be named Maryland (see MARYLAND, COLONY) after Charles I's Roman Catholic wife Henrietta Maria, and the grant was then made to Cecilius as heir.

Desirous of fulfilling his father's wish of establishing a colony where Roman Catholics were secure, Cecilius sent out two ships, the *Ark* and the *Dove*, to Maryland the following year under the governorship of his brother Leonard Calvert. This group was comprised of 30 gentlemen, 200 mostly Protestant laborers, and two Jesuit priests, who would perform the first public mass in British North America.

To preserve the peace Cecilius directed his brother to allow complete religious freedom to all Christians. The Catholics also were warned to avoid antagonizing their fellow colonists and not to practice their religion too publicly. As added insurance against conflict Calvert attempted to control the activities of the Jesuits, extracting from the Jesuit General the ruling that all priests must conform to the colony's laws and gaining veto power over appointments of priests to the colony.

Hostility from English Protestants who opposed a colony ruled by a Catholic and from the colonists who chafed under the absolute

Cecilius Calvert, the second Lord Baltimore, established the colony of Maryland where his fellow Roman Catholics and all Christians could worship freely. *(Enoch Pratt Free Library)*

rule of the proprietor forced Cecilius to grant a measure of self-government to the colony, retaining only the right of veto over the colony's laws. This brought little respite, however, and until his death, Cecilius's energies were expended in attempting to control the colony. After a period of armed rebellion in the early 1640s, he reestablished his control in 1647. In 1649 Leonard's successor, the Protestant William Stone, attempted to establish peace by convincing the colonial assembly to pass an "Act Concerning Religion," otherwise known as the Toleration Act of 1649 (see ACT OF TOLERATION, MARYLAND), that allowed religious freedom for all those not denying the Trinity and made it illegal to disparage anyone's religion.

This act did not have the desired effect. In 1650, Protestants gained control over the colony's government and in 1654 forced the assembly to disfranchise all Catholics and to outlaw "popery, prelacy, and licentiousness." The Calverts once again regained control of the colony in 1658. For the next 17 years, until Cecilius's death on November 30, 1675, Maryland remained relatively peaceful and stable, and the proprietorship passed to his son George.

The "Glorious Revolution" of 1688 in England, which deposed the Roman Catholic James II and replaced him with the Protestants William and Mary, marked the end of the Catholic proprietorship in Maryland. Galvanized by the revolution, a group of Maryland Protestants seized control of the government. In 1691 King William III relieved the Calverts of their grant, and Maryland became a royal colony, thereby ending one of America's earliest experiences in religious liberty.

(See also COLONIAL PERIOD.)

EQ

Bibliography: William H. Browne, *George Calvert and Cecilius Calvert: Barons Baltimore of Baltimore* (New York: Dodd, Mead, 1890); John Tracy Ellis, *Catholics in Colonial America* (Baltimore, Md.: Helicon, 1965); James Hennesey, S.J., *American Catholics: A History of the Roman Catholic Community in the United States* (New York: Oxford University Press, 1981).

Calvinism   A theological tradition that began with Swiss Protestant reformer John Calvin, Calvinism is based upon the principle of God's absolute sovereignty and initiative in granting eternal salvation to human beings. English Calvinism, which found expression within the Puritan (see PURITANISM) movement of the 16th and 17th centuries, decisively shaped religious life in early America. Indeed, Calvinism has been the single most important force in religious thought in the United States, having influenced perhaps three-quarters of all American Christians in the years prior to the War for Independence.

John Calvin (in French, Jean Cauvin) was born in France in 1509. Sometime around the year 1533 or 1534, Calvin underwent a profound experience of religious conversion. He broke away from the Roman Catholic Church in May 1534 and dedicated himself to restoring Christianity to what he conceived to be the purity of biblical times. In the same period, he also began to write his *Institutes of the Christian Religion*, which would become one of the most important statements of Protestant belief. Calvin completed the first edition of the *Institutes* in 1536, the same year he arrived in Geneva, Switzerland, to begin the reformation of the church in that city. Over the next three decades until his death in 1564, he devoted himself to transforming Geneva into (in the words of Scottish reformer John Knox) "the most perfect school of Christ."

Eventually, nearly 5,000 Protestant refugees from other countries flocked to Calvin's Geneva in the mid-16th century. Harassed in their own homelands, these exiles were attracted both by Calvin's intellectual stature and by the safety his city offered them. Between 1553 and 1558, many English Protestants, fleeing persecution in the reign of the Catholic Queen Mary, were among the group of refugees in Geneva. There they imbibed Calvin's ideas on creation, divine redemption, history, and politics, which they brought back to England after Mary's death. Thanks to the tutelage of those English exiles under Calvin, most serious Protestants in England were committed to Calvinist theology by the end of the 16th century.

Calvin had borrowed heavily from the ideas of Augustine of Hippo, the great Christian theologian of the fourth century. In his writings about the church, Augustine distinguished between its visible and invisible manifestations. Only God knew, on the one hand, who belonged to the invisible church. God had chosen the members of that church, Augustine said, even before the creation of the world. The visible church, on the other hand, was the human institution known on earth. While insisting that membership in the visible church was no guarantee of eternal salvation, Augustine acknowledged that God's elect (see ELECTION) almost invariably belonged to the visible church during their lifetimes.

Calvin adopted Augustine's emphasis on the omnipotence of God and the passivity of humankind, and he employed those ideas as the foundation of his religious thought. Without divine grace, Calvin wrote, no person could repent and become a Christian. Yet God's grace was a gift that only the elect received. Calvin also denied the freedom of the human will. Humans were "free" to sin but not to save themselves. The credit for salvation belonged solely to God who, from eternity, had predestined the fate of the soul. Only God knew who would be saved and who would be damned. Although his teaching on predestination appeared to undercut participation in the visible church, since no amount of piety or faithfulness could ever change God's eternal decrees, Calvin contended that the elect would inevitably lead pious, Christian lives. He counseled people not to dwell on their failings, but simply to trust in the all-sufficient grace of God.

In the early 17th century, Dutch theologian Jacobus Arminius advanced a conspicuous challenge to Calvin's teachings on predestination (see ARMINIANISM). Arminius, who doubted that God would have arbitrarily chosen to save some human beings and damn others, wished to reaffirm the importance of the human will in spiritual matters. After Arminius's death, his followers formally disputed the deterministic logic of Calvinism. The "Arminians" argued that God foreknew, but did not foreordain, who would be saved and gave all people the grace to accept eternal salvation. Orthodox Calvinists vigorously counterattacked and at the Synod of Dort in 1619 officially condemned Arminianism. The *Canons* of the Synod of Dort promulgated what

are now recognized as the five principal tenets (popularly summarized by the acronym TULIP) of Calvinism:

1. total depravity (human beings are wholly sinful and entirely incapable of saving themselves);
2. unconditional election (God predestined some human beings for salvation without regard to their individual merits or possible good works);
3. limited atonement (Christ suffered and died on the cross to save only those whom God had already chosen for salvation);
4. irresistible grace (God's chosen ones can never reject salvation);
5. perseverance of the saints (the chosen will never fall away from their state of grace).

At the same time that Calvin's disciples on the Continent were debating his doctrines, Calvinists in England had also become engaged in a controversy. Arminians such as William Laud, the archbishop of Canterbury, desired to return participation in the sacraments of the church to the center of the process of salvation. Calvinists, called "Puritans" after the 1620s, continued to emphasize God's initiative and devalued human endeavors. Arguing about a number of important issues, including the role of bishops in church government, the use of vestments in worship, and the meaning of the church's sacraments, Arminians and Puritans in the Church of England eventually went their separate ways. Between 1620 and 1640, approximately 20,000 Puritans left England and migrated to New England, thereby conveying Calvinism to the New World.

In the century and a half between the arrival of the Pilgrims in Plymouth, Massachusetts, in 1620 and the start of the American Revolution, Calvinism became well established in America. Thousands of continental Calvinists belonging to the Dutch Reformed, German Reformed, and French Reformed (or Huguenot) traditions followed the English

Puritan migration and streamed into the American colonies. British Calvinism was strengthened, moreover, by the arrival of Scottish and Scotch-Irish immigrants in the late 17th century. And, although the revivals of the GREAT AWAKENING often aroused violent controversies within the American churches in the mid-18th century, Calvinism provided the theological foundation on which the value and meaning of the Awakening was debated.

By the late 18th century, however, Calvinist hegemony in America began clearly to decline. The fatalism implicit in the doctrine of predestination, for example, appealed less and less to a society that prized freedom of action and the opportunity for self-improvement. The view of the human condition advanced by the "Consistent Calvinists" like Congregational theologian Samuel HOPKINS, who claimed he would be willing "to be damned for the glory of God," appeared too harsh to increasing numbers of Americans. Extreme Calvinism placed believers in a moral quandary. They never could be sure whether or not they should *try* to be good. As a popular ditty of the day put it:

> *You can and you can't,*
> *You shall and you shan't;*
> *You will and you won't.*
> *You're damned if you do,*
> *And damned if you don't.*

The SECOND GREAT AWAKENING of the early 19th century further undercut Calvinism's authority. American evangelicals (see EVANGELICALISM), even those who belonged to denominations like the Presbyterians and the Congregationalists that had once wholeheartedly affirmed Calvinist theology, reacted strongly against the notion of predestination. Anyone *could* achieve salvation by undergoing a spiritual rebirth. Presbyterian revivalist Charles G. FINNEY was renowned for pleading with men and women to change their hearts and surrender to God. His most famous sermon, "Sinners Bound to Change Their Own Hearts," argued that God required people to act for themselves. Despite the Calvinist insistence that men and women were morally unable to choose between heaven and hell, Finney taught that common sense showed they had the God-given power to make up their own minds.

Despite such noteworthy modifications, Calvinism did not entirely die out in the United States in the 19th century. In fact, the threat to it made some theologians even more vigilant in upholding the essential truth of Calvin's teachings. Among Presbyterians, the theological tradition cultivated at Princeton (see PRINCETON THEOLOGY) Seminary in New Jersey was the most resistant to altering Calvinist orthodoxy in any way. While some Presbyterians sought a flexible version of Calvinism more in accord with revivalism and religious emotions, the Princeton theologians held firm. As Princeton professor Charles HODGE remarked about his school, "a new idea never originated in this Seminary." The Princeton Theology continued to influence conservative Presbyterians and other evangelicals throughout much of the 19th and 20th centuries.

Despite revisions and resistance to change, Calvinism has dominated American Protestantism, especially denominations within the REFORMED TRADITION. While the direct heirs of colonial Presbyterianism and Congregationalism, the Presbyterian Church (U.S.A.) and the United Church of Christ, no longer emphasize strict Calvinist beliefs, smaller denominational bodies such as the Orthodox Presbyterian Church and the Presbyterian Church in America militantly maintain Calvinist orthodoxy. Moreover, among members of the Dutch Reformed tradition, represented by the Reformed Church of America and the smaller, more conservative Christian Reformed Church, faithfulness to the traditional confessions of Calvinism is strictly preserved. And since many Baptists, Episcopalians, and members of various other independent churches also adhere to the principles of Calvinism today, the breadth of commitment to this theological tradition remains indisputable.

GHS, Jr.

Bibliography: Bruce Kuklick, *Churchmen and Philosophers from Jonathan Edwards to John Dewey* (New Haven: Yale University Press, 1985); John T. McNeill, *The History and Character of Calvinism* (1954; New York: Oxford University Press, 1967).

Cambridge Platform   Adopted in August 1648, the Cambridge Platform set forth the basic doctrines and church polity of the Puritan (Congregational) churches (see PURITANISM; CONGREGATIONALISM) in New England. The document was the first official statement of these churches and made explicit what previously had only been implied in the writings of Puritan theologians. It remained the basis for Congregationalism until the 1830s.

The adoption of the Cambridge Platform was the result of many forces. During the 1630s, the colonies had been threatened by individuals whose teachings challenged their religio-political unity, which led to the calling of a ministerial synod by the Massachusetts General Court in September 1646.

The Cambridge Synod, as it was known, drew delegates from all the Massachusetts churches, except Concord, as well as from New Hampshire, Plymouth, and Connecticut. Among the Connecticut delegates was Thomas HOOKER, who had pushed for such a gathering for five years. The synod's deliberations continued intermittently until August 1648. Its result, "A Platform of Church Discipline Gathered out of the Word of God," combined the church polity of Hooker with the theology of John COTTON and Richard Mather. It duly affirmed the Westminster Confession of Faith as the fundamental expression of doctrine and then turned to its major points.

The first was limited church membership. The church was to be composed of those who could give evidence of a conversion experience. The children of these members could be bap-

tized, but full membership would await their own conversion experience (see HALF-WAY COVENANT). The autonomy of the individual congregation was proclaimed, as well as its freedom from coercion by any synod or association of churches.

Religious and civil authorities were to be separate but mutually reinforcing. The civil authorities were not to hinder the churches but to "help and further them." In return, the churches should seek the approval of magistrates at every legitimate opportunity. While the state could not compel church membership, it was to enforce uniformity and punish persons guilty of idolatry, blasphemy, and heresy. Finally the magistrates were allowed to call synods "to counsell & assist them in matters of religion."

The Cambridge Platform was the crowning glory of the first generation of Puritans. A succinct and coherent statement of Puritan beliefs and practices, it created a solid and stable system for subsequent generations of believers. Although requiring some adjustments in later years, the platform stood the test of time as a defining statement of Congregationalism for nearly two centuries.

EQ

Bibliography: Darren Staloff, *The Making of an American Thinking Class: Intellectuals and Intelligentsia in Puritan Massachusetts* (New York: Oxford University Press, 1998), Williston Walker, *The Creeds and Platforms of Congregationalism* (New York: Pilgrim Press, 1991).

camp meetings   The camp meeting was the most distinctive feature of religious life on the American frontier in the first decades of the 19th century. A notable offshoot of the SECOND GREAT AWAKENING and a highly effective means of evangelizing unsettled areas, camp meetings were interdenominational revivals (see REVIVALISM) held in the open air over several days. While a revival was taking place, most participants, who had often traveled great distances,

A popular method of evangelization, camp meetings spread Protestantism to the scattered frontier population in the 18th and 19th centuries. *(Library of Congress)*

camped at the site where the religious exercises were held.

Although the camp meeting was popularized in the United States, the phenomenon itself originated in Scotland and northern Ireland. Scottish Presbyterians had developed a pattern of assembling once or twice a year to celebrate the Lord's Supper and hear sermons stressing the need for repentance. These gatherings lasted for several days, during which worshipers prepared themselves spiritually before sharing bread and wine at large tables. Presbyterians transported their "communion

seasons" to the New World. That practice provided the basis for the revivals that began to occur on the American frontier in the 1790s.

Presbyterian minister James McGready of Logan County, Kentucky, is generally regarded as the person who initiated the camp meeting technique in America. He led a well-attended four-day revival at Red River, Kentucky, in June 1800 and repeated his success a month later at Gasper River, Kentucky. At the Red River revival, McGready, two other Presbyterians, and two Methodist clergy exhorted the men and women present to renounce their sins and let God reign over their hearts. Worshipers began to shout for mercy as the preachers moved among them, and scores reportedly sank to the ground in religious ecstasy. The outdoor setting, the welcome break from the ordinary routines of farm life on the frontier, and a genuine sense of their own sinfulness made many responsive to the preachers' appeals for spiritual conversion.

Barton W. STONE, whom McGready had earlier influenced, attended the Gasper River revival and determined to duplicate what he had seen there. Stone summoned thousands to his own church at Cane Ridge, Kentucky, in early August 1801. The CANE RIDGE REVIVAL proved to be the largest and most successful camp meeting ever held, as over 10,000 people—more than five times the size of the largest settlement in Kentucky at the time—assembled for a week under Stone's direction. The unusual bodily motions of those caught up in the religious enthusiasm at Cane Ridge (e.g., falling, dancing, jerking, laughing, and even barking) forever marked revivalism in the popular mind. While critics pointed to that event as an example of the shocking delusions and excesses camp meetings inspired, defenders simply noted the extraordinary number of converts and new members revivals brought into churches on the frontier.

Camp meetings like the Cane Ridge revival, however, proved to be relatively short-lived. Although McGready and Stone, the earliest proponents of the camp meeting, were Presbyterians, Americans who belonged to that denomination tended to value order over enthusiasm and quickly withdrew support for outdoor revivals. Baptists also soon abandoned camp meetings in favor of protracted revival services held inside church buildings in towns and cities. As a result, by 1840 the camp meeting became the almost exclusive domain of the Methodist denomination. Moreover, as the scattered populace and isolation found on the frontier were replaced by settled communities and organized church life, the urgent evangelistic impulses that had shaped the first camp meetings became institutionalized and domesticated. Instead of the frenzied excitement of the frontier revivals, the next generation of camp meetings were carefully controlled, dignified affairs. Methodists transformed the grounds where gatherings were held into permanent Bible camps, conference centers, and summer resorts, such as at Chautauqua, New York, and Oak Bluffs, Massachusetts.

Camp meetings again became a vital feature of religious life in the United States as the Holiness movement emerged out of American evangelicalism in the late 19th century. In 1867 several Methodist ministers issued a call for a camp meeting to be held at Vineland, New Jersey. After that gathering, many who had been involved in it formed the National Camp Meeting Association for the Promotion of Christian Holiness, which sponsored more than 50 meetings over the next 15 years. Camp meetings continue to be associated with the Holiness movement today. A 1987 directory published by Asbury College in Kentucky, for example, listed 114 meetings that were to be held that year. Camp meetings still provide an opportunity for believers to leave behind their ordinary routines and come together for extended periods of worship and Bible study.

GHS, Jr.

Bibliography: Dickson D. Bruce, Jr., *And They All Sang Hallelujah: Plain-Folk Camp-Meeting Religion, 1800–1845* (Knoxville: University of Tennessee Press, 1974); Leigh Eric Schmidt, *Holy Fairs: Scot-*

Alexander Campbell, a Scotch-Irish missionary and cofounder of the Disciples of Christ. His "restoration" of the Gospel had wide appeal to 19th-century Americans.

tish Communions and American Revivals in the Early Modern Period (Princeton: Princeton University Press, 1989).

Campbell, Alexander (1788–1866)

Alexander Campbell was a Protestant minister and, with his father, Thomas, cofounder of the CHRISTIAN CHURCH (DISCIPLES OF CHRIST). He was also the most influential figure of American "restorationism" (see RESTORATION MOVEMENT), the religious movement that sought to return 19th-century Protestantism to the beliefs and practices of New Testament times.

Alexander Campbell was born at Ballymena, Ireland, on September 12, 1788. His early education was at home under the tutelage of his father, then a Presbyterian clergyman, and he later studied at the University of Glasgow in Scotland. When Thomas migrated to the United States in 1807, Alexander followed him, eventually settling in Pennsylvania in September 1809.

Disturbed by petty theological quarrels among his fellow Presbyterians in America, Thomas decided to withdraw from his denomination and promote unity among members of all Christian traditions. In 1809 he founded a new religious fellowship, called simply the "Christian Association of Washington" (Pennsylvania). Guided by principles that Thomas outlined, the Christian Association adopted a single, biblically based creed: "Where the Scriptures speak, we speak; where the Scriptures are silent, we are silent." In 1811, Thomas and Alexander together organized a church at Brush Run, Pennsylvania, and served as its clergy. Because of the Campbells' belief that immersion was the only proper form of the Christian baptismal rite, their church joined the local Redstone Baptist Association in 1813, an affiliation that lasted until 1827.

Alexander soon assumed sole leadership of the church, and he began to travel extensively over what is now the Midwest and upper South to win members for the nondenominational movement he championed. He formed groups called "Disciples of Christ," which became one of the fastest-growing religious organizations of the time. Campbell emphasized a Christianity based upon the New Testament, a faith both free from doctrinal hairsplitting and broad in focus. Noted for his detailed expositions of the structures and practices of primitive Christianity, he insisted that 19th-century Americans could, if they wished, reconstruct the first-century church and thereby transform their society.

Tension over a number of theological matters led eventually to the withdrawal of the Brush Run Church from the Redstone Baptist Association. After meeting Barton Stone in 1830 and finding common ground with Stone's "Christians," Campbell brought his Disciples of Christ into fellowship with Stone's group. On January 1, 1832, 12,000 of Campbell's "Disciples" and 10,000 of Stone's "Christians" came together for a meeting at Lexington, Kentucky. While its internal organization was not completed until 1849, a new denomination emerged out of the self-consciously nondenominational movements that both Campbells and Stone had launched. The Disciples of Christ grew from 22,000 members in 1832 to almost 200,000 in 1860. Alexander Campbell chartered Bethany College in Bethany, Virginia (now West Virginia), in 1840. Under his leadership as president from 1840 to 1866, the college provided an educated ministry for his rapidly expanding church.

Campbell remained active, writing and teaching for many years to come. He had already published an English translation of the New Testament in 1827. Later, he wrote other books on the Bible, baptism, and primitive Christianity. He also expounded his theological views over the course of five decades in two successive monthly journals: *The Christian Baptist,* published from 1823 to 1830, and *The Millennial Harbinger,* published from 1830 until 1866. The authority of Campbell's teachings in the denomination he helped found continues strong today. He died at Bethany on March 4, 1866.

GHS, Jr.

Bibliography: Denton Ray Lindley, *Apostle of Freedom* (St. Louis: Bethany Press, 1957).

Campbell, Thomas   See CAMPBELL, ALEXANDER.

Campbell, Will D.   See COMMITTEE OF SOUTHERN CHURCHMEN.

Cane Ridge revival   The Cane Ridge revival (see REVIVALISM), a gathering of at least 10,000 people at Cane Ridge, Kentucky, in August 1801, was the largest and most memorable of the frontier CAMP MEETINGS of the early 19th century. For a week, hundreds of men and women prayed, sang, and proclaimed their new faith in Jesus Christ.

James McGready, a Presbyterian minister who took charge of three churches in southwestern Kentucky in 1796, was the first great frontier revivalist. At Red River, Kentucky, in June 1800 and at Gasper River, Kentucky, the next month, McGready and his associates gathered worshipers from as far as 100 miles away. They exhorted people to "let the Lord Omnipotent reign in their hearts," and many responded by shouting for mercy and by falling to the floor in spiritual ecstasy. Barton W. Stone, a Presbyterian minister who had been converted by McGready and attended the Gasper River revival, soon adopted the same methods. Stone announced that a great meeting would be held at the small church at Cane Ridge, where he served as pastor.

Wooden preaching platforms were hastily constructed and a rough clearing made for the revival. Ministers of the Presbyterian, Baptist, and Methodist churches all came together and cooperated in a common, nonsectarian effort. Since nearby Lexington, then Kentucky's largest city, had fewer than 2,000 residents, the volume of people attending the Cane Ridge meeting was itself stupendous. After the revival ended, some participants referred to the experience at Cane Ridge as the greatest outpouring of the Holy Spirit since the biblical day of Pentecost.

The gathering was a scene of milling crowds and immense confusion. Everyone walked about, assembled in small groups, and listened to ministers shouting at them simultaneously from several preaching platforms. The traditional process of religious conversion that had once required months, even years, of spiritual preparation was forgotten. Instead, at Cane Ridge all was compressed into mere hours, as believers passed rapidly through stages of guilt, despair, hope, and finally assurance of the forgiveness of their sins. The psychological stress caused by the tremendous throng of preachers and believers forced those who were wavering to respond immediately. Outbursts of religious emotion punctuated the affair: people sobbing, screaming, dancing, and jerking their limbs spasmodically.

Cane Ridge symbolized the tremendous religious changes occurring in the United States in the early years of the new republic's life. Camp meetings became the principal means by which Protestantism spread on the western frontier during the period of the SECOND GREAT AWAKENING. Over the next three years especially, similar revivals were held throughout Kentucky, Tennessee, and southern Ohio, and thousands of previously unchurched settlers were incorporated into Christian denominations. While all churches in these areas gained new members in the wake of the revivals, the most insistently democratic denominations, the Baptists and the Methodists, expanded the most rapidly over the next decades. As a result of the enthusiasm Cane Ridge helped inspire, Baptists and Methodists soon became the largest church bodies in the United States.

GHS, Jr.

Bibliography: Paul K. Conkin, *Cane Ridge: America's Pentecost* (Madison: University of Wisconsin Press, 1990).

Carolinas (colonial period)

The religious life of the Carolinas during the COLONIAL PERIOD was quite mixed. The early history of both colonies manifested much religious diversity, but while attempts to establish the Church of England (see ANGLICANISM) in North Carolina were unsuccessful, South Carolina eventually managed not only an establishment but legislation requiring religious conformity as well.

The earliest attempts at colonization in what is now the Carolinas were made by the Spanish (see NEW SPAIN). In 1526, Spanish colonies were planted in both modern-day North and South Carolina, but they soon failed. The French (see NEW FRANCE) made the next attempt, establishing a settlement at what is now Parris Island, South Carolina, in 1562. This settlement was equally unsuccessful, and despite repeated attempts at revitalization it was abandoned by 1680.

North Carolina saw the first British attempt at colonization in North America as well as the creation of an American legend, when Sir Walter Raleigh established a colony at Roanoke Island in 1585. This colony survived only with constant resupply from England, and when the threat of a Spanish invasion interrupted British shipping between 1587 and 1590, the colony disappeared and with it the first English child born in North America.

No other formal attempts at colonization took place until the 1660s, although northern Carolina had begun to receive some settlement by Virginians (see VIRGINIA) who migrated south during the 1650s. Carolina was organized as a proprietary colony along feudal lines with the settlers required to pay fees to the proprietors. Despite this feudal form, its constitution—which John Locke (see ENLIGHTENMENT, THE) supposedly helped write—allowed religious tolerance in a bid to encourage settlement.

Settlement in the northern part was slow, but South Carolina soon developed into a thriving colony, and by 1681 Charleston had an Anglican Church. In 1704 the colonial assembly established the Church of England and required conformity with its laws and rites. By 1723 there were 13 parishes in the colony, most of which were prosperous and well served.

Despite the existence of an established church, colonial South Carolina contained significant religious diversity. Beyond the pockets of Native Americans who survived European diseases and war to maintain their traditional religious beliefs, South Carolina had one of the largest populations of Africans in the colonies. Many of these enslaved Africans retained their traditional religious beliefs or merged them with the incipient Christianity they received. Given the high mortality rate among slaves in the rice and indigo plantations of the colony, South Carolina imported more recently enslaved Africans who helped to maintain the traditions longer there than in most other colonies.

European diversity was also marked. The colony's first governor was a Puritan (see PURITANISM), and many of its earliest settlements had distinctively Baptist leanings (see BAPTISTS). Quakers (see FRIENDS, THE RELIGIOUS SOCIETY OF [QUAKERS]) were also well represented in the colony, and one, John Archdale, served as colonial governor from 1694 to 1695. A group of Huguenots—French Protestants—arrived in 1680, and in 1730 German and Swiss Lutherans settled in the colony. Charleston was also the center of colonial Judaism, with the largest Jewish population (500) in the colonies at the beginning of the American Revolution.

One group markedly absent from both northern and southern Carolina was the Roman Catholics. Strictly enforced laws against their presence, Catholic priests, and the performance of the Mass prevented any noticeable Roman Catholic migration to the colonies.

Religious life in colonial North Carolina was equally diverse, albeit much less regularized. Settlement was slow in North Carolina, and the colony had no incorporated town until 1706, when Bath was organized by a group of Huguenot settlers. Religious diversity in North Carolina owed a lot to the stringent religious laws of Virginia, which led many dissenters to migrate south.

From the earliest time, North Carolina included large numbers of Quakers, Baptists, Presbyterians (see PRESBYTERIANISM), and the unchurched, along with the indigenous peoples and enslaved Africans. Attempts to establish the Church of England in the colony met with much resistance and even violence. In 1701 the colonial assembly officially established the Church of England and followed this in 1705 with a law for tax support for Anglican churches. Both of these met with much opposition, and the proprietors quickly vetoed the establishment law while an armed rebellion forced the repeal of the support law.

North Carolina reverted to royal control in 1729. This led to greater stability in the colony, although it was still prone to numerous insurrections. The Church of England was officially established in 1741, and while this put dissenters on an unequal political footing, it did little to end the colony's religious diversity. In the 1750s a group of Moravians established Salem, and their presence, along with that of the Quakers, has had a lasting influence on the religious ethos of that part of the state.

More importantly, however, has been the Baptist role in the history of both the colony and later the state. Baptists were among the earliest settlers of the colony, joining Quakers who drifted south from Virginia. These Baptists received a major organizational boost in 1751 when the Baptist missionary Shubal Stearns settled in Sandy Creek, North Carolina. There he organized several churches which formed the Sandy Creek Association, with 10 churches by 1760. This growth continued for the next decade, but increasing religious persecution and political conflicts soon forced many Baptists to flee the colony. This was especially true after 1771 when government troops crushed the Regulator movement at the Battle of Alamance. The Regulators, who were in revolt against the eastern aristocracy, were particularly strong in Baptist-dominated areas, and Baptist hostility remained great, resulting in widespread Baptist support for the revolution and, later, support for laws guaranteeing religious liberty.

While their small populations and distance from the center of colonial development have resulted in little attention being paid to them, the Carolinas provide an interesting example of colonial religious diversity. As such they served to demonstrate the peace that is possible in the absence of religious coercion and, in the North Carolina case, the hostilities and animosities that emerge when it is attempted on a varied population.

EQ

Bibliography: S. Charles Bolton, *Southern Anglicanism* (Westport, Conn.: Greenwood Press, 1982); Samuel S. Hill, ed., *Encyclopedia of Religion in the South* (Macon, Ga.: Mercer University Press, 1984); Charles H. Lippy, *A Bibliography of Religion in the South* (Macon, Ga.: Mercer University Press, 1985).

Carroll, John (1735–1815)

The first bishop of the Roman Catholic Church (see ROMAN CATHOLICISM) in the United States, John Carroll laid an admirable foundation for the church's growth and stability. More importantly, he set the example for future American Catholic bishops by his support for the U.S. political system and its commitment to religious liberty.

John Carroll was born on January 8, 1735, to a wealthy and distinguished Maryland Catholic family. His father, Daniel, an Irish immigrant, was a successful merchant and tobacco farmer, while his mother, Eleanor Darnall, was from an old Maryland Catholic family. Through her, John was related to the most important Catholics in the country.

Despite their social and economic standing, Catholics in Maryland lived under legal restrictions. Public celebration of the Mass and the building of churches were illegal. Even Bohemia Manor, the Jesuit school Carroll attended beginning at age 12, was unlawful. Sent to Europe the following year for further study, he attended St. Omer's in French Flanders and graduated in 1753. At this time Carroll entered the Society of Jesus (see JESUITS) and spent the next several years training at Jesuit seminaries in France and Belgium. After his ordination around 1769, he taught philosophy and theology at several Jesuit schools and served as a tutor to English Catholics touring the European continent.

The suppression of the Jesuits by Pope Clement XIV in 1773 hit the young man hard. His life and dreams shattered, Carroll returned home to the America he had not seen in a quarter-century. Settling at his mother's estate at Rock Creek, Maryland, he began a small mission church and ministered to the needs of local Catholics.

The American Revolution saw Carroll a committed patriot. With his cousin, Charles Carroll of Carrollton (the wealthiest man in America and the only Catholic signer of the Declaration of Independence), and Benjamin Franklin, he undertook an ultimately unsuccessful diplomatic mission to Canada designed to gain French Catholic support for the Revolutionary cause.

While American victory in the Revolution eased most legal burdens on American Catholics, it left the Church in the United States with no administrative center. No longer could it take directives from London, or anywhere on the continent for that matter. The Church needed its own bishop. In 1783 Carroll and five other priests petitioned the Pope to provide some structure for the American church by appointing a leader from among its members.

In response, the Pope appointed Carroll superior of the American church. Disturbed by the lack of consultation in the appointment and the limited authority vested in the position, Carroll delayed acceptance. Only after receiving an expansion in authority and the title of vicar apostolic, did Carroll accept, undertaking the job of imposing order upon a weak church spread over a vast nation.

This job was made somewhat easier when, in 1789, Pius VI appointed Carroll bishop of the diocese of Baltimore, which covered most of the United States from Vermont to Louisiana. The selection had followed Carroll's suggestions. He had been chosen by the priests in the United States and his name submitted to Rome for approval. This was consistent with Carroll's view of the Church. For him the Roman Catholic Church was a combination of national churches united by doctrine and belief under the headship of the pope. As long as each national church was consistent with Rome in faith and doctrine, it should be allowed to organize its own affairs according to its traditions and national character. For Carroll this meant an American church committed to religious liberty and to American democracy.

To increase the number of clergy in America, he encouraged European orders to establish themselves in the United States. In this he was aided by the French Revolution, during which many French priests and nuns emigrated to America. Most visible among these were the Sulpicians, who would form the bulk of America's second generation of Roman Catholic leaders.

Most importantly, Carroll recognized that the Roman Catholic Church in the United States needed a complete infrastructure of institutions and organizations. This included the creation of American religious orders, like Elizabeth SETON's Sisters of Charity. Education was preeminent in the mind of this former professor, and he was instrumental in the creation of what is now Georgetown University (1789), Mount St. Mary's College (Annapolis, Maryland, 1792), and St. Joseph's College (Emmitsburg, Maryland, 1809).

Carroll also established his authority over individual parishes, ending a long conflict about the ability of parish trustees to choose their own priests and control church money. At the Synod of Baltimore (1791) and the Provincial Council of 1810 he oversaw the first codification of Church law for the United States.

Although many of his dreams for the American Church would not be realized—Carroll was both the first and last American bishop chosen by the priests—Carroll created an admirable foundation for the growth of Roman Catholicism in the United States. At his death on December 3, 1815, the American Church had four bishops and one archbishop, numerous schools and colleges, as well as a growing population. More importantly, it had an American character and ethos that aided it during the next 150 years as it struggled to respond to massive immigration and growth.

EQ

Bibliography: Joseph Agonito, *The Building of an American Catholic Church* (New York: Garland Press, 1988); Peter Guilday, *The Life and Times of John Carroll, Archbishop of Baltimore, 1735–1815,*

2 vols. (New York: The Encyclopedia Press, 1922); Annabelle M. Melville, *John Carroll of Baltimore: Founder of the American Catholic Hierarchy* (New York: Scribner, 1955); John Gilmary Shea, *The Life and Times of the Most Rev. John Carroll, Bishop and First Archbishop of Baltimore* (New York: J. G. Shea, 1900).

Carter, Jimmy (James Earl, Jr.) (1924–)

Perhaps the most conventionally and actively religious U.S. president since Woodrow Wilson, Jimmy Carter brought to the broader American public a new sight: a southern, evangelical Protestant, comfortable with African Americans, committed to civil rights, and outspoken in his religious faith. He brought the term "born again" into the pages of the *New York Times* and turned a large but relatively unnoticed reality (with the exception of the Billy GRAHAM crusades) into front page news.

Born on October 1, 1924, in Plains, Georgia, and raised in the small town of Archery, Carter led a life typical of many small-town white boys in the rural South. His father worked a family farm and ran a small business; his mother was a registered nurse. After finishing public schools in Plains, Carter attended Georgia Southwestern College and Georgia Tech University before graduating from the U.S. Naval Academy in Annapolis, Maryland, in 1946. Shortly after his graduation and receiving his commission in the U.S. Navy, he married Rosalynn Smith.

Carter was well on the way toward a successful naval career, having served in both the Pacific and Atlantic fleets and under Admiral Hyman Rickover, the father of the nuclear navy. This career was cut short by the death of Carter's father in 1953. As a result, Carter abruptly resigned his naval commission, returning home to run the family farm and, with his wife, Carter's Warehouse, a local feed and seed store.

Carter became a regular member of the local Southern Baptist (see SOUTHERN BAPTIST CONVENTION) congregation and an active participant in community affairs. During this time his political career began. He was elected to the county school board and served as president of the Georgia Planning Commission. In 1962 he successfully campaigned for a state senate seat, only to lose the 1966 gubernatorial race. The defeat did not deter him, and he ran again in 1970. This time he was successful and became Georgia's governor in January 1971.

Carter became a rising star in the national Democratic Party, serving as Democratic National Committee campaign chairman for the 1974 congressional elections. In December of that year he announced his candidacy for president of the United States. He built a strong grassroots base throughout the country, which propelled him to victory in the Democratic presidential primaries and eventually in the presidential election.

Carter's presidency was a period of much domestic and international turmoil. Domestic economic woes and the Iranian takeover of the U.S. embassy in Tehran led to the increasing polarization of American politics. Despite these difficulties and an overwhelming defeat in the 1980 election, Carter's presidency had numerous successes, including the Panama Canal treaty, the peace treaty between Egypt and Israel, the SALT II treaty with the Soviet Union, and the establishment of U.S. diplomatic relations with the People's Republic of China. Domestically, the deregulation of energy, transportation, communications, and finance and the establishment of the Departments of Education and Energy left their mark on the country.

Carter also made human rights part of the international and domestic agendas. After his presidency, disregard of this issue was no longer possible. The human rights agenda reflected in many ways Carter's moralistic approach to politics. While this approach would cause him numerous difficulties, as it did Woodrow Wilson, it set him apart from the Kissinger-inspired realpolitik of the previous eight years and made him a distinctive personality in

American politics. It also would serve him well after his defeat in 1980.

Perhaps no former president since John Quincy Adams has had a more active and successful public life. Unlike Adams, who spent his post-presidential years in the House of Representatives, Carter has worked in the worlds of religion and nongovernmental organizations, notably HABITAT FOR HUMANITY. Carter and his wife have also taken leadership roles in the areas of international peace and health, both through the work of the Carter Center—the combination Carter library and research center located in Atlanta—and as election observers. Carter also has been an active negotiator for peace in many of the world's trouble spots.

Religion continues to play a major role in his life. Carter still teaches Sunday school at his local church and speaks readily of the importance of faith to his life. One of his books, *Sources of Strength* (1977), is a compilation of his weekly Sunday school lessons. His disagreement with the SBC's increasingly conservative views, especially on the role of women, led to Carter's formal break with the Southern Baptist Convention in October 2000.

While a final verdict on Carter's public life must wait for future historians, it is clear that he set the standard for speaking comfortably about religion in the public realm. Carter's words about his faith never seemed forced or false. He also seemed willing both in and out of government to live through his faith. His work for Habitat for Humanity, the ease with which he spoke of his personal struggles, and his passionate commitment to PEACE all served to elevate Carter in the public eye to heights he never reached while president.

(See also HUMAN RIGHTS.)

EQ

Bibliography: Douglas Brinkley, *The Unfinished Presidency: Jimmy Carter's Journey Beyond the White House* (New York: Penguin USA, 1999); Jimmy Carter, *The Blood of Abraham* (Fayetteville: University of Arkansas Press, 1993); ———, *A Government as Good as Its People* (Fayetteville: University of Arkansas Press, 1996); ———, *Keeping Faith: Memoirs of a President* (Fayetteville: University of Arkansas Press, 1995); ———, *Sources of Strength* (New York: Times Books, 1997); ———, *Why Not the Best?* (Fayetteville: University of Arkansas Press, 1996); Jimmy Carter and Rosalynn Carter, *Everything to Gain: Making the Most of the Rest of Your Life* (Fayetteville: University of Arkansas Press, 1995).

Cartwright, Peter (1785–1872)   An itinerant Methodist minister and frontier preacher, Peter Cartwright served for nearly 70 years, first, in a circuit covering Kentucky, Tennessee, Ohio, and Indiana and, later, in Illinois. Cartwright's evangelistic zeal, coupled with his wit and homespun sermons, contributed greatly to the expansion of Methodism throughout the Midwest and upper South in the first half of the 19th century.

Cartwright was born in Amherst County, Virginia, on September 1, 1785. His family moved to Kentucky when he was five years old. Cartwright had little formal education, and he later said he reveled in the horse races and gambling then so common in Kentucky society. Converted to Christianity, however, at a camp meeting (see CAMP MEETINGS) in 1801, Cartwright was licensed the next year as an exhorter of the Methodist Episcopal Church. He became a circuit rider in 1803, and having mastered extemporaneous preaching, he preached an average of more than a sermon a day for the next 20 years. He was ordained a deacon in 1806 and an elder in 1808. After serving as presiding elder of the Methodists' Cumberland District from 1821 to 1823, Cartwright was transferred in 1824 to the Illinois Conference, where he was a presiding elder for most of the next 50 years.

Cartwright scorned religious formalism and believed that daily Bible reading and regular prayer were the keys to the spiritual life. He preached a simple message of free salvation and rigorous moral conduct—hallmarks of early American Methodism. He also claimed that Methodist ministers could set the world on fire while other clergy were still earning degrees and negotiating their salaries. However, over the course of Cartwright's career, Methodism itself began to change, gradually abandoning its former simplicity. In his 1856 autobiography, Cartwright lamented that Methodists had turned their backs on the popular enthusiasm that once had fueled their movement. He feared that Methodist clergy, too, had become "downy doctors and learned presidents and professors," while lay men and women desired only wealth, fashion, and material comforts.

Cartwright's own successful political career in many ways exemplifies the rising respectability and influence he decried among members of his denomination. He was elected twice to the Illinois state legislature, representing his district from 1824 to 1840. He also ran for United States Congress in 1846 but was defeated by Abraham Lincoln. As the question of slavery began to divide the nation, Cartwright emerged as an important opponent of the slave system. When the Methodist General Conference of 1844 debated the question of slaveholding, Cartwright attempted to hold the two factions in his church together. When the split came and the Methodist Episcopal Church, South was formed in 1845, he sided with the antislavery party and remained loyal to the continuing Methodist denomination in the northern states.

Cartwright is said to have preached nearly 15,000 sermons and baptized almost 10,000 converts over the course of his long career. Although Methodism evolved culturally in that time and his methods became outdated before his death, he still maintained his plain manner and homey preaching style. Cartwright died in Pleasant Plains, Illinois, on September 25, 1872.

GHS, Jr.

Bibliography: Peter Cartwright, *The Autobiography of Peter Cartwright*, ed. Charles L. Wallis (Nashville: Abingdon Press, 1956).

Catholic Worker movement   Founded in 1933 by Dorothy DAY and Peter Maurin to "popularize and make known the encyclicals of the Popes in regard to social justice," the Catholic Worker movement was a Roman Catholic (see ROMAN CATHOLICISM) lay movement committed to the participation of all in the mystical body of Christ. Maurin, the leading theoretician of the movement, called for a "green revolution" that would combine sacramental piety, farming communes, voluntary poverty, houses of hospitality for the urban poor, and pacifism (see PEACE REFORM). The eventual goal was the establishment of a communitarian society free of the profit motive where the divine value of each human being could be grasped. Through its newspaper, also called the *Catholic Worker*, the movement drew on Day's journalistic experience to spread its message widely throughout American Catholicism.

At its height the movement had established more than 50 houses of hospitality and communal farms. Numerically strongest during the 1930s, when it touched thousands affected by the Great Depression, it lost ground during WORLD WAR II as a result of its pacifism. During the 1950s and 1960s its influence rebounded as numerous priests and laypeople who had done stints in the houses of hospitality moved into positions of authority. This influence was strengthened by the fact that despite constant conflicts with governmental authorities, the movement rarely challenged Church authority and was accepted, albeit grudgingly, by even the most conservative bishops.

Although Catholic social action in the United States has tended to reject the agrarianism and "Christian anarchism" of the Catholic Worker, by challenging people to live out the claims of the Gospels, the Catholic Worker remains a significant moral force among American Catholics.

(See also REFORM, SOCIAL.)

EQ

Bibliography: Anne Klejment and Alice Klejment, *Dorothy Day and the Catholic Worker: A Bibliography and Index* (New York: Garland Press, 1986); Mel Piehl, *Breaking Bread: The Catholic Worker and the Origin of Catholic Radicalism in America* (Philadelphia: Temple University Press, 1982); Nancy L. Roberts, *Dorothy Day and the "Catholic Worker"* (New York: SUNY Press, 1985); www.catholicworker.org/roundtable (Catholic Worker).

Catholicism   See ANGLO-CATHOLICISM; ROMAN CATHOLICISM.

Central Conference of American Rabbis (CCAR)

The professional association of Reform Jewish rabbis (see REFORM JUDAISM) in the United States and Canada, the Central Conference of American Rabbis is the oldest and largest rabbinical association in North America. Organized in 1892 under the watchful eye of Isaac Mayer WISE, the founder of Reform Judaism in the United States, the CCAR has long been the central defining institution of Reform thought and doctrine.

Historically, this rabbinical dominance has hindered Reform Judaism's ability to respond to changed conditions. In its early years the CCAR's control by rabbis whose cultural and linguistic homeland was Germany resulted in its failure to adjust to the needs and attitudes of the eastern European Jews who dominated Jewish immigration from 1890 to 1927. Although willing to aid them materially, the CCAR's membership had little respect for their religious orthodoxy (see ORTHODOX JUDAISM). As Wise wrote in 1894, "the Central Conference at once rejected all illiberal elements, and stands only . . . for the American Israel of the liberal and progressive school . . ."

This commitment to an "American Israel" also led the CCAR to adopt a hostile stance toward ZIONISM and to reject the traditional Jewish prayers for the return of the Jews to Israel and the restoration of the temple. The rise of Nazism and the horrors of the Holocaust, however, forced a revision of that policy. In 1937 the CCAR adopted a policy of neutrality on the issue of Zionism. After WORLD WAR II its position became even stronger when it adopted a resolution announcing its solidarity with Israel, declaring that "their triumphs are our triumphs. Their ordeal is our ordeal. Their fate is our fate." This shift became institutionalized two years later when the CCAR made Israeli Independence Day part of Reform Judaism's religious calendar.

By the late 1940s and early 1950s there was growing pressure within the CCAR to move toward more traditional forms of Judaism. Led primarily by the descendants of the eastern European immigrants, this movement produced some major changes within the organization. These included greater use of Hebrew within worship, the restoration of Jewish symbols and customs, and the inclusion of a prayer for Israel in the prayer book.

Despite the increased traditionalism in religious forms, the CCAR remained committed to its purpose of creating an American Judaism attuned to the needs and realities of the modern world. Significantly the CCAR was the first rabbinical association to ordain a woman as rabbi, in 1972. The CCAR also has been the only rabbinical association to vocally support the religious rights of gays and lesbians, including the recognition of same-sex unions.

While many of these changes would have been inconceivable to the founders of classical Reform Judaism, in enacting them the CCAR continues to express its connections with those founders as it struggles to make the ancient religion speak anew to the world.

EQ

Bibliography: Nathan Glazer, *American Judaism*, 2d ed., rev. (Chicago: University of Chicago Press, 1972); Beryl Harold Levy, *Reform Judaism in America: A Study in Religious Adaptation* (New York: Ph.D. dissertation, Columbia University, 1933); Julian Morgenstern, *As a Mighty Stream: The Progress of Judaism Through History* (Philadelphia: Jewish Publication Society, 1949); Kerry M. Olitzky, Lance J. Sussman, and Malcolm A. Stern, eds., *Reform Judaism in America: A Biographical Dictionary and Sourcebook* (Westport, Conn.: Greenwood Press, 1993); W. Gunther Plaut; *The Rise of Reform Judaism,* 2 vols. (New York: World Union for Progressive Judaism, 1963–65); www.ccarnet.org (Central Conference of American Rabbis).

Channing, William Ellery (1780–1842)

William Ellery Channing is generally acknowledged to be the most important representative of the Unitarian movement that emerged out of New England Congregationalism in the early 19th century. Channing's greatest contribution to Unitarian thought is contained in an ordination sermon he preached in 1819. There he spoke out against such traditional Protestant beliefs as the threefold nature of God, the deity of Jesus Christ, and the total sinfulness of human beings.

Born in Newport, Rhode Island, on April 7, 1780, Channing graduated from Harvard College in 1798 and served briefly as a private tutor in Richmond, Virginia. After a course of theological study, he was ordained to the Congregational ministry in 1803 and assumed the pastorate at Federal Street Church in Boston. Although Channing said he had long been troubled by the extreme CALVINISM he learned as a youth, he did not emerge as a spokesman for Unitarian theology until 1815. In "A Letter to the Rev. Samuel C. Thacher," however, Channing responded to fellow Congregationaliat Jedidiah Morse's attack on liberals such as himself. Channing also published two open letters to Samuel Worcester, a conservative minister in Salem, who had entered the fray in support of the anti-Unitarian position.

The sermon Channing preached at the ordination of Jared Sparks in Baltimore, Maryland, in 1819, later published under the title "Unitarian Christianity," outlined the intellectual bases for the theological liberalism he and other Unitarians were championing. Channing declared that the New Testament taught God's essential oneness, not threeness, that is, God as Unity rather than as Trinity. While he believed

William Ellery Channing, the "Luther of Boston," led the flowering of Unitarianism in antebellum New England. *(Painting by Gilbert Stuart)*

that Jesus had been inspired by God to effect the moral and spiritual deliverance of humankind, Channing denied the prevailing Calvinist doctrine that Jesus' death had paid a price to atone for humanity's innate guilt. Channing spoke of the essential similarity between God and humankind. The significance of Jesus' ministry, he thought, was his leading men and women toward perfection and bringing them into closer communion with God their Father.

Most of Channing's published work was in the form of lectures and sermons, not systematic theological treatises. His faith, like Unitarianism itself, was not entirely novel but a restatement of many beliefs already implicit within the Christian theological tradition. He emphasized the benevolence of God and, rejecting the doctrine of human depravity, underscored the divinely given potential within every human being. He also criticized others such as the transcendentalists (see TRANSCENDENTALISM) for moving too far away from accepted Christian beliefs. Channing's thought perpetuated a liberal religious outlook reminiscent of the late 18th century, and he helped bring stability and respectability to the new Unitarian denomination that first took shape in 1825.

Toward the latter stages of his life, Channing's trust in human perfectibility impelled him into increasing devotion to causes relating to social reform, especially the nascent antislavery movement. He published an important indictment of the slave system in "Slavery" in 1835, and his last work, the "Address at Lenox" (1842), sought to arouse abolitionist sentiment in the North. In identifying theology with ethics, Channing exemplified, according to many, the best of the New England religious culture of his day, and a number of American reformers in the middle years of the 19th century were to be counted among his disciples.

Although Channing served at the Federal Street Church for his entire ministerial career, he gradually withdrew from his pastoral responsibilities when his health began to decline. He died at Bennington, Vermont, on October 2, 1842.

GHS, Jr.

Bibliography: Andrew Delbanco, *William Ellery Channing: An Essay on the Liberal Spirit in America* (Cambridge, Mass.: Harvard University Press, 1981).

Charismatic movement   Among the distinguishing marks of the Charismatic movement is the claim that the *charismata* ("spiritual gifts" in Greek) manifested by Christians in the apostolic age can still be enjoyed by Christians today. These gifts, which are typically bestowed through the ritual of the baptism in the Spirit, include spiritual healing, prophecy, and, most notably, glossolalia, or "speaking in tongues."

Most Charismatics, as participants in the movement are called, tend toward conservative Christian positions on doctrinal matters such as the Trinity, biblical inspiration, and the atoning death and physical resurrection of Jesus Christ. What draws Charismatics together, however, is not a common theology but a shared experience of baptism in the Spirit and a shared commitment to renewing and expanding the Christian church through the exercise of a wide range of spiritual gifts. These gifts are especially evident in Charismatic worship services, which typically emphasize praising God rather than the Eucharist or preaching.

Charismatics trace their origin back to the biblical day of Pentecost, when spiritual gifts, most notably speaking in tongues, were bestowed by the Holy Spirit on the early Christians. Historians view the Charismatic movement as a more recent creation that emerged out of PENTECOSTALISM in the 1960s and 1970s. For this reason, it is sometimes referred to as "Neo-Pentecostalism."

Charismatics differ from Pentecostals in at least two respects. First, Charismatics tend to be white and middle class, and Pentecostals African American and working class. Second, Charismatics have not typically withdrawn from their churches in order to form separate denominations. The Charismatic movement, therefore, represents a transplantation of the Pentecostal impulse from the storefront churches of working people and minorities into the sanctuaries of white, middle-class members of the Roman Catholic Church and Protestant mainstream denominations.

One person who facilitated this shift to respectability was Oral ROBERTS, who through his broadcasting empire did much to introduce non-Pentecostals to spiritual healing and speaking in tongues. Another key figure was Demos Shakarian, who in 1951 in Los Angeles founded the Full Gospel Business Men's

Fellowship International. Members of this fellowship were, like Shakarian himself, both lay Pentecostals and successful businesspeople. The success of their well-publicized meetings signaled a shift in Pentecostalism toward middle-class, mainline respectability and away from clerical authority.

The Charismatic movement participated in these broader trends in Pentecostalism. It first received public attention in 1960, when the Reverend Dennis Bennett announced from his pulpit at St. Mark's Episcopal Church in Van Nuys, California, that he had received the spiritual gift of speaking in tongues. Bennett's revelation split his church, and he was soon exiled to a less prestigious post at St. Luke's Episcopal Church in Seattle, Washington. Bennett's new church expanded rapidly, testifying to the strength of the Charismatic movement.

From Bennett's Episcopal churches in California and Washington, the movement spread during the 1960s to Methodist, Lutheran, and Presbyterian congregations in the West, the Midwest, and New England. Charismatics enjoyed particular success on college campuses. In 1963 and again in the early 1980s, speaking in tongues broke out at Yale University among members of the Intervarsity Christian Fellowship, an evangelical student group.

The Charismatic movement first emerged among Roman Catholics at Duquesne University in Pittsburgh in 1966. From there it spread through networks of Catholic student groups to other college campuses, including the University of Notre Dame and the University of Michigan. Roman Catholic authorities warned against divisive tendencies within the movement, but they have nonetheless made a place in their church for Charismatics. Like leaders in other, more sacramental Protestant denominations, however, they have tended to view baptism in the Holy Spirit not as a second experience of grace, as many Charismatics claim, but as an event coterminous with water baptism.

In 1994, the Charismatic movement received a boost when congregants at a small church called Toronto Airport Vineyard in Toronto, Ontario, Canada, began experiencing what would come to be known as "holy laughter" or the "Toronto Blessing." While some parishioners wept or spoke in tongues in typical Charismatic style, others laughed uncontrollably. Soon this new form of Charismatic practice spread throughout the United States. And while it won the endorsement of such luminaries as Oral Roberts, many evangelical Christians and some Charismatics denounced "holy laughter" as unbiblical nonsense.

Members of conservative denominations, including the SOUTHERN BAPTIST CONVENTION, opposed not only the "Toronto Blessing" in particular but also the Charismatic movement in general as overly emotional and even demonic. Still, the Charismatic movement has enjoyed considerable success. The "gifts of the Spirit," almost unknown at the turn of the 20th century, are widely practiced in America at the start of the 21st.

SRP

Bibliography: Edith Blumhofer, Russell Spittler, and Grant Wacker, eds., *Pentecostal Currents in American Protestantism* (Urbana: University of Illinois Press, 1999); Michael L. Brown, *From Holy Laughter to Holy Fire: America on the Edge of Revival* (Shippensburg, Pa.: Destiny Image Publishers, 1996); Thomas J. Csordas, *Language, Charisma, and Creativity: The Ritual Life of a Religious Movement* (Berkeley: University of California Press, 1997); Richard Quebedeaux, *The New Charismatics: The Origins, Development, and Significance of Neo-Pentecostalism* (Garden City, N.Y.: Doubleday, 1976).

Chauncy, Charles (1705–1787)

In his 60-year ministry at the prestigious First Church of Boston, Charles Chauncy made liberal theology the dominant force in that city to such an extent that it became the prevailing orthodoxy. While not as radical as his younger contemporary and friend Jonathan MAYHEW, Chauncy espoused a reasonable, enlightened version of Christianity that set the stage for the emergence of Unitarianism (see UNITARIAN CONTROVERSY) in the next century.

Chauncy, born January 1, 1705, was not a cold-hearted rationalist but one who believed that human reason served as the integrative source of religious experience. This view gave him a positive vision of the role of human activity and human will in doing good. In this position Chauncy found himself as the defender of the status quo, a leader of the "Old Lights" against the revival movement known as the GREAT AWAKENING.

Chauncy viewed the revivals as a resurgence of the antinomian and enthusiastic heresies that his Puritan forefathers had crushed the century before. George WHITEFIELD he viewed as a theologically ignorant ranter. He felt that Jonathan EDWARDS's congregation in Northamptom suffered from insanity.

The emotionalism and passion of the revivals demanded a response. Chauncy provided one in his *Seasonable Thoughts on the State of Religion in New England* (1743). This book, beyond providing a catalog of the emotional and behavioral excesses of the revivals, detailed Chauncy's view of human reason as the center of religious faith. He did not reject religious emotions but argued that they must be subordinated to reason if chaos, disorder, and schism were to be avoided.

Jonathan Edwards responded with *A Treatise Concerning Religious Affections* (1746), one of the most significant works on religion ever written in America. Chauncy ignored it, having dismissed Edwards as a "visionary enthusiast not to be minded in anything he says."

While his opponents preached human sin and weakness, placing all in the hands of an omnipotent God, Chauncy had turned the sermon into a lecture designed to expound religious truths and the moral obligations of humanity. His emphasis on the reasonableness of Christianity led him to a study of the doctrines of election and eternal damnation. These he could reconcile neither with reason nor with the existence of a benevolent deity. The conclusion to Chauncy was unavoidable. Salvation would be granted to all. By 1762 he had become convinced of this view, known as UNIVERSALISM, but hesitated making it known. Not until 1784, just three years before his death on February 10, 1787, would he publish his book on the subject, *The Salvation of All Men*, and then only anonymously in London.

Chauncy's views represented a transition from the Puritan theology of the 17th century toward the development of Unitarianism in the 19th century. The result would be a major alteration in the religious and social makeup of New England and especially Massachusetts.

EQ

Bibliography: Edward M. Griffin, *Old Brick: Charles Chauncy of Boston, 1705–1787* (Minneapolis: University of Minnesota Press, 1980); Charles Lippy, *Seasonable Revolutionary: The Mind of Charles Chauncy* (Chicago: Nelson Hall, 1981); Conrad Wright, *The Beginnings of Unitarianism in America* (Boston: Starr King Press, 1955).

Chicago-Lambeth Quadrilateral See EPISCOPAL CHURCH.

Christadelphians An outgrowth of Alexander Campbell's RESTORATION MOVEMENT and the Adventism of William MILLER, the Christadelphian movement has been more successful in Great Britain than in the United States, where it claims only a few thousand members. The movement is a significant example, however, of these two influential impulses in American religious life.

The founder of Christadelphianism was John Thomas (b. 1782), a medical doctor who immigrated from England to Cincinnati, Ohio, in 1832. There Thomas was introduced to the restorationist theology of Alexander CAMPBELL. Convinced that it was the duty of 19th-century believers to restore the Christian church to its apostolic purity, Thomas was rebaptized and became a member of the Disciples of Christ (see CHRISTIAN CHURCH [DISCIPLES OF CHRIST]). Soon he was traveling across the country as an itinerant preacher for the Campbellite cause and editing a series of Campbellite periodicals, beginning with the *Apostolic Advocate* (established in 1834).

Thomas eventually split from Campbell over what he saw as a lack of attention to a key principle of the Christian movement: the imperative to restore the contemporary church to the primitive purity of apostolic Christianity (see PRIMITIVISM). "Disfellowshipped" by Campbell in 1837, Thomas turned an eager ear to the millennial and apocalyptic teachings of William Miller's Adventists. Thomas then creatively combined themes from Miller and Campbell into his mature theology, which he articulated in a series of books, beginning with *Elpis Israel: An Exposition of the Kingdom of God with Reference to the Time of the End and the Age to Come* (1850).

The first Christadelphian "ecclesia" (Christadelphians prefer not to refer to their associations as "churches") emerged in 1852 in New York City. That group initially called itself the Royal Association of Believers. Not until 1864, when his followers needed to demonstrate their membership in a bona fide religious organization to justify their opposition to military service in the Civil War did Thomas refer to his movement as "Christadelphian" ("Brethren in Christ").

Like other religious sectarians, Christadelphians draw a sharp distinction between those who are "in the truth" and those who are not. One way they articulate their separation from the evils of the world is through their refusal to participate in government. Typically, Christadelphians are pacifists. They generally refuse to join political parties, vote, hold political office, or sit on juries. Each of these refusals, along with their taboo against marrying outside the Christadelphian fold, helps to insure their purity in the midst of what they believe is a polluted world.

Christadelphian theology is based on the Bible, which according to believers is the infallible word of God. But Christadelphians interpret the Bible through the writings of their founder. They tend, as a result, to emphasize prophetic books, such as Daniel and Revelation, which they read alongside and in light of accounts of important historical events, especially military clashes, that signify in their view the imminence of the Second Advent of Christ.

Christadelphians distinguish themselves from other restorationist and Adventist groups by their preference for Unitarianism over trinitarianism. Jesus is embraced as King of Israel and Son of God, but Christadelphians insist that he was "adopted" by God and thus did not exist before the creation of the world. In 2000, there were 5,700 Christadelphians in 180 ecclesias in the United States.

SRP

Bibliography: Charles H. Lippy, *The Christadelphians in North America* (Lewiston, N.Y.: Edwin Mellen Press, 1989).

Christian and Missionary Alliance   See HOLINESS MOVEMENT.

Christian Broadcasting Network   See ELECTRONIC CHURCH.

Christian Church (Disciples of Christ)
The Christian Church (Disciples of Christ) traces its roots to the RESTORATION MOVEMENT of the early 19th century. The restoration movement, an outgrowth of the SECOND GREAT AWAKENING, was composed of diverse religious elements all seeking to reestablish the primitive (see PRIMITIVISM) Christianity of New Testament times. Restorationism was marked by one primary goal: the reunification all churches under the lordship of Jesus Christ and the absolute authority of the Bible.

In 1831 the two major restorationist strands in the United States joined forces when many of Barton W. STONE's "Christians" merged with Alexander CAMPBELL's "Disciples." While its internal organization was not completed until 1849, a new body emerged out of the self-consciously nondenominational movements Campbell and Stone launched. Since Campbell preferred the name "Disciples of Christ," that became the label usually applied to the movement after 1831. (Stone's term, "Christian Church," while equally proper, was less commonly used.) Despite the fact that there was never perfect uniformity among the Disciples, emphasis on a New Testament precedent for all beliefs and practices was central to the united movement.

Although the Disciples for many years refused to call themselves a denomination, because they believed such a designation was unbiblical, they still became the fastest-growing church in America in the 19th century. They competed with the Baptists and the Methodists in seeking the allegiance of common people on the western frontier. The Disciples were most successful in what is now the Midwest and the upper South. During the 1840s, they established two important institutions. Alexander Campbell founded Bethany College in western Virginia (West Virginia today) in 1840, and the Disciples created the American Christian Missionary Society, the movement's first semi-official organization, in 1849. The sixth-largest religious body in the United States on the eve of the Civil War, the Disciples contained 192,000 members in 1860.

Since most of the church's leaders were border state moderates, the Civil War, which was so disruptive of other Protestant denominations, did not seriously threaten the Disciples' unity. In fact, the Disciples were one of the few American churches that did not split during the Civil War. However, a number of other factors, including continued growth, sociological diversity, and doctrinal disputes, soon threatened their unity after 1865. The inherent tension in the restoration movement between primitivism, which demanded a literalistic interpretation of the Bible, and inclusivity, which allowed openness to the modern world, split the Disciples apart early in the 20th century.

The first schism was officially recognized in 1906, when the United States Census Bureau differentiated between the Disciples of Christ and the CHURCHES OF CHRIST, a group of highly

conservative congregations. The use of pipe organs and instrumental music in churches, as well as the role of missionary societies and other ecclesiastical agencies, were cited as the reasons for the breakup. The issue dividing the two religious bodies, however, actually went far deeper than that. The true conflict was over how biblical teachings in general were to be applied to the present-day life of the church. Conservative congregations, of which the majority were located in the South, refused to follow what they believed were the more liberal, modern theological tendencies adopted by the church's leadership in the upper Midwest.

The Disciples' congregations that remained after the defection of their ultraconservative brethren were by no means wholly united in belief. While few questioned the old verities of 19th-century restorationism, many of the denomination's leaders actively embraced new theological trends. In the early 20th century, in fact, the *Christian Century*, a Disciples journal that had begun as the *Christian Oracle* in 1884, became the most prominent forum of liberal Protestant opinion in America. This trend toward liberalism further exacerbated denominational ties already stretched to the breaking point by intellectual controversies over Darwinism and biblical criticism.

During the heyday of the dispute between fundamentalists and theological liberals in American Protestantism, conservatives within the Disciples of Christ accused their leadership of undercutting the traditional authority of the Scriptures. When the traditionalists did not think their concerns had been given a fair hearing, they formed their own alternative denominational body, the North American Christian Convention, in 1927. The boundary line between the Disciples and the new association of independent Christian churches was not always clear. The publication of a directory of the conservative congregations in 1955, however, clearly denoted where the division had occurred. And when the Disciples restructured themselves in 1968 and created a regional and national structure akin to the organization of other mainline Protestant (see MAINLINE PROTESTANTISM) denominations, an estimated 2,000 conservative congregations refused to acknowledge the change.

Throughout their history, the Disciples of Christ have maintained most of the practices common to the early restoration movement: baptism by immersion for the forgiveness of sins as a condition for church membership, the celebration of Communion every Sunday, and the local autonomy of individual congregations. The Disciples also continue the tradition of having "no creed but the Bible." Always proponents of church unity, they were active in founding the Federal Council of Churches (1908), the World Council of Churches (1948), and the Consultation on Church Union (1962). Typical of all the mainstream denominations since the 1960s, moreover, the church has experienced a slight numerical decline in the last quarter-century. Some attribute the apparent defection of members to various liberal social pronouncements made by the national leadership in recent years.

While the denomination reported more than 2 million members in the late 1940s, those figures have now been cut in half. The Christian Church (Disciples of Christ) listed approximately 4,000 congregations and slightly fewer than 1 million members at the end of 20th century.

GHS, Jr.

Bibliography: David Edwin Harrell, *Quest for a Christian America: The Disciples of Christ and American Society to 1866* (Nashville: Disciples of Christ Historical Society, 1966); David Edwin Harrell, *The Social Sources of Division in the Disciples of Christ, 1865–1900* (Atlanta: Publishing Systems, 1973); D. Newell Williams, ed., *A Case Study of Mainstream Protestantism: The Disciples' Relation to American Culture, 1880–1989* (Grand Rapids, Mich.: Eerdmans, 1991); www.disciples.org (Disciples of Christ).

Christian Churches and Churches of Christ   See CHURCHES OF CHRIST.

Christian Coalition   See CHRISTIAN RIGHT.

Christian Commission   See CIVIL WAR, THE.

Christian Connection   See RESTORATION MOVEMENT.

Christian Holiness Association   See HOLINESS MOVEMENT.

Christian Methodist Episcopal Church
Originally known as the Colored Methodist Episcopal Church in America until its name change in 1954, the Christian Methodist Episcopal Church (C.M.E.) has known a very different history from the two other historically black Methodist denominations. Like them, it owes its existence to disgust with racism, but whereas the AFRICAN METHODIST EPISCOPAL CHURCH (A.M.E.) and AFRICAN METHODIST EPISCOPAL ZION CHURCH (A.M.E. ZION) emerged out of northern Methodism before the Civil War, the C.M.E. emerged from the Methodist Episcopal Church, South, in the period following the war.

This separation, part amicable and part hostile, was symptomatic of the exodus of the former slaves from the churches of their erstwhile masters. African Americans' dissatisfaction with inferior status in the white church made them exceedingly susceptible to the missionary activity of the A.M.E. and A.M.E. Zion churches, and by 1870 only 40,000 blacks remained in the southern Methodist church. In December of that year, with the blessing of the leadership of the Methodist Episcopal Church, South, the Colored Methodist Episcopal Church was organized. The senior bishop and three ministers of the southern Methodist Church presided over the new denomination's organization, and the bishop consecrated the C.M.E.'s first two bishops, William H. Miles and Richard H. Vanderhorst.

Throughout the 19th century the C.M.E. remained a primarily southern denomination, centered mostly in Alabama, Tennessee, Georgia, and Mississippi. The increasing migration of southern blacks to the North meant that the church also migrated and by 1945 had expanded to 18 northern states. It remains the smallest of the three black Methodist churches, however, numbering about 800,000 in the United States in 2000. The denomination operates five colleges—Miles, Paine, Texas, Lane, and Mississippi Industrial—and one seminary, Phillips, which is affiliated with the Interdenominational Theological Center in Atlanta.

(See also AFRICAN-AMERICAN RELIGION; METHODISM.)

EQ

Bibliography: Katherine Dvorak, *An African-American Exodus: The Segregation of the Southern Churches* (Brooklyn, N.Y.: Carlson Publishing, 1991); Othal H. Lakey, *The History of the C.M.E. Church* (Memphis, Tenn.: C.M.E. Publishing House, 1996); ———, *The Rise of Colored "Methodism": A Study of the Background and Beginnings of the Christian Methodist Episcopal Church* (Dallas: Crescendo Book Publications, 1972); ———, *God in My Mama's House: The Women's Movement in the CME Church* (Memphis, Tenn.: C.M.E. Publishing House, 1994); C. H. Phillips, *The History of the Colored Methodist Episcopal Church* (New York: Arno Press, 1972); www.c-m-e.org (Christian Methodist Episcopal Church).

Christian Reformed Church   The Christian Reformed Church was created out of the wave of Dutch immigrants who came to the American Midwest from 1840 to 1920 and were dissatisfied with the Dutch Reformed churches (see REFORMED CHURCH IN AMERICA) already established there. The denomination had its institutional beginnings in April 1857 among a small group of settlers at Zeeland, Michigan, who formed the True Holland Reformed Church, later called the Christian Reformed Church. Most of the new Dutch settlers who entered Michigan and Iowa in the 1840s had already separated from the state church of the Netherlands over its supposed theological laxity. Refusal to join the main Reformed Dutch denomination, therefore, merely continued that separatist trend in America.

Earlier in the 19th century, some Dutch Reformed clergy had already expressed fears that the spread of revivalism would erode the doctrinal conservatism that consistently had been the hallmark of the REFORMED TRADITION. To resist this trend, Solomon Froelich and other Dutch Reformed ministers in New York and New Jersey seceded from their church and formed the True Dutch Reformed Church in 1822. A later dispute within the Reformed Church in America over the propriety of its members being Freemasons led to another exodus of dissidents in 1882. Finally, in 1890, both the True Dutch Reformed Church and the 1882 secession movement were subsumed into the Christian Reformed Church. Dutch immigration to the United States helped this united denomination grow steadily into the early 20th century.

Although the language of its worship was changed to English in the 1930s, the denomination continues to be profoundly marked by its Dutch heritage. Maintaining an unceasing struggle against theological liberalism but rejecting narrow-minded FUNDAMENTALISM, the Christian Reformed Church maintains a heartfelt piety mingled with strict adherence to the traditional confessions of CALVINISM. A strong emphasis on intellectual matters has led members to support both the largest Protestant private school system in the United States and a heritage of theological education exemplified by Calvin College and Theological Seminary in Grand Rapids, Michigan. Still, the denomination has been doggedly insular and sectarian, refusing even to engage in ecumenical activity with a Christian body as compatible as the Reformed Church in America. An old proverb has sometimes been applied to explain this denomination's combative character: "One Dutchman a church, two Dutchmen a denomination, three Dutchmen a schism."

Consisting of about 250,000 members in more than 700 churches in 2000, the Christian Reformed Church seeks to be a solid bastion of conservative doctrine and church discipline in 21st-century America.

GHS, Jr.

Bibliography: Peter De Klerk and Richard De Ridder, eds., *Perspectives on the Christian Reformed Church: Studies in Its History, Theology, and Ecumenicity* (Grand Rapids, Mich.: Baker Book House, 1983).

Christian Right Composed of groups of theologically and socially conservative Americans, the Christian Right, which first emerged during the 1920s, is an influential force in politics in the United States today. The roots of the Christian Right are found primarily within the most politically active segments of the American fundamentalist (see FUNDAMENTALISM) movement. Some fundamentalists have fought not only against the theological liberalism of mainline Protestant churches, but also against evils they see threatening America's moral and spiritual heritage, most notably atheistic communism, secular humanism, and the sexual (see SEXUALITY) revolution of the 1960s.

Fundamentalist preacher Gerald B. Winrod was one of the earliest figures of the Christian Right. He founded the Defenders of the Christian Faith in 1925 to oppose the teaching of evolution and used his organization's journal, *The Defender Magazine*, to bring his political message to thousands of American Protestant households. A believer in the imminent return of Jesus Christ, Winrod studied prophetic themes in the Bible and pondered the place of the Jewish people in God's plans. Increasingly anti-Semitic (see ANTI-SEMITISM), he concluded that a Jewish conspiracy lay behind many world events, and he blamed the Jews for World War I, Bolshevism, and the Great Depression. Winrod became involved in American politics when he supported Prohibition and opposed the presidential candidacies of Alfred E. Smith and Franklin D. Roosevelt. He later charged that Roosevelt's New Deal was part of the Jewish conspiracy.

Gerald L. K. Smith, a Disciples of Christ minister, was a major figure of the Christian Right in the 1940s and 1950s. As the pastor of a church in Shreveport, Louisiana, Smith established a reputation for social reform and became one of the chief advisers of Louisiana's populist governor Huey Long. He delivered a memorable eulogy after Long's assassination in 1935. After World War II, Smith transferred his base to Michigan, where he organized the Christian Nationalist Crusade. Arguing that Christian character is the basis of all "real Americanism," Smith developed a political program that included segregationist (see SEGREGATION), anti-Communist, and anti-Semitic ideas. His magazine *The Cross and the Flag* insisted that "the Jews, the pagans and the Communists realize that they cannot capture America . . . as long as we remain a Christian nation."

Not solely the preserve of Protestant fundamentalists, the so-called Old Christian Right also included Roman Catholic priest Charles E. COUGHLIN. One of the earliest preachers to exploit the potential of the electronic (see ELECTRONIC CHURCH) media, Coughlin began a highly effective radio ministry in 1926. By 1930 he had turned from discussing religious topics to promoting political causes. Credited with aiding the election of Franklin D. Roosevelt as president in 1932, Coughlin turned against him as the 1930s progressed. His preaching became so pro-Nazi and anti-Semitic that he was eventually forced off the air by church authorities in 1942.

Carl McIntire, who had founded the Bible Presbyterian Church in 1939 and bitterly opposed liberal trends in American Protestant theology, emerged as a leading clerical opponent of Communism in the 1950s. Through his daily radio broadcast, the "Twentieth-Century Reformation Hour," and through the *Christian Beacon* newspaper, McIntire disseminated a combination of religious fundamentalism and political extremism. He urged Bible-believing American Christians to keep themselves free from entanglement with an increasingly godless society. However, never fearful himself of involvement in political affairs, McIntire passionately supported the United States war effort in Vietnam and organized several "Marches for Victory" in Washington, D.C., in the 1960s.

Billy James Hargis of Tulsa, Oklahoma, was another fundamentalist minister who led the anti-Communist crusade in the 1950s and 1960s. Preaching over the radio and publishing a monthly journal entitled *The Christian Crusade Newspaper,* Hargis took the phrase "For Christ and Against Communism" as his motto. Still active today, Hargis has consistently advocated free enterprise, limited government, and the restoration of what he believes are American Christian principles. He also opposes the United Nations, which he condemns as a fundamentally anti-Christian institution.

Dominion theology, also known as Christian Reconstructionism, provides an intellectual foundation for the political activities of some members of the Christian Right today. Developed under the leadership of R. J. Rushdoony in the 1960s, dominion theology is based upon three fundamental presuppositions. First, truth is available only through God's revelation in the Bible. Second, Old Testament laws are fully applicable to contemporary American culture. And third, believers should work to Christianize the society in which they live. As a result, Reconstructionists lobby to make the death penalty in the United States applicable to the same offenses it covered in biblical times: homosexuality, Sabbath-breaking, and other violations of the Ten Commandments. Although a small minority within the American fundamentalist community, Reconstructionists in recent years have spread their ideas through the media and fielded candidates for political office.

A new conservative religious movement arose in the 1970s that, despite its sympathy with many positions of the Old Right, must be sharply distinguished from it. While the Old Right often focused narrowly on anti-Communism and was not hesitant to advance blatantly anti-Semitic and racist views, the New Religious Right has attempted to appeal to a broad range of social and ethnic groups. The New Religious Right closely mirrors the portion of the Republican party that most enthusiastically supported Ronald Reagan's successful presidential campaigns in 1980 and 1984.

The New Religious Right surfaced in the 1970s in reaction to many of the social developments of the tumultuous 1960s. Three important events triggered the renewal of political activity by conservative Protestants in that period. First, many religious Americans viewed *Roe v. Wade,* the 1973 Supreme Court decision legalizing abortion, as both an affront to the Judeo-Christian reverence for life and an explicit sanction of the sexual revolution. Second, the Bicentennial celebration in 1976 provided a public occasion in which conservatives could appeal for a return to their nation's allegedly Christian heritage. Third, the election of Ronald Reagan in 1980 demonstrated the effectiveness of mobilizing conservative Christians of different denominational traditions in a common political cause.

Several religious figures, skillful in the use of the electronic media, emerged as key spokesmen for Reagan's political revolution. Baptist minister Jerry FALWELL, who founded the political action group known as the MORAL MAJORITY in 1979, was one of the most prominent leaders of the New Religious Right. Pastor of Thomas Road Baptist Church in Lynchburg, Virginia, and televangelist on the "Old-Time Gospel Hour," Falwell entered the American political arena in 1976, staging "I Love America" rallies during the Bicentennial. Falwell envisioned his Moral Majority as a coalition of God-fearing Americans dedicated to undertaking the moral reform of society. Committed to battling "amoral and secular humanists and other liberals . . . destroying the traditional family and moral values" on which their country was built, Moral Majority members opposed abortion, homosexuality, pornography, feminism, and a host of similar "evils."

Evangelist and Republican presidential candidate Pat ROBERTSON heads the flourishing Christian Broadcasting Network in Virginia Beach, Virginia. Believing that Christians could be mobilized for political action, he obtained the signatures of 3 million Americans who promised to provide financial support and prayer for his run for the presidency in 1988. Although his campaign met with only limited success, he established a central place for the Christian Right in the Republican Party.

Robertson also helped found the Christian Coalition in 1989. This organization, which now has 350,000 members and more than 750 chapters nationwide, claims to have won more than 1,000 local elections since its inception. According to Ralph Reed, the Coalition's one-time executive director, the switch to the grass roots was a key decision. "We tried to change Washington when we should have been focusing on the states," he said in 1992. "The real battles of concern to Christians are in the neighborhoods, school boards, city councils, and state legislatures."

Critics of Falwell, Robertson, and Reed have consistently argued that their mixture of religion and politics violates the separation of church and state guaranteed by the Bill of Rights. Opponents of the Christian Right also believe that it attempts to undermine the cultural and religious PLURALISM on which American democracy is based. The conservative movement has been further criticized for being too simplistic in its ethical analyses, positions that are merely ideological and political, while ignoring such genuine social evils as racism and poverty. Finally, sociologists and scholars of American religion suggest that the Christian Right receives more attention than it deserves, representing as it does only a minority of theologically conservative Christians, who are themselves only a minority of the American population.

Conservative leaders succeeded in mobilizing a segment of the electorate that, until recently, had not been engaged in the American political process. Even as late as 1965 Jerry Falwell, when commenting on the CIVIL RIGHTS MOVEMENT, insisted that Christian churches should be concerned only with "the pure saving Gospel of Jesus Christ," and not with any worldly concern, "including fighting Communism." On the other hand, the wholehearted embrace of the Republican Party by the New Religious Right may have harmed rather than helped Republicans in the 1992 elections. Many Americans, even many conservatives, said they were repulsed by the Christian Right's militant support of candidates such as former president George H. W. Bush.

Moreover, despite intense lobbying for the passage of a constitutional amendment banning abortions or for the reinstatement of prayer in public schools, the Christian Right has failed thus far to achieve the major legislative goals it set more than a decade ago. This was well seen in the 2000 presidential election. Although George W. Bush barely defeated Al Gore, his Democratic rival, he minimized the power and influence of the religious right in doing so.

(See also ELECTRONIC CHURCH, THE.)

GHS, Jr.

Bibliography: Walter H. Capps, *The New Religious Right: Piety, Patriotism, and Politics* (Columbia: University of South Carolina Press, 1990); Matthew C. Moen, *The Transformation of the Christian Right* (Tuscaloosa: University of Alabama Press, 1992); Leo P. Ribuffo, *The Old Christian Right: The Protestant Far Right from the Great Depression to the Cold War* (Philadelphia: Temple University Press, 1983).

Christian Science Christian Science was one of the most successful new religious movements of 19th-century America. Incorporated by Mary Baker EDDY (1821–1910) in 1879, the Church of Christ (Scientist) distinguished itself from contemporaneous American religious creations such as THEOSOPHY and Mormonism (see CHURCH OF JESUS CHRIST OF LATTER-DAY SAINTS) by insisting that all healing should be accomplished by spirit and mind without the aid of drugs or doctors. Christian Science has exerted an important influence not only on adherents but also on NEW THOUGHT and the POSITIVE THINKING tradition popularized after WORLD WAR II by Norman Vincent Peale.

Mary Baker Eddy was born Mary Morse Baker in rural New Hampshire in 1821. She suffered from a series of physical and nervous ailments and was an invalid for much of her early life. In 1862 Eddy met Phineas P. QUIMBY (1802–1866), an itinerant mesmerist whose nonpharmaceutical cures relieved Eddy from many of her ailments. Soon Eddy was studying Quimby's theories regarding the mental origins of disease and using terms such as *Christian Science* and *science of health*.

Following Quimby's death in 1866, Eddy slipped on ice and severely injured her back. "On the third day" after this "fall," Eddy reportedly cured herself and "rose again" from her bed. Eddy later described this resurrection experience as the founding moment of Christian Science. From that point forward, she devoted herself to developing and spreading her own version of Quimby's science of health.

Eddy organized the first Christian Science service at her home in Lynn, Massachusetts, in 1875. That same year she published the first edition of her most important book, *Science and Health, with Key to the Scriptures.* Eddy organized the Christian Science Association in 1876 and incorporated the Church of Christ (Scientist) three years later. In 1881 she moved the church's headquarters to Boston, where in 1895 the spectacular "Mother Church" was built.

Led by Eddy (now "Mother" to the faithful), Christian Scientists publicized their theories and practices through a monthly, the *Christian Science Journal* (established in 1883), a weekly, the *Christian Science Sentinel* (1908), and a daily, the *Christian Science Monitor* (1908). Between 1881 and 1899 converts were taught and practitioners were trained at Eddy's Massachusetts Metaphysical College. Under its founder's firm direction, the church grew from a small band who followed a charismatic heal-

er to a large and bureaucratic international institution. By the time of Eddy's death in 1910, the church boasted nearly 100,000 members. Her *Manual of the Mother Church* still functions as the movement's charter.

Any discussion of the theology of Christian Science must begin with Eddy's *Science and Health*, the distinctive scripture of the Church of Christ (Scientist). *Science and Health* is read alongside the Bible at Christian Science services, and in deference to the final and incontestable authority of both texts, no sermon is incorporated into the liturgy.

Eddy described the awakening in her of Christian Science as both a "discovery" and a "revelation," and, in keeping with her view that revelation was both natural and ongoing, she revised her life-work numerous times. Earlier versions of that text include references to HINDUISM, for example, while later versions do not. In all its iterations, however, *Science and Health* represents a decisive turn away from the modified CALVINISM of Eddy's youth. All editions of the book portray a friendly cosmos in which God is All and All is Mind. Only the spiritual world is real. Like matter itself, sickness, sin, pain, and death are illusions that can be manipulated by mental and spiritual means. Thus Eddy urged her followers to shun both drugs and doctors and to rely on faith for their well-being and on Christian Science practitioners for healing.

Eddy moved beyond Quimby, who ignored theology in favor of therapy, to develop a theology for the science of health. But Christian Science still seems to appeal to its members more for its this-worldly benefits than for its otherworldly promises. More than everlasting salvation in a life to come, the church offers its members health, happiness, and prosperity here and now. Many Christian Scientists have apparently achieved at least some of those fruits. Members of the Church of Christ (Scientist) consistently rank very high in the United States in wealth per capita. A disproportionate number of Christian Scientists are, like their founder, women.

Christian Science has been described as a form of religious liberalism, and Eddy's theories do bear important resemblances to the TRANSCENDENTALISM of Ralph Waldo EMERSON and the pragmatism of William JAMES. Like Emerson, Eddy shunned Calvinist verities such as the absolute sovereignty of God and the total depravity of humans in favor of a more optimistic and egalitarian worldview in which humans who are fundamentally good are united to a decidedly nonthreatening God. Eddy joined James in justifying her truths primarily on the pragmatic ground that they worked.

Christian Science has been called a "harmonial religion," but this description ignores Eddy's fundamental disagreements with practitioners of more unabashed forms of harmonialism such as NEW THOUGHT. Eddy proved herself at least a bit more gloomy than her optimistic New Thought contemporaries when she insisted that human beings, at least in their unregenerate state, are not with God but against God. It is through Jesus Christ that Scientists (as members of the movement are called) are able to penetrate the illusions that keep them separate from God and so live a life of freedom from sickness and sin. Eddy further distinguished Christian Science from New Thought by her abiding conviction that the human mind was capable not only of healing through "animal magnetism" but of injuring through "malicious animal magnetism."

Since Eddy's death in 1910, Christian Science has grown into an international organization with hundreds of churches and centers and a publishing empire that includes a highly acclaimed daily newspaper, the *Christian Science Monitor*. Despite these successes, however, Christian Scientists have not managed to work their way fully into the mainstream of American religious life. A number of recent court cases have resulted in manslaughter convictions for parents within the church who have refused to treat their children with medical sci-

ence. Still, Christian Science remains both the religion and the science of choice for roughly 200,000 Americans.

SRP

Bibliography: Gillian Gill, *Mary Baker Eddy* (Reading, Mass.: Perseus, 1998); Stephen Gottschalk, *The Emergence of Christian Science in American Religious Life* (Berkeley: University of California Press, 1973); Donald Meyer, *The Positive Thinkers: Religion as Pop Psychology from Mary Baker Eddy to Oral Roberts* (New York: Pantheon Books, 1980); www.christianscience.org/SAH.html (Science and Health online).

Christmas Conference See METHODISTS.

church and state, relationship between

The relationship between religion and the state in the United States is an issue that has engaged the minds of some the nation's best thinkers, from Thomas JEFFERSON to the late Supreme Court Justice Hugo Black. The governments of the United States and of the states must constantly find a balance between two phrases in the FIRST AMENDMENT to the CONSTITUTION. One forbids the government from making any law respecting the establishment of religion, the other forbids any limits on the free exercise of religion. The need to interpret and apply these phrases to an increasingly complex religious landscape has made the federal judicial system the final arbiter of what is and is not allowable.

During the colonial period an established church was the accepted ideal—in NEW SPAIN and NEW FRANCE, Roman Catholicism, in British America, Protestantism, either the Church of England or its congregational version known as Puritanism. In the short-lived New Sweden and New Netherland, Lutheranism and the Dutch Reformed Church were established as well. These churches were supported by taxes, and membership in them often was required for the exercise of full civil rights—voting, holding public office, serving on juries. The strength and power of these establishments varied

The first prayer in Congress illustrates the complex relation of religion and government in the United States. *(Billy Graham Center Museum)*

according to the will, circumstances, and resources of the colonies and their leaders.

Of all the colonies in British America, none was so scrupulous in maintaining its religious character as Massachusetts (see MASSACHUSETTS BAY COLONY). The Puritans (see PURITANISM) desired religious and social uniformity and used the civil law to enforce religious behavior. While ministers held less real power than they had in most of Europe, they exercised a strong influence over public opinion. The persecution of one of its inhabitants, Roger WILLIAMS, led to the creation of Rhode Island, the first colony to guarantee religious tolerance. The colony of Maryland (see MARYLAND [COLONY]) also allowed some religious leeway, although not as great as that permitted in Rhode Island. Founded as a refuge for English

Catholics, Maryland allowed civil equality for everyone who did not deny the Trinity.

The period of the American Revolution changed this. The need to rally all segments of the population to support the war weakened the religious establishments. The hostility to the established churches by nonconforming groups and the growing influence of Enlightenment ideas strengthened this tendency. This was especially true in Virginia, where a coalition of Deists, BAPTISTS, and PRESBYTERIANS ended the colony's religious establishment with the passage of Thomas Jefferson's "Bill for Establishing Religious Freedom."

This same coalition was instrumental in forcing the adoption of a Bill of Rights to the U.S. Constitution guaranteeing what is known as religious liberty. The Constitution originally applied only to the national government, however, and several states, primarily in New England, retained established churches. While such establishments were often merely nominal, they conferred influence and respectability to a particular church. These states could not stand against the tide, and the churches were slowly disestablished. Massachusetts was the last to yield, giving up its Congregational establishment in 1833.

That the early 19th century saw few judicial decisions on church-state issues does not mean there were no conflicts over religion and political affairs. Indeed, in these years a semi-official religious establishment emerged. This was the heyday of the Protestant empire, when Protestant civilization and democratic values seemed coextensive. By midcentury the growing influx of Catholic immigrants challenged the nation's Protestant predominance, resulting in numerous conflicts. A main source of contention was schools. Catholics objected neither to religious instruction nor Bible reading in the public schools. They did object to Protestant instruction and Protestant Bibles. Opposition to Protestant dominance sparked riots and violence in many states (see ANTI-CATHOLICISM).

Jews also suffered under this quasi establishment. Maryland, North Carolina, and New Hampshire retained colonial laws denying them full civil rights (holding state office, serving on juries) into the 19th century, although the evidence suggests enforcement was lax (see ANTI-SEMITISM).

With the passage of the FOURTEENTH AMENDMENT the number of legal challenges to state laws increased. Swelling immigration weakened the Protestant empire by diluting its numbers. By the 20th century the federal courts were forced to arbitrate debates touching on religion.

There were several reasons for this. The first was the growing willingness of the federal courts to apply the First Amendment guarantees to the states through the use of the Fourteenth Amendment. The second reason was the

dramatic increase of different religious groups in the nation. Attending this were growing conflicts among different religious perspectives. Finally, greater federal involvement in education, medical care, and social programs brought the national government (and tax money) into increasing contact with religious organizations.

The expansion of conflicts over religion in the 20th century has forced the federal courts to decide what is and is not acceptable. During this century the courts and especially the Supreme Court have groped slowly for a method of applying the First Amendment. The Court has declared numerous activities to be unconstitutional violations of the establishment clause. These have included the use of public schools for religious instruction even after school hours (*McCollum v. Board of Education*), government-sponsored prayer in school (*Engel v. Vitale*), and Bible reading in school (*Abington School District v. Schemp, Murray v. Curlett*).

The courts have had to determine when laws undermined the free exercise of religion. Most of these decisions guaranteed protection to religious minorities. Many involved the JEHOVAH'S WITNESSES, and the Court has overturned laws limiting their ability to distribute literature and upheld their right to refuse to salute the flag (*Cantwell v. Connecticut, West Virginia State Board of Education v. Barnette*).

In the last quarter of the 20th century the issue of free exercise took a surprising turn. Many conservative religious organizations that previously opposed attempts to remove religion from the public schools began to argue that their free exercise of religion was violated by the introduction of secular-humanistic religion into the public schools, primarily through the teaching of evolution (see CREATIONISM). While the federal courts have not accepted such arguments, they have been more inclined to allow tangential involvement between governments and religion based on the free-exercise clause. Resulting decisions have allowed the placement of nativity scenes and menorahs in city halls and state capitols.

The end of the 20th and beginning of the 21st century found the conflicts over church and state intense in many ways and confused in others. Concern about the perceived relaxation of the Supreme Court's standard of review in determining whether a law unduly burdened religious liberty issues led Congress to pass the Religious Freedom Restoration Act (RFRA) in 1993. Supported by religious groups from across the political spectrum, it was declared unconstitutional in 1997 as a violation of both separation of powers and federalism.

Additionally, the tendency of politicians of all stripes to look to faith-based service providers to address seemingly intractable social problems led to a relaxation of the limitations under which some thought these agencies suffered when accepting government funds. While the implications of this "Charitable Choice" provision of the welfare reform bill of 1996 remain hidden, the thinking behind it played a major role in the 2000 presidential elections as both major candidates made strong pleas for greater involvement by religious communities in meeting social needs. In fact, one of the first actions of the newly inaugurated George W. Bush was the establishment of the Office of Faith-based Community Organizations.

The perception that the United States was beset by unending social evils—school shootings, drug abuse, single motherhood—led to increased demands for a greater religious presence in schools. Everything from a return to prayer in schools to posting the Ten Commandments in schools and other public places was demanded as a way of fighting this seeming moral decay. The result was greater litigation in local courts, with some of the cases eventually finding their way to the Supreme Court. These cases concerned prayer during graduation ceremonies and the funding of religious newspapers at public universities. The decisions in these cases have not demonstrat-ed a coherent First Amendment jurisprudence at the beginning of the 21st century, making it increasingly difficult to discuss the developments in what already was a confused arena.

There is no conclusion to the issues involving church and state in the United States. Social and political attitudes change, as do the members of the Supreme Court. New situations arise. Because of all these factors the struggle to determine the delicate balance between what constitutes an establishment and what violates the right to free exercise will continue.

EQ

Bibliography: Maureen Harrison and Steve Gilbert, *Freedom of Religion Decisions of the United States Supreme Court* (San Diego: Excellent Books, 1996); Leonard W. Levy, *The Establishment Clause: Religion and the First Amendment* (New York: Macmillan, 1986); William Miller, *The First Liberty: Religion and the American Republic* (New York: Knopf, 1986); Leo Pfeffer, *Church, State, and Freedom*, Rev. ed. (Boston: Beacon Press, 1967); Anson Phelps Stokes, *Church and State in the United States*, Rev. ed. (Westport, Conn.: Greenwood Press, 1975).

Church of England   See ANGLICANISM.

Church of God (Anderson, Indiana)
See HOLINESS MOVEMENT.

Church of God (Cleveland, Tennessee)
The Church of God (Cleveland, Tennessee) is the second-oldest Pentecostal (see PENTECOSTAL-ISM) denomination in the United States. The origins of the church lie in a revival that occurred in east Tennessee in 1886, when eight Baptists joined together and dedicated themselves to the ideal of restoring primitive Christianity. Organized in 1902 as the Holiness Church of Camp Creek (North Carolina), the denomination moved to Cleveland, Tennessee, and adopted its present name in 1907.

The Pentecostal movement emerged out of American Protestantism in the early 20th century. The AZUSA STREET REVIVAL, a period of intense religious excitement at a storefront church in Los Angeles, sparked Pentecostalism's growth after 1906. Part of a diverse movement that eventually inspired millions, Pentecostals were united by one central conviction: the belief that religious conversion must be followed by a second miraculous experience known as the baptism of the Holy Spirit. The ability to speak in tongues, that is, uttering ecstatic languages intelligible only to God (also known as glossolalia), was generally considered evidence that a person had received Spirit baptism.

The Church of God originated in the late 19th century in the mountainous region that covers eastern Tennessee and western North Carolina. The Tennessee Baptists who united in 1886 merged with a similar group of North Carolinians who had spoken in tongues at a revival held near Camp Creek, North Carolina, in 1896. The two groups adopted a formal church government in 1902.

The Camp Creek organization might well have remained in obscurity if it had not been for the leadership of A. J. TOMLINSON, an itinerant preacher and erstwhile Sunday school superintendent. In 1889 Tomlinson had organized a congregation that advocated Holiness doctrines of entire sanctification and Christian PERFECTIONISM. After several years of missionary work spreading these teachings in the Tennessee and North Carolina mountains, Tomlinson encountered and quickly assumed control over the Camp Creek church. He renamed the organization the Church of God to emphasize that it was the only true church, a community in continuity with the church of New Testament times. In 1909 Tomlinson was elected general moderator (later called general overseer) of the new denomination.

The acceptance of faith healing and glossolalia quickly set the Church of God apart from other churches in the area. After learning of the doctrine of divine healing taught by Pentecostal minister Carrie Judd Montgomery, Tomlinson began praying for the healing of the sick in his revival services. His ideas about Christian holiness convinced him that God would not merely help believers overcome sin in the present life, but would bring them physical healing as well. In January 1908 Tomlinson underwent a tremendous spiritual experience that was the Spirit baptism he longed to receive. From that point on, he looked upon the ability to speak in tongues as evidence of divine favor, and glossolalia became a regular feature of worship in the Church of God.

A general assembly of the denomination's ministers met yearly in various locations between 1906 and 1920. In 1920 a new auditorium was built in Cleveland, Tennessee, and while the general assembly has since gathered in a number of places, the church's headquarters have remained in Cleveland. After the creation of the post of general overseer, Tomlinson held the position and also edited the denomination's official journal, *The Church of God Evangel*. However, his refusal to share power with other church officers alienated his colleagues and led to a schism in the church. Accused of financial mismanagement, Tomlinson was deposed from his position in 1923.

Tomlinson took about 2,000 adherents with him to form a new denomination, which he also named "Church of God." Following a lengthy period of litigation, the original denomination retained its name, and Tomlinson's denomination eventually accepted the designation Church of God of Prophecy. Although this church also split when Tomlinson died in 1943, his son Milton retained control over the main body. Tomlinson's Church of God of Prophecy, like the Church of God, maintains its headquarters in Cleveland and now has around 73,000 members.

In 1948 the Church of God formulated an official declaration of faith professing such conservative theological beliefs as the verbal inspiration of the Bible and the premillennial (see PREMILLENNIALISM) return of Jesus Christ. The church also affirmed the distinctive doctrines of Pentecostalism, namely, the availability of divine healing and the belief that the baptism of the Spirit is evidenced by speaking in tongues. The denomination's strength remains in the region of the South where it was first formed, being heavily concentrated in Tennessee and North Carolina. In 2000 the Church of God reported approximately 750,000 members in more than 5,800 congregations.

GHS, Jr.

Bibliography: Mickey Crews, *The Church of God: A Social History* (Knoxville: University of Tennessee Press, 1990).

Church of God in Christ   The Church of God in Christ (COGIC) is the oldest Pentecostal (see PENTECOSTALISM) denomination in the United States today. Founded in Mississippi in 1897 by Baptist ministers C. H. Mason and Charles Price Jones and composed primarily of African Americans, COGIC has grown over the years from a small sect into a substantial denomination. Today it is the largest black Pentecostal body in the world.

The Pentecostal movement, which emerged out of American Protestantism in the early 20th century, has produced more than 300 denominations and several million adherents. One conviction unites all members of this otherwise diverse movement: the belief that religious conversion must be followed by a second transforming experience called the baptism of the Holy Spirit. The ability to speak in tongues, that is, employing ecstatic, incoherent forms of speech intelligible only to God, is considered evidence that a person has been baptized in the Spirit.

The AZUSA STREET REVIVAL in Los Angeles is commonly considered the birthplace of American Pentecostalism. The revival was started in 1906 by William J. SEYMOUR, a black Holiness preacher. Seymour had earlier espoused the doctrine of entire sanctification, the belief that Christians could be set free from the power of sin and attain holiness in the present life. In 1905 he accepted that speaking in tongues was proof of sanctification, and in April 1906 the group he led experienced its first outbreak of glossolalia. When the private home he used became too small for the crowds flocking to his revival, Seymour moved the meetings to an old building at 312 Azusa Street in a rundown section of Los Angeles.

At the height of the revival excitement, worship at the Azusa Street Mission was held three times a day, beginning at midmorning and continuing past midnight. Miraculous healings and a general spiritual delirium marked the event. The revival was also noted for its interracial makeup, a feature some observers saw as a special sign of divine favor. Thousands flocked to Azusa Street. Seymour's ministry, furthermore, helped spark important growth in the Pentecostal movement, because many visitors who participated in the Los Angeles revival took its message back to their local churches.

C. H. Mason, then pastor of a Holiness congregation in Memphis, Tennessee, was among the people who came to the West Coast in that period. Mason, who had undergone a dramatic religious experience in 1880, was licensed as a Baptist preacher in 1893. Two years later, Mason met another Baptist preacher, Charles Price Jones of Jackson, Mississippi. Jones and Mason worked closely together for several years and formed a loose confederation of Holiness congregations that they named the Church of God in Christ. After hearing about worshipers speaking in tongues at the Azusa Street revival, Mason traveled to Los Angeles to witness the event firsthand. In March 1907, he himself experienced the baptism of the Holy Spirit and spoke in tongues. Mason stayed in Los Angeles for five weeks, before returning home to report on what had occurred.

At his church in Memphis, Mason began to hold meetings lasting from 7:30 in the evening until 6:30 the next morning. Soon even the city's white newspapers took notice of this activity as people came to Mason's church to witness to their faith, to be healed of their illnesses, and to speak in tongues. Although Jones disapproved of Mason's Pentecostal practices and eventually parted company from him, most of their nascent denomination remained loyal to Mason. Mason's group kept the name Church of God in Christ and incorporated itself in the fall of 1907. Mason was elected general overseer of the church, a post he held until his death in 1961.

After Mason's death, the issue of authority surfaced and for a time COGIC was divided into three contending factions. Each group claimed to be Mason's genuine successor, and all adopted the same denominational name. Six years of litigation led to the convening of a constitutional convention, which determined that an elected board of bishops would oversee the work of the church. James O. Patterson, Mason's son-in-law, was elected presiding bishop, and despite some defections, most dissident ministers and their congregations returned to the main fold.

The complexity of the denomination's governance sets it apart from the generally loose associations typical of other Pentecostal churches. The denomination also is far more concerned with addressing social problems than are most white Pentecostals. Although its membership statistics may be somewhat inflated, its influence in the African-American community is unquestionably immense. Still headquartered in Memphis, COGIC reported more than 6 million members in more than 15,000 congregations in 2000.

(See also HOLINESS MOVEMENT.)

GHS, Jr.

Bibliography: Arthur E. Paris, *Black Pentecostalism: Southern Religion in an Urban World* (Amherst: University of Massachusetts Press, 1982); James O. Patterson et al., *History and Formative Years of the Church of God in Christ* (Memphis: Church of God in Christ Publishing House, 1969); www.cogic.org (Church of God in Christ)

Church of God of Prophecy   See CHURCH OF GOD (CLEVELAND, TENNESSEE).

Church of Jesus Christ of Latter-day Saints

The Church of Jesus Christ of Latter-Day Saints (LDS) is the largest denomination of the Mormon movement. One of America's most successful and controversial new religious traditions, Mormonism emerged in the 1830s out of Christianity in much the same way that Christianity emerged from Judaism—by claiming to fulfill the promises of the tradition out of which it emerged even as it reformed that tradition's doctrines, practices, and institutions. Mormons accept the Bible ("so far as it is correctly translated") as divinely inspired Scripture, but they have added to the Christian tradition new scriptures (including the BOOK OF MORMON), new doctrines (e.g., the plurality and corporeality of gods and the "eternal progression" of humans toward divinity), and new practices, such as polygamy, marriage for eternity, and baptism for the dead by proxy. Because of these and other innovations, Mormonism is seen by some scholars not as another Christian denomination but as an entirely new religious creation. Mormons, however, typically describe themselves as Christians.

Mormonism first appeared publicly in 1830, the year that Joseph SMITH, Jr., published the Book of Mormon and organized the Church of Jesus Christ in Fayette, New York. This church is now known as the Church of Jesus Christ of Latter-day Saints because of Smith's conviction that the saints of God were living in the last days before the return of Jesus Christ. Smith's new scripture and new church synthesized venerable Jewish and Christian themes with the 19th-century concerns of the BURNED-OVER DISTRICT of western New York state. Like other liberal religious traditions that prospered in that region, Mormonism rejected harsh Calvinist orthodoxies such as predestination and original sin in favor of more modest accounts of divine sovereignty and more generous accounts of human character. It also participated in the populist strain of other Burned-Over District religious movements by downplaying the distinction between clergy and laity.

The Temple in Salt Lake City, Utah, is a mecca for Mormons worldwide. *(Library of Congress)*

The Book of Mormon presents itself as a historical work narrating the New World drama of two ancient Hebraic peoples who sailed to the Americas long before Columbus. Both these groups eventually died out, but one left Native Americans as a remnant. Another claim of the book is that after his death and resurrection Jesus Christ came to America, where he preached, performed miracles, ordained disciples, and established a Christian church. These early Christians eventually turned from God and thus disappeared, but they left behind a secret history of their New World experiences engraved on gold plates by a father named Mormon (hence "Mormonism") and a son, Moroni. Moroni developed over time from a human into an angel and eventually led Smith to this hidden historical treasure.

In their early history the Latter-day Saints moved frequently, largely as a result of anti-Mormon propaganda and persecution. Wherever they settled, Mormons were greeted by debunkers who denounced Mormonism as heresy and the Book of Mormon as fraud. On a number of occasions, this criticism precipitated violence. Smith typically responded to this violence by uprooting his church and moving west. He transplanted his church from New York to Kirtland, Ohio, in 1831, then to locations in Missouri, and, finally, to Nauvoo, Illinois, in 1839.

The Mormons experienced both economic prosperity and demographic growth in Nauvoo, but in the early 1840s Smith announced a series of new beliefs and practices that solidified brewing anti-Mormons sentiment and secured his own martyrdom. The most controversial such practice was "plural marriage," or polygamy. In January of 1844 he announced himself as a candidate for the United States presidency. Later that same year, anti-Mormon sentiment erupted into violence. Smith and his brother Hyrum were arrested and imprisoned in Carthage, Illinois. On June 27, 1844, an anti-Mormon mob sacked the jail and killed Smith and his brother.

After Smith's death a struggle ensued over the leadership and direction of the Mormon movement. This battle resulted in the division of Mormonism into its two main groups: the Church of Jesus Christ of Latter-day Saints (also known as the Utah Mormons), which followed Brigham YOUNG and affirmed controversial practices such as polygamy, and the much smaller REORGANIZED CHURCH OF JESUS CHRIST OF LATTER-DAY SAINTS (the Missouri Mormons), which followed Joseph Smith III and denied polygamy and other Nauvoo innovations as both unbiblical and contrary to the Book of Mormon.

Young's most celebrated act as Smith's successor was his spearheading of a massive Mormon migration, between 1846 and 1848, to the state of "Deseret" in the basin of the Great Salt Lake in present-day Utah. There, under Young's tenure as territorial governor and superintendent of Indian affairs, the Mormons prospered as they once had in Nauvoo under Smith. Initially they emphasized their distinctiveness from the rest of American religion and culture, but after midcentury the Mormons felt more and more pressure to conform. A federal law passed in 1862 made polygamy illegal; in 1879 the U.S. Supreme Court upheld anti-polygamy laws as constitutional; and an 1882 act disfranchised all polygamists. As a result of these actions, a number of Utah Mormons were imprisoned in the early 1880s. Finally, in 1890, LDS president Wilford Woodruff announced a new revelation against plural marriage. This change, accompanied by the abandonment of a nascent Mormon political party, paved the way for Utah statehood in 1896.

In the 20th century, Mormons established themselves both as a distinctive subculture in the United States and as an intensely patriotic people. During the 1960s and 1970s the group drew fire for its refusal to ordain African Americans to the priesthood—a policy reversed by a new revelation in 1978. Today a few Mormons continue to practice polygamy, but most distinguish themselves from other Americans not so much by their esoteric beliefs and controversial practices as by their strict ethics and their continuing support of missions. They typically abstain from tobacco, alcohol, tea, and coffee; they adhere to a strict sexual ethic; and they have played major roles in opposing both the Equal Rights Amendment and abortion rights. Mormons also sustain a massive missionary movement that continues to make converts in the United States and abroad.

The LDS Church is one of the fastest-growing American denominations. At the turn of the third millennium it claimed approximately 5 million members in the United States and 10 million worldwide.

SRP

Bibliography: Claudia L. and Richard L. Bushman, *Mormons in America* (New York: Oxford University Press, 1999); Daniel H. Ludlow, *The Encyclopedia of Mormonism* (New York: Macmillan, 1992); Richard N. Ostling, *Mormon America: The Power and the Promise* (San Francisco: HarperSanFrancisco, 1999); Jan Shipps, *Mormonism: The Story of a New Religious Tradition* (Urbana: Illinois University Press, 1985); www.lds.org (Church of Jesus Christ of Latter-day Saints).

Church of the Brethren (Dunkers)

The Church of the Brethren is an anticreedal, pietist denomination of German origin that stands alongside the Quakers (see FRIENDS, THE RELIGIOUS SOCIETY OF [QUAKERS]) and the MENNONITES as one of America's three major "peace churches."

Like other Anabaptist groups, the Brethren are primitivists (see PRIMITIVISM) who aim to restore at least a remnant of modern Christianity to its ancient purity. They practice a number of rituals attributed to the apostolic church, including foot-washing, the holy kiss, the love feast, and anointing of the sick. They live simply and avoid drugs and alcohol. The Brethren follow other Anabaptist groups in rebaptizing adult converts, but their method of adult baptism is distinctive. Typically they immerse the initiate three times, face first, in running water. Because of this practice of "trine immersion," members of the Church of the Brethren are popularly referred to as Dunkers, from the German *tunken* ("to dip or immerse").

The founder of the Church of the Brethren was Alexander Mack, Sr. (1679–1735), a radical pietist (see PIETISM) who in 1708 in Schwarzenau, Germany, called the first group of Brethren out of the German Reformed tradition in which he (and most of them) had been reared. The eight founding members of the group devoted themselves to Bible study, prayer, and fellowship. In typically pietist fashion, they minimized the importance of Christian doctrine and eschewed creeds. They incorporated ostensibly apostolic rituals such as foot-washing into their Holy Communion services. Like other Anabaptists, they rebaptize adult members and manifest their withdrawal from the world by refusing to take oaths, fight wars, or otherwise participate in government. Initially, they also practiced celibacy and a form of Christian communism, but those practices later fell away.

Largely because of their pacifism and unyielding commitment to the separation of church and state, the Dunkers were persecuted in Europe. The first group of Brethren migrated to America in 1719, seeking religious freedom. A second group came with Mack 10 years later, virtually emptying Europe of Dunkers. Like other German sectarian groups, these members of the Church of the Brethren settled in Germantown, Pennsylvania, where they enjoyed a climate of greater tolerance and established the first New World congregation.

One of the most famous of the German-born Dunkers was Christopher Sauer (1693–1758), who came to America in 1724. Like Mack, Sauer was educated at the University of Halle. He worked as a medical doctor in Germantown and a farmer in Lancaster County, Pennsylvania, before turning to printing, the profession that would bring him fame. He began publishing the *Hoch-Deutsch Pensylvanische Geschichts-Schreiber* for the benefit of German-speaking Americans in 1739. In 1743 he produced a German edition of Luther's Bible, the first western-language version of the Christian Scriptures printed in the Americas.

The Dunkers, who like the Mennonites eventually left urban areas for rural lives devoted to agriculture, existed in North America for nearly 200 years before they came to be known officially as the Church of the Brethren. Like other pietistic sects of German origin, they have suffered multiple schisms. Between 1881 and 1883 both a progressive and an ultraconservative faction split off from the main body of Brethren. The progressive group, whose members sought to downplay their German roots by accommodating themselves to American culture, formed the Brethren Church (Progressive Dunkers). The ultraconservative schismatics established the Old German Baptist Brethren (Old Order Dunkers), which objected to practices, including the payment of salaries to ministers and the establishment of church-based schools and missionary societies, that in their view contravened apostolic models.

Another important offshoot of the Church of the Brethren was the EPHRATA COMMUNITY, a monastic group established in 1732 at Ephrata, Pennsylvania, by Conrad Beissel (1691–1768), a German-born pietist inclined toward solitude and asceticism. Because of their observation of the Sabbath on Saturday rather than Sunday, Beissel's followers came to be called the German Seventh-day Baptists.

The Church of the Brethren has endured its schisms by maintaining a middling position between its progressive and ultraconservative offspring. A member of both the NATIONAL COUNCIL OF CHURCHES and the WORLD COUNCIL OF CHURCHES, it has roughly 200,000 congregants in the United States. Like other peace churches, the Church of the Brethren maintains voluntary associations devoted to assisting its conscientious objectors. Other voluntary associations, such as Brethren Volunteer Service, provide humanitarian relief to the needy both at home and abroad.

SRP

Bibliography: Donald F. Durnbaugh, ed., *The Brethren Encyclopedia*, 3 vols. (Philadelphia: Brethren Encyclopedia, Inc., 1983–84); Donald F. Durnbaugh, *Fruit of the Vine: A History of the Brethren, 1708–1995* (Elgin, Ill.: Brethren Press, 1997).

Church of the Nazarene   The Church of the Nazarene is the largest American denomination to emerge out of the HOLINESS MOVEMENT of the 19th century. It was founded in 1908 through the union of several religious bodies, including Phineas F. Bresee's Church of the Nazarene in southern California and the eastern-based Association of Pentecostal Churches. The denomination emphasizes the doctrine of entire sanctification as a "second blessing" that comes to believers after conversion. Nazarenes believe that, by the action of divine grace, Christians can be freed from inbred sin, brought into a state of full devotion to God, and enabled to adopt a lifestyle reflecting "holiness of heart."

Phineas Bresee had been a Methodist clergyman and pastor of the First Methodist Church in Los Angeles. He first encountered the Holiness movement during his ministry at that church. Some members of the congregation requested Bresee to call evangelists from the National Holiness Association, an organization founded in 1867 to help lead Methodists back to John Wesley's teachings on Christian perfection (see PERFECTIONISM). Bresee soon underwent an experience of sanctification and began conducting revivals with the aid of Holiness preachers. Conflict with his bishop over these activities, however, eventually forced Bresee to withdraw from the Methodist ministry in 1895.

Holiness leaders like Bresee believed in the importance of opposing the worldliness they saw spreading within American Methodism. Attempting to revive the simplicity of the early Wesleyan movement, they organized churches that welcomed, rather than rejected, the poor. With such goals in mind, Bresee founded a congregation known as the Church of the Nazarene in Los Angeles in 1895. Similar in some ways to the SOCIAL GOSPEL then being preached in mainline Protestant denominations, Bresee's ministry offered both spiritual and material care to modern city-dwellers. The Church of the Nazarene proved to be hugely successful, and the organization quickly grew.

The eastern branch of the future Church of the Nazarene began when several independent congregations merged into the Association of Pentecostal Churches in 1896. Many of these churches were led by clergy who had left the Methodist Episcopal Church because of opposition to their teachings on sanctification and Christian perfection. Representatives of the association met with Bresee, and in 1907 the two groups united at Chicago to form the Pentecostal Church of the Nazarene. The following year, this church also accepted the Holiness Church of Christ, a southern group, into its membership at a meeting in Pilot Point, Texas. By 1915, the new church numbered nearly 35,000 members. The title "Pentecostal" was dropped in 1919 in order to avoid confusion with groups that spoke in tongues, a practice the Nazarenes did not embrace.

Since the Church of the Nazarene emerged out of American Methodism, its beliefs reflect many features of the WESLEYAN TRADITION. Like Methodist founder John Wesley, Nazarenes teach that their faith necessarily has a social component. True to Wesley's perfectionist moral ideals, they pledge themselves to assisting the poor, hungry, and sick, while refraining from the use of alcohol, tobacco, or drugs. Their Articles of Faith (contained in the denomination's *Manual*) also condemn the "indulging of pride" in either behavior or dress. Finally, Nazarenes are committed to missionary work both in American cities and in more than 80 locations outside the United States.

Headquartered in Kansas City, Missouri, the Church of the Nazarene reported in 2000 an American membership of approximately 600,000 people in nearly 5,200 congregations.

GHS, Jr.

Bibliography: Timothy L. Smith and W. T. Purkiser, *Called Unto Holiness; The Story of the Nazarenes,* 2 vols. (Kansas City: Nazarene Publishing House, 1962–1983); www.nazarene.org (Church of the Nazarene).

Church of the United Brethren in Christ

See UNITED METHODIST CHURCH.

Churches of Christ

The Churches of Christ (Noninstrumental) and the Christian Churches and Churches of Christ (Independent) are associations of churches that represent the most conservative wing of the RESTORATION MOVEMENT. In 1831 the major American restorationist strands, under the leadership of Barton STONE and Alexander CAMPBELL, together formed a single denominational body called the Disciples of Christ (see CHRISTIAN CHURCH [DISCIPLES OF CHRIST]). In the early 20th century, this coalition broke apart as two large groups of theologically conservative congregations left separately and organized their own quasi-denominational organizations.

Thomas Campbell, one of the early leaders of the restoration movement, coined the phrase that best describes the restorationists' original intent: "Where the Scriptures speak, we speak;

where the Scriptures are silent, we are silent." Alexander Campbell, Thomas's son, believed that the Bible contained a clear description of those aspects of the early church that ought to be reconstructed. He thought Christians should reject the empty theological divisions that separated them and reunite to restore the purity of the apostolic age. Barton Stone was committed to similar goals, though he was less interested in structures than in simple holiness. Stone's followers tended to reject "worldly" concerns and were generally antimodern in their intellectual outlook. While these dissimilarities were overlooked when Stone and Campbell brought their groups together in the 1830s, they presaged a later conflict.

A critical figure in the breakup of the restoration movement was Tennessee preacher David LIPSCOMB. Lipscomb stressed three important teachings. First, he thought loyalty to the plain teachings of Scripture required that believers take no active role in politics or in other earthly affairs. He looked forward to the return of Christ, when all human governments would be destroyed and the thousand-year reign of Christ would be inaugurated. Second, Lipscomb attacked the use of instrumental music. (Hence, the term *noninstrumental* as a title for the churches that followed his leadership). He considered church organs as worldly contrivances with no warrant either in the Bible or in the worship of the early church. Third, Lipscomb opposed missionary societies and other ecclesiastical agencies. He feared they only routinized the sacred and detracted from genuine Christian spirituality.

The popularity of Lipscomb's positions in the late 19th century symbolized that a clear division had taken place within his denomination. In 1906, after prodding by Lipscomb, the United States Census Bureau officially recognized the existence of two separate organizations: Lipscomb's militantly antimodern Churches of Christ (Noninstrumental) and the more mainstream Disciples of Christ. The census of 1906 also revealed marked sectional dif-

ferences between the two groups. Of the Churches of Christ's 159,000 members, 100,000 lived in states that had seceded from the Union in 1860 and 1861. Even today, four-fifths of the membership of the Churches of Christ live within 200 miles of a line drawn from Chattanooga, Tennessee, to El Paso, Texas.

Other social divisions also split restorationist groups in the 20th century. The census of 1936, for instance, showed that, while the majority of the members of the northern-dominated Disciples of Christ lived in urban areas, more than half of the Churches of Christ's members were affiliated with rural churches. Lipscomb had earlier articulated what that distinction meant for him: His conservatives wanted people to come to Christ, but "the society folks" (i.e., the Disciples) only desired "fine houses, fashionable music, and eloquent speeches."

The Churches of Christ grew rapidly during the early 20th century, thanks largely to their evangelistic fervor. They spread their message with virtually no denominational organization or financial support for their preachers. Religious periodicals proved to be a unifying force in the movement, especially Lipscomb's *Gospel Advocate.* The Churches of Christ also founded a number of colleges that acted as centers of influence: David Lipscomb College in Nashville; Harding College in Searcy, Alabama; Abilene Christian University in Abilene, Texas; and Pepperdine University in Los Angeles.

The focus on biblical authority, the impulse that initially persuaded the Churches of Christ to separate themselves from the Disciples of Christ, however, tended to encourage further sundering of the conservative movement. In the 1930s, for example, Louisville preacher Robert H. Boll took a strong premillennialist (see PREMILLENNIALISM) stand. When the majority of the church rejected his position, approximately 100 congregations became alienated from the Churches of Christ. Recent disputes have concerned such matters as marriage and divorce, the covering of women's heads in worship, and the number of cups used in Communion services. The search for the purity of the early church, therefore, has often led members of the Churches of Christ into bitter controversy with one another.

The Christian Churches and Churches of Christ (Independent) are a second group of conservative congregations that drifted away from the Disciples of Christ early in the 20th century. During the heyday of the battle between fundamentalists (see FUNDAMENTALISM) and theological liberals in American Protestantism, conservatives within the Disciples accused their leadership of undercutting the traditional authority of the Bible. When the traditionalists did not think their concerns had been given a fair hearing, they formed their own denominational body, the North American Christian Convention, in 1927. Although the boundary line between the Disciples and the new association of independent Christian Churches was not originally clear, the publication of a directory of conservative congregations in 1955 helped denote where the division had occurred. And when the Disciples restructured themselves in 1968 and created a regional and national structure akin to the organization of other mainline denominations, an estimated 2,000 conservative congregations officially withdrew their names from the Disciples *Year Book*.

The Christian Churches and Churches of Christ (Independent) have much in common with American EVANGELICALISM. They believe that the Bible is divinely inspired, and they are opposed to most forms of theological and social liberalism. They have been distinguished as well by their belief in the necessity of baptism by immersion as a condition for church membership. These churches are divided, however, over the question of whether the forgiveness of sins occurs before or during the act of baptism.

The Churches of Christ (Noninstrumental) is the largest of the three denominational bodies that presently compose the American restoration movement. It reported more than 14,400 congregations and nearly 1.8 million members in 1990. The Christian Churches and Churches of Christ (Independent), which is approximately equal in size to the Christian Church (Disciples of Christ), now contains more than 14,000 congregations and about 1.1 million members.

GHS, Jr.

Bibliography: David Edwin Harrell, *The Social Sources of Division in the Disciples of Christ, 1865–1900* (Atlanta: Publishing Systems, 1973); Richard T. Hughes, "The Apocalyptic Origins of Churches of Christ and the Triumph of Modernism," *Religion and American Culture* 2 (1992), 181–214; http://church-of-christ.org (Churches of Christ).

civil religion   The phrase "civil religion," used by the French philosopher Jean-Jacques Rousseau in *The Social Contract* (1762), has come to refer to the processes by which most modern states attempt to gain legitimacy and support from their populations. American civil religion draws upon biblical religion as well as the traditions of Greek and Roman political life. Often expressed most clearly during times of crisis or war, American civil religion seems to ebb and flow in its ability to contribute to social cohesiveness.

The phrase *civil religion* has been subjected to considerable debate since sociologist Robert N. Bellah first brought it into academic and public discourse in 1967. Bellah claimed that Americans had developed "alongside of and rather clearly differentiated from the churches an elaborate and well-institutionalized civil religion." Bellah was particularly concerned to show that while this form of religion often served to legitimatize the state's conduct, it also provided a means whereby the state could be held subject to a higher law. Historians and sociologists have argued over how constant and how "well institutionalized" such a religion might be; theologians have debated its value. Other terms, such as *public religion, religious nationalism,* or *patriotic faith* are preferred by some scholars. And one may well question the extent to which civil religion maintains a distinctive institutional form. Bellah himself eventually abandoned the term. Nevertheless, the concept points to some extremely important features of religious life in modern societies.

The historical roots of American civil religion are twofold. One thread comes from the Hebraic tradition of the Bible, brought to American shores by Puritans in the early 17th century (see PURITANISM). Puritans often spoke of themselves as "a chosen people," selected by the biblical God to accomplish a great work—the creation of a righteous society, a "city on a hill" as John WINTHROP put it, which would serve as a moral beacon for the rest of the world. Puritans read their own experience of migration and settlement in a land already populated by indigenous people as a repetition of the biblical story of the Exodus. Thus, they were the "new Israel," led out into the American wilderness, a proving ground that they often viewed as the haunt of Satan and his children, the Algonquin tribes. And like the Jews of old, many Puritans were aware that their position as God's chosen people required of them a willingness to suffer for their righteous goals. Such suffering for the faith came in the form of external threats from papist European states or neighboring tribes, and from the internal threats of their own sinfulness.

The second thread in the development of American civil religion emerged out of the revolutionary era (see AMERICAN REVOLUTION), and it, too, consisted of an effort by self-conscious Americans to understand their own experience of creating a new society by seeking parallels with that of another ancient tradition: Greco-Roman republican politics. American revolutionaries certainly drew upon their Puritan heritage in their struggle with Britain, often viewing the conflict itself as the millennial battle between Christ and Satan foretold in the Bible. But, as did many during the ENLIGHTENMENT, American leaders and educated citizens discovered enormous intellectual resources in

the Greco-Roman heritage. In particular, in striving to create a new form of government, they found instructive and inspirational parallels between their own attempt to unify a number of ethnic and religious groups under one political structure and that of the Roman Empire. As a consequence, one finds significant borrowings from ancient Rome in many aspects of American culture, ranging from the political ideal of liberty to the production of political rituals such as those for the inauguration of George Washington in 1789 (often referred to by his contemporaries as the "American Cincinnatus," after the famous Roman citizen/general) or the processions accompanying the heroic Marquis de Lafayette in 1824 and 1825. The Roman thread is perhaps most visible in such shared features of American life as the architectural designs common to public buildings, in which post offices and court houses often look like Greek or Roman temples, or in the engraving styles found on American currency. The dollar bill, with its Latin phrases *e pluribus unum* ("one out of many") and *novus ordo seclorum* ("new order of the ages"), has become an icon of the Roman influence on the formation of American civil religion.

Over the years the civil religion emerging out of the country's birth struggles has changed. Certain elements have come to provide a core. Americans follow a ritual calendar of holidays, ranging from overtly political celebrations such as July 4th and Labor Day to the more family-centered holidays of Christmas and Thanksgiving. A set of sacred scriptures has emerged, including the Constitution (1789), the Declaration of Independence (1776), speeches by leaders such as Washington, Abraham LINCOLN, Franklin Delano Roosevelt, and John F. Kennedy, and perhaps even a few Supreme Court decisions, such as *Brown v. Board of Education* (1954). But these "core elements" just as easily suggest that if there is a civil religion in the United States, it remains far distant from the realities of most citizens' lives.

A more fruitful way of discerning the patterns of civil religion might be found by focusing on the functions or problems for which Americans have drawn on religious expressions in their public life. Two particular problems, first faced by citizens of the early republic, have continued to shape the development of American civil religion and account for its episodic appearance. The first is the problem of *national integration*, the creation of common sentiment capable of binding together a population of diverse ethnic, geographic, and religious backgrounds and interests. Elites have thought such sentiment was needed to assure the priority of national loyalty over more immediate, deeply felt regional, ethnic, or religious ties. This dimension of American civil religion often remains weak, especially in the ordinary ebb and flow of political life. Symbols such as Uncle Sam, the American eagle, the Great Seal, or the commemorative holidays of Memorial Day or July 4, lose their power and focus over time, or only resonate within certain segments of the population. In addition, the basic task of insuring the priority of national over more immediate loyalties has been steadily resisted by many Americans, who often seek to downplay the symbolic presence of the federal government in their daily lives.

But if Americans have resisted the nationalization of sentiment in ordinary times, they have been much more willing to respond positively under circumstances of danger or threat, a function that we could label *national mobilization*. American civil religion has been far more successful when developed in response to extraordinary times. On occasion, social crises (the Great Depression), natural disasters (the Chicago Fire), or even technological breakdowns (the Challenger explosion in 1986) have triggered the development and expression of civil religion. In the face of such crises Americans have urged each other to put aside their differences and unite to stave off threat or loss. But it is especially the potential or necessity of war that has most consistently shaped the mobilizing tenor of civil religion.

Having seen in both European and Native American military power a kind of demonic attack on their divinely inspired goals, Americans in the colonial, revolutionary, and early republican eras found the most compelling rationale for national unity arising out of their perceptions of violent threats to their common life. Thus Thomas JEFFERSON in the Declaration of Independence (1776) spoke of those who possessed the natural (divinely given) rights of "life, liberty and the pursuit of happiness" as also having the duty to take up arms against those forces who would try to deprive a people of those rights. Jefferson's language of duty has given rise to a longstanding tradition in which those who possess liberty are required to be ever-vigilant and ready for personal sacrifice in liberty's defense.

Throughout American history the occasion of war has served to link Jefferson's themes of liberty and sacrifice (see CIVIL WAR, WORLD WAR I, WORLD WAR II). During the period of western expansion (see MANIFEST DESTINY), Americans viewed their losses of life and property stemming from wars with numerous Native American tribes as sacrifices. General George Armstrong Custer, defeated by Lakota, Cheyenne, and Arapahoe warriors at the Little Big Horn in 1876, became a national martyr, dying a Christlike death for the advancement of civilization. Abraham Lincoln in his Gettysburg Address (1863) spoke forcefully about the blood spilled by American soldiers as providing the means of "a new birth of freedom" for the nation.

If civil religion has grown strongest during times of war, it also showed its limits during the VIETNAM WAR, a time of widespread national self-examination. In subsequent years civil religion has not faded away, as some predicted. Increased ideological conflict with the Soviet Union during the 1980s, undergirded by a continued threat of nuclear war, was interpreted by both supporters and opponents of

American policy in terms consistent with the tradition of civil religion. In a 1983 address, President Ronald Reagan spoke of the Soviet Union as "evil incarnate in the modern world." Large numbers of church members active in the widespread anti–nuclear weapons movement at the time saw American military expansion and increased support of counterinsurgency efforts by Third World governments (see LIBERATION THEOLOGY) as violating America's fundamental identity as a country based on the ideals of liberty.

Americans have most frequently used civil religion to help sustain a sense of their own uniqueness in relation to an outside power. The collapse of the Soviet Union brought not an end of the tradition but another shift in its form. In initiating the Persian Gulf War in 1991, President George H. W. Bush demonized Iraqi leader Saddam Hussein as part Satan and part Hitler. He also elicited sympathy for the Kuwaitis, whose land had been occupied by Iraqi forces, as people yearning for liberty. Finally, President Clinton led a troubled North Atlantic Treaty Organization (NATO) coalition in an air war against Serbian president Slobodan Milosevic in 1999, maintaining solidarity in that campaign by claiming that NATO was waging war in defense of human rights. Both presidents drew from the Declaration of Independence in justifying their actions and characterizing their opponents. As post-Vietnam policy makers, however, both Bush and Clinton were keenly aware that Americans had become suspicious of sacrifice of the nation's young people, even for some combination of God and country.

MG

Bibliography: Robert N. Bellah, *Beyond Belief: Essays on Religion in a Post-Traditional World* (New York: Harper and Row, 1970); Edward Tabor Linenthal, *Sacred Ground: Americans and Their Battlefields* (Urbana: University of Illinois Press, 1991); John F. Wilson, *Public Religion in American Culture* (Philadelphia: Temple University Press, 1979); Wilbur Zelinsky, *Nation Into State: The Shifting Symbolic Foundations of American Nationalism* (Chapel Hill: University of North Carolina Press, 1988).

civil rights movement   The civil rights movement, the struggle for the universal application of legal and social rights in the United States, was a milestone in American religious, social, and political history. The term has two meanings, one narrow and one wide. The narrow meaning—which many intend when they refer to "the Movement"—defines the struggle for black political equality that leapt into public view in the 1950s and continued through the late 1960s.

The wider meaning includes all the struggles and attempts to ensure that political rights are applied equally to all Americans regardless of religion, background, color, sex, heritage, and other extraneous factors. In this sense the civil rights movement never ended. Its roots permeate human history in all the places where individuals suggested that equality before the law was a natural right.

The roots of the movement for black civil rights are long and deep. It is not unreasonable to suggest that the roots began when the first African resisted the process of enslavement by revolting, running away, or committing suicide rather than submitting to captivity. Similar forms of resistance marked the entire slave period. From work slowdowns to poisonings, from feigning illness to staging rebellions, slaves resisted enslavement and worked to affirm their human dignity and independence.

Such actions were not confined to the slaves alone. Freed blacks also resisted the social and legal constraints under which they labored. Racism in the churches led many into separate black churches and even denominations (see AFRICAN-AMERICAN RELIGION, AFRICAN METHODIST EPISCOPAL CHURCH, AFRICAN METHODIST EPISCOPAL ZION CHURCH). Discrimination in social services and fraternal organizations led blacks to create their own institutions, which voiced black dissatisfaction with second-class status. In many of these organizations, religious leaders took the lead.

Not all institutions working to overcome the limitations under which blacks were forced to live were black institutions. Some, like the Quakers (see FRIENDS, RELIGIOUS SOCIETY OF), were composed of a majority of white members. While these predominantly white institutions might oppose slavery, organize schools for blacks, and even accept that blacks and whites were equal before God, they could do little to overcome the increasingly entrenched mores and laws that relegated blacks to the status of second-class beings.

ABOLITIONISM, the struggle to end slavery, would become the most institutionalized of the early attempts to recognize the dignity and equality of blacks. The abolitionist movement was a precursor of the civil rights movement in form, in its level of integration, and also in its internal conflicts and disagreements. Bursting on the scene with the first issue of William Lloyd Garrison's *The Liberator*, the abolitionist movement had been long in coming. Preceded by the so-called Negro conventions organized by Bishop Richard ALLEN of the A.M.E. Church and black opposition to the American Colonization Society, formed to convince slaveholders to free their slaves and then return them to Africa, abolitionism brought blacks and whites into an integrated sociopolitical movement for the first time.

For many this crusade was driven by a perfectionist religiosity emerging from the SECOND GREAT AWAKENING, and took the form of a moral suasion, nonaccommodation to evil, and nonviolence. This was the route of Garrison, Theodore Dwight WELD, Angelina and Sarah GRIMKÉ, and, for a while, the black abolitionists Frederick Douglass and Charles Lenox Remond. Some abolitionists favored the political approach. Still others, eventually including Douglas and Remond, favored ballots if possible and bullets if necessary.

Speeches, testimonies by fugitive slaves, escapes along the Underground Railroad, and aborted rebellions all attested to the struggle against slavery and to the refusal of African Americans to accept second-class citizenship. As the black abolitionist Samuel Cornish declared, "[B]rethren! You are COLORED AMERICANS. The Indians are RED AMERICANS, and the white people are WHITE AMERICANS, and *you are as good as they, and they are no better than you.*"

As abolitionist efforts waxed and waned, the country divided and moved closer to the conflict that would define the nation for nearly a century. If the Civil War decided the question of slavery, the period of Reconstruction attempted to settle the question of black political equality. The so-called Reconstruction amendments (see FOURTEENTH AMENDMENT) abolished slavery, defined citizenship, and forbade limitations on voting imposed solely because of color. But as Reconstruction faded due to political compromise, the promise of equality was replaced with the reality of white political and social domination known as Jim Crow (see SEGREGATION). This was enshrined in law by the Supreme Court's decision in *Plessy v. Ferguson*, which established the legal acceptability of separate but allegedly equal facilities for blacks and whites. In reality it established an entire system of white domination and black subjection, white power and black degradation, a white world and a black one. It was this world that the civil rights movement challenged and changed.

The struggle for black civil rights in the 20th century is an incomplete struggle in two parts. The first part encompasses the work of men like W. E. B. DU BOIS, A. Philip Randolph, and Roy Wilkins, and organizations like the National Association for the Advancement of Colored People (NAACP), Congress on Racial Equality, and the Fellowship of Reconciliation. The second part was the work of men like Martin Luther KING, Jr., Bob Moses, Ralph ABERNATHY, and new organizations such as the SOUTHERN CHRISTIAN LEADERSHIP CONFERENCE (SCLC) and STUDENT NONVIOLENT COORDINATING COMMITTEE.

The first half of the 20th century saw increasing institutionalization of segregation. Laws were written to meet new conditions as well as older situations that had not been covered. This included enforced segregation in airport waiting rooms, for example, as well as laws such as the one passed by the Birmingham, Alabama, city council forbidding whites and blacks to play checkers together or in the presence of each other.

Simultaneously, the institutionalized political and social inequality of blacks was under growing attack. At the turn of the 20th century the leadership of black America was firmly in the hands of Booker T. WASHINGTON, an accomodationist who was the most powerful black leader America had ever seen. Republican administrations made no appointments of blacks, and few if any of whites in the South, without his approval. But Washington was challenged by newer and younger black leaders who rejected Washington's accomodationism. These men organized the NAACP in 1909 and used its journal, *The Crisis,* as their voice. Edited by W. E. B. Du Bois, *The Crisis* articulated the need for a concerted attack on legal segregation and the training of a black elite (the "talented 10th") who could lead the black masses to social equality.

Under the direction of Walter White, who served the organization from 1918 until 1955, and who was so light-skinned that he traveled through the South by passing as a white man, the NAACP documented the number and gruesomeness of lynchings. Blacks' increasing political strength was illustrated by the ability of the African-American community to prevent Senate approval of Judge William Parker to the Supreme Court due to his support for laws that restricted black suffrage. Under White and his successor, Roy Wilkins, the NAACP became the organizational center for black opposition to segregation. The NAACP remained, however, an elite organization centering its work on legal and political remedies.

More in touch with working-class blacks was A. Philip Randolph, longtime president of the Brotherhood of Sleeping Car Porters. Randolp had a long and distinguished career. He fought with W. E. B. Du Bois over the latter's suggestion that blacks should fight in World War I and with John Lewis, chairman of SNCC, over his speech at the 1963 March on Washington. Randolph was a working man, and his concerns always extended beyond race to include issues of economic justice. Not only Randolph but leaders within the Pullman Porters Union like E. D. Nixon in Montgomery, Alabama, would provide much of the local work for civil rights prior to the 1950s.

The 1940s and 1950s saw growing successes by both of these organizations in the area of civil rights. Franklin D. Roosevelt showed a greater interest in black concerns than any president since Theodore Roosevelt and had his own black "kitchen cabinet." His wife, Eleanor, had an even more active concern with civil rights issues, serving on the executive committee of the NAACP.

Black activists themselves also achieved marked success in this period. Randolph's threat to march against Washington in 1943 forced Roosevelt to issue an executive order integrating all war industries. During this time as well the NAACP's legal challenges were beginning to bear fruit, as its lawyers won a series of cases striking down "whites-only" primaries and segregation in higher education. This work culminated in 1954 with the Supreme Court decision in *Brown v. Board of Education of Topeka, Kansas,* declaring public school segregation illegal.

To have the courts overturn legal segregation was not the same as ending it in fact. During the next two decades the civil rights movement tried to achieve in practice what law and the courts had said were their rights. This struggle would be long, savage, and bloody. Also, more than any period since the abolitionist movement, it would be rooted in religion.

During this time the drive for civil rights became a mass movement, due primarily to the work of Martin Luther King, Jr. When he and others formed the Montgomery Improvement Association in 1955 to end unfair treatment on city buses, the movement was born. Preaching a message of justice and nonviolence, King and his colleagues, working through the SCLC, slowly began to peel away the layers of racism and economic exploitation under which African Americans labored. The struggle was difficult, but included dramatic successes in places like Birmingham and Selma, Alabama, where the viciousness of the attacks upon peaceful demonstrators galvanized public opinion, ultimately helping to end legalized segregation and paving the way for the Voting Rights Act of 1965.

The SCLC was a churchly organization, drawing its strength from the power of the African-American religious tradition. Rooted in the call for justice announced by the prophets in the Hebrew Bible, symbolized in the Exodus story of Moses leading the Israelites from slavery in Egypt to freedom in Canaan, and organized around Jesus' Sermon on the Mount, the SCLC spoke eloquently to the African-American situation and powerfully of their claims for justice.

King, Ralph Abernathy, and the SCLC taught that only through nonviolence could blacks win their rights. For them nonviolence was more than a tactic, it was the strategic use of divine love and power. For King and his colleagues nonviolence embodied the Gospel by effecting both CONVERSION and forgiveness. While this message dominated the movement during the early 1960s, others began to question both nonviolence and white involvement.

Some of this opposition came from expected critics, primarily MALCOLM X. Other critics of nonviolence included Roy Wilkins of the NAACP, who urged that blacks should be willing to shoot back in self-defense. More surprising was the change in the attitude of SNCC. Organized as a younger, more active, and less clergy-driven counterpart to the SCLC, SNCC achieved its greatest visibility in 1964 with the creation of the Mississippi Freedom Summer and the formation of the Mississippi Freedom Democratic Party, which tried to unseat the regular (all-white) Democratic party at the 1964 presidential convention. Freedom Summer brought students (primarily white northerners) into Mississippi to teach black children, participate in organizing, and fight segregation. One of the most shocking results of this endeavor was the brutal murder of James Chaney, Andrew Goodman, and Michael Schwerner in May 1964. This killing, accomplished with the participation of the local police, went far to radicalize SNCC.

King's assassination on April 4, 1968, with the resulting riots and violence, also weakened the appeal of nonviolence. There were increasing calls for aggressive response to racism and injustice. These voices included the Black Panthers advocating armed rebellion on one hand and the Conference of Black Churchmen demanding reparations on the other. As nonviolence gave way to Black Power, "We shall overcome" became "Burn, baby, burn." The refusal of entrenched white power structures to change and the violence with which they defended their bastions led to an increasing militancy among blacks. This militancy led to numerous violent confrontations with police and increasing violence in America's cities.

Richard Nixon's election as president in November 1968 did little to ease the calls for increasing militancy. The Republican administration's apparent lack of concern for African Americans, the Vietnam War, and increasing social conflict diverted attention from civil rights. Although this revived somewhat during the presidency of Jimmy Carter, President Ronald Reagan's administration was particularly hostile to advances on the civil rights front.

Equally significant was the fact that after the ending of legal segregation and the guaranteeing of voting rights, the more complex and tedious issues of economic justice were not amenable to traditional mass protests and legal challenges. Declining economic fortunes also led increasingly to situations where economic justice for blacks was seen as an economic threat by poorer whites, thus exacerbating racial tensions and animosities.

By the 1980s and 1990s, questions surrounding race in the United States seemingly had become more complex and less amenable to straightforward legal solutions. The scourge of drug abuse and the rise of what seemed to be a permanent underclass composed primarily of people of color made many individuals question traditional approaches to racial issues. Opinion polls showed that blacks and whites in the United States had widely divergent views on the continuing power of racism and its affects on individuals' daily lives. Some commentators even claimed that the civil rights leadership intentionally favored policies designed to keep blacks subservient to the government in order to further their own ends. While such opinions remained minority views, their emergence suggested the apparent intractability that certain aspects of race had taken on. Additionally, questions surrounding police brutality and racial disparity in the application of the death penalty continued to show the lingering vestiges of racial inequity in American society.

The period of the civil rights movement remains a symbol of America's struggle to realize its most deeply held values. It had a particular appeal because of its religious thrust, its nonviolence, and its martyred leader. The religious dimension of King's vision and that of his colleagues stirred chords in the hearts of many Americans and helped to bring an end to racial divisions enforced by law.

EQ

Bibliography: Taylor Branch, *Parting the Waters: America in the King Years, 1954–1963* (New York: Simon & Schuster, 1988); W. E. B. DuBois, *The Souls of Black Folk* (New York: New American Library, 1961); John Hope Franklin, *From Slavery to Freedom: A History of African-Americans* (New York: McGraw-Hill, 1994); Vincent Harding, *Hope and History: Why We Must Share the Story of the Movement* (Maryknoll, N.Y.: Orbis, 1990); C. Eric Lincoln, *The Black Experience in Religion* (Garden City, N.Y.: Anchor Press, 1974); Walter Dean Myers, *Now is Your Time: The African-American Struggle for Freedom* (New York: HarperCollins, 1991); Peter Paris, *The Social Teaching of the Black Churches* (Philadelphia: Fortress Press, 1985); Clarence Taylor and Jonathan Birnbaum, eds., *Civil Rights Since 1787: A Reader* (New York: New York University Press, 2000).

Civil War, the (1861–1865)   The Civil War, the bitter four-year struggle between the North and the SOUTH, proved as traumatic for American religion as it was for the nation as a whole. The Civil War era was profoundly shaped not only by competing political ideologies, but also by religious ideas expressed within the churches of both the Union and the Confederacy.

Several decades before the bloodshed began, debates over SLAVERY had caused the country's three largest denominations to divide on regional lines. The Presbyterians were the first to split apart, when in 1837 the southern-oriented "Old School" faction expelled the northern-oriented "New School" from its fellowship. Next, the northern section of the Methodist Episcopal Church adopted an antislavery position so offensive to southern whites that a new Methodist denomination was formed in the South in 1845. Finally, a firm stand by northern Baptists against appointing slaveholders as missionaries led to the organization of the SOUTHERN BAPTIST CONVENTION in 1845.

When the election of Abraham LINCOLN in November 1860 helped impel the southern states to secede from the Union, many conservative northern ministers urged caution by the government. Those with strong commitments to ABOLITIONISM even argued that the departure of the South might be beneficial, freeing the United States of the taint of slavery. But when war broke out in April 1861 and Union-held Fort Sumter surrendered to southern forces in

Charleston, South Carolina, virtually all religious bodies of the North (with the exception of historic peace churches such as the Mennonites and the Church of the Brethren) blessed the Union war effort.

Millennialism (see POSTMILLENNIALISM) became a strong theme in northern preaching during the Civil War. The United States was envisioned as a political paragon that would aid in the reformation of world civilization and prepare the way for the entrance of God's kingdom on earth. Most northern Christians complacently trusted that final victory over the Confederacy would be the judgment of a righteous God against the wickedness of the rebellious, slaveholding southern states. Julia Ward HOWE expressed this idea most vividly in her "Battle Hymn of the Republic," portraying Union soldiers as actors in a cosmic struggle between God and the forces of evil.

The formation of the two great wartime philanthropic organizations (see PHILANTHROPY), the United States Christian Commission and the United States Sanitary Commission, epitomized the blending of practical and spiritual concerns that characterized northern religious efforts. The Christian Commission was the fullest institutional expression of 19th-century religious benevolence. Organized in November 1861 under the guidance of the New York YMCA, the commission was intended to help northern chaplains lead worship and distribute religious tracts. The conversion of Union soldiers was its initial aim. After the first year of the war, however, commission agents increasingly found themselves ministering in practical ways to the physical needs of the troops, acting as nurses on battlefields and in hospitals. George H. Stuart, a Philadelphia merchant and Presbyterian lay leader who was its president, once replied to critics who wished his commission to deal solely with soldiers' spiritual concerns, "there is a good deal of religion in a warm shirt and a good beefsteak."

The Sanitary Commission, the largest and most tightly organized American philanthrop-

Frederick Douglass, slave-born and self taught, escaped slavery to become the most eloquent American advocate of abolitionism. *(Library of Congress)*

ic body of its time, was formed in June 1861 under the direction of Henry Whitney Bellows, a prominent Unitarian minister in New York City. Bellows conceived its mission to be the dispatching of salaried inspectors to the Union armies to oversee general medical care during the war. Although less forthrightly pious than the Christian Commission, the Sanitary Commission had prominent members of the more liberal denominations among its leadership, men and women who viewed their charitable labors as essentially religious in character. Novelist Louisa May Alcott, a Unitarian, for example, sewed shirts for the Sanitary Commission and wrote about the organization in her 1863 book, *Hospital Sketches.* And as "Mother" Mary Ann Bickerdyke, an agent who labored tirelessly with wounded soldiers, said to an army surgeon who inquired about her nursing qualifications, "I have received my authority from the Lord God Almighty!"

The Sanitary Commission eventually won the cooperation of the War Department and the army's Medical Bureau and was able to become involved in all aspects of aid to the troops. The Christian Commission was even more popular. It evolved into a vast interdenominational fellowship, supporting a hierarchical structure that reached to more than 5,000 volunteers stationed throughout the Union armies. It also raised and distributed more than 6 million dollars in money and supplies over the course of the war. Both the Sanitary Commission and the Christian Commission accomplished their wartime goals and disbanded when the conflict ended.

Clergy and lay people in the South, no less than their northern counterparts, were almost unanimously convinced that their national cause was holy and just. The new Confederacy, they said, had a special mission to maintain biblical values and the ideals of ordered liberty, which the North had perverted in the prewar period. Clergy also saw proof of their national righteousness in the constitution of the Confederacy for, unlike the United States Constitution, the southern document explicitly recognized a national dependence on God. White southern Christians, too, had their own millennialist interpretation of the struggle: Slavery symbolized the divinely ordained pattern for the relationships of capital to labor and of a superior to an inferior race. As Stephen Elliott, the Episcopal bishop of Georgia, declared, "We do not place our cause upon its highest level until we grasp the idea that God has made us the guardians and champions of a people whom he is preparing for his own purposes."

Clergy actively supported the war by serving both as military chaplains (approximately 2,300 in the Union army and roughly a third that number in the Confederate army) and—in a few notable cases—as soldiers. Holding worship services was the only duty specifically assigned to chaplains, but ministers performed many other useful tasks: teaching men how to read and write, delivering mail and writing letters home for wounded and dead soldiers, distributing Bibles and religious tracts, and serving as nurses during battles.

For some clergy, especially those of the depleted southern armies, the temptation to pick up a rifle and fight, or to serve as a line or staff officer, was strong. Leonidas Polk, for example, was the Episcopal bishop of Louisiana, but having been trained at West Point before entering seminary, he accepted a general's rank in the Confederate army. William Nelson Pendleton, an Episcopal clergyman in Lexington, Virginia, also had been educated for military service. He commanded the artillery forces of the Army of Northern Virginia in the war and was said to have prayed for the souls of his opponents before opening fire on them in battle.

Major religious revivals broke out in the armies over the course of the war. Among the northern troops, between 100,000 and 200,000 soldiers were said to have converted to Christianity, while at least 100,000 were similarly converted in the smaller southern forces—approximately 10 percent of all the men engaged in the Civil War. Soldiers viewed the army revivals as intensely spiritual experiences in which, amid the dangers and often random violence of the battlefield, they were able to feel God's providence guarding and guiding them. One Virginia soldier wrote in his wartime diary: "Oh Lord, if we should go into battle, be thou our shield & hiding place." And as an African-American soldier in the Union army was heard to pray, "Let me live with the musket in one hand and the Bible in the other,—that . . . I may know I have the blessed Jesus in my hand, and have no fear."

The revivals among the Civil War soldiers had a particularly lasting effect on Christianity in the South, where after 1865 little seemed to be left *except* religion. Two former Confederate chaplains wrote books detailing the religious life of the southern forces. In 1877, William W. Bennet, a minister who had headed the Methodist Soldiers' Tract Association, published *A Narrative of the Great Revival Which*

Prevailed in the Southern Armies. Bennett believed the Confederate army camp had been "a school of Christ," in which pious generals like Robert E. Lee and Stonewall Jackson led their men both in battles and in prayer meetings. Religion had become the "'silver lining' to the dark and heavy cloud" of the South's defeat. Popular Baptist minister J. William JONES described his own experiences and those of other chaplains in Lee's army in a book entitled *Christ in the Camp* (1887). He thought that the soldiers converted during the war had been able to look beyond their misfortunes and set to work rebuilding southern society after the Confederacy's crushing defeat.

Protestants in both sections hoped that the Civil War would be what they termed a "baptism of blood" for Americans, reconsecrating them for a high and holy mission. Horace BUSH-NELL, a Congregational minister in Hartford, Connecticut, explored this theme in sermons and addresses throughout the war. Only by the path of suffering could the United States be purged of its sinfulness and attain a more perfect national identity, Bushnell preached. Abraham LINCOLN's death symbolized for northern clergy a final ritualized meaning of the war. His assassination on Good Friday in 1865, like Jesus' sacrifice at Calvary, redeemed a people from their sins and brought them new life.

White southerners, on the other hand, fashioned an interpretation of the war that transformed military loss into a glorious spiritual triumph, also akin to the crucifixion of Jesus Christ. Through the formulation of what came to be known as the myth of the Lost Cause (see LOST CAUSE MYTH), southern whites spoke of the moral benefits they gained from adversity. While temporal prosperity made a people arrogant and seduced them into thinking they did not need God (witness the North in the Gilded Age, southern clergy argued), the hardships endured by the South taught forbearance and genuine Christian humility.

In the haze of nostalgic romanticism and myth making that shrouded the nation in the last few years of the 19th century, the fallen Confederacy soon became—in the eyes of whites in North and South alike—a paragon of moral virtue. Victor and vanquished clasped hands of friendship over the bloody chasm of war and tacitly agreed to ignore the material needs and political rights of the newly emancipated slaves. As a result, the deeper ethical issue of slavery that once had divided American Christians was forgotten by all but African Americans and a few conscientious whites. The lynching of black men reached epidemic proportions throughout the South, and discriminatory Jim Crow laws were created to keep African Americans socially subservient. The moral rebirth many Christians had hoped the Civil War would bring never materialized. Not until the CIVIL RIGHTS MOVEMENT of the 1950s and 1960s were the larger moral concerns first raised during the Civil War era finally addressed by American society.

(See also AMERICAN MISSIONARY ASSOCIATION; PROSLAVERY THOUGHT; VEROT, JEAN PIERRE AUGUSTIN MARCELLIN.)

GHS, Jr.

Bibliography: David C. Chesebrough, ed., *God Ordained This War: Sermons on the Sectional Crisis, 1830–1865* (Columbia: University of South Carolina Press, 1991); James H. Moorhead, *American Apocalypse: Yankee Protestants and the Civil War, 1860–1869* (New Haven: Yale University Press, 1978); Gardiner H. Shattuck, Jr., *A Shield and Hiding Place: The Religious Life of the Civil War Armies* (Macon, Ga.: Mercer University Press, 1987).

Clarke, James Freeman (1810–1888)

James Freeman Clarke was a mid-19th century Unitarian minister and transcendentalist (see TRANSCENDENTALISM). He is credited with providing the classic summary of Unitarian beliefs: "The fatherhood of God, the brotherhood of man, the leadership of Jesus, salvation by character, and the progress of mankind onward and upward forever."

Clarke was born at Hanover, New Hampshire, on April 4, 1810. Stepson of James

Freeman, who had led King's Chapel, Boston, into Unitarianism in 1785–1787, Clarke thoroughly imbibed optimistic religious rationalism as a youth. He graduated from Harvard College in 1829 and from Harvard Divinity School in 1833, then went west to serve in a new Unitarian congregation in Louisville, Kentucky, from 1833 to 1840. During that period, Clarke also edited a monthly religious magazine, the *Western Messenger* (1836–1839) and became involved in the growing antislavery movement. He returned to New England and in 1841 organized the Church of the Disciples in Boston. Clarke's greatest work was *Ten Great Religions*, a two-volume examination of the world's religions that appeared in 1871 and in 1883. These books exemplified the fascination with Asian thought that surfaced in American religion during the 19th century.

Like fellow Unitarian minister Frederic Henry Hedge, Clarke represented the moderate, churchly side of the transcendentalist movement. Although many transcendentalists were openly hostile to organized Christianity, Clarke was an irenic advocate of liberal religion who sought to keep Unitarianism a Christian denomination. He was a reformer who envisioned a "Church of the Future" that would combine all the best elements of the many branches of the Christian tradition. After 1867, he served as an adjunct member of the faculty at Harvard Divinity School, and as both a teacher and minister he had a profound impact on the shape of Unitarianism in his day. Trusted by both radicals and conservatives, he was also an important figure in the formation of the National Conference of Unitarian Churches, which in 1865 established a denominational bureaucracy and a regular assembly to set church policy.

With the exception of a period of convalescence and travel between 1850 and 1854, Clarke served at the Church of the Disciples from 1841 until his death more than four decades later. He died in Boston on June 8, 1888.

GHS, Jr.

Bibliography: Arthur S. Bolster, *James Freeman Clarke, Disciple to Advancing Truth* (Boston: Beacon Press, 1954).

Clarke, William Newton (1841–1912)

A Baptist minister and one of the leading systematizers of theological MODERNISM in his day, William Newton Clarke believed that religious experience, not religious belief, was the essence of faith. The textbook he published in 1898 *(An Outline of Christian Theology)* became the essential handbook of late-19th-century liberal Protestant ideas.

Clarke was born in Cazenovia, New York, on December 2, 1841. After graduation from Madison College and from Hamilton Seminary (both now Colgate) in 1861 and 1863, respectively, Clarke worked in short-lived pastorates at churches in New Hampshire, Massachusetts, Canada, and New York. He was professor of New Testament at Toronto Baptist College from 1883 to 1887. In 1891 he came to Colgate Seminary as professor of theology and remained there until his death.

Christian theology, Clarke consistently taught, should not view the Bible as a book filled with irrefutable facts or as a proof-text for doctrinal statements, the position on which conservative biblical interpretation was based. The Scriptures were the inspiration for theological inquiry rather than the objects of that study. Clarke's thinking followed the arguments German theologian Friedrich Schleiermacher had advanced in the 1820s concerning "the religious sentiment." Since the quest for the divine that both Clarke and Schleiermacher celebrated was a universal human attribute, every religion was assumed to contain some measure of truth. Although Clarke was unwilling to abandon the missionary enterprise entirely or repudiate traditional claims about the uniqueness and superiority of Christianity, a simpler, more realistic, and scientific faith (he argued in *A Study of Christian Missions* in 1900) needed to be carried to foreign lands.

Clarke resigned his professorship at Colgate in 1908 but continued to lecture on Christian ethics. Failing health led him to spend winters in Deland, Florida, where he died on January 12, 1912.

GHS, Jr.

Bibliography: William Newton Clarke, *Sixty Years With the Bible: A Record of Experience* (New York: Charles Scribner's Sons, 1912); William R. Hutchison, *The Modernist Impulse in American Protestantism* (1976; Durham, N.C.: Duke University Press, 1992).

Coke, Thomas (1747–1814) Thomas Coke was an English Methodist minister and one of the first two superintendents of the Methodist Episcopal Church in the United States. Always desirous of extending Methodism's evangelistic outreach, Coke spent most of his career fostering the growth of his denomination not only in America, but also throughout the world.

Coke was born in Brecon, Wales, on October 9, 1747. Educated at Jesus College, Oxford, from which he received a doctorate in civil law in 1775, he was ordained to the Anglican ministry and held a parish position between 1771 and 1777. He was ejected from his parish in 1777 because of his enthusiastic preaching and activities on behalf of the Methodist movement then emerging within the Church of England. Coke's religious fervor, however, won the attention of Methodist founder John Wesley (see WESLEYAN TRADITION, THE), and he soon became his trusted associate. He served for six years as a minister in London. In 1784 Wesley chose Coke to undertake work in the newly independent United States, and he appointed him as a superintendent, a title later changed to bishop, with authority over the American church.

Coke traveled to the United States on nine occasions between 1784 and 1803. After arriving in America for the first time, he joined with Francis Asbury and other Methodist leaders in the critical "Christmas Conference," held in Baltimore in December 1784, at which the new Methodist Episcopal Church was organized. Although Coke had Wesley's authority to ordain Asbury as his joint superintendent without further consultation, he acquiesced to the democratic inclinations of the Americans who wished to elect Coke and Asbury themselves. Following that election, Coke and two other English Methodist clergymen ordained Asbury to the ministry.

Coke attempted to maintain cordial relations with Asbury and other Methodists in the United States, despite increasingly successful American efforts to escape from English supervision. Like Wesley, who referred to human slavery as "the sum of all villainies," Coke opposed slaveholding and threatened to exclude those who owned slaves from the church. While American Methodists gradually modified their original antislavery stance, Coke himself refused to compromise. By the early 19th century, Coke's conflict with church members under his charge reached a point of crisis over a number of issues. Although he remained nominally an American bishop for the remainder of his life, he gave up virtually all his institutional responsibilities in the United States after 1808.

Filled with a zeal for foreign missions, Coke continued to direct his energies into building up churches in England's overseas colonies. En route to Ceylon during a missionary journey, he died at sea on May 3, 1814.

GHS, Jr.

Bibliography: John A. Vickers, *Thomas Coke: Apostle of Methodism* (Nashville: Abingdon Press, 1969).

Cold War Following the conclusion of WORLD WAR II in August 1945, tensions between two former allies, the United States and the Soviet Union, grew quickly as their leaders grappled with a new postwar international order in which they had clearly emerged as the two leading powers. The term *Cold War* refers to the long period of struggle between the two countries for dominance in world politics, beginning with the partition of Europe after World War II and ending with the erosion of COMMUNISM in Eastern Europe between 1989 (the fall of the Berlin Wall) and 1991 (the collapse of the Soviet Union).

Although never engaging in a "shooting war," the United States and the Soviet Union each developed massive military capabilities, pursued armed conflict through networks of client states, and sought to direct the course of global development through foreign aid, propaganda, and covert operations. Such a commitment of energy and resources required the nearly perpetual mobilization of their own populations. In America this mobilization took the form of a religious crusade, supported initially by most religious organizations and the majority of the population. Over time, however, the nearly mythical vision of American identity worked out at the beginning of the nuclear age came under increased scrutiny by Americans of many religious and intellectual perspectives. As a consequence, while America exercised great global influence and developed the world's largest economy during the Cold War, the nation was also beset by social and cultural crises that at times threatened America's self-identity as "God's Country."

While the Cold War was about many things—economics, spheres of influence, and the uses of power—its participants framed it primarily as a conflict over ideas of national identity and purpose. For Americans, those ideas had developed over the course of time into a CIVIL RELIGION. Americans were already used to seeing their own country as the embodiment of divine will and their enemies as demonic. But in contrast to earlier wars (see AMERICAN REVOLUTION; CIVIL WAR; WORLD WAR I), in which the tide of patriotic fervor rose and fell within a period of time limited by the conduct of actual war, the Cold War seemed to many a struggle that would continue indefinitely, creating a problem of sustaining long-term support for militarization among a people who historically saw little benefit in standing armies.

The Cold War began in the failure of the Allies at Yalta to agree on the partitioning of postwar Europe. Its tenor, however, emerged in the shock waves of the atomic bombs dropped on the Japanese cities of Hiroshima and Nagasaki, August 6 and 8, 1945. To many Americans "the Bomb" marked not only the ending of World War II, but also a transition into a completely new period in history, and perhaps the end of history as well. Thus the bomb became a potent symbol of the risks and responsibilities facing Americans during the ensuing economic, territorial, and ideological struggle with the Soviet Union. President Harry S. Truman, in his August 10th announcement of his decision to bomb Hiroshima and Nagasaki, said "we thank God it has come to us instead of to our enemies, and we pray that He may guide us to use it in His ways and for His purposes." Truman combined the traditional civil religious idea of America as a redeemer nation, carrying out God's will, with the new idea that nuclear technology was itself a divine gift.

While a number of Americans, including Protestant Reinhold NIEBUHR and Catholic Paul Furfey, questioned the morality of the bombings, most were content to view them in the terms set by Truman, and "the Bomb" rapidly became a symbol of American power and national identity. During the decade from 1945 to 1955, images of the bomb's cloud appeared everywhere, as a marketing device, in popular music, literature, science fiction films, sermons, and theological works. The equation of technological achievements with divine providence gave Americans the symbolic substance to sustain their advance into an uncertain postwar future.

But at the same time as the new technology provided a positive symbol, its horror was inescapable, and Americans frequently vacillated between hope and fear. When the Soviet Union detonated its own atomic bomb in 1949, and a hydrogen bomb in 1954, widespread confidence in America's divine mission slackened, as it became clear to many that the mission might entail the potential end of civilization.

To some religious leaders such a catastrophe called for caution, and commissions conducted by the NATIONAL COUNCIL OF CHURCHES and the WORLD COUNCIL OF CHURCHES urged American leaders to restrain their growing tendency to see themselves locked in an eternal struggle with the demonic Soviet Union. Catholics, with large groups of immigrants from Eastern Europe, did tend to support the growing ideology of anti-Communism, but even John Courtney MURRAY argued that the conflict should be fought with ideas, not nuclear arsenals. Among Jews, initial pride over the prominence of Jews among the scientists who developed atomic weapons and hopes that general recognition of their achievement would help erase ANTI-SEMITISM largely eroded by 1946. National organizations such as the Synagogue Council of America and the CENTRAL CONFERENCE OF AMERICAN RABBIS supported never-implemented plans to subject nuclear weapons to international control, thus echoing the growing critical concern among the nuclear scientists themselves. By contrast, Protestant premillennialists (see PREMILLENNIALISM) often spoke of the bomb as the culmination of biblical prophecy concerning the end of the world and for the next few decades produced an enormous popular literature correlating prophecy and Cold War developments.

During the 1950s anti-Communism affected domestic American life in a number of ways. American Catholics were confirmed in their opposition to Communism by the Soviet Union's treatment of Eastern European Catholics, and while Catholics tended to avoid social activism during the decade, Catholic students organized large rallies in support of persecuted Czech and Hungarian Catholics. Fulton SHEEN and other leaders campaigned actively against Communist expansion and domestic influence. Wisconsin's Senator Joseph McCarthy, who organized growing fears into a purge of Communist influence in the federal government, received widespread, though not uniform, support from fellow Catholics.

The stridency of Cold War anti-Communism issued from a remarkable American consensus contrasting with the social turmoil of preceding decades. Postwar abundance, shared by a growing middle-class of mostly white Americans, suggested America really was favored by God, as Puritan forebears had thought (see PURITANISM). Vice president Richard Nixon argued with Soviet premier Nikita Khrushchev in their famous "Kitchen Debate" about the merits of American household appliances at a trade show in 1959. Under these conditions of affluence, and for the first time in American history, the major faiths achieved a harmony of purpose, leading Jewish sociologist Will Herberg to speak in his popular *Protestant-Catholic-Jew* (1955) of an "American Way of Life" cherished by all.

At times playing upon and at times ignoring the "doomsday" political climate, embodied most clearly in the Soviet construction of the Berlin Wall in 1961 and the Cuban missile crisis of 1962, during which nuclear war seemed imminent, religion was everywhere. Religious groups grew at remarkable rates during the 1950s, church membership climbing from 86.8 million to 114 million between 1950 and 1960 as Americans moved to suburbs and took on the largest campaign of church-building in American history. *Time* magazine proclaimed Billy GRAHAM the best-known religious leader in the world, apart from the pope. Books by Trappist monk Thomas MERTON sold widely. Hollywood produced *The Ten Commandments* and other enormously popular Bible spectacles. Radios played "Big Fellow in the Sky." Americans thought positively (see POSITIVE THINKING), extending Norman Vincent Peale's own program by purchasing titles such as *Pray Your Weight Away* and *The Power of Prayer on Plants*. In 1954 Congress officially approved the slogan "In God We Trust" for American currency and inserted "under God" after "one nation" in the Pledge of Allegiance. The prevalent assumption that religion and America went hand in hand appeared in a remark frequently attributed to President Eisenhower: "Our government makes no sense unless it is founded in a deeply felt religious faith—and I don't care what it is."

The consensus established during the Cold War's first decade dissolved gradually during the late 1950s, as racial tensions increased and various intellectuals, "Beats," and young people came to regard the consensus as stifling (see BEAT MOVEMENT; COUNTERCULTURE). By the mid-1960s, racial tensions and the United States entry in the VIETNAM WAR unleashed a torrent of protests and riots (see CIVIL RIGHTS MOVEMENT).

In response to these crises, new cultural divisions appeared, no longer along denominational lines, but across the older religious divides of Catholic, Jewish, Protestant, and secular. Likewise new interfaith alliances appeared; the relevant religious dividing lines became those between liberals and conservatives, traditionalists and modernists of all faiths. At the same time a wide variety of racial and ethnic groups asserted their cultural independence (see ETHNICITY; PLURALISM). In the wake of Vietnam, religion grew increasingly political, as liberals and conservatives fought over whose vision was sufficient to guide the country out of national turmoil and perceived decline. While American leaders grappled with a changing world order during the 1970s and 1980s, citizens found themselves struggling not only with division over the nation's foreign role, but also over basic goals at home. Thus when the Cold War apparently ended with the collapse of the Soviet Union in 1991, Americans were left without the external threat that had provided the symbolic basis for national consensus in the years since World War II.

MG

Bibliography: Paul Boyer, *By the Bomb's Early Light: American Thought and Culture at the Dawn of the Atomic Age* (New York: Pantheon, 1985); Margaret A. Henriksen, *Dr. Strangelove's America: Society and Culture in the Atomic Age* (Berkeley: University of California Press, 1997); J. Ronald Oakley, *God's Country: America in the Fifties* (New York: Dembner Books, 1986); Robert Wuthnow, *The Restructuring of American Religion: Society and Faith Since World War Two* (Princeton: Princeton University Press, 1988).

colonial period   The colonial period of American history constituted one of the most innovative in terms of religious development and organization. This outcome is surprising considering that all the European powers that colonized what is now the United States desire to recreate their religious establishments in this land.

Both the French and Spanish colonies established Roman Catholicism as the state church, and the Spanish colonies implemented the Inquisition as a means of guaranteeing religious conformity (see NEW FRANCE; NEW SPAIN). Even the small and short-lived colonial possessions of Sweden and the Netherlands (see NEW NETHERLAND) attempted to ensure that the Church of Sweden (Lutheran) and the Dutch Reformed Church would be established in the colonies. Similarly, in the British colonies, such as VIRGINIA and MASSACHUSETTS BAY, religion was established by law, and religious uniformity was the goal.

In British North America, however, this goal was thwarted by many different realities. The first was the fact that many English colonies were established by groups seeking to escape the religious persecution they experienced at home and in America. Colonies such as Rhode Island, PENNSYLVANIA, and MARYLAND allowed for a diversity of religious views and practices unknown back in England. Pennsylvania actually encouraged diverse religious groups to settle there and drew to it many small sects that eventually would be wiped out in Europe.

Even a colony like Massachusetts Bay helped make British North America a religiously plural society. Although the Puritans' (see PURITANISM) opposition to bishops was at odds with the ideal of the British monarchs, the Puritans believed they were establishing the Church of England, albeit in a more perfect form. This led to conflict with those Puritans, the Separatists, who favored a complete break with the established church. Most notable among these opponents was Roger WILLIAMS, whose clashes with the colonial authorities in Massachusetts led him to establish Rhode Island on the basis of religious tolerance.

Similarly, persecution of Quakers (see FRIENDS, RELIGIOUS SOCIETY OF [QUAKERS]) both in England and in North America led to the formation of Pennsylvania, primarily as a refuge for that group, but with religious toleration as one of its guiding principles. Its founder, William PENN, actually encouraged numerous small sects to come to the colony, which soon became a haven for all religious groups, including Roman Catholics.

Like Pennsylvania, Maryland was originally designed as a refuge for another religious group persecuted in England, Roman Catholics. The colony's proprietors, the Calvert family (see CALVERT, CECILIUS), recognized that the existence of the colony as a refuge was dependent upon a policy of religious tolerance for all Christians and instituted such a policy at the colony's founding. This was extended by the colonial legislature with the passage of its "Act Concerning Religion" in 1649 (see TOLERATION, ACT OF [MARYLAND]). The act had a fitful existence, however, as the colony's Protestant majority overthrew the proprietary government and outlawed public religious services by Catholics. Restored in 1657, the act was finally abrogated in 1689 when, following the English overthrow of the Catholic king, James II, Protestants took permanent control of the colony's government.

The other source of opposition to the Puritan model were those who desired to see the establishment in North America of the Church of England in all its forms. Although the Puritan colonies, including those with both Congregational and Presbyterian leanings (see CONGREGATIONALISM; PRESBYTERIANISM), were capable of preventing such inroads until the formation of the Union of New England in 1686 placed them under royal control, other colonies were established with the intention of making the Church of England, as it truly existed in England, the established church.

Virginia and South Carolina were perhaps the most successful at this, with Georgia and North Carolina slightly less so. In these colonies the organization of parishes with resident priests was the goal. There also was occasional talk of appointing a bishop for the colonies, although this came to naught. Despite the laws, the Church of England never received the level of establishment and organization in these colonies as it did back in England. Anglicanism, moreover, was severely damaged by its association with England and loyalism during the Revolutionary War. The future of American religion lay with those smaller and more despised sects that were just coming into their own during the late 18th century. These groups, among them the Baptists and the Methodists, would soon sweep over the land, and while the descendants of the Puritans, the Congregationalists, would continue in their strength in New England and make some inroads into the Midwest, the colonial troika of Congregationalism, Anglicanism, and Presbyterianism would soon lose religious dominance.

FQ

Bibliography: Jon Butler, *Religion in Colonial America* (New York: Oxford University Press, 2000); David D. Hall, *Faithful Shepherd: A History of the New England Ministry in the Seventeenth Century* (Chapel Hill: University of North Carolina Press, 1972); ———, *Worlds of Wonder, Days of Judgment* (New York: Knopf, 1989); Perry Miller, *The New England Mind: From Colony to Province* (Cambridge, Mass.: Harvard University Press, 1953); ———, *The New England Mind: The Seventeenth Century* (Cambridge: Harvard University Press, 1939); Edmund Morgan, *Visible Saints: The History of a Puritan Idea* (New York: Oxford University Press, 1963).

Colored Methodist Episcopal Church

See CHRISTIAN METHODIST EPISCOPAL CHURCH.

Columbus, Christopher (1451?–1506)

Five hundred years after he landed on the island of San Salvador (Watling Island) in the Caribbean in October 1492, Christopher Columbus has become more important as a symbol than as a historical figure. Although not the first European to land in the Americas—he had been preceded by the Vikings and probably English fishermen—Columbus opened up an entirely new phase in European exploration. He died believing he had landed in Asia (the Indies), but Columbus truly "discovered" America for Europe. Some view him as an exemplar of European and Christian advance, while others see his career as the archetype of European violence and rapaciousness.

Since Columbus, more than any other individual, was responsible for opening up the Western hemisphere for European settlement, his name has become linked inextricably with the evils and horrors that accompanied it. During the 1980s and 1990s, as the 500th anniversary of his first expedition neared, he became vilified increasingly and took on, in an almost mythological way, the sins of all Western culture. As a result there has been an increasing tendency to relegate the historical Columbus to the sidelines and replace him with the Columbus of metaphor. Despite this tendency, he was very much a man, a man who had marked strengths and weaknesses, both of which appeared during his four expeditions to the West.

Born in Genoa, modern-day Italy, probably in the year 1451, Christopher Columbus grew up in a family of skilled laborers. His father was a weaver, and Columbus appears to have followed this trade while young. He went to sea during his teens and by his mid-20s had traveled to Tunis and Marseilles. In 1476, while on a voyage to Flanders and England, his ship was sunk by French privateers. Columbus made his way to Portugal, where he was taken in by a Genoese family in Lisbon. While there he gained what formal education he had, learning to speak, read, and write Portuguese and Castilian (Spanish). He also learned some Latin and improved his knowledge of sailing and navigation.

During his time in Portugal, Columbus became a successful merchant captain and was financially secure enough to marry into the lower nobility (1479). His wife, Felipa Perestrello e Moniz, had property in Madeira, where Columbus moved following their marriage. In the following year Felipa gave birth to Columbus's only legitimate son, Diego.

Columbus left Madeira in the 1480s for at least one expedition, this time sailing to West Africa. After observing the trade in slaves, gold, and goods, he was convinced that a fortune could be made trading in the East.

Deeply religious, Columbus was increasingly concerned with the Muslim control of Jerusalem and with the prophetic books of the Bible, notably Daniel and Revelation. He became convinced that by sailing west he could arrive at Cathay (China) and Cipangu (Japan), thereby avoiding the Arab middlemen who controlled the China trade and creating a base from which Christian Europe could move to liberate Jerusalem.

Contrary to decades of mythology, Columbus did not create the view that the world was round. This had been known and accepted by learned men since the ancient Greeks. What Columbus did was underestimate its circumference and overestimate the size of China. According to his calculations, the distance from Europe to Japan—actually 10,000 miles—was 3,000 nautical miles. This shorter distance made the trip a relatively easy affair, convincing Columbus that it could be done.

Looking for financial backing, Columbus took these convictions to the Portuguese court in 1484, but the early successes of Portuguese navigators on the Africa route to India led to a rejection. He also offered the idea to Henry VII of England. Again he was rebuffed. There followed another attempt with Portugal, but the news that Bartholomew Diaz had rounded the Cape of Good Hope ended these negotiations as well.

Following this rejection, Columbus turned his attention to the Kingdoms of Castille and Aragon—Spain. There he also met early disappointment, especially when a panel of experts dismissed his estimation of the earth's circumference and recommended against the trip. Columbus persisted, however, and with the aid of King Ferdinand's keeper of the privy purse, Luis de Santangel, won over the monarchs. Ferdinand and Isabella, ebullient over the surrender of the Moorish Kingdom of Granada and the unification of Spain under Christian control, granted Columbus numerous subsidies for the expedition. The ships and salaries were paid for from royal funds, as were the supplies. Columbus himself was to receive numerous concessions if the trip was successful, including a title and coat of arms, appointment as Admiral of the Ocean Sea, and a percentage of all the wealth obtained.

The expedition set sail on August 3, 1492, from the Spanish port of Palos, the country's major port of Cadiz being overwhelmed by the Spanish Jews who had been expelled from the kingdom. After a stop in the Canary Islands for water and some minor repairs, Columbus and his crew would sail for 33 days before sighting land on October 12, 1492. Columbus and the crew went ashore on the Island of San Salvador and took possession of it in the name of the Spanish monarchs, believing that they had landed on an island west of the Japanese archipelago. Convinced that he had missed Japan, Columbus continued sailing west in hopes of finding Cathay, China. But the wreckage of his main ship, the *Santa Maria*, forced him to return home with a little gold and several Arawaks from the island of Hispaniola (the island consisting of present-day Haiti and the Dominican Republic).

He arrived in Spain to a hero's welcome and was soon preparing for a second voyage.

The colony planted by this expedition on Hispaniola suffered from neglect by Columbus, who spent his time exploring Cuba, which he believed was a peninsula of China. Although increasingly suspicious of Columbus's abilities, the monarchs outfitted a third expedition in 1498 under his leadership. On this expedition, Columbus first sighted the South American continent, reporting to the king and queen his belief that it was the terrestrial paradise. Reports of his highhandedness and a revolt among the Spanish colonists at Hispaniola led to an investigation, and Columbus was returned to Spain in chains.

Although the monarchs restored his titles and income, he was removed from any position of real power in the West Indies and had difficulty securing permission for a fourth expedition that left in May 1502. On this expedition he made land in modern-day Honduras and explored the Central American coast down to the Isthmus. Conflict with the natives and the loss of two ships forced his return to Hispaniola in April 1503. By this time the ships were no longer seaworthy and had to be beached on the Jamaican coast. Requests for assistance from Hispaniola were ignored for a year, and Columbus and his companions did not return to Spain until November 1504.

Although this expedition had been the most financially successful, Columbus was ignored by the monarchs. Not until 1505 was he granted an audience with the king, who was growing weary with Columbus's demands. Increasingly ignored and engaged in numerous lawsuits, Columbus died on May 20, 1506. His remains were buried in Valladolid and then reinterred in Seville in 1509. Following the wishes of his son Diego's will, they were again removed and buried in Santo Domingo in 1541. At the time of this writing, their location is a matter of much dispute.

EQ

Bibliography: Silvio A. Bedini, ed., *The Christopher Columbus Encyclopedia*, 2 vols. (New York: Simon & Schuster, 1991); Miles H. Davidson, *Columbus*

Then and Now: A Life Reexamined (Norman: University of Oklahoma Press, 1997); Felipe Fernandez-Armesto, *Columbus* (New York: Oxford University Press, 1991); Samuel Eliot Morison, *Admiral of the Ocean Sea*, 2 vols. (Boston: Little, Brown & Co., 1942); ———, ed. and tr., *Journals and Other Documents on the Life and Voyages of Christopher Columbus* (New York: Heritage Press, 1964); Stephen Summerhill, ed., *Sinking Columbus: Contested History, Cultural Politics, and Mythmaking During the Quincentenary* (Gainesville: University Press of Florida, 2000); John Noble Wilford, *The Mysterious History of Columbus: An Exploration of the Man, the Myth, the Legacy* (New York: Knopf, 1991).

Committee of Southern Churchmen

A small, nondenominational Christian service organization based in Nashville, Tennessee, and led by Baptist minister Will D. Campbell, the Committee of Southern Churchmen was formed in 1964 out of the remnants of an earlier religious movement, the Fellowship of Southern Churchmen. Like the fellowship before it, the committee was dedicated to working for interracial justice and social reform in the South.

The Fellowship of Southern Churchmen (originally named the Conference of Younger Churchmen) was founded at a gathering in Monteagle, Tennessee, in May 1934. By the early 1950s, the fellowship had approximately 400 members, of whom roughly 80 percent were white and 20 percent African American. Ministers and teachers represented the largest portion of the membership. The fellowship emphasized a neo-orthodox position, that is, it synthesized traditional theological beliefs about God, sin, and the Christian gospel with a liberal, sometimes radical, political commitment to the poor. Aware of the South's hostility to "outside agitators" from the North, the fellowship restricted its membership almost exclusively to the southern-born.

Until the 1950s, the fellowship's members, like most southern liberals of the time, seemed confident that their policy of gradual racial integration would result in worthwhile social progress for African Americans. However, as matters turned out, the decade witnessed a devastating counteroffensive by conservative whites. The fellowship was unable to adjust to changing circumstances, as segregationists sought to block the forward strides southern blacks had made throughout the region. The fellowship's membership dwindled, and its funds became depleted. Although individuals such as Presbyterian writer James McBride Dabbs and Will Campbell focused their attention on the emerging black-led CIVIL RIGHTS MOVEMENT, the fellowship ceased to exist as an organization by the end of 1957.

Then serving with the National Council of Churches, Campbell had been among those who escorted African-American children through jeering mobs in Little Rock, Arkansas, in 1957. That same year, he was the only white to participate in the establishment of Martin Luther King's SOUTHERN CHRISTIAN LEADERSHIP CONFERENCE. Campbell resigned his post with the National Council of Churches and returned to the South in 1963. Seeking justice for downtrodden whites as well as for African Americans, he helped form the Committee of Southern Churchmen in 1964. Campbell believed that the overthrow of the idea of white supremacy and the success of the civil rights movement represented the South's reconciliation with God. The judging and classification of groups by race, he said, denied God's sovereignty over humankind.

Campbell's committee was a smaller, more conservative association than the Fellowship of Southern Churchmen. While it continued the earlier group's emphasis on the SOCIAL GOSPEL, it also recognized the limitations imposed upon any social reform program by the reality of human sinfulness. The committee has emphasized, therefore, the need for individual as well as collective action in addressing the problems of society. During the VIETNAM WAR, the group ministered to draft resisters and antiwar activists. From 1975 to

1983, the group published a theological journal called *Katallagete—Be Reconciled*, which mirrored the committee's emphasis on sin, forgiveness, and Christian service. Campbell has argued that the real enemies of human rights in the South have been the government and the business community. Those institutions, he thought, have traditionally oppressed blacks and poor whites together.

GHS, Jr.

Bibliography: Thomas Lawrence Connelly, *Will Campbell and the Soul of the South* (New York: Continuum, 1982); John A. Salmond, "The Fellowship of Southern Churchmen and Interracial Change in the South," *North Carolina Historical Review* 69 (1992), 179–99.

Common Sense Philosophy   See SCOTTISH COMMON SENSE REALISM.

Communism

Communism, broadly defined, is a social theory advocating the holding of property in common rather than individually. As a worldview of history, Communism became a powerful alternative to the capitalism shaping western Europe and the United States in the 19th century. Undergirding a global wave of revolutions in the 20th century, Communism, despite its avowed atheism, often appeared to foster a religious dedication among its followers. In the United States, where Communist activities remained marginal, the movement gave rise to a far more powerful worldview of anti-Communism, arising in conjunction with early 20th-century IMMIGRATION. Anti-Communism, similar in form to the NATIVISM that inspired the persecution of many non-Protestant groups in American life, became prominent during the "Red Scare" following WORLD WAR I. However, it was not until the COLD WAR that anti-Communism gained a lasting hold in America, shaping political life, religious understandings, and popular culture.

Communism shared a millennarian desire quite widespread in the 19th century: to establish a perfect society based on the norms of community rather than manipulation (see MILLENNIALISM; COMMUNITARIANISM). Such desire for a perfect society, going back into the foundations of Western thought, also played an important role in the creation of America (see PURITANISM; AMERICAN REVOLUTION).

Communism emerged out of debate and controversy among a number of thinkers but was best expressed by Karl Marx (1818–1883), a secular German Jew drawn to the budding workers movement after studying philosophy and law. In *Critique of the Gotha Program* (1875) Marx summed up the young movement's goal: "From each according to his abilities, to each according to his needs." Arising in opposition to the industrial capitalism radically reshaping Europe in the early 19th century, Communism envisioned a future in which private property, and the state's protection of it, would be abolished and humans freed from the bondage of wage-labor. To accomplish this Marx envisioned the emergence of a universal class. In Marx's writings, the proletariat, unlimited by particular interests in preserving privilege, and fully aware of the alienation caused by private property, would unite to emancipate all by exercising universal suffrage. Only by altering "the relations of production"—that is, private ownership of the productive process—could emancipation proceed. Marx consequently dismissed the efforts of socialists and trade unionists to redistribute the fruits of production.

European revolutionary movements remained unsuccessful until the Russian Revolution of 1917. The victorious Bolsheviks, under the leadership of Vladimir Illych Lenin (1870–1924), seriously modified Marx's social theory and in the process built a centralized state that took on the task of abolishing many features of traditional Russian culture, including its ORTHODOX CHRISTIANITY.

Communist ideals, present in some form in 19th-century America among communitarian groups such as the SHAKERS, the Mormons (see CHURCH OF JESUS CHRIST OF LATTER-DAY SAINTS), and Oneida Community (see NOYES,

JOHN HUMPHREY), have attracted the support of Americans troubled by the social inequality that became prominent as a result of industrialization after the CIVIL WAR. SOCIAL GOSPEL preachers, such as Walter RAUSCHENBUSCH and Solomon Washington GLADDEN, were critical of entrenched features of American capitalism and thought genuine religious faith impelled believers to seek the abolition of social injustice. Indeed, some form of radical critique of capitalism has characterized many American religious and secular political viewpoints throughout the century (see CATHOLIC WORKER MOVEMENT; COUNTERCULTURE; KING, MARTIN LUTHER, JR.; NIEBUHR, REINHOLD; SOJOURNERS FELLOWSHIP). In organized form, however, the Communist Party of the United States, present since 1919, has remained weak, garnering only 102,000 votes in the 1932 election, its highest percentage ever.

But if organized Communism is mostly invisible, its specter has been everywhere. In the wake of post–WORLD WAR I labor strikes and several bomb threats, U.S. Attorney General A. Mitchell Palmer employed the wartime Sedition Act to curb dissent, rounding up 4,000 suspected radicals on January 1, 1920. Most of those detained, primarily Jewish immigrants from eastern Europe, were eventually released, but the "Red Scare" spawned widespread concern about foreigners polluting American life.

Many American intellectuals developed favorable views of Soviet efforts to construct a classless society during the years of the Great Depression, and official anti-Communism declined as a result of the American alliance with the Soviet Union during WORLD WAR II. But by the late 1940s, as the Soviets sat in control of eastern European lands liberated from the Germans, President Harry Truman (1884–1972) and his administration came to view Soviet leader Joseph Stalin (1879–1953) as intent on world conquest. In addition to military and diplomatic efforts to "contain" the spread of Communism, Americans turned increasingly to ferreting out its influence at home. While the

earlier Red Scare had been a predominantly Protestant enterprise, the anti-Communism of the Cold War united Protestants with Catholics and Jews, all of whom now identified themselves as partakers in the "American Way of Life." Both America and the Soviet Union came to stand for opposed millennial ideals, one divine, the other diabolical.

Anti-Communism increasingly took on a powerful role in shaping the worldview of American culture during the Cold War. Fear of Communist subversion and infiltration fostered by the opportunistic Catholic senator Joseph R. McCarthy spread across the society. States passed laws making criticism of the government illegal, and even pleading the Fifth Amendment became proof of Communist Party membership. Prior to their execution for espionage in 1950, Ethel and Julius Rosenberg claimed during their well-publicized trial that they were victims of ANTI-SEMITISM. The House Un-American Activities Committee launched full-scale investigations of Hollywood in 1947, "blacklisting" hundreds of actors and directors because of presumed connections to the Communist Party. Nearly 40 feature films were produced echoing the fear of Communist subversion. Anti-Communism also targeted education as a seedbed of Communism. Libraries were purged of material critical of the American way of life and several hundred college professors were dismissed. Ecumenical organizations such as the NATIONAL COUNCIL OF CHURCHES were suspect.

While the purges ended in the late 1950s, the fear continued to be an active force in American political and religious life throughout the next three decades. The dissolution of the Soviet Union in 1991 in effect curtailed the force that anti-Communists have seen activating the spread of Communism.

In serving as a counterimage to what America is supposed to represent, Communism enabled several generations of Americans to retain the originally Protestant faith that America is *the* Christian nation. It has also enabled many non-Protestant Americans to gain status in American society by demonstrating their own commitment to the American way of life. With Communism's collapse outside the Third World, and its apparent diminution as a threat, the question to be asked is what will take its place.

MG

Bibliography: Albert Fried, *Communism in America: A History in Documents* (New York: Columbia University Press, 1997); John Earl Haynes, *Red Scare or Red Menace?: American Communism and Anticommunism in the Cold War Era* (Chicago: Ivan R. Dee, 1996); Harvey Kleher, *The Heyday of American Communism: The Depression Decade* (New York: Basic Books, 1984).

communitarianism   The practice of communitarian living, usually signifying a community in which there is some degree of sharing common resources and property, has a long history in Judeo-Christian cultures. The term is sometimes also used to indicate a system in which social reform is attempted through small communities. In practice, these two meanings have often overlapped: Many communities constitute themselves and share goods with the express purpose of providing a template for society as a whole. Thus, communitarian groups often have utopian aims (see UTOPIANISM).

The most enduring American communitarian enterprises have been explicitly religious, motivated by the conviction that believers must separate from the world and renounce certain aspects of their former lives in order to practice their religion in its pure and authentic form. Persecution from outsiders has often added to the sense that spiritual purity cannot be maintained in society at large. All communitarian religious groups assume that purity of beliefs and practices is possible in this world and that their particular social form is best suited to the maintenance of holiness. Such communities are frequently characterized by the meticulous ordering and

ritualizing of all aspects of life, including work patterns, diet, sexual practices, and even the definition of family.

Communitarianism can be traced back to the ancient Essenes, a male, celibate order in Palestinian Syria that emerged sometime before the birth of Christ. Some 4,000 members held property in common and observed strict religious rituals, but they lived scattered in various towns and villages. Early Christian groups, similarly, advocated the sharing of resources and property, although it is less clear that the apostolic church constituted itself this way. Nonetheless, many later communitarian movements were inspired by the biblical formulation of the Book of Acts 4:32–35, "they had all things in common," a passage that describes the intimate connection between sharing resources and sharing spiritual goals. Christian movements therefore have frequently construed communitarian living as a spiritual restoration, a return to the model of the early church.

Traditional renderings of the communitarian impulse move rather quickly from the early church to several medieval European communities, including the Albigenses and the Waldenses, and on to the flowering of sectarianism catalyzed by the Protestant Reformation. The Cathars in France, the English Lollards, the Labadists in Holland, and the Anabaptists in central Europe all shared in the desire to create a purified religious community and to separate themselves from a sinful world. With the European discovery of the "New World" of America, new sectarian communities were afforded the land and the relative freedom to fashion their own religious havens.

Communitarianism in America flourished most noticeably between the AMERICAN REVOLUTION and the CIVIL WAR. The opening of western lands, the social possibilities unleashed by the severing of traditional political and religious ties, a pervasive sense of the latent perfectibility of both individuals and society, millennialist prophecies, and growing qualms about an unabashed cultural commitment to the individualistic and competitive world of the capitalist marketplace led to the appearance of dozens of communitarian enterprises in this period. During the course of the 19th century, more than 100,000 people scattered in more than 100 colonies experimented with alternative social forms. This enthusiasm peaked in the 1840s with the emergence of groups such as Hopedale, Bethel-Aurora, Bishop Hill, Amana, Oneida (see NOYES, JOHN HUMPHREY), Brook Farm, Fruitlands, and the SHAKERS. Interest waned rapidly in the late 1860s and 1870s, as Americans struggled to recover from the devastating effects of the Civil War, but communitarians continued to follow the line of westward settlement, seeking new opportunities for purity and further separation from the perceived sinfulness of American life. Other eras, most recently the late 1960s and early 1970s, have witnessed a resurgence of many of the same impulses.

Although many American communes have looked back nostalgically to earlier periods or "golden ages," such as the Garden of Eden or the apostolic church, for their models of communal living, communitarians most often characterize their experiments as progressive and bold ventures, not as retreats from the "real" world. Many see themselves setting an important example as pioneers, using the small community model to force upon the wider society certain kinds of spiritual and/or social reforms. The communitarian template offers a noncoercive path to societal change, whether characterized as a "city upon a hill," a garden in the midst of the wilderness, or a pad where people can "discover" themselves.

Nonetheless, by focusing on communitarianism primarily as a consequence of the radical Reformation, historians have often ignored the many other social experiments in America that are also communitarian in nature. A most obvious example can be seen in Roman Catholic religious orders (see ROMAN CATHOLICISM), small communities of believers who often share resources and possessions, who live lives of ritual observance, and who have renounced key aspects of secular life. More recently, African Americans (see AFRICAN-AMERICAN RELIGION), Hasidic Jews (see HASIDISM), and Buddhists (see BUDDHISM) have established communitarian enterprises in the United States. Few scholars have analyzed these social experiments in the same detail that has been applied to Euro-Protestant or quasi-Protestant examples, but such study would undoubtedly enrich and perhaps qualify our assessments of communitarianism as a whole.

LMK

Bibliography: Lawrence Foster, *Religion and Sexuality: Three American Communal Experiments of the Nineteenth Century* (New York: Oxford University Press, 1981); John A. Hostetler, *Communitarian Societies* (New York: Holt, Rinehart, and Winston, 1974); Charles H. Lippy, "Communitarianism," in Charles H. Lippy and Peter W. Williams, eds., *Encyclopedia of the American Religious Experience* (New York: Charles Scribner's Sons, 1988); Donald E. Pitzer, ed., *America's Communal Utopias* (Chapel Hill: University of North Carolina Press, 1997).

Congregational Christian Churches   See UNITED CHURCH OF CHRIST.

Congregationalism   Congregationalism is a form of church government that evolved out of the English Puritan (see PURITANISM) movement of the 16th century. As distinct from episcopacy (governance by bishops) and presbyterianism (governance by ministers and elected laity), classic Congregational polity maintains that local Christian congregations may govern themselves without reference to any wider church authority or hierarchy.

Beginning in the late 16th century, groups of radical Puritans called Separatists broke away from the parish churches of the Church of England and established their own independent congregations. They believed that church membership should be restricted exclusively to those who were convinced believers in Jesus Christ. They also taught that each congregation was given authority by God to determine who might participate in its institutional and sacramental life. The PILGRIMS who settled Plymouth, Massachusetts, in 1620 were Separatists and the first adherents of Congregationalism to come to America. After 1629, other Puritans under the leadership of John WINTHROP found the Massachusetts Bay Colony a welcome outlet to escape from the English parish system. By the end of the 17th century, Congregationalists, the dominant religious group in New England, had effectively become a new Protestant denomination.

The government of the Congregational Churches in America received its first official definition at a church synod convened at Cambridge, Massachusetts, between 1646 and 1648. The CAMBRIDGE PLATFORM of 1648 established a system of independent local churches in which members and their elected officers shared equal authority. A half century later, a synod meeting in Saybrook, Connecticut, in 1708 further systematized Congregational government. The SAYBROOK PLATFORM, adopted in four Connecticut counties, provided that lay and clerical representatives of the churches would meet and offer judgments in disputes between local congregations. Ministerial associations were also created to approve candidates for ordination and oversee clergy. However, because the Saybrook Platform undercut the principle of absolute congregational independence and favored a modified connectional system, many churches both in Connecticut and in Massachusetts refused to be bound by its provisions.

Congregationalism next endured two major schisms that significantly altered its membership between 1735 and 1825. First, following the revivalist fervor of the GREAT AWAKENING of the 1730s and 1740s, some New England Congregationalists insisted that their clergy and fellow church members lacked true piety. Many of these dissidents, called New

Lights (see NEW LIGHTS/OLD LIGHTS), eventually split from the Congregational establishment and later reorganized themselves as Baptist congregations. Second, in the early 19th century, the emerging Unitarian (see UNITARIAN CONTROVERSY) movement caused nearly 100 more parishes in the Boston area to break formally with Congregationalism. These liberal churches allied themselves with one another and in 1825 formed the American Unitarian Association, the forerunner of the modern-day UNITARIAN UNIVERSALIST ASSOCIATION.

Official Congregational polity continued to develop after these defections, although because of the principle of strictly independent church bodies, a true denominational bureaucracy did not emerge until the late 19th century. The first state conference of Congregational churches was held in Maine in 1822, but only in 1871 were Congregationalists organized fully on a national level, when the National Council of Congregational Churches was founded. In 1865, the Boston Platform also superceded the two-century-old Cambridge Platform. The Boston Platform reaffirmed the idea that the local congregation, which derives its authority directly from Jesus Christ, is also sole basis of the church. However, the Boston Platform also allowed the conferring of ministerial standing and the installation of clergy to be shared by associations and conferences.

While the UNITED CHURCH OF CHRIST, formed by a union of the Congregational Christian Churches with the Evangelical and Reformed Church in 1957, is the most direct heir of the Puritan Congregational impulse today, many other churches in the United States trace their ecclesiastical lineage back to 16th-century English Congregationalism. These include the several Baptist denominations, the Unitarian Universalist Association, the Conservative Congregational Christian Conference, and a number of independent churches that still maintain a self-governing Congregational polity.

GHS, Jr.

Bibliography: Stephen Foster, *The Long Argument: English Puritanism and the Shaping of New England Culture, 1570–1700* (Chapel Hill: University of North Carolina Press, 1991); John von Rohr, *The Shaping of American Congregationalism* (Cleveland, Ohio: Pilgrim Press, 1992); J. William T. Youngs, *The Congregationalists* (New York: Greenwood Press, 1990).

Conservative Baptist Association See BAPTISTS.

Conservative Congregational Christian Conference See UNITED CHURCH OF CHRIST.

Conservative Judaism Although the division of JUDAISM into three "denominations," or branches, is an American phenomenon, Conservative Judaism claims to be the "authentic American Judaism." While perhaps overstated, there is some basis for this claim.

Unlike REFORM JUDAISM and ORTHODOX JUDAISM, which have their roots in Europe as institutions, Conservative Judaism is an indigenous phenomenon brought about by American conditions and circumstances. Conservative Judaism attempts to follow the "middle way" between Reform and Orthodoxy, adapting to new realities when necessary but committed to the preservation of the tradition. Although a definite minority in the 19th century and without organizational form until 1913, by 2000 Conservative Judaism had more than 850 congregations representing 1.5 million members.

The beginning of this major movement can be traced to a minor event that occurred in 1883 at a banquet honoring the first graduating class of Hebrew Union College in Cincinnati. The school, although dominated by Reform thinking, had been established to serve the entire American Jewish community. Knowing that several members of the college's board of directors followed *kashrut*, the Jewish dietary laws, the banquet's planners hired a Jewish caterer. When the first course was set before the participants, several rabbis stalked from the room, for on their plates were shrimp, one of the forbidden foods. This event demonstrated to the traditionalists that they could not work with the reformers. The magnitude of their differences became obvious two years later when the Reform group issued its statement of principles. In this statement, the PITTSBURGH PLATFORM, so much of Jewish tradition was rejected that for many traditionalists accommodation was impossible.

While the "*trefa* banquet" (*trefa* is Hebrew for forbidden food) was the immediate occasion for a separation between the more traditionally minded Jews and the reformers, it was not the sufficient cause. Conservative Judaism has its roots in the historical development of Judaism in the United States and in European intellectual currents.

Not all Jews in the United States were comfortable with the radical break with Jewish tradition represented by the reformers. This group, composed of more Orthodox immigrants and members of America's older Sephardic Jewish community, was concerned with retaining their Jewish identity, Jewish dietary laws, and the traditional religious rituals—including the use of Hebrew. This group, led by Isaac LEESER, Sabato MORAIS, Henry Pereira MENDES, Marcus Jastrow, and Benjamin Szold, rejected the complete disregard for tradition and Jewish law they saw among the reformers—as exemplified by the *trefa* banquet and the Pittsburgh Platform. These men stood for the maintenance of the dietary laws (which the Reform leader Isaac Mayer WISE disparaged as "kitchen Judaism"), the exilic character of the Jewish people, and unity with Jews throughout the world.

Many of these traditionalists agreed with the reformers that the 16th-century codification of Jewish law by Joseph Caro in the *Shulhan Arukh* needed alteration. The dead letter of the books had replaced the living letter of rabbinical synods. They rejected, however, what they saw as Reform's emphasis on utility—the attitude that the laws needed alteration not because they were tried and found wanting, but were tried and found difficult.

These men, generally referred to as the Historical School, were influenced by the thought of Rabbi Zechariah Frankel of Dresden. Frankel, affiliated with the *Wissenschaft des Judentums* (Science of Judaism) movement, felt that precise scholarship on the tradition was demanded, but unlike the reformers he used this scholarship not to denigrate tradition but to infuse it with new life.

Frankel desired to place Judaism on its "positive historical foundations." Rather than emphasizing the negative, he desired to see how the traditions expressed the living faith of a people. For Frankel, and for Conservative Judaism generally, the traditions were valuable because they were living vehicles of the religious expressions of the Jews. Not every element of the tradition was ordained by God; many were simply the creations of their age and location. But any alteration of that tradition would be equally so. As long as a tradition expressed the religious will of the Jewish people, it should be retained. If a practice no longer functioned as a source of religious value and meaning, then change was permissible, but only as an expression of the "total popular will." Rabbi Alexander Kohut of Ahavath Chesed in New York expressed the ideals of this movement in his first sermon (1885): "I desire a Judaism full of life . . . a Judaism true to itself and its past, yet receptive of the ideas of the present."

The emphasis on the totality of the community, *klal Yisrael* ("universal Israel"), has been dominant within Conservative Judaism. In fact, those involved in its formation viewed themselves as creating a religious organization that would bring together all Jews. The result, as so often happened in American history, was the formation of one more denomination.

It is telling that such a group first formed not a denominational organization, but a seminary—Jewish Theological Seminary in New York. Organized "to impart the love of the Hebrew language, and a spirit of fidelity and devotion to the Jewish law," the first class met on January 2, 1887 in the Shearith Israel synagogue in New York. Although its first graduate went on to become chief rabbi of the British Empire, the seminary struggled during its early years. By 1901 the school was close to folding.

The school was saved by the activities of Cyrus ADLER, who convinced a large number of Jewish laymen to re-endow the school. Even more important was Adler's ability to convince Solomon SCHECHTER to accept its presidency. Schechter, a Romanian-born rabbi and professor of Hebrew at the University of London, transformed the fortunes of the school and of the Conservative movement itself. Schechter viewed the school as a "theological center which should be all things to all men, reconciling all parties, and appealing to all sectors of the community." While it failed to achieve this goal—the Reformed and Orthodox went their own ways—it provided a middle way between the accommodationism of Reform and the parochialism of the Orthodox.

Giving organizational form to this middle way took some time. In 1901 an Alumni Association of Jewish Theological Seminary was formed, then reorganized in 1919 as the Rabbinical Assembly of America, with the responsibility for ordaining rabbis and overseeing issues of Jewish law and practice within the movement.

Not until 1913 did an institution bringing together all like-minded congregations form. Its very name expressed the universality desired by the movement: the United Synagogue of America (see UNITED SYNAGOGUE OF CONSERVATIVE JUDAISM). Originally comprised of 60 congregations, by 1980 it had become the largest branch of American Judaism. It owed this growth to the huge numbers of eastern European immigrants who swept into America between 1880 and 1924. As they and their children drifted away from traditional orthodoxy, some became nonobservant, others became Reform, but many joined the Conservative movement as a compromise. In institutional terms this middle way has served Conservatism well.

The fusion of tradition and change, however, has made it impossible for Conservatism to adopt either the majoritarian decision-making of Reform or the authoritarianism of the Orthodox. Its commitment to tradition resulted in the secession of its more liberal members, who founded RECONSTRUCTIONIST JUDAISM—a fourth branch of American Judaism. Its commitment to change has led to growing tensions with the Orthodox community.

Over no issue has this conflict with orthodoxy been greater than over the role of women within Judaism. The abolition of the barrier (*mehitzah*) separating women from men was only the first of many conflicts; the introduction of mixed seating in many synagogues was an even greater breach of traditional practice. The worst violations of Jewish law from the Orthodox perspective were changes allowing greater participation of women within religious services. Some of these were relatively minor, allowing women to read from the Torah during services, for example. Others were major transformations of Jewish tradition.

The first was the 1973 issuance of a *takhanah* ("legislative enactment") by the Rabbinical Assembly's law committee allowing women to be counted in a *minyan,* the 10 Jewish adults necessary to conduct services. There followed a decade-long conflict over whether to accept women in the rabbinate. This debate closed in 1983, when the faculty of Jewish Theological Seminary voted 34-8 to admit women to the rabbinical school. In May 1985, Amy Eiberg became the first woman ordained by the Rabbinical Assembly.

The conflict over the role of women led to the formation of the Union for Traditional Conservative Judaism, composed of those opposed to women's ordination. Whether this will lead to another split within the denomination, or whether these more conservative rabbis and laymen will drift into the Orthodox camp, remains to be seen.

There are other ongoing tensions within the movement. The first of these is the traditionalism of the seminary faculty and the realities of life as a Conservative rabbi. While the movement itself is committed to the observance of the dietary laws, more than 60 percent of its members do not keep kosher homes, and Conservative rabbis have little authority to oppose this nonobservance.

Lack of authority is the source of yet more conflict between a traditionally trained rabbi and a less traditionally minded congregation. Power rests in the hands of the latter. While the rabbi can condemn, demand, and plead, there is little she or he can do. People can always leave or dismiss the rabbi. Many Conservative rabbis find themselves in the position of being their congregations' representative of tradition.

The 1970s and 1980s were difficult years for Conservative Judaism. A more traditionally oriented Reform movement attracted many of its liberal members, and an increasingly aggressive Orthodoxy appealed to the more conservative. There also was vigorous criticism from within, especially from those raised in the movement. Younger members criticized the sterile and impersonal nature of the synagogues, adaptation to middle-class values, as well as lax observance. Many founded *havuroth,* religious communities based on the pharisaic brotherhoods of the Roman era. While favoring more traditional observances, these *havuroth* also pushed for a greater involvement of women and increased social concern.

In the last quarter of the 20th century, the Conservative movement struggled to find a way to reinvigorate itself. Attempting to articulate a positive identity, the movement issued a statement of beliefs and principles in 1988, Emet Ve-Emunah, that placed Conservative Judaism religiously between the Reform on the left and Orthodox on the right. It expressed Conservatism's commitment to the normativity of the Halakhah (Jewish law) and the Jewish tradition, while noting the role of development and change within the Halakhah. Most significantly, it recognized the role of religious authorities within the Conservative movement to interpret and adjust Jewish law, thereby rejecting the Orthodox claim that the law cannot be altered. To a great extent, the Emet Ve-Emunah simply restated officially the premises upon which Conservative Judaism is based. The statement does, however, explicitly separate the movement from both the Reform and Orthodox. The last decade of the 20th century saw Conservative Judaism at a crossroads. Seemingly outflanked on the left by Reform and on the right by the Orthodox, Conservative Judaism appeared to lack a clear focus. Interestingly, this difficulty saw a solution in changing demographics.

By focusing increasingly on serving local congregations and addressing the needs of the growing numbers of young professional couples with children, Conservative Judaism found a new population eager for structure and strong religious learning. Many of these families were products of "mixed" Jewish marriages, where one spouse had been raised in a more religious household and the other in a less observant environment. For them a Conservative synagogue provided an alternative comfortable to both.

Although no longer the largest movement within American Judaism, the Conservative movement remains strong. Its deep historical roots and its commitment to using the power of the religious tradition to answer pressing contemporary concerns and to adjust to new realities keeps it both vibrant and grounded. For these reasons alone it should continue to find its membership among large numbers of American Jews.

EQ

Bibliography: Gerson D. Cohen, *Jewish History and Jewish Destiny* (New York: Jewish Theological Seminary of America, 1997); Moshe Davis, *The Emergence of Conservative Judaism: The Historical School in Nineteenth-Century America* (Westport, Conn.: Greenwood Press, 1977); Daniel Judah Elazar, *The Conservative Movement in Judaism: Dilemmas and Opportunities* (Albany: State University of New York Press, 2000); Pamela Susan Nadell, *Conservative Judaism in America: A Biographical Dictionary* (New York: Greenwood Press, 1980); Herbert Rosenblum, *Conservative Judaism: A Contemporary History* (New York: United Synagogue of America, 1983); Marshall Sklare, *Conservative Judaism: An American Religious Movement* (Glencoe, Ill.: Free Press, 1955); Jack Wertheimer, *Tradition Renewed: A History of the Jewish Theological Seminary* (New York: Jewish Theological Seminary of America, 1997); www.uscj.org (United Synagogue of Conservative Judaism); www.jtsa.org (Jewish Theological Seminary); www.rabassembly.org (Rabbinical Assembly of America); www.mercazusa.org (International Organization of Conservative Judaism).

Consistent Calvinism   See NEW DIVINITY.

Constitution (U.S.)   The Constitution of the United States of America is the fundamental law of the nation. It provides the country with the basis for its national government, setting forth the government's functions, powers, and roles. The genius of the document rests in its flexibility. Rather than legislate for all contingencies, the Constitution is formulated on broad principles that allow for responses to changing situations and conditions. The Constitution is specific, however, when it enumerates the limits of governmental power. These limits serve to prevent the rise of a despotic and tyrannical government.

Based on the philosophical and political ideas of the ENLIGHTENMENT, the Constitution is preeminently the work of James MADISON, although the text as adopted was penned by Gouverneur Morris of New York. Between May and September 1787 delegates from 12 of the 13 states then composing the United States of America met in Philadelphia to find some way to strengthen the existing federal government. The instructions given the delegates by the various states empowered them only to modify the existing fundamental law of the land, the Articles of Confederation. Under the leadership of Madison, however, those present took it upon themselves to write a completely new constitution. When they had finished, 39 of the 42 delegates signed the new document, which they then presented to the people for ratification. By June of 1788 ratification by the people of the required nine states had been secured, and the Constitution took effect as the basis for the national government.

Religious issues played an insignificant role in the drafting of the Constitution. None of the delegates suggested that the document allow for a religious establishment. In fact, the only mention of religion in the document, in Article VI, Section 3—adopted over the objections of the delegates from Maryland, North Carolina, and Connecticut (North Carolina being the only one to finally vote against it)—expressly forbids the requirement of religious tests for the holding of political office.

During the debates over ratification some objected to this clause, fearing that it would allow Catholics and pagans to hold political office. The biggest fear, however, was from the other position, that the document did not sufficiently protect religion from governmental meddling. This and related fears led to the adoption of the first 10 amendments to the Constitution: the Bill of Rights. Of these amendments one specifically deals with religion. The FIRST AMENDMENT states that "Congress shall make no law respecting the establishment of religion, or prohibiting the free exercise thereof; . . . ."

These amendments, however, applied only to the national government and not to the various state governments. Several states retained their pre-Revolutionary religious establishments well into the 1800s. The relationship of the state governments to religion was a matter only of state law, not constitutional guarantees.

This eventually changed due to the adoption of the FOURTEENTH AMENDMENT. This amendment, ratified in 1868, was designed primarily to protect the newly freed slaves from political abuse by their former masters. Among its various provisions the amendment

states that "No State shall make or enforce any law which shall abridge the privileges and immunities of citizens of the United States."

Through the use of this amendment the federal courts, and the Supreme Court as the ultimate arbiter of the Constitution's meaning, began to apply the freedoms guaranteed in the Bill of Rights to the states. The first Supreme Court decision to apply the "free exercise" clause of the First Amendment to the states was in *Cantwell v. Connecticut* in 1940. In 1947 the Supreme Court for the first time applied the "establishment clause" of the First Amendment to the states via the Fourteenth Amendment in its decision in *Everson v. Board of Education*.

Beyond its legal and political importance the Constitution has deeper significance in the United States as one of the icons of America's CIVIL RELIGION. An overwhelming majority in the United States pays homage to the document. Those who have never bothered to read the Constitution esteem it as one of the greatest works of the ages. All politicians favor it, and the epithet "unconstitutional" is often hurled at legislation the speaker opposes. This level of reverence for the Constitution, illustrates its importance in American society. Everyone fights over the Constitution, and people with opposing views claim its support. While the desire of so many to wrap themselves in the Constitution does not necessarily honor it, the fact that the Constitution protects so many under its banner does. The constitutional guarantees to religious equality and religious freedom, despite the occasional lapses in application, cannot be overestimated in importance. They have made it possible for the United States to become a religiously pluralistic nation with a minimum of religious violence and bloodshed. Despite prejudice, hostility, and sporadic violence, the United States has been spared the large-scale conflicts that have marked other diverse nations. This must be attributed primarily to the guarantee of free religious exercise and prohibition of a religious establishment in the Bill of Rights.

(See also CHURCH AND STATE, RELATIONSHIP BETWEEN.)

EQ

Bibliography: Michael Kammen, ed., *The Origins of the American Constitution: A Documentary History* (New York: Penguin, 1986); Joseph M. Lynch, *Negotiating the Constitution: The Earliest Debates Over Original Intent* (Ithaca, N.Y.: Cornell University Press, 1999); Forrest McDonald, *Novus Ordo Seclorum: Intellectual Origins of the American Constitution* (Lawrence: University Press of Kansas, 1989); John Witte, *Religion and the American Constitutional Experiment: Essential Rights and Liberties* (Boulder, Colo.: Westview Press, 2000).

conversion The word *conversion* derives from the Latin *conversio*, which means "a turning round" or "revolution." In religious terminology, the word implies a change from one type of life to another—in Christianity, a rejection of sin and the acceptance of a new life in Jesus Christ. Emphasis on conversion and ongoing spiritual regeneration has always been a hallmark of EVANGELICALISM in America. Evangelicals traditionally regarded the experience of religious conversion as a mark of the genuine Christian.

The willingness to testify to one's conversion experience was a central feature of the Puritan movement of the late 16th and early 17th century. Most Puritans believed that conversion was a gradual process. PURITANISM encouraged prolonged and continual self-analysis, a process in which believers searched their hearts for evidences of divine grace. After the Puritan migration to New England, candidates for church membership were required to undergo an examination about their conversion. When a person requested membership, the petitioner would be asked to describe how the results of God's grace were first perceived and then acceded to.

As the original fervor of first-generation Puritanism waned, more and more New Englanders failed to recognize in themselves signs of the experience of saving grace that their parents and grandparents had known. Although most were professing Christians and tried to lead moral lives, these unconverted persons increased dramatically in number and presented a critical spiritual problem for the Congregational churches of New England. At the end of the 17th century, prominent clergy such as Increase MATHER and Solomon STODDARD introduced periods of intense preaching in their churches. Their goal was the inauguration of a "revival" (see REVIVALISM), that is, a time when people would experience conversion, feel their hearts changed, and enter full church membership.

During the GREAT AWAKENING, the religious explosion that shook the American churches in the middle decades of the 18th century, the need for conversion became an overarching theme in the preaching of revival leaders. Jonathan EDWARDS, for example, minister of the Congregational church in Northampton, Massachusetts, was alarmed by the spiritual complacency he perceived among many of his parishioners. To counter this, he preached a series of sermons on JUSTIFICATION by faith alone in 1734. He soon noticed important changes in his people: Religious interest and conversions began to increase markedly.

As Edwards realized, however, there was an inherent tension in the way preachers such as he approached the task of evangelism. Orthodox Calvinists knew that, from eternity, God had arbitrarily chosen to save some human beings and damn others without regard to actual merit. Calvinists believed that God would inevitably awaken faith within the hearts of the predestined elect (see ELECTION), while those predestined to damnation would simply never experience a conversion. Yet if conversion were solely a divine action, indeed an event foreordained by God before creation itself, there would seem to be little justification for pressing a sinner to repent. To stress the importance of the human will in conversion not only was inappropriate, but might even signal a lack of faith in divine grace.

Despite Calvinist misgivings, pressing for conversion rapidly became a highly successful recruiting technique for churches during the Great Awakening. Conversion changed from being a purely individual affair to being a mass concern. By the time of the SECOND GREAT AWAKENING in the early 19th century, emphasis on the use of one's free will, coupled with pressure tactics about the need for acceptance of God's grace, began to dominate American evangelical ideas on conversion. Charles G. FINNEY, arguably the greatest revivalist of all time, exemplified the attitude of that period. Finney was renowned for pleading with men and women to change their hearts and surrender to God. His most famous sermon, "Sinners Bound to Change Their Own Hearts," argued that God had given people power to make up their own minds and act for themselves. Anyone who wanted *could* undergo a spiritual rebirth and attain salvation.

Later in the 19th century, revivalist Dwight L. MOODY combined Gilded Age optimism with classic theological ARMINIANISM. He urged the crowds that flocked to hear him to effect salvation by giving their hearts to God. Moody's message was a simple one. Through an act of will, a person could accept divine grace and instantly be saved. Moody would hold up a Bible and assure his congregations that eternal life was available for the asking. All people had to do was "come forward and t-a-k-e, TAKE!"

This form of conversion that Moody popularized is typical of conservative Protestantism in the United States today. Evangelicals believe that individuals must welcome God's saving grace into their hearts in order to authenticate any claim to being a Christian. Conversion, feeling "born again" or "saved," therefore, remains the central experience by which a person enters into a life of religious commitment.

GHS, Jr.

Bibliography: Jerald C. Brauer, "Conversion: From Puritanism to Revival," *The Journal of Religion* 58 (1978), 227–43; Patricia Caldwell, *The Puritan Conversion Narrative: The Beginnings of American Expression* (Cambridge, Mass.: Harvard University Press, 1983).

Conwell, Russell Herman (1843–1925)

Russell Conwell was a Baptist minister and popular lecturer of the late 19th and early 20th century. The most celebrated clerical spokesman for the GOSPEL OF WEALTH movement, he was famed for the lecture "Acres of Diamonds," in which he admonished listeners that it was their Christian "duty to get rich." Conwell also founded Temple University in Philadelphia to educate working men and women who were unable to attend a traditional college but still wished to better themselves. He served as Temple's first president between 1888 and 1925.

Conwell was born in South Worthington, Massachusetts, on February 15, 1843. He studied at Yale College for two years before serving as an officer in the Union army during the Civil War. He graduated in 1865 from the School of Law at Albany University in New York and practiced law in Minneapolis, Minnesota, from 1865 to 1868. Although wounds he received in the war forced him into a two-year convalescence period, Conwell returned to work in 1870 and found employment as a traveling journalist, lawyer, and businessman. The death of his first wife in 1879 led him to consider the ministry as a new career. Having taught Bible classes in local churches and having worked with the YMCA, he was called to a Baptist church in Lexington, Massachusetts, where he was ordained in 1880.

In 1882 Conwell came to Grace Baptist Church, a struggling congregation in Philadelphia. Conwell soon won renown not only for his preaching and evangelistic fervor, but also for his promotion of educational and social concerns. His ministry in Philadelphia reflected a mixture of religion and social activism that paralleled aspects of the SOCIAL GOSPEL movement. By 1893 Conwell's church, then called the Baptist Temple, contained more than

Russell Herman Conwell, the founder of Temple University. His "Acres of Diamonds" spoke of a Christian "duty to get rich."

3,000 members and had become one of the most active Protestant congregations in the country. A new building was built with a gymnasium, Sunday school, and reading rooms—the perfect model of the "institutional church" of the period, not simply a place of worship, but a community center as well. Conwell provided free night-school classes in the basement of his church, and in 1888 this venture evolved into Temple University.

Conwell was undoubtedly best known for the speech "Acres of Diamonds," which he delivered on over 6,000 occasions. Conwell believed that God gave everyone opportunities for material advancement. All people have "diamonds" in their own backyards, he declared, and they can uncover them if they look hard enough. When he was asked why he did not preach a less worldly gospel but only exhorted people to get rich, Conwell replied that "to make money honestly is to preach the gospel." A self-made man who amassed a fortune, Conwell did take seriously the idea of Christian stewardship. He believed in civic responsibility and charity, and he used his money to aid poor students at Temple.

Conwell's opinions on industriousness, self-help, and the universal potential for success struck a responsive chord in the minds of many Americans in the Gilded Age. He remained active both as minister of the Baptist Temple and as president of the university until the end of his life. He died at Philadelphia on December 6, 1925.

GHS, Jr.

Bibliography: Agnes Rush Burr, *Russell H. Conwell and His Work: One Man's Interpretation of Life* (Philadelphia: John C. Winston Company, 1926).

Cotton, John (1584–1652) John Cotton was one of the leading ministers of the MASSACHUSETTS BAY COLONY. His theological and social views helped form the "New England Way"—the religious and political structures of the Puritan colonies (see PURITANISM). This was an interesting role for someone so bookish that he daily spent 12 hours in his study and was heard to remark, regarding the many interruptions a minister suffers, that he found it much more rewarding to converse with the dead (in books) than with the living.

For Cotton, the road to America was not a direct one. Born in Derby, England, on December 4, 1584, Cotton attended Trinity College, Cambridge, where he received his B.A. degree in 1603 and his M.A. degree in 1606. In 1607 he became chief lecturer and dean of Emmanuel College, a position he held until 1612, when he took religious orders, receiving his B.D. degree from Emmanuel College the following year.

In the year of his ordination Cotton received the prestigious appointment to St.

John Cotton, a Cambridge University graduate and Boston minister whose preaching and writing shaped New England Puritanism. *(Boston Public Library)*

Botolph's in Boston, England. The way to advancement seemed assured to the scholarly and accomplished minister. By 1615, however, Cotton had become a Puritan and brought the worship services at St. Botolph's into line with Puritan views. A lenient bishop allowed Cotton his ways for 18 years, but the king's opposition to Puritanism was stronger than the indifference of a bishop, and in 1632 Cotton was ordered to appear before the Court of High Commission (Star Chamber) to answer for his views. He went into hiding in London, where he remained until his departure for America in September 1633.

Cotton's arrival in Massachusetts was welcomed. (It was rumored that Boston had been given its name in hope of increasing the likelihood of his emigration.) The church of Boston appointed him teacher, the ministerial post responsible for supervising doctrine and delivering sermons. His influence in the colony was felt immediately. Cotton began a series of sermons on the Covenant of Grace, warning people against falling into the belief that their actions could aid in bringing about their salvation.

Because of this strong belief in human inability regarding salvation, Cotton helped give birth to the ANTINOMIAN CONTROVERSY of 1636–1637. In fact, Cotton was the ministerial idol of Anne HUTCHINSON, the leader of the so-called antinomians. Cotton initially supported Hutchinson, but he eventually acquiesced in her banishment, partially in response to pressure from his fellow ministers.

Although Cotton gave some support to Hutchinson, he firmly opposed another dissenter, Roger WILLIAMS. Williams's belief that religious affairs should be removed from civil enforcement was something Cotton could not countenance either theologically or socially, and Cotton led the movement to banish Williams from the colony (1635). This did not end the conflict, however, and the two carried on a pamphlet war over the issue during the 1640s and 1650s.

In his works, primarily *The Bloudy Tenent, Washed, And made White in the Bloud of the Lambe* (1647), Cotton sets forth his view that the secular government must enforce religious uniformity. For Cotton, obedience to true religion was necessary for a functioning society. God judged societies on their godliness. Societies that allowed the existence of heretics and blasphemers called divine retribution down on themselves. Also, diversity of religious views led to conflict within society that threatened its existence. For these reasons Massachusetts could not suffer the existence of those who deviated from Puritan orthodoxy; to do so imperiled the colony's continued existence. Those who did not conform must be made to do so or be removed from the colony.

Until his death on December 23, 1652, Cotton was most influential in setting the religious standards of Puritan New England. At his insistence, the churches of Massachusetts adopted (between 1635 and 1640) the testimony of a conversion experience as a requirement for church membership. He prepared the standard catechism, *Milk for Babies* (1646), setting out for children the basic doctrines of Puritanism. Finally in 1648, along with Richard Mather, Cotton drafted the CAMBRIDGE PLATFORM, the document that would serve as the basis for the polity and doctrine of CONGREGATIONALISM until the 19th century.

EQ

Bibliography: John Cotton, *Of the Holinesse of Church-members* (London: Printed by F. N. for Hanna Allen, 1650); ———, *A Treatise of the Covenant of Grace,* 3rd ed. (London: Peter Parker, 1671); Everett H. Emerson, *John Cotton,* rev. ed. (Boston: Twayne, 1990); Larzer Ziff, *The Career of John Cotton: Puritanism and the American Experience* (Princeton, N.J.: Princeton University Press, 1962).

Coucouzes, Iakovos (1911–)

During a long career begun in 1939, Archbishop Iakovos Coucouzes has become the most familiar public representative of Orthodox Christianity and the longest-serving Orthodox hierarch in American history.

The future leader of the GREEK ORTHODOX ARCHDIOCESE OF NORTH AND SOUTH AMERICA was born Dimitrios Coucouzes on the Aegean island of Imvros in 1911. Educated at the Ecumenical Patriarchate's seminary at Halki near Istanbul, he was ordained to the diaconate in 1934 and took the monastic name Iakovos.

He immigrated to the United States in 1939 and joined a small circle of clerics who helped Archbishop Athenagoras SPYROU forge a centralized and unified Greek Orthodox Church in North America. Closely associated with the founding of the Holy Cross Greek Orthodox School of Theology, Iakovos was ordained to the priesthood in 1940 and served several parishes, including an influential pastorate in Boston from 1942 to 1954.

Consecrated a bishop in 1954, he played an important role in the ECUMENICAL MOVEMENT. He represented the patriarchate at the World Council of Churches in Geneva from 1955 to 1959 and eventually served the council as co-president.

Enthroned as archbishop of North and South America in 1959, Iakovos returned to the United States at a point when the children of the first generation of Greek immigrants were coming to maturity. His style of leadership was activist, and he was determined to claim a visible place for the Orthodox in American life.

Iakovos soon became a familiar figure at public events, offering prayers at presidential inaugurations and other such gatherings. A photograph of Iakovos standing with Martin Luther KING, Jr., at Selma, Alabama, in 1965 became one of the best-known symbols of the ecumenical movement during the 1960s.

His major administrative achievement was the sweeping reorganization of the archdiocese in 1978, when the centralized structure adopted during the 1930s was replaced by a more traditional Orthodox system in which a synod of diocesan bishops sits under the leadership of the archbishop.

During the 1960s and 1970s, Iakovos also emerged as an important ethnic leader, rallying Greek Americans against the Turkish intervention in Cyprus and the persecution of the patriarchate in Istanbul. Although his 1972 candidacy for the patriarchate was vetoed by the Turkish government, Iakovos eventually served as an effective advocate of the patriarchate with the Turks.

In 1994, Iakovos chaired a meeting of all the nation's Orthodox bishops in Ligonier, Pennsylvania. The group issued an unprecedented declaration that the process of uniting all Orthodox jurisdictions into a single North American church had already begun. The Ecumenical Patriarchate reacted angrily, viewing the Ligonier Declaration as a threat to its own position in North America. Patriarch Bartholomew announced in 1995 that he had accepted Iakovos's resignation. Iakovos retired reluctantly in 1996.

AHW

Bibliography: George Poulos, *A Breath of God: Portrait of a Prelate, A Biography of Archbishop Iakovos* (Brookline, Mass.: Holy Cross Press, 1984).

Coughlin, Charles E. (1891–1979)

A Roman Catholic priest and radio personality, Charles Edward Coughlin was one of the many people who gained notoriety during the Great Depression with their views on how to solve the country's economic problems.

Born in Hamilton, Ontario, on October 25, 1891, Coughlin grew up in a Catholic

Father Coughlin's social protest during the Great Depression at first won the radio priest wide popularity. He eventually was silenced by the bishop of Detroit for his isolationist, pro–Axis advocacy. *(Library of Congress)*

neighborhood surrounded by Roman Catholic institutions. After attending St. Michael's College, Toronto University (Ph.D., 1911), he taught philosophy and English at Assumption College in Sandwich, Ontario.

Ordained in 1916, he served various pastorates in the Detroit diocese. In 1926, sent to found a parish at Royal Oak, Michigan, he established the Shrine of the Little Flower. A cross-burning on the lawn of his newly completed church, combined with parish financial problems, led Coughlin to turn to radio as a means of explaining Catholicism and soliciting money for his church.

He soon developed a wide following and in 1930 signed a contract with the CBS radio network. With the onset of the Great Depression his talks became increasingly political and his attacks on international bankers, unregulated capitalism, and the wealthy drew a large audience. It is estimated that 40 million listeners tuned in each Sunday afternoon, and Coughlin received more mail than any American of his time. This popularity did not save him in 1931 when his criticism of President Herbert Hoover became too extreme and CBS removed him from the air.

Coughlin responded by developing a network of independent radio stations and in the election of 1932 threw his support behind Franklin Roosevelt. During this time Coughlin's radio talks became increasingly anti-Semitic (see ANTI-SEMITISM) and supportive of the policies of Mussolini and, later, Hitler. In 1934 he organized the National Union for Social Justice, whose principles included the abolition of private banking, the nationalization of major resources, and price controls. Increasingly opposed to Roosevelt, he supported the newly formed Union Party in 1936, vowing that he would leave the air if its nominee, William Lemke, received fewer than 9 million votes.

His 40 million listeners delivered few votes, however, and the Union Party garnered only 1 million ballots. True to his word, Coughlin left the airwaves for seven weeks.

When he returned, he continued his anti-Semitic and anti-Roosevelt diatribes, speaking of a British-Roosevelt-Jewish conspiracy to drag the United States into war.

After the bombing of Pearl Harbor, Coughlin continued his isolationist and pro-Axis views, steadily losing listeners and stations. In 1942, the U.S. government barred his magazine from the mails for violating the Espionage Act, and the bishop of Detroit gave him the choice of keeping silent on social issues or leaving the priesthood. Coughlin chose the former and continued as pastor of the Shrine of the Little Flower until his retirement in 1966. Although he ceased his involvement in politics, he did continue to write pamphlets opposing Communism and, later, Vatican II until his death on October 27, 1979.

EQ

Bibliography: Ronald H. Carpenter, *Father Charles Coughlin: Surrogate Spokesman for the Disaffected* (Westport, Conn.: Greenwood Press, 1998); Albert Fried, *FDR and his Enemies* (New York: St. Martin's Press, 1999); Sheldon Marcus, *Father Coughlin: The Tumultuous Life of the Priest of the Little Flower* (Boston: Little, Brown, 1973); Donald Warren, *Radio Priest: Charles Coughlin, the Father of Hate Radio* (New York: Free Press, 1996).

counterculture   The term *counterculture* refers to a diffuse set of movements, individuals, ideas, and practices that emerged in self-conscious opposition to dominant trends in American culture during the 1960s and early 1970s. With roots in the BEAT MOVEMENT of the 1950s, the counterculture flourished during a period of severe social tensions (see VIETNAM WAR, CIVIL RIGHTS MOVEMENT). While spawning an intense conservative reaction during the 1980s and 1990s (see MORAL MAJORITY), the counterculture left a lasting impact on American values, religious life, politics, and popular culture.

The counterculture was born in the era of affluence following the end of WORLD WAR II. Although the COLD WAR years of the 1950s are often seen as a time of cultural conformity and revived mainstream religion, they also contained a significant current of dissent emerging from various marginal ethnic and racial groups within the culture (see ETHNICITY) as well as intellectuals such as Erich Fromm and Herbert Marcuse, many of them refugees from Nazi Europe, who were dissatisfied with what they saw as the country's shift to suburban conformity. In addition to fueling the growing frustration over continued racial inequality, African-American influence also appeared in the popular culture, particularly in the musical forms of rock and roll and jazz. "Beatniks," such as poet Allen Ginsberg, often combined the language and marijuana-smoking of the "hip" jazz subculture of urban blacks, the intellectual critiques of Western culture coming from psychoanalysis and existentialism, and popularized forms of Asian religion (see WATTS, ALAN WILSON) in an effort to articulate a worldview more satisfying than that available from the cultural mainstream.

In 1964 the dissent percolating through the previous decade exploded, fed by the increased political hostility over civil rights, the emerging "Free Speech Movement" in Berkeley, California, and growing American involvement in Vietnam. Increasingly, young people in their teens and 20s saw themselves separated from their elders by a "generation gap"—making the politically and culturally relevant dividing line in America one of age, not class, race, or religion. Hence the popular slogan: "Don't trust anyone over 30." During the 1960s young people took their awareness of this generation gap in two occasionally related directions. Some university students, inspired directly by the civil rights movement and the critiques of mass society developed by emigré intellectuals such as Herbert Marcuse, turned to politics. Members of the New Left characterized their efforts to oppose the war, support oppressed people in the United States and abroad, and create a new egalitarian politics as laying the groundwork for "revolution." Their youthfulness itself often seemed to guarantee that, unlike the Old Left, they would not falter for lack of will.

The counterculture itself ran along different lines. Its members were of more mixed origins than the New Left, and while equally inclined to see themselves as revolutionary, they tended to regard politics itself as part of the malaise affecting American culture, since politics by nature perpetuates the power of some versus others. By contrast, the counterculture sought harmony and, when not sharing the New Left's disdain for history, turned to THOREAU and WHITMAN rather than Karl Marx for inspiration. Sharing some of the same disdain for a culture based on the "Protestant ethic" as their transcendentalist forebears, members of the counterculture rallied to the cry of "turn on, tune in, drop out." Assuming the larger society would simply disintegrate if left alone, "hippies" sought alternatives to replace the moribund and, above all, "square" beliefs, practices, and values of middle-class American culture.

The counterculture viewed the human self as inherently creative, once freed from the shackles of conformity; thus individuals were encouraged to "do your own thing." Valuing hedonism over hard work, spontaneity over planning, the new over the old, the "intuitive" over the "rational," the counterculture appeared to outsiders as dangerously chaotic, threatening the framework of American society.

While counterculturists themselves agreed with this assessment, there were nevertheless significant patterns that gave the movement coherence, as well as continuity with long-standing trends in American life, in particular the great currents of revival and reform that periodically sweep American life (see REVIVALISM; SOCIAL GOSPEL). For instance, downplaying political change, counterculturists emphasized social transformation through individual self-realization. Whereas earlier reformers had urged individual Americans to take up the Gospel, counterculturists urged the taking of "dope"—psychedelic drugs. To "feed your head," as the Jefferson Airplane sang, would

alter consciousness and pave the way for religious enlightenment. Or in the words of Harvard psychiatrist Timothy Leary, an early experimenter with LSD (lysergic acid diethylamide): "Your only hope is dope." While dope provided the medium for ecstatic religious experience, counterculturists also developed their understanding of reality by generally abandoning the religious traditions of their parents, turning instead to popularized versions of BUDDHISM, HINDUISM, or NATIVE AMERICAN traditions.

In addition to self-realization, the counterculture endeavored to create new forms of communal experience, thereby preparing the way for the dissolution of dominant social institutions. Like the utopian movements of the 19th century (see COMMUNITARIANISM), many "dropped out" completely in order to create a new social order from the ground up, creating communes like The Farm in Tennessee, and "getting back to nature." The communal spirit also animated spontaneous gatherings, such as the San Francisco "Be-ins" held during the 1967 "Summer of Love." Rock concerts, and festivals such as Woodstock in 1969 promoted both communal solidarity and ecstatic experience, which even at the time were characterized as similar to the CAMP MEETINGS of the great 19th-century revivals. As a form of music, rock was seen to have the power to permeate individual senses, and its lyrics provided the counterculture with a language, a set of images, and stories that helped form personal as well as generational identity.

The counterculture's communalism also gave rise to new forms of social and economic relations, some of which paralleled those of earlier utopian movements. Regarding existing middle-class sexual norms as repressive and outmoded, counterculturists advocated sexual liberation and experimentation and the abandonment of the nuclear family, which many saw as an institution based not on love but on property. Sexual pleasure unconstrained could itself lead to social transformation, as suggested by the slogan "Make Love, Not War."

Like the SHAKERS, counterculturists also redefined the meaning of work. Condemning the growth of corporate capitalism, which despoiled the earth and produced mindless jobs for alienated workers, counterculturists instead viewed work as self-expression. Indeed, many ridiculed the "Establishment" view of economic rewards. The Diggers, for instance, a group of street actors based in San Francisco's mecca, the Haight-Ashbury district, viewed love as the basic economic principle. To that end, during 1967's "Summer of Love" they ran free stores, handed out free food, drugs, and money, and fed the large crowds gathered for free rock concerts in Golden Gate Park. Other enterprising counterculturists developed a counter economy, centered around arts and crafts production, health food stores, and cooperatives of all sorts.

The fate of the counterculture is difficult to trace. Hippies themselves mourned "The Death of Hip" at the end of the Summer of Love. Certainly the nation's climate changed. Continuing escalation of the Vietnam War was accompanied by an increasingly hostile domestic scene: racial hostility and riots, "hippie-bashing," and the debacle of the 1968 Democratic National Convention. But in spite of growing violence, the counterculture did not die at the hands of "rednecks" or enraged parents. Many of the central themes of countercultural life—self-expression, harmony with nature, sexual freedom, the monotony of the "treadmill"—began to appear in the everyday concerns of large numbers of Americans. The history of alternative religious groups such as the utopian communities, the Shakers, or the Mormons (see CHURCH OF JESUS CHRIST OF LATTER-DAY SAINTS) suggest that it is difficult to maintain a stance of opposition to the dominant American culture. In part this is due to the power of the idea of individual freedom upon which the culture is based. While the counterculture came into existence as a movement

opposed to the dominant culture, at the same time, its members were basically trying to extend the scope of individual freedom, not replace it.

MG

Bibliography: Todd Gitlin, *The Sixties: Years of Hope, Days of Rage* (New York: Bantam Books, 1987); Timothy Miller, *The Hippies and American Values* (Knoxville: University of Tennessee Press, 1991); Douglas G. Rossinow, *The Politics of Authenticity: Liberalism, Christianity, and the New Left in America* (New York: Columbia University Press, 1998); Theodore Roszak, *The Making of a Counter-Culture* (Garden City, N.Y.: Doubleday, 1969).

Covenant Theology   Covenant, or Federal, Theology (from the Latin *foedus*, "covenant"), was the most original theological doctrine developed by the Puritans (see PURITANISM). Designed to reconcile the doctrine of election with a doctrine of divine justice, covenant theology interpreted God's intercourse with humanity as operating under two covenants, or promises. The first was the "Covenant of Works." Here God offered Adam complete happiness and material fulfillment in return for Adam's perfect obedience to the divine law. With the fall of Adam and Eve, God offered Adam the "Covenant of Grace." This covenant is effected by Christ's complete fulfillment of the divine law. The Covenant of Grace offers salvation on the basis of faith, and God makes it possible for the elect to believe, since in their fallen condition human beings are unable to will that belief themselves.

Although the covenant is at God's initiative and hence a work of divine power, it was accepted by Adam. Divine activity is not cold and impersonal but intimately linked to our acceptance of it in faith and is thereby very personal. One can rely on God to fulfill the divine promise. For this reason one need not fear the whimsy of some immovable power that damns us for no reason.

The Covenant of Works is not abrogated, however, by the Covenant of Grace. It is no longer something the literal fulfillment of which is demanded of us but a goal toward which the saint (the redeemed individual) must constantly strive, and toward which the saint will strive because of her or his being numbered among the elect.

The question remained as to how one could know whether one had received the imputing of grace necessary for salvation. It is one thing to know that God will fulfill God's side of the bargain, another to know that one has done so oneself. The depravity of humanity is such that one "will bend the truth to his mind though he break it," according to Thomas Hooker. The Puritans believed that the human capacity for self-delusion was immense, to think that one is good when one is not is common. How does one know whether she is among the elect or not?

The Puritans never developed a completely satisfactory answer to this question. The answer they provided was intimately related to their views of society and morality. The desire for faith, the striving to fulfill the demands of the Covenant of Works, could be viewed as a demonstration of the presence of grace within an individual. This desire or striving does not bring about the presence of grace but shows that grace is already present. This is at best a partial demonstration of the existence of grace, given humanity's ability for falsehood and hypocrisy. It was, however, useful for determining the obviously degenerate. The hypocrites, even if not discovered by the human community, were known to God.

Covenant Theology was a doctrine of election that avoided antinomian interpretations and their disruptive effects on the community (see ANTINOMIAN CONTROVERSY) while easing the apparent severity and randomness of the doctrine of election. It simultaneously maintained the necessity and priority of divine action in the saving act and room for human activity.

EQ

Bibliography: John D. Eusden, tr. and ed., *The Marrow of Theology: William Ames, 1576–1633* (Philadelphia: Westminster Press, 1968); Kenneth B. Stoever, *"A Faire and Easie Way to Heaven": Covenant Theology and Antinomianism in Early Massachusetts* (Middletown, Conn.: Wesleyan University Press, 1978).

creationism   For more than a century, the teaching of EVOLUTION has been the battleground for a bitter conflict between SCIENCE AND RELIGION in the United States. The creationist, or creation-science, movement regards the theory of biological evolution, popularized in the mid-19th century by Charles Darwin, as antithetical to the biblical idea of creation described in the Old Testament Book of Genesis. According to the creationist view, a literal reading of Genesis 1–2 reveals that God created the universe by fiat in six 24-hour days. Creationists reject any other premise as contrary not only to Christian belief, but also to science itself.

Although the publication of Darwin's *On the Origin of Species* in 1859 sparked this debate, his theories of evolution were not immediately challenged by traditional Christians. Harvard scientist Asa Gray, America's first great proponent of Darwinism, for example, remained an orthodox Congregationalist. He argued that nothing in Darwin's evolutionary scheme necessarily contradicted the possibility of divine guidance over natural processes. Even George Frederick Wright, a colleague of Gray, who in 1912 contributed an essay to the conservative series *The Fundamentals* (see FUNDAMENTALISM), believed that evolution might well be consistent with God's creative designs and a method by which God exerted providential care over history.

Over time, however, the original tolerance Christian conservatives evinced toward Darwinism eroded. During the early 1920s, antievolution articles began to appear in the *Princeton Theological Review,* a journal that had earlier carried cautiously supportive views of evolution. The well-publicized SCOPES TRIAL of 1925, moreover, also served to focus attention on the question of evolution. The dismissive reaction of many American agnostics to William Jennings Bryan's defense of the Book of Genesis forced conservatives to choose sides in the debate. And in 1926, George McCready Price, a Seventh-day Adventist who had earlier inspired Bryan's questioning of Darwinism, declared that belief in evolution was essentially atheistic. Price and his successors helped devise "flood geology," the theory that all plants and animals were created in the six days of Genesis, with the fossils being formed during Noah's flood.

Advocates of the creationist position have argued in recent years that biological and geological evolution are unproved hypotheses with no basis in scientific fact. Henry M. Morris, a close friend of Price, helped found the Institute for Creation Research in 1972. While Morris's concerns clearly were as much theological as scientific (he blamed Satan for inspiring the idea of evolution), his principal attacks against evolution were based on scientific grounds. The public school edition of his *Scientific Creationism* (1974), for instance, discussed the question of creation without reference to the Bible or any other religious text. Morris offered as an alternative to evolution the theory that the universe is only 10,000 years old. Although geological findings would seem to undermine this thesis, Morris argued that a universal flood might just as well explain the observable data.

Scholars of fundamentalism point to two main intellectual principles supporting the creationist viewpoint: an inerrantist (see INERRAN-CY) interpretation of the Bible and acceptance of the Scottish Common Sense philosophical system (see SCOTTISH COMMON SENSE REALISM). As Morris insisted in his aptly titled article "The Bible *Is* a Textbook of Science," anyone who wishes to know about creation ought to look first in the Bible, which is the "sole source of true information" and the "textbook on the science of Creation." The inerrantist view is based on the belief that, since the Bible is the very Word of God, it must be accurate in all

matters, in science and history as well as in theological doctrine. When combined with the rationalism of the Common Sense philosophy (an 18th-century philosophical school that emphasized how supernatural truth is discoverable through empirical study), inerrancy leads believers to great intellectual confidence. In the minds of creationists, as in the minds of fundamentalists generally, the Bible is a book of facts, a collection of precise propositions about reality and a dependable repository of scientific truths.

Despite considerable resistance from the regular scientific community and from most mainline American denominations, creationists won a number of legislative victories for their teaching. In 1981 both the Arkansas and the Louisiana legislatures enacted laws that would have given equal treatment in the public schools to "evolution science" and to "creation science." The Arkansas law countered the standard evolutionary view of natural development by positing "a relatively recent inception of the Earth and of living things." When opponents of those state laws argued that they were introducing religious beliefs into the curriculum of public schools, the courts concurred and struck down the laws as unconstitutional.

Creationists continue to insist that what they teach is essentially a scientific premise, not a religious view. They emphasize that since hundreds of scientists with academic doctorates are part of their movement, creation science, though certainly debatable, cannot be dismissed as altogether unscientific. Furthermore, an important result of this controversy has been the increasing awareness among Americans that Darwinism is only a hypothesis, albeit a favored one, about the origins of life on earth.

Following these defeats in court, the creationists developed a strategy to influence education at the local level by winning election to local and state school boards. Perhaps the most successful example of this was their attainment of a majority of the state school board in

Kansas. From this position they managed to remove evolution as a required curriculum topic in that state's schools. The ridicule heaped on the state nationally and internationally led to a backlash, and in the 2000 elections enough of the creationist members were defeated to result in a 7-3 majority in favor of restoring evolution to the curriculum.

Despite the almost universal opposition to creationism in the scientific community, creationists continue to insist that their position is science, not religion. They claim that hundreds of scientists with academic doctorates are a part of their movement, a claim that is minimized by the fact that the overwhelming majority of their scientists are engineers, computer specialists, and physicians, along with the occasional chemist. They number few biologists among their members.

In the more than 70 years since the Scopes trial, the ongoing fight over evolution is a reminder of the power of religious stories on people's lives. It also demonstrates that religious controversies can and do reappear, even when they were thought to be solved.

GHS, Jr./ELQ

Bibliography: Tim M. Berra, *Evolution and the Myth of Creationism: A Basic Guide to the Facts in the Evolution Debate* (Stanford, Calif.: Stanford University Press, 1990); Ronald L. Numbers, *The Creationists* (New York: Knopf, 1992); Robert T. Pennock, *Tower of Babel: The Evidence Against the New Creationism* (Cambridge, Mass.: MIT Press, 1999); George W. Webb, *The Evolution Controversy in America* (Lexington: University of Kentucky Press, 1994).

Crummell, Alexander (1819–1898)

Of the many notable 19th-century African Americans bypassed by historians, Episcopal clergyman Alexander Crummell is perhaps the most fascinating. In his abilities, and in the tragedies of his life, he is reminiscent of W. E. B. DU BOIS, who in many ways continued Crummell's legacy.

Born in 1819 in New York City of an African-born father and a free-black mother,

Crummell grew up in an African-American community that valued both education and religion. After distinguishing himself in elementary and high school, Crummell was sent to the newly opened Noyes Academy in Canaan, New York. Angered by the presence of black students and the school's abolitionist leanings, the local farmers hitched the school building to a team of 90 oxen and dragged it into a nearby swamp, ending its attempt to integrate education.

The abolitionist dream did not die, however, and the next year (1836) Crummell entered Oneida Academy (Whitesboro, New York), run by the abolitionist Beriah Green. After graduating in 1839, he applied for admission to the General Theological Seminary in New York City to prepare for the Episcopal priesthood, only to be rejected because of his race. Disheartened, he persevered, studying privately with clergymen in Providence and Boston.

Ordained in 1842, Crummell served in Providence until 1844, when he applied for admission to the diocese of Philadelphia. There the bishop refused his application because of his color. Stung by this refusal, Crummell left for New York City, where he organized a congregation among working-class blacks. Although he formerly shunned political activity, he became active in the Negro Convention Movement and abolitionist activities, where he was closely associated with Frederick Douglass.

Encouraged by friends to travel to England to solicit funds for a church building, Crummell left America for a quarter-century. He arrived in 1848 to an England that welcomed and honored him. For three years he traveled and preached, raising money for his church. In 1851, with the patronage of Sir William Dodie, he entered Queen's College, Cambridge, graduating in 1853.

Rather than return to America, Crummell looked to his ancestral home of Africa and sailed for Liberia. He founded several churches throughout that country, and soon expanded his work to include education, becoming master of the country's leading high school in 1858 and a professor at the newly formed Liberia College in 1861. In great demand as a speaker for religious and national events, Crummell—who viewed himself as a public teacher—used these occasions to speak for racial pride and moral strength. However, Crummell's racial views antagonized Liberia's caste-conscious mulatto elite, who looked down on African-born and darker-skinned Liberians. When a coup restored the mulattoes to power, Crummell was threatened and his son jailed. Disillusioned, he returned to America in 1873.

Settling in Washington, D.C., he founded St. Luke's Church, where he served until 1894 as senior minister. Until his death in September 1898, Crummell's major concerns were the role of blacks within the Episcopal Church and the development of a black intellectual elite. To further these goals he founded the Conference of Church Workers among Colored People (1883) and the American Negro Academy (1897). In his demand for educated blacks to lead in the redemption of the race, Crummell anticipated Du Bois's call for an educated class that pursued knowledge not for its own purposes but with a practical intent—the elevation of the race.

Crummell established an organized African-American presence within the Episcopal Church and supported the expansion of black churches and priests. He also created a tradition of black scholarship in the United States through the formation of the American Negro Academy. Finally, Crummell was a "public theologian," calling blacks to racial pride and moral strength, while demanding that whites recognize that racism violated their own higher religious and political values.

(See also AFRICAN-AMERICAN RELIGION.)

EQ

Bibliography: Alexander Crummell, *Destiny and Race: Selected Writings, 1840–1898* (Amherst: Uni-

versity of Massachusetts Press, 1992); W. E. B. Du Bois, "Of Alexander Crummell," in *The Souls of Black Folk* (New York: New American Library, 1961); Gregory U. Rigsby, *Alexander Crummell in Nineteenth Century Pan-African Thought* (New York: Greenwood Press, 1987); Otey M. Scruggs, *We the Children of Africa in the Land: Alexander Crummell* (Washington, D.C.: Howard University, Department of History, 1972).

cults See ANTICULT MOVEMENT.

Cumberland Presbyterian Church See PRESBYTERIANISM.

Cushing, Richard James (1895–1970)

Perhaps no one embodied the nature of American ROMAN CATHOLICISM, at least in its Irish and northeastern version, than Richard James Cushing, archbishop of Boston from 1944 until his death on November 2, 1970. At ease both with his faith and with American society, Cushing was a jovial figure whose free-and-easy air attracted friends and admirers among all classes and religions.

Born in Boston to working-class Irish immigrant parents on August 24, 1895, he early developed the inclination toward the priesthood. After two years at Boston College (1913–1915) he transferred to St. John's Seminary in Brighton, Massachusetts, graduating in 1921. Following his ordination in that year he took over a parish but was transferred to the Boston office of the Society for the Propagation of the Faith, becoming its director (and a monsignor) in 1928. Cushing, long interested in foreign missions, soon turned the Boston office of the society into the most active and effective in the nation. His success as an administrator led to his appointment as auxiliary bishop of Boston in 1939. In 1944 he succeeded Cardinal William O'Connell as archbishop of Boston.

Cushing's episcopacy was a marked contrast from that of his predecessor. Where O'Connell had been an aristocratic and urbane

Catholic separatist, Cushing was an informal man of the people who took pride in his humble origins. No separatist, he spoke in Protestant churches as well as synagogues, and was responsible for the establishment of a Catholic chapel at predominantly Jewish Brandeis University, to the horror of many Catholic conservatives. He even arranged for the midnight mass at St. John's Seminary to be televised, with a commentary, so that non-Catholics could understand what was happening.

Although often criticized for his ecumenicity, he refused to back down, declaring in a speech at Harvard in 1963, "I'm all for Catholics being identified with Protestants and Jews . . . in every possible friendly way. Nobody is asking them to deny their faith and they shouldn't be asking anybody to deny their faith." He pressed these views during the second Vatican Council (see VATICAN COUNCIL II) where, although his weak Latin led him to absent himself from most deliberations, he was deeply involved in the discussions leading up to the declaration on religious liberty and on Roman Catholic relations to other faiths.

Cushing welcomed the results of Vatican II as long overdue, seeing them as a legitimate memorial to John XXIII, with whom he identified. He was less favorably disposed toward Paul VI and felt that the encyclical *Humane Vitae* was an unfortunate public proclamation about matters of private conscience.

Despite this, his responses to the council were as contradictory as his responses to other political and social occurrences. A longtime member of the NAACP, he shared the view of his fellow Catholic, J. Edgar Hoover, that Martin Luther KING, Jr., was a dangerous subversive. Outspoken in his support for labor unions, he also supported the John Birch Society due to its strong anti-Communism.

As a bishop, Cushing greatly expanded the work within the diocese. Eighty churches were built during his episcopate, along with three colleges, the first airport chapel, a seminary for older men seeking ordination, and the first diocesan center for radio and television in the country. His interest in missions continued unabated. He founded the Missionary Society of St. James the Apostle and allowed his diocesan priests to serve in South America.

His greatest concern was for the poor and the weak. The diocese built six new hospitals during his reign, and Cushing made frequent pastoral visits to Boston's jails. In 1947 he established St. Coletta's School for mentally retarded children. This was his special project, and he arranged to be buried on its grounds. Not one for ceremony, during his visits to homes for the elderly he gleefully joined in the singing or dancing. Cushing saw himself as one of the people, and he took great pride in his free and easy interchange with the poor and the weak.

Although he identified with the working-class Irish of Boston, his influence extended into the ranks of the rich and powerful as well. He often called upon Joseph Kennedy to aid the diocese's fund-raising and became friendly with the young John F. Kennedy. When Kennedy announced his candidacy for president, Cushing, although doubtful that the United States was ready for a Catholic president, assisted the campaign. Here Cushing asserted his most common theme, the compatibility of American values and Catholicism, as well as the inviolability of the human conscience, asserting in one statement that, "Whatever may be the custom elsewhere, the American tradition, of which Catholics form so loyal a part, is satisfied simply to call to public attention moral questions with their implications, and leave to the conscience of the people the specific political decision which comes in the act of voting."

Cushing's later years were difficult ones. Cancer, asthma, and ulcers left him drained and weak. He also watched as the numerous institutions he had built pushed the diocese into financial decline. Recognizing the need for new leadership, he resigned in September 1970 and died shortly thereafter on November 2, 1970.

Cushing's significance for the American church was twofold. First was his leadership in calling for the Church to recognize that it lived in a dynamic world to which it must respond. Certainly the Church had its unchanging essentials, "but beyond these," he said in 1961, "there must always be innovation, enterprise, new vision." Before leaving to attend the 1963 conclave to elect a successor to John XXIII (Cushing had been made a cardinal in 1958) he admitted that the Church had not always recognized that fact, expressing his desire that "the new Pope will be living in the twentieth century, and will think the twentieth century, and not the fourteenth or sixteenth century."

Cushing stood in the line of earlier bishops, most notably John CARROLL and James GIBBONS, who proclaimed the compatibility of Catholicism and American political values. The United States had a distinctive political and cultural tradition to which European models did not apply and that held that a person's Catholicism in no way affected her or his ability to be a good citizen or a servant of the general welfare. Cushing felt comfortable around non-Catholics and did much to break down the remaining elements of suspicion that they harbored toward the Roman Church (see ANTI-CATHOLICISM).

Personable, warm, and unpretentious, forward-looking but not cerebral, Cushing had the personality to make American Catholics confront the realities of the time and to cause non-Catholics to see the human, nonthreatening face of the Church. For these reasons he was one of its most popular and loved representatives.

EQ

Bibliography: John Henry Cutler, *Cardinal Cushing of Boston* (New York: Hawthorn Books, 1970); Joseph Dever, *Cushing of Boston: A Candid Portrait* (Boston: Bruce Humphries, 1965); John H. Fenton, *Salt of the Earth: An Informal Portrait of Richard Cardinal Cushing* (New York: Coward-McCann, 1965).

D

Dabney, Robert Lewis (1820–1898)

Robert Lewis Dabney was a Presbyterian minister, theologian, and one of the most articulate defenders of the defeated South in the post–Civil War period. Chosen during the war to be chief of staff to Confederate General Thomas J. "Stonewall" Jackson, a pious Presbyterian, Dabney published the first major biography of Jackson.

Dabney was born in Louisa County, Virginia, on March 5, 1820. He was educated at Hampden-Sydney College (1836–1837), the University of Virginia (1842), and Union Theological Seminary, Virginia (1846). After serving as pastor of the Presbyterian church in Tinkling Spring, Virginia, and as headmaster of a classical academy, Dabney returned in 1853 to Union Seminary, where he taught for the next 30 years. Although he had cautioned political moderation prior to the outbreak of the Civil War, Dabney became a strong advocate of the Confederacy once the fighting began. He was present as the chaplain of a Virginia regiment at the first battle of Manassas in 1861 and served for a few months in 1862 as Jackson's chief of staff. After Jackson's death in 1863, Dabney gathered materials for his biography. *The Life and Campaigns of Lieut.-Gen. Thomas J. Jackson,* published in 1866, celebrated both the military and the religious virtues of the southern military leader.

After the war ended in 1865 and for the rest of his long life, Dabney kept alive the South's LOST CAUSE MYTH. In *A Defence of Vir-ginia, and Through Her of the South* (1867), he defended slavery and the Confederate war effort and reminded his people of the miseries they were suffering at the hands of Yankee "invaders." He was a special critic of the emerging industrial capitalism of the "New South," a trend popularized by Atlanta editor Henry Grady and Methodist educator and minister Atticus G. HAYGOOD. In a commencement address at Hampden-Sydney in June 1882, Dabney argued that the outcome of the war was a providential tragedy, and he lamented the fact that many were seeking to remake the South with a materialistic northern mold. He feared that southerners would make temporal wealth their "idol, the all in all of sectional greatness," thus leading their region and its people into the worship of false gods.

Dabney's reputation as a theological scholar and polemicist brought him a place of prominence in his denomination. Known for his conservative CALVINISM, in his best-known academic work, *The Sensualist Philosophy of the Nineteenth Century* (1875), Dabney attacked various forms of modernist (see MODERNISM, PROTESTANT) theology. Consistently pro-southern even in church debates, Dabney also opposed all efforts to reunite southern Presbyterianism with the church in the North.

Dabney fell ill with bronchitis in 1882, and poor health forced him to leave Virginia the next year. He assumed the professorship of moral philosophy at the University of Texas in 1883 and helped found Austin Theological

Seminary, serving on the faculty there until just before his death. Although he had entirely lost his eyesight by 1890, Dabney continued to lecture from memory for several more years. He died in Victoria, Texas, on January 3, 1898.

GHS, Jr.

Bibliography: Thomas Cary Johnson, *The Life and Letters of Robert Lewis Dabney* (Richmond: Presbyterian Committee of Publication, 1903); David H. Overy, "When the Wicked Beareth Rule: A Southern Critique of Industrial America," *Journal of Presbyterian History* 48 (1970), 130–42.

Dalai Lama (1935–)

Dalai Lama is, strictly speaking, a title rather than a proper name. The phrase means "teacher whose wisdom is as wide as the ocean," and it refers to the spiritual leader of what is commonly called the Yellow Hat sect of Tibetan BUDDHISM. Since the 17th century, however, Dalai Lamas have also served as the political rulers of Tibet. Followers view them as incarnations of Avalokiteshvara, the bodhisattva ("enlightenment being") of compassion. Each successive Dalai Lama, moreover, is believed to be a reincarnation of his predecessor.

The current Dalai Lama, the 14th, was born Llamo Dhondrub in 1935 into a peasant home in Taktser, a village in eastern Tibet. At the age of two he was recognized as the reincarnation of the 13th Dalai Lama and given the name of Tenzin Gyatso. At six, he began his education under the tutelage of Tibetan monks. In 1950, when he was only 15, the Chinese army invaded Tibet, and the Dalai Lama assumed his current duties as the spiritual and political leader of Tibet. In 1959, the Chinese army put down a large independence demonstration in the Tibetan capital of Lhasa, and the Dalai Lama fled into exile in India. Roughly 100,000 followers eventually joined him, and together they established a Tibetan government in exile in Dharamsala, India. For his nonviolent struggle for the survival of the Tibetan people and the preservation of Tibetan culture, the Dalai Lama was awarded the Nobel Peace Prize in 1989.

In the United States, the Dalai Lama plays two key roles. First, he personifies Buddhism. Just as SWAMI VIVEKANANDA exemplified HINDUISM in the United States a century ago, the Dalai Lama is the most famous Buddhist in contemporary America. As recognizable as he is revered, he is known and respected by Buddhists and non-Buddhists alike. Second, the Dalai Lama personifies the Tibetan struggle for autonomy. His charismatic personality has inspired many Americans to embrace not only Buddhism but also the cause of Tibet. That cause has found institutional form in the United States in organizations such as Students for a Free Tibet, a campus-based grassroots movement, and the Milarepa Fund, an organization led by Adam Yauch, a musician with the hip-hop group the Beastie Boys (and a Buddhist himself).

The leader of the Tibetans in exile who fled the Chinese invasion, the Dalai Lama has been a leading advocate for Buddhism, peace, and ecology. *(Photo credit: Dan Farber for The Way of Freedom, HarperSanFrancisco)*

Though shunned for decades by American leaders (who have never recognized Tibet as a sovereign state), the Dalai Lama has met with Presidents George H. W. Bush and Bill Clinton and addressed the U.S. Congress. He has also been active in the United States in Buddhist-Christian and Buddhist-Jewish dialogue. Among his many bestselling books are *The Good Heart: A Buddhist Perspective on the Teachings of Jesus* (1996) and *Ethics for the New Millennium* (1999).

SRP

Bibliography: Roger Hicks and Ngakpa Chogyam, *Great Ocean: An Authorized Biography of the Buddhist Monk Tenzin Gyatso, His Holiness the Fourteenth Dalai Lama* (New York: Penguin, 1990); His Holiness the Dalai Lama, *Freedom in Exile: The Autobiography of the Dalai Lama* (New York: HarperCollins, 1990); Sidney Piburn and Claiborne Pell, eds., *The Dalai Lama, a Policy of Kindness: An Anthology of Writings by and About the Dalai Lama* (Ithaca, N.Y.: Snow Lion Publications, 1990); http://www.tibet.com (Tibetan government in exile).

Daly, Mary (1928–   )

Mary Daly is America's most widely known and controversial feminist philosopher and theologian. A prolific writer, Daly has published many books that offer sharp criticisms of patriarchal religions and attempt to construct not only a new post-patriarchal feminist theology but also a new language in which to conduct that enterprise.

Born on October 16, 1928, in Schenectady, New York, Mary Daly attended Catholic schools in a working-class neighborhood. She attended the College of Saint Rose in Albany and received an M.A. in English at the Catholic University of America in Washington, D.C. She earned three Ph.D.s: in religion at St. Mary's College (1954) and in theology (1963) and philosophy (1965) at the University of Fribourg. Her dissertation in philosophy is entitled *Natural Knowledge of God in the Philosophy of Jacques Maritain*.

In 1966 Daly began teaching in the Theology Department at Boston College. She was an assistant professor from 1966 to 1969, when she was named an associate professor. She became the first chair of the Women and Religion section of the American Academy of Religion in 1971. Despite the support of professional societies and much student protest, she was not granted promotion to full professorship at Boston College. Daly was forced into retirement in 1999 after a male student insisted on enrolling in one of her courses and Daly insisted on an all-female class. A legal fight between Daly and Boston College ensued and was settled in 2001.

Since the publication of her *The Church and the Second Sex* in 1968, which criticized sexism in the Christian church but did not aim to move beyond Christianity, Daly has been at the forefront of FEMINIST THEOLOGY and philosophy. Daly was the first woman to be invited to preach at Harvard University's Memorial Chapel, but in 1971 she and others walked out of that church, calling for an exodus from patriarchal religion. This event marked the beginning of Daly's post-Christian work as well as the initiation of "sisterhood as antichurch," a term which she later changed to "Sisterhood as Cosmic Covenant" in *Beyond God the Father: Toward a Philosophy of Women's Liberation* (1973).

In addition to developing her own feminist theology, Daly has developed her own feminist vocabulary, most notably in the *Websters' First New Intergalactic Wickedary of the English Language* (with Jane Caputi, 1987). Daly has also been at the forefront in raising lesbian concerns in feminist theologizing.

Mary Daly continues to be a major force in religious studies. Her autobiography, *Outercourse*, shows the importance to feminist theology of the narrative retelling of women's experiences. In *Quintessence*, Daly offers a radical, feminist philosophical response to the millennial world of genetics, cloning, and environmental destruction.

TP

Bibliography: Mary Daly, *Beyond God the Father* (Boston: Beacon Press, 1973); ———, *The Church and the Second Sex* (New York: Harper and Row, 1968); ———, *Outercourse: The Be-Dazzling Voyage* (San Francisco: HarperSanFrancisco, 1992); ———, *Quintessence—Realizing the Archaic Future: A Radical Elemental Feminist Manifesto* (Boston: Beacon Press, 1998); Sarah Lucia Hoagland and Marilyn Frye, eds., *Feminist Interpretations of Mary Daly (Re-Reading the Canon)* (University Park: Pennsylvania State University Press, 2000).

Darby, John Nelson   See DISPENSATIONALISM.

Darwinism   See CREATIONISM; EVOLUTION; SCIENCE AND RELIGION.

Davies, Samuel (1723–1761)   Samuel Davies was a Presbyterian minister, educator, and advocate of religious freedom before the AMERICAN REVOLUTION. He was instrumental in establishing the Hanover (Virginia) presbytery in 1755, his denomination's first association of churches in the South. A preacher of great power, Davies was a successful evangelist during the GREAT AWAKENING of the mid-18th century.

Davies was born near Summit Ridge, Delaware, on November 3, 1723. After studying at Samuel Blair's academy in Pennsylvania, he was licensed to preach in 1746. In 1748 he moved to Hanover County, where, as a dissenting clergyman in the midst of Virginia's Anglican religious establishment, he faced severe restrictions on his ministerial activities. At that time, pious men and women whose religious needs were not met by the services of the Church of England could gather only in private at their homes. Davies fought a lengthy legal battle on behalf of the seven Virginia Presbyterian churches he served. Arguing that the Toleration Act of 1689, which permitted freedom of worship in Great Britain, applied to the British colonies as well, Davies eventually won a favorable ruling in 1755. After that date, Presbyterians were free to organize their own churches.

Davies traveled throughout Virginia to help build up Presbyterianism in the colony. His sympathies lay with the pro-revival faction within his denomination, and his sermons contributed to the final, southern phase of the Great Awakening. Davies attracted such fame as an evangelist that he was elected to the presidency of the College of New Jersey (now Princeton University) in 1759. His move to New Jersey, however, left no educated Presbyterian minister in Virginia, a fact that caused his church to enter a period of decline.

In poor health, Davies served only briefly at Princeton. He died on February 4, 1761, just 18 months after assuming the office of college president.

GHS, Jr.

Bibliography: George W. Pilcher, *Samuel Davies: Apostle of Dissent in Colonial Virginia* (Knoxville: University of Tennessee Press, 1971).

Davis, Andrew Jackson (1826–1910) The career of Andrew Jackson Davis as the greatest philosopher of American SPIRITUALISM began when, at the age of 17, he attended a lecture by an itinerant mesmerist and discovered that he possessed the power of clairvoyance. In 1844, Davis went into a hypnotic trance and learned that he could diagnose and cure diseases, converse with the spirits of deceased luminaries such as Emmanuel Swedenborg (see SWEDENBORGIANISM), and even travel to spiritual worlds. Dubbed the "Poughkeepsie Seer," Davis became America's first and most successful professional medium. Through voluminous writings and an occult healing practice, he helped to precipitate the Spiritualist boom of the mid-19th century.

Born in Blooming Grove, New York, to a family of farmers, weavers, and shoemakers, Davis received little formal education. So he attributed his insights into higher truths not to his own work but to the influence of spirits. Davis first outlined his beliefs and practices in a series of lectures that he delivered, supposedly while in a trance. Those lectures were published in 1847 as Davis's first book, *The Principles of Nature, Her Divine Revelation and a Voice to Mankind.* Davis published many more books, including his five-volume magnum opus, *The Great Harmonia* (1850–1855). His writings also appeared in *The Univercoelum* (1847–1849), a New York weekly friendly to Spiritualism. In addition to writing and lecturing, Davis practiced medicine. He received a medical degree from the United States Medical College in New York City in 1886.

Although Davis was undoubtedly the most important thinker in 19th-century American Spiritualism, his tendencies toward mysticism and philosophy distinguished him from many of his fellow Spiritualists, who lacked interest in theorizing about their experiences and claimed to mistrust anything that they could not demonstrate empirically.

Davis's "harmonial philosophy," which drew on Swedenborgianism, MESMERISM, and other romantic currents, postulated six ascending spheres of existence. According to Davis, humans progressed onward and upward through these spheres until they met God, whom Davis equated with the power of love and wisdom that resided in the Great Celestial Center. This divine power manifested itself, he believed, in all human beings, who were in his view only emanations of the Divine Mind.

Davis demonstrated his kinship with other philosophers of "harmonial religion" by rejecting the reality of both evil and sin. Davis's cosmic optimism was most apparent in his theory of "Summerland," a heavenly abode where people go after death and where the season is always summer.

Davis's theories were not entirely otherworldly. Like other universal reformers of his time, Davis believed that the transformation of individuals would result in sweeping social reforms. Ever the optimist, he looked forward to a utopian social order in which all plants, animals, and human beings would work together harmoniously for their common benefit.

Late in his life Davis ran a bookstore and conducted a private medical practice in Boston. He died in 1910, but his legacy lives on in 21st-century America in the popular practice of channeling the spirits of the dead.

SRP

Bibliography: Andrew Jackson Davis, *The Principles of Nature, Her Divine Revelation and a Voice to Mankind* (New York: S.S. Lyon & W. Fishbough, 1847); Robert W. Delp, "Andrew Jackson Davis: Prophet of American Spiritualism," *Journal of American History* 54 (June 1967) 43–56.

Day, Dorothy (1897–1980)

One of the most fascinating people in American religious history, Dorothy Day stood in a long line of American converts to ROMAN CATHOLICISM whose faith and life made a lasting impact on that church and on society. As the driving force in the CATHOLIC WORKER MOVEMENT, she inspired many, both Catholics and non-Catholics, to an active Christianity devoted to the poor and to peace.

The third of five children of John and Grace (Satterlee) Day, Dorothy Day was born in Brooklyn, New York, on November 8, 1897. Her father's work took the family to San Francisco in 1903, and the 1906 earthquake drove them to Chicago in 1907. While living in Chicago, the sensitive and studious Day read Upton Sinclair, whose graphic descriptions of work in the Chicago stockyards moved her deeply.

A Hearst scholarship sent her to the University of Illinois, Urbana, in 1914. While there, her radical politics and unconventional lifestyle increasingly alienated her from her family, and Day had to work as a maid to support herself. Often she was poorly clothed and hungry. These difficulties did little to stifle her intellect and much to deepen her compassion for the poor and unfortunate.

Leaving the university in 1916, she moved to New York, where she became a journalist. She worked on the *Call, Masses,* and *Liberator,* all leading left-wing magazines. Active in radical politics and living a rather bohemian life,

Day became pregnant and had an illegal abortion in 1919. These personal upheavals—along with political turmoil, including the crackdown on radicals during World War I—distressed Day greatly. The source for her only novel, *The Eleventh Virgin* (1924), they drove her to greater introspection.

Drawn increasingly toward religion despite herself, she had her daughter Tamar (born in 1927) baptized despite the objections of Tamar's father. Required to take religious instruction as part of Tamar's baptism, Day began to consider being baptized herself, to which she submitted on December 28, 1927. The long struggle she experienced over this process of conversion is described in her book, *The Long Loneliness*, which stands alongside Thomas MERTON's *The Seven Storey Mountain* as a classic American Catholic conversion narrative.

While her conversion brought Day internal peace, it led to her estrangement from her friends, who viewed religion as an oppressive superstition. Neither was she at ease among her new community. Day's political ideas made her uncomfortable with what she saw as the Church's complacency with an unjust social order. The ability to merge her politics and her faith occurred after a meeting with Peter Maurin. A French-born Catholic philosopher, Maurin called for a process of social reconstruction known as the "green revolution." Based upon communal farming and the establishment of houses of hospitality for the urban poor, this revolution was driven by the idea of correlating the spiritual with the material. Those concerned with the poor were to become one with them, not doing *for* the poor and weak but *with* the poor and weak.

These ideas found their voice in the newspaper Maurin and Day founded in 1933. The *Catholic Worker* expressed the ideas of economic justice, pacifism, and racial equality that were the hallmark of Maurin's and Day's thought. In the following year they founded the first house of hospitality, St. Joseph's, in New York City. This was followed by houses in other cities, as well as communal farms where volunteers lived lives of voluntary poverty with the poor and homeless.

During World War II the movement suffered as a result of its PACIFISM, which cost it much support. Day herself was repeatedly jailed for refusing to participate in New York's compulsory civil defense drills. The Catholic Worker movement supported conscientious objectors and offered alternative service at one of its farms in upstate New York.

Until her death on November 29, 1980, Day continued her struggle for a just social order, a struggle rooted in her belief in divine love as the ultimate transfiguring value. She believed that by literally living out Christ's command to love one's neighbor, the world would be transformed. Day's books, articles, and speeches took the message of the Catholic Worker movement to nearly all American parishes, and there were few areas where these views had not touched some members. Her influence reached Protestants and atheists as well. At the time of her death, Day was revered as America's most influential Roman Catholic voice calling for peace and social transformation.

EQ

Bibliography: Dorothy Day, *The Long Loneliness: An Autobiography* (New York: Harper & Brothers, 1952); Anne Klejment and Alice Klejment, *Dorothy Day and The Catholic Worker: A Bibliography and Index* (New York: Garland Press, 1986); Mel Piehl, *Breaking Bread: The Catholic Worker and the Origin of Catholic Radicalism in America* (Philadelphia: Temple University Press, 1982); Nancy L. Roberts, *Dorothy Day and the "Catholic Worker"* (Albany: SUNY Press, 1985).

"death of God" theology In April 1966 a a cover of *Time* magazine was headlined "Is God Dead?" Needless to say, such a public question met with much consternation and dismay, for it identified one of the most extreme, misunderstood, and perplexing periods in

20th-century theology, the so-called radical or "death of God" theology. Never a coherent movement, in fact many of those associated with it meant different things by the term, this theological phase was an attempt to take seriously the contemporary situation in light of the work of the century's leading theologians.

The roots of "death of God" theology lay in 20th-century NEO-ORTHODOXY, specifically the work of Karl Barth, Dietrich Bonhoeffer, and Paul TILLICH. Although all three would have disavowed the use put to their thought, radical theology took seriously Barth's claim that Christianity was not a religion, Tillich's claim that God does not exist as a being, and Bonhoeffer's cryptic comments about the role of Christianity in a "world come of age."

Theologians such as Gabriel Vahanian, Paul Van Buren, and William Hamilton wondered how humanity in the last half of the 20th century could relate to God when humanity had lost all sense of transcendence. For Vahanian, whose 1961 book *The Death of God* gave the movement its name, this was *the* issue. People whose lives were void of any feeling of the transcendent, who lived in societies with no underlying religious significance, and who existed in historical time without any sense of providence were not people capable of experiencing the divine presence. For such a people and society God was effectively dead. While Vahanian never concluded that God did not exist, he did believe that unless there were a radical transformation of Western culture, a transcendent God could not be a living, vibrant reality.

Others, however, were not so reticent. Paul Van Buren and William Hamilton took the fact of Western society's absence of transcendental meaning as determinative rather than descriptive. For them, the absence of transcendental values in society demonstrated that there was no God. In place of God, however, was the true humanity of the person Jesus, whose all-embracing love—demonstrated by his treatment of others and his death on the cross—showed us how we should live.

Richard Rubenstein, emerging out of the Jewish tradition, also used the existing historical context as the basis for his conclusion that neither God nor religion as traditionally understood were possible. The evil wrought by the Nazis in the Holocaust prevented one from proclaiming the existence of God and God's covenant with the Jewish people. It also prevented one from believing that individual and social life have any meaning beyond that which individuals and groups create themselves. Any meaning to be found in the life of the Jewish people must be made by the Jewish people themselves in the act of creating their own state and culture.

Perhaps the most extreme and undoubtedly the most flamboyant of the radical theologians was Thomas J. J. Altizer. In his book *The Gospel of Christian Atheism* (1966), Altizer drew on the German philosopher Georg W. F. Hegel to develop a radical incarnational theology. Altizer took seriously the traditional Christian claim that in Jesus, God had become man, or in Hegelian terms, the Universal had become specific and concrete. Once the Universal is concretized, however, it loses its Universal character. God become human in the world is no longer God as transcendent reality independent of the world. At the crucifixion, God as God truly dies. In this act, however, we are shown how to live out our lives in the world.

The extreme language used by some of these theologians and the sensational coverage they received in the popular press gave them a notoriety not often accorded to serious theological reflection. While as a major mode of theological development the "death of God" theology was short-lived, the challenges it presented increased theological reflection on doctrines of God, the nature of the incarnation, and the implications of social realities for doing theology.

EQ

Bibliography: Thomas J. J. Altizer, *The Gospel of Christian Atheism* (Philadelphia: Westminster Press, 1966); ——— and William Hamilton, *Rad-*

ical Theology and the Death of God (Indianapolis: Bobbs-Merrill, 1966); Langdon Gilkey, *Naming the Whirlwind: The Renewal of God-Language* (Indianapolis: Bobbs-Merrill, 1969); Richard Rubenstein, *After Auschwitz: Radical Theology and Contemporary Judaism* (Indianapolis: Bobbs-Merrill, 1966); Paul Van Buren, *The Secular Meaning of the Gospel* (New York: Macmillan, 1963); Gabriel Vahanian, *The Death of God: The Culture of Our Post-Christian Era* (New York: G. Braziller, 1961).

deep ecology   Norwegian philosopher Arne Naess (b. 1912) coined the term "deep ecology" in a 1973 article, "The Shallow and the Deep, Long-Range Ecology Movements." The phrase has since become the most widely accepted label for an important branch of the global environmental movement.

Deep ecologists trace their sentiments to personal experiences of "ecological consciousness," which they describe as an intuitive, affective perception of the sacredness and interconnectedness of all life. A person who has experienced the "ecological self" transcends the limitations of ego, viewing the self not as separate from and superior to all else but rather as a small part of the divine cosmos. From this perspective, all life and even ecosystems themselves have inherent value, even if they are not plainly useful to humans. Deep ecologists credit Aldo Leopold with expressing this idea succinctly in his landmark "Land Ethic" essay, published posthumously in *A Sand County Almanac* (1949). There Leopold argued that humans ought to act only in ways designed to protect the long-term flourishing of all ecosystems. Deep ecologists now call this perspective *ecocentrism* (or sometimes *biocentrism*) and trace today's environmental crises to anthropocentrism: the perspective in which nature is valued exclusively in terms of its usefulness to humans. Deep ecologists conclude that only by "resacralizing" our perceptions of the natural world can we put ecosystems above narrow human interests and thereby learn to live harmoniously with the natural world and avert human-caused ecological catastrophe.

While these spiritual sentiments and ecocentric ethics make it possible to speak of a shared deep ecology tradition, differences about the proper means to promoting ecosystems have increasingly led to differentiation within the movement.

One important North American branch is bioregionalism. Envisioning communities of creatures living harmoniously and simply within the boundaries of distinct ecosystems, bioregionalism stands against large, growth-based industrial societies, preferring small, self-sufficient, and ecologically sustainable economies along with decentralized political self-rule. Deep ecology is best known, however, as the philosophy underpinning the work of radical environmentalists and Earth First! activists. Adding radical political analyses ("democracy is a sham") to ecological science ("we are in the midst of an unprecedented extinction crisis exacerbated and perhaps caused by human overpopulation") and spiritually based moral sentiments ("all life is sacred"), radical environmentalists believe that it is inadequate to focus exclusively on developing bioregionally sustainable communities. Ecocide must be resisted, they argue, by diverse means, including extralegal tactics and even sabotage. Finally, many deep ecologists believe that the root of the ecological crisis is spiritual. So they promote transformation of consciousness through ritual, poetry, and music designed to evoke wild, authentic, and ecological selves in spiritually dead humans.

In the early 1980s, deep ecology "road shows" resembling itinerant revival meetings began serving as recruiting grounds for the most important ritual process invented by deep ecologists: the Council of All Beings. The council was created primarily by two practicing Buddhists, Joanna Macy and John Seed (who now calls himself a pagan) and functions as a "ritual of inclusion" helping people to feel kinship with other life forms and ecosystems. In council rites, humans are imaginatively or shamanically possessed by the spirits of nonhuman entities (animals, rocks, soils, rivers), allowing those entities to verbalize their anger at being so poorly treated by people and to cry out for fair treatment and harmonious relations among all ecosystem citizens. The humans in these rites seek personal transformation and empowerment for their ecological activism—through the gifts of special powers granted by the nonhuman entities in their midst. More recently, Seed and others have developed workshops that use meditative breath work and evocative music to deepen still further the participants' experiences of their ecological selves.

Today the Council of all Beings can be found at Earth First! wilderness rendezvous, festivals of NEOPAGANISM, and sometimes at NEW AGE gatherings and meetings of environmentalist Christians. What distinguishes deep ecology from other forms of contemporary spirituality seeking to resacralize nature, however, is that deep ecologists are much less optimistic about the capacity of humans to change their ways. They do not share the optimism of many New Age practitioners. They also tend to be much more critical of the nation-state and of consumer capitalism than either New Age or neopagan devotees. In fact, deep ecologists tend to view modern industrial societies as incompatible with ecologically appropriate lifeways, preferring decentralized political self-rule and low-technology economic alternatives.

Deep ecology has found fertile ground in North America, particularly within the COUNTERCULTURE that began with the BEAT MOVEMENT in the 1950s and exploded during the 1960s and 1970s. (Beat poet Gary Snyder is now an honored "elder" of the deep ecology movement.) Deep ecology promises to grow significantly in the foreseeable future, in part because its leaders have thus far resisted a key liability of many millennial movements: predicting events that never come to pass. If environmental pressures increase, as deep ecologists predict, this movement and its pessimistic apocalypticism will only grow.

(See also John MUIR.)

BRT

Bibliography: Bill Devall and George Sessions, *Deep Ecology* (Salt Lake City, Utah: Gibbs Smith, 1985); Alan Drengson and Y. Inoue, eds., *The Deep Ecology Movement: An Introductory Anthology* (Berkeley, Calif.: North Atlantic, 1985); Arne Naess, *Ecology, Community and Lifestyle* (New York: Cambridge University Press, 1989); John Seed and others, *Thinking Like a Mountain: Towards a Council of All Beings* (Philadelphia: New Society, 1988); George Sessions, ed., *Deep Ecology for the 21st Century* (Boston: Shambhala, 1995); Bron Taylor, ed., *Ecological Resistance Movements: The Global Emergence of Radical and Popular Environmentalism* (Albany: State University of New York Press, 1995).

Dewey, John (1859–1952)

John Dewey, philosopher and educator, set many of the terms for discussing liberal approaches to religion, political life, science, and education in America for several decades.

Dewey was born to middle-class parents Archibald and Lucina Rich Dewey in Burlington, Vermont, on October 20, 1859. Dewey grew up in a household devoted to religious and philanthropic concerns, undergirded with a love of learning. In 1875 he enrolled at the University of Vermont. Teaching high school upon graduation in 1879, Dewey grew frustrated with the problems of classroom discipline and left for graduate studies at Johns Hopkins, where he enrolled in 1882.

He took his first academic position at the University of Michigan in 1884, becoming chair of the philosophy department in 1888. At Michigan, Dewey, who had inherited his mother's passion for social reform, focused much of his energy on reconciling his New England Protestantism and what he saw as the democratic potential of American life with the modern evolutionary thought of such Europeans as Charles Darwin, Auguste Comte, and Karl Marx.

A member of the Ann Arbor Congregational Church, Dewey regularly taught Bible classes and served on church committees as well as the board of trustees for the Student Christian Association there. During this time he married

Alice Chipman, a free-thinking student who was to have a lasting impact on both his social concerns and his theological perspective. The German philosopher G. W. F. Hegel and his English followers, such as T. H. Green, also heavily influenced Dewey during his graduate training. In these years he spoke of Christian themes in a language that, like Hegel's, sought to emphasize the immanence of the divine within both the natural world and human social life. In Ann Arbor he focused his sights on economic and social problems, defending the rights of workers in the wake of Chicago's Haymarket Square riots in 1887 and calling for government regulation of industry and business. While Dewey had much in common with other liberal Protestant reformers of his day (see SOCIAL GOSPEL), his Hegelianism led him to conclude that the religious and the secular were inseparable and that humans themselves would eventually make the Kingdom of God visible in the democratic community as a whole. Thus he told students in 1892, "The function of the church is to universalize itself and pass out of existence."

By the time he moved to the University of Chicago in 1894, Dewey was leaving liberal Protestantism behind. In his Chicago years he spoke of religion in the modern world as best expressed through democracy, science, and art and abandoned the project of reconciling Christianity itself with modernity. Increasingly, he also strove to separate naturalism and empiricism from Hegel's philosophical absolute "Spirit." As he matured he spoke most frequently of authentic religion as "natural piety," an experience available apart from the authoritative power of religious traditions and institutions.

At the core of Dewey's philosophical approach was a deep belief in the power of education and the need for "reconstruction" in both intellectual and social life. At Chicago he was responsible for the university's educational work, creating a Department of Pedagogy and an experimental elementary school. Working with progressives such as Jane Addams of Hull House and the National Education Association, Dewey was in the vanguard of a movement to reconstruct public education around the insights obtained from the social sciences and psychology, a movement that had a lasting, and often controversial, impact on American education throughout the 20th century. Angered over Chicago's lack of support for his experimental approach to education, Dewey accepted a position at Columbia University's Teachers College and Department of Philosophy in 1904.

Apart from a two-and-a-half-year stay in China and Japan after World War I, Dewey remained at Columbia until he retired in 1930. In the years between his return from Asia and the end of World War II, Dewey was prolific, producing books on art, epistemology, education, political theory, and religion. He was also extremely active in politics throughout this period. A trip to the Soviet Union in 1928 gave him hope that socialism could become a viable force in American life, and while he soon became an adamant anti-Stalinist, he never abandoned the hope that socialism and democracy could be combined successfully.

In the 1930s his faith in the potential of a democratic, scientific culture was attacked by a number of intellectuals on both left and right, the foremost being Reinhold NIEBUHR. A signer of the HUMANIST MANIFESTO, Dewey expressed his religious ideas most clearly in *A Common Faith* (1934), in which he sought to separate the natural "religious" quality of human experience from any association with historic religions, which he saw as limited expressions of such experience at best. In that work he also attacked the resurgent emphasis on human sin common among Christian theologians and preachers influenced by Niebuhrian NEO-ORTHODOXY.

While his significance endures in many fields, during the 1940s Dewey's fellow philosophers became absorbed with questions far removed from those of freedom, democracy, and creativity, the concerns that Dewey saw as philosophy's central contribution to modern society. Active until the end of his life, Dewey died of pneumonia on June 1, 1952.

MG

Bibliography: John Dewey, *The Works of John Dewey,* 37 vols. (Carbondale: Southern Illinois University Press, 1969–89); David Fott, *John Dewey: America's Philosopher of Democracy* (Lanham, Md.: Rowman & Littlefield, 1998); Steven C. Rockefeller, *John Dewey: Religious Faith and Democratic Humanism* (New York: Columbia University Press, 1991).

Dharmapala, Anagarika (1864–1933)

The first Buddhist missionary to the United States and the founder of the Maha Bodhi Society was born David Hewivitarne to a middle-class family in Colombo, Ceylon (now Sri Lanka) in 1864. In his early adulthood, he took the name Anagarika Dharmapala, which means "homeless defender of the Buddhist doctrine."

Though his parents were practicing Sinhalese Buddhists, they sent him to Christian schools where he attended church and endured compulsory Christian education. Following a much-publicized Buddhist-Christian riot, likely precipitated by Catholics who turned a Buddhist procession into a brawl, Hewivitarne left his Christian schooling behind.

Impressed with the pro-Buddhist and anti-Christian lectures delivered during an 1880 tour of Ceylon by the Theosophists Helena Petrovna BLAVATSKY and Henry Steel OLCOTT, Dharmapala joined the Theosophical Society (see THEOSOPHY). He was soon working alongside Olcott in Ceylon, where they labored to raise money for Buddhist education, and in other parts of Asia, where they endeavored to unite northern and southern Buddhists into one ecumenical International Buddhist League.

Influenced by the lamentations of the Victorian poet Edwin Arnold over the degradation of Bodh Gaya, India, the place of the Buddha's enlightenment, Dharmapala traveled to Bodh Gaya in 1891. There he vowed to restore the site and transform it into a sacred space that would be for Buddhists what Jerusalem is to Christians. To accomplish this task and to rescue other Buddhist sites from ill repair, Dharmapala organized the Maha Bodhi Society in 1891.

Dharmapala achieved international renown when he traveled to Chicago in 1893 as a delegate to the WORLD'S PARLIAMENT OF RELIGIONS. There he advocated a Theosophical version of the Theravada ("Way of the Elders") Buddhism of southern Asia that acknowledged important similarities between BUDDHISM and Christianity and urged all people of faith to practice religious tolerance. He also established an American branch of the Maha Bodhi Society.

Days after the parliament, Dharmapala officiated at a rite in which C. T. Strauss, a Swiss-born Theosophist of Jewish descent, became the first westerner formally and officially to convert to Buddhism on American soil. Dharmapala returned to the United States for lecture tours on several occasions after 1893. In 1897 he presided over America's first celebration of Wesak, the festival of the Buddha's birthday.

Although he began his public career as a religiously tolerant Theosophist, Dharmapala's Buddhist rhetoric sharpened over time. By the turn of the 20th century, he spoke far more about Buddhism's superiority over all other religions than he did about the fundamental unity of religious traditions. In 1905, Dharmapala severed his long association with the Theosophical Society. "Buddhism is absolutely opposed to the teachings of other existing religions," he concluded, and "Theosophy is irreconcilable with Buddhism."

Dharmapala died in 1933 near the place of the Buddha's first sermon in Sarnath, India. He is recognized worldwide as a champion of a nonsectarian United Buddhist World and at home in Sri Lanka as a leader of a major revival of Buddhism.

SRP

Bibliography: Ananda Guruge, ed., *Return to Righteousness: A Collection of the Speeches, Essays and Letters of Anagarika Dharmapala* (Colombo, Ceylon: Government Press, 1965).

Dickinson, Emily Elizabeth   See LITERA-
TURE AND CHRISTIANITY.

Disciples of Christ   See CHRISTIAN CHURCH
(DISCIPLES OF CHRIST); RESTORATION MOVEMENT.

disestablishment   See ESTABLISHMENT, RELI-
GIOUS.

dispensationalism   Dispensationalism is a
form of prophetic teaching and biblical interpretation that first became popular among
American Protestants following the CIVIL WAR
(1861–1865). Dispensationalists rejected the
optimistic POSTMILLENNIALISM of the day, the
belief that human beings could establish God's
kingdom through their own moral efforts. Dispensationalists placed virtually no value on
human achievement, stressing instead the
absolute sovereignty of God over history.

Dispensationalism was developed by John
Nelson Darby, an Anglican minister who left
the Church of Ireland and in 1831 helped found
the movement known as the Plymouth
Brethren. Darby emphasized that Christianity
as it then existed was hopelessly corrupt, and
he urged individuals to remove themselves from
it. His central tenet was that the Bible explained
historical change as a system of eras, or "dispensations," in which God tested humanity by different plans of salvation. There were seven
dispensations in all, and in each one humanity
failed and catastrophe and divine intervention
ensued. The first five dispensations had already
concluded with the expulsion from Eden, the
Flood, the Tower of Babel, the Exodus, and the
crucifixion of Jesus. The present era, the church
age, was soon to end with the RAPTURE of the
church to heaven, and following a period of
tribulation, Jesus Christ would return to earth
and the millennium (Christ's thousand-year
reign) would begin.

Dispensationalism was the virtual antithe-
sis of the modernist creed that also attained
prominence in late 19th-century American
Protestantism. While modernism was opti-

mistic about social progress, dispensationalism
was pessimistic. While modernists tended to
emphasize evolutionary development, dispensationalists accentuated the supernatural and
God's intervention in historical processes. And
while modernism analyzed the Bible in relation to human life and experience, dispensationalism interpreted all human activity
exclusively through the lens of the Bible. Dispensationalists believed that human beings
were participating in a grand cosmic struggle,
the details of which were not only outside their
control, but also ordained by God at the beginning of creation.

Darby's teachings arrived in the United
States in the 1870s and quickly spread through
Bible and prophecy conferences, week-long
summer meetings in which participants assembled for Bible study and prayer. His emphasis
on supernatural causation was consistent with
most Christian interpretations of history
advanced prior to the mid-19th century. What
was novel about Darby's views was not his
stress on God's control over history, but his
unique system of classification by eras. Darby
won over a number of theological conservatives
such as Reuben A. Torrey, A. C. Dixon, and—
most importantly—Cyrus Ingerson SCOFIELD,
whose *Reference Bible* (1909) became the standard text for American dispensationalists.

This tradition has proved to be tremendously influential in evangelical circles and is
the most accepted teaching about Christ's second coming in American fundamentalist
churches today. Dispensationalism received its
greatest exposure in the 1970s, when Hal Lind-
sey's *The Late Great Planet Earth* reached mass-
market paperback bookshelves across the
United States. This popular dispensationalist
tract has now sold close to 20 million copies.
(See also ESCHATOLOGY; PREMILLENNIALISM.)

GHS, Jr.

Bibliography: Ernest R. Sandeen, *The Roots of Fundamentalism: British and American Millenarianism,
1800–1930* (1970; Grand Rapids, Mich.: Baker
Book House, 1978).

Divine, Father (1877/82?–1965)   Little is known about the early life of the man who, as Father Divine, was worshiped as God by his followers in the Peace Mission Movement begun in 1914. Apparently he was born George Baker on Hutchinson Island, Savannah River, Georgia, sometime between 1877 and 1882. His parents were sharecroppers, and his early life was that of a poor farm boy. Around 1900 he moved to Baltimore, where he worked as a gardener and an itinerant preacher. There he fell in with several self-proclaimed messiahs, including one Samuel Morris (the Father Eternal, Father Jehovah) who anointed Baker "God in the Sonship degree."

This title gained Baker his own followers in Baltimore, who traveled with him to Valdosta, Georgia, in 1914, where he founded a community and proclaimed himself God. After a legal conflict in which he was accused of being a public menace, he and his followers returned to the North, settling in a black section of Brooklyn, where he used the name Major J. Devine. There his wife, "Sister Penny," began serving meals to all comers—a major practice of the movement—and by 1919 Father Divine had formulated the central beliefs of the Peace Mission Movement. His followers were to refrain from sex, alcohol, and drugs, as well as cosmetics, movies, and tobacco. Segregation and prejudice were forbidden.

These were not merely formal requirements, for Father Divine gathered both black and white followers, including many who were quite wealthy and highly educated. The movement was prosperous. By 1919 Father Divine purchased a house in Sayville, Long Island (New York) in a previously all-white area. Here his closest followers lived, and he dispensed the meals, money, and jobs that made him a legend throughout the black community. Conflict with his neighbors, who objected either to the crowds or to their color, led to his arrest in 1931. Convicted of disturbing the peace, on June 5, 1932, he was sentenced to a year in jail. He served three days before the judge—supposedly in perfect health and the prime of life—dropped dead. Divine reportedly remarked, "I hated to do it." This event seemed to some to validate his claim of divinity. In January 1933 the New York Supreme Court overturned the conviction, and Father Divine was a free man.

Following his release from prison, he moved the Peace Mission to Harlem, from where the movement had drawn most of its members. By that time his followers were so numerous that Fiorello La Guardia sought his endorsement during the New York mayoral campaign. At this time the Peace Mission Movement probably had 2 million members across the globe, although the movement claimed 20 million. It also had businesses spread throughout the world. Centered primarily in New York (including a 25-acre estate next door to President Roosevelt's home), the church owned properties in California, Pennsylvania, and Switzerland. The businesses included farms, barbershops, bakeries, and stores. At both the movement's center in Harlem and in its extensions through the world, members were provided with shelter, food, and clothing.

Father Divine and the Peace Mission Movement suffered severe setbacks in the late 1930s as a result of scandals involving the two issues most anathema to the movement—sex and money. A wealthy white follower was arrested in California on charges of violating the Mann Act prohibiting transportation of individuals across state lines for immoral purposes. Around the same time one of Divine's most important followers circulated tales of orgies. Finally a New York court ordered him to return $5,000 to a member declared to be mentally incompetent. Divine refused, and to avoid imprisonment moved his headquarters to Philadelphia.

Although weakened by these scandals, the loss of his traditional power base in Harlem, as well as his marriage to a white Canadian follower in 1946 (Sister Penny died in 1937), he retained the loyalty of most members and managed to solidify the movement in Philadelphia.

The last 29 years of Father Divine's life were nearly as hidden as his first 24. Although retaining leadership of the movement, he withdrew from the public eye. In 1953 he shifted his headquarters to Woodmont, a 73-acre estate outside Philadelphia. There he lived until his death on September 10, 1965. Control of the movement, and its $10 million in property, fell to his wife, Mother Divine, who continues to direct the Peace Mission Movement. Although smaller than in the past, the Peace Mission Movement continues the tradition of feeding the hungry and preaching racial equality begun by Father Divine in 1914.

(See also AFRICAN-AMERICAN RELIGION.)

EQ

Bibliography: Arthur H. Fauset, *Black Gods of the Metropolis: Negro Religious Cults of the Urban North* (New York: Octagon Books, 1970); Sara Harris and Harriet Crittenden, *Father Divine: Holy Husband* (Garden City, N.Y.: Permabooks, 1971); John Hoshor, *God in a Rolls Royce: The Rise of Father Divine, Madman, Menace, or Messiah* (New York: Hillman-Curl, 1936); William M. Kephart, ed., *Extraordinary Groups: An Examination of Unconventional Life-styles* (New York: St. Martin's Press, 1994); Jill Watts, *God, Harlem U.S.A.: The Father Divine Story* (Berkeley: University of California Press, 1992); Robert Weisbrot, *Father Divine and the Struggle for Racial Equality* (Urbana: University of Illinois Press, 1983); www.libertynet.org/fd/pmm (Peace Mission Movement).

Dixon, Amzi Clarence (1854–1925)

A. C. Dixon was a Southern Baptist (see SOUTHERN BAPTIST CONVENTION) minister, evangelist, and one of the early leaders of the conservative Protestant movement known as FUNDAMENTALISM. The most notable contribution he made to the fundamentalist cause was his work as the initial editor of *The Fundamentals*, the 12-volume series paperback that gave the movement its name.

Dixon was born in Shelby, North Carolina, on July 6, 1854. He graduated from Wake Forest College in 1874 and studied briefly at the Southern Baptist seminary in Greenville,

South Carolina, in 1875 and 1876. Following his ordination to the ministry, Dixon had a lengthy and well-traveled career as a pastor of churches not only in the South, but also in Baltimore, Boston, Chicago, Brooklyn, and London, England. Committed to the tasks of evangelism and conversion, he viewed each new pastorate as a means for reaching more lost souls with the message of Christian salvation. In 1893, Dixon preached with Dwight L. MOODY, the most highly regarded revivalist of the day, during Moody's evangelistic campaign at the Chicago World's Fair. Later, in 1906, Dixon was called to be pastor of Moody's church in Chicago, where he served until 1911.

Because he was interested primarily in the conversion of individual sinners, Dixon engaged in few debates about either doctrinal or social issues during the first decades of his ministry. His displeasure with the increasing respectability of theological modernism and the threats Darwinian evolutionary thought and biblical criticism posed to the Christian Gospel, however, eventually led Dixon to become a spokesman for the fundamentalist movement. When wealthy California businessman Lyman Stewart asked him in 1909 to aid in compiling a series of books setting forth the basic principles of Christianity, Dixon readily agreed. The first book in *The Fundamentals* series appeared the next year. Dixon oversaw the publication of five out of 12 volumes, all of which were sent free of charge to ministers, missionaries, and Sunday school teachers throughout the English-speaking world. Although Dixon resigned from his editorial position in 1911 when he left to become pastor of a church in London, he considered that to have been one of the most significant accomplishments of his half-century ministry.

After returning to the United States in 1919, Dixon spent a number of months traveling across the country as an itinerant evangelist and Bible teacher. In 1921, he accepted a call to the University Baptist Church, Baltimore.

That was to be Dixon's last pastorate, for he died in Baltimore on June 14, 1925.

GHS, Jr.

Bibliography: Helen Cadbury Alexander Dixon, *A. C. Dixon: A Romance of Preaching* (New York: Putnam's, 1931); Ernest R. Sandeen, *The Roots of Fundamentalism: British and American Millenarianism, 1800–1930* (1970; Grand Rapids: Baker Book House, 1978).

dominion theology   See CHRISTIAN RIGHT.

Drew, Timothy (Noble Drew Ali) (1886–1929)   As Noble Drew Ali, Timothy Drew, born January 8, 1886 in North Carolina, began the first of several U.S. movements to identify African Americans with ISLAM. This he did with the formation of the Moorish Science Temple of America.

Although a recipient of a poor education, as was often the case of American blacks, Drew received some knowledge of Eastern thought and Islam. He claimed to have traveled to the Middle East, where he received the title "Ali" from Abdul Aziz ibn Saud during a visit to Mecca.

Returning to the United States, Drew preached that blacks were Asiatics rather than Africans. Their true ancestral homeland was Morocco, and they properly should be called Moors. Ali developed an elaborate genealogy and history for blacks. Prior to the American Revolution blacks had been conscious of their nationality as Moors. The Continental Congress had stripped them of this identity, declaring them to be Negro, colored, and Ethiopian, assigning them to slavery in 1779.

Drew opened his first Moorish Temple in Newark, New Jersey, in 1913. This was followed by others in Detroit, Pittsburgh, and several other cities. In 1925 he established his headquarters in Chicago and incorporated the Moorish Temple of Science in the following year. (The latter was later changed to Moorish Science Temple.)

The beliefs of the Moorish Science Temple are set down in *The Holy Koran*, not to be confused with the Qur'an. In 64 pages of small print, Drew set out a strange combination of Islam, Christianity, and SPIRITUALISM, much of it lifted from *The Aquarian Gospel of Jesus Christ*, written by the spiritualist Levi Dowling.

As the movement expanded, problems developed within and without. Devotees' newfound identity and liberation from fear led to numerous altercations with whites. These conflicts reached such proportions that Drew was forced to issue a statement against provocation, although not before tensions had reached a point where the mention of the "Moors" could turn many a midwestern police chief apoplectic.

Internally, many saw the movement as an occasion for self-aggrandizement and began peddling such items as Old Moorish Healing Oil and Moorish Purifier Bath Compound. When Drew attempted to end such practices, conflict erupted, resulting in the murder of his business manager. Drew was arrested, despite being out of the city at the time of the killing.

Released on bond, he died a few weeks later, July 20, 1929, under mysterious circumstances. While some claim his death was the result of a beating received in police custody, most accept that he was murdered by opponents within the Moorish Science Temple.

EQ

Bibliography: Arthur H. Fauset, *Black Gods of the Metropolis: Negro Religious Cults of the Urban North* (New York: Octagon Books, 1970); C. Eric Lincoln, *The Black Muslims in America*. 3rd ed. (Grand Rapids: Eerdmans, 1994); Frank T. Simpson, "The Moorish Science Temple and Its 'Koran,'" *Moslem World* (January 1947): 56–61.

Du Bois, W. E. B. (1868–1963)   Arguably one of America's greatest intellects, William Edward Burghardt Du Bois holds a distinctive position in African-American thought and life. Decades ahead of his time in advocating black educational and economic opportunity, racial pride, and political equality, Du Bois was a man whose life was destined for frustration and bitterness, despite great individual ability and even success.

Born in Great Barrington, Massachusetts, on February 23, 1868, Du Bois attended the local Congregational church, where, as at school, he was often the only black student. His accomplishments at school were many, and following his graduation from high school, the local church's aid enabled him to attend Fisk University in Nashville, Tennessee. There he encountered firsthand the harshness of the South's caste system and came in contact with the vitality and plurality of black America.

Du Bois excelled at Fisk and, after graduating in 1888, refused a scholarship to study for the ministry in order to attend Harvard. Entering Harvard as a junior, he attracted the attention of the historian Albert Bushnell Hart and the philosopher and psychologist William JAMES. He frequently visited the James house, where he encountered secular and liberal thought far removed from the religious intensity of Fisk. His contact with James, Du Bois later claimed, turned him from philosophy to social analysis.

He graduated from Harvard College in 1890 and began his doctoral work under Hart. He was preparing to leave for a research trip to Europe in 1892, but a conflict over the availability of research money for minority students led Du Bois to write an "impudent" letter to the president accusing him of bad faith. The money was found, and Du Bois spent the next two years studying at the University of Berlin.

Returning to "nigger hating America" in 1894, he was appointed professor of Greek, Latin, German, and English at Wilberforce University in Ohio. While there, he completed his dissertation, receiving his Ph.D. in 1895. The thesis, *The Suppression of the African Slave Trade to the United States,* was the first book issued in the Harvard Historical series and landed him a one-year appointment at the University of Pennsylvania, where he was assigned to write a

study of Philadelphia's black community. The result, *The Philadelphia Negro* (1899), ran counter to the academic tide. Its detailed analysis debunked the "scientific racism" of the time that attributed everything to genetic factors. Du Bois's work found that the problems of poverty, crime, and degradation among Philadelphia's urban blacks resulted from historical and environmental factors rather than any racial deficiency of African Americans. In 1897 he accepted an appointment as professor of economics and history at Atlanta University. Here Du Bois published several more books, including *The Souls of Black Folk.*

Considered by many his finest work, *The Souls of Black Folk* is a lyrical and reflective essay on the life, burdens, and religious vitality of American blacks, as well as the first scholarly reflection on black religious music. The book's ominous prophecy that the "problem of the Twentieth Century is the problem of the color line" proved all too true.

The book also marked Du Bois's public break with Booker T. WASHINGTON over the issue of political equality for blacks. Du Bois became increasingly involved in political affairs. In 1900 he had served as secretary of the first Pan-Africanist Conference meeting in London and in 1905 organized the Niagara Movement, as a black opposition group to Washington's accommodationism. In 1909 he helped found the National Association for the Advancement of Colored People (NAACP), leaving Atlanta University the following year to assume the editorship of its magazine, *The Crisis.* Underappreciated and volatile, he gave offense as easily as he took it, and conflicts with colleagues over the direction of the NAACP and *The Crisis* led to his resignation as editor in 1934.

He returned to Atlanta University, where he continued to publish works on the history and culture of African Americans. His increasingly radical views led to his retirement from the university in 1944. He returned to the NAACP as director of special research until 1948, when his support for Henry Wallace and the Progressive

Party—despite the NAACP's official support for Harry Truman—resulted in his firing.

His views on race, world peace, and economics ran counter to the views of 1950s America. He suffered increasing harassment by the United States government, including arrest for acting as an unregistered agent of a foreign power and revocation of his passport.

Buffeted by the racist society around him, Du Bois grew increasingly bitter and angry. Despairing of any change in American society and hopeful about the emerging independent nations of Africa, he accepted the invitation of Ghanaian president Kwame Nkrumah to assume the editorship of the *Encyclopedia Africana*. He applied for membership in the Communist Party of the U.S.A., to which he was officially admitted on October 13, 1961, a week after he had left for Ghana. In February 1963 he took on Ghanaian citizenship, and at his death on August 27th of that year was given a state funeral.

In the decades since his death, American society has caught up to many of Du Bois's views. Not only is his *Souls of Black Folk* considered a classic interpretation of American culture, his *Black Reconstruction in America* (1935) has been validated by recent scholarship that demonstrates that the period of Reconstruction in the South was riddled neither with political corruption nor black violence but was a period when many southern states had the most representative and efficient governments in their histories. Du Bois must also be credited with a major role in the establishment of the African-American intellectual tradition in the United States. His seminal scholarship, support of black artists and scholars both personally and in the pages of the *Crisis,* and opposition to Booker T. Washington's emphasis on manual labor, helped pave the way for future black intellectuals. Perhaps it was fitting that Du Bois died on the day of the March on Washington, D.C., organized by the leaders of the CIVIL RIGHTS MOVEMENT. His sometime nemesis at the NAACP, Roy Wilkins, said of Du Bois's life, ". . .

it is incontrovertible that at the dawn of the twentieth century his was the voice that was calling you to gather here today in this cause." (See also AFRICAN-AMERICAN RELIGION.)

EQ

Bibliography: W. E. B. Du Bois, *The Autobiography of W. E. B. Du Bois: A Soliloquy on Viewing My Life from the Last Decade of Its First Century* (New York: International Publishers, 1968), ———, *W. E. B. Du Bois on Race and Culture: Philosophy, Politics, and Poetics* (New York: Routledge, 1996); ———, *The Souls of Black Folk* (New York: New American Library, 1961); Robert Michael Franklin, *Liberating Visions: Human Fulfillment and Social Justice in African-American Thought* (Minneapolis: Fortress Press, 1990); David L. Lewis, *W. E. B. Du Bois— Biography of a Race, 1868–1919* (New York: Henry Holt, 1993); Paul G. Partington, *W. E. B. Du Bois: A Bibliography of His Published Writings* (Whittier, Calif.: Partington, 1979); Ross Posnock, *Color & Culture: Black Writers and the Making of the Modern Intellectual* (Cambridge, Mass.: Harvard University Press, 1998); Shamoon Zamir, *Dark Voices: W.E.B. DuBois and American Thought, 1888–1903* (Chicago: University of Chicago Press, 1995); Phil Zuckerman, ed., *DuBois On Religion* (Walnut Creek, Calif.: Alta Mira Press, 2000).

DuBose, William Porcher (1836–1918)

William Porcher DuBose was an Episcopal clergyman and professor at the University of the South in Tennessee. The most important theologian in the history of the Episcopal Church, DuBose reflected the theological liberalism that gained ascendancy among American Protestants in the late 19th century. However, unlike the modernist (see MODERNISM) theologians of the North, DuBose's vivid sense of God's presence within human suffering and adversity reflected his critical experience as a white southerner living in the aftermath of the Civil War.

DuBose was born on April 11, 1836, in Winnsboro, South Carolina. The DuBoses were prominent plantation owners descended from Huguenots who had settled the low country of South Carolina in the 17th century. DuBose graduated from the Military College of South Carolina (the Citadel) in 1855 and earned an M.A. at the University of Virginia in 1859. Although he entered the Episcopal diocesan seminary at Camden, South Carolina, in October 1859, the outbreak of the Civil War forced him to withdraw and join the Confederate army instead. He was wounded in battle and spent two months in a Union prisoner-of-war camp. After the war, he was ordained in 1866 and served briefly as rector, first at St. John's Church Winnsboro, and later at Trinity Church, in Abbeville, South Carolina. DuBose came to Sewanee, Tennessee, as chaplain of the University of the South in 1871. After the establishment of a department of theology at the university, he resigned his chaplaincy position in 1882 to devote himself to teaching. He also held the position of dean of Sewanee's School of Theology between 1894 and 1908.

In his spiritual autobiography, *Turning Points in My Life* (1912), composed for the celebration of his 75th birthday, DuBose explained how his theological position had evolved over the years. He believed that the Civil War had been pivotal in shaping his development as a theologian. In the fall of 1864, when he came to the realization that the Confederate cause was lost, he sensed the ultimate futility of worldly concerns and dedicated himself from then on to the work of the church. Laying particular stress on the doctrine of the incarnation, DuBose taught that God was immanent in his creation, in human imperfection and suffering, and in the ongoing life of the Christian church. While Jesus Christ was the particular incarnation of God, all humanity participated generically in the incarnation of the divine.

Geographically isolated from the mainstream of American theology in his day and relatively unappreciated amid the dominant theological conservatism of the South, DuBose began to receive recognition for his progressive orthodoxy only in the 20th century. He published six major theological books as well

William Porcher DuBose, a Confederate Army veteran who became the Episcopal Church's most influential theologian.

as numerous essays over the course of his teaching career. Having lived at Sewanee for nearly five decades, DuBose died there on August 18, 1918.

GHS, Jr.

Bibliography: *William Porcher DuBose: Selected Writings,* ed. Jon Alexander (New York: Paulist Press, 1988); Robert Boak Slocum, *The Theology of William Porcher DuBose: Life, Movement, and Being* (Columbia: University of South Carolina Press, 2000); John Morris Wilson, *I Have Looked Death in the Face: A Biography of William Porcher DuBose, Soldier, Philosopher, Theologian* (Kingston, Tenn.: Paint Rock Publishing, 1996).

Dwight, Timothy (1752–1817) Grandson of Jonathan EDWARDS, precocious, and wealthy through inheritance, Timothy Dwight had all of life's advantages. He did not waste them. Dwight early became a leading figure in the religious and political life of New England.

Born on May 14, 1752, in Northampton, Massachusetts, Dwight entered Yale at the age of 13. He spent the next 12 years of his life there, first as a student and then as a tutor. In 1777 he joined the American Revolution as a military chaplain. Resigning in 1779 to take charge of family property, he spent the next 16 years as farmer, legislator, teacher, and minister. In 1795 he became president of Yale and in that role made his greatest contributions.

His achievements prior to that time as an epic poet, hymn writer, and preacher were not insignificant, but as president of Yale Dwight found the "bully pulpit" he desired. He revived the flagging fortunes of the school, augmenting the faculty and adding professional departments in medicine and theology. Dwight also brought a new religious fervor to the school. He began a series of lectures on the Christian religion that led to a revival among the Yale students. Considered one of the harbingers of the SECOND GREAT AWAKENING, this revival not only infused new religious life into the college, but led to the formation of societies for moral uplift.

Foreign missions (see MISSIONS, FOREIGN) engaged Dwight's passion, and he encouraged his students to take the Gospel to heathen lands. He spoke of his hope that one day soon not a cathedral, mosque, or pagoda would remain standing. Dwight was one of the first religious leaders to favor total abstinence from alcohol, rather than moderation.

Domestic religious and political enemies attracted most of Dwight's energy. He feared the spread of irreligion and the Jeffersonians (see JEFFERSON, THOMAS). As a teacher and a public figure he spent much of his time combating what he saw as the blasphemous views of Thomas PAINE, Thomas Jefferson, and their followers. A staunch Federalist, Dwight believed that the party of John Adams provided the one bulwark against the inevitable results of the infidels, results seen in the atheism, violence, and chaos of the French Revolution.

In his defense of revealed religion Dwight showed himself as an heir of his grandfather, with some modification. Dwight, much more than Edwards, emphasized the moral demands of religion and the ability of human beings to act upon those responsibilities. This human action was possible because the moral truths of religion were grounded in the revelation of God manifested in the resurrection of Christ. Dwight, until his death on January 11, 1817, affirmed this truth against the skeptics and in doing so helped initiate a new period of religious activity in the United States.

EQ

Bibliography: Charles E. Cunningham, *Timothy Dwight, 1752–1817: A Biography* (New York: Macmillan, 1942); John R. Fitzmier, *New England's Moral Legislator: Timothy Dwight, 1752–1817* (Bloomington: Indiana University Press, 1998); Kenneth Silverman, *Timothy Dwight* (New York: Twayne Publishers, 1969); Annabelle S. Wenzke, *Timothy Dwight 1752–1817* (Lewiston, N.Y.: Edwin Mellen, 1989).

Dyer, Mary (1591?–1660) Quaker dissenter Mary Dyer's death by hanging on Boston Common ended her long-running conflict with the rulers of the MASSACHUSETTS BAY COLONY. The conflict began with her outspoken support for Anne HUTCHINSON. It ended in her persistent attempts to spread her Quaker beliefs (see FRIENDS, THE RELIGIOUS SOCIETY OF) within the colony.

Nothing is known of Mary Dyer's early life, the first mention of her being in 1633, when the marriage of Mary Barrett to William Dyer was recorded in London. Two years later the couple joined the Puritan (see PURITANISM) migration to New England, where they became accepted members of the Boston community and the Boston church. This period of harmony soon ended as the entire colony became embroiled in the so-called ANTINOMIAN CONTROVERSY.

The Dyers supported the group led by Anne Hutchinson and John Wheelwright. When the colonial authorities moved against them in 1637, William Dyer was among those disfranchised and disarmed. This did not dissuade Mary, who remained loyal to Anne Hutchinson throughout her trial. This stance led to Mary Dyer's excommunication by the Boston Church as well.

Moving to Rhode Island, she joined other dissenters from Massachusetts. During a visit to England in 1650, Mary became a Quaker. Fired with missionary zeal, she returned to Boston in 1657 to spread the Quaker message. Massachusetts authorities rewarded her concern by imprisoning her. Her husband, who had not adopted Mary's Quakerism, gained her release. Imprisonment did not dampen her spirit. She returned to Boston in the summer of 1659. The authorities again expelled her upon pain of death for reentering the colony. When she returned in September, she and her two companions, William Robinson and Marmaduke Stephenson, were tried and condemned to death. The noose had already been placed round her neck when the last-minute intercession of her son with the colonial authorities, who did not wish to execute a woman, gained her yet another reprieve.

Incapable of ignoring the divine will that called her to preach in Massachusetts, Dyer reentered the colony in May 1660. This time she had tried the colony's patience once too often. Condemned to death at the end of May, she was hanged on June 1, 1660. In death she joined numerous Quaker and religious martyrs who refused to allow human laws to restrict religious belief and action.

EQ

Bibliography: Deborah Crawford, *Four Women in a Violent Time: Anne Hutchinson 1591–1643, Mary Dyer 1591?–1660, Lady Deborah Moody 1600–1659, Penelope Stout 1622–1732* (New York: Crown, 1970); Horatio Rogers, *Mary Dyer, the Quaker Martyr that Was Hanged on Boston Common June 1, 1660* (Providence: Preston & Rounds, 1899).

E

Eastern Orthodoxy See GREEK ORTHODOX ARCHDIOCESE OF NORTH AND SOUTH AMERICA; ORTHODOX CHRISTIANITY; ORTHODOX CHURCH IN AMERICA.

Eastern religions See BAHÁ'Í; BUDDHISM; HINDUISM; JAINISM; TAOISM; ZEN.

ecumenical movement The ecumenical movement—the desire for a return to the unity of the Christian church—has been a major element of 20th-century Christianity. The word ecumenical, deriving from the Greek *oikumene* meaning the "inhabited world," or more precisely the known world of Greco-Roman culture, however, has a long history. *Oikumene* appears 15 times in the New Testament, eight of them in Luke and Acts, speaking of the world into which Christians must spread the Gospel. In the early church the word signified the church universal. The seven general church councils from 325 to 787, those that included representatives from throughout the *oikumene* as distinct from local assemblies, were referred to as "ecumenical."

The church universal, however, was soon the church divided. There were repeated ruptures within the early church culminating with the great split between the eastern Orthodox Church and the western Roman Church in 1054. The divisions caused by the Reformation of the 16th century helped to splinter Christianity even more. By the 19th century the unbroken body of Christ had been torn into innumerable pieces.

Credit must be given to these divided churches in that they recognized that the divisions were sinful, to use theological language. The refusal of each church to change its version of the truth while demanding that others do so made solving this problem impossible.

This attitude began to change during the 19th century, primarily in the area of missions. In fact, the missionary movement gave birth to the modern ecumenical movement. To a great extent this new era of interdenominational cooperation began in the United States. The task of meeting the religious needs of a constantly expanding nation was beyond the scope of any one denomination. Denominations combined to meet those needs, creating the American Board of Commissioners for Foreign Missions (1810), the American Bible Society (1816), the American Sunday School Union (1824), and the American Home Missionary Society (1826). Equally significant was the PLAN OF UNION between the Presbyterians and Congregationalists.

While many of these organizations collapsed over doctrinal conflicts and none were completely inclusive, they set the tone for interdenominational cooperation. Cooperation was to be based upon actions, upon what the churches could do together. Theological and doctrinal issues would be ignored while the denominations cooperated on general enterprises such as missions, charity, combatting infidelity, and moral reform. Following the Civil War there was an increase in the numbers of these organizations, especially among young people of college age: YMCAs and YWCAs (see YOUNG MEN'S CHRISTIAN ASSOCIATION and YOUNG WOMEN'S CHRISTIAN ASSOCIATION) in the United States, the Interseminary Missionary Alliance, and the Student Volunteer Movement for Foreign Missions. Organized on an international level in 1895 as the World's Student Christian Fellowship, the last had a major impact on the ecumenical movement, for it created a core of educated, able, and adventurous young people committed to interdenominational cooperation.

In the United States these movements came together in 1908 with the formation of the Federal Council of Churches of Christ in America (see NATIONAL COUNCIL OF CHURCHES). The ability of 33 denominations to join together in Christian work provided a major impetus for further developments. The first of these was the International Missionary Conference in Edinburgh in 1910. The conference, generally considered the birth of the worldwide ecumenical movement, grew out of the earlier World's Student Christian Fellowship and other organizations devoted to foreign missions. In fact, the founder of the WSCF, John R. MOTT, chaired the committee organized to continue the work begun at Edinburgh. The most visible result of the Edinburgh conference was the founding in 1921 of the International Missionary Council, whose function was to stimulate thinking about the missionary enterprise and to coordinate the activities of the various Christian churches in the mission field so that they, where possible, could engage in cooperative rather than competitive action.

The emphasis on the churches combining for shared action was continued by the calling of the Universal Christian Conference on Life and Work in Stockholm, Sweden, August 19–30, 1925. More than 600 delegates representing 91 denominations and 37 countries met to discuss economic, educational, and international issues. While responses to the conference were mixed, there was sufficient

support to create a Continuation Committee to carry on the work of the conference. This committee, later reconstituted as the Life and Work Committee, and its organization of a second Life and Work Conference dealing with church, community, and the state marked a turning point for the ecumenical movement. At this conference (Oxford, July 1937) the idea of merging the Life and Work Commission with the Faith and Order Commission was approved. This approval paved the way for the eventual creation of the WORLD COUNCIL OF CHURCHES (WCC) following WORLD WAR II.

Cooperation on religious action, what is known in the ecumenical movement as life and work, has been the easiest but not the only element of the struggle for Christian unity. Issues of doctrine, of faith and order, have troubled serious thinkers. If there is one truth, then how can there be several churches?

While missions, moral reform, and social service could cause division among churches, nothing divided like questions of doctrine and church governance. For this reason most interdenominational organizations forbade or severely limited discussions of doctrine. Some viewed this limitation as hindering rather than aiding Christian unity. By an odd historical coincidence three denominations in the United States took up this issue within days of each other in October 1910. In that month the Protestant Episcopal Church, the Disciples of Christ, and the Congregational Churches independently adopted resolutions calling for a world conference of Christian churches "for the consideration of questions touching Faith and Order," as the Episcopal resolution read. Committees formed to implement these resolutions found their work interrupted by WORLD WAR I. Not until 1927 was the first Conference on Faith and Order held in Lausanne, Switzerland.

Like the Life and Work Conference, Faith and Order organized a Continuation Committee to carry on the work of the conference. While little had been solved at the conference, its mere occurrence, including representatives from the Orthodox and Ancient Eastern churches (see ORTHODOX CHRISTIANITY), marked a major shift in religious discussion. The second Faith and Order Conference, held in Edinburgh in 1937, resulted in a general agreement about the "grace of our Lord Jesus Christ" but little else except a decision to merge with the Life and Work Conference. The result of this merger was the formation in 1948 of the World Council of Churches.

This development, along with the 1951 reorganization of the Federal Council as the National Council of Churches of Christ in the USA, was a significant development for the ecumenical movement. For the first time there existed organized institutions with denominational connections whose purpose was to pursue Christian unity, both in terms of action and doctrine. While few solutions have come from these discussions, they have illuminated similarities previously obscured.

Ecumenism, however, has not been limited to the formation of interdenominational institutions. One of the biggest obstacles to Christian unity has been the refusal of the Roman Catholic Church to join either the NCC or the WCC. Changes within the Roman church during the 1960s encouraged greater opening toward other Christian bodies. The Second Vatican Council (see VATICAN COUNCIL II) was most significant in this regard. At this conference not only were Protestant, Anglican, and Orthodox bodies invited to send observers, but the adoption of several documents on the relationship of the Roman Church to other Christian denominations and a statement on religious liberty went far toward lessening mutual hostility and suspicion.

The last quarter of the 20th century, while seeing a retrenchment of ecumenism on many levels, did see some movement toward union on bilateral levels. Discussions between numerous Lutheran denominations in the United States led to the formation of the EVANGELICAL LUTHERAN CHURCH IN AMERICA, which undertook a series of negotiations with the Episcopal Church leading to a mutual recognition of each other's orders and sacraments. On an international level, discussions between Lutherans and Roman Catholics led to a fair degree of agreement on what had been hotly contested doctrinal differences.

Struggling with their own doctrinal and theological differences also made Christians more aware of the complexity of their relationship to the wider world. This has caused many Christian churches to reexamine their traditional attitudes toward non-Christian religions, especially Judaism. The Vatican II document, "The Relationship of the Church to Non-Christian Religions" transformed the traditional Catholic view of other religion, and explicitly rejected Jewish responsibility for the crucifixion of Jesus. The WCC and NCC have held numerous conferences dealing with the relationship of Christianity to other religions.

What began as a movement toward greater Protestant unity has become a movement of worldwide scope. While no one envisions a religiously united world, the ecumenical movement has produced a greater willingness to meet others in discussions based on mutual concern and appreciation. For this, if nothing else, its historical significance is assured.

EQ

Bibliography: *Dictionary of the Ecumenical Movement* (Geneva: World Council of Churches; Grand Rapids, Mich.: Eerdmans, 1991); Ruth Rouse and Stephen Neill, *A History of the Ecumenical Movement.* 2 vols. (Philadelphia: Westminster Press, 1967, 1970); Nicholas Sagovsky, *Ecumenism, Christian Origins, and the Practice of Communion* (Cambridge: Cambridge University Press, 2000); Geoffrey Wainwright, *The Ecumenical Moment: Crisis and Opportunity for the Church* (Grand Rapids, Mich.: W. B. Eerdmans, 1983).

Eddy, Mary Baker (1821–1910)

The founder of CHRISTIAN SCIENCE and the woman who presided over its remarkable growth, Mary Baker Eddy stands among a handful of American religious reformers who have demonstrated both the charisma necessary to give birth to a new religious movement and the organizational skills to insure its long life. Her theories and practices, institutionalized in the Church of Christ (Scientist) (established 1879), have found their way into "harmonial religions" such as NEW THOUGHT and the POSITIVE THINKING tradition of Norman Vincent PEALE.

Eddy was born Mary Morse Baker into a farming family in Bow, New Hampshire, in 1821. She received little formal education but was reared in the NEW DIVINITY theology developed by the followers of the Puritan divine Jonathan EDWARDS. She married three times: in 1843, to George Washington Glover, who died one year later; in 1853, to a dentist, Dr. Daniel Patterson, whom she left after 20 unhappy years; and, finally, in 1877, to Asa Gilbert Eddy, who passed away in 1882.

Eddy's early life was marked by a never-ending battle with physical and nervous disorders, including the near-ubiquitous 19th-century malady of neurasthenia. These ailments left Eddy largely incapacitated. Her life took a new turn, however, when she traveled to Portland, Maine, in 1862 to meet Phineas P. QUIMBY (1802–1866). A clockmaker by trade, Quimby was by avocation an itinerant healer who traveled across New England diagnosing diseases and dispensing cures. Long before Eddy, he used terms such as *Christian science* and *science of health* and theorized that sickness resulted from mental rather than physical disorders and so could be healed through techniques that gave mind priority over matter.

Eddy's health improved dramatically after treatments by Quimby. She moved to Portland later in 1862 in order to continue her treatments and to apprentice under him. Shortly after her mentor's death in 1866, Eddy slipped on ice outside her new home in Lynn, Massachusetts, suffering severe injuries. This incident, which would soon be enshrined in the lore of Christian Science as Eddy's famous "fall," confined her to bed rest until "on the third day" she miraculously "rose again"—a completely

Mary Baker Eddy, the 19th-century religious reformer, founded Christian Science and wrote *Science and Health. (First Church of Christ, Scientist, Boston)*

healed and completely new woman. Eddy had cured herself, but more importantly she had discovered Christian Science.

After her fall and resurrection in 1866, Eddy supported herself as an itinerant healer and worked out the theological implications of her discovery. She convened the first gathering of Christian Scientists at her home in Lynn in 1875 and in 1879 incorporated the Church of Christ (Scientist). Boston became Eddy's headquarters in 1881. The spectacular "Mother Church" was completed there in 1895.

Eddy described the awakening in her of Christian Science not only as a "discovery" but also as a "revelation," and it was consistent with her view that revelation was both natural and ongoing that on numerous occasions she revised the distinctive scripture of Christian Science, *Science and Health, With Key to the Scriptures* (1875). In all its versions, however, *Science and Health* represented a decisive turn away from the modified CALVINISM of Eddy's youth.

Eddy, like her pious Puritan forebears, read the Bible regularly and prayed enthusiastically, but she grew to prefer a loving and immanent deity to the Puritans' radically transcendent and wrathful God. Like many of her contemporaries in Gilded Age America, she moved away from Calvinist orthodoxy and toward religious liberalism.

Eddy's thought incorporated but moved far beyond Quimby's theory that sickness and health are mental rather than physical. Eddy distinguished herself from Quimby by developing a detailed theology and by devoting considerable efforts to interpreting the Bible in light of Christian Science. God, she argued, was Mind. The "mortal mind" reflected but was inferior to this "divine Mind." Humans were by no means utterly distinct from God, but they were separated from God nonetheless by illusions of pain and sickness, sin and death. By turning to Jesus Christ, however, people could break through their illusions and live, in union with God, a life marked by health, happiness, and prosperity.

Eddy's unorthodox theories earned her a coterie of critics. The most famous was the humorist Mark Twain, who turned Eddy-bashing into sport. Although Twain delighted in deriding God for committing grievous grammatical errors in Eddy's revelatory *Science and Health,* he saved his most biting invective for what he saw as her dictatorial leadership style. In a book called *Christian Science* (1907), he predicted (incorrectly) that Christian Science would sweep the country, enslaving all Americans under "the most insolent and unscrupulous a tyrannical politico-religious master . . . since the palmy days of the Inquisition."

Though most of Eddy's converts remained faithful to their founder, whom they affectionately referred to as "Mother," Eddy was criticized by some members of her own movement. Emma Curtis HOPKINS, who had served as editor of the monthly *Christian Science Journal,* broke away from Eddy in the mid-1880s and opened the Christian Science Theological Seminary in Chicago as an alternative to the Eddy-controlled Massachusetts Metaphysical College. Hopkins would eventually become one of the most important leaders of the New Thought movement.

Refusing to succumb to her critics, Eddy skillfully steered her way through internal schisms and around outsider contempt. In the process, she built not only a church but also a media empire. When she died in 1910 she left behind a highly acclaimed daily newspaper, the *Christian Science Monitor* (established 1908) and a church of nearly 100,000 members.

SRP

Bibliography: Gillian Gill, *Mary Baker Eddy* (Reading Mass.: Perseus, 1998); Robert Peel, *Mary Baker Eddy: The Years of Discovery* (New York: Holt, Rinehart and Winston, 1966);———, *Mary Baker Eddy: The Years of Trial* (New York: Holt, Rinehart and Winston, 1971);———, *Mary Baker Eddy: Years of Authority* (New York: Holt, Rinehart and Winston, 1977); Mark Twain, *Christian Science* (New York: Oxford University Press, 1996).

education, public school   American public schools began in the early 19th century, shifting in focus over time as Americans turned to education in order to meet what they saw as the changing needs of society.

Public education was crucial to the general program of reform stemming from the SECOND GREAT AWAKENING. Reformers saw free, universal education as the best way to create the sort of responsible, religiously and morally grounded citizenry required to preserve the young republic. With heavy emphasis on moral instruction, education developed a noticeably Protestant flavor. By century's end, a second wave of Progressive Era reformers sought to recast education to conform to the needs of a more secular, urban society. Ensuing decades have been marked by continuing tension between those who see education as technical or professional preparation for participation in economic life and those who see it as developing the moral and intellectual insight necessary for citizenship.

Americans in the COLONIAL PERIOD took education seriously, though not always formally. Revolutionary leaders such as Thomas JEFFERSON and Thomas PAINE saw education as the crucible out of which a genuinely new, fully American person would emerge, the basis for a population of what Benjamin Rush called "republican machines." But in the years following the AMERICAN REVOLUTION, Americans conceived of education broadly, being achieved through a variety of means, such as the press, the churches, the family, and public debate, and pursued throughout an individual's life.

The specific impetus to create public schools came in response to a general demographic change in the early 19th century: the creation of childhood as a distinct phase in human life. As mortality rates decreased, adults began to look on children as unique individuals who required the special attention of parents. The family became a center of nurture and care rather than a center of production. Mothers became idealized for their new role as the dominant family figure. As one minister intoned: "When our land is filled with virtuous and patriotic mothers, then it will be filled with virtuous and patriotic men."

But with a burgeoning population, including immigrants from a variety of countries, reformers in the early 19th century sought to create institutions more capable of providing a uniform education than could be guaranteed by individual families. Expanding upon the educational goal of private evangelical academies (see EVANGELICALISM) and the growing SUNDAY SCHOOL movement, religious leaders as diverse as Horace BUSHNELL and Lyman BEECHER campaigned for common schools to supplement education from home and church. Beecher, in his famous *Plea for the West*, called for an educational system capable of insuring America could meet its millennial task: to "lead the way in the moral and political emancipation of the world." In spite of the deep theological divisions at the time, Beecher, Bushnell, and other Protestants united around the goal of creating a public system based on Christian, republican values, where all classes could learn the skills and responsibilities necessary to sustain the expanding American nation.

Since the federal Constitution nowhere mentioned education, states reserved to themselves the right to develop their own approaches, making the creation of public schools an erratic and variable process. In Massachusetts, New York, and some western states, public institutions were well established by the 1830s; but in Virginia a public system did not emerge until after the CIVIL WAR. Without a clear separation between public and private, 19th-century American education consisted of a patchwork of institutions: local primary schools, state-authorized universities, and church-supported academies and colleges. Controversies over state control, public funding, and the sorts of knowledge taught troubled Americans from early in the century. However, by the 1850s a general pattern of public control had emerged, influenced greatly by the nonsectarian views of Horace MANN.

The idea of compulsory, publicly controlled, publicly funded education evolving during the 19th century was contested by many Americans, particularly Catholics, who found themselves being denied funding as the notion of "public" spread. Catholics in New York City and elsewhere argued that "public" really meant Protestant and that the local schools were fomenting anti-Catholic sentiments. Unable to rectify the situation, by the late 1840s Catholics were forced to establish their own school system, attached to local parishes (see ROMAN CATHOLICISM).

These conflicts were as much over symbolic issues of patriotic loyalty and national identity as they were over funding and structure. In the many decades since their creation, public schools have changed along with the rest of society, but they have also remained an important battleground in American culture. Originally a Protestant vehicle for forging a national consensus of values, they have become a crucial arena for the expression of public conflict, as can be seen in the bitter controversies over racial equality and desegregation that began in the 1950s (see CIVIL RIGHTS MOVEMENT). Religious, ethnic, and ideological groups of all stripes have sought to secure their own view of the world by incorporating it into the school curriculum, or else to insure that they, too, have sufficient access to the resources and opportunities provided by the schools.

In the early 20th century, associates of John DEWEY sought to transform education, contending that the traditional Protestant, rural values and skills enshrined by the schools needed replacement by the more modern values of humanism and the teaching of scientific and technical skills appropriate to an urban, industrial society (see SECULAR HUMANISM; SCIENCE AND RELIGION; SCOPES TRIAL). But there also have been conflicts among the modernists who inherited Dewey's vision, some seeing schools as providing a technically trained, competent workforce for an advanced economy, others arguing for their role in creating critically minded democratic citizens. The struggle between traditionalists and modernists has endured as well, although in recent decades the traditionalists have come to include Catholics and Jews as well as conservative Protestants. While CREATIONISM, prayer, and religious assembly in public schools remain primarily Protestant issues, the schools' response to changing sexual standards unites Protestants with conservative Catholics and Jews. Even as the 21st century dawned, schools continued to reflect profound disagreements inherent in American public life.

MG

Bibliography: Lawrence A. Cremin, *American Education: The National Experience, 1783–1876* (New York: Harper and Row, 1980);———, *American Education: The Metropolitan Experience, 1876–1980* (New York: Harper and Row, 1988); James R. Durham, *Secular Darkness: Religious Right Involvement in Texas Public Education, 1963–1989* (New York: P. Lang, 1995); Ward McAfee, *Religion, Race, and Reconstruction: The Public School in the Politics of the 1870s* (Albany: State University of New York Press, 1998).

Edwards, Jonathan (1703–1758)

One of America's greatest religious thinkers, Jonathan Edwards was deeply influenced by both Neoplatonism and the philosophy of John Locke (see ENLIGHTENMENT, THE). Edwards devised a theology at once orthodox and scientific, logical and mystical.

Edwards was born October 5, 1703, in East Windsor, Connecticut, into two families of notable Congregationalist ministers. He graduated from Yale College in 1720. After two years of graduate work he served a pastorate in New York, returning to Yale as a tutor in 1724. Two years later he joined his grandfather Solomon STODDARD at the church in Northampton, Massachusetts, as a junior colleague, becoming the senior minister after Stoddard's death in 1729.

At Northampton, Edwards was immersed in parish duties, although he found some time for writing. To Edwards's surprise, in 1734, during a series of sermons against ARMINIANISM, the belief that human activity could help effect salvation, his parish underwent a religious revival that is generally considered the start of the GREAT AWAKENING.

Although Edwards was the spokesman for a renewal of traditional CALVINISM and orthodox doctrine, he defended these doctrines with the new learning. In doing so he became a leading exponent of "religious experience." In his *A Treatise Concerning Religious Affections* Edwards argues that true religion is more than mere assent to religious knowledge or doctrine. It is the complete possession of the individual, "driven by love which is the first and chief . . . and the fountain of all affections."

Continued reflection on the nature of God's majestic presence led Edwards to an increasing awareness of the seriousness of both church membership and the sacraments. In response to this awareness, he attempted to reverse some of the practices instituted by his grandfather. Edward's tightening of the criteria for BAPTISM and admission to the Lord's Supper met with increasing hostility from his congregation. His desire to deliver a series of sermons on the latter subject in 1748 met not only with disapproval, but also with a request for his resignation. The conflict lasted until the summer of 1750, when the church voted 200-53 for dismissal. He delivered his farewell sermon July 1, 1750.

Thrown adrift with a wife and seven children, he received a call from the frontier town of Stockbridge, where his duties included services to both whites and the Housatonic Indians. The years spent in Stockbridge proved the most productive of Edwards's life. He continued his arguments on behalf of the traditional doctrines of Calvinism—the supremacy of God, the depravity of humanity, and the bondage of will. Edwards was no arid dogmatist, however. His writings have a sense of feeling and mysticism that seems almost Romantic. He also defended these traditional doctrines with a most complex use of the new, enlightened, and liberal learning of the time. John Locke's psychology and philosophical idealism became Edwards's weapons against the Lockeans. It is unfortunate that Edwards is known chiefly (if at all) through his widely anthologized sermon, "Sinners in the Hands of an Angry God," one of the very few threatening and condemnatory sermons he ever gave.

In 1757 he was asked to fill the presidency of the College of New Jersey (later Princeton University) following the death of his son-in-law Aaron Burr, who was president. After some hesitation, he accepted the position in January 1758. While there his interest in science and modern thought ended his life. Firmly believing in the usefulness of the new

Jonathan Edwards, the eminent American theologian who deeply influenced the 18th-century revival of religion known as the Great Awakening.

science, he submitted himself to a smallpox inoculation. Complications resulted and he died March 22, 1758.

EQ

Bibliography: Alexander V. G. Allen, *Jonathan Edwards* (Boston: Houghton Mifflin, 1889); Conrad Cherry, *The Theology of Jonathan Edwards: A Reappraisal* (Garden City, N.Y.: Anchor Books, 1966); Leon Chai, *Jonathan Edwards and the Limits of Enlightenment Philosophy* (New York: Oxford University Press, 1998); Jonathan Edwards, *A Faithful Narrative of the Surprising Work of God* (New Haven: Yale University Press, 1972);———, *Letters and Personal Writings* (New Haven: Yale University Press, 1998);———, *A Treatise Concerning*

Religious Affections (New Haven: Yale University Press, 1959); Douglas J. Elwood, *The Philosophical Theology of Jonathan Edwards* (New York: Columbia University Press, 1960); Sang Hyun Lee, *The Philosophical Theology of Jonathan Edwards* (Princeton: Princeton University Press, 2000); Gerald R. McDermott, *Jonathan Edwards Confronts the Gods: Christian Theology, Enlightenment Religion, and Non-Christian Faiths* (New York: Oxford University Press, 2000); Perry Miller, *Jonathan Edwards* (New York: W. Sloane Associates, 1949); Ola E. Winslow, *Jonathan Edwards* (New York: Collier Books, 1940).

Einhorn, David (1809–1879)

David Einhorn was, as his son-in-law Kaufmann KOHLER called him, "the Reform theologian *par excellence*." Already a major figure in German REFORM JUDAISM before his 1855 arrival in the United States, Einhorn provided American Reform Judaism with an intellectual basis for its beliefs and actions. A theological radical, he had little patience with Isaac WISE's moderate reform and organizational concerns or with Wise's attempt to create an Americanized Judaism. For Einhorn, Reform Judaism was a German phenomenon, dependent upon the German language and German philosophy.

Born in Dispek, Germany, on November 10, 1809, Einhorn studied at an Orthodox yeshiva, receiving his rabbinical certificate in 1826. He then took the radical step of attending several secular universities. This, along with his increasingly unorthodox views, led to a reaction among the Orthodox rabbis, who prevented his appointment as a rabbi for a decade. He finally obtained a position in Mecklenburg-Schwerin and later in Pesth, Hungary. Following the failure of the Hungarian revolution (1848–1849), however, his temple was closed due to his support for the revolution and the hostility of his Orthodox colleagues.

Einhorn came to the somewhat freer atmosphere of America in 1855 as rabbi of Temple Har Sinai in Baltimore. Even there his views caused problems, and in 1861 he left after being attacked for his abolitionist views. Einhorn served as rabbi of Keneseth Israel in Philadelphia (1861–1866) and Adath Jeshurun (later Temple Beth-El) in New York (1866–1879) until his death on November 2, 1879. During this time he continued his theological work of placing Reform Judaism on a sound intellectual basis.

David Einhorn was the radical thinker of American Reform Judaism. For him, Judaism needed a drastic restructuring. It had become too encrusted with useless and unnecessary rituals and rules. For Einhorn the goal was to locate and retain the eternal essence of Judaism and remove all that was temporary. As he said, "Like man himself the divine law has a perishable body and an imperishable spirit." This imperishable spirit lay in Judaism's monotheistic God and in the ethical commandments. These were eternal, while the ritual obligations were deemed to be merely reflections of the spirit of the time that created them.

David Einhorn's teachings about religion dominated Reform Judaism for nearly seven decades. They included a rejection of the ritual law and the idea of a separate Jewish people. Judaism was a religion whose universal mission was to bring ethical monotheism to all. The dispersal of Jews throughout the world was not an exile for sin but a necessary part of this mission. Since the Jewish people were not in exile they did not look toward a messianic restoration of the Jewish state, but viewed the messianic age as one of universal peace and justice. Incorporated after his death into the PITTSBURGH PLATFORM of 1885, these views dominated American Reform Judaism until 1937.

EQ

Bibliography: Eitel Wolf Dobert, *Einhorn and Szold: Two Liberal German Rabbis in Baltimore* (Baltimore: Society for the History of the Germans in Maryland, 1956); David Einhorn, *Dr. David Einhorn's 'Olat Tamid: Book of Prayers for Jewish Congregations.* (Chicago: Press of S. Ettlinger, 1896); Nathan Glazer, *American Judaism.* 2d ed., rev. (Chicago: University of Chicago Press, 1972); W. Gunther Plaut, *The Rise of Reform Judaism: A Sourcebook of*

Its European Origins. 2 vols. (New York: World Union of Progressive Judaism, 1969); Howard M. Sachar, *A History of the Jews in America* (New York: Knopf, 1992).

election The word *election* is derived from the Latin *electio*, which means "a choice." In a religious setting, the term has traditionally referred to God's choice of certain people to receive forgiveness of sins and eternal salvation. The concept of election appears in the New Testament in the writings of St. Paul, who refers to those whom God "chose . . . before the foundation of the world to be holy and blameless before him" (Ephesians 1:4). Emphasis on election has been a hallmark of CALVINISM and the REFORMED TRADITION.

Fundamental to belief in election is the concept of divine grace. The idea of grace is widespread throughout the Bible and generally denotes the favor God shows to undeserving, sinful human beings. In the fourth century, Christian theologian Augustine of Hippo chose to emphasize divine grace and denigrate the importance of human responsibility in the process of salvation. So strong was Augustine's accent upon the divine, rather than the human, will that he believed God had foreordained the salvation of men and women before the creation of the world. God had predestined from eternity, therefore, the election of some souls to salvation.

Sixteenth-century reformer John Calvin adopted Augustine's emphasis on the omnipotence of God and the passivity of humankind. He made the doctrine of predestination the foundation of his theological system. Without divine grace, Calvin wrote, no person could repent and become a Christian. Yet God's grace was a gift that only the elect received. The credit for salvation belonged solely to God, who had predestined the fate of human souls, gratuitously granting irresistible salvation to some and inescapable damnation to others. Although his teaching on election appeared to undercut the need for moral effort, since no amount of piety or faithfulness could ever change the divine eternal plan, Calvin counseled people simply to trust in the all-sufficient grace of God.

In the early 17th century, Dutch theologian Jacobus Arminius advanced a pivotal challenge to Calvin's teachings on election. Arminius, who doubted that God's choice could ever have been as arbitrary as Calvin suggested, wished to reaffirm the importance of the human will in spiritual matters. Arminius's followers formally disputed Calvin's fatalism and argued that, by God's grace, all people might potentially attain everlasting salvation. Orthodox Calvinists vigorously counterattacked and at the Synod of Dort in 1619 officially condemned ARMINIANISM. The *Canons* of the Synod of Dort asserted that divine election was unconditional. God had predestined some human beings for salvation, Calvinists triumphantly proclaimed, regardless of individual merit or good deeds.

The Puritan movement that emerged in England in the late 16th century also wrestled with the implications of Calvin's doctrine of election. While never directly contradicting Calvin's teaching on predestination, Puritan theologians still sought some gauge by which ordinary believers might be assured that they were numbered among the elect. Puritans came to believe that there were four stages through which a true Christian would pass: effectual calling, justification, sanctification, and glorification. The third stage, SANCTIFICATION, was the key. At that point believers might note their good works, thereby coming to a realization that God had chosen them and that they were, in fact, saved.

The Puritans carried these ideas about election to New England in their migration in the mid-17th century. Using the idea of the heart's preparation for grace, Puritan theologians intended to keep Arminianism at bay. However, allowing believers to observe the steps they took toward conversion insinuated that the soul's regeneration was more a gradual, contemporary process than a sudden and ancient divine decree. "Preparationism," therefore, helped further Arminian notions about self-reliance in America. Despite Calvin's commonly recognized authority, and even despite the emphasis placed upon divine sovereignty by theologian Jonathan EDWARDS, predestination was not to be the principal focus of later American teaching on divine election.

The person most responsible for overthrowing Calvinist determinism and stressing the free human will in Protestant thought was Methodist founder John Wesley. Wesley transformed Arminian themes and adapted them to the new religious movement he led. While earlier Protestant reformers had emphasized God's role in choosing some women and men for salvation, Wesley underscored the responsibility of human beings in appropriating the salvation that God graciously extended to them. Wesley's theology fit the self-reliant spirit of the young American republic, and by the middle of the 19th century the Methodists had become the largest denomination in the United States.

A democratic Arminian emphasis on free will dominated the revivals of the SECOND GREAT AWAKENING. Revival leaders assumed that individuals had the innate ability to reform themselves, and they exhorted sinners to abandon evil and come to God. Anyone who wanted, they said, could be converted and attain salvation. New School Presbyterian clergyman Charles G. FINNEY exemplified the era. Finney taught that ordinary reason revealed that God had given people power to make up their own minds. In an exuberantly democratic era that celebrated the importance of the "common man," when politicians pressed citizens for votes, Finney conceived that the Christian evangelist's primary job was convincing Americans to cast their spiritual ballots for God.

By the late 19th century, the emphasis American evangelicals placed, not on God's choice of the individual but on the individual's obligation to choose Jesus Christ, signified the triumph of Arminianism over the Calvinist understanding of election. While Calvin had once asserted that the most pious Christians could not save themselves nor the most heinous sinners damn themselves, the vast majority of Calvin's spiritual heirs in the United States today assume that the prerogative of accepting or rejecting eternal salvation rests entirely with them.

GHS, Jr.

Bibliography: John T. McNeill, *The History and Character of Calvinism* (1954; New York: Oxford University Press, 1967).

electronic church   *Electronic church* is a term used in recent years to describe various religious broadcasting programs, organizations, and leaders who regularly employ the electronic media. Despite the long history of religious broadcasting in the United States, the term *electronic church* usually refers to television programs produced by conservative Protestant figures from the fundamentalist, evangelical, and Pentecostal traditions. The prominence gained in the 1980s by televangelists such as Jerry FALWELL, Pat ROBERTSON (see also CHRISTIAN RIGHT), Jim and Tammy Bakker, and Jimmy Swaggart generated unprecedented attention to this type of religious broadcasting.

The first wireless transmission of the human voice took place on Christmas Eve in 1906. The program included Bible readings and a rendition of "O Holy Night." The first regularly scheduled religious programming began at station KDKA in Pittsburgh in 1921, when Calvary Episcopal Church broadcast its Sunday evening service. Radio broadcasting developed rapidly in the 1920s. Church leaders soon realized radio's potential advantages for evangelism, and by 1925 about 10 percent of all American radio stations were owned by religious organizations.

Two of the earliest popularizers of religious broadcasting were highly controversial. Aimee Semple MCPHERSON, the flamboyant founder of the International Church of the Foursquare Gospel, was one of the first evangelists to recognize the potential of radio. The radio, she observed in 1924, carried "on the winged feet of the winds, the story of hope, the words of joy, of comfort, of salvation." Roman Catholic priest Charles COUGHLIN began his highly effective radio ministry in 1926. By 1930 he had turned from discussing religious topics to promoting political causes. Credited with aiding the election of Franklin D. Roosevelt as president in 1932, Coughlin turned against him as the 1930s progressed. His preaching became so vitriolic that he was eventually forced off the air by church authorities in 1942.

Charles E. Fuller, a more conventional religious figure than either McPherson or Coughlin, was the most successful radio evangelist of the late 1930s. Fuller started teaching Bible lessons over the air at a radio station owned by the Bible Institute of Los Angeles in the 1920s. By 1930 he was broadcasting services from the church where he served as pastor. He moved to a national audience in 1937, and his program, *The Old Fashioned Revival Hour*, was heard on 30 stations with an estimated 10 million listeners. By mid-1943, *The Old Fashioned Revival Hour* and a second program, *The Pilgrim's Hour*, were broadcast on more than a thousand stations at an annual cost of $1.5 million. Fuller, who helped found Fuller Theological Seminary in Pasadena, California, in 1947, continued his radio ministry until shortly before his death in 1968.

The first religious television broadcast was on Easter Sunday in 1940. Soon, the Federal Council of Churches, an ecumenical association of Protestant denominations, arranged religious programming for NBC. Its initial production, *I Believe*, featured a discussion by leading theologians about religion's applicability to everyday life. In the early 1950s, several conservative denominations launched television ministries. The SEVENTH-DAY ADVENTIST CHURCH began its *Faith for Today* program in 1950, with its star, William A. Fagal, assuming the role of television's first on-air pastor. The LUTHERAN CHURCH—MISSOURI SYNOD started its dramatic

series *This Is the Life* in 1951. And in 1954 the SOUTHERN BAPTIST CONVENTION initiated a series of films based on the parables of Jesus.

Roman Catholic bishop Fulton J. SHEEN was the first true superstar of religious television broadcasting. Sheen was already well known to Americans as an author. He had been the featured speaker on *The Catholic Hour* radio program since 1930. His *Life Is Worth Living* television program, which ran from 1951 until 1957, reached approximately 30 million viewers each week. Sheen's cassock and cape and the twinkle that shone in his eye impressed a faithful audience of Protestants as well as Catholics. Testimonials to his success included both an Emmy award and an appearance on the cover of *Time* magazine in 1952.

Despite Sheen's early prominence, religious television broadcasting was to become the almost exclusive preserve of evangelical preachers (see PREACHERS, PROTESTANT). Evangelist Rex Humbard began this trend in 1952 with broadcasts of Sunday services at his church in Akron, Ohio. "I saw this new thing called television," Humbard later remarked, "and I said, 'That's it.'" He believed God wished preachers to use television to spread the Christian gospel throughout the United States. Pentecostal evangelist and faith healer Oral ROBERTS also helped establish the religious broadcasting movement. He decided in 1954 to telecast the healing services he held in Tulsa, Oklahoma. Another significant event in the use of television by conservative Protestants was the coast-to-coast broadcast of Billy GRAHAM's 1957 preaching crusade in New York City.

The real breakthrough for the new wave of televangelists occurred in 1960. The Federal Communications Commission, which regulates the broadcasting industry, ruled that a station's legal obligation to provide air time for "public service" broadcasts could be met by paid, as well as by free, programming. This decision, coupled with the heightened militancy of conservative Protestantism and the rise of the New CHRISTIAN RIGHT in the 1970s, enabled the electronic church to emerge as a significant force in American life. Given the chance to buy air time, evangelicals soon gained a virtual monopoly over religious broadcasting, purchasing more than 90 percent of all programming related to religious topics.

Evangelicals also developed television networks that offered a combination of family-oriented and religious programs. Evangelist Pat Robertson's Christian Broadcasting Network (CBN), which first went on the air in October 1961, was the most successful of these and became the second-largest cable television operation in the United States. Located in Virginia Beach, Virginia, Robertson's network had an annual budget of more than $200 million in 1987 and reached more than 190 stations throughout the world. Robertson even founded CBN University in 1978, offering courses in communications as well as in law, education, and theology. Although his 1988 and 2000 campaigns for the United States presidency met with limited success, Robertson's television ministry has established him in a position of considerable influence in the Republican party.

After Robertson, the most notable televangelist of the 1980s was MORAL MAJORITY leader Jerry Falwell. Falwell, a Baptist minister, organized the Thomas Road Baptist Church in Lynchburg, Virginia, in 1956. There he launched, first, a daily radio program and, later, a weekly television broadcast of his Sunday morning services (*The Old-Time Gospel Hour*). These ministries became a springboard for the creation of Moral Majority, an educational and fund-raising organization dedicated to lobbying on behalf of conservative political causes. The organization blended fundamentalist religious beliefs with rigidly conservative views on a host of ethical issues that troubled late-20th-century American society. At the height of Falwell's fame in 1983, yearly contributions to his *Old-Time Gospel Hour* totaled more than $52 million.

Two other popular television ministries that gained great prominence in the 1980s

later collapsed in the wake of sexual scandals. Jim Bakker, a minister of the ASSEMBLIES OF GOD and a former host on Pat Robertson's Christian Broadcasting Network, developed his own television show, *The PTL Club*, which by 1987 reached 13 million homes on cable TV. Along with his wife Tammy, Bakker also built a Christian theme park and resort, Heritage USA, outside Charlotte, North Carolina. However, financial improprieties and revelations of Jim Bakker's affair with his secretary led to his resignation in disgrace in 1987. Jimmy Swaggart, an Assemblies of God evangelist like Bakker, began a weekly television broadcast in 1973. By the late 1980s *The Jimmy Swaggart Show* was broadcast nationwide from his headquarters in Baton Rouge, Louisiana. After bringing charges of adultery against Jim Bakker in the spring of 1987, Swaggart was publicly exposed for his own sexual encounters with a prostitute. He was defrocked by his denomination in 1988.

One other prosperous television ministry of recent times has been the *Hour of Power* broadcasts of Robert Schuller, a minister of the REFORMED CHURCH IN AMERICA. Schuller began telecasting Sunday worship services at his Garden Grove Community Church in southern California as early as 1970. By the mid-1970s, the program was aired nationally in major cities. Schuller dreamed of building a church that would serve both a walk-in and a drive-in congregation. This hope was realized in 1980 with the completion of the spectacular Crystal Cathedral, erected at a cost of nearly $20 million. Fashioning an optimistic theology he called "possibility thinking," Schuller recast the Christian Gospel into a form that appealed to the age-old human quest for self-esteem and worldly success.

At present, about 16 million people, or roughly 8 percent of the national television audience, regularly listen to religious broadcasts. The number of syndicated religious programs increased dramatically between 1970 and 1975, jumping from 38 to 66. This figure further increased to nearly 100 by the early 1980s. Most of the audience of the electronic church is also active in local congregations. These viewers tend to believe that the religious broadcasts they watch are supplements to their Sunday morning churchgoing. Their financial giving to the television ministries is unquestionably substantial. The total annual revenue for religious broadcasting in the United States exceeds $1 billion.

Despite the lurid scandals of recent years, most religious broadcasters certainly believe the Gospel they preach on radio and television. Like many popular religious leaders throughout American history, the televangelists insist that Christianity was never intended to be an obscure creed intelligible only to the intellectually sophisticated. Rather, it contains a plain message that anyone can understand. The electronic church simply provides an effective means, they say, of spreading the Gospel widely throughout modern American society.

GHS, Jr.

Bibliography: Razelle Frankl, *Televangelism: The Marketing of Popular Religion* (Carbondale: Southern Illinois University Press, 1987); Jeffrey K. Hadden and Charles E. Swann, *Prime Time Preachers: The Rising Power of Televangelism* (Reading, Mass.: Addison Wesley, 1981).

Eliot, John (1604–1690)

Among the Puritans (see PURITANISM) who fled to America in order to escape increasing persecution was one whose labors among the Algonquin-speaking Indians would earn him the title "Apostle to the Indians." John Eliot (born in Winford, England, in August 1604) labored among the Wampanoag and Massachusetts Indians for 44 years, only to see most of his work destroyed by war.

Like most of the Puritan ministers who came to New England, Eliot had been educated at Cambridge University. While there he was deeply influenced by the work of Thomas HOOKER, whom he assisted in operating a school at Little Boddon. When Hooker was summoned before the Court of High Commission (Star Chamber) in 1630 for his religious beliefs, Eliot—sensing danger—wisely emigrated to the MASSACHUSETTS BAY COLONY the next year.

Upon arriving he served as a supply minister in Boston until 1632. In that year he was called to a church in Roxbury. There Eliot combined work among the English with a growing concern for the Native Americans. He eventually would devote all his energy to the latter.

With the aid of native tutors, he slowly learned the Algonquin language, producing an alphabet, dictionary, and grammar and delivering his first sermon in that language in 1646. Eliot had the consuming Puritan interest in doctrine and the Bible. This led him to produce an Algonquin catechism (1653) and a translation of the Bible. This would be the first Bible printed in America, the New Testament in 1661 and Old Testament in 1663.

Eliot's labors among the Indians bore fruit slowly but steadily. His efforts led to the chartering of the Society for the Propagation of the Gospel in New England by the British Parliament in 1649 to support missions among Native Americans. In 1651 a group of Eliot's converts formed the town of Natick. By 1674, 1,100 of these "Praying Indians" were organized into 14 self-governing towns, many with their own native ministers. In these towns, the converts were transformed socially into Englishmen and women. They conformed to English modes of dress and economics, settling into permanent villages with the men engaged in agriculture and the women in domestic activities.

The outbreak of King Philip's War (1675–1676) virtually destroyed these communities. Racism and suspicion led the New England colonists to vent their fury on these Christianized Indians, who were more accessible than the elusive Metacomet (King Philip) and his warriors. Their towns were burnt and hundreds died in concentration camps. By the end of the war only four towns remained intact. Eliot's work never recovered, although he continued to work among the scattered and demoralized Indians until his death on May 21, 1690.

EQ

Bibliography: David Chamberlain, *Eliot of Massachusetts, the Apostle to the Indians* (London: Independent Press, 1928); Richard W. Cogley, *John Eliot's Mission to the Indians Before King Philip's War* (Cambridge, Mass.: Harvard University Press, 1999); Ola E. Winslow, *John Eliot: Apostle to the Indians* (Boston: Houghton Mifflin, 1968).

Emerson, Ralph Waldo (1803–1882)

Inheriting a mixture of the declining PURITANISM and nascent Unitarianism (see UNITARIAN CONTROVERSY) of his New England ancestors, Emerson gained a considerable reputation as a gifted speaker and an original mind in his own day, becoming the central figure in the school of thought known as TRANSCENDENTALISM.

Emerson was born in Boston to William and Ruth Haskins Emerson on May 25, 1803. His father, who was the pastor of Boston's First Unitarian Church, died of tuberculosis while Emerson was quite young. Emerson grew up under the Calvinist (see CALVINISM) influence of his aunt, Mary Moody Emerson. As a boy Emerson studied Latin, Greek, mathematics, and writing, eventually enrolling at Harvard College in 1817. In addition to the classics, he immersed himself in the works of Shakespeare, Montaigne, and contemporary European authors. After graduating in 1821, he began teaching at a private school for young women run by his brother William. Having decided on the ministry, he entered Harvard Divinity School in 1824.

His vocational choice provided a ready vehicle for his writing. Following his return from a trip to Florida, taken to recover from rheumatism, Emerson preached regularly in a number of neighboring Massachusetts towns. In 1829, after his marriage to Ellen Tucker (who died in 1831), he was called to the pulpit of Boston's Second Church. However, he found the Unitarianism of his day too confining, writing in his journal, "It is the best part of the man,

I sometimes think, that revolts against his being the minister. His good revolts against official goodness." After requesting that he be permitted to forego administering Communion to his congregation and being refused by the church board, he announced his resignation following a sermon on "The Lord's Supper," September 9, 1832, and sailed to Europe on Christmas Day. During travels in England he met Samuel Taylor Coleridge, William Wordsworth, John Stuart Mill, and Thomas Carlyle, with whom he formed a lasting friendship.

After his return he settled in Concord, marrying Lydia Jackson in 1835, and began receiving invitations to preach and lecture. Emerson loved conversation, and the informal Transcendental Club meeting in his home brought together a number of important intellectual figures: Bronson ALCOTT, William Ellery CHANNING JR., Margaret FULLER, and Henry David THOREAU. As his reputation grew, lecturing became increasingly lucrative, and Emerson spent several decades delivering lectures throughout the United States and in England. Emerson also edited the transcendentalist organ, *The Dial*, for several years and produced a number of volumes of collected essays and poems.

In line with the concerns for social reform common in his circle (see LIBERALISM, THEOLOGICAL) Emerson spoke out on a number of public issues, denouncing the forced removal of the Cherokees from Georgia in the late 1830s and the Mexican War (1846–1848). As tensions between North and South mounted, he adopted the cause of ABOLITIONISM. After the outbreak of the CIVIL WAR he voiced frequent support for President Abraham LINCOLN. In later life, conservationist John MUIR also sought to enlist him in the cause of wilderness preservation, though without much success. In the 1870s declining health forced him to cut back on his writing, which remained sporadic up to the time of his death on April 27, 1882.

Emerson was a dynamic thinker, led by the fluidity of language to question everything he asserted. "A foolish consistency is the hobgob-

Ralph Waldo Emerson, the sage and seer of 19th-century transcendentalism who preached self-reliance as the cardinal virtue. *(Engraving by J. A. J. Wilcox)*

conformism of New England's intellectual life led him to explore not only the leading European thinkers Kant, Hegel, Schiller, and Goethe, but also classics of Asian thought, such as the *Bhagavad Gita* (see HINDUISM) and to seek direct connection with the divine through nature. While his originality is sometimes questioned, his relentless passion to encounter "the currents of the Universal Being" in the midst of mind, nature, society, art, language, and individual life ensures Emerson a lasting influence on American thought.

MG

Bibliography: John MacAleer, *Ralph Waldo Emerson: Days of Encounter* (Boston: Little, Brown, 1984); Joel Porte and Saundra Morris, *The Cambridge Companion to Ralph Waldo Emerson* (New York: Cambridge University Press, 1999); David Robinson, *Apostle of Culture: Emerson as Preacher and Lecturer* (Philadelphia: University of Pennsylvania Press, 1982); Stephen E. Whicher, *Freedom and Fate: An Inner Life of Ralph Waldo Emerson* (Philadelphia: University of Pennsylvania Press, 1971).

Enlightenment, the   The Enlightenment, which has exerted a tremendous influence on religion in the United States since the beginning of the republic, refers to an intellectual movement in the modern West devoted to utilizing reason to improve society, politics, and religion. Enlightenment thinkers believed deeply in the perfectibility of human beings and the possibility of social progress. Their scientific spirit inclined them toward skepticism and tolerance in religion but only in exceptional cases to infidelity.

The German philosopher Immanuel Kant described the Enlightenment as "man's emergence from his self-incurred immaturity." Kant's definition sums up a diffuse set of intellectual currents accompanying the broad-scale transformations through which medieval Europe became a modern society. Revolutions in science, political and economic life, philosophy, and religion all emerged after the 130 years of religious war and colonial expansion that

lin of little minds," he claimed in "Self Reliance" (1847). Urging independence of mind, he attacked what he saw as the stale conformity of New England, especially its religion. Invited to speak by Harvard students, he encouraged them in his famous "Divinity School Address" to reject the formalism of the existing church and to think: "Yourself a newborn bard of the Holy Ghost—cast behind you all conformity, and acquaint men at first hand with Deity." In the same way he urged Americans to think the sort of new thoughts demanded by their unique position in history and by the unique continent they were conquering. His own efforts to cast off what he saw as the

followed in the wake of the Protestant Reformation (1519–1564). The beginnings of the Enlightenment are often traced to England during the Glorious Revolution (1688), a point in time close to the publication of such influential works as Isaac Newton's *Principia Mathematica* (1687) and John Locke's *An Essay Concerning Human Understanding* (1690). Its roots certainly extend even earlier to the work of Francis Bacon (1561–1626) and Réné Descartes (1596–1650). For these founders of the modern scientific world view, true knowledge was not guaranteed by religious authority or tradition but rather by individual rational effort. The power of reason was sufficient to expose the errors of tradition.

The potential for human reason to cast doubt upon revealed religious truth enabled Enlightenment thinkers to expand and splinter into various, often conflicting, parties. In England the materialist political philosopher Thomas Hobbes (1588–1679) and John Locke (1632–1704), whose political theories played a role in sharpening the revolutionary ideas of American colonists, remained loyal members of the Church of England. In France, on the other hand, with an entrenched aristocracy and a powerful Catholic Church, Enlightenment themes of the triumph of human reason over superstition often took on a much sharper anticlerical tone, eventually culminating during the French Revolution in the movement to confiscate Church lands and in French *philosophe* Denis Diderot's complaint that "mankind shall not be free until the last king is strangled with the entrails of the last priest."

Enlightenment thinkers differed sharply over correct scientific method, whether political rule ought to be invested in the people or a sovereign, whether all religion was merely superstition, and whether progress in human affairs was really possible. However, they shared a conviction that human reason or will, once released from the bonds of authority and tradition, could be relied upon as the surest guide to human happiness and the improvement of society.

Americans at first were simply recipients of enlightened ideas arising in England. Much of Puritan social theory, biblical interpretation, and theology was dependent upon the Neoplatonic metaphysics the Protestant reformers had inherited from the Middle Ages. But a number of Puritan intellectuals in America were able to form at least some links between their CALVINISM and the new faith in reason. Beginning in the late 17th century, students at Harvard had begun reading directly or indirectly the works of Descartes, Locke, John Tillotson, and to some extent Sir Isaac Newton. John Ray's *Wisdom of God Manifest in the Works of Creation* (1691), an inquiry into nature as a source of knowledge about divinity, became a popular introduction to "natural theology." Cotton MATHER drew on Newton's argument for an ordered universe in *Reasonable Religion* (1700) and *The Christian Philosopher* (1721). Locke's plea for religious tolerance, *The Reasonableness of Christianity* (1695), was read and appreciated far more than his theory of knowledge, though Jonathan EDWARDS drew heavily on Locke's views of human knowledge.

During the second half of the 18th century, moderate versions of Enlightenment ideas spread across America's upper classes. Anglicans (see ANGLICANISM) in both southern and northern colonies backed up their rejection of revivals and religious enthusiasm (see GREAT AWAKENING) by portraying their own religion as the most reasonable. John Witherspoon, a Scottish Presbyterian convinced of the harmony between Christian faith and the new "natural philosophy," brought the "common sense" ideas of fellow Scots Dugald Stewart and Thomas Reid, as well as those of Adam Smith and even skeptic David Hume, into the curriculum at the College of New Jersey, now Princeton University.

In addition to efforts within church circles to stem the enthusiastic tide of popular religion, others who doubted Christianity were also using the new faith in reason to diminish Christianity's hold on colonial minds. Outright skeptics were few. Benjamin Franklin may have been the only American comfortable in the anticlerical salons of Parisian society during the revolutionary years, and few colonists were familiar with the work of French authors. Another Enlightenment movement, Deism, played a more prominent role in American life.

In general, deists, originating in England, expanded upon the work of Locke and Newton, and spoke of the world as a rational order, created by a rational God. Calvinists had often spoken of divine sovereignty, meaning that God's freedom was not subject to the laws of nature. Consequently, God could only be known through faith. Deists, however, thought the creator was bound by the same standards of rationality and morality visible in the natural order. Accordingly, deists were suspicious of biblical accounts of miracles and claims of the Bible's supernatural authorship. Deists did tend to approve the concept of an afterlife, which served as an anchor for moral rectitude.

While deist clubs formed in many colonial towns, the movements as a whole lacked organizational power. Deists found their most congenial home in the lodges of FREEMASONRY, spreading throughout the colonies and often developing a relation of tolerance with Protestant liberals. The rituals and symbols used by the Masonic brotherhood showed a strong Enlightenment influence. The sun symbolized both reason's inner light and natural order. Such architectural symbols as the compass and square signified both the rational order of nature and the human capacity to design and build a well-ordered, just society.

Deists were an ideologically diverse group, although many deists played an influential role in the formation of revolutionary sentiment. Deist talk of the reasoning powers of all human beings, the possibility of human perfectibility, and of universal moral standards serving to judge the actions of states and rulers all shaped the discourse of colonists bent on revolution. Thomas JEFFERSON's Declaration of Independence is perhaps the most recognizable state-

ment of deist values. Fifty-two of its 56 signers were deists, although the vast majority also were faithful Anglicans. Most members of the Continental Congress and many generals in the Continental Army were deists as well.

In the years following the Revolution a number of more radical Enlightenment voices were raised, many of them deist, but some, such as that of English immigrant Joseph Priestley, took hold within the growing camp of Unitarianism (see UNITARIAN CONTROVERSY). Priestley forged a unique blend of French materialism, scientific insight, dissenting Protestantism, and a deep commitment to the justness of the American Revolution. Tom PAINE's *The Age of Reason* (1794–1796) and *Reason the Only Oracle of Man* (1784) by Ethan Allen gained notoriety for their attacks on Christianity. Rationalist Elihu Palmer drew on the rhetoric of French *philosophes* to portray a postrevolutionary world stripped of priests and kings, a millennial republic of justice and peace built on the foundation of human reason. Virginia's College of William and Mary, where Jefferson had earlier abolished the chairs of divinity, became the leading center of radical learning.

The radical deist influence declined sharply in the first years of the 19th century. In more theologically and politically moderate forms the Enlightenment lived on in the thought of Protestant liberals and New England Unitarians. But the radical republican vision of Paine and Palmer, which had looked to France for revolutionary inspiration, suffered as Jacobin forces there turned the revolution in a more extreme direction. In the midst of an America undergoing an enthusiastic Protestant revival (see SECOND GREAT AWAKENING), influential Calvinist clergy such as Timothy DWIGHT of Yale increasingly portrayed deists as part of an international conspiracy, threatening the foundations of Christian civilization.

In the long term, Enlightenment ideals played a crucial role in the rise of a more secular American culture (see SECULARISM; DEWEY,

JOHN). The language by which Americans speak of their faith in science, their conviction that the future is one of progress, and the value of religious and political liberty is rooted in the worldview of the Enlightenment. At times Americans have been able to blend the Enlightenment with the Bible. But throughout American history followers of the two traditions also have repeatedly clashed.

MG

Bibliography: Peter Gay, *The Enlightenment, an Interpretation*, 2 vols. (New York: Alfred A. Knopf, 1966–1969); Henry F. May, *The Enlightenment in America* (New York: Oxford University Press, 1976).

Ephrata Community An 18th-century monastic order, the Ephrata Community offered its members simple lives of solitude and piety. The community, an offshoot of the CHURCH OF THE BRETHREN, was founded by Johann Conrad Beissel (1691–1768), a devoted German pietist who emigrated to Germantown, Pennsylvania, in 1720.

From his rebaptism in 1722 until he left the group in 1728, Beissel was officially a member of the Church of the Brethren. But community life among the Dunkers, as members of the Church of the Brethren were popularly called, proved too much for the solitary Beissel, who frequently withdrew from church fellowship for long periods of isolation. By 1732, Beissel had gathered around him enough like-minded pietists (see PIETISM) to form a monastic group in Ephrata, Pennsylvania.

Among the distinctive practices of the Ephrata Community was its observation of the Sabbath on Saturday rather than Sunday. Because of this practice, Beissel's followers came to be known as the German Seventh-Day Baptists. Members of Beissel's community also engaged in daily spiritual warfare with the temptations of the flesh, practicing continence in all things. Celibacy and poverty were key ideals, and segregation of the sexes and asceticism key practices.

Beissel's community soon began attracting converts not only from the Brethren but also from the much larger German Reformed community of Pennsylvania. Perhaps because of its successes, the Ephrata Community experienced tensions with other German pietists in the area. But more than anything else, Beissel's inclination toward the solitary life of the ascetic led to the group's demise. Administrative affairs were not the pietist's forte; his resolve to rule with an iron fist created conflicts among community members.

Following his death in 1768, Beissel was succeeded by John Peter Miller (1710–1796), who like most Dunkers had been raised in the German Reformed tradition. Miller was able to hold the group together for a time, but shortly after his death in 1796 the Ephrata experiment dissolved. Despite its short life, this community stands as a conspicuous example of monastic living in lay-oriented America.

SRP

Bibliography: E. G. Alderfer, *The Ephrata Commune: An Early American Counterculture* (Pittsburgh: University of Pittsburgh Press, 1985); Walter C. Klein, *Johann Conrad Beissel: Mystic and Martinet* (Philadelphia: Porcupine Press, 1973).

episcopacy Episcopacy is a form of church government in which authority is centered in the office of bishop. The word itself derives from the Greek *episkopos*, meaning "overseer" or, as it is traditionally translated when it appears in the New Testament, "bishop." By the end of the second century, a threefold order of bishops, priests, and deacons had been established as the governing hierarchy of the Christian church. The bishop, whose authority was said to derive directly from the apostles of Jesus, presided as chief pastor and administrator of a geographic district known as a diocese. He alone was sanctioned to perform the sacramental rites of ordination and (by the Middle Ages) confirmation.

Between the second and the 16th centuries, Christianity everywhere was organized on this episcopal system, which Roman Catholic and Eastern Orthodox churches maintain today. However, at the time of the Reformation, most Protestant denominations abolished the episcopate, denouncing it as a corrupt institution. They adopted instead either a presbyterian (governance by clergy and elected laity) or a congregational (governance by local congregations) structure. Only Anglicans continued to govern according to the medieval episcopal system. A few Protestant denominations, namely, Methodists, Lutherans of Scandinavian heritage, and Moravians, while still formally maintaining the bishop's office, modified its pre-Reformation functions.

Episcopacy became a source of conflict at one critical juncture in American history. Although the episcopate was central to the governance of the Church of England, no Anglican bishop resided in America during the colonial period. An uproar arose in the 1760s, when some Anglicans in the colonies began to press for their own bishop. Since bishops in England held temporal as well as ecclesiastical powers, American Congregationalists, Presbyterians, and even a few Anglicans reacted negatively to the proposal, fearing it represented an imposition of British tyranny similar to the Stamp Act of the same period. American resistance was successful, and no Anglican bishop was consecrated in America until after the War for Independence. But as patriot leader John Adams later remarked, "the apprehension of Episcopacy" contributed significantly to the outbreak of the AMERICAN REVOLUTION.

Episcopalians, Methodists, and Roman Catholics were the three major denominations with bishops in the United States at the time of the founding of the country. Samuel SEABURY of Connecticut was consecrated in Scotland in 1784 as the first bishop of the Episcopal Church. Thomas COKE was ordained by John Wesley in 1784 as the first bishop (or superintendent, the term Wesley preferred) of the Methodist Episcopal Church. And John CAR-

ROLL of Baltimore, the first Roman Catholic bishop, was consecrated in 1790.

GHS, Jr.

Bibliography: Carl Bridenbaugh, *Mitre and Sceptre: Transatlantic Faiths, Ideas, Personalities, and Politics, 1689–1775* (New York: Oxford University Press, 1962); William Telfer, *The Office of a Bishop* (London: Darton, Longman & Todd, 1962).

Episcopal Church Originally known as the Protestant Episcopal Church in the United States of America, the Episcopal Church is a member of the Anglican (see ANGLICANISM) Communion, the worldwide fellowship of churches that trace their historical roots to the Church of England. The Episcopal Church was organized in October 1789, when its first General Convention adopted a constitution, ratified a set of church canons, and authorized a Book of Common Prayer for use in services of worship.

Anglicanism came to America in the first half of the 17th century. The English settlers who established colonies in Massachusetts and Virginia were members of the Church of England, and though the New England settlements rapidly adopted a congregational form of church government (see CONGREGATIONALISM), those in Virginia continued loyal to the episcopal (see EPISCOPACY) polity and liturgical forms of Anglicanism. While Virginia remained the great center of Anglican strength throughout the colonial period, Anglicanism had spread throughout all 13 colonies before the AMERICAN REVOLUTION. The founding of two missionary organizations in England, the Society for Promoting Christian Knowledge (1698) and the SOCIETY FOR THE PROPAGATION OF THE GOSPEL IN FOREIGN PARTS (1701), also helped revitalize Anglican spiritual life and led to the establishing of many new churches in America.

Anglicanism suffered tremendously during the Revolution. Since the clergy, especially those in the northern colonies, tended to be loyal to the English crown and preferred to close their church buildings rather than alter their services and pray for the American cause, many were forced to return to England or emigrate to Canada during the war. Most Anglicans in the southern colonies were sympathetic to the revolt from Great Britain. Two-thirds of the signers of the Declaration of Independence were Anglican laymen.

After the Revolution and during the early national period, the new Episcopal Church struggled to reestablish its institutional life. Its principal concern was creating a denomination that was indigenous to America and independent of the English king, the "supreme governor" of the Church of England. Because

Barbara Harris is the first woman to become a bishop in the Episcopal Church. She was elected Bishop of the Diocese of Eastern Massachusetts, the largest in the United States, in September 1988. *(Photo credit: David Zadig, Episcopal Church Times)*

the sacramental rites of ordination and confirmation (confirmation being a prerequisite for admission to Holy Communion) could not be performed without a bishop, the procuring of an American bishop was absolutely essential. In November 1784, Samuel SEABURY, a Connecticut clergyman, was consecrated as the first American bishop by three bishops of the Scottish Episcopal Church. And after the British Parliament passed legislation allowing the consecration of clergymen who were not British subjects, William White of Pennsylvania and Samuel Provoost of New York were consecrated as the second and third American bishops in July 1789.

During the 19th century, the Episcopal Church (like most American denominations) grew rapidly, increasing from roughly 30,000 to more than 700,000 members between 1830 and 1900, and from about 600 to more than 6,200 churches in the same period. In that century, three separate church "parties" emerged, each emphasizing distinctive theological and liturgical views of the Christian life. Bishop John Henry HOBART of New York and Bishop John Stark Ravenscroft of North Carolina were representative of the high church party (later called ANGLO-CATHOLICISM), which stressed the apostolic succession of bishops and the historic catholicity of the church. Alexander Viets Griswold, bishop of the Eastern Diocese (the New England states except Connecticut) and William Meade, bishop of Virginia, represented the low church, or evangelical party. Episcopal evangelicals, similar to American Protestants generally, emphasized the importance of individual conversion and a disciplined moral life. And the broad church, or liberal party, which developed after the Civil War, sought a faith that was open to modern intellectual and social trends. Phillips BROOKS of Trinity Church, Boston, and William Porcher DUBOSE, a theologian at the University of the South, were leading spokesmen for broad church Episcopalians.

Disagreements over "churchmanship" led to the only major schism the Episcopal Church has ever suffered. When George David Cummins, the assistant bishop of Kentucky, was censured by high church Episcopalians for participating in a Protestant Communion service, he resigned his position and helped organize the Reformed Episcopal Church (REC) in December 1873. The leaders of the new REC adopted a Prayer Book and rules of order similar to those of the Episcopal Church, but envisioned a closer relationship with other Protestant denominations than had been feasible within the increasingly Catholic-oriented Episcopal fold. Although in recent years the REC and the Episcopal Church have discussed the possibility of reunion, the REC remains a separate denomination with roughly 6,000 members.

The Episcopal Church (despite its internal diversity) has engaged in dialogue with other Protestant churches with some hesitation. In 1886, for example, William Reed Huntington convinced Episcopal bishops to accept a four-fold position as the basis for Christian reunion. Afterwards known as the Chicago-Lambeth Quadrilateral, the document Huntington proposed affirmed the following starting points for ecumenical discussions: 1) the Holy Scriptures as the Word of God; 2) the Nicene Creed as an acceptable statement of the Christian faith; 3) the two sacraments instituted by Jesus—baptism and the Lord's Supper; and 4) the historic episcopate. The episcopate remained a subject of controversy in Episcopal ecumenical ventures, but Huntington's document helped open an era of interchurch cooperation that began in the early 20th century and peaked in the 1960s.

The second half of the 20th century proved to be tumultuous for the Episcopal Church. Beginning in 1949 and culminating in 1979, Episcopalians studied and approved the most radical revision of the Book of Common Prayer since the introduction of an English-language prayer book in 1549. Although many traditionalists clung to the Elizabethan English used throughout the earlier 1928 edition of the American Prayer Book, scholars insisted that the new

prayer book of 1979, which replaced the 1928 book, represented the best liturgical thinking of the day. The place of women in the church was another area of disagreement, as barriers to female participation in the church were gradually removed after 1964. In 1976, church canons were altered to allow the ordination of women to the priesthood. And Barbara Harris, consecrated suffragan (assistant) bishop of Massachusetts in 1989, became the first female bishop of the Anglican Communion, an event marked by protest from theological conservatives.

Liberals in the Episcopal Church in the 1960s struggled to relate the Gospel to the realities of the modern world. James Pike, the bishop of California, for instance, denied the virgin birth of Jesus and questioned the relevance of the doctrine of the Trinity for his time. He was eventually censured by his fellow bishops, who objected to his tendency to vulgarize and caricature the "great expressions of the faith." In the 1980s, Bishop John Spong of the diocese of Newark likewise wondered whether the language of the Bible should still inform the thinking of 20th-century Christians. Spong challenged the church's sexual mores when he ordained a homosexual to the priesthood in 1989, an action later repudiated by his fellow bishops.

The organization of the Episcopal Church today is substantially shaped by the American democratic experience of the late 18th century. Although the church derives its name from the bishops who preside over its liturgy and governance, actual authority is divided equally among bishops, clergy, and laity. Each diocese (usually conforming to the boundaries of a state) is administered by one or more bishops and an annual convention of clergy and delegates from local parishes. A General Convention of bishops and elected clerical and lay representatives from each diocese meets every three years to decide church policy. Within the General Convention there are two houses: the House of Bishops and the House of Deputies, and consent from both bodies is required before a legislative proposal can be enacted. An elected presiding bishop and executive council carry on the work of the national church between meetings of the General Convention.

The Episcopal Church occupies a somewhat anomalous position in American religion, permitting great latitude in belief but defining unity quite rigidly through worship and polity. On the one hand, it holds to the ancient creeds of Christendom and through its prayer book maintains uniform orders of worship and preserves the liturgical heritage of Catholic Christianity. On the other, a wide variety of interpretation of both biblical texts and theological tradition has often been tolerated.

One of the most important developments for the Episcopal Church during the late 20th century was dialogue with the Evangelical Lutheran Church of America about developing a relationship of full communion. These discussions were concluded in the summer of 2000 when the two denominations adopted a "Call to Common Mission" that committed them to enter into full communion where each denomination would recognize the legitimacy of the other's baptism and ordination on an equal footing with its own. While not a merger of the two denominations, it did bring them into a close theological and working relationship when it became effective at the beginning of 2001.

The Episcopal Church grew numerically through the middle of the 20th century, experiencing a growth of about a million members between 1950 and 1965. After 1965, and paralleling the declines in other mainline Protestant denominations over the same period, membership slipped by 1 million. In 2000, there were more than 2.5 million members of the church in 7,500 parishes.

GHS, Jr.

Bibliography: David L. Holmes, *A Brief History of the Episcopal Church* (Valley Forge, Pa.: Trinity Press International, 1993); Robert W. Prichard, *A History of the Episcopal Church* (Harrisburg, Pa.: More-house Publishing, 1991); www.ecusa.anglican.org (Episcopal Church).

Episcopal Synod of America See ANGLO-CATHOLICISM.

eschatology Eschatology is the study of "last things," or the "end-times" (from the Greek *eschaton*). When employed in American religion, this term usually refers to events Christians believe will occur at the time of the second coming of Jesus Christ. Eschatology has roots within the Jewish and Christian traditions, particularly in the Hebrew Bible Book of Daniel and the New Testament Book of Revelation. Moreover, eschatological beliefs have generally been expressed in relationship to expectations of a coming millennium, a 1,000-year period of unprecedented peace and righteousness alluded to in the 20th chapter of the Book of Revelation.

Scholars of American religion divide Christian millennialism into three main categories:

1. Postmillennialists (see POSTMILLENNIALISM) believe that God's kingdom will be established on earth by the faithful actions of the church. It is the duty of Christians to labor to transform human society until the golden age begins, at which time Christ will return and inaugurate his reign. In the estimation of postmillennialists, therefore, Christ's second coming can only take place *after* the millennium.
2. Premillennialists (see PREMILLENNIALISM), on the other hand, argue that a radical break must occur between the present age and the establishment of the kingdom of God. They expect that the coming of Christ will *precede* the millennium and that the supernatural Christ, not the church alone, can reform human society. One form of premillennialism that has achieved enormous popularity over the past hundred years is called DISPENSATIONALISM, a division of cosmic time into various dispensations, or stages, in which God reveals himself.
3. Amillennialists (that is, those who believe in "no millennium") do not interpret biblical references to the 1,000-year reign of Christ

literally but believe instead that goodness will simply develop naturally in the world until the second coming of Jesus. Amillennialists also tend to emphasize the presence of the kingdom of God within the institutional church and the hearts of faithful believers.

The optimistic period before the Civil War was the heyday of postmillennial beliefs in the United States. These progressive religious ideas were manifested principally within Protestant REVIVALISM and numerous reform movements, such as antislavery, peace, and temperance. After the Civil War and amid the widespread disillusionment of the Gilded Age, however, premillennialism gained the upper hand. It heavily influenced the fundamentalist movement that emerged late in the century and is widely accepted among most conservative Christian groups in 20th-century America. And since millennialism is seldom discussed at present by the leadership of either the mainline Protestant denominations or Roman Catholicism, the amillennial interpretation of the Bible may be said to dominate that portion of American Christianity today.

The 18th and 19th centuries witnessed a burgeoning interest in eschatology and the proliferation of millennial movements in America. Major denominations that trace their historical roots to the millennialism of that era are the Disciples of Christ, the Seventh-day Adventists, the Mormons, and the Jehovah's Witnesses. The Shakers as well (originally named the United Society of Believers in Christ's Second Coming), although tiny now, had a significant impact on American religion after the Revolutionary War. Eschatology, thus, remains a key concept not only for understanding American religion in the past, but also for interpreting developments in the present day.

GHS, Jr.

Bibliography: Paul Boyer, *When Time Shall Be No More: Prophecy Belief in Modern American Culture* (Cambridge, Mass.: Harvard University Press, 1992); Ernest Lee Tuveson, *Redeemer Nation: The Idea of America's Millennial Role* (Chicago: University of Chicago Press, 1968); Timothy P. Weber, *Living in the Shadow of the Second Coming: American Premillennialism, 1875–1982,* enl. ed. (1979; Chicago: University of Chicago Press, 1987).

establishment, religious   The phrase *religious establishment* refers to the practice in colonial America that granted privileged status to a single Christian denomination in a colony or, later, a state. Prior to the AMERICAN REVOLUTION, nine of the original 13 colonies had religious establishments. In Virginia, Maryland, North Carolina, South Carolina, Georgia, and portions of New York, ANGLICANISM was the state-supported faith. In Massachusetts, Connecticut, and New Hampshire, the Congregational churches were officially established. Only Rhode Island, Pennsylvania, New Jersey, and Delaware had no established churches.

Providing government support for Christianity had a long history prior to the settling of North America. In the early fourth century, the Roman emperor Constantine, after a military victory he attributed to the Christian God, granted patronage to the church and established Christianity as the official religion of the empire. The idea that church and society should constitute a unified entity continued throughout the Middle Ages. Christianity was viewed as the foundation upon which the medieval European social world was constructed. Despite challenges, church-state unity remained intact even in areas affected by the Reformation of the 16th century.

The American colonial religious establishments grew out of the religious situation in England in the 1530s. After overthrowing the authority of Roman Catholicism in his realm, Henry VIII had declared that he, not the pope, was "Supreme Head" of the English church. Thereafter, the monarch was to have power to appoint the bishops who administer and lead Anglican church affairs, and the government was to raise taxes to support clergy and maintain the church's property. The English settlers who came to Virginia in 1607 brought this heritage with them. As early as 1619, the Virginia legislature made provision for assistance to Anglican clergy. Parish boundaries were legally fixed, farmlands (called glebes) were set aside for the support of ministers, and lay vestries (committees that administered parishes) were given broad powers over ecclesiastical and charitable affairs in the colony.

Although Puritans chafed at the restrictions the Anglican establishment placed upon them in England, they carried a similar vision of what a unified Christian society should be to New England in the 1630s. While a polity based upon the autonomy of local congregations replaced the episcopacy of the Church of England, Puritan churches still functioned like English parishes. Town governments assessed taxpayers for the support of a minister and maintenance of the meetinghouse. All residents were also expected to attend worship services, even those who were not formal church members.

Three of the early American colonies, on the other hand, followed their own distinctive religious paths. Rhode Island was settled in the late 1630s by Roger WILLIAMS and others who had been driven out of Massachusetts by the Puritan leadership. Rhode Island was to prove a haven for BAPTISTS, Quakers, and other dissenting religious groups throughout the colonial period. Maryland was founded in 1634 under the auspices of a Roman Catholic proprietor, Cecilius CALVERT, who instructed that all settlers were to be granted religious liberty. This stipulation was codified in 1649 by the Act of Toleration (see TOLERATION, ACT OF), which granted legal protection to all Christians who believed in the doctrine of the Trinity. And William PENN's colony, which he received from Charles II in 1688, was founded upon the principle that true religion flourished best where there was no coercion about matters of faith.

After the Glorious Revolution of 1688, the English monarchy sought to expand its authority over the American colonies. One means of accomplishing this political end was the establishment of the Church of England in colonies where it had not been the official faith. The joint monarchs William III and Mary II and their successor, Anne, instructed royal governors to lobby colonial legislatures to establish Anglicanism. The policy at first met only limited success. The royal governor of New York, for instance, persuaded the colonial assembly in 1693 to provide six "good sufficient Protestant" ministers to serve the four counties around New York City. The first church officially chartered under this act, however, was a Dutch Reformed church. The policy proved more effective in Maryland and South Carolina, where the Church of England was established in 1702 and 1706, respectively, and—several decades later—in Georgia (1758) and North Carolina (1765).

Despite Anglican and Puritan intentions, the GREAT AWAKENING of the mid-18th century presented a radical challenge that started to topple the colonial religious establishments. In the Congregational churches of New England, the revivals of the 1740s created severe tension, as revivalist "New Lights" began to insist that their fellow church members and clergy lacked genuine piety. Some New Lights withdrew from their parishes, founded new churches, and pressed for tax relief. Isaac BACKUS, the principal spokesman of this group, argued that state-supported churches corrupted true Christianity. In his most famous work, *An Appeal to the Public for Religious Liberty Against the Oppression of the Present Day* (1773), he pressed for the full separation of church and state.

In the South, Presbyterian minister Samuel DAVIES became one of the principal dissenters against the Anglican establishment during the Great Awakening. At that time, pious non-Anglicans in Virginia were only allowed to gather for worship within their own homes. Davies fought a lengthy legal battle on behalf of the Presbyterian churches he served. He argued that the Toleration Act of 1689, which permitted freedom of worship in Great Britain, applied to the British colonies as well. He won a favorable ruling in 1755, and after that date Presbyterians were free to organize their own churches.

The American Revolution eventually made the position of the Anglican colonial establishments untenable. Since Anglican clergy were bound by their ordination oaths to support and pray for the English king, colonial legislatures after 1776 were loath to support ministers opposed to the patriot cause. Thus, southern legislatures finally acceded to requests by dissenting Baptists and Presbyterians and suspended payment of the salaries of Anglican clergymen—in Maryland, Virginia, and North Carolina in 1776, in Georgia in 1777, and in South Carolina in 1778. Yet because these legislatures often retained their traditional controls over the licensing and selection of ministers, the clergy as well became vocal advocates of disestablishment. They quickly realized the advantages of regulating church affairs entirely free of governmental control.

After the war ended, Virginia legislator Patrick Henry made one last effort to support a religious establishment by championing a "General Assessment" that would distribute funds impartially among all Christian churches. Baptist minister John LELAND was one of the key figures fighting Henry's plan. Because of their earlier refusal to comply with the Anglican religious establishment, Baptist preachers in colonial Virginia had been imprisoned and their worship services disrupted. This experience led Leland to believe that governments could best assist Christianity by leaving it alone. He thought religious establishments had done more to harm the cause of Jesus Christ than all the persecutions of Christianity combined.

In alliance with statesmen such as nominal Anglicans Thomas JEFFERSON and James MADISON, Leland eventually saw his position vindicated. Madison argued in his *Memorial and Remonstrance* of 1784, for example, that

religion was best served when it was taken entirely out of the hands of the state. Jefferson's Bill for Establishing Religious Freedom, which was adopted by the Virginia House of Burgesses in 1786, began with the premise that "Almighty God hath created the mind free." The Virginia legislative assembly resolved that citizens should never be compelled against their wishes to worship in or support a church.

When delegates gathered in Philadelphia in 1787 to draft a constitution for the new nation, the role of religion in government received consideration. Article Six of the Constitution provided, for instance, that no religious test would be required for holding a federal office. Madison and Jefferson also wanted the Constitution to make a positive statement about the freedom of religion. Madison, therefore, helped guide the Bill of Rights through the first Congress in 1789 and gave religious liberty the solid base he sought. The FIRST AMENDMENT codified Madison and Jefferson's beliefs: The government of the United States would neither favor nor inhibit the exercise of religious beliefs.

The First Amendment established religious freedom as a binding policy for the nation. However, the restrictions of the federal Bill of Rights did not at that time apply to the individual states, and thus weak Congregational establishments were able to survive in Connecticut, New Hampshire, and Massachusetts for several more decades. The Massachusetts constitution of 1780, for example, continued a truncated version of the prerevolutionary religious establishment, in which towns were required to elect their own "public teachers of piety, religion and morality." As political power passed out of the hands of Congregationalists in New England, however, the last state establishments fell. In Connecticut in 1818, a coalition of Baptists, Methodists, Anglicans, and nonbelievers passed a new state charter that stipulated "no preference shall be given by law to any Christian sect." New Hampshire passed a similar law in 1819, and in 1820 Maine, originally part of Massachusetts, entered the union as a state with no established church.

The UNITARIAN CONTROVERSY, which tore apart Congregational parishes into Trinitarian and Unitarian factions early in the 19th century, led at last to disestablishment in Massachusetts. Since the "public teachers" elected by towns were not required to be either orthodox Congregationalists or ordained ministers, voters in some localities started to choose Unitarians to fill those positions. Divisions between Unitarians and Trinitarians became so heated that law suits resulted. In the famed "Dedham Decision" of 1820, the Unitarian-dominated Supreme Court of Massachusetts ruled that control of church property and the right to call a minister belonged to the parish (that is, to the town) rather than to the communicant membership of the local church. The effects of this decision were far-reaching, for it meant there was no further reason for orthodox Congregationalists to support their own established status. Numerous Congregationalists withdrew, formed separate churches, and in 1833 joined forces with other dissenters to abolish the religious establishment.

Connecticut Congregationalist Lyman BEECHER offered one of the most perceptive comments about the end of the old religious system in New England. When Connecticut disestablished Congregationalism, Beecher at first felt depressed. But when he later reflected on the revolution that had occurred, he observed that Christianity had actually gained far more than it had lost by being thrown entirely upon its own resources. The American churches had learned to exert far more spiritual influence through voluntary (see VOLUNTARYISM) societies and revivals, he concluded, than through all the "queues and shoe-buckles, and cocked hats, and gold-headed canes" of former days.

(See also CHURCH AND STATE, RELATIONSHIP BETWEEN.)

GHS, Jr.

Bibliography: Rhys Isaac, *The Transformation of Virginia, 1740–1790* (Chapel Hill: University of North Carolina Press, 1982); William G. McLoughlin, *New England Dissent, 1630–1833: The Baptists and the Separation of Church and State*, 2 vols. (Cambridge, Mass.: Harvard University Press, 1971); Edmund S. Morgan, *Visible Saints: The History of a Puritan Idea* (Ithaca, N.Y.: Cornell University Press, 1963.

Ethical Culture   The Society for Ethical Culture embodied the concerns of advocates of REFORM JUDAISM dissatisfied with the limitations of the Reform movement itself. Seeking to establish a group committed to moral principles and the need for social improvement, the society was unable to expand beyond a base group of intellectual supporters.

SECULARISM played a large role in the years after the CIVIL WAR, thoroughly reshaping American life. At the institutional level, new organizations emerged—public universities, modern business corporations, and professional bodies, all able to function without reference to the evangelical assumptions about society so entrenched in the war. At the level of ideals, many prominent people in American culture began to speak publicly about the superior value of a secular society. While some of these figures, such as Samuel Clemens (Mark Twain) and Colonel Bob INGERSOLL, railed against the influence of religion in any form, others sought to provide the new secular outlook with the same support religious institutions were able to provide their members.

One organization, the Free Religious Association (see FROTHINGHAM, OCTAVIUS BROOKS), arose in 1867 out of postwar Unitarian efforts to formulate a liberal position in a changing social environment (see UNITARIAN UNIVERSALIST ASSOCIATION; LIBERALISM, THEOLOGICAL). The second organization, the Society for Ethical Culture, began under the leadership of Felix ADLER, who first served as president of the Free Religious Association. Adler's battles for free thought, however, were waged against his own Jewish tradition, not against liberal Protestantism.

Groomed for the rabbinate by his father and the congregation at New York's prestigious Temple Emanu-El, Adler chose teaching instead, taking a position at Cornell University in 1871 after completing his Ph.D. at Heidelberg University in Germany. At Heidelberg, exposure to new methods of biblical scholarship shattered his faith. He replaced religious belief with philosopher Immanuel Kant's conviction in the supremacy of a moral law. However, Adler was not satisfied with simply bypassing the influence of his Reform background.

Returning to New York City in 1876, he presented a lecture on May 15 in which he proposed creating a religious society free from creedal concerns. The Society for Ethical Culture, as this new group came to be called, provided secular-minded Jews with an alternative to the Reform synagogue and what he saw as spurious debates within the Reform movement over how to accommodate Jewish religious identity to American culture.

The society was underwritten by Gentiles like John D. Rockefeller, Jr., as well as wealthy New York Reform Jews, some of whom belonged to Adler's father's synagogue. Reflecting the impact of the Protestant SOCIAL GOSPEL, Ethical Culture adopted the Sunday morning hour for its meetings, where lectures showing "the supreme importance of the ethical in life" became the alternative to traditional ritual and prayer, and the motto "Deed not Creed" replaced doctrinal debate with social concern.

Eventually applauded by liberal Protestants, the movement received considerable criticism in its early days. Conservative Protestants denounced it from one side, while those more secular than Adler attacked it as being "vaguely idealistic." Expanding somewhat in spite of these attacks, local groups formed in Boston, Philadelphia, Chicago, and St. Louis and banded together in 1889 to form the American Ethical Union. The union served as a clearing-house for information and also began publishing a journal, eventually known as the *International Journal of Ethics*. In 1896 the

movement became international, holding congresses in Zurich and Germany over the next several years that attracted leaders from academia and several European governments.

If the impetus for Ethical Culture lay in repudiating Judaism, Adler insured that it would retain a Jewish identity, and thus a limited potential for growth. Joseph Seligman, the society's first president, attracted many young Reform Jews. With a Jewish board of directors, Adler continued to address the issues faced by east European immigrant Jews entering America on the bottom rung. Adler denied his link to Judaism while at the same time attracting other Jews disenchanted with the religion. Thus, by the turn of the century, a new generation of leadership among Reform Jews was able to marshal the growing concern for social justice that Adler had seen as the impetus behind Ethical Culture. In spite of organizing numerous activities to attract members, including a series of summer camps for children and a variety of cultural activities, membership never grew substantially. After more than 100 years, the American Ethical Union claims only a few thousand members.

MG

Bibliography: Edward L. Ericson, *The Humanist Way: An Introduction to Ethical Humanist Religion* (New York: Unger, 1988); Benny Kraut, *From Reform Judaism to Ethical Culture: The Religious Evolution of Felix Adler* (Cincinnati: Hebrew Union College Press, 1979); www.aeu.org (American Ethical Union).

ethnicity   Ethnicity has long been a powerful force in the United States, often closely tied to religion, race, and class, although historians and sociologists find it difficult to define. One problem is that most definitions of ethnicity, implicitly or explicitly, rest on the idea of an "other" set against a normative center.

For instance, one century-old meaning of *ethnic* in the English language refers to those not Jewish or Christian, that is, pagan or heathen. This meaning lasted well into the 19th century, when Hinduism, Buddhism, or Islam were considered "ethnic" religions by Protestant Christians. But a secondary meaning became increasingly important. *Ethnic* was often used among Anglo-American Protestants as a rough, if somewhat dismissive, synonym for "picturesque" or "exotic" when referring to those peoples, Christian or otherwise, who displayed a degree of local color, remained embedded in folkways, and were not acculturated to the progressive ideals of urban-industrial society. This usage is still current today, although gaining a more universal application. On one hand, *ethnics* as a noun still tends to refer to non-British peoples who came to the United States during the migrations of the 19th century and later. On the other hand, Anglo-Saxon is itself increasingly understood to denote a discrete system of folkways, an ethnicity among American ethnicities.

Ethnicity also tends to evoke ideas of kin, common blood, or race, when in fact an ethnic group is often a flexible, constructed fiction, especially in highly mobile, immigrant societies such as the United States. For instance, "Anglo-Saxon" was only clearly defined as a group toward the end of the 19th century, when Jews and Catholics from south and central Europe arrived in numbers sufficient to prompt earlier arrivals to define themselves distinctly. Anglo-Saxon then was taken to mean an amalgam of British and Continental peoples with common roots and interests—Normans, Picts, Jutes, Saxons, Angles, Scots, and Welsh, but also Protestant Teutons, Irish, and French. At about the same time, people with regional identities such as Calabrese, Milanese, Sicilian, or Piedmontese found themselves struggling to define themselves as Italian or Italian American. The need to redefine oneself in the United States—whether the particular example is the varied Africans who have been transformed into African Americans or the Indonesians, Saudis, and Moroccans who are laboring to build a Muslim-American community—helps to account for the imprecise nature of ethnic communities' boundaries. The task of building ethnic American identities has been further complicated by the question of who has the power to define. Newly arriving immigrants have often found themselves forced into synthetic categories such as "Asian" or "Latino," when in fact their own sense of self-identity rests on regional, religious, or tribal affiliations. No small part of the history of ethnic groups in America has been the effort to seize the power to define their own identity, a struggle nowhere more marked than in the case of the African-American community.

The relationship between ethnicity and religion is intimate. Religion often supports ethnicity by providing an institutional setting for the maintenance of tradition, but at the same time ethnic identity can also supersede religion as the source of individual and group identity, particular in a highly secularized culture. Religion and ethnicity often share the same fate in a fluid society, where the pressure to assimilate is strong. When individuals seek to assimilate, they will often reject the religion with which their ethnicity is most closely identified. Other individuals, having struggled free from an ethnic background, have later found traditional religious values and folkways to be important sources of coherence and identity. Ethnicity, like religion, has become for many a matter of choice, one source among others to draw upon in the process of creating an American identity. For still others, ethnicity and religion, particularly when closely tied to race, have become highly politicized and are used as effective tools both to support identity and to work for change in the dominant society.

Since the opening up of immigration in 1965 and the ethnic revival that followed, ethnicity and ethnic identity have been celebrated, decried, and politicized, so there is currently much debate over what role they should play in American society. This is particularly evident in the controversy concerning the teaching of multiculturalism in the primary and secondary schools. One line of thought tends to favor a culture-blind approach to education, to stress the "classics," and to see ethnic identity as emotional and clannish—a threat to the rational individualism at the heart of American democracy. This position is dismissed by ethnic group activists and many religious minorities as an attempt to maintain older, Anglo-Protestant forms of cultural authority. A second line favors a form of education in which the highly varied experiences of different ethnic and religious groups are all accounted for in a curriculum that emphasizes the vitality and texture, as well as the perennial conflicts, in a multicultural and democratic society. Many cultural conservatives see this as caving in to special interests.

RHS

Bibliography: Martin E. Marty and R. Scott Appleby, eds., *Religion, Ethnicity, and Self-Identity: Nations in Turmoil* (Hanover, N. H.: University Press of New England, 1997); William Peterson, Michael Novak, and Philip Gleason, *Concepts of Ethnicity* (Cambridge, Mass.: Harvard University Press, 1982); Werner Sollors, ed., *Theories of Ethnicity: A Classical Reader* (New York: New York University Press, 1996).

Evangelical Lutheran Church in America

The Evangelical Lutheran Church in America (ELCA) is the largest Lutheran (see LUTHERANISM) denomination in the United States. Organized in 1987, it represents the merger of two major Lutheran bodies, the Lutheran Church in America (LCA) and the American Lutheran Church (ALC), and the smaller Association of Evangelical Lutheran Churches (AELC). Since American Lutheranism contains what church historian Martin Marty called a "crazy-quilt pattern" of separate ethnic, geographic, and theological traditions, the background of the ELCA is, to say the least, variegated. Both the LCA and the ALC themselves resulted from earlier mergers of several small Lutheran denominations in the 1960s, while the AELC was formed after a split in the ranks of the conservative LUTHERAN CHURCH—MISSOURI SYNOD in the 1970s.

The ELCA's heritage reaches back to the ministry of Pennsylvania pastor Henry Melchior MUHLENBERG. In 1742 Muhlenberg emigrated from Germany to undertake missionary work among Lutheran settlers in the New World. Arriving in Pennsylvania, he discovered Lutheran church life thoroughly entwined with that of the German Reformed population, whose members were committed to the liturgical and doctrinal teachings of John Calvin. Lutherans and Reformed, who shared a common language, also tended to use the same clergy, form "union churches," and worship together. Proselytizers belonging to German sectarian groups such as the MORAVIANS and the Dunkers (see CHURCH OF THE BRETHREN) further confused Lutheran denominational identity and even falsely posed as Lutheran clergy.

Muhlenberg wished to regularize American Lutheranism, keeping it loyal to the teachings of German reformer Martin Luther. The most effective step he took toward attaining that ideal was forming in 1748 the Pennsylvania Ministerium, the denomination's first permanent governing body. A constitution was prepared that gave the laity a voice in church government but subordinated them to the clergy. A new book of worship drew upon Lutheranism's rich liturgical heritage.

In the late 18th century, German Lutherans in the mid-Atlantic states began to move southward along the Shenandoah Valley to the Carolinas and westward across the Appalachians to Ohio, Kentucky, and Tennessee. The Pennsylvania Ministerium soon was incapable of providing for those distant settlements. As a consequence, new synods (federations of local congregations with the power to ordain clergy) were founded in South Carolina (1787), North Carolina (1791), New York (1792), and Ohio (1818). Language also became a matter for debate, as German Americans moved away from their original ethnic enclaves. Although Lutherans living in isolated rural locations continued to use German, new English-speaking congregations appeared in relatively populated

Old Lutheran Church in Philadelphia, 1880. *(Library of Congress)*

areas where Germans mingled with British ethnic groups.

By the early 19th century, leaders in the various state synods were seeking a national body to unite them and make corporate decisions about worship and doctrine. Despite resistance to the principle of a centralized hierarchy, which some church members viewed as too much like Roman Catholicism, the formation of the General Synod of the Evangelical Lutheran Church in 1820 gave a new direction to Lutheranism in the eastern United States. In the transitional period that followed, Samuel SCHMUCKER, president of the General Synod's new seminary at Gettysburg, Pennsylvania, provided his denomination with critical leadership.

Schmucker wished to see Lutheranism integrated into the Protestant evangelical movement that dominated the religious landscape of the United States. He thought that Lutherans, who had initiated the Reformation in the 16th century, should also play a dominant role in spreading the Christian Gospel in America. Schmucker opposed the narrow doctrinal conservatism of the "Old," or "Historic," Lutherans, who insisted upon staunch adherence to classic Lutheran creedal statements. He believed that Americans should not have to be bound either to antiquated ecclesiastical documents or simply to "the minutiae of any human creed." He argued, moreover, that the genius of the new "American Lutheranism" would lie in its ability to adapt to changing cultural and religious circumstances.

Under Schmucker's direction, the General Synod gathered together two-thirds of the Lutherans in the United States by 1860. But two schisms soon shook the church and radically undermined Schmucker's dream of a broad, unified Lutheran front. First, during the Civil War, five synods in the seceding southern states organized themselves separately as the Evangelical Lutheran Church in the Confederate States of America. After the war, this denomination became known as the United Synod South. Second, in 1867, five other synods that were formerly part of the General Synod withdrew and formed themselves into the General Council of the Evangelical Lutheran Church. Led by Charles Porterfield KRAUTH, the General Council, unlike the General Synod, demanded full subscription to the Augsburg Confession, the 16th-century statement of Lutheran beliefs.

The General Synod, General Council, and United Synod South were all centered in the East. Meanwhile, thousands of other Lutherans from Scandinavia and Germany flooded into the Midwest between 1830 and 1914. They, too, established their own synods along ethnic lines. Some 60 new Lutheran church bodies were started by Swedes, Norwegians, Danes, Finns, Germans, and others between 1840 and 1875. Although the largest midwestern Lutheran organization, the Lutheran Church—Missouri Synod, remains distinct from the ELCA, the other ethnically divergent, but often theologically congruent, traditions gradually began to coalesce into a single denominational stream in the early 20th century.

With the outbreak of World War I, the process of Lutheran unification started in earnest. The war not only suspended the flow of immigrants to the United States but also heightened a self conscious "Americanism" among many recently arrived ethnic groups. Lutheran bodies chose to band together and coordinate their labors in ministering to Amer-

ican troops in 1917 and 1918. With the exception of the Missouri Synod, most Lutherans recognized the value of an agency that would be able to represent their common interests. As a result, the National Lutheran Council was formed in 1918. It represented eight Lutheran groups in the United States, roughly two-thirds of all American Lutherans. Besides undertaking traditional foreign and home missionary work, the council provided material relief to Europeans during World War I and World War II.

Several mergers of independent Lutheran synods into larger denominational bodies occurred between World War I and the 1960s. First, three Norwegian groups joined in 1917 to create the Evangelical Lutheran Church. This denomination was centered at Luther Seminary in St. Paul, Minnesota. Next, the eastern-based Lutherans of the General Synod, General Council, and United Synod South reunited in 1918 and formed the United Lutheran Church in America. The Slovak Zion Synod and the Icelandic Synod joined this church in 1920 and 1940, respectively. Third, the synods of Ohio, Iowa, Texas, and Buffalo united in 1930 as the American Lutheran Church. The midwestern-oriented ALC was joined by the Norwegians of the Evangelical Lutheran Church and of the Lutheran Free Church, and by the Danes of another small denomination, the United Evangelical Lutheran Church, in 1960 and 1963, respectively. Finally, the United Lutheran Church in America joined with the Swedish Augustana Synod, the Finnish Evangelical Lutheran Church, and the Danish American Evangelical Lutheran Church to form the Lutheran Church in America in 1962.

By the mid-1960s, many Lutherans believed that the former divisions within American Lutheranism were about to end, as the LCA, the ALC, and theologically moderate elements of the Missouri Synod began to discuss one last, universal merger. Although a radically conservative theological movement soon took control of the Missouri Synod and stopped that dialogue, the new Association of

Evangelical Lutheran Churches, founded in 1976 by 110,000 former Missouri Synod members, continued unification talks. These discussions focused on two principal concerns: preserving the distinctive doctrinal emphases that had often kept Lutheran churches separate, while providing the organizational stability needed to further Lutheran evangelistic efforts in the late 20th century. An accord was reached at a meeting in Columbus, Ohio, in April–May 1987, and the 2.9-million-member LCA, the 2.3-million-member ALC, and the AELC were officially united on January 1, 1998.

An important development in the history of the new denomination took place in the late 1990s when it began discussions with the Episcopal Church regarding the possibility of shared communion. These discussions came to a successful conclusion in the summer of 2000 when the two denominations adopted a "Call to Common Mission" committing them to full communion with each other at the beginning of 2001. While this was not a complete merger, each denomination recognized the validity of the other's baptism and ordination and allowed a sharing of the sacraments.

As with most of the denominations that constitute mainline Protestantism today, the ELCA is experiencing internal strain. There is theological skirmishing between progressive and conservative groups whose interests were necessarily slighted during the process of merging. The church continues to engage in ecumenical discussions with other denominations. It has considered, but did not approve, union with the Episcopal Church, whose worship and beliefs closely resemble those of Lutheranism. The ELCA is now the third-largest (after the Southern Baptist Convention and the United Methodist Church) Protestant denomination in the United States. In 2000 it reported about 5.2 million members organized into 65 geographical synods and containing more than 11,000 congregations.

GHS, Jr.

Bibliography: L. DeAne Lagerquist, *The Lutherans* (Westport, Conn.: Greenwood, 1999); E. Clifford Nelson, ed., *The Lutherans in North America* (Philadelphia: Fortress Press, 1975); Todd W. Nichol, *All These Lutherans: Three Paths Toward a New Lutheran Church* (Minneapolis: Augsburg, 1986); Abdel Ross Wentz, *A Basic History of Lutheranism in America* (Philadelphia: Fortress Press, 1964); www.elca.org (Evangelical Lutheran Church of America).

Evangelical Synod of North America
See GERMAN REFORMED CHURCH.

Evangelical United Brethren Church
See UNITED METHODIST CHURCH.

Evangelical United Front

The term *Evangelical United Front* refers to the coalition of single-issue organizations working for social reform during the first half of the 19th century.

Based on a shared ideology of Christian benevolence, a multitude of groups coordinated their efforts in the areas of religious education and home and foreign missions (see MISSIONS, FOREIGN; MISSIONS, HOME). Another more-perfectionist wave arising in the late 1820s turned to PEACE REFORM, TEMPERANCE, and ABOLITIONISM. The coalition, which enabled Protestants to see themselves as upholding the demands of both the gospel and patriotism, underscored the dominant influence of Protestantism as an unofficial religious establishment. The socially conservative nature of many of the earlier groups proved to be a limitation, as the front collapsed with the rise of the antislavery movement in the late 1830s.

At the beginning of the 19th century, evangelical reform swept the country, emanating out of a New England affected by the optimistic religious fervor stemming from the SECOND GREAT AWAKENING. Evangelical faith assumed that individuals transformed by conversion would necessarily make a dramatic impact on society. Evangelicals, influenced by the NEW DIVINITY of Samuel HOPKINS, Timothy DWIGHT, and Lyman BEECHER, organized numerous missionary enterprises, such as the American Tract Society, the American Bible Society, the American Sunday School Union, and the American Home Mission Society to convert the poor, the unbelieving rationalists, and the heretics and to bolster declining moral standards. These organizations, often lay-led and inspired by the work of British organizations, focused on single issues, frequently attracting a multidenominational membership, particularly Presbyterians (see PRESBYTERIANISM) and Congregationalists (see CONGREGATIONALISM), but also including METHODISTS and other evangelicals. Independently chartered along various lines, the organizations embodied the principle of VOLUNTARYISM that was to become so crucial in American life.

A second wave of reform emerged in the 1820s, associated with the revivals of Charles FINNEY (see REVIVALISM). In contrast to the darker views of an earlier CALVINISM, already somewhat abandoned by Lyman Beecher, Finney and his followers preached the possibility of a moral perfection that could be attained in this life and then prompt individuals with this dramatic "change of heart" to contribute to the creation of a morally pure society. In this second wave of reform, evangelicals sought not simply to shore up society's moral standards, but to remove social evils as well.

In the 1830s the front foundered, splintered by a number of tensions. Conservative reformers remained most interested in promoting personal piety, but perfectionists took their desire to stamp out sin in radical directions. Abolitionism, the movement to eradicate slavery immediately, spread beyond the confines of the Quakers (see FRIENDS, THE RELIGIOUS SOCIETY OF) with the conversion of Theodore Dwight WELD to the cause in 1835 in Cincinnati. Abolitionists helped spread the desire to take dramatic action to remove social evils to the temperance and peace reform movements as well. Both William Lloyd Garrison (1805–1879), anarchist editor of the more radical organ *Liberator*, and the Grimké sisters

(see GRIMKÉ, ANGELINA EMILY AND SARAH MOORE) pushed existing organizations to accept women's leadership, hence raising the social stakes of reform. Increasingly, convictions such as those voiced by Garrison in a warning to the American Colonization Society in 1829—"the terrible judgment of an incensed God will complete the catastrophe of republican America"—worked to split the society in two.

The front dissolved in the sectional crisis preceding the CIVIL WAR, but its impact in the antebellum period can be measured by considering the financial resources raised by member groups. By 1828 the federal government was spending only $700,000 more than was gathered by the largest benevolent organizations. By 1840, the front's combined budget exceeded that of the federal government. The front's continuing influence lies in the fact that the evangelical hopes of a Christian America have never been completely abandoned by subsequent generations of reform-minded Protestants.

(See also CHRISTIAN RIGHT; SOCIAL GOSPEL.)

MG

Bibliography: Charles I. Foster, *Errand of Mercy: The Evangelical United Front, 1790–1837* (Chapel Hill: University of North Carolina Press, 1960); William G. McLoughlin, *Revivals, Awakenings and Reform: An Essay on Religion and Social Change in America, 1607–1977* (Chicago: University of Chicago Press, 1978).

evangelicalism Evangelicalism is a general term for a religious and cultural movement that has played a predominant role in American history. Unlike Europe—where evangelical simply means "not Catholic"—in the United States it conjures up both more sweeping and more particular meanings emphasizing individual conversion, the authority of scripture, and moral and social reform.

While most American evangelicals look to the 17th and 18th centuries as the time of religious orthodoxy in America, the 19th was truly the evangelical century. During this time, with the notable exceptions of Episcopalians and Unitarians, most Protestants were evangelicals. The 19th century also provided the evangelical movement with the source of much of its strength—REVIVALISM. Although revivalism had earlier beginnings, primarily in the first GREAT AWAKENING (roughly 1734–1764), in the 19th century it became a major part of the American religious landscape. No one represented this better than Charles Grandison FINNEY, who transformed revivalism from an event to a technique. For Finney revivals could be brought about by human activity and planning without denying their divine source.

This emphasis on human ability, called ARMINIANISM from the Dutch theologian Jacob Arminius (1560–1609), argues that the individual has the ability to accept or reject God's grace—to choose or refuse salvation. Arminianism's strength in the United States constituted a major shift in Protestant thinking—away from the earlier insistence on predestination and the inability of fallen individuals to choose the good—both of which remain tenets of the Reformed churches and Presbyterianism.

The insistence on human activity also created the impetus for the moral and social reform movements of the 19th century. Among the many movements supported by evangelicals in this period were ABOLITIONISM, women's rights, and TEMPERANCE. Evangelicals also spent much effort on education, and the fruits of those labors include the founding of hundreds of colleges.

In the last half of the 19th century new intellectual and scientific movements from Europe arrived in the United States. Two of these, EVOLUTION and biblical criticism, had a tremendous impact upon religious thought in the United States, and the responses to them served to define and create 20th-century evangelicalism.

The publication of Charles Darwin's *On the Origin of the Species by Means of Natural Selection* (1859) troubled many evangelical thinkers. The increasing acceptance of Darwin by the scientific community and the publication of his *The Descent of Man* (1871) (along with the more radical views of Darwin's popularizers) threatened religious beliefs. Not only did the theory of evolution deny the biblical account of creation, it contradicted the belief in the special, divine creation of human beings as well. This, along with the higher biblical criticism that challenged the literal truth of the Bible, menaced traditional Christian views of the world.

The development of evolution and biblical criticism broke American Protestants into two opposing camps. There were ministers and theologians who accommodated Christian beliefs to the new scholarship and science. This movement was known as theological liberalism (see LIBERALISM, THEOLOGICAL; MODERNISM) and generally ceased to use the term evangelical.

FUNDAMENTALISM arose among those Protestants who rejected the higher criticism of the Bible and Darwinian evolution in defense of what they saw as traditional Protestant orthodoxy. The doctrines they defended included the literal acceptance of the virgin birth, the resurrection of Jesus, miracles, and the unquestionable authority of Scripture. Conflict between modernists and fundamentalists marked most of the first quarter of the 20th century. While a few denominations remained aloof from both modernism and fundamentalism during this time, many, like the Presbyterians and northern Baptists, were torn by conflict.

Fundamentalism inherited the mantle of American evangelicalism, and during the late 19th and early 20th century fundamentalism and evangelicalism were basically synonymous. The years after the 1920s saw definite growing differences. While fundamentalists and evangelicals agree on many doctrinal issues, there is much separating them. In the late 1920s some theological conservatives emerged from the modernist-fundamentalist conflicts with a distaste for the rigid sectarianism of the fundamentalists. This group, which included Harold John OCKENGA, Edward

John Carnell, and Carl F. H. HENRY, differed mainly in attitude and tone from the fundamentalists. These neo-evangelicals, as they called themselves, were more open and flexible in their relations to others. They felt that the partisanship and fighting of the 1920s hurt the image of Christian orthodoxy. The efforts of these men during the 1940s and 1950s basically defined and organized 20th-century evangelicalism.

Twentieth-century evangelicalism came about primarily through the founding of three institutions: the NATIONAL ASSOCIATION OF EVANGELICALS (1942), the magazine *Christianity Today* (1956), and the Evangelical Theological Society (1949). A fourth element in the growth and strength of evangelicalism in the 20th century was Billy GRAHAM and the Billy Graham Evangelistic Association. Through a combination of doctrinal orthodoxy and intellectual effort, these institutions gave a new respectability to theological conservatism in the 1950s and 1960s. *Christianity Today* demonstrated to a wide audience that religious conservatives were not anti-intellectual boobs. The massive crusades led by Billy Graham, along with his moral stature, provided tremendous numbers of people with a view of evangelicalism at its most personable level. Carl F. H. Henry's *The Uneasy Conscience of Modern Fundamentalism* (1947) did much to develop social concern among evangelicals.

Neo-evangelicals maintained a moderate conservatism in political views, another position separating them from most fundamentalists. The late 1960s and 1970s saw the growth of a more radical and activist wing of evangelical thought. The most prominent example of this was the appearance of the magazine *Post-American* in 1971 (later *Sojourners;* see SOJOURNERS COMMUNITY) under the editorship of Jim Wallis. In the 1980s the organization HABITAT FOR HUMANITY, dedicated to providing affordable housing both in the United States and internationally, became a visible manifestation of the social concern of some evangelicals due

primarily to the involvement of former president Jimmy CARTER.

The resurgence during the late 1970s and early 1980s of an activist and politically conservative fundamentalism served to overshadow the evangelical movement. Despite this event and despite the fact that many people, including the media, lump evangelicals and fundamentalists together, 20th-century evangelicalism remains an important force in American Christianity. From centers like Wheaton College in Illinois, Calvin College in Michigan, and Fuller Theological Seminary in California, evangelicalism continues to define itself as a distinctive form of American Protestantism, separate from both fundamentalism and liberalism.

EQ

Bibliography: Randall Balmer, *Blessed Assurance: A History of Evangelicalism in America* (Boston: Beacon Press, 1999); *Mine Eyes Have Seen the Glory: A Journey into the Evangelical Subculture in America.* 3rd ed. (New York: Oxford University Press, 2000); Nancy Hardesty, *Women Called to Witness: Evangelical Feminism in the Nineteenth Century.* 2nd ed. (Knoxville: University of Tennessee Press, 1999); James Davison Hunter, *American Evangelicalism* (New Brunswick, N.J.: Rutgers University Press, 1983); Christine Leigh Heyrman, *Southern Cross: The Beginnings of the Bible Belt* (New York: Knopf, 1997); George M. Marsden, ed., *Evangelicalism and Modern America* (Grand Rapids, Mich.: Eerdmans, 1984); William G. McLoughlin, ed., *The American Evangelicals, 1800–1900, an Anthology* (New York: Harper & Row, 1968); Leonard I. Sweet, *The Evangelical Tradition in America* (Macon, Ga.: Mercer University Press, 1984).

evolution   The theory of evolution contends that humans and the world they inhabit evolved over a long period of time as a result of the gradual process of natural selection. This theory appears to contradict traditional readings of the Book of Genesis, namely that God created humans and the world in six days at the beginning of time.

The publication in 1859 of Charles Darwin's *On the Origin of Species* popularized this theory and represents a pivotal event in the relationship between SCIENCE AND RELIGION in the United States. Although Protestants since the 17th century had assumed that faith, reason, and science were all compatible, the dissemination of Darwin's theories on organic evolution in the decades after the Civil War challenged that earlier synthesis.

The radical impact of Darwin's thought, however, was not immediately apparent to American Christians. While he was the first to present a plausible mechanism (natural selection) by which one species might gradually be transformed into another, Darwin was not unique in suggesting the possibility of evolution. Most theologians, in fact, initially accepted his evolutionary hypothesis. They had already harmonized the six "days" of creation to which the biblical Book of Genesis refers with the eons actually required for the earth's geological development. They believed, therefore, that evolution could also be made consistent both with God's creative activities described in Genesis and with God's ongoing, providential care of worldly events.

Harvard scientist Asa GRAY, for example, became a prominent proponent of Darwinism while remaining an orthodox Congregationalist. He suggested that nothing in Darwin's biological theories necessarily contradicted the idea of a divine direction over the evolutionary processes. Even as conservative a figure as Princeton Seminary professor Benjamin WARFIELD, the theologian who coined the term *inerrancy* to describe the literal truth of the biblical text, thought that evolution might well have provided the means by which God guided creation. And George Frederick Wright, who contributed an essay on evolution to the landmark series *The Fundamentals*, did not think his defense of Protestant orthodoxy precluded evolutionary notions of divine creativity.

Nevertheless, over the years, many conservatives came to question Darwinism, perceiving the threat that natural selection posed to traditional Christian belief about divine sovereignty. This opposition was best articulated by Charles HODGE, the scholar who had trained Warfield at Princeton. Hodge's critique was stated succinctly in his 1874 book *What Is Darwinism?*, in which he attacked Darwin's rejection of divine design. Hodge concluded that Darwin's refusal to acknowledge that God, not mere chance, guided the evolution of species was tantamount to atheism. At the same time, many of Darwin's agnostic supporters also began to appreciate the critical significance of this point. They eagerly pressed Darwin's theories in hopes of driving an immovable wedge between Christianity and science.

By the 1920s, antievolution had become one of the principal touchstones of theological conservatism in America. Under the leadership of statesman and politician William Jennings BRYAN, the growing fundamentalist movement articulated the manifold threats Darwinism posed to traditional Christian civilization. Fundamentalist leaders feared that evolution undermined faith in the Bible as the source of truth and would inevitably lead Americans into immorality and atheism. Despite Bryan's successful prosecution of John T. Scopes (see SCOPES TRIAL) for violating the Tennessee antievolution law in the famed "Monkey Trial" of 1925, Bryan won, as it turned out, only a Pyrrhic victory. His inept attacks on Darwinism raised such an outcry of indignation and ridicule from the national press that FUNDAMENTALISM itself soon appeared thoroughly discredited.

Despite the embarrassing aftermath of the Scopes trial, most conservative Christians remained quietly loyal to Bryan's views on evolution over the next half-century. The rise of CREATIONISM in the 1970s reveals, moreover, that fundamentalist opposition to Darwin's controversial theory is as strong as ever. Creationists wish to preserve the idea that God controls the processes of creation and natural development, and they argue that Darwin's evolutionary theory is not the only viable hypothesis that explains the origins of life on earth. They also hope "creation science" will one day be taught as a legitimate scientific theory. Creationism even won a short-lived victory when the Arkansas and Louisiana state legislatures in 1981 both passed laws (later declared unconstitutional) giving equal treatment to "evolution science" and to "creation science" in the curricula of public schools.

Following these defeats in court, opponents of evolution developed a strategy to influence education at the local level by running for local and state school boards. Perhaps the most successful example of this was their attainment of a majority of members on the state school board in Kansas. From this position they managed to remove evolution as a required curriculum topic in that state's schools. The ridicule heaped on the state nationally and internationally as a result of these actions led to a backlash, and in the 2000 elections several of the antievolution members of the school board were defeated. A 7-3 majority voted in favor of returning evolution to the curriculum in January 2001.

Darwin's theory and the conflicts it has engendered continue to have tremendous significance for the interaction of religion and American culture. Although no amount of scientific evidence will ever prove or disprove whether an all-powerful God directs the universe, agnostics and fundamentalists together agree that evolution is critical to their understanding of how the world came into being.

GHS, Jr.

Bibliography: Edward J. Larson, *Summer for the Gods: The Scopes Trial and America's Continuing Debate over Science and Religion* (New York: Basic Books, 1997); David N. Livingstone, *Darwin's Forgotten Defenders: The Encounter between Evangelical Theology and Evolutionary Thought* (Grand Rapids, Mich.: Eerdmans, 1987); Jon H. Roberts, *Darwinism and the Divine in America: Protestant Intellectuals and Organic Evolution, 1859–1900* (Madison: University of Wisconsin Press, 1988).

F

Falwell, Jerry (1933–) As founder of the MORAL MAJORITY (1979–1987), Jerry Falwell was one of the leaders responsible for the politically active conservative Christianity that emerged in the 1970s. Born on August 11, 1933, in Lynchburg, Virginia, Falwell was one of twins. His father, Carey, a successful businessman, and his mother, Helen, provided a financially secure and prosperous home life where Falwell was doted on by his parents and much older siblings.

His father suffered from a drinking problem, however, and this undoubtedly contributed to his early death when Falwell was only 15. The last days of his father's life seem to have affected Falwell tremendously. He often speaks of how moved he was by his father's acceptance of Christ just days before his death and the way in which this changed his father.

During high school Falwell was successful and popular. He captained the school's football team, edited the school newspaper, and graduated as class valedictorian. Despite this, his mischievous nature often got him into trouble, and he was not allowed to deliver the valedictory address at graduation.

Falwell attended Lynchburg College, where he became a Christian and first felt the call to the ministry. The call became so strong that he transferred to Baptist Bible College in Springfield, Missouri, in 1952. After finishing bible college, Falwell served various pastorates until being called to Thomas Road Baptist Church in Lynchburg in 1956. He has remained the church's pastor ever since, and from there he built his massive religious and political empire.

Falwell first came to public prominence with his "Listen America" rallies during the nation's bicentennial in 1976. At these rallies, Falwell urged Americans to turn from what he viewed as their moral laxity and to embrace truth and virtue. Falwell also spoke of returning the United States to what he saw as its Christian, or at least godly, roots. He railed against the Supreme Court's ruling forbidding state-sponsored prayers in public schools, against liberal politicians, and, as the issues became prominent, against homosexuality and abortion. In 1979 Falwell and other conservative Christians established the Moral Majority, an organization designed to give a political voice to the views of political and social conservatives. To a great extent this coalition helped mobilize sufficient voters to help elect President Ronald Reagan and to produce the eventual Republican majority in the U.S. House of Representatives and the Senate.

Nonetheless, the Moral Majority had little success in driving through most of its political positions. Falwell, claiming it had served its purposes, disbanded the organization in 1989 to devote his efforts to his ministries. Along with serving as senior minister at Thomas Road, Falwell also oversees Liberty University and *The Old-Time Gospel Hour* television program.

(See also ELECTRONIC CHURCH; RELIGIOUS RIGHT; RIGHT TO LIFE MOVEMENT; SOUTHERN BAPTISTS.)

EQ

Bibliography: Jerry Falwell, *Falwell: An Autobiography* (Lynchburg, Va.: Liberty House, 1997); ———, *Listen America* (New York: Bantam Books, 1981); Susan Harding Friend, *The Book of Jerry Falwell: Fundamentalist Language and Politics* (Princeton: Princeton University Press, 2000); Arthur Frederick Ide, *Evangelical Terrorism: Censorship, Falwell, Robertson & the Seamy Side of Christian Fundamentalism* (Irving, Tx.: Scholars Books, 1986); www.falwell.com (Jerry Falwell); www.listenamerica.net (Listen America); www.otgh.org (Old Time Gospel Hour).

Fard, W. D. (?–1934?)

The founder of the NATION OF ISLAM (NOI), Black Muslims, W. D. Fard remains as mysterious today as when he first appeared in the black section of Detroit on July 4, 1930. There—known by various names Wallace Fard, Wali Farrad, Professor Ford, Farrad Mohammed, and F. Mohammed Ali—he made his living as an itinerant peddler.

Many stories circulated about Fard's early life. He claimed he had been born in Mecca to a wealthy family of the tribe of Koreish (Quraysh)—the tribe of Muhammad (the founder of ISLAM)—and had attended college in England, or at the University of Southern California, where he had been groomed to enter the diplomatic service of the Kingdom of the Hejaz (modern-day Saudi Arabia). He had abandoned this career, however, in order to bring religious truth and freedom to his "Uncle," the black man living in the "wilderness of North America."

As a peddler in Detroit he told people that his silks "were the same kind that our people used in their country . . .," according to an early convert. When asked to tell about this country, he explained that the so-called Negroes were the original humans who had been stolen from their home by the "white devils." Blacks needed to separate themselves from these "subhumans" and return to their true religion, Islam.

When they did so Allah would unleash his fury on the whites and restore blacks to their rightful place as his chosen.

Fard made a large impression on recent black immigrants from the rural South and soon gained several thousand followers. He produced two basic texts for his followers, *The Secret Ritual of the Nation of Islam*, which was passed on orally, and *Teaching for the Lost Found Nation of Islam in a Mathematical Way*. Fard also organized several auxiliaries to the Nation of Islam, including a school, a girls' training class, and a security organization—the Fruit of Islam.

The NOI soon came to the attention of the police, who were troubled by Fard's apparent emphasis on human sacrifice as a means of expiating sin, as well as his teaching that every follower was to sacrifice four Caucasian "devils." Newspaper stories of human sacrifice among Nation of Islam followers, known to the police as the "Voodoo Cult," brought the movement to the attention of white Detroit—attention that was increased by the attempted sacrifice of two white welfare workers that was widely reported in the Detroit press and caused much fear among white Detroiters.

Objections to sacrifice led to one of the many divisions within the movement. Others involved conflicts over loyalty to the U.S. flag and Constitution, Communist and Japanese infiltration, and an attempt by the Ethiopian government to use the NOI as a channel for funds. Despite these divisions Fard achieved a remarkable degree of organizational stability in a relatively short time. Starting in 1933 he began to recede into the background, decreasing his public appearances and leaving affairs to his assistant ministers. Fard disappeared completely on June 30, 1934.

His disappearance led to a series of violent leadership conflicts, the magnitude of which was sufficiently high to force one group to flee to Chicago. This group, led by Elijah MUHAMMAD, established its own temple in Chicago, and Elijah Muhammad declared himself the legitimate successor to Fard. Although considered schismatic and minor as late as 1937, Muhammad's group eventually became the dominant branch of the NOI.

Under Elijah Muhammad's leadership the NOI transformed Fard's status. Fard was revealed to have been Allah himself in human form, who came to save his people. Fard had passed on his teaching to Elijah Muhammad, who remained as Allah's messenger on earth, to teach American blacks their true religion and their true nature as the superior race. These teachings remained the cornerstone of the Nation of Islam throughout the life of Elijah Muhammad and were central to the movement's expansion during the 1950s and 1960s.

EQ

Bibliography: Doanne Beynon Erdman, "The Voodoo Cult Among Negro Migrants In Detroit," *American Journal of Sociology* 43 (July 1937–May 1938), 804–907; C. Eric Lincoln, *The Black Muslims in America.* 3rd ed. (Grand Rapids, Mich.: Eerdmans, 1994).

Farrakhan, Louis Abdul (1933–   )   Born

Louis Eugene Wolcott in the Bronx, New York, in 1933, Louis Farrakhan, as head of the reconstituted NATION OF ISLAM (NOI), had become by the 1990s the most visible spokesman for African-American separatism in the United States. As a result he received much media attention, especially during Jesse JACKSON's 1984 run for the presidency, when the NOI provided security guards for Jackson's campaign, and when Farrakhan issued a veiled death threat against a black newspaperman who reported that Jackson called New York "Hymietown." Despite his visibility, Farrakhan remains a mystery to most Americans.

Although born in New York, Wolcott grew up in Boston, where he was raised by his mother, a West Indian immigrant. Deeply religious, he attended an Episcopal church and served as an altar boy. He graduated with honors from Boston English High School, where

he also ran track. Wolcott also played the violin and piano.

In 1951 he began college at Winston-Salen (North Carolina) Teachers College but dropped out after two years to pursue a musical career playing calypso and country music in nightclubs. In 1955 Farrakhan met MALCOLM X, who recruited him for the NOI (Black Muslims). The influence of Malcom X and, later, a personal meeting with the Honorable Elijah MUHAMMAD led Wolcott to adopt the "X" as his last name, signifying the lost names of his African ancestors and proclaiming his existence as an ex-Negro, "ex-slave, ex-Christian, ex-smoker, ex-drinker, ex-mainstream American."

Louis X soon became a significant part of the NOI, and Elijah Muhammad himself bestowed the name "Abdul Farrakhan" on the young man. Farrakhan wrote the only play, *Orgena* ("a Negro" spelled backward), and song, "A White Man's Heaven is a Black Man's Hell," sanctioned by the NOI. He served as Malcolm X's assistant at Temple No. 7 in Harlem before being appointed head minister of the Boston Temple.

When Malcolm broke with the NOI, Farrakhan replaced him as national representative and also led the attack upon Malcolm within the movement. Although denying any direct involvement by the NOI in Malcolm's assassination, he has admitted that verbal attacks on Malcolm may have created a climate that led to his murder.

Following the death of Elijah Muhammad in 1975 and the actions of his son and successor Warith Deen MUHAMMAD in transforming the NOI into an orthodox Sunni Muslim group that renounced racial separatism (the World Community of Al-Islam in the West), Farrakhan led a breakaway movement in 1978. In this schismatic movement, which retained the name Nation of Islam, Farrakhan returned to the religious and racial views of Elijah Muhammad. These include the beliefs that W. D. FARD was Allah come to earth, that Elijah Muhammad was his apostle, that blacks were the first humans, and that whites are devils and inferior beings created by a mad scientist. Farrakhan also expanded upon Elijah Muhammad's view that UFOs are emissaries from a giant "mothership" come to rescue blacks from the apocalypse that will destroy the earth and all the wicked people.

Farrakhan has been given to extremist views. His flaming oratory has included calling Hitler a "great man" (albeit wickedly so), describing Judaism as a "gutter religion," and complaining about the "Jewish-controlled media." His references to "white devils" and his avowed racial separatism also brought him much attention. As a result, many black political leaders have been under some pressure to disavow him. Some, among them Tom Bradley and David Dinkins, have been quick to do so, while others have resisted.

Farrakhan's work to reestablish the Nation of Islam was fairly successful. By the mid 1990s its membership was close to 60,000, and he had repurchased both the NOI's former headquarters, Temple No. 2 (which he renamed Temple Maryam), and Elijah Muhammad's home in Chicago, from which he bases his work. Farrakhan also has attempted to realize the NOI's vision of black self-sufficiency and economic development, primarily through the Power Pac cosmetic line.

The Nation of Islam's strong moral code and its teaching of black self-respect and independence offered a powerful message to an African-American community hit hard by poverty, drug abuse, and declining public concern for civil rights. Like both Elijah Muhammad and Malcolm X, Farrakhan's message reached far beyond the members of the NOI. At public rallies he regularly spoke to audiences numbering in the thousands, and many African Americans opposed to both his theology and his racial separatism reacted warmly to his message of black pride and independence. As the leader of the longest-lived of all black separatist groups, Farrakhan seemed poised to bring the message into a new day and a new audience.

Beginning in 1990, however, Farrakhan appeared to be moving the NOI into a new direction. He encouraged Black Muslims to participate in local and national politics, an activity that was anathema to Elijah Muhammad and a source of much frustration to Malcolm X. Farrakhan also made some overtures toward orthodox Islam. In autumn 1990 at the General Meeting of the Continental Council of the Masjid of North America, he publicly recited the *Shahadah*, the orthodox Muslim profession of faith. The result was his acceptance into the Muslim fold by Warith Deen Muhammad. Some suspected that this action was solely undertaken with an eye toward the Saudi and Gulf sheikdom monies that Warith Muhammad controlled. While the suspicions seemed to be proven by Farrakhan's actions in the early 1990s, there was a hint of change.

Following a bout with life-threatening cancer, Farrakhan emerged a transformed man in the eyes of many. The result was that the hinted changes became solidified. In spring 2000, at the annual Savior's Day event, Farrakhan publicly expressed his commitment to Orthodox Sunni Islam and his desire to bring the NOI into an active engagement with mainstream Islamic institutions. Sharing the dais with him that day were Imam Warith Deen Muhammad and the leaders of several American Muslim organizations, including the secretary general of the ISLAMIC SOCIETY OF NORTH AMERICA. All of this appeared to be more than rhetoric, as members of the NOI soon became a common presence at Orthodox Islamic meetings and conferences throughout the United States.

EQ

Bibliography: Joseph D. Eure and Richard M. Jerome, eds., *Back Where We Belong: Selected Speeches by Minister Louis Farrakhan* (Philadelphia: PC International Press, 1989); ———, *In the Name of Elijah Muhammad: Louis Farrakhan and the Nation of Islam* (Durham, N.C.: Duke University Press, 1996); Mattias Gardell, *Countdown to Armageddon: Louis Farrakhan and the Nation of Islam* (London: Hurst, 1996); Florence Hamlish Levinsohn,

Looking for Farrakhan (Chicago: Ivan R. Dee, 1997); C. Eric Lincoln, *The Black Muslims in America.* 3rd ed. (Grand Rapids, Mich.: Eerdmans, 1994); Arthur J. Magida, *Prophet of Rage: A Life of Louis Farrakhan and His Nation* (New York: Basic Books, 1996); Malcolm X with Alex Haley, *The Autobiography of Malcolm X* (New York: Grove Press, 1964).

feminist theology   Feminist theology is theology that denies male domination and seeks to empower women. It is difficult to offer a more precise definition of feminist *theology* because there are in fact many different feminist *theologies.* Feminist theologians disagree, for example, about whether Judaism, Christianity, and Islam are essentially sexist. They agree, however, on the need to criticize the biases against women inherent in patriarchal theologies and the urgency of pressing beyond those theologies to articulate views that affirm and empower women.

Although rooted in the 19th-century women's rights movement, feminist theology first emerged forcefully around the midpoint of the 20th century. In the 19th century, social and religious reformers such as Angelina and Sarah GRIMKÉ, Elizabeth Cady STANTON, Matilda Joslyn Gage, and Susan B. Anthony moved in the direction of feminist theology when they reinterpreted Genesis 1–3, arguing that this foundational creation myth argued for the original equality of men and women (Gen. 1:27) and honored the place of Eve as the "mother of all living" (Gen. 3:20) (see WOMAN'S BIBLE, THE).

Today many feminist theologians continue to focus their interpretive energies on Genesis. Phyllis Trible, for example, has argued that Genesis 2–3 cannot be interpreted to justify the domination of men over women, and Elaine Pagels has criticized the misogynist tendencies of church fathers (in particular, Augustine), who read the creation narratives as an indictment of women for bringing sin into the world.

An important year in the development of feminist theology was 1968. Two books published in that year outlined the patriarchal institutions of religion and the history of their sexist teachings: Kari Borresen's *Subordination and Equivalence: The Nature and Role of Woman in Augustine and Thomas Aquinas* and Mary DALY's *The Church and the Second Sex.* In an attempt to expose the hierarchical assumptions of the patriarchy, these two Roman Catholic women argued that traditional Christian theology wrongly dictates that women are the "lesser sex" and are to be submissive to men. Women are, they contended, prohibited from leadership, teaching, or ritual roles in many religious groups. Daly's work developed into a widely influential, radical feminist theology that moved from being Christian to being post-Christian and has since settled in a location outside male-defined religion altogether.

Since 1968, feminist theologians have followed two broadly defined paths. The first led to liberal feminist theologies that work within a particular religious tradition in an effort to reform and reconstruct the roles and images of women in it. The second path led to radical feminist theologies that, viewing traditional organized religions as irredeemably misogynist, align themselves with a variety of goddess- and earth-based religions.

Among the reconstructionist theologians working to reform Christianity is Rosemary Radford Reuther, who aims not only to expose patriarchy as a system oppressive to both sexes but also to describe the parameters of a liberating church. From her work was born the "women-church" movement, which presents a gender-inclusive model of the worshipping Christian community.

Feminist biblical scholarship has also largely followed this reconstructionist path. Phyllis Trible's work on the Hebrew Scriptures and Elisabeth Schuessler Fiorenza's on the New Testament are major examples of scholarship that criticizes the history of patriarchal exegesis even as it celebrates the roles of women in the biblical text and as scriptural interpreters.

Although reconstructionists argue that their religious traditions have become patriarchal, they do not typically believe that their religions are essentially so. Thus the scriptural work of Judith Plaskow aims to move beyond the historical exclusion of women from Judaism by putting women back into the covenant God made with Israel (Exodus 19:15) in order to be "standing again at Sinai." And Rachel Adler pushes this vision further by seeking a more inclusive Judaism still rooted in traditions. Riffat Hassan, who argues for a "post-patriarchal Islam," reinterprets the Qur'an to find what she sees as the originally intended equality between the sexes in Islam. Buddhist feminists such as Rita Gross are also working within their tradition to refashion a religion connected to its sacred scripture and traditions but separate from patriarchy and its alleged sexism and misogyny.

Womanist theologians (see WOMANIST THEOLOGY) have also retold their stories, pointing not only to the bankruptcy of traditional theologies but also to the limitations of white, European-American feminism. Jacqueline Grant and Katie G. Cannon have traced the history of African-American women through slavery to the present. Biblical scholars Renita Weems and Clarice Martin reclaim the presence of Africa and Africans in the biblical text and decry racist and sexist biblical interpretation.

Finally, some lesbian theologians aim to reconstruct their respective religious traditions to include the erotic power of the divine. Jewish lesbian feminists, such as Rebecca Alpert, are reforming their faith by finding their own interpretive strategies and critical voices. In the Christian tradition Carter Heyward criticizes not only the sexism but also the heterosexism of the Christian church and points to the need for repentance and reform.

Other theologians, most notably Mary Daly, have chosen the second, more radical path of feminist theology, rejecting their inherited religious traditions and seeking older roots for women's spirituality. Many of these theologians (or "thealogians") define themselves as post-biblical, post-Christian, post-Jewish, or in newer terms utterly disconnected from the Jewish or Christian traditions. Sallie McFague represents a type of radical feminist theology that is concerned with the environment and with creating new metaphors or models of God (e.g., mother, lover, and friend). McFague wants to build from the base of Christianity but considers herself "post-Christian."

Other feminists, such as Starhawk and Carol Christ, turn away from the Christian and Jewish traditions in search of older, goddess-centered religions. Spirituality, ritual, and social justice are central to feminist theologies that are reclaiming their goddess heritage. NEOPAGANISM and witchcraft (or the "Craft") are names for the movement back to spiritualities that affirm either one Goddess or multiple goddesses.

Feminist theologians disagree about many things, but they do share some common features: an interest in language and symbols, a concern for social justice and political reform, a desire to provide a spiritual base for environmental activism, and a hope for the creation of a global feminism that allows for and affirms differences in race, class, ethnicity, and sexual orientation.

TP

Bibliography: Rachel Adler, *Engendering Judaism: An Inclusive Theology and Ethics* (New York: Jewish Publication Society, 1989); Rebecca Alpert, *Like Bread on the Seder Plate: Jewish Lesbians and the Transformation of Tradition* (New York: Columbia University Press, 1997); Nancy Falk and Rita Gross, *Unspoken Worlds: Women's Religious Lives* (Belmont, Calif.: Wadsworth Publishing Company, 1989); Paula Cooey, William Eakin, and Jay McDaniel, eds., *After Patriarchy: Feminist Transformations of the World Religions* (Maryknoll, N.Y.: Orbis Books, 1991); Rosemary Radford Ruether, *Sexism and God-Talk: Toward a Feminist Theology* (Boston: Beacon Press, 1983).

Finney, Charles Grandison (1792–1875)

Charles G. Finney was the premier figure in American EVANGELICALISM before the Civil War and the greatest revivalist of the SECOND GREAT

AWAKENING, the period of intense spiritual excitement that spanned the first three decades of the 19th century. After undergoing a sudden religious conversion in 1821, Finney abandoned his career as a lawyer and set to work as an itinerant missionary in upstate New York. Over the next decade, he introduced controversial revival techniques known as the "new measures," which not only helped shape religious belief and practice in the new United States but also had a profound impact on American social views. Finney hoped that winning souls for Christ would help Americans establish the millennial kingdom of God on earth.

Finney was born in Warren, Connecticut, on August 29, 1792. His parents were farmers, and the shortage of land in Connecticut forced the Finney family to move westward two years after his birth. The Finneys eventually settled in Hanover (now Kirkland), New York. Charles returned to Connecticut to attend Warren Academy in 1812 and then planned to enroll at Yale College. However, he was dissuaded from going to Yale and instead taught school for two years in New Jersey. In 1818 he entered a legal apprenticeship in Adams, New York.

By his own account, Finney was a sinful, worldly man until his conversion on October 10, 1821. Walking to his office that morning, he received the startling insight that salvation was available to anyone who would consent to receiving it. According to his own account, Finney stopped in the middle of the street and felt God's Holy Spirit descend upon him. The next day, when a deacon of his church reminded him of a court case he was scheduled to plead for him in court, Finney responded: "I have a retainer from the Lord Jesus Christ to plead his cause, and I cannot plead yours." After studying theology with George Gale, the Presbyterian pastor at Adams, Finney was licensed to preach in December 1823. He was ordained to the Presbyterian ministry in July of the following year.

Finney had remarkable physical characteristics that he put to good use in his ministerial work. He was over six feet in height and possessed piercing, hypnotic eyes. A commanding figure in the pulpit, he spoke in plain language to everyone who gathered to hear him. Finney also was not afraid to address people directly by name. In the revivals he led, he pleaded with men and women to change their hearts and surrender to God. He called them forward to the "anxious bench," a front pew where they publicly struggled to acknowledge their sins and seek forgiveness. There, friends and neighbors stood close by to "pray them through" the experience.

Finney was immediately successful as villages, towns, and eventually cities "caught fire" during revivals he organized. He held protracted meetings, that is, community-wide revivals, prepared in advance, lasting for several weeks—urban events akin to the exuberant CAMP MEETINGS on the frontier. In 1825 he moved through the Mohawk Valley of New York. Attracting national attention, he went to Wilmington, Delaware, and Philadelphia in 1827, and the next year he ministered in New York City. Finney's revival campaign achieved its greatest success in Rochester, New York, in the winter of 1830–1831. Although resisted at first by many clergy who resented the disruption he caused in their churches, he eventually won over even his most bitter foes. New England Congregationalist leader Lyman BEECHER, for example, who once swore that he would "call out all the artillerymen, and fight [Finney] every inch of the way to Boston," actually welcomed him to the city in late 1831. Only illness stopped Finney. He curtailed his itinerant activities in 1832 and accepted a permanent pastorate at the Second Free Presbyterian Church in New York City.

In spite of all his well-meaning evangelistic efforts, Finney fostered divisions within his own Presbyterian denomination. Those who opposed him tended to focus their attacks on three key features of his revivalistic work: his willingness to allow women to preach and pray in public; his admitted abandonment of traditional Calvinist (see CALVINISM) teachings about the workings of divine grace; and his openness to social reform. The latter two issues especially were to become critical factors in the NEW SCHOOL/OLD SCHOOL dispute that split the Presbyterian Church in 1837.

For many women in Finney's day, simply coming forward to the "anxious bench" to offer a public testimony about their faith could well represent a form of social and psychological emancipation. And the heavenly promises they received when they were spiritually reborn might also become the beginning of a new earthly life. On a purely mundane level, Finney employed women as assistants in the organizational work of his revivals, and he created women's auxiliaries that assured female participation in church work both locally and nationally. Some women gave such moving accounts of their conversion that they were invited to serve as traveling evangelists, speaking wherever revivals were held.

Finney's most notable theological innovation was the emphasis he placed on the human, rather than the divine, role in effecting religious transformation. As he declared in 1835 in his practical manual *Lectures on Revivals*, a "revival is not a miracle," but simply "the right use of the constituted means." In opposition to earlier teaching dating from the GREAT AWAKENING of the 18th century, when clergy argued that a revival should only be viewed (in Jonathan EDWARDS's phrase) as "a surprising work of God," Finney believed that human beings could and should strive to seek divine blessing. Despite the Calvinist insistence that men and women were morally unable to choose between heaven and hell, Finney taught that God had given them power to make up their own minds. The title of his most famous sermon epitomizes the message Finney continually preached: "Sinners Bound to Change Their Own Hearts." In the exuberantly democratic era that celebrated the rise of Andrew Jackson and the "common man," when American politicians were not embar-

rassed to garner votes for their party, Finney conceived that the revivalist's work was likewise convincing sinners to cast their spiritual ballots for God.

Increasingly optimistic about the progress of revivals across the country and about the growth in church membership, Finney predicted in 1835 that the start of the millennium, the thousand-year reign of Christ on earth, was only three years away. Finney's teaching on free will had always suggested the possibility of a person's attaining moral perfection in the present life. He was at first hesitant, however, about applying those theological beliefs to the political sphere, for he believed that society could be reformed only when human beings had been fully transformed from within. Thus, in 1830 he identified drinking alcohol as a sin to be eradicated by conversion, not by prohibition laws. Still, his emphasis on the need to dedicate oneself to the advancement of God's kingdom certainly was open to concrete social interpretations. In New York City in 1832, Finney concluded that slaveholding was sinful, and he refused membership in his church to anyone involved with the slave system. The next year, he allowed William Lloyd Garrison's new American Anti-Slavery Society to use his church building as a meeting place. And in the same period, he inspired Theodore Dwight WELD, a young revivalist he had converted, to organize an abolition crusade in western New York and Ohio.

Although Finney's career changed course in 1832, he remained an influential figure in American Protestantism. After working for a brief period as a pastor in New York City, he accepted an appointment to the professorship of theology at newly founded Oberlin College in Ohio in 1835. Later, he served as president of the college from 1851 to 1866, and as pastor of the First Congregational Church in the town from 1837 to 1872. Finney's presence at Oberlin assured that the college would become a national center not only for revivalism, but also for antislavery and other reform movements.

Besides *Lectures on Revivals,* Finney's most important writings were *Lectures on Systematic Theology* (1846), which reflects the modifications he made of traditional Calvinist orthodoxy, and his informative *Memoirs,* published the year after he died. Although he resigned his pastorate at the church in Oberlin in 1872, Finney remained active as a lecturer at the college until shortly before his death. He died at his home in Oberlin on August 16, 1875.

GHS, Jr.

Bibliography: Richard A. G. Dupuis and Garth M. Rosell, eds., *The Memoirs of Charles G. Finney: The Complete Restored Text* (Grand Rapids, Mich.: Academic Books, 1989); Keith J. Hardman, *Charles Grandison Finney, 1792–1875: Revivalist and Reformer* (Syracuse, N.Y.: Syracuse University Press, 1987); Charles E. Hambrick-Stowe, *Charles G. Finney and the Spirit of American Evangelicalism* (Grand Rapids, Mich.: Eerdmans, 1996).

First Amendment Adopted in 1791 to meet the objections that certain freedoms were not protected by the new Constitution, the First Amendment and the nine others ratified with it form what is commonly known as the Bill of Rights. They are understood to guarantee to the inhabitants of the United States rights the national government cannot infringe.

The First Amendment to the U.S. CONSTITUTION is arguably the most familiar, at least in broad outline, and the most important of the constitutional amendments. In this amendment are written all the legal guarantees that make freedom a meaningful term and democracy possible. "Congress shall make no law respecting an establishment of religion, or prohibiting the free exercise thereof; or abridging the freedom of speech, or of the press; or of the right of the people peaceably to assemble, and to petition the government for a redress of grievances."

In terms of religion the amendment has two distinct clauses. One prohibits Congress from making any law respecting the establishment of religion. The other clause prevents Congress from passing any law prohibiting a person from the exercise of her or his religious beliefs. Originally applicable only to the federal government, these clauses were first applied to the state governments by the Supreme Court in the 1940s as among those rights protected by the FOURTEENTH AMENDMENT.

The meaning and application of these two clauses is for the Supreme Court to decide. The Court's duty is to apply these important yet vague formulations to specific situations. This task has increased in complexity since the Court's 1940 decision in *Cantwell v. Connecticut* in which it argued that the "free exercise" clause of the amendment was binding on the states due to the Fourteenth Amendment. The Supreme Court has attempted to apply the religious clauses to legal statutes through the use of various metaphors. These have included "excessive entanglement," "wall of separation," and "legitimate secular purpose."

The need for such complex schemes of interpretation illustrates the difficulty in applying the "establishment" and "free exercise" clauses to particular cases. Nearly everyone would agree that human sacrifice should be punished as murder regardless of whether one's religion required it. But what of animal sacrifice? Is it unconstitutional for a city or state to outlaw animal sacrifices? In the case of *The Church of Lukumi Babalu Aye v. City of Hialeah* (1993) the Supreme Court apparently has decided that it is, if the ordinance is solely directed at a religious practice. Can a state pay for bus transportation for children attending religious schools? Yes, according to the Supreme Court in *Everson v. Board of Education* (1947). Such activity falls within the legitimate police powers of the state to protect citizens. Other CHURCH AND STATE issues decided by the Court have involved polygamy (no) (see CHURCH OF JESUS CHRIST OF LATTER DAY SAINTS), compulsory public school prayer (no), compulsory school Bible reading (no), and Sunday closing laws (yes) (see SABBATARIANISM).

As one can see from this short list the questions allow no easy answers and are bound to become more difficult. As the varieties of religious beliefs in the United States increase, scholars believe that the cultural hegemony of the Christian or Judeo-Christian tradition will be increasingly challenged. The federal courts will be called upon to decide the issues. In this role they will struggle to determine the appropriate application of the "free exercise" and "establishment" clauses of the First Amendment to the new realities of America's religious landscape.

EQ

Bibliography: E. J. Dionne, Jr., and John J. DiIulio, Jr., eds., *What's God Got to Do With the American Experiment?* (Washington, D.C.: Brookings Institution Press, 2000); Marjorie Garber and Rebecca L. Walkowitz, eds., *One Nation Under God?: Religion and American Culture* (New York: Routledge, 1999); Maureen Harrison and Steve Gilbert, *Freedom of Religion Decisions of the United States Supreme Court* (San Diego: Excellent Books, 1996); Leonard W. Levy, *The Establishment Clause: Religion and the First Amendment* (New York: Macmillan, 1986); William Miller, *The First Liberty: Religion and the American Republic* (New York: Knopf, 1986).

Fosdick, Harry Emerson (1878–1969)

A renowned Baptist preacher, theological liberal (see LIBERALISM, THEOLOGICAL), and social activist, Harry Emerson Fosdick was one of the most visible religious leaders of his day. Born in Buffalo, New York, on May 24, 1878, Fosdick converted at the age of seven and soon thereafter expressed a desire to serve as a missionary.

For the 1900–1901 school year Fosdick attended Colgate University, where he was influenced deeply by the liberal Baptist theologian William Newton CLARK, who emphasized the need to separate the eternal substance of the Christian message from its transient historical forms. After a year at Colgate Seminary, Fosdick entered Union Theological Seminary in New York. His education there strengthened

his liberal leanings. He also became a strong advocate of the SOCIAL GOSPEL, maintaining that the churches had a definite role to play in the creation of a more just social order. After graduating from Union in 1904, Fosdick took the pulpit at Montclair Baptist Church in New Jersey, where he developed a reputation as an outstanding preacher. He also taught at New York's Union Seminary, originally as a part-time instructor and later as professor of practical theology.

Upon returning from chaplaincy work in Europe in 1918 for the YOUNG MEN'S CHRISTIAN ASSOCIATION, the young Baptist minister accepted a call to a Presbyterian pulpit at First Presbyterian Church in New York City. While there, Fosdick preached his most famous sermon. "Shall the Fundamentalists Win?" was both a plea for less hostility between liberals and fundamentalists (see FUNDAMENTALISM) and a public refutation of major fundamentalist doctrines, including the virgin birth, which he claimed was inessential; the inerrancy of the Bible, which was in his view incredible; and the belief in the second coming of Christ, which he believed needed reevaluation. Published as "The New Knowledge and the Christian Faith," the sermon made Fosdick a lightning rod for fundamentalist attacks, especially in the PRESBYTERIAN CHURCH (U.S.A.). Many wanted the denomination to force Fosdick out of his Presbyterian pulpit. Although these attempts failed, he left the church in 1924.

At the urging of John D. Rockefeller, Fosdick was hired by Park Avenue Baptist Church, which five years later moved to its new building, Riverside Church. Nonsectarian and mission-driven, Riverside Church became a center of liberal Protestantism and the social gospel. Among the numerous activities sponsored by the church was a job placement agency organized during the Great Depression of the 1930s.

Fosdick's message extended far beyond his church. A highly popular radio show, *National Vespers*, and his many books brought his message to millions. Perhaps even more significant was the effect he had on the students in his classes on practical theology at Union Seminary.

After retiring from his pastorate in 1946, Fosdick led an active life promoting social and economic justice, racial harmony, and world peace. Although he had been a strong supporter of American entry in WORLD WAR I, even writing an enormously successful defense of American intervention—*The Challenge of the Present Crisis* (1917)—he became a convinced pacifist during the 1920s, a position he would hold the remainder of his life, even during WORLD WAR II. Despite his concern with the apparent intractability of evil, which made him less optimistic in his later years, Fosdick remained committed to the idea that human participation with God's activity in history was all that was necessary to overcome sin and evil. Although slowed by arthritis and a heart condition, Fosdick continued to be active until his death on October 5, 1969.

EQ

Bibliography: Harry Emerson Fosdick, *The Living of These Days: An Autobiography* (New York: Harper and Row, 1969); Robert Moats Miller, *Harry Emerson Fosdick: Preacher, Pastor, Prophet* (New York: Oxford University Press, 1985).

Foursquare Gospel See MCPHERSON, AIMEE SEMPLE; PENTECOSTALISM.

Fourteenth Amendment The Fourteenth Amendment, adopted in 1868, is one of the three amendments to the United States CONSTITUTION adopted during the Reconstruction era. Along with the Thirteenth Amendment outlawing SLAVERY and the Fifteenth guaranteeing the right to vote regardless of race, color, or previous conditions of servitude, the Fourteenth Amendment was designed primarily to protect newly freed slaves from political and legal abuse.

The amendment has five sections. The second through fifth deal with issues emerging from the Civil War. They outline the punishments for states that disfranchise blacks, for-

bid the paying of Confederate war debts, and disbar Confederate leaders from elective office.

The first section, however, is by far the most important. It declares all persons born in the United States citizens of that nation and of the state in which they reside. It also forbids the states from passing any laws that "abridge the privileges and immunities" of United States citizens and from denying any of its citizens due process and equal protection under the laws.

This is significant because it seems to guarantee to the citizens of the various states the same rights they have as United States citizens. It was some time, however, before the implications of this amendment became part of American law. This happened through what is known as the incorporation doctrine, which states that within the "due process" clause of the amendment are included particular rights and liberties. The first time a Supreme Court majority took this position and incorporated (or included) sections of the FIRST AMENDMENT into the Fourteenth Amendment's due process clause was in *Gitlow v. New York* (1925). In the majority opinion Justice Edward Sanford wrote, "For the present purposes, we may and do assume that freedom of the speech and of the press . . . are among the fundamental rights and 'liberties' protected by the due process clause of the Fourteenth Amendment." Few recognized the significance of this point until the Court's decision in *Stromberg v. California* (1931) struck down a California statute prohibiting the display of a red flag as an emblem of anarchism. In the majority decision, Chief Justice Charles Evans Hughes wrote, "It has been determined that the conception of liberty under the due process clause of the Fourteenth Amendment embraces the right of free speech."

In its decision in *Cantwell v. Connecticut* (1940), the Supreme Court broadened the incorporation doctrine to embrace the "free exercise" clause of the First Amendment. The incorporation of the "establishment" clause occurred in the Court's decision in *Everson v. Board of Education* (1947).

These latter decisions brought state and local laws touching on religion under the examination of the federal courts. The result was a proliferation of court cases as the implications of these rulings were worked out. Clearly, the Fourteenth Amendment and the incorporation doctrine have been very significant. They have protected the liberties and freedom of the citizens of the various states and prevented the suppression of unpopular opinions and religious views.

EQ

Bibliography: Leonard W. Levy, *The Establishment Clause: Religion and the First Amendment* (New York: Macmillan, 1986); Michael J. Perry, *We the People: The Fourteenth Amendment and the Supreme Court* (New York: Oxford University Press, 1999); Leo Pfeffer, *Church, State, and Freedom,* rev. ed. (Boston: Beacon Press, 1967); Anson Phelps Stokes, *Church and State in the United States,* rev. one-volume ed. (Westport, Conn.: Greenwood Press, 1975).

Free Church Tradition   See AMISH, THE; CHURCH OF THE BRETHREN (DUNKERS); HUTTERITES; MENNONITES; MORAVIANS; PIETISM.

Free Methodist Church   See METHODISTS.

Free Religious Association   See FROTHINGHAM, OCTAVIUS BROOKS.

free thought   See ATHEISM.

Free Will Baptists   See BAPTISTS.

Freemasonry   A moral and religious fraternal practice within the Judeo-Christian family, Freemasonry (or Masonry) arose in Britain early in the 18th century and quickly spread to the European continent and American colonies. The movement derives its name from the work of the masons of King Solomon's temple, whose physical labor in constructing this biblical house of worship is taken as a model for the task of building one's character in the modern world.

The precise origins of Freemasonry remain obscure. Many followers trace the roots of their tradition to King Solomon himself, or to still earlier biblical figures. From these beginnings Masonry is said to have been kept alive by builders' guilds in ancient Rome and the Middle Ages as well as by the Knights Templar, a 12th-century military order that participated in the Crusades to regain Jerusalem, with its temple site, for Christianity. Some Masons, together with most scholars, distinguish between these sacred mythological origins and the rise of the movement in early-18th-century England and Scotland, when middle-class men, imbued with the new optimistic faith of the Enlightenment, began joining moribund lodges of operative Masons and turned them into spiritual chambers of ritual and symbolism. Organized Masonic history, in any case, dates from the formation of the Grand Lodge of England in 1717.

Freemasonry immediately became popular in colonial towns and cities in North America. By the time of the Revolution, perhaps several thousand Americans, including such leading political figures as Benjamin Franklin and George Washington, belonged to the brotherhood. Indeed, for a few years following the Revolution, Freemasonry supplied many of the beliefs and symbols of the new nation's CIVIL RELIGION. (One legacy from this period is the national seal of the United States, containing the Masonic symbol of the All-Seeing Eye placed at the apex of an Egyptian pyramid, that appears today on the one-dollar bill). But the faith of the Enlightenment was not to rule America. The rise of evangelical Protestantism in the early 19th century brought sharp attacks on the fraternity for its secrecy, exclusivity, and alleged idolatry, causing three-fourths of the lodges to close and membership to plummet. By 1850, however, Masonry had begun to recover and entered its period of greatest growth, reaching close to 1 million members by the year 1900, and its high point of about 4 million by the mid-1950s.

As products of the moderate British Enlightenment, Freemasons believe in many of the same tenets of rational religion shared by most Episcopalians and Unitarians: God (often referred to as "The Great Architect of the Universe") created everything in the universe but does not intervene directly in its operation; the human soul is immortal; reason provides adequate means to apprehend the laws of God in nature and morality; the highest duty of humankind is to obey the laws of morality. Freemasons part company with Episcopalians, Unitarians, and all other Christians, however, in omitting the story of Jesus. They do this in the belief that Freemasonry teaches only those principles held in common by all the world's religions and thus can unite all men regardless of background. Not surprisingly, Jews have found such a universalistic faith hospitable, and they have been received into many, though not all, Masonic lodges. Nevertheless, a strong, though disguised, Christian element can be found in the most sacred of Masonic stories, that of Hiram Abif, King Solomon's master builder, who is murdered for his virtue and miraculously resurrected. Masons also celebrate the holidays of the Christian saints John the Baptist and John the Evangelist, and there exists a Masonic subgroup (the Order of Knights Templar) that explicitly reveres the Christian Trinity.

Beliefs alone, however, tell less than half the story of Freemasonry. The devotional life of Masonry centers around a series of rituals called "degrees," which progressively initiate members into the spiritual wisdom imparted by the tradition. This gnostic form of the brotherhood's practice raises the question of Freemasonry's connection with the occult. Scattered references to the ancient mystery religions of the Middle East, Egypt, and Greece, as well as to various European strains of mysticism and magic (hermeticism, Rosicrucianism [see ROSICRUCIANS], and alchemy), can be found in the earliest records of the fraternity, and some of these themes achieved greater elaboration as Masonry developed. But whereas the leading traditions of the occult aim to lead a follower to a mystical experience of oneness with the sacred forces of the universe, Freemasonry seeks no such communion. Rather it uses its ties to pre-Christian faiths simply to support its claim to universalism and to enhance the ceremonial appeal of its beliefs.

Considering the significant differences that separate the fraternity from the mainstream of Protestant evangelical and liberal faith in the United States, Masonry has had a remarkably large influence on American life. In addition to attracting an enormous membership of its own, the brotherhood has spawned women's auxiliaries and youth groups for boys and girls. It has also stimulated the emergence of a vast number of fraternal organizations, from the Independent Order of Odd Fellows to the Benevolent Protective Order of Elks, the religious meanings of whose practices remain unexplored but may well hold much in common with the outlook of Freemasonry.

TF

Bibliography: Steven C. Bullock, *Revolutionary Brotherhood: Freemasonry and the Transformation of the American Social Order, 1730–1840* (Chapel Hill: University of North Carolina Press, 1996); Mark C. Carnes, *Secret Ritual and Manhood in Victorian America* (New Haven: Yale University Press, 1989); Lynn Dumenil, *Freemasonry and American Culture, 1880–1930* (Princeton: Princeton University Press, 1984); Anthony D. Fels, "The Square and Compass: San Francisco's Freemasons and American Religion, 1870–1900," (Ph.D. dissertation, Stanford University, 1987); Dorothy Ann Lipson, *Freemasonry in Federalist Connecticut, 1789–1835* (Princeton: Princeton University Press, 1977).

Frelinghuysen, Theodorus Jacobus (1691–1748)

Theodorus J. Frelinghuysen was one of the founders of the Dutch Reformed Church in America. A minister in the Raritan Valley of New Jersey, he achieved notoriety for his insistence on the necessity of conversion and living a godly life. As a result of this evangelical emphasis, Frelinghuysen is now generally regarded as the herald of the remarkable series of mid-18th century revivals known as the GREAT AWAKENING.

Frelinghuysen was born near the Dutch border at Hagen, Germany, in November 1691. The son of a Reformed pastor and educated at the University of Lingen, he was profoundly influenced by continental PIETISM, a religious movement that stressed personal holiness. Frelinghuysen served briefly in two separate pastorates in the Netherlands following his ordination. In 1720 he migrated to America where, as a Reformed clergyman, he was under the jurisdiction of the Dutch Reformed Church. He served churches in New Jersey for almost three decades.

Because many of his clerical colleagues considered him more troublesome than saintly, Frelinghuysen's persistent emphasis on heartfelt piety made him an influential, but unpopular, figure in church affairs in the New World. Overturning the cold formalism that characterized Reformed churches at that time, he laid down strict requirements for admission to Communion. Frelinghuysen demanded that the "unconverted" be excluded from the Lord's table until they could testify to their genuine repentance and reliance on the Holy Spirit. He criticized the ecclesiastical hierarchy back in Amsterdam, moreover, for failing to send pietist clergy to America. Since he also encouraged lay participation in church life, which soon fostered growth in the areas where he ministered, leaders of the Great Awakening such as Gilbert TENNENT, Jonathan EDWARDS, and George WHITEFIELD later testified to Frelinghuysen's influence on their evangelistic work.

Frelinghuysen trained several young men for the ministry and caused a considerable stir in his denomination when he ordained them himself, without obtaining permission from church headquarters in Holland. Seeking local autonomy for Dutch churches, he helped organize the first coetus (organization of churches) in America in 1747. Although he did not live to see this movement come to fruition, Frelinghuysen's leadership was critical to the eventual formation of an independent Dutch Reformed Church in 1755.

The exact date and place of Frelinghuysen's death are unknown. He is assumed to have died in New Jersey in about 1748.

GHS, Jr.

Bibliography: Theodorus Jacobus Frelinghuysen, *Forerunner of the Great Awakening: Sermons by Theodorus Jacobus,* ed. Joel R. Beeke (Grand Rapids, Mich.: Eerdmans, 2000); James R. Tanis, *Dutch Calvinistic Pietism in the Middle Colonies: A Study in the Life and Theology of Theodorus Jacobus Frelinghuysen* (The Hague, Netherlands: Martinus Nijhoff, 1968).

French Reformed   See HUGUENOTS.

Friends, The Religious Society of (Quakers)   The Religious Society of Friends, popularly known as the Quakers, dates its founding to 1652, when George Fox, standing on Pendle Hill in northwest England, received a vision from God. This vision lifted Fox out of his frustration with the failures of the numerous contending religious groups that had emerged in England during the Puritan revolution. Long a searcher for religious truth, Fox was near despair when he heard the voice of God telling him that "there is one even Jesus Christ who can speak to your condition." Fox interpreted this message to mean that the immediacy of the spiritual presence was the source of all religious truth. This became the basis for the Quaker doctrine of the inner light—the spirit of the transcendent God perceptibly entering into human consciousness.

Fox took this message throughout England, preaching the need for complete and true obedience to Christ. This obedience included pacifism, a rejection of oaths, and the refusal to make prescribed signs of respect—such as removing one's hat—to social superiors. Such attitudes often brought the Quakers into conflict with political and religious authorities both in England and in the American colonies.

The first Quakers came to British America in July 1656, when Mary Fisher and Ann Austin arrived in Boston aboard a ship from Barbados. The colonial authorities quickly arrested them on charges of witchcraft and shipped them back. No sooner had this happened than another group arrived to meet the same welcome. In response to this growing influx of religious enthusiasts, the colony barred ships from landing Quakers in the colony. In response Quakers started settling in the religiously tolerant colony of Rhode Island. From there they continued their attempts to take their religious message to the MASSACHU-SETTS BAY COLONY, where the authorities were driven to increasingly extreme measures in response, including the execution of four Quakers on Boston Common.

The founding of Pennsylvania (see PENN-SYLVANIA [COLONY]) in 1681 by the Quaker William PENN provided a place of refuge for English Quakers, as well as persecuted religious groups throughout Europe. Under Quaker leadership the colony became prosperous and successful, but the demands of running the colony, especially during the French and Indian War, threatened their religious tenets and led Quakers to remove themselves from the colony's assembly.

Quakers in the United States held their first General Meeting in 1681 in Burlington, New Jersey. In 1685 it merged with the Philadelphia annual meeting to become "The General Yearly Meeting for Friends of Pennsylvania, East Jersey, and of the Adjacent Provinces." Now known as the Philadelphia Yearly Meeting, it is the oldest Quaker group in the United States.

Although Quakers early settled in the Southern states, their growing opposition to slavery made them increasingly unwelcome there. As tension between proslavery and antislavery forces intensified, Quakers increasingly left the South for the newly opened regions of Ohio and Indiana, giving the Midwest a fairly large Quaker population, but a minuscule presence south of the Ohio River.

One significant element of Quaker history that should not be overlooked is that from the beginning women had an equal role in the community's activity. Knowing that God was no respecter of persons, Quakers recognized that the divine spirit could settle anywhere, and so women have played a major role in the denomination's history. Equally significant was the fact that this equality within the denomination led Quaker women such as Susan B. Anthony and Lucretia Mott to leadership roles in the struggle for women's rights.

Although there are fewer than 115,000 Friends in the United States, they are divided into three main theological groupings. The largest, the Friends United Meeting, most resembles mainstream Protestantism with its programmed meetings and hired ministers. Numbering around 45,000, they consider themselves to be the continuation of the "orthodox" Friends who did not separate during the numerous schisms of the 1800s.

The Friends General Conference is a result of the Hicksite controversy in Quakerism. In the 1820s a Quaker minister named Elias Hick began to condemn the growing worldliness and formalism of the Quakers. After several years of controversy Hick's followers withdrew from the Philadelphia Yearly Meeting to organize what became the General Conference. The churches affiliated with the Friends General Conference do not prepare worship services but wait for the divine spirit to lead one to speak. The conference numbers about 35,000 members and is the most active in social issues.

The Evangelical Friends Alliance, with roughly 38,000 members, was formed in 1965 by Friends meetinghouses influenced by EVAN-GELICALISM. It brought together congregations that had recently adopted evangelical practice with older congregations formed by the schism created when the British Quaker John Gurney visited the United States in 1837–1840 and urged the adoption of revivalistic methods and a salaried ministry.

The remaining Quakers are joined in several different meetings that are not affiliated with any of the above conferences. Despite these differences in affiliation, most of the conferences are on good terms with each other and join in numerous activities, primarily social action, through such bodies as the American Friends Service Committee and the Friends Committee for National Legislation.

EQ

Bibliography: Margaret Hope Bacon, *Mothers of Feminism: The Story of Quaker Women in America* (San Francisco: Harper & Row, 1986); ———, *The Quiet Rebels: The Story of the Quakers in America* (New York: Basic Books, 1969); Thomas D. Hamm, *The Transformation of American Quakerism: Orthodox Friends, 1800–1907* (Bloomington: Indiana University Press, 1988); H. Larry Ingle, *First Among Friends: George Fox and the Creation of Quakerism* (New York: Oxford University Press, 1994); Rufus Jones, *The Quakers in the American Colonies* (New York: Russell & Russell, 1911); ———, *The Later Periods of Quakerism* (1921; Westport, Conn.: Greenwood Press, 1970); D. Elton Trueblood, *The People Called Quakers* (New York: Harper & Row, 1966); www.quaker.org/fgc (Friends General Conference); www.fum.org (Friends United Meeting); www.evangelical-friends.org (Evangelical Friends Alliance).

frontier A term broadly applied to areas of social, cultural, political, and economic contact, the *frontier* has traditionally indicated a line of advance that marked the gradual process by which European-American migrants settled and "civilized" western regions of the North American continent, rendering order from apparent chaos. Following the thesis posited by Frederick Jackson Turner in the 1890s, many scholars have seen the social transformation that occurred on the American frontier as directly responsible for the creation of a distinctive American identity. In recent years this paradigm of westward movement has been the focus of considerable debate and revision, as historians have acknowledged the drawbacks of viewing American history solely from the perspective of European-American migration.

Drawing upon Turner's thesis, scholars until recently have depicted religion on the frontier almost solely in terms of the spread of Protestant Christianity westward, focusing on the characteristic forms that religious adherence assumed in an environment of continuous social formation. William Warren Sweet, the best-known scholar of "frontier religion," has argued that the institutions and practices that came to be most closely associated with American evangelical religion in the 19th century were largely a product of a frontier culture. The individualism, emotionalism, pragmatism, anti-intellectualism, and egalitarianism that came to characterize evangelical religion were attributed to the needs and desires of a mobile, sparsely settled, and largely agrarian population.

The most widespread and best-known of these religious practices was REVIVALISM, the periodic gathering of participants and observers for the purpose of encouraging emotionally charged religious fellowship and individual conversions to Christianity. Although revivals had characterized evangelical Protestantism during the GREAT AWAKENING of the 18th century, they became an intrinsic aspect of religious life during the early 19th century, as European-American migrants settled territories west of the original 13 states.

In 1801, Cane Ridge, Kentucky, was the site of a large revival (see CANE RIDGE REVIVAL) in which some 3,000 participants experienced tremendous outpourings of enthusiastic spiritual expression, including dancing, singing, barking, jerking, and rolling. Such CAMP MEETINGS also gave rise to a particular brand of itinerant preacher, men and women who could "stir up" the passions of individuals, create a strong sense of religious community with little regard to denominational affiliation, and evoke from their listeners the desire to repent and convert. Charles Grandison FINNEY, the most famous frontier itinerant, preached throughout New York State and instituted a series of "new measures," practices that set the pattern for revivalism into the 20th century. Finney's innovations included praying for individuals by name, encouraging women to speak in public, and using an "anxious bench" at the front of the assembly so that participants considering conversion could come before the entire congregation. In construing a revival as a function of human practices and passions, Finney also downplayed the role of God as the initiator of conversion and heightened the importance of individual enterprise and assent.

This pattern of frontier revivalism, instigated in New York, Kentucky, and other areas encompassing the line of European-American settlement, set the stage for evangelical practices on frontiers farther west throughout the 19th century. Camp meetings, sometimes lasting three to five days, provided social interaction and the foundations of community organization for settlers who had left their homes and families back east. Denominational structures were transformed to meet the needs of the westward migration, and revivalism favored those organizations, especially BAPTISTS and METHODISTS, that were flexible enough to adjust to a variety of social and cultural settings.

But if the frontier has provided a setting for the extension of Protestant religious groups westward, it has also promoted experimentation and syncretism. European Americans who had severed their ties with eastern communities and churches were often more likely to entertain new religious ideas and practices. Just as Finney's new measures thrived in the environment of western New York, so too did new religions such as Mormonism, Shaker communities, and a variety of utopian experiments find rich soil and ready believers. New religious groups, seeking further distance from a society that often barely tolerated their practices, proved instrumental in the subsequent development of American frontiers.

Scholars in recent years have chosen to look at frontiers not simply as lines of European-American settlement, but as places of intercultural contact among a variety of migrants, including Native Americans and settlers with roots in Europe, Africa, Asia, and Latin America. In this view, a frontier does not necessarily imply a movement from social chaos to order, but instead indicates meetings, negotiations, and often confrontations among a multiplicity of cultures about what constitutes community life. Additionally, it has been argued persuasively that even European-American settlement never followed a continuous, slowly advancing cultural front, but instead functioned in a variety of ways, giving rise to urban, agricultural, mining, timber, and ranching frontiers, all with different forms of social and religious organization. Rather than seeing in these newer definitions of the frontier a loss of religious coherence, some scholars view them as an opportunity to explore religious beliefs and practices in myriad circumstances, and indeed to expand more traditional concepts of what constitutes religion itself.

LMK

Bibliography: Robert V. Hine, *Community on the American Frontier: Separate But Not Alone* (Norman: University of Oklahoma Press, 1980); Laurie F. Maffly-Kipp, *Religion and Society in Frontier California* (New Haven: Yale University Press, 1994); Patricia Nelson Limerick, *The Legacy of Conquest: The Unbroken Past of the American West* (New York: W. W. Norton, 1987); David J. Weber, *The Spanish Frontier in North America* (New Haven: Yale University Press, 1994).

Frothingham, Octavius Brooks (1822–1895)

Octavius B. Frothingham was a Unitarian minister and first president of the Free Religious Association, an ultraliberal theological movement that (in Frothingham's words) went "beyond Christianity." His ministry and growing disenchantment with theistic beliefs symbolized a general transition within American Unitarianism as a whole after the Civil War. In the second half of the 19th century, Frothingham's denomination changed from being a recognizably Christian church to a religious organization with an essentially humanistic focus.

Frothingham was born in Boston on November 26, 1822. Following his graduation from Harvard College (1843) and Harvard Divinity School (1846), he became the pastor of the North Church in Salem, Massachusetts, where he served for eight years. He next led churches in Jersey City, New Jersey (1855–1859), and in New York City (1859–1879), eventually transforming New York's Third Unitarian Society into the so-called Independent Liberal Church. In 1872 he published *The Religion of Humanity,* one of the classic expressions of naturalistic religious thought in postbellum America. Frothingham also wrote *Transcendentalism in New England* (1876), an insider's view of that movement and the earliest history of TRANSCENDENTALISM.

When the National Conference of Unitarian Churches was organized in 1865 with a constitution that officially committed the denomination to the "Lordship of Christ," Frothingham and other religious radicals began to make plans to cut their institutional ties with Unitarianism. Instrumental in founding the Free Religious Association in 1867, he was elected its president, a post he held until 1878. Frothingham also contributed numerous articles to *The Index,* the association's journal. The Free Religion movement was short-lived and by the end of the century had been reabsorbed into Unitarianism. However, Unitarianism itself had changed and was far more compatible with religious humanism (see SECULAR HUMANISM) than it had been a half-century before.

Because of ill health, Frothingham retired from the Independent Liberal Church in 1879, and the congregation soon disbanded after his departure. Still active as a writer in retirement, he died in Boston on November 27, 1895.

(See also MODERNISM, PROTESTANT.)

GHS, Jr.

Bibliography: J. Wade Caruthers, *Octavius Brooks Frothingham, Gentle Radical* (University: University of Alabama Press, 1977); Octavius Brooks Frothingham, *Transcendentalism in New England,* ed. Sydney E. Ahlstrom (1876; New York: Harper, 1959).

Fuller, Sarah Margaret (1810–1850)

Writer, reformer, literary critic, and acclaimed conversationalist, Margaret Fuller synthesized the convictions of TRANSCENDENTALISM and the concerns of early women's rights activists. Though dismissed during her lifetime as a second-rate author, Fuller's *Woman in the Nineteenth Century* (1845) survives as a classic in the tradition of Mary Wollstonecraft's *Vindication of the Rights of Woman* (1792) and Simone de Beauvoir's *The Second Sex* (1953). Fuller's thought also lives on in contemporary FEMINIST THEOLOGY.

Fuller was born in 1810 in Cambridgeport, Massachusetts, where her facility with languages such as Latin, Greek, Italian, and French earned her a reputation as a child prodigy. Her family moved to Groton, Massachusetts, in 1833. They relocated in 1839 to Jamaica Plain, Massachusetts, where in that same year Fuller organized a conversation circle for prominent Boston women, many of them transcendentalists. In 1840 Fuller became editor-in-chief of *The Dial,* an organ for transcendentalist thought and literature. She served in that post for four years. Fuller moved in 1844 to New York City, where she worked as a literary critic at Horace Greeley's reform-minded paper, the *New York Tribune.* She relocated in 1846 to Europe, where she mingled with such luminaries as Thomas Carlyle, William Wordsworth, and George Sand. In Italy, she met and married Giovanni Angelo, Marquis Ossoli. During the European revolutions of 1848, she served as a nurse and chief administrator at the Hospital of the Trinity to the Pilgrims, which served Roman soldiers. After the French took Rome in 1849, she and her husband fled with their newborn child to a mountain village and, eventually, to Florence. From there Fuller

Margaret Fuller, transcendentalist writer whose *Woman in the Nineteenth Century* (1845) was the first philosophical statement of feminism by an American woman.

decided, in the spring of 1850, to return with her family to the United States. Tragically, the boat that was carrying Fuller, her husband, and her child ran aground off Fire Island, just short of their New York destination, and all three perished on July 19, 1850.

Fuller once confided to transcendentalist William Henry CHANNING her "secret hope" that women would some day contribute significantly to the American literary tradition, and her own work helped to transform that hope into a reality. During her lifetime, however, Fuller was noted more as a conversationalist than as an author. Though the universal reformer Thomas Wentworth Higginson praised Fuller as "the best literary critic whom

America has yet seen," detractors from James Russell Lowell to Perry Miller dismissed her as a woman whose ego far outweighed her capacities as a thinker and as a writer.

A new generation of scholars has begun to challenge this consensus. The book they esteem most highly is *Woman in the Nineteenth Century*, a feminist manifesto that in their view provided much of the inspiration and intellectual foundation for the women's movement. Fuller's *Woman* shared much with Mary Wollstonecraft's earlier work, *A Vindication of the Rights of Woman*. But whereas Wollstonecraft grounded her feminist views in Enlightenment notions of rights, Fuller proceeded from Romantic notions such as the glories of the cultivation of the individual soul. Among "the prophets of the coming age" whom *Woman* conjured up were the socialist Charles Fourier, the seer Emmanuel Swedenborg (see SWEDENBORGIANISM), and the German romantic Johann Wolfgang von Goethe.

Transcendentalism was, however, the most notable philosophical and religious influence on Fuller's work. Along with intimates such as Ralph Waldo EMERSON and James Freeman CLARKE, Fuller affirmed such transcendentalist verities as human perfectibility, historical progress, and self-reliance. She, too, trusted spirit more than matter, intuition more than reason. Because she believed that women were "intuitive in function, spiritual in tendency," she found room in her work to heap praise on her sex.

Fuller belied the title of her most famous book by examining the roles and images of women from ancient to modern times. She discussed in *Woman* both the Madonna and Isis and drew on Hindu myths and European folklore as well as the Bible. Among the theological affirmations of the book was Fuller's insistence that God was immanent in both women and men. Women should devote their lives first and foremost, Fuller argued, to God, not men. Fuller shocked many of her readers by discussing frankly taboo subjects such as prostitution and by her insistence that Christianity had done little to improve the lot of women.

Though Fuller's *Woman* was largely forgotten in the first half of the 20th century, it inspired a generation of early American feminists. In July 1848, three years after the book appeared, friends of Fuller organized the first woman's rights convention at Seneca Falls, New York. Their Declaration of Sentiments owed much, of course, to the Declaration of Independence; but it may have owed more to Fuller's *Woman*.

SRP

Bibliography: Eve Kornfeld, *Margaret Fuller: A Brief Biography with Documents* (Boston: Bedford, 1997); Marie Mitchell Olesen Urbanski, *Margaret Fuller's Woman in the Nineteenth Century: A Literary Study of Form and Content, of Sources and Influence* (Westport, Conn.: Greenwood Press, 1980); David Watson, *Margaret Fuller: An American Romantic* (New York: St. Martin's, 1988).

Fuller, Charles E. See ELECTRONIC CHURCH.

fundamentalism (Protestant) Fundamentalism—a form of Protestant Christianity distinguished by its commitment to biblical INERRANCY, DISPENSATIONALISM, strict morality, and religious separatism—slowly emerged out of the mainstream of American evangelical Protestantism (see EVANGELICALISM) during the last third of the 19th century. By the 1920s, when the term was first used, fundamentalism was a separate and recognizable religious movement whose adherents viewed themselves as heirs of orthodox Christianity. In the late 19th and early 20th century this was at least partially true. During that time fundamentalists had not separated from other conservative evangelical Christians with whom they shared an opposition to EVOLUTION, biblical criticism, and MODERNISM and liberalism.

But fundamentalists were not true heirs. They adopted new ideas and new concepts as transformative of the Christian tradition as the modernists they opposed. The new ideas were dispensationalism, PREMILLENNIALISM, and biblical inerrancy. While all three had antecedents in the history of Christianity, they had never been dominant. Within fundamentalism, however, they became determinative for judging a believer's orthodoxy.

Premillennialism cut across the grain of American Protestantism. Historically American Protestantism was postmillennial (see POSTMILLENNIALISM), meaning that most Protestants believed Christ's return would occur after the millennium, the thousand years of peace and prosperity. This belief fit well with the optimism that marked the United States. Premillennialism presented a different face entirely. Premillennialists rejected the possibility of progress, asserting that this world was destined for decline and decay.

This version of premillennialism was based on a theory of biblical interpretation known as dispensationalism. Originating in England, dispensationalism was formalized in the United States by Cyrus Scofield's *Scofield Reference Bible*. Dispensationalism claims that world history is divided into various periods of time, dispensations. These periods, of which there are seven, are marked by changing relationships between humanity and God and are foreshadowed in the Bible.

If the biblical description of historical events determined the understanding of humanity's relationship to God, the Bible had to be true, inerrant. For fundamentalists this term contained the idea that the Bible was not only reliable but also precise. Seven days meant seven days. This level of precision meant the Bible was completely adequate on all issues. Anything contradicting the Bible was wrong. The Bible contained facts, not theories.

This conviction brought fundamentalists into sharp conflict with their opponents, who tried to harmonize the Bible and science. Evolution and biblical criticism were not demonstrably true, claimed the fundamentalists, but mere hypotheses. In fact, evolution directly contradicted their view of science as the collection and cataloging of facts. Evolution was a theory which adapted facts to fit it.

Fundamentalists were fighting a cultural battle as well—a battle against America's Gilded Age. They feared that American society had lost all sense of the spiritual nature of human beings who were nothing more than objects to be bought and sold, and social Darwinism demonstrated that the losers deserved to fail. Combined with these more reflective views were the confusion and fear of those who suffered during that period of rapid industrialization, urbanization, and immigration.

No event served to solidify fundamentalism as much as WORLD WAR I. For fundamentalists the war was the result of the ideas of Charles Darwin, Friedrich Nietzsche, and biblical criticism. Germany was the source of both biblical criticism and the Nietzschean superman. In the popular fundamentalist mind, the violence and rapacity of the Germans resulted directly from their rejection of Biblical truth. To the fundamentalists the war demonstrated what would happen to the world when morality and Christianity were undermined.

The fusion of these ideas into a powerful movement occurred during the 1920s, when the sniping between religious conservatives and moderates became an all-out war. The modernists were better organized and better established. In 1919, fundamentalists found a unified voice in the World Christian Fundamentals Association. This organization, explicitly premillennial and dispensational, was formed to combat the spread of modernism within the denominations.

The following year a broader group of conservatives within the Northern Baptist Convention organized a Fundamentals group to remove modernists from the denomination. One of this group's leaders, Curtis Lee Laws, editor of the denomination's *Watchman-Examiner*, and neither a dispensationalist nor an inerrantist, coined the term *fundamentalist*.

As the fundamentalists attempted to remove the corrupt from the fold, they found themselves increasingly isolated, antagonizing their allies as much as their opponents. Rather than maintain alliances with theological conservatives, they insisted upon acceptance of dispensationalism, premillennialism, and inerrancy as marks of orthodoxy. By this categorization Laws himself was excluded.

During the 1920s the Presbyterians (both North and South), the Northern and Southern Baptist Conventions, the Disciples of Christ, and to a lesser extent other denominations were dominated by conflicts with the fundamentalists. With their insistence upon dispensationalism, premillennialism, and inerrancy as proof of right belief, fundamentalists often alienated their allies and allowed their opponents to frame the debate over the issues of tolerance and inclusiveness. By 1926 fundamentalism was a spent force within the major denominations. The more militant fundamentalists left to found new denominations or centered their activities in interdenominational fundamentalist organizations, thus beginning the history of fundamentalism as one of sectarianism and separatism.

The failure to purge the denominations of modernists signalled the death knell for fundamentalism within mainstream Protestant evangelicalism. The trial of John Scopes (see SCOPES TRIAL) for teaching evolution discredited fundamentalism as a cultural movement. The eventual conviction of Scopes was lost amidst the carnival atmosphere of the trial. Led by H. L. MENCKEN, the nation's media reported the defeat of a crusade, a defeat that drove the fundamentalists underground. For the next several decades fundamentalists' despair over the world led to a rejection of both American culture and politics.

Fundamentalism did not die following the defeats of the 1920s, but merely retrenched. Some fundamentalists, disgusted with sectarianism and conflict, left the movement. Calling themselves neo-evangelicals, they became the respectable face of conservative Protestantism. Others followed a path of increasing sectarianism. J. Frank Norris, Bob JONES, and Carl McIntire are only three who opted for strict separatism.

By the mid-1950s separatism, the refusal to have anything to do with nonfundamentalists, had become the final element in defining fundamentalism. In 1957 Billy GRAHAM, until that time a darling of the fundamentalists, accepted the sponsorship of the ecumenical Protestant Council for his New York crusade. This split the fundamentalist movement and narrowed the term's use to strict separatists. Separatism increasingly isolated the movement in the 1950s and 1960s.

What many in the 1920s saw as a dead movement returned in the late 1970s and 1980s. The social dislocation of the 1960s sent many people into the fundamentalist fold. Patriotism, morality, and security were the traditional values to which fundamentalists appealed.

These themes were combined with a message of a supposedly simpler time—a time when drug use and abortion were shameful secrets, and people could walk the streets safely. Fundamentalists made sophisticated use of the media and developed effective organizations. No one managed this better than Jerry FALWELL, who from his church in Lynchburg, Virginia, created a political movement, the MORAL MAJORITY, that touched resonant chords even among those opposed to his religious views. These chords played the music that helped to elect Ronald Reagan president in 1980.

While Falwell eventually would increasingly remove himself from the political fray, his place was taken by others, including Pat Robertson. The strength fundamentalists had shown in developing their organizations was put at the service of political goals, and by the 1990s, fundamentalists had become a major, if not the major, force within the Republican Party.

The fundamentalist resurgence had a significant impact in the religious realm as well. Serious questions about doctrine affected two

The Moody Bible Institute is a major center that has trained generations to interpret the Bible as the literal word of God. *(Billy Graham Center Museum)*

denominations historically aloof from such debates—the Southern Baptist Convention and the Lutheran Church—Missouri Synod. During the 1970s these denominations experienced the controversies other denominations had suffered during the 1920s. This time, however, the fundamentalists emerged victorious. While the effect within the Missouri Synod was not that visible, given its historical tradition of separatism and its confessional basis, the opposite was the case for the Southern Baptists. Its size, the diversity within it, and the resulting rejection of many historical doctrinal views transformed the denomination into something new and different.

(See also EVANGELICALISM; *FUNDAMENTALS, THE.*)

EQ

Bibliography: Norman K. Furniss, *The Fundamentalist Controversy, 1918–1931* (New Haven, Conn.: Yale University Press, 1954); Louis Gasper, *The Fundamentalist Movement, 1930–1956* (Grand Rapids, Mich.: Baker Book House, 1963); Michael Lienesch, *Redeeming America: Piety and Politics in the New Christian Right* (Chapel Hill: University of North Carolina Press, 1993); George Marsden, *Fundamentalism and American Culture: The Shaping of Twentieth Century American Evangelicalism, 1870–1925* (New York: Oxford University Press, 1980); ———, ed., *The Fundamentals: A Testimony to Truth* (New York: Garland, 1988); Martin Marty, ed., *Fundamentalism and Evangelicalism* (Munich: K.G. Saur, 1993); Ernest R. Sandeen, *The Roots of Fundamentalism: British and American Millennarianism, 1800–1930* (Chicago: University of Chicago Press, 1970).

Fundamentals, The *The Fundamentals* was a 12-volume paperback series of books published between 1910 and 1915 in defense of what its authors believed was traditional Christian orthodoxy. Intended simply as a "testimony to the truth" (as the subtitle of the books puts it), the series gave shape and intellectual substance to the conservative theological movement now called FUNDAMENTALISM that had emerged in England and America at the end of the 19th century.

The project was the brainchild of Lyman Stewart, a wealthy California businessman who financed the publishing venture with the aid of his brother and partner, Milton. Stewart hired well-known Baptist evangelist Amzi Clarence DIXON, then pastor of Dwight L. MOODY's church in Chicago, as the editor of the first five volumes. Dixon later edited a four-volume edition in 1917 as well. The work was eventually completed by Reuben Archer TORREY and Louis Meyer, and it contained 90 articles written by many of the most distinguished conservative theologians and Bible scholars of the day. The Stewarts mailed some three million free copies of *The Fundamentals* to Protestant leaders throughout the English-speaking world in an attempt to spread their views.

The essays tended to be quite moderate in tone and discussed a variety of popular and scholarly topics. The articles carefully avoided the most pressing political issues of the day, including Prohibition, and assumed that the church should remain entirely aloof from social concerns. The books, moreover, made virtually no mention of controversial theological beliefs about the second coming of Christ, then popular among some conservative Protestants. And despite opposition to Darwinist theories about biology and the origins of humankind, a few essayists even made room for a theistic form of evolution, that is, the possibility that God had directed the evolutionary development of life on earth.

In terms of the subject matter of the series, about a third of the articles dealt with the Bible and defended it against attacks by liberal critics who rejected the validity of portions of its text. The authors of *The Fundamentals* believed that the Scriptures were not only scientifically and rationally verifiable, but also wholly without error. Another third of the essays discussed traditional theological questions such as the doctrine of the Trinity and teachings about sin and salvation. The rest of the writings are somewhat more difficult to classify; some contained condemnations of various modern "heresies" (Mormonism, CHRISTIAN SCIENCE, JEHOVAH'S WITNESSES, and SPIRITUALISM), and others made appeals to readers to engage in missionary and evangelistic work.

The immediate response to *The Fundamentals* was surprisingly muted, and neither serious theological journals nor popular religious magazines gave the books more than passing notice. It is now clear, however, that the series, which coined the term later identified with a broad, antimodern movement in the 20th century, represented an important transitional phase in the development of a new religious phenomenon. Although for a time "fundamentalism" remained only a loose alliance of Protestant traditionalists, by the 1920s the movement had become more militant and had begun to jettison the moderate positions espoused by its earliest proponents. Thus, while the initial reception of *The Fundamentals* was meager, the long-term significance of those volumes for American Protestantism has been and continues to be immense.

GHS, Jr.

Bibliography: Ernest R. Sandeen, *The Roots of Fundamentalism: British and American Millenarianism, 1800–1930* (Grand Rapids, Mich.: Baker Book House, 1978); Reuben A. Torrey and Amzi C. Dixon, eds., *The Fundamentals: A Testimony to the Truth* (Grand Rapids, Mich.: Baker Books, 1993).

Furman, Richard (1755–1825)

Richard Furman was a Baptist minister and prominent religious leader in South Carolina in the early 19th century. A strong advocate of centralized authority in ecclesiastical affairs, he was the first president of the Triennial Convention, the original national body of BAPTISTS. Known among his colleagues as the "apostle of education," he developed an educational plan for his denomination in 1817, and Furman University, the first Baptist college in the South, was named in his honor.

Furman was born in Esopus, New York, on October 9, 1755. His family moved to the South shortly after his birth. Although he had little formal education, he was a bright student who was able to learn a good deal by studying at home. He was converted by revival-oriented Separate Baptists in 1771 and immediately began work as an evangelist. Furman won renown for his preaching while he was still a teenager, serving as a Baptist pastor near Charleston, South Carolina, after 1774. Although his support of the American cause during the War for Independence forced him to flee from the British in South Carolina, he was able to return home after the war. In 1787 he became minister of the First Baptist Church in Charleston, then the most prominent Baptist church in the South.

Furman's organizational ideas emphasized the importance of centralized missionary and educational efforts. When Baptists formed the General Missionary Convention (soon known as the Triennial Convention) to give needed support to Baptist overseas missionaries, Furman was chosen as its initial president in 1814. He was elected to a second three-year term in 1817. Furman also was active in the organization of the South Carolina Baptist Convention, the denomination's first state convention. He headed the South Carolina organization between 1821 and 1825. In addition, he served as moderator of the Charleston Baptist Association for more than 25 years.

Furman's most lasting contribution to his church was in the field of education. While the early Baptist movement tended to disparage the importance of education, Furman insisted that meeting educational needs, especially training young men for the ministry, would be essential for the denomination's long-term success. He founded a committee to raise funds for education, and he directed it for 34 years. He also urged Baptists in Georgia and the Carolinas to build a college and theological school, which were established shortly after his death.

Furman held the pastor's position at the First Baptist Church from 1787 until his death nearly four decades later. He died at High Hills, South Carolina, on August 25, 1825.

GHS, Jr.

Bibliography: James A. Rogers, *Richard Furman: Life and Legacy* (Macon, Ga.: Mercer University Press, 1985).

G

Garvey, Marcus (1887–1940) Marcus Garvey organized the first mass movement of blacks in the United States by emphasizing racial pride, self-sufficiency, and unity. Although the movement collapsed following his deportation from the United States in 1927, he laid the groundwork for the demands of black empowerment that emerged in the 1960s and 1970s.

Born in St. Anne's Bay, Jamaica, on August 17, 1887, Marcus Garvey was the youngest of 11 children. Of African descent, Garvey suffered under Jamaica's strict three-color caste system of whites, creoles (those of mixed race), and blacks. Despite this social discrimination, his father's descent from Maroons—escaped slaves who successfully defended their freedom against both the Spanish and English—gave the young Garvey pride in being black.

Forced by poverty to leave school at the age of 14, Garvey became a printer's apprentice and in 1904 went to Kingston, where he participated in an unsuccessful printer's strike in 1907. Following his debacle he bounced around the Caribbean and Central America, working as a journalist and fruit picker. Angered by the exploitation and mistreatment of his fellow workers, he complained to British consular officials, whose indifference convinced Garvey that blacks could not rely on whites for justice and aid.

He traveled to England in 1912, where he met Africans for the first time. This led to an interest in African affairs, and he began to write for the *Africa Times and Orient Review.* During this period, Garvey read Booker T. WASHINGTON's autobiography, *Up from Slavery.* Although he opposed Washington's political quiescence, Garvey was drawn to Washington's plea for black economic independence and self-sufficiency.

In 1914 he returned to Jamaica, where, on August 1, he organized the Universal Negro Improvement and Conservation Association and African Communities League (U.N.I.A.), designed to draw the race together through education, commercial development, and racial pride. Invited to the United States by Booker T. Washington to discuss a trade school the U.N.I.A. had opened in Jamaica, he arrived on March 23, 1916. By this time Washington was dead and Garvey was alone and unknown in America.

During that summer Garvey organized a chapter of the U.N.I.A. in Harlem. Although its membership was originally drawn from the West Indian community, it soon included large numbers of American blacks, and Garvey's speaking tours to black churches and groups throughout the United States generated national support. In January 1918 he began publishing the *Negro World*, which became one of the leading African-American weeklies, with a circulation of more than 200,000 and sections in Spanish and French for the benefit of subscribers in Africa, Latin America, and the West Indies.

Blacks flocked to Garvey's movement, and the 1920 international meeting of the U.N.I.A.

brought several thousand delegates from every state in the union and dozens of countries to New York City. The convention was marked by parades, mass meetings, and displays by the various arms of the U.N.I.A., including the paramilitary African Legion and the Black Cross Nurses.

Much excitement had been generated by the formation of the Black Star Line in the previous year. This steamship company, owned, operated, and manned by blacks, was to be Garvey's downfall. Although successful at raising funds, the company was hampered by antiquated equipment and soon faced financial collapse. Garvey and three associates were arrested in 1922 on charges of mail fraud in connection with the company's failure. Acting as his own attorney, Garvey used the trial as a forum for his racial and political views. Although his codefendants were acquitted, Garvey was convicted and sentenced to five years in prison and fined $1,000.

During his appeal Garvey attempted to restructure the steamship company as part of a larger back-to-Africa movement that included settlements in Liberia. This effort collapsed in 1924, when the Liberian government—under pressure from France and England—closed the settlements. The following year the Supreme Court refused to hear Garvey's appeal, and on February 8, 1925, he entered the federal penitentiary in Atlanta.

The movement dwindled during his imprisonment, although the campaign for his release revived it somewhat. In 1927 President Calvin Coolidge commuted Garvey's sentence and ordered him deported. Returning to Jamaica, he presided over the 1929 convention of the U.N.I.A., the movement's last great moment. Weakened in the United States by Garvey's absence, and throughout the world by the Great Depression, the U.N.I.A. declined rapidly.

Moving in 1935 to London, where he published the magazine *Black Man*, Garvey labored to keep the movement alive, but asthma, aggra-vated by pneumonia, weakened him severely. In 1940 he suffered two strokes that paralyzed his right side and resulted in his death on June 10, 1940.

Although moribund at the time of his death, "Garveyism" has had a long-lived significance. The first person to develop a mass following among American blacks, Garvey did so by appealing to racial pride and black nationalism. These would reappear in the Black Power movement, and MALCOLM X could claim that the Black Muslims were reaping the seeds Garvey had sown.

Garvey used the black churches as vehicles for transmitting his ideas. He also urged blacks to think of God as one of them. The motto of the U.N.I.A., "One God! One Aim! One Destiny!" contained within it the implication that God was with the blacks in their struggle for independence and justice, and even black himself. Although he avoided antagonizing the established churches, Garvey and several of his followers urged the creation of an all-black church with a black Christ and black images. In response, the African Orthodox Church was founded under Garvey's auspices with a former U.N.I.A. chaplain and Episcopal priest consecrated as its first bishop. Its journal, the *Negro Churchman*, attempted to develop a religiosity freed from European symbols and white dominance. Although rejected by most African Americans, Garvey's views were a precursor of the black theology of the later 20th century.

(See also AFRICAN-AMERICAN RELIGION; CIVIL RIGHTS MOVEMENT; NATION OF ISLAM [BLACK MUSLIMS]).

EQ

Bibliography: Jules Archer, *They Had a Dream: The Civil Rights Struggle, from Frederick Douglass to Marcus Garvey, to Martin Luther King, and Malcolm X* (New York: Viking, 1993); Randall K. Burkett, *Garveyism as a Religious Movement: The Institutionalization of Black Civil Religion* (Metuchen, N.J.: Scarecrow Press, 1978); Edmund D. Cronon, *Black Moses: The Story of Marcus Garvey and the Universal Negro Improvement Association* (Madison: University of Wisconsin Press, 1955); Elton C. Fax, *Garvey: The Story of a Pioneer Black Nationalist* (New York: Dodd, Mead, 1972); Amy Jacques-Garvey, *Garvey and Garveyism* (Kingston, Jamaica: n.p., 1963); Theodore G. Vincent, *Black Power and the Garvey Movement* (Berkeley: Ramparts Press, 1971).

German Reformed Church   The roots of the German Reformed Church in the United States can be traced to late-17th-century immigration, principally from the Palatinate, an area along the Rhine in southern Germany. German settlement in America began with the founding of Germantown, Pennsylvania, in 1683 and continued throughout the 18th century until, by the eve of the Revolution, Germans numbered more than 225,000 in the 13 colonies. Although most German Protestants were Lutherans, the German Reformed community was distinguished by its adherence to the Heidelberg Catechism of 1563. The catechism, commissioned by Elector Frederick William III of the Palatinate, sought to mediate between the theological teachings of Swiss reformer John Calvin (see CALVINISM) and the ideas of Martin Luther, whose thought dominated Germany.

John Philip Boehm was the principal organizer of the German Reformed Church in America in the first half of the 18th century. A schoolmaster in Germany, Boehm settled in Pennsylvania in 1720 and in 1729 was ordained to the ministry of the Dutch Reformed Church. Because of the similarity between the beliefs of the Dutch Reformed and German Reformed Churches, the church in the Netherlands originally provided assistance to both Dutch and German emigrants in America. Geographical distance as well as differences in language and culture, however, eventually made this relationship a difficult one to maintain. As a consequence, German Reformed congregations often lacked clergy and had to learn to improvise with lay leadership.

The initial coetus (that is, the representative body containing ministers and lay elders from several local congregations that is essential to the governance of the Reformed Church) was organized by Michael Schlatter in 1746. By then numbering approximately 80 congregations, the church adopted a constitution in 1748 and thus brought itself within the emerging denominational system of the colonies. During the War for Independence, pastors and congregations actively supported the patriot cause, and in 1791, inspired by the ideals of civil independence, the German Reformed Church officially separated from the Dutch and claimed the right to ordain clergy without approval from the Netherlands. The Synod of the Reformed German Church in the United States of America, consisting of 178 congregations and more than 50,000 adherents, assembled for the first time in 1793.

The westward movement of German settlers carried the church into western Pennsylvania and Ohio in the early 19th century, but latent divisions within the denomination accompanied them. Disputes about worship, including the use of English and revivalistic techniques, for example, raised serious questions about the church's ability to adapt to both the secular and the religious culture of America. A short-lived schism, moreover, occurred during the same period. Although pastors had always been allowed to train candidates for the ministry, this system was halted in 1820 with the adoption of a plan for a denomination-wide seminary. Lebrecht Frederick Herman organized the Synod of the Free German Reformed Congregations of Pennsylvania in an attempt to maintain theological education as the local congregation's prerogative.

The most significant developments in the German Reformed Church, however, were centered at the denomination's seminary, opened in 1825 at Carlisle, Pennsylvania, and finally established at Mercersburg, Pennsylvania, in 1837. There, faculty members John Williamson NEVIN and Philip SCHAFF became architects of a movement known as the Mercersburg Theology. Nevin and Schaff criticized the superficiality of popular American revivalism and highlighted instead the spiritual depth of their church's historic liturgy and creeds. These teachings not only stirred controversy about "Romanism" within the German Reformed ranks, but also undermined proposals of merger with the Dutch Reformed, the Presbyterians, and the Lutherans, who feared that Catholic tendencies had emerged in their sister denomination.

On average, approximately 40,000 Germans entered the United States each year between 1830 and 1845, and the majority settled in the Midwest. The eastern and Ohio synods of the German Reformed Church established the first General Synod of the German Reformed Church in the United States in Pittsburgh in 1863 (with 230,000 members, 1,200 congregations, and 500 ministers). However, most new German settlers remained aloof from that church, opposing it on a variety of grounds, and they organized instead the German Evangelical Synod of North America in 1872. The Evangelical Synod's strong identification with German culture in the Midwest greatly benefited the church for a time, as immigration from Germany to the United States surged in the 1880s. Slow to accommodate itself to American society, the synod provided strong ethnic cohesiveness well into the 20th century. Although it adopted an English-language catechism in 1892 and an English hymnal in 1898, it continued to use German in its minutes until 1925.

In ironic contrast to this inward-looking focus, the German Evangelical Synod profoundly influenced American religious life by nurturing two of the United States's most distinguished theologians, Reinhold NIEBUHR and H. Richard NIEBUHR. Educated at the synod's college in Elmhurst, Illinois, and at Eden Theological Seminary in St. Louis, the Niebuhr brothers helped shape 20th-century Protestant thought by their ability to relate traditional theological concepts to the political realities of the modern era.

H. Richard Niebuhr's 1951 book, *Christ and Culture,* for instance, is now considered the classic exposition of how Christians interact with the world. Reinhold Niebuhr, active throughout his life in politics, was founder and editor of the magazine *Christianity and Crisis,* which brought religion to bear on social justice concerns.

In the early 20th century, the Reformed Church in the United States and the Evangelical Synod (having dropped "German" from their names in 1869 and 1927, respectively) consciously sought to reach beyond their narrow ethnic base and attract English-speaking members. In this they were largely unsuccessful. After merger attempts with the United Brethren in Christ and the Presbyterian Church in the United States fell through, the two German Reformed bodies united in 1934 to form the Evangelical and Reformed Church. This new church contained 600,000 members and 3,000 congregations predominantly in Pennsylvania, the Midwest, and the Plains states. Despite expanding to 800,000 members during the 1950s, a period of unprecedented growth in mainline American Protestantism, the Evangelical and Reformed Church not only was unable to keep pace with the population growth of the nation as a whole, but also had fewer congregations in the 1950s than it had 20 years earlier.

As part of the ecumenical impulse of the time, discussions of merger with the Congregational Christian churches had begun in 1944. A number of obstacles immediately presented themselves. Reinhold Niebuhr characterized the theology of the Congregational Christian churches as "modern liberalism shading off to Unitarianism," while his own denomination tended to be conservative in its theological orientation. And while the Congregational Christian churches staunchly upheld the independence of individual congregations, the Evangelical and Reformed had a strong sense of connectedness between congregations, a pattern typical of churches with a presbyterian (see PRESBYTERIANISM) form of church governance. In spite of these difficulties, a merger into a new, 2-million-member denomination called the UNITED CHURCH OF CHRIST was eventually effected in June 1957.

Unlike the continuing denominational tradition of the Dutch Reformed churches, whose institutional life they had once roughly paralleled, the German Reformed churches so radically altered themselves in the 20th century that their former identity was virtually extinguished. No longer the church of an immigrant people, indeed, no longer even a church, the German Reformed surrendered the distinctive ethnic heritage that had earlier marked them and adapted to the tolerant theological and social milieu of contemporary mainline Protestantism.

GHS, Jr.

Bibliography: David Dunn, *A History of the Evangelical and Reformed Church* (Philadelphia: Christian Education Press, 1961); www.ucc.org (United Church of Christ).

Ghost Dance   The Ghost Dance, which spread rapidly across the western states in 1889, is the best known example of an extensive series of Native American religious movements, in which members of indigenous cultures used ritual and prophetic means to revive their traditional worlds in the wake of conflict with encroaching colonial or American society. Although many saw the massacre of Lakotas at Wounded Knee, South Dakota, in December 1890 as marking the end of the dance as a social movement, it continued among other Plains tribes (see NATIVE AMERICAN RELIGIONS: PLAINS) for a number of years and has occasionally resurfaced among groups of Native American social activists.

In its best-known form the Ghost Dance emerged from a vision given to WOVOKA, a member of the Tovusi-dokado band of Nevada's Northern Paiutes (Paviotso), during an eclipse of the sun on January 1, 1889. Wovoka's own religious influences included several forms of the millennialism common in 19th-century America, including a native Paiute tradition of the world's end; the evangelical PRESBYTERIANISM of his employer, David Wilson; Mormonism; and perhaps some beliefs of native prophets active to the north (see NATIVE AMERICAN RELIGIONS: CALIFORNIA/INTERMONTANE), such as the Wanapum leader Smoholla or John Slocum, a Squaxin prophet from the Warm Springs reservation in Oregon. Wovoka's vision also resembles that of an earlier movement, involving his father, that spread after 1869 from the Walker River Paiutes in western Nevada to members of several northern California tribes, including the Pomo, Modoc, Klamath, Shasta, and Karok.

The Ghost Dance is notable because of its rapid diffusion during a period of great social stress. Between 1889 and the early 1890s, the new movement spread west and east to other Great Basin tribes: Washoes, Western Shoshones, Bannocks, and Utes; to California and southward to the Mojaves; east across the Plains to the Kiowas, Comanches, Caddos, and Pawnees in Indian territory (Oklahoma); and northeast among the Arapahos, Wind River Shoshones, Cheyennes, Assiniboines, Lakotas, and others.

In its basic form, the Ghost Dance taught by Wovoka grew out of the traditional Paiute Round Dances that provided the people with an opening to spiritual influence. Men, women, and children would join hands, moving in a clockwise direction to symbolize the sun's trajectory across the sky. Wovoka came to see the Round Dance as the right vehicle for enabling the living to communicate with the dead, as he had in his vision. The dance took on an ecstatic character as dancers fell in trances, taken to the land of the dead. Returning to this world, they could also testify that both the dead and depleted game would soon return as part of the world's renewal.

In spreading throughout much of the West, the dance provided a symbolic and ritual means for tribal members to create an alternative future to the one they were being offered by missionaries, the Office of Indian Affairs, and the United States army—a future in which the only way to survive was to cease living as members of distinct cultures (see ASSIMILATION AND RESISTANCE, NATIVE AMERICAN). In a period marked by drought and malnutrition, rapid land loss, forced relocation, and religious persecution (see AMERICAN INDIAN RELIGIOUS FREEDOM ACT), many Indian people sought ways to construct a future in which they were not the passive beings envisioned within the myth of the dominant culture (see MANIFEST DESTINY).

News of the prophet's activities spread from tribe to tribe across telegraph lines and postal networks. Many tribes sent representatives to Nevada to meet the new prophet, whose power was evident to all in the fact that he could communicate with groups from various tribes in their own separate languages. Many of these leaders understood themselves to have been initiated into a new movement or way of life. The dance spread as these leaders returned to their reservations, bearing symbols of Wovoka's blessing. Given the wide gap between the Paiute worldview and that of other tribes, Ghost Dance preachers had to select elements from Wovoka's teachings that might mix creatively with the worldviews of their own tribes. By amalgamating these elements with their own traditions about the future, combined with elements common to the evangelical Christianity present among the agencies, the various tribal practitioners created a ceremonial and mythical means for transforming a disturbing present into a hopeful future.

The version of the Ghost Dance practiced by the Lakotas (western Sioux) receives continued attention from historians, journalists, and the public, largely due to the United States army massacre of Big Foot and his band (among whom were many dancers) at Wounded Knee, South Dakota, on December 29, 1890. Wounded Knee has consequently become a powerful symbol of the end of the FRONTIER, the near-extinction of the Indian, and the birth of modern America. In typical fash-

ion, many interpreters emphasize the irrationality of Lakota Ghost Dancers. Both popular and scholarly treatments portray the Ghost Dancers as warding off an inevitable future by a last-ditch futile effort to dream away their powerlessness. Lakota leaders of the dance, such as Kicking Bird or Short Bull, appear to be religious fanatics or opportunists, eager to increase their own political prestige, clinging blindly to the hopes that bullet-proof ghost shirts would make them invincible as they rose to battle the army.

However, this interpretation ignores both the complexity of cultural diffusion and the legitimacy of the dance as a religious movement. Lakota dancers were not irrational, but rather began to practice the new dance because it promised to renew the religious ritual forms under which Plains culture had historically flourished. Lakotas traditionally understood the annual return of the bison herds to be dependent upon the petitions to the powers, *wakan tanka*, that sustained life. The annual Sun Dance, prohibited under 1883 Office of Indian Affairs regulations, provided Lakotas with the primary ritual means by which to purify themselves in order to insure that the bison would be willing to return. Consequently, it was not the near extinction of the great herd by 1883, under pressure from encroaching Americans, that provoked a fundamental crisis among Lakotas, since they understood the periodic absence of bison as a ritually reversible process. Instead, the prohibition of the Sun Dance created a religious crisis, resolved only by introduction of the new dance, which Lakotas recast to resemble the Sun Dance as closely as possible.

While many groups abandoned the dance itself in the wake of Wounded Knee, other tribes, such as the Pawnees and a group of Canadian Dakotas (eastern Sioux) retained it into the 20th century. Some claim it continued to lead an underground existence for several decades, reemerging among American Indian Movement activists in the early 1970s.

While the attention devoted to the Ghost Dance suggests that it is a unique movement, it remains simply one example of a series of efforts by native peoples to transform their lives under the impact of European-American colonialism by the renewal of traditional religions.

MG

Bibliography: Raymond J. DeMallie, "The Lakota Ghost Dance: An Ethnohistorical Account," *Pacific Historical Review* 51 (1982): 385–405; Michael Hittman, *Wovoka and the Ghost Dance* (Lincoln: University of Nebraska Press, 1998); Alice Beck Kehoe, *The Ghost Dance: Ethnohistory and Revitalization* (New York: Holt, Rinehart and Winston, Inc., 1989); Joel W. Martin, "Before and Beyond the Sioux Ghost Dance: Native American Prophetic Movements and the Study of Religion," *Journal of the American Academy of Religion* 59 (April 1991): 667–701.

Gibbons, James (1834–1921)

During his long tenure as the leading member of the Roman Catholic Church's hierarchy in the United States (see ROMAN CATHOLICISM), James Gibbons, Cardinal Archbishop of Baltimore, guided the church through a period of turmoil, change, and challenge. Although often accused of vacillation and indecision, Gibbons's prudence held the church together. As an interpreter of America to Rome and Catholicism to Americans, Gibbons gained the respect both of presidents and popes.

Unlike most of his peers, James Gibbons was born in the United States, in Baltimore, on July 23, 1834, of Irish immigrant parents. His father was a moderately successful clerk. The elder Gibbons's poor health led him to leave for Ireland with the family in 1837. In 1853, six years after his father's death, Gibbons's mother returned to the United States, settling with her son in New Orleans.

In January 1854 a mission sermon piqued Gibbons's interest in the priesthood, and the following year he entered St. Charles College outside of Baltimore, graduating in 1858. He continued his studies at St. Mary's Seminary, receiving his ordination on June 30, 1861.

Gibbons served for four years as a priest in Baltimore, his tenure spanning the Civil War. He demonstrated great pastoral, administrative, and diplomatic skill. Personally pro-Union, he served as chaplain to the troops garrisoned at Forts McHenry and Marshall while avoiding conflicts with his predominantly pro-Confederate parishioners and neighbors.

These abilities brought the young Gibbons to the attention of the archbishop of Baltimore, Martin SPALDING, who asked the young priest to become his secretary. Gibbons accepted and was soon involved in the preparations for the Second Plenary Council of Baltimore (1866) (see BALTIMORE, COUNCILS OF). As assistant chancellor for the council, he so impressed the members of the hierarchy that when the vicariate apostolic of North Carolina was created (in 1868), the 32-year-old Gibbons was named bishop.

Consecrated on August 16, 1868, Gibbons, the youngest of 1,200 bishops in the Roman Church, was responsible for a 50,000-square-mile diocese of 1 million inhabitants with only 700 Catholics, 3 priests, and no Catholic institutions. While head of this diocese Gibbons developed the manner and tone that later served him well. He was a forceful yet tolerant proponent of Catholic doctrine, a fighter for converts and for strong Catholic institutions. Simultaneously, he cultivated warm relations with non-Catholics and argued that American political institutions were not hostile to Catholicism but conducive to its strength and expansion.

His duties expanded in 1872, when he was named administrator and then bishop (1873) of the diocese of Richmond. During this time he wrote his most famous book, *The Faith of Our Fathers* (1867). This soon became the most popular explanation of the Catholic faith in America, with nearly 2 million copies in circulation by the time of Gibbons's death. Popular outside the United States as well, it was translated into six different European languages.

The ailing archbishop of Baltimore, James Roosevelt Bayley, often called upon Gibbons for assistance. Recognizing the need for a smooth transition of authority in the nation's premier see, Bayley asked Gibbons to become his co-adjutor. After much hesitation Gibbons accepted in May 1877. Five months later Bayley was dead, and Gibbons, age 43, became the head of the most important archdiocese in America.

His first nine years as archbishop of Baltimore were relatively uneventful. He successfully directed the third Plenary Council of Baltimore (1884), which set in place the framework for the parochial school system and the operations of the American church for the next three decades. This earned him the support of all the nation's bishops as well as the commendation of Leo XIII, and it was widely rumored that he soon would receive a cardinal's cap. This he did on June 30, 1886.

The next 15 years of Gibbons's episcopacy would be among the most troubled for the American church, as it attempted to respond to the needs of its predominantly immigrant members and to the difference between European and American realities. Although early in the papacy of Leo XIII Gibbons was able to use his influence to forestall papal condemnation of the Knights of Labor and the writings of the economist Henry George by arguing that such condemnation was alien to American realities, by the 1890s this influence was on the wane as the commitment of Gibbons, John IRELAND, John Keane, and other bishops to the American cultural and social ethos increasingly appeared suspect in Roman eyes.

Since the 1790s the Church had allied itself with the conservative regimes of Europe and had suffered under revolutionary and democratic governments, most notably in France and Italy. To Rome the United States looked like the mother of all these threats. Certainly the Church did not experience state persecution in the United States, but it received no financial or legal aid, and ANTI-CATHOLICISM was not unknown. The state upheld religious liberty, democratic ideals, a free press, and was predominantly Protestant in ethos. In addition, it

was an upstart nation that presumed to have a moral superiority over the nations of Europe. This growing papal concern about the influence of American society on the American church became visible with Leo XIII's encyclical LONGINQUA OCEANI (1895), rejecting the view that the American model of church-state separation should be universally adopted.

This conflict culminated on January 22, 1899, when Leo addressed the apostolic letter *Testem Benevolentiae* to Gibbons. This letter informed Gibbons that rumors had reached the pope that some American clerics held questionable views regarding the nature of the church and belief. These supposed beliefs were that there should be increased freedom in the Church, and that to respond to the modern age the Church needed to change not only externals but doctrine as well (see AMERICANISM).

Gibbons informed Leo that such views were condemned by the Church's hierarchy. Although no one was singled out for punishment, this letter, along with Leo's condemnation of Catholic modernism in 1907, ended creative thought within the United States Roman Catholic Church until the late 1950s.

After guiding the American Church through two difficult decades, Gibbons's last decades were filled with peace and public honors. His assistance in easing conflicts in the Philippines over the property owned by religious orders, along with his support for the creation of the National Catholic War Council (1917) and its transformation into the National Catholic Welfare Conference (1919), earned him the praise of many. Gibbons served as an unofficial adviser on Catholic affairs, including the concerns of the papacy, to several presidents and went far in demonstrating the compatibility of Roman Catholicism to the American governmental system. In 1917 Theodore Roosevelt lauded him as "the most respected and venerated and useful citizen of our country."

At the time of his death on March 24, 1921, Gibbons could look back with satisfaction on his life. He had shepherded the Roman Catholic Church in the United States through dangerous times. A church that could have been shattered by ethnic tensions was unified. A church that could have been marginalized by its association with reactionary European political currents was accepted, albeit grudgingly, as a legitimate part of American culture, due primarily to Gibbons's efforts.

EQ

Bibliography: John Tracy Ellis, *The Life of James Cardinal Gibbons: Archbishop of Baltimore, 1834–1921* (Milwaukee: Bruce Publishing Co., 1963); James Gibbons, *Collections and Recollections in the Life and Times of Cardinal Gibbons* (John Reilly, ed. 10 vols. (Martinsburg, W.V.: Herald Press, 1890–1904); ———, *The Faith of Our Fathers* (Baltimore: J. Murphy Co., 1904); ———, *A Retrospect of Fifty Years.* 2 vols. (Baltimore: J. Murphy, 1916); Allen S. Will. *The Life of Cardinal Gibbons, Archbishop of Baltimore.* 2 vols. (New York: E. P. Dutton, 1922).

Gideons International   See BIBLE SOCIETIES.

Gladden, Solomon Washington (1836–1918)

In the years of reconstruction, industrialization, and expansion following the Civil War, Solomon Washington Gladden was one of the first Protestant clergy to emphasize social justice as the basis for Christian responses to the changing society. His views gained widespread influence for the SOCIAL GOSPEL among fellow clergy, policy makers, and citizens during a career spread over half a century.

Born February 11, 1836, and raised on a farm outside Oswego, New York, Gladden received a B.A. from Williams College in 1859. Apart from a stint on the New York–based editorial staff of *The Independent,* an abolitionist organ that became the nation's leading church paper after the Civil War. Gladden's career focused on pastoral ministry. He served churches in New York and Massachussetts until appointed pastor of the First Congregational Church of Columbus. Ohio, in 1882, where

Solomon Washington Gladden, a pioneer of the Social Gospel movement in the Gilded Age. *(First Congregational Church, Columbus, Ohio)*

he remained until retirement in 1914. He died in Columbus on July 2, 1918.

Gladden was not a trained theologian, nor did he try to approach favorite topics such as race, economics, or religious divisions in a systematic way. But in the course of writing more than 38 books and many articles, sermons, and speeches, he offered exacting critiques of the social injustices he saw embedded in the fabric of American society. Gladden's inspiration owed much to the work of theological liberals such as his friend Horace BUSHNELL, who sought to reconcile Darwinian science and Christian faith and emphasized an immanent God active in the development of nature and society. But whereas many representatives of the new theology were social conservatives,

Gladden came to interpret the Christian faith, embodied in Jesus' teachings about love, as requiring substantial reconstruction in American society. A pastorate in Springfield, Massachussetts (1875–1882), involved him in the affairs of the labor movement. Unlike Walter RAUSCHENBUSCH, he did not become socialist. He did, however, advocate many policies running counter to the *laissez faire* attitudes of the day, such as public ownership of railroads and utilities and the rights of labor (including cooperative corporate ownership), policies that he saw contributing to the coming of the kingdom of God. He also played a role in improving race relations. Influenced first by Booker T. WASHINGTON and later by W. E. B. DU BOIS, he came to see that political as well as economic enfranchisement was necessary to overcome the legacy of slavery.

Gladden, like many of his contemporaries, linked the advance of the Christian faith to the growth of American civilization, concluding that "a considerable part of the life of civilized society is controlled by Christian principles." For Gladden, this meant that the churches could best aid the cause of the kingdom by securing social reform in those areas of society not yet ruled by principles of Christian love.

Thinking that progress required Christians to abandon their denominational animosities, Gladden was also an advocate of ecumenical cooperation, becoming an early leader in the Federal Council of Churches (see NATIONAL COUNCIL OF CHURCHES). He saw Jews and Catholics as potential allies in the effort of social justice. He argued that those who had truly heard the Gospel would see the vital relationship between individual and social salvation. Thus he refused to support the work of evangelists such as Billy SUNDAY. There were also other limits to cooperation. Although he denounced the application of social Darwinian ideas about the survival of the fittest to economic life, he used that language to describe the relationships between the world's religions. He had no doubt that morally superior American Christianity could best meet the needs of modern human nature.

MG

Bibliography: Jacob Henry Dorn, *Washington Gladden: Prophet of the Social Gospel* (Columbus: Ohio State University Press, 1967); Solomon Washington Gladden, *Applied Christianity: Moral Aspects of Social Questions* (1886; Salem, N.H.: Ayers Co., 1977); Robert T. Handy, ed., *The Social Gospel in America, 1870–1920* (New York: Oxford University Press, 1976).

glossolalia   See PENTECOSTALISM.

Gospel of Wealth   In its most recognized form, the Gospel of Wealth was a philosophy of stewardship promoted by the great steel magnate Andrew Carnegie. In an article entitled "Wealth," published in the June 1889 edition of the *North American Review*, Carnegie set forth his view that those who have accumulated great fortunes possess an obligation to dispense with some of their money to benefit their "poorer brethren." The immigrant bobbin boy, whose rise to riches constituted one of the most spectacular success stories of late-19th-century America, believed that the concentration of wealth in the hands of a relatively few leading industrialists was "not only beneficial but essential to the future of the race." These highly qualified individuals possessed the skills and capacities necessary to bring order and efficiency to the nascent industrial system, upon whose output depended the welfare of the mass of the populace.

Nevertheless, the rich had an obligation to expend part of their fortunes on worthy public projects. Most prominent among Carnegie's own philanthropies were the hundreds of libraries he subsidized all over the United States and in some foreign countries. His benefactions also supported scientific research, the advancement of teaching, and international peace. Carnegie's Gospel of Wealth emerged directly out of his adherence to the notion of social Darwinism, which had widespread public support during the decades after the Civil War. Applying Charles Darwin's evolutionary theories to society, social Darwinists preached the virtues of competition, confident that in the "struggle for survival" the fittest would survive (see EVOLUTION). Progress would naturally emanate from the relentless competition that occurred in the economic arena.

Other prominent Americans simultaneously promoted ideas that bolstered Carnegie's Gospel of Wealth. The Philadelphia Baptist minister and founder of Temple University, Russell CONWELL, preached his sermon "Acres of Diamonds" 6,000 times to an estimated audience of 13 million people. His message: Everyone not only has a right to be, but has an obligation to be, rich. The signs of visible wealth, he told his audiences, were evidence of the godliness of their bearers. Episcopal bishop William Lawrence asserted that it was God's will that some should attain great wealth. In his words, "Godliness is in league with riches."

If some were entitled to riches, others were condemned to poverty. Poverty, preached supporters of the Gospel of Wealth, results from laziness, improvidence, vice, and, in some cases, misfortune. It was basically not a result of social conditions or broad economic forces but rather an indicator of individual failure.

As a justification for social inequality, the Gospel of Wealth lost most of its power with the rise of the new Progressive intellectual currents around the turn of the 20th century, but as a motive for philanthropy it retained considerable force. In the last decades of the 20th century the Gospel of Wealth took on new forms with the flourishing of the computer software industry and the Internet. Software and Internet entrepreneurs such as Steve Jobs of Apple and Bill Gates of Microsoft adopted a prophetic stance, delivering a message of the new millennium as a technological promised land. They also engaged in philanthropic activities, donating computers to poor school districts and communities, funding medical research

and public health projects, and establishing scholarships for minority children. Some information technology entrepreneurs continued to harken back to Carnegie's reasoning and biblical principles to spur their philanthropy and justify their wealth. But others, informed by BUDDHISM, HINDUISM, or the NEW AGE (all in the air in Silicon Valley), fashioned a new Gospel of Wealth on very different grounds. Like Carnegie's 19th-century theology, however, those new Gospels of Wealth all stressed the importance of technology and learning as the basis for social progress and viewed capitalism as a moral and spiritual force.

MG

Bibliography: H. W. Brands, *Masters of Enterprise: Giants of American Business from John Jacob Astor and J. P. Morgan to Bill Gates and Oprah Winfrey* (New York: Free Press, 1999); Andrew Carnegie, *The Andrew Carnegie Reader* (Pittsburgh: University of Pittsburgh Press, 1992).

Grace, Sweet Daddy (Charles Emmanuel) (1881–1960)

Founder of the United House of Prayer for All People and a prominent black religious leader, Charles Emmanuel "Sweet Daddy" Grace left little information about his early life. He was born in Brava, Cape Verde Islands, on January 25, 1881, of mixed African and Portuguese parentage. Although he denied being a Negro and often talked disparagingly of blacks, the membership of his United House of Prayer for All People was overwhelmingly composed of poor, urban blacks.

Grace, probably an assumed name, although some authorities argue that his birth name was Marcelino Manoel de Graca, came to the United States about 1900. He apparently spent 25 years working as a railroad cook before organizing his first house of prayer in Charlotte, North Carolina, in 1926, although some claim that Grace started his first House of Prayer in Wareham, Massachusetts, in 1921.

Grace did not claim to be divine, but his role with the church overshadowed that of the deity. He was known to tell his followers, "Never mind about God. Salvation is by Grace only. . . . Grace has given God a vacation and since God is on his vacation, don't worry him. . . . If you sin against God, Grace can save you, but if you sin against Grace, God cannot save you."

Other than its veneration of Bishop Grace as the mediator between God and humanity (and a strong emphasis on raising money for him), the church shared many characteristics with other Pentecostal-Holiness churches (see PENTECOSTALISM; HOLINESS MOVEMENT). It emphasized ecstatic worship, including speaking in tongues and dancing, and forbade drinking, smoking, and the "beautification of the person."

Church membership also provided concrete benefits. Grace was often compared to Father DIVINE, and Grace's House of Prayer, like Divine's Peace Mission Movement, provided meals at church-run cafeterias, and it owned several residences and retirement homes. Most important, however, was its emphasis on healing. Testimonies gathered from members of the church by Arthur Fauset for his book *Black God of the Metropolis* invariably cited healing as the reason for joining the church. The church's *Grace Magazine* when placed upon the chest was said to cure colds and even tuberculosis. The various items sold by the church to raise funds, including cold creams, hair pomades, toothpaste, and soaps, were equally invested with curative powers.

The sale of these items as well as frequent personal donations from members provided the money to run the church and to keep Grace in a rather princely style. Daddy Grace lived a royal and flamboyant life—royal enough to receive the attention of the Internal Revenue Service, which led him to leave the country for several years during the 1930s. Big cars, fancy jewelry, and expensive clothes were part of his mystique—along with an 84-room mansion in Los Angeles and an estate in Cuba.

At the time of his death in Los Angeles on January 12, 1960, the United House of Prayer for All People claimed a membership of 3 mil-lion. Although this number is probably inflated, the church had a significant membership, and unlike many other religious movements dominated by a single charismatic individual, retained much of its membership after Grace's death and even experienced some growth.

(See also AFRICAN-AMERICAN RELIGION.)

EQ

Bibliography: Lenwood G. Davis, *Daddy Grace: An Annotated Bibliography* (New York: Greenwood Press, 1992); Arthur H. Fauset, *Black Gods of the Metropolis: Negro Religious Cults of the Urban North* (New York: Octagon Books, 1970).

Graham, Billy (William Franklin) (1918–)

Billy Graham was born on November 7, 1918, the eldest child of William Franklin and Morrow Graham in Charlotte, North Carolina. By the mid-1960s he had become America's preeminent evangelist (see EVANGELISM), a friend of presidents, and one of the most admired men in the country. He would hold this position throughout the century, and in the 1990s he would deliver both the invocation at the inauguration of President Bill Clinton (1992) and the eulogy at the funeral of former president Richard Nixon (1994).

Graham was raised in a conservative Southern Presbyterian (see PRESBYTERIANISM; SOUTH) household and internalized the values of that society, including a rejection of alcohol, pre- and extramarital sex, and profanity. In 1934, during a revival (see REVIVALISM) in Charlotte led by the itinerant evangelist Mordecai Ham, Graham underwent a CONVERSION experience and shortly afterwards decided to become a preacher.

In the fall of 1936 he entered Bob Jones University in Columbia, South Carolina, but found the atmosphere too stifling and transferred in January 1937 to Florida Bible Institute. Doing so earned him the animosity of Bob Jones, Sr., and as Graham showed openness to nonfundamentalist Christians (see FUNDAMENTALISM) during the 1950s, this hostility would become more pronounced. While attending Florida Bible Institute in Tampa, Graham first joined a Baptist church. This began a longstanding and mutually beneficial connection between Graham and the SOUTH-ERN BAPTIST CONVENTION. While at Florida Bible Institute Graham experienced a period of emotional turmoil, including a broken engagement and an internal struggle about whether to enter the ministry. This struggle came to an end in 1938, when Graham surrendered to the call and committed himself to the ministry.

After finishing at the institute, Graham entered Wheaton College (Wheaton, Illinois) in the autumn of 1940. There he met Ruth Bell, whom he married in 1943. After graduation Graham began his ministry as pastor of the United Gospel Tabernacle in Wheaton. He resigned that position in 1945 to take up full-time evangelistic work with Youth for Christ. Between 1945 and 1949 Graham led Youth for Christ rallies in England and throughout the United States. He also served as president of Northwestern Bible College in Minneapolis (1947–1951) after being personally chosen for that position by the school's retiring founding president, William B. Riley.

In 1949, one of the two events occurred that served to make Graham's career. The 1949 revival campaign in Los Angeles was accompanied by William Randolph Hearst's famous directive to his newspaper staff to "Puff Graham!" This favorable treatment in the media, including *Life, Time,* and *Newsweek,* and the conversions of several celebrities during the crusade generated tremendous amounts of publicity for the young evangelist. Eight years later Graham's 1957 New York City crusade brought the evangelical movement to a central position on the American scene. It was during the New York crusade that Graham committed himself and his organization to working with all the Christian denominations in the community. By including representatives of mainline Protestantism, Graham earned the ire of many of his fundamentalist supporters, who felt that he had seriously compromised Gospel truth by associating with liberals (see LIBERAL-ISM, THEOLOGICAL). This action, which became the norm for all of Graham's later crusades, demonstrated his willingness to change his mind as he confronted new realities and new situations. Similarly, Graham was one of the first evangelists to insist that his crusades in the American South, and later in South Africa, not be segregated by race.

During the 1950s and 1960s Graham did more than anyone to bring evangelicals into the mainstream of American public culture. A symbol of this was Graham's access to numerous American presidents. Although he managed to antagonize President Truman by reporting some of his conversation with the president, Graham was close to both Dwight Eisenhower and then Vice President Richard Nixon, whose candidacy he obliquely supported in 1960. Lyndon Johnson also attracted Graham as both a southerner and a man of working-class roots, and Johnson convinced Graham to support his War on Poverty. In 1968 and 1972 Graham again supported Richard Nixon. The revelations of Nixon's activities during the Watergate crisis and Nixon's extreme vulgarity on the tapes caused Graham a great deal of personal pain. While he rejected the claim made by some that he was used intentionally by Nixon to further Nixon's political goals, Graham became increasingly leery of politicians. Graham also was close to Ronald Reagan, however, and—surprisingly to some—to President Clinton as well. Interestingly, Jimmy Carter, the president closest to Graham in religious orientation and social background, held the evangelist at a distance.

During the 1980s Graham, and the evangelical movement in general, were overshadowed by the resurgence of a militantly political fundamentalism. Although Graham ceased to hold center stage in the media, this did not end his evangelistic work. He continued to preach throughout the United States and the world, including visits to the Soviet Union and Eastern Europe. He also spoke out in favor of nuclear disarmament, another position that distanced him from many fundamentalists.

During the 1990s, however, Graham regained much of his earlier visibility. His appearance at President Clinton's inauguration and Richard Nixon's funeral were highly visible illustrations of his public stature. Evangelistic trips to China and North Korea during times when the United States's relations with those countries were quite tense illustrated Graham's tendency to place evangelistic concerns over political ones.

Billy Graham's work is funded through the Billy Graham Evangelistic Association (BGEA), an organization he founded in 1950. Graham receives an annual salary from the BGEA and has little involvement with its operation. Although there have been some criticisms of the way the BGEA has allocated its money, the organization has been a model of fiscal responsibility and public accountability, another fact that has separated Graham from many other evangelists. This was especially true during the 1980s when several highly visible television evangelists were brought down by evidence of financial and personal irregularities.

By the late 1990s, Graham increasingly began to withdraw from the overall management of the BGEA. In 1995, his son Franklin Graham became the first vice chairman of BGEA. Despite his age and occasional health problems, however, Graham continued to lead crusades, retaining his massive following and high level of respect.

Graham's ministry is firmly within the evangelical tradition. He is strongly committed to the authority of the Bible, and his belief in the centrality of a conversion experience provides the basis for the "crusades" he has led throughout the world. Associated with the group of people known as neo-evangelicals, Graham helped to start the magazine *Christianity Today* and has helped to make his alma mater, Wheaton College, a center for evangelical scholarship. No one living has preached before as many people as Graham, and it is esti-

mated that more than 2 million people have been converted by Graham. Graham has also reached wide audiences through numerous books and newspaper columns and through television and radio. All this activity as well as his integrity and deep personal humility have made him one of the most visible and respected figures in American religion.

EQ

Bibliography: Marshall Frady, *Billy Graham, A Parable of American Righteousness* (Boston: Little, Brown, 1979); Billy Graham, *The Collected Works of Billy Graham* (New York: Arrowood Press, 1993); ———, *Just as I Am: The Autobiography of Billy Graham* (San Francisco: HarperSanFrancisco, 1999); William C. Martin, *A Prophet with Honor: The Billy Graham Story* (New York: William Morrow, 1991); William C. McLoughlin, Jr., *Billy Graham, Revivalist in a Secular Age* (New York: Ronald Press, 1960); John Charles Pollock, *Billy Graham, Evangelist to the World: An Authorized Biography of the Decisive Years* (San Francisco: Harper & Row, 1979); ———, *To All the Nations: The Billy Graham Story* (San Francisco: Harper & Row, 1985); Sherwood Eliot Wirt, *Billy: A Personal Look at Billy Graham, the World's Best-loved Evangelist* (Wheaton, Ill.: Crossway Books, 1997); www.bgea.org (Billy Graham Evangelistic Association).

Graham, Franklin (1952–)

Born July 14, 1952, outside Asheville, North Carolina, William Franklin Graham III is the fourth of the five children of Ruth Bell Graham and the evangelist William Franklin Graham (see GRAHAM, BILLY). Franklin became the successor to his father as the head of the Billy Graham Evangelistic Association.

This choice, however, was not foreordained. To a great extent, Franklin Graham was a true prodigal son, given to motorcycle riding, gun toting, and, rumor had it, even drinking. Most of this came to an end one night in 1974. Sitting alone in a hotel room in Jerusalem, Franklin Graham underwent a conversion experience and dedicated his life to Jesus Christ. The possibilities for service provided by the combination of Franklin Graham's personality and

Billy Graham (right), the leading evangelist of the second half of the 20th century, with his son and presumptive successor to head the Billy Graham Evangelical Association, Franklin Graham. *(Billy Graham Center Museum)*

his conversion were quickly recognized by Bob Pierce, the founder of World Vision, an evangelical relief agency, who invited Graham to join him on an Asian tour on behalf of Samaritan's Purse, an evangelical Christian relief agency. That experience convinced Graham that his calling was to serve those whose lives had been disrupted by war, famine, epidemics, and natural disasters.

His dedication to such service led Graham to join the board of Samaritan's Purse in 1978. With Pierce's death the following year, he was elected president of the organization. Currently Graham serves as president and chief executive officer, overseeing Samaritan's Purse's relief work in more than 100 countries.

This work led to an even bigger set of obligations as his rapprochement with his father and his father's legacy led Graham eventually to undertake his own evangelistic career, conducting his first crusade in 1989. Now comfortable with his own calling, he committed himself to spending 10 percent of his time as an evangelist, conducting crusades on behalf of his father's Billy Graham Evangelistic Association (BGEA).

His abilities as an administrator and his gifts as an evangelist soon made it apparent that he would be a worthy successor to his father as head of the BGEA. This was formalized in 1995 with his election as first vice chairman and the designated successor to the chairman of the BGEA.

While this designation may not seem surprising—the rebellious youth fits in well with the traditional conversion process (and even has a significant psychological basis given the pressures Franklin must have felt as Billy Graham's son)—Franklin Graham's trajectory illustrates something more. The way he entered the evangelical movement, through international relief work, cannot be overestimated as a significant phenomenon. The importance of evangelical relief agencies, of which World Vision is perhaps the best known, must be understood as a major development in American evangelicalism. They provide a major source of activism and commitment, not to mention financial support. The fact that Graham has refused to decrease that work shows how important active service to others is in the life of a committed evangelical.

Additionally, this major difference may serve Graham well when he succeeds his father as head of BGEA. As he recognized early in his youth, few could fill his father's shoes, but Franklin Graham brings a distinctive style and experience with him that will help deflect unproductive comparisons. People already know what he is and what he is not. This should give him the freedom to build on BGEA's success without feeling a need to make radical changes in order to place his own stamp on the organization, or to keep things exactly as they are for fear of criticism. That said, his succession to the leadership of the BGEA will signify a major generational shift in American EVANGELICALISM.

EQ

Bibliography: Franklin Graham, *Living Beyond the Limits: A Life in Sync with God* (Nashville, Tenn.: Thomas Nelson, 1998); ———, *Rebel With A Cause: Finally Comfortable Being Graham* (Nashville, Tenn.: Thomas Nelson, 1995); www.bgea.org (Billy Graham Evangelistic Association).

Graves, James Robinson (1820–1893)

A Southern Baptist preacher and editor of *The Tennessee Baptist*, then the largest Baptist weekly in the world, James Robinson Graves was also the dominant figure in the controversy over the "old landmarks," a set of ecclesias-

tical principles that disrupted the SOUTHERN BAPTIST CONVENTION at the turn of the century.

Graves was born on a farm near Chester, Vermont, on April 10, 1820. Although he had little opportunity to receive a formal education, he studied privately and later found employment as a schoolteacher in Kingsville, Ohio (1840–1842), and in Jessamine County, Kentucky (1842–1843). Graves joined a Baptist church when he was 15 years old and was ordained to the Baptist ministry in 1842. He served as the pastor of churches in Ohio between 1843 and 1845. Graves left Ohio to take a teaching position in Nashville, Tennessee, and by 1846 he had become editor of *The Tennessee Baptist*. Grave's paper was enormously successful and had some 13,000 subscribers by the eve of the Civil War.

In 1848 Graves began to publish articles defending what he regarded as the distinctive tenets of the Baptist faith. Although the term "landmark" (from Proverbs 22:28, "Do not remove the ancient landmark that your ancestors set up") was coined in 1854 by James M. Pendleton, a Baptist pastor in Bowling Green, Kentucky, Graves popularized the idea. He convened a mass meeting at Cotton Grove, Tennessee, in 1851 that drafted the precepts of Landmarkism and emerged as a leader of the movement. Basic to Landmarkism was the belief that adult BAPTISM by immersion and the independence of the local congregation were the distinguishing marks of the true church of Jesus Christ. There had been an unbroken line of Baptist churches observing these practices, Graves said, that extended from apostolic times to the present day. The corollary of Graves's position was that any deviation from the landmarks nullified a church's claim to being a "church." Thus, Graves dismissed the Methodists and Disciples of Christ as mere "religious societies" and condemned all fellowship with them.

Landmarkism became a potent force in the Southern Baptist Convention, especially in the region known as the Old Southwest, during the last half of the 19th century. The movement stimulated a new denominational self-consciousness, hindered pulpit exchanges with ministers of other denominations, and generally negated attempts at rapprochement with other southern Protestants. Landmarkism eventually gave rise to a splinter group represented today by the American Baptist Association, a small denomination organized in Arkansas in 1905.

Graves moved his paper from Nashville to Memphis after the Civil War, and from that base in west Tennessee he toured the South with his message. He published several books, the most important being *Old Landmarkism: What Is It?* (1880), which contains the classic pronouncements about the doctrine. After suffering a stroke that confined him to a wheelchair, Graves entered retirement in 1889. He died at Memphis on June 26, 1893.

GHS, Jr.

Bibliography: Hugh Wamble, "Landmarkism: Doctrinaire Ecclesiology among Baptists," *Church History* 33 (1964), 429–47; James E. Tull, *Shapers of Baptist Thought* (Valley Forge, Pa.: Judson Press, 1972); http://www.abaptist.org (American Baptist Association).

Gray, Asa (1810–1888) Asa Gray was the most distinguished American botanist of his generation. An orthodox Congregationalist, he was also an amateur theologian and advocate for Darwinism. In contrast to the agnosticism held by many of Darwin's interpreters, Gray taught that EVOLUTION was God's method of effecting biological and moral progress in the world. Untroubled by new scientific findings advanced during the second half of the 19th century, Gray combined an essentially tolerant Protestant faith with his work as a scholar and teacher.

Gray was born at Sauquoit, New York, on November 18, 1810. After graduating from Fairfield Medical School with an M.D. in 1831, teaching high school at Utica, New York, and traveling abroad on research for several years, he began a long career as a professor at Harvard in 1842. Following the publication of Charles Darwin's *On the Origin of Species* in 1859, Gray favorably reviewed the book in the March 1860 issue of the *American Journal of Science*. As Gray argued in his 1876 collection of essays, *Darwiniana*, the theory of evolution did not necessarily contradict Christian doctrine, for God's purposes could well be understood in evolutionary terms. Gray's acceptance of Darwinism proved a boon to liberal theologians. Despite a negative initial response to Darwin among American Christians, and contrary to Darwin's own explicit dissent, Protestant modernists (see MODERNISM, PROTESTANT) considered the doctrine of evolution as simply one of many manifestations of the divine presence in the natural world.

Gray retired from his teaching duties at Harvard in 1873, but he continued to hold his professorship and remained active as a scholar until his death. After suffering a stroke, he died at his home in Cambridge, Massachusetts, on January 30, 1888.

(See also SCIENCE AND RELIGION.)

GHS, Jr.

Bibliography: A. Hunter Dupree, *Asa Gray, 1810–1888* (New York: Atheneum, 1968).

Great Awakening Used to describe the wave of religious revivals that shook American churches in the mid-18th century, the term *Great Awakening* first appeared in 1842, when Joseph Tracy employed it as the title of his book on the quickening of religious interest in the colonial period. Scholars since Tracy's time have generally considered the series of revivals that started in the late 1720s, peaked in 1740, and continued into the 1770s to have been part of a single historical phenomenon. The Great Awakening marks the beginning of the dominance of EVANGELICALISM (a movement emphasizing the need for conversion and acceptance of Christ as personal savior) within American Protestant churches.

The awakening was heralded by local revivals that developed under the leadership of Dutch Reformed minister Theodorus J. FRELINGHUYSEN in northern New Jersey around the year 1726. In an attempt to eliminate the formalistic worship he perceived in churches in his area, Frelinghuysen demanded that his parishioners be excluded from Communion until they could testify that they had repented of their sins and relied entirely upon the Holy Spirit. This position soon fostered growth where Frelinghuysen ministered, and many leaders of the awakening later testified to his influence on their own evangelistic work.

William Tennent, Sr., and his sons Gilbert, John, and William, Jr., were key figures in the outbreak of revivals in the Presbyterian denomination. When Gilbert TENNENT was called to the Presbyterian church at New Brunswick, he and Frelinghuysen quickly recognized that they had similar spiritual interests. Frelinghuysen encouraged Tennent to regard an experience of regeneration, followed by inward assurance of divine grace, as the sole mark of a true Christian. In the late 1720s and early 1730s, Tennent was also involved with the "Log College" his father had founded to train clergy. Despite being derided for its lack of academic credentials by those who opposed the revivals, the Log College turned out a group of ministers who continued the tradition of the awakening within Presbyterianism.

A more significant stage of this religious excitement developed under the leadership of Jonathan EDWARDS, minister of the Congregational church in Northampton, Massachusetts. Edwards was alarmed by the spiritual complacency he perceived among his parishioners and by their acceptance of ARMINIANISM, that is, belief in the human ability to obtain God's grace. To counter these threats, Edwards preached a series of sermons on JUSTIFICATION by faith alone in 1734. He soon noticed important changes in his people: religious interest and conversions began to increase, and by 1736 the revival had spread to neighboring

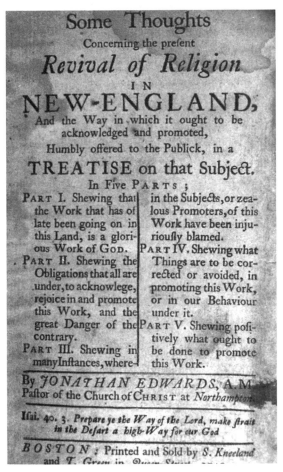

The Great Awakening was a movement of revivals and conversions that swept the American colonies in the mid-18th century. Title page of . . . *Revival of Religion in New England* by Jonathan Edwards. *(Billy Graham Center Museum)*

towns in the Connecticut River valley. Edwards recorded the events in *A Faithful Narrative of the Surprising Work of God,* which was published in London in 1737. Edwards's book had a tremendous influence on Anglican clergymen John Wesley and George WHITEFIELD, inspiring their efforts to evangelize the masses in England and America.

Whitefield had studied at Oxford University, where he befriended the Wesley brothers, John and Charles. Although he remained a

Calvinist (see CALVINISM) in theological orientation and rejected the Wesleys' emphasis on the freedom of the human will, Whitefield absorbed their ideas about the need for heartfelt piety and spiritual regeneration. Whitefield's restlessness and religious enthusiasm eventually led him to North America. Although his initial American trip to Georgia in 1738 was a modest success, his next tour, which lasted from 1739 to 1741, represented a crucial moment for the growth and spread of the Great Awakening.

Whitefield, known as "the Grand Itinerant," arrived in Philadelphia in November 1739. He hurried up and down the eastern seaboard, from town to town, from crowded church to busy market, wherever people would listen to his message. He estimated that 20,000 people heard him preach on Boston Common in October 1740. At Northampton, his preaching made Jonathan Edwards weep. And back at Philadelphia a year later, he preached to thousands in an auditorium specially built for his visit. Even the skeptical Benjamin Franklin was impressed with Whitefield and the good effect he had upon the people of his city.

Despite such praise, some clergy in America soon began to resent his mission and the awakening in general. Timothy Cutler, an Anglican minister in Boston, complained that the enthusiasm Whitefield generated amounted almost to madness. His evening sermons were said to be "attended with hideous yellings, and shameful revels, continuing . . . till break of day." Worst of all, Cutler reported, Whitefield encouraged laity to turn against their proper ecclesiastical leaders and question established religious beliefs and customs.

While Whitefield's American tour was upsetting his fellow Anglicans, a storm of opposition to the Awakening also broke out among the Presbyterians. Gilbert Tennent, who had been asked by Whitefield to accompany him and lead revivals, brought about the Presbyterian rupture by his sermon on "The Danger of an Unconverted Ministry," which he

preached in March 1740. In contrast to what he called the "carnal security" of routine churchgoing and unexamined adherence to creeds, Tennent summoned men and women to genuine repentance and an experience of God's power over their lives. He had gone too far. Using the issue of ministerial education and the inadequacy of the preparation of the revival-oriented Log College men, the conservative "Old Side" party (see NEW SIDE/OLD SIDE) ejected Tennent's New Brunswick presbytery in 1741 from the Synod of Philadelphia. The "New Side" Presbyterians, as the revival party was known, responded by organizing a church of their own. This division, a direct result of the Great Awakening, continued until 1758, when the Presbyterian factions came together again under the dominance of the New Side.

Further opposition to the awakening was aroused by Congregational minister James Davenport, pastor of the church at Southold, Long Island. Following Whitefield and Tennent to Connecticut in the summer of 1741, Davenport stirred the revival excitement while lambasting the ministers of the colony with unrelenting personal invectives. He claimed to be able to distinguish infallibly between God's elect and the damned, and he sang publicly as he walked the streets on the way to places of worship. Davenport was arrested both in Connecticut in 1741 and in Massachusetts the next year. His bizarre antics helped turn opinion in New England against the revivals.

Congregationalist Charles CHAUNCY, leader of the emergent anti-revival, or "Old Light," (see NEW LIGHTS/OLD LIGHTS), faction in his denomination, blasted the Awakening from his pulpit at the First Church in Boston. In *Seasonable Thoughts on the State of Religion in New England*, a lengthy work published in 1743, Chauncy catalogued what he believed were the worst features of the revivals. Although George Whitefield had been feted at Harvard College during his earlier visit to Boston, Chauncy convinced the Harvard faculty to close their doors to Whitefield in 1744.

Radical "New Light" Congregationalists in New England, on the other hand, insisted that many of their fellow church members and clergy, Chauncy being a prime example, lacked true piety. Called "Separates," this group was led by Isaac BACKUS of Norwich, Connecticut. Backus had been brought to "a saving knowledge of the truth" at a local revival in 1741. In 1748 he accepted a call to minister to a Separate church in Middleborough, Massachusetts. Disturbed over the question of baptism, Backus and six others were later rebaptized after a profession of faith in Jesus Christ. This was the beginning of a tremendous surge in growth among BAPTISTS in New England. Eventually, the awakening encouraged more than a hundred congregations to split from the Congregational establishment, and close to 80 of these eventually reorganized themselves as Baptist churches.

In the southern colonies, the Great Awakening developed far more slowly than in the North. Although Whitefield had preached to large numbers of people during his evangelistic tours of the South, the hostility of the Anglican religious establishment, as well as the general lack of settled population centers, prevented revivals from developing. Whitefield blazed a trail for the spread of the awakening, but he himself was unable to consolidate it into a widespread movement as he had done in the North.

The earliest discernible outbreak of religious enthusiasm in the South appeared in Hanover County, Virginia, where William Robinson, a graduate of William Tennent's Log College, was sent by New Jersey Presbyterians on a missionary tour in 1742. Other itinerant revivalists followed Robinson and kept the spiritual interest alive. In 1747 Samuel DAVIES succeeded Robinson at Hanover County. Davies fought a lengthy legal battle against the Anglican establishment on behalf of toleration for the seven Virginia Presbyterian churches he served, and he attracted fame as a successful evangelist. He traveled throughout Virginia to

help build up Presbyterianism. Called to the presidency of what is now Princeton University in 1759, his departure for New Jersey left no educated minister of his denomination in Virginia. As a consequence, the cause of revivalism among southern Presbyterians quickly declined.

The Baptists emerged as the most prominent evangelical force in Virginia. In 1754, Shubal Stearns and Daniel Marshall came to Virginia from Connecticut, where they had been converted by Whitefield. The two clergymen introduced several key evangelical elements: a free church without any hierarchy, a ministry that depended upon the call of God as its single credential, and the baptism of adult believers only. Although Stearns soon left for North Carolina and Marshall went on to Georgia, they had helped form a strong coterie of Baptists in Virginia. As an Anglican leader remarked in 1759 about the headway the Baptists were making, their "shocking delusion . . . threatens the entire subversion of *true religion* in these parts."

Anglicans gained their own revival party when Devereux JARRATT was installed as rector at Bath, Virginia, in 1763. He had been influenced by both Whitefield and the Wesleys. Under his preaching, churches became so crowded that he was compelled to hold services outside. Jarratt also began to move outside the geographic boundaries of his parish, and large assemblies gathered to hear him in the open air. In 1773, he joined forces with the "METHODISTS," evangelical societies forming within Anglicanism, and cooperated with them in revivals that occurred just prior to the American Revolution. After the war, when those societies left Anglicanism and formed the Methodist Episcopal Church, Jarratt felt he had been betrayed. Remaining within the Anglican fold, he contributed greatly to the growth of the evangelical party within the newly organized Episcopal Church.

With the beginning of the War for Independence, the Great Awakening effectively came to an end, as Americans were forced to consider matters even more pressing than the eternal states of their souls. The awakening, a spontaneous religious movement that swept across all colonial boundaries and spanned more than three decades, introduced a new sense of cohesiveness to the American people. Although no one is able to give an exact estimate of the number of people who joined churches in that period, the impact upon all the Protestant denominations was unquestionably immense. The awakening, in fact, while building up churches, also tended to minimize denominational distinctions. John Wesley exemplified this element in the revivals when he declared he would make no distinction between men and women of different denominations who still acknowledged "the common principles of Christianity." "Dost thou love and fear God?" he asked. If the answer were positive, he concluded: "It is enough! I give thee the right hand of fellowship."

As a result of this understanding about the relative unimportance of denominations, the Protestant churches of the new United States were able to develop a certain functional unity. This sense of fellowship, an essential harmony existing beneath the diversity of outward ecclesiastical forms, bore even greater fruit in the 19th century in the creation of a system of voluntary societies for the promotion of various religious causes. During the burst of renewed evangelical fervor, now called the SEC-OND GREAT AWAKENING, that appeared in the late 1790s, American Protestants successfully channeled their efforts into many common tasks, including building new churches and Christian schools and establishing numerous agencies of moral and social reform.

GHS, Jr.

Bibliography: John M. Bumsted and John E. Van de Wetering, *What Must I Do To Be Saved? The Great Awakening in Colonial America* (Hinsdale, Ill.: Dryden Press, 1976); Edwin Scott Gaustad, *The Great Awakening in New England* (New York: Harper and Row, 1957); Harry S. Stout, *The New England Soul: Preaching and Religious Culture in Colonial New England* (New York: Oxford University Press, 1986).

Greek Orthodox Archdiocese of North and South America   The Greek Orthodox Archdiocese of North and South America is the largest organization of Greek Orthodox Christians in the United States. Although established in 1922, its roots go back to the late 19th century.

Only a few Greeks lived in the United States before the 1880s, but immigration surged after 1890, and Greeks began to organize Orthodox parishes to preserve their religious and ethnic identity. The nation's first Greek Orthodox parish, Holy Trinity in New Orleans, began in 1864 as a pan-Orthodox venture. Purely Greek communities began to form later, led by New York's Holy Trinity in 1892 and Chicago's Assumption in 1893. Early parishes were typically organized by lay societies, which at the time petitioned the Church of Greece or the Ecumenical Patriarchate of Constantinople for priests. This informal approach persisted until 1918, even though the Church of Greece exercised formal authority over Greek churches in America after 1908. This long period of fluidity made it difficult to impose hierarchical authority later.

When efforts to organize a Greek diocese finally began, they were compromised immediately by political struggles. Meletios Metaxakis, the liberal archbishop of Athens, visited the United States in 1918 and assigned a bishop to gather the approximately 150 Greek parishes then existing into a diocese. But soon after returning to Greece, Meletios was deposed by royalists, who sent a conservative bishop to America to counter Meletios's efforts.

Meletios returned briefly to the United States, but in 1921 he was unexpectedly elected Patriarch of Constantinople. One year later he established the Greek Orthodox Archdiocese of North and South America. The royalists reacted vigorously, and the 1920s were marked by extended tumult in America, including rival hierarchies, parish schisms, and numerous lawsuits. Peter Kourides, a lay official, later recalled that "police were stationed

After 1890, Greek immigrants organized churches, such as this Greek Orthodox Church in Amoskeag, New Hampshire, to preserve their religion and ethnic culture. *(Library of Congress)*

at strategic positions within some of the churches to prevent bloodshed."

The worst period of strife ended in 1930, when the patriarchate and the Church of Greece agreed to remove all the contending bishops and to send a new archbishop to America. Athenagoras SPYROU arrived in 1931 to take up the task of healing divisions. The persuasive Athenagoras spent more than a decade working to mend the divisions of the 1920s, traveling around the United States and knitting together a highly centralized archdiocese.

Despite the exigencies of the Great Depression, the archdiocese made progress, and a number of crucial national institutions, including a theological seminary, were established. Athenagoras also championed Greek identity and fostered the development of an

extensive network of language and catechetical schools for children.

Elected Ecumenical Patriarch in 1948, he left behind an archdiocese basking in what one historian has called the Greek-American community's "era of respectability." Expansion continued during the 1950s under the leadership of Archbishop Michael Constantindes, who had served earlier as Metropolitan of Corinth in Greece. In 1959, Michael was succeeded by Archbishop Iakovos COUCOUZES, who had spent most of his career as a priest in the United States.

Under Iakovos, the archdiocese played a significant role in ecumenical activities and began to address the increasing acculturation of its members. In 1970, the 20th archdiocesan Clergy-Laity Conference approved the use of English in the liturgy, but the proposal was rejected decisively by Patriarch Athenagoras.

A stormy and unresolved debate over language followed. The struggle was fueled after 1965 by the resumption of Greek immigration, which created a renewed pastoral need for ministry in Greek. Despite this controversy the expansion of the archdiocese continued, and it achieved recognition as the largest, best organized, and most affluent Orthodox jurisdiction in North America.

It now claims about 2 million members in North and South America. In the early 1990s, its approximately 600 parishes were organized into eight dioceses in the United States. The archdiocese also serves Canada and significant communities in Latin America. Iakovos also supervises smaller American jurisdictions of Carpatho-Russian, Ukrainian, and Albanian Orthodox on behalf of the Ecumenical Patriarchate.

AHW

Bibliography: John H. Erickson, *Orthodox Christians in America* (New York: Oxford University Press, 1999); George Papaioannou, *The Odyssey of Hellenism in America* (Thessaloniki: Patriarchal Institute for Patristic Studies, 1985); Theodore Salutos, *The Greeks in America* (Cambridge, Mass.: Harvard University Press, 1964); http://www.goarch.org (Greek Orthodox Archdiocese of America).

Grimké, Angelina Emily (1805–1879) and Sarah Moore (1792–1873)

Sarah and Angelina Grimké were the first women born into a slaveholding family in the South to speak out forcefully for the abolition of slavery. They were also among the first women to agitate for the right of women to speak in public. Breaking through the separate domestic sphere allotted to them as Victorian females, the Grimké sisters argued on biblical grounds that God saw both the enslavement of African Americans and the bondage of women as sin.

The Grimkés were born in Charleston, South Carolina, to an affluent family that included 14 children and numerous slaves. Because of their personal experience with the "peculiar institution" of Southern slavery, the Grimké sisters were particularly useful to ABOLITIONISM. Neither Sarah nor Angelina received much formal education, but both were eager readers who became convinced after reading the Bible that slavery was contrary to the will of God. Though raised in the EPISCOPAL CHURCH, both sisters were spiritually restless, affiliating themselves at one time or another with PRESBYTERIANISM, Quakerism (see FRIENDS, THE RELIGIOUS SOCIETY OF [QUAKERS]), and SPIRITUALISM.

The Grimkés' odyssey out of the slaveholding South began in 1819, when Sarah traveled with her ailing father to Philadelphia, where he subsequently died. On her solitary way home, Sarah met some Quakers and was introduced to the Society of Friends. One year later she became a Quaker herself, and in 1821 she moved to Philadelphia. Angelina joined her sister in 1829 and the two soon began attending antislavery lectures and Quaker meetings.

The Grimkés first captured widespread attention on September 19, 1835, when radical abolitionist William Lloyd Garrison published Angelina's antislavery letter in *The Liberator*. Calling abolitionism "a cause worth dying for," Angelina emphasized that she wrote on the basis of "what I have seen, and heard, and known in a land of slavery, where rests the darkness of Egypt, and where is found the sin of Sodom."

In 1836 the Grimkés traveled to New York City, where they began speaking to groups of women about slavery, first in private parlors and later in larger and more public venues. In that same year both Angelina and Sarah produced their first of many abolitionist pamphlets based on their firsthand knowledge of slavery. Angelina's *An Appeal to the Christian Women of the South* (1836) and Sarah's *Epistle to the Clergy of the Southern States* (1836) both refuted biblical arguments for slavery popular among Southerners and contended that slavery was contrary to the will of God and the principles of the Declaration of Independence.

In 1837 Angelina and Sarah made their way to Boston, where their historic decision to address "mixed" audiences precipitated a great controversy about the right of women to speak in public. Among those who objected to the Grimkés' forthrightness were the Congregational ministers of Massachusetts, whose "Pastoral Letter" denounced on New Testament grounds females "who so far forget themselves as to itinerate in the character of public lecturers and teachers." Also objecting was Catharine Beecher, the first daughter of preacher Lyman BEECHER, who like her father was not as radical a reformer as the Grimkés. While Catharine Beecher argued in an open letter to Angelina that slaves should be freed gradually and settled in an African colony, Angelina insisted that slaves should be granted immediate emancipation followed by full suffrage. Angelina also rejected Beecher's suggestion that women should exercise their influence in the private sphere of the home.

The Grimkés' public career took an important turn on May 14, 1838, when Angelina married Theodore Dwight WELD. On the following day in New York City, both Grimkés attended the Anti-Slavery Convention of American Women. At that gathering, the Grimkés and fellow female abolitionists were taunted by anti-abolitionist mobs who burned their meeting place to the ground.

Whether they were frightened by this mob violence or cajoled by the more moderate Weld is not certain, but the Grimkés subsequently withdrew from public view. After producing *American Slavery As It Is* (1839) with Weld, the Grimkés concluded their public careers. In 1840 both Angelina and Sarah moved with Weld to a farm in Belleville, New Jersey, where they devoted themselves to teaching and educational reform. In 1864 the sisters settled in Hyde Park, Massachusetts. Sarah died in 1873 and Angelina in 1879.

Though their public agitation on behalf of slaves and women lasted only from 1835 to 1839, the Grimkés did much to link women's rights with abolitionism and to convince Americans that the enslavement of African Americans and the bondage of women were contrary to both the design of nature and the commandments of God.

SRP

Bibliography: Larry Ceplair, ed., *The Public Years of Sarah and Angelina Grimké: Selected Writings 1835–1839* (New York: Columbia University Press, 1989); Gerda Lerner, *The Grimké Sisters From South Carolina: Pioneers for Woman's Rights and Abolition* (New York: Oxford University Press, 1998); Anna M. Speicher, *The Religious World of Antislavery Women: Spirituality in the Lives of Five Abolitionist Lecturers* (Syracuse, N.Y.: Syracuse University Press, 2000).

H

Habitat for Humanity   Perhaps few undertakings better deserve the term *phenomenon* than does the organization Habitat for Humanity International. Its fusion of religion, self-help, PHILANTHROPY, a former United States president, and an all-embracing ethos together make it a fascinating enterprise.

Strangely, Habitat for Humanity is even more intriguing for its history. Founded by Millard and Linda Fuller in conjunction with Clarence JORDAN and other members of KOINONIA FARM, Habitat for Humanity is a combination of evangelical Christianity, civil rights, and personal transformation.

The transformation that helped to give Habitat for Humanity its birth was that of Millard and Linda Fuller. Born and reared in Alabama, the Fullers had built up their marketing company to the point where they were millionaires while still in their 20s. But success took a major toll on their health and personal lives.

Following a period of reflection, they concluded that they had lost track of the essence of their Christianity and rededicated themselves to God. This rededication began with selling their possessions and giving away all their money to the poor. Eventually, they found their way to Koinonia Farm, an interracial Christian agricultural community established in Georgia by Clarence Jordan in 1942.

While there, they developed the idea of establishing "partnership housing," a scheme in which those in need of homes would work with volunteers to build simple, affordable, decent housing. Funding for these houses would be provided by a revolving loan fund capitalized by donations, fund-raising activities, house payments, and no-interest loans from supporters. The first letter from Koinonia Farm described it:

> What the poor need is not charity but capital, not caseworkers but co-workers. And what the rich need is a wise, honorable and just way of divesting themselves of their over-abundance. The Fund for Humanity will meet both of these needs. Money for the fund will come from shared gifts by those who feel they have more than they need and from non-interest bearing loans from those who cannot afford to make a gift but who do want to provide working capital for the disinherited. . . . The fund will give away no money. It is not a handout.

The first homes were built near Americus, Georgia, where Koinonia was located in 1968. This was followed by a move to Africa in 1972, where the Fullers attempted to put their ideas into practice in Zaire. Success there convinced the Fullers that their vision could and should be expanded. They returned to the United States in 1976, where at a meeting of supporters Habitat for Humanity International was formed with the goal of providing quality housing internationally.

The idea met with a remarkable reception, aided to some extent by the commitment that Jimmy and Rosalynn CARTER, longtime supporters and neighbors in Americus, brought to the project. Such publicity helped. But the vision and commitment of the Fullers and others, the belief that people can help others help themselves, and the romance of the "flash builds," where people join together to build a home for real people whom they can meet and see, spoke to something deep not only within the American psyche, but also to people around the world. A home—an idea that resonates with shelter, warmth, and security—is not an idea anyone can oppose. The "sweat equity" of the soon-to-be owners also makes the work appealing.

Habitat for Humanity, which is unabashedly Christian, even evangelical, in its vision also shows how values and commitments readily cross religious lines when a common good is perceived. By focusing on service, "the theology of the hammer," as Millard Fuller put it, religion becomes a force for bringing people of all and no religious beliefs together.

While Habitat alone may not solve the world's housing problems, it has been remarkably successful, building more than 95,000 houses that shelter more than 475,000 people in some 2,000 communities worldwide. It now ranks as one of the 20 largest home-builders in the United States and the largest nonprofit builder. Millard Fuller has said, "My responsibility is to use what God has given me to help His people in need."

EQ

Bibliography: Millard Fuller, *More than Houses: How Habitat for Humanity is Transforming Lives and Neighborhoods* (Dallas: Word Books, 1999); ———, *The Theology of the Hammer* (Macon, Ga.: Smith & Helwys, 1994); Frye Gaillard, *If I Were a Carpenter: Twenty Years of Habitat for Humanity* (Winston-Salem, N.C.: John F. Blair, 1996); www.habitat.org (Habitat for Humanity).

Half-way Covenant Adopted in 1662, the Half-way Covenant was basically an adjustment of the criteria for BAPTISM and full membership in the New England Congregational churches (see CONGREGATIONALISM). Its adoption and effects have led it to receive many interpretations from scholars. Some have argued that it was necessitated by declining religious fervor, others attribute it to increased religious scrupulousness. Still others viewed it as a response to decreasing numbers of eligible voters.

While the adoption of the Half-way Covenant resulted in the eventual transformation of New England PURITANISM, it was not caused by any major change in religious belief, nor by concerns over the franchise. In fact, of the four colonies involved—MASSACHUSETTS BAY COLONY, New Haven, PLYMOUTH, and Connecticut—only the first two made full church membership a requirement for full citizenship and the franchise, and by 1665 they had eliminated it as a voting requirement.

The Half-way Covenant was necessitated by requiring testimony of regeneration (a CONVERSION experience) for full membership in the Congregational churches of New England. This requirement, adopted by nearly all the churches between 1635 and 1640, had unexpected results. While it did not affect the "first generation" of Puritans in America—since they had been accepted into church membership solely on the bases of not living a scandalous life and assenting to the doctrines of the church—their children, the "second generation," felt the implications strongly. Many never felt the working of grace in their souls that marked the experience of regeneration and, as a result, never became full church members. Since baptism was limited to those infants who had at least one parent as a full member, many of their children—the "third generation" of Puritans—could not be baptized.

This troubled many ministers who, understanding God's covenant as eternal, saw no reason why it should be cut off in the third generation. As early as 1645 Richard Mather argued that the children of baptized persons should be eligible for baptism themselves, but no official action was taken on his suggestion until June 1657, when a ministerial assembly in Boston recommended that children of baptized members be eligible for baptism. When several ministers attempted to implement this recommendation, they faced opposition from church members, and the question languished for another five years.

In 1662 the ministers took up the issue again at a meeting now known as the Half-way Synod. After meeting in four sessions throughout that year, it issued recommendations at the end of September. Over the objections of the president of Harvard, Charles Chauncy, and Richard Mather's sons Increase and Eleazar (see MATHER, INCREASE), the synod recommended that churches accept children of all baptized members. As they phrased it, "Church-members who were admitted in minority, understanding the Doctrine of Faith, and publickly professing their assent thereto; not scandalous in life, and solemnly owning the convenant before the Church, wherein they give themselves and their children to the Lord, and subject themselves to the Government of Christ in the Church, their children are to be baptized."

The General Court of Massachusetts urged the churches to adopt these recommendations. They met much opposition from the laity, however, who were strengthened in their opposition by the Mather brothers and John Davenport of New Haven. As late as 1672 only two-fifths of the churches in Massachusetts had implemented the change. By that time Increase Mather had accepted it (1671), but his brother, Eleazar, went to an early grave (1669) still opposed. In Connecticut, the conflicts were so great that the General Court announced in 1669 all positions were acceptable until new light fell on the subject.

Eventually, even the most recalcitrant were reconciled, and the Half-way Covenant became an accepted part of the New England way. For many, however, it remained a symbol of the decline of the colonies from their earlier purity and religiosity. More appropriately, this change should be understood as part of the ongoing attempt of Puritan congregationalism to create a workable doctrine of the church.

(See also CAMBRIDGE PLATFORM; COVENANT THEOLOGY.)

EQ

Bibliography: Robert Pope, *The Half-Way Covenant: Church Membership in Puritan New England* (Princeton: Princeton University Press, 1969); Darren Staloff, *The Making of an American Thinking Class: Intellectuals and Intelligentsia in Puritan Massachusetts* (New York: Oxford University Press, 1998); Williston Walker, *The Creeds and Platforms of Congregationalism* (Philadelphia: Pilgrim Press, 1960).

Handsome Lake (Ganio'dai'io) (1735–1815)

Handsome Lake, a religious visionary and political leader, rallied his people, the Seneca nation of the Iroquois, during a time of economic dislocation and political disruption in the early 19th century. His evangelistic efforts to revive his culture produced a new religion that played a continuing role in Iroquois life.

Born in 1735, Handsome Lake lived in the western part of the Iroquois Confederacy, the Haudenosaunee, in the Genesee River village of Gano'wages, in what is now New York State. In the years prior to the French and Indian Wars, Iroquois land extended from Lake Erie to the Hudson River. Their actual realm of influence stretched from the Mississippi River to the Atlantic seaboard, as they controlled both trade and the delicate balance between European powers competing for access to furs in the Ohio country. Handsome Lake came of age as this era of Iroquois dominance in the northeast ended. He took an active role in Iroquois efforts to retain their regional control, fighting against the British prior to the 1763 Treaty of Paris, which removed the Iroquois's French ally, and with the British during the American Revolution under the leadership of the Mohawk Joseph Brant. After the war, Handsome Lake, now a Seneca chief, took part in several delegations to Washington, ultimately failing in their efforts to stop American settlements advancing onto Haudenosaunee land, much of which was eventually sold to the Americans.

With the effective destruction of the Iroquois Confederacy's power, a loss of population due to war and disease, and the rising influence of Christian missionaries, many Iroquois, including Handsome Lake, despaired over the dissolution of traditional ways of life. Living in the Seneca village led by his brother Cornplanter, who turned to Quaker missionaries to find help coping with the new society, Handsome Lake began receiving visions in the spring of 1799.

After succumbing to illness, and assumed dead by his relatives, Handsome Lake awoke and described a visit by three angels, dressed in Iroquois ceremonial clothing. Handsome Lake's visions, which combined both traditional Iroquois and Christian symbolism, became the basis of an oral tradition, handed down into the present. He claimed the angels told him that the Iroquois should retain traditional festivals, such as the early-summer strawberry festival, and refrain from the evils of whiskey, witchcraft, love-magic, and abortion/sterility medicine. In visions received over the next year, Handsome Lake was taken by another angel on a tour of heaven and hell. On a journey to the sky, Handsome Lake said he met George Washington and Jesus, who spoke to him about the frustrations of ministry among the white people who had crucified him. During these visions Handsome Lake received numerous instructions about proper Iroquois responses to white culture. The early visions placed a great deal of emphasis upon the need for personal confession and salvation, and in the latter there was corresponding concern for social renewal.

By creatively adapting aspects of American culture and resisting others, Handsome Lake took a leading hand in negotiating the path for his people's continued identity in American society. To some extent, this leader's visions legitimized certain cultural and economic transformations: He opposed the pre-dominant matrilineal power in Iroquois family life, and he supported the agricultural labor and domestic power of men, thus replacing traditional Iroquois division of labor and family structure with a model similar to that advocated by the Quaker missionaries. In addition, his ritual of confession incorporated the missionaries' ideas of sin and salvation. But he also denounced many white practices and upheld tribal ownership of land, gift-giving as the preferred mode of exchange, and much of traditional mythology and ceremony (apart from those practices associated with shamanism and witchcraft). The new religion spread widely as Handsome Lake preached in councils of Iroquois leaders, to visiting delegations from other tribes, and in many Iroquois towns.

Made leader of the Iroquois nations in 1801, Handsome Lake was less successful at politics than evangelism, becoming embroiled in controversies over witchcraft and competition with other Seneca leaders, such as his brother Cornplanter and Red Jacket. He died on August 10, 1815, without having achieved his goal of political unity among the Iroquois, which he hoped to accomplish by strengthening his own visionary role at the expense of other chiefs. By 1850 the accounts of Handsome Lake's visions had been incorporated into an oral tradition called the *Gaiwiio*, the "good word," or the Code of Handsome Lake. The "Longhouse Religion," or "the Old Way of Handsome Lake," endures today, remaining the primary form of traditional Iroquois religious life.

MG

Bibliography: Anthony F. C. Wallace, *The Death and Rebirth of the Seneca* (New York: Vintage, 1972).

Harkness, Georgia Elma (1891–1974)

A social activist, poet, and ecumenist, Georgia Elma Harkness was America's first professional female theologian and the first woman to teach theology at a major Protestant seminary in the United States. Harkness was an early advocate of women's rights in the church even

Dr. Georgia Harkness was the first woman theologian to teach in a seminary in the Unites States (Garrett Theological Seminary, 1940–1950). With Reinhold Niebuhr, Paul Tillich, Bishop Angus Dun, John Bennett and other male church leaders, she served on the Federal Council of Churches commission in 1950 to consider the implications of obliteration bombing. *(John C. Bennett Archives)*

as she demonstrated the ability of women to do theology and to teach in areas outside the traditional female sphere of religious education.

Born on a family farm in Harkness in the Lake Champlain region of New York, Harkness was raised by METHODISTS. She had a conversion experience at the age of 14 and became a church member. She graduated from Cornell University in 1912 and for the next six years worked as a schoolteacher in New York State. She then resumed her education at Boston

University, where she earned an M.A. degree in religious education in 1920 and a Ph.D. in philosophy in 1923.

Harkness was hired in 1922 as an assistant professor of religious education at Elmira College, a woman's school in Elmira, New York. She taught in the philosophy department there from 1923 until 1937. After spending time at Union Theological Seminary in New York City in the mid-1930s, Harkness decided that her calling was theology rather than philosophy. In 1937 she was hired as an associate professor in the Department of the History and Literature of Religion at Mount Holyoke College (also a woman's school), but after only two years there she accepted a position as professor of applied theology at Garrett Biblical Institute (now Garrett-Evangelical Theological Seminary) in Evanston, Illinois. Harkness's last academic position was as professor of applied theology at Pacific School of Religion, where she served from 1949 until her retirement in 1961.

During her long and distinguished teaching career, Harkness traveled widely, frequently as a delegate to ecumenical conferences (see ECUMENISM). She wrote 40 books on topics ranging from social ethics to devotional poetry. Critics described her theological work as insubstantial, but admirers applauded Harkness for making theology accessible to laypeople.

Harkness described herself as an "evangelical liberal" who based her progressive political stances and her Christocentric theology on biblical teachings. She believed that both sin and salvation were social, and she saw it as every Christian's duty to usher in the kingdom of God here and now.

A self-described pacifist and socialist, she opposed wars from WORLD WAR II to the VIETNAM WAR and criticized capitalism as anti-Christian. In 1950 she served alongside Reinhold NIEBUHR, Paul TILLICH, and seven other male theologians on the Commission of Christian Scholars appointed by the Federal Council of Churches (see NATIONAL COUNCIL OF CHURCHES) to consider the morality of nuclear weapons. Although the majority decided that Christian ethics did not proscribe the first use of nuclear weapons, Harkness dissented, contending according to the commission's report "that God calls some men to take the way of non-violence."

Despite her controversial commitment to pacifism, Harkness is best remembered as an early champion for the rights of women in the church, including the right to full ordination. Though radical in her aims on women's issues, she was moderate in her means. When urged in the 1970s to refer to God as "She," Harkness refused. Yet she publicly lamented the fact that the church remained "the most impregnable stronghold of male dominance." As early as 1924, she was deriding the reluctance of Christian denominations to ordain women as "a deep-seated relic of medievalism," and she continued to agitate for the full ordination of women in her own Methodist denomination until that right was granted in 1956. In 1948 Harkness achieved wide acclaim when she debated neo-orthodox theologian Karl Barth (see NEO-ORTHODOXY) at a meeting of the WORLD COUNCIL OF CHURCHES in Amsterdam. Harkness argued that Genesis asserted that male and female were created equal and in the image of God; Galatians, moreover, established the fact that Christ did not discriminate between men and women. Her views on women and Christianity are detailed in *Women in Church and Society* (1972), a book she wrote at the age of 81.

Harkness retired in 1961 and moved to Claremont, California. In 1975, Garrett-Evangelical Theological Seminary established a Georgia Harkness Chair in Applied Theology in recognition of Harkness's pioneering contributions.

SRP

Bibliography: Georgia Harkness, *Women in Church and Society: A Historical and Theological Inquiry* (Nashville, Tenn.: Abingdon, 1971); Rosemary Skinner Keller, *Georgia Harkness: For Such a Time as This* (Nashville, Tenn.: Abingdon, 1992).

harmonial religion   See CHRISTADELPHIANS; CHRISTIAN SCIENCE; MESMERISM; NEW AGE RELIGION; NEW THOUGHT; POSITIVE THINKING; ROSICRUCIANS; SCIENTOLOGY; SPIRITUALISM; THEOSOPHY; TRANSCENDENTAL MEDITATION.

Hasidism   A mystical strain of JUDAISM that emerged in Poland and the Ukraine during the 18th century, Hasidism has played an important role in American Judaism only since World War II. Composed of various sects, or dynasties, contemporary Hasidism emphasizes piety, strict ritual observance, and withdrawal from the wider world. Easily recognizable by their distinctive dress, Hasids have settled primarily in the Williamsburg and Crown Heights sections of New York City, where they live a relatively insulated existence.

The roots of Hasidism are traceable to the teachings of Israel Ben Eliezer (1700–1760), the Baal Shem Tov or Besht (Master of the Good Name). Around 1735 he began to wander around Poland teaching that study of the Talmud and asceticism were not the only ways to gain divine knowledge, but that God could be known through the feelings. He emphasized joy and happiness, claiming that God hallowed all passions and all activities if done with piety, devotion, and purity. He and his disciples also emphasized the mystical tradition known as the Kabbala, especially the divine light or spark that is present in creation.

As the movement grew it engendered a reaction among the rabbinic leaders. Despite this opposition, Hasidism gained wide popular support, and it reached its height following legal recognition by the Russian government in 1804. By the mid-1800s, nearly half of eastern Europe's Jews were affiliated with one of the Hasidic dynasties.

The most distinctive feature of Hasidism is the role played by the *zaddikim* (righteous ones) or the rebbes. Unlike the traditional rabbis, whose honor resulted from their learning, the *zaddikim* drew followers due to their mystical power and charismatic personalities. Because of his righteousness the *zaddik*, who is without sin, mediates between his followers and the divine, effecting forgiveness of their sins and transforming the evil within them into good. As Hasidism became institutionalized the *zaddikim* tended to pass on their leadership roles to close disciples, usually relatives, breaking up the movement into various sects and creating the Hasidic "dynasties" that exist today.

Although individual Hasids came to the United States during the late 19th century, there was no organized Hasidic community until the 20th century, when the earliest rebbes, scions of the Stoliner and the Chernobyler (named for the towns where the original founder lived), came to the United States after the Russian Revolution. The greatest influx of Hasids into the United States came after the rise of Nazism. Some, like the Lubavitcher rebbe Menachem Mendel SCHNEERSON, came during the war; others who survived the Holocaust and the Soviet occupation of Eastern Europe arrived later. There are now nearly 20 Hasidic dynasties in the United States, mostly centered in Brooklyn, although some have established communities in upstate New York, where they can live in greater isolation from the modern world.

Of all the Hasidic groups in the United States, the two most significant are the Satmars and the Lubavitchers. These groups differ radically in their approaches to the wider world. The Satmars, the largest group in the United States, were founded only in the 1920s, although the founder Rebbe Yoel Teitelbaum (1886–1982) descends from a long line of Hasidic rebbes. The most distinctive element of the Satmars is their virulent opposition to the state of Israel. Believing that the Jewish state can be restored only by the Messiah, they view the secular state of Israel as blasphemous. The present rebbe, a nephew of the movement's founder, exercises strict control over his followers, along with several smaller Hasidic groups of Hungarian origin that lost their rebbes during the Holocaust.

The Lubavitchers, the most visible of all Hasids, differ greatly from other Hasidic groups. With their origins in Lithuania, they fell heir to the studiousness of the Lithuanian Jewish tradition. The founder, Rabbi Schneur Zalman (1748–1812), formulated the movement known as Habad, an acronym drawn from *Hochma* (wisdom), *Binah* (reason), and *Da'at* (knowledge), giving Lubavitch Hasidism the other name by which it is known. Although a Lubavitch community was organized in the United States during the 1920s, it remained small until 1940. In that year, the rebbe Joseph

Isaac Schneerson (1880–1950) arrived in the United States. He settled in the Crown Heights neighborhood in Brooklyn with hundreds of his followers, most of whom were also refugees. After his death he was succeeded by his son-in-law, Menachem Mendel Schneerson.

The younger Schneerson turned the movement into the most organizationally sophisticated of all the Hasidic groups. Unlike most other Hasids, the Lubavitchers actively proselytize among other Jews. One of the rebbe's greatest desires was to bring nonobservant Jews into observance. Since the Lubavitchers' mystical theology emphasizes the divine spark within everyone, if nonobservant Jews begin to observe one of the religious laws (*mitzvoth*), the spark will grow, driving them to greater religious observance until they are consumed by religious fire. Lubavitchers see this as a necessary part of entering the messianic age. There are nearly 40 Lubavitcher yeshivas (religious schools) in the United States, 100 Habad houses in college communities, and numerous summer camps. The movement also sends members to serve the needs of Jews around the world.

During the late 1980s and early 1990s Schneerson's followers began increasingly to view him as the messiah. This seemed to be borne out by his predictions, among them that the 1991 Gulf War would be short and Israel spared, that the Soviet Union would collapse, and that Russian and Ethiopian Jews would undertake an exodus to Israel. This expectation received a setback in the winter of 1992, when Schneerson suffered a stroke, but as he slowly recovered, his followers' expectations continued to rise. Even his death in 1994 did little to cool the messianic fervor of some Lubavitchers, and tensions emerged between those who continued to expect his return as the messiah and those who were willing to postpone their expectations, suggesting a possible rift in the organization.

Although the fastest-growing of all movements in American Judaism due to a high birth rate and active proselytizing, all Hasidic groups in the United States combined contain fewer than 200,000 members. Their impact is much wider than those numbers suggest. The traditions and tales of Hasidism have entered into the religious and cultural fabric of American Judaism. Hasidism also has infused greater life into ORTHODOX JUDAISM in particular. Self-consciously strict in its interpretations of Jewish law, Hasidism has served to pull American Orthodoxy to the right. Its unabashed difference from society provides a countervailing element to the tendency toward accommodation that marked "modern Orthodoxy" in the United States.

Even many secularized Jews, anxious about their failure to maintain the religious laws, view the Hasids as faithful maintainers of Jewish tradition and provide them with a great deal of financial support. In doing so they perhaps take the concept of the *zaddik* to its logical, albeit extreme, conclusion: Hasidism exists to atone for the failings of the secularized community.

EQ

Bibliography: Martin Buber, *Tales of the Hasidim*. 2 vols. (New York: Schocken, 1947–1948); Lis Harris, *Holy Days: The World of a Hasidic Family* (New York: Simon & Schuster, 1995); Edward Hoffman, *Despite All Odds: The Story of Lubavitch* (New York: Simon & Schuster, 1991); David Landau, *Piety and Power: The World of Jewish Fundamentalism* (New York: Hill & Wang, 1993); Jerome R. Mintz, *Hasidic People: A Place in the New World* (Cambridge, Mass.: Harvard University Press, 1992); Solomon Poll, *The Hasidic Community of Williamsburg: A Study in the Sociology of Religion* (New York: Schocken, 1967); Harry M. Rabinowicz, *Hasidism: The Movement and Its Masters* (Northvale, N.J.: J. Aronson, 1988); Gershom Scholem, *The Messianic Idea in Judaism and Other Essays on Jewish Spirituality* (New York: Schocken, 1971); www.chabad.org (Lubavitch [Chabad] Hasidism); www.breslov.org (Breslover Hasidism).

Hawthorne, Nathaniel   See LITERATURE AND RELIGION.

Haygood, Atticus Greene (1839–1896)

Atticus G. Haygood, Methodist bishop and educator, was one of the first white church leaders in the postbellum South to protest the mistreatment of African Americans. Known for his paternalistic racial attitudes, Haygood wanted his region to look toward the future and leave its past, especially the crippling effects of slavery, behind.

Haygood was born on November 19, 1839, in Watkinsville, Georgia. He graduated from Emory College, then in Oxford, Georgia, in 1859 and subsequently was ordained to the ministry of the Methodist Episcopal Church, South. After serving as a Confederate chaplain, he rose to prominence in his denomination after the Civil War. He became president of Emory in 1875 and editor of the influential *Wesleyan Christian Advocate* in 1878.

Although newspaperman and Atlanta *Constitution* editor Henry Grady popularized the phrase *New South*, Haygood originated the term, employing it as the title of a sermon on Thanksgiving Day in 1880. Published by a New York financier and widely circulated in the North, Haygood's sermon spoke of how southern whites were much better off in 1880 than they had been before the war. Haygood continued his attack on what he considered the false virtues of the LOST CAUSE MYTH in his pathbreaking book, *Our Brother in Black* (1881). Although he believed divine providence had allowed Africans to be brought to America to Christianize and civilize them, he rejoiced that God had destroyed slavery. Confederate defeat, he said, had provided many benefits to both white and black southerners, including the educational work of the northern churches in the South after the Civil War ended. *Our Brother in Black* won considerable praise from philanthropists in the North, and within a year Haygood was named the executive agent of the newly created Slater Fund, an organization dedicated to the industrial education of blacks. He was a moving spirit, too, in the creation of Paine College in Augusta, Georgia, another African-American educational institution.

Haygood resigned from the Slater Fund to accept election as bishop of California and missionary bishop of Mexico in 1890, taking up residence in Los Angeles. After contracting a fever on a visit to Mexico, he returned to Georgia in 1893. Embittered by the lack of acceptance of his views on race, Haygood lived in a weakened condition in Oxford, Georgia, for two more years. He died there on January 16, 1896.

GHS, Jr.

Bibliography: Harold W. Mann, *Atticus Greene Haygood: Methodist Bishop, Editor, and Educator* (Athens: University of Georgia Press, 1965).

Haystack Prayer Meeting

Often described as the founding event of the Protestant foreign missions movement in the United States, the Haystack Prayer Meeting (1806) was a fabled gathering of students who later gained renown for their commitment to evangelical missions abroad. While seeking shelter from a summer thunderstorm in a hayloft, a group of Williams College students, including Samuel J. Mills, James Richards, Francis Robbins, Harvey Loomis, Gordon Hall, Luther Rice, and Byron Green, dedicated themselves to foreign missionary labors and subsequently formed the Society of the Brethren (1808), adopting the motto, "We can do it if we will." Joined at Andover Theological Seminary by Adoniram JUDSON, Samuel Newell, and Samuel Nott, Jr., the group advocated organized, interdenominational mission efforts that would spread the Gospel to all parts of the globe. In 1810 they sought counsel from the Congregational General Association of Massachusetts. In response, and due largely to the groundswell of support among seminary students, Congregational ministers in New England founded the American Board of Commissioners for Foreign Missions (1810). Judson and Rice were among the first group of missionaries to leave for India in 1812 under the auspices of the newly established organization. For later generations of evangelicals, the Haystack Prayer Meeting served as an enduring symbol of the power of youthful initiative and popular support for the early organization of foreign missions.

LMK

Bibliography: Courtney Anderson, *To the Golden Shore: The Life of Adoniram Judson* (Boston: Little, Brown, 1956).

healing   See CHARISMATIC MOVEMENT; HOLINESS MOVEMENT; PENTECOSTALISM.

Heaven's Gate   On March 26, 1997, news began to break of a mass suicide among a group of young people who shared a house in Rancho Santa Fe, California. Thirty-nine people had died, most of them computer professionals and all of them members of a religious group known as "Heaven's Gate." The suicides were occasioned by the appearance of the comet Hale-Bopp and the group's belief that the comet was accompanied by a spaceship that would take them from this world to a higher and better place. This spiritual place required them to leave behind their "outer shells"—their bodies.

Horrified, Americans were immediately reminded of the Jonestown Massacre (see JONES, JIM) and wondered what would compel people to such an act. In this case it was religious belief formed by a fusion of Christianity, Theosophy, gnosticism, belief in UFOs, and desire for spiritual self-actualization.

In this fusion, Heaven's Gate was not exceptionally bizarre. For more than a century similar movements have traveled the United States religious landscape. The suicides, however, were, if not unique, at least a major aberration. Despite the dispassionate view of scholars about NEW RELIGIOUS MOVEMENTS, many spoke out again against the dangers of "cults," renewing the debate about whether certain religions are illegitimate and deserving of special suspicion.

Heaven's Gate was the product of the religious visions of Marshall H. Applewhite (1931–1997) and Bonnie Lu Trusdale Nettles

(1928–1985), known at various times as Bo and Peep, Do and Ti, and The Two. The couple met while Applewhite was in a Houston hospital and Nettles, one of his nurses, urged him to join her at several Theosophical meetings. The twosome soon began holding their own meetings throughout the western United States, promising their followers celestial bliss and escape in a UFO.

Initially they called their group Human Individual Metamorphosis, or HIM, and convinced a small group of fairly successful and talented individuals to give up their possessions, friends, and families to prepare for their departure into the heavens. In 1975 they and their followers left Oregon, where they had been living, and moved to eastern Colorado, where they believed a spaceship would meet them and take them away.

When the ship did not come, the group ceased its public activities and did not resurface until 1993. In that year they purchased an advertisement in *USA Today* claiming that the earth's present civilization was about to be "recycled" and "spaded under." By this time Nettles had died, and Applewhite had assumed sole leadership.

His preaching about celestial or extraterrestrial beings who had imparted to him knowledge of a high level of human consciousness attracted a small following composed primarily of information technology professionals who eventually gathered with Applewhite in a house in Rancho Santa Fe, California. The house was rented in October of 1996 by Applewhite, who told the owner that his group was composed of Christian-based angels who had been sent to earth.

The appearance of the Hale-Bopp comet and the rumor that it was being followed by a spaceship was a momentous occasion for the group. This spaceship, which purportedly had been detected by an amateur astronomer, was widely discussed on talk radio. The group viewed its appearance as their chance to be taken up to a higher spiritual plane.

As the message on their website said:

Whether Hale-Bopp has a "companion" or not is irrelevant from our perspective. However, its arrival is joyously very significant to us at "Heaven's Gate." The joy is that our Older Member in the Evolutionary Level Above Human (the "Kingdom of Heaven") has made it clear to us that Hale-Bopp's approach is the "marker" we"ve been waiting for—the time for the arrival of the spacecraft from the Level Above Human to take us home to "Their World"—in the literal Heavens. Our 22 years [from 1975, the year of the failed appearance] of classroom here on planet Earth is finally coming to conclusion—"graduation" from the Human Evolutionary Level. We are happily prepared to leave "this world" and go with Ti's crew.

All that was needed was to remove their earthly shells, the only things that still held them back. This they did by committing mass suicide on March 26, 1997. The comet continued on its course, and the spaceship turned out to be only a fairly dim star lurking behind the comet.

EQ

Bibliography: Ted Daniels, *A Doomsday Reader: Prophets, Predictors, and Hucksters of Salvation* (New York: New York University Press, 1999); Bill Hoffman, *Heaven's Gate: Cult Suicide in San Diego* (New York: HarperPaperbacks, 1997); Catherine Wessinger, *How the Millennium Comes Violently: From Jonestown to Heaven's Gate* (New York: Seven Bridges, 2000).

Hecker, Isaac (1819–1888)

Roman Catholic convert, founder of the Paulists, and defender of the American political system, Isaac Hecker was, with his friend and confidante Orestes BROWNSON, the most ardent early-19th-century articulator of ROMAN CATHOLICISM to Protestant America and of America to the Roman Catholic hierarchy.

The son of German immigrants, Hecker was born in New York City on December 18, 1819. Originally baptized a Methodist (see

Influenced by Orestes Brownson, transcendentalist Isaac Hecker converted to Roman Catholicism and began the Paulist Order to promulgate Catholicism among American Protestants. *(Painting by G. P. A. Healy, Paulist Communications)*

METHODISM), by his mid-teens he had embarked upon the intellectual and spiritual quest that would take him from Methodism to Unitarianism (see UNITARIAN UNIVERSALIST ASSOCIATION), Mormonism (see CHURCH OF JESUS CHRIST OF LATTER-DAY SAINTS), socialism, TRANSCENDENTALISM, and finally Catholicism. The last he found under the guidance of Brownson, whom Hecker would later call his "spiritual parent."

At the age of 24, Hecker joined the transcendentalist commune at Brook Farm but was disenchanted with the extreme individualism and solitariness of transcendentalism. A stay at Bronson Alcott's Fruitlands community did little to ease this feeling. In 1844 he lived with Henry David THOREAU and his family, continuing the study in philosophy and theology that he had begun in the 1830s while working in his family's bakery.

Naturally contemplative and increasingly influenced by Continental Romanticism, Hecker was drawn to the Catholic Church, with its emphasis on tradition, coherence, and order. In this Brownson led the way intellectually, but it was Hecker who made a commitment first. More than two months before Brownson, Hecker was baptized in the Roman Catholic Church on August 2, 1844.

The next year Hecker and two other converts sailed for Europe to begin their novitiate in the Redemptorist order. After four years of training in Belgium and Holland, in 1849 Hecker was ordained as a Roman Catholic priest in London, where he served for two years before returning to America as a missionary. A successful and widely traveled evangelist, Hecker quickly made an impact on the Roman Catholic Church in America, so much so that in the early 1850s he was nominated to become bishop of Natchez, Mississippi.

A change in the Redemptorists' leadership in the United States ended this evangelical work, however, and the increasing insularity of the predominantly German order began to disturb Hecker and his fellow American convert priests. These men desired to found a distinctly American house for the order, where English rather than German would be the language and whose mission would be to serve the rapidly Americanizing immigrants.

Chosen to plead their case in Rome, Hecker sailed to Europe in 1857. Incensed by this failure of obedience, the rector major of the Redemptorists expelled him from the order. Hecker had made a sufficiently strong case that Pius IX nullified the expulsion and released Hecker and his compatriots from their vows, granting them permission to create a new order aimed at the conversion of Protestants.

Upon returning to New York in July 1858, Hecker and his colleagues organized the Missionary Priests of St. Paul the Apostle (Paulists), with Hecker as superior. Although seriously debilitated by leukemia after 1872, he remained as superior until his death on December 22, 1888.

Until that time, Hecker was a tireless exponent of Catholicism. Through the pages of the *Catholic World* (founded 1865) and in the tracts published by the Catholic Publication Society (1866, now Paulist Press), Hecker and his order argued for the compatibility of Roman Catholicism with American life and sought to convince the Church of the need to accept the modern world of political democracy, religious liberty, and scientific advance. These views would later be central to the Americanist controversy (see AMERICANISM) within the Roman Catholic Church. Although Hecker had been dead for a decade, his life would be at the center of the controversy, when the French translation of Hecker's biography suggested (approvingly) that Hecker sought the creation of a separate American Catholic Church, or at the very least the democratization of the existing Church.

While these views, condemned by Leo XII in 1899, were not truly Hecker's, they did contain the kernel of Hecker's thought. During the papacy of John XXIII (1958–1963), Hecker's call for an openness to the modern world would be heard, and his belief that the Church's truths have nothing to fear from science, democracy, or freedom would be affirmed.

EQ

Bibliography: Walter Elliott, *The Life of Father Hecker* (New York: Columbus Press, 1891); John Farina, *An American Experience of God: The Spirituality of Isaac Hecker* (New York: Paulist Press, 1981); Vincent F. Holden, *The Yankee Paul: Isaac Thomas Hecker* (Milwaukee, Wisc.: Bruce Publishing Co., 1958); David J. O'Brien, *Isaac Hecker, An American Catholic* (New York: Paulist Press, 1992); William L. Portier, *Isaac Hecker and the First Vatican Council* (New York: Edwin Mellen Press, 1985).

Henry, Carl Ferdinand Howard (1913–   )
Carl Henry is a Baptist minister, educator, and the first editor of the influential magazine *Christianity Today*. Today he is considered to be the senior statesman of American EVANGELICALISM.

Born in New York City on January 22, 1913, Henry grew up on Long Island. Although he took a position as a newspaper reporter after high school, a conversion experience led him to enroll at Wheaton College, the evangelical college near Chicago, from which he graduated in 1938. He received graduate degrees at Wheaton and at Northern Baptist Seminary in Chicago in 1941 and 1942, and he was ordained to the Baptist ministry in 1941. Henry taught theology at Northern Baptist from 1940 through 1947. During his summers, he also taught at Gordon College in Massachusetts and studied for a Ph.D., which he received from Boston University in 1949.

Henry moved to Pasadena, California, in 1948 to serve on the faculty at Fuller Theological Seminary, an institution founded the year before through the efforts of radio evangelist Charles E. Fuller. Although Henry and his colleagues affirmed the infallibility of the biblical text and were respectful of the doctrinal militancy of FUNDAMENTALISM, they also desired to overcome the narrow sectarianism that often typified evangelicals in that era. The faculty became representative of the "neo-evangelicalism," a term Fuller president Harold Ockenga coined to describe "fundamentalism with a social message." Henry's 1947 book, *The Uneasy Conscience of Modern Fundamentalism*, deplored conservative Protestants' emphasis on personal morality at the expense of a positive social program. He argued that the collapse of Western civilization, as evidenced by post–World War II Europe, provided the church with a tremendous opportunity to which evangelicals were generally failing to respond.

By 1955, Henry had been invited by evangelist Billy GRAHAM to become the editor of a new magazine, *Christianity Today*. Graham wished the publication to become the evangelical community's alternative to the *Christian Century*, the organ of mainline Protestantism. Henry moved to Washington, D.C., to take the new position. He served as editor for a 12-year period in which the circulation of *Christianity Today* surpassed that of its liberal rival. Henry's magazine became recognized as the intellectual voice of the new evangelicalism he championed. Still, Henry eventually lost his job to Harold Lindsell in 1968, because he failed to meet the standards of political conservatism imposed by J. Howard Pew, the magazine's most important financial backer.

After leaving *Christianity Today*, Henry began work on his six-volume *God, Revelation and Authority*, completed in 1983. At the same time, he accepted a position at Eastern Baptist Theological Seminary in Philadelphia, teaching there from 1969 to 1974. In 1974, he became a lecturer-at-large for World Vision, the nondenominational evangelical relief organization. Henry retired in 1978 but continues to write and give speeches.

GHS, Jr.

Bibliography: Carl F. Henry, *Confessions of a Theologian: An Autobiography* (Waco, Tx.: Word Books, 1986); George M. Marsden, *Reforming Fundamentalism: Fuller Seminary and the New Evangelicalism* (Grand Rapids, Mich.: Eerdmans, 1987).

heresy   The term *heresy*, derived from the Greek *hairesis*, meaning "choice" or "religious school," refers to the denial of accepted doctrines and the teaching of erroneous beliefs. Since the earliest days of the church, Christian leaders have claimed the prerogative of distinguishing between truth and falsehood in matters of theology. In the 19th century especially, numerous heresy trials were conducted in the United States, as Christian denominations, most notably the Presbyterians, grappled with the religious implications of new and changing intellectual trends.

One of the earliest theological controversies occurred when Old and New School (see

NEW SCHOOL/OLD SCHOOL) Presbyterian factions fought over the significance of REVIVALISM in their denomination. Philadelphia pastor Albert Barnes, a New School minister, was renowned for adapting his beliefs to fit the loose theological standards typical of the revival movement. After preaching and publishing a sermon that criticized the Westminster Confession, the classic expression of Presbyterian orthodoxy, Barnes was charged with heresy. The doctrinally rigid Old School party accused Barnes of questioning several key Presbyterian beliefs. Although the New School party had enough votes to acquit Barnes when he was tried in 1831, he was charged with heresy again in 1835 and at that time convicted.

In 1835, Lyman BEECHER, then one of the most famous clergymen in the United States, was also arraigned for heresy by the Presbyterians. Influenced by revivalism and highly optimistic about American social advances, Beecher began to question traditional Calvinist teachings about sin and increasingly emphasized the possibility of human progress. As a result, three indictments for heresy were brought against him, charging that he failed to uphold orthodox Presbyterian beliefs about human depravity. But efforts to censure Beecher failed, and he was acquitted.

Although controversies over race, slavery, and the Civil War distracted Americans in the middle decades of the 19th century, concern about theological and intellectual issues returned to the churches by century's end. More than any other Protestant denomination, Presbyterians were shaken by disputes between doctrinal conservatives and so-called modernists, leaders who wished to reconcile religious beliefs with developments in modern culture.

The first highly publicized heresy trial of the postwar period involved Presbyterian pastor David Swing of Chicago. Swing argued that religious creeds, like all human expressions, were imperfect and might contain errors. "A creed is only the highest wisdom of a particular time and place," he declared. Francis Pat-

ton, professor of theology at the Presbyterian seminary in Chicago, compiled a list of Swing's alleged heresies. The basic issue, as Patton and his followers saw it, concerned doctrinal integrity: If you profess a creed, you should either stand by it in every detail or renounce it entirely. Swing's allies perceived the problem differently. In their minds, even Jesus Christ himself would not have been doctrinally pure enough for rigid Presbyterians like Patton. Tried for heresy in 1874, Swing was acquitted but still withdrew from his denomination and established an independent congregation.

An even more bitter controversy engulfed Presbyterian clergyman Charles Augustus BRIGGS, who had taught at his denomination's Union Theological Seminary in New York since 1876. In 1891 Briggs was inducted into the chair of biblical studies at Union. In his inaugural address on "The Authority of Holy Scripture," Briggs denied both the verbal inspiration of the Bible and the doctrine of INERRANCY, beliefs that were the linchpins of conservative teaching on the Bible. Briggs's address led the Presbyterian General Assembly, the highest decision-making body of the denomination, to veto his professional appointment and charge him with heresy. His trial extended over three years, and in 1893 he was suspended from the Presbyterian ministry. Briggs, however, retained his position at Union, for the seminary severed its relationship with Presbyterianism, and he soon joined the Episcopal Church.

Despite the widespread internal strife that Presbyterians in the North experienced over charges of heresy, other Protestant denominations in the 19th century, though not untouched by controversy, suffered fewer serious divisions. Congregationalists and Baptists, for example, with their loose ecclesiastical structures, did not have the means to enforce doctrinal conformity and thus offered a relatively free field for the growth of liberal ideas. While both the Episcopal Church and the Methodist Episcopal Church possessed the organizational cohesion to prevent theological innovation, neither had an ethos attuned to hunting down suspected heretics. Episcopalians had traditionally adopted a policy of theological comprehensiveness, and Methodists were more concerned with proper behavior and heartfelt devotion than with correct beliefs. Finally, in the conservative South, the few outbreaks of apparent heresy (e.g., Crawford Toy among the Southern Baptists and James Woodrow among the southern Presbyterians) were squelched so swiftly that orthodoxy remained virtually unsullied in the region as a whole.

In American Protestant circles, accusations of heresy that agitated churches in the 19th century—questions of biblical authority and subscription to traditional creeds—surfaced again in the fundamentalist (see FUNDAMENTALISM) controversy of the 20th century. Protestants continued to divide into liberal and conservative camps and debate the meaning of their beliefs. Roman Catholics also faced controversies about heresy in that same period. Unlike Protestants, whose debates centered on interpretations of the Bible, Roman Catholics considered the appropriate relationship of their church to American society and to the modern age.

In an apostolic letter entitled *Testem Benevolentiae*, addressed to Cardinal James GIBBONS of Baltimore in 1899, Pope Leo XIII condemned a heresy he called AMERICANISM. According to the letter, Americanism was an unfortunate outgrowth of the political liberties that citizens of the United States enjoyed. Leo repudiated the idea that the Church should either adapt itself to its secular environment or introduce greater individual freedom of belief. Four years earlier, in the encyclical *LONGINQUA OCEANI*, the pope had cautioned Catholics against thinking that the separation of church and state Americans celebrated was a desirable arrangement for Roman Catholicism generally. This was to counter the statements of bishops of the time who had expressed enthusiastic opinions

about their church's relationship with American culture. However, since Cardinal Gibbons later responded that no church leader ever held the exact position Leo condemned, Americanism has often been dismissed by American Catholics as a "phantom heresy."

GHS, Jr.

Bibliography: George H. Shriver, ed., *American Religious Heretics: Formal and Informal Trials* (Nashville, Tenn.: Abingdon Press, 1966).

Heschel, Abraham Joshua (1907–1972)

A leading Jewish theologian and social activist, Abraham Joshua Heschel bridged the gulf between traditional religious practice and modern society. Heschel understood that the problem of secular society was not unbelief, but the inability to believe. This inability caused individuals to focus on themselves. To overcome that self-absorption, Heschel formulated a theology that articulated traditional Jewish understandings in light of modern philosophical and psychological concepts.

Born in Warsaw, Poland, in 1907, and descended from a long line of religious scholars and Hasidic (see HASIDISM) rabbis, Heschel's vocation as a theologian now seems predestined. Following a traditional religious education in which he immersed himself in the study of the Talmud and the Kabbala, Heschel undertook a secular education, first at a Yiddish *gymnasium* in Lithuania, and later at the Hochschule fur die Wissenschaft des Judentums and the University of Berlin. Expelled from Germany in 1938, he returned to his native Poland. An offer of a professorship at Hebrew Union College found Heschel out of the country when the Nazis invaded Poland, thereby saving him from experiencing firsthand the horrors of the Holocaust.

Arriving in the United States in 1940, Heschel taught at Hebrew Union College (Cincinnati, Ohio) for five years, leaving in 1945 for the more traditional and congenial atmosphere of Jewish Theological Seminary. There he served as professor of Jewish ethics and mysticism until his death on December 23, 1972.

During the early 1950s Heschel's work began to attract widespread popular attention, beginning with the 1951 publication of *Man Is Not Alone*. Already a respected interpreter of the Jewish tradition, Heschel addressed in his theological work the existential questions of modern humanity, primarily the problem of meaninglessness. Meaninglessness, for Heschel, resulted from modern humanity's inability to encounter the God of the Bible. Cut off from community and skeptical of supernaturalism and miracles, modern humanity lacks the location, experience, and language necessary to experience God as a concerned creator.

The fact that God was a living God, not some impersonal being or unmoved mover, was central to Heschel's theology. The living God of the Bible was an empathic God who needed humanity and expressed that need in demands made upon humanity. Faith is humanity's way to respond to these demands. In responding to divine demands, humanity simultaneously experiences itself as the object of divine concern. From this interchange faith and religious feeling, and thereby meaning, emerge.

Heschel's significance for contemporary American Judaism was not limited to his theological work. He was a public figure, perhaps the preeminent public figure in traditional Judaism. Heschel was among the earliest to voice his support for Soviet Jews, demanding that they be allowed to practice their religion and to emigrate. Heschel's advice was significant in the negotiations behind the declaration on the Jews that emerged from VATICAN COUNCIL II. This "Declaration on the Relationship of the Church to Non-Christian Religions" (*Nostra aetate*) was a turning point in the Roman Catholic Church's understanding of Jews and Judaism. It rejected the view that Jews were responsible for the death of Jesus and condemned anti-Semitism.

Heschel's social views were not limited to Jewish issues, however. He was a vocal supporter of the CIVIL RIGHTS MOVEMENT, labeling racism a cancer of the soul and an unmitigated evil. Heschel marched with Martin Luther KING, Jr., at Selma and was jailed for his activities. He opposed the VIETNAM WAR and added his voice to those demanding American withdrawal.

This combination of traditional religious views and social action was a hallmark of Heschel's theology. As a traditionalist he took the reality of evil seriously. He wrote, "There is one line that expresses the mood of the Jewish man throughout the ages: *'The earth is given into the hand of the wicked'*" (Job 9:24). Humanity cannot ignore responsibility, however, for we are commanded to love good and hate evil. "At the end of days evil will be conquered by the One; in historic times evils must be conquered one by one."

(See also CONSERVATIVE JUDAISM; JUDAISM.)

EQ

Bibliography: Robert G. Goldy, *The Emergence of Jewish Theology in America* (Bloomington: Indiana University Press, 1990); Abraham Joshua Heschel, *Between God and Man: An Interpretation of Judaism* (New York: Free Press, 1965); ———, *God in Search of Man: A Philosophy of Judaism* (New York: Farrar, Straus & Cudahy, 1955); Edward K. Kaplan and Samuel H. Dresner, *Abraham Joshua Heschel: Prophetic Witness* (New Haven: Yale University Press, 1998); ———, *Holiness in Words: Abraham Joshua Heschel's Poetics of Piety* (West Fulton: State University of New York Press, 1996); John Merkle, *The Genesis of Faith: The Depth Theology of Abraham Joshua Heschel* (New York: Macmillan, 1985).

high-church tradition See ANGLO-CATHOLICISM.

Higher Christian Life movement The Higher Christian Life movement originated in the late 19th century among American Protestants who believed in the possibility of Christian PERFECTIONISM. Although the perfectionist ideal was first espoused by the HOLINESS

MOVEMENT that emerged out of American Methodism, many members of non-Methodist denominations both in Great Britain and in the United States were influenced by it. The spirituality embodied in the Higher Christian Life was further articulated in the Keswick teachings, a related religious movement that began in England in 1876.

The idea of Christian perfection was originally popularized in the 1830s by Presbyterian revivalist Charles G. FINNEY and his colleague Asa MAHAN, a Congregational minister and first president of Oberlin College in Ohio. Both Finney and Mahan had read Methodist founder John Wesley's *Plain Account of Christian Perfection* and believed absolute obedience to God's laws was possible in the present life. Mahan applied Christian perfectionism to social reform activities, notably the campaign against slavery. In the same period, Methodist evangelist Phoebe PALMER stressed the importance of entire SANCTIFICATION, a religious experience by which the Christian became consecrated wholly to God.

The urban revivals of 1857 and 1858, with their noontime prayer meetings and interdenominational lay leadership, helped spread perfectionism throughout much of the United States. In the optimistic moral climate of mid-19th century America, the expectation that a Christian *could* overcome sin seemed completely reasonable. In 1858 Presbyterian minister William E. Boardman, a frequent participant in Palmer's "Tuesday Meetings for the Promotion of Holiness," published *The Higher Christian Life*. This book furnished a classic statement of how a Christian might win victory over sin. Boardman was instrumental in attracting his fellow Presbyterians, as well as Quakers, Congregationalists, and Baptists, to the growing Holiness revival.

Immediately following the 1857–1858 revival, both Finney and Palmer conducted revivals in the British Isles. A few years later, the husband-and-wife team of Robert Pearsall and Hannah Whitall Smith further spread Holiness teaching in Great Britain. Raised as Quakers, the Smiths had each experienced an emotional "baptism of the Holy Spirit" after attending Methodist camp meetings in the late 1860s. On a trip to England in 1872, they spoke publicly about those experiences of sanctification and soon became popular speakers at Holiness meetings. Hannah Smith's *The Christian's Secret of a Happy Life*, published in 1875, also became an important devotional guide. She summarized her beliefs in an analogy that compared Christians to clay in God's hands: "In order for a lump of clay to be made into a beautiful vessel, it must be entirely abandoned to the potter, and must lie passive in his hands."

In the early 1870s, Hannah and Robert Smith joined William Boardman in promoting Holiness teaching in England. Later, at Oxford in the summer of 1874, the Smiths, Boardman, and Asa Mahan participated in an influential convention. Anglican clergyman T. D. Harford Battersby, who had attended the Oxford convention, organized an open-air conference at his parish in Keswick, a small town in northwest England. The first Keswick conference took place in July 1875. An annual event thereafter, it became one of the principal institutions of the Holiness movement. Keswick teachings were imported back to the United States in the 1880s by American revivalist Dwight L. MOODY, who had conducted successful revivals in Great Britain from 1881 to 1884.

Americans always were influential at Keswick, and in 1913 a separate American organization was born under the leadership of Charles G. Trumbull and Robert C. McQuilkin of Pennsylvania. Trumbull had experienced an intense conversion to what he called the "Victorious Life" in 1910. As editor of the weekly *Sunday School Times*, Trumbull transformed that journal into an organ of Keswick teaching. Trumbull and McQuilkin, then associate editor of the periodical, created Victorious Life conferences, a series of summer gatherings held at various locations along the East Coast beginning in 1913. In 1924 the Victorious Life conference was moved to its present home at Keswick Grove, New Jersey.

Unlike other groups within the Holiness movement, the Higher Christian Life and Keswick circle never formed a separate denomination but remained simply a conglomerate of individuals committed to common ideals. This group was distinctive because it owed far more to CALVINISM than to the ARMINIANISM espoused by most Holiness advocates. Although the Arminian tradition, which typified the Methodist churches, tended to stress that Christians might overcome all conscious sin by their cooperation with God, Calvinists customarily underscored believers' continuing sinfulness and the passivity of the process of sanctification. Thus, Keswick leaders spoke of "yielding" to God's grace and accepting the "suppression," not the eradication, of one's sinful proclivities. The result of sanctification was not merely a pure heart but visible Christian service as well.

The Higher Christian Life movement, like the Holiness movement generally, offered Christians a sense of the certainty of their salvation. This idea became popular in many segments of American Protestantism. It spread throughout the Protestant churches in the early 20th century and is now a distinguishing feature of EVANGELICALISM in the United States.

GHS, Jr.

Bibliography: Steven Barabas, *So Great Salvation: The History and Message of the Keswick Convention* (Westwood, N.J.: Fleming H. Revell, 1952); Melvin E. Dieter, *The Holiness Revival of the Nineteenth Century* (Metuchen, N.J.: Scarecrow Press, 1980).

higher criticism   See BIBLICAL INTERPRETATION.

Hinduism   Hinduism, one of the world's major religious traditions, exists in the United States both as the faith of Asian Indian immigrants and their descendants and as a religious tradition that has influenced European-American sympathizers and adherents.

Hindu immigrants came to the United States later than their Buddhist counterparts from China and Japan, yet Hinduism preceded Buddhism as an intellectual influence. American interest in Hinduism dates back at least to *India Christiania*, written by the Puritan divine Cotton MATHER in 1721. The first sympathetic treatment of Hinduism appeared in *An Alphabetical Compendium of the Various Sects* (1784) by the Unitarian Hannah Adams. Widespread American interest in Hinduism was not sparked, however, until after English translations of Hindu religious texts such as Charles Wilkins's *Bhagavad Gita* (1785) and Sir William Jones's *The Laws of Manu* (1794) began to appear in the last two decades of the 18th century. One influential book that used these translations was *A Comparison of the Institutions of Moses with Those of the Hindoos and Other Ancient Nations* (1799) by the British Unitarian Joseph PRIESTLEY.

Although scholars in the nascent field of academic Orientalism used their newfound knowledge of Sanskrit to produce translations of Hindu scriptures throughout the 19th century, nothing did more to popularize Hinduism in America during those hundred years than New England TRANSCENDENTALISM. Ralph Waldo EMERSON was introduced to Asian religious traditions at a young age by his aunt Mary Moody Emerson, a Unitarian who saw in the Hindu monotheism of the Indian reformer Rammohun Roy a faith that mirrored her own. Emerson's writings did not begin to reflect his Asian interests until the appearance, beginning in the 1840s, of poems such as "Hamatreya" and "Brahma" and essays like "Oversoul," "Illusions," and "Compensation."

While Emerson was moved most deeply by the *Bhagavad Gita*, an epic narrative, Henry David THOREAU, another transcendentalist, was more influenced by *The Laws of Manu*, a work of Hindu ethics. Thoreau scoffed at the thought of joining any organized religion, but he came close to referring to himself as a Hindu when, after his experiment at Walden Pond, he

Indians who came to America brought their religious practices and customs with them. Hindu Festival of India, Edison, New Jersey, July 1991. *(Photograph by Steven Gelberg. Pluralism Project of Harvard University)*

affirmed, "To some extent, and at rare intervals, even I am a yogin."

Perhaps more than Emerson and Thoreau, so-called lesser transcendentalists such as James Freeman CLARKE helped to transform Hinduism into a legitimate religious alternative in America. Both Clarke's *Ten Great Religions: An Essay in Comparative Theology* (1871) and Samuel Johnson's *Oriental Religions and Their Relation to Universal Religion* (1872) attempted to portray Hinduism in a favorable light, though both ultimately opted for a form of Christian liberalism.

Theosophists (see THEOSOPHY) like Helena Petrovna BLAVATSKY and Henry Steel OLCOTT built upon the transcendentalists' interest in Asia. Unlike Emerson and Thoreau, Blavatsky

and Olcott actually moved to India and immersed themselves in Hindu culture. The Theosophists were initially attracted more to Buddhism than to Hinduism, but Annie Wood Besant changed that when she succeeded Olcott as president of the Theosophical Society in 1907. A British socialist turned Theosophist, Besant championed Hinduism as the religion par excellence for the modern West. Indian nationalists recognized her in 1917 for her efforts on behalf of their country and its traditions by electing her the only Western president of the Indian National Congress. Her books and lectures educated a generation of American Theosophists and Theosophical sympathizers about Hinduism.

Another Theosophically-inclined Hindu, the Indian-born Mohandas K. Gandhi (1869–1948), had a more profound effect on American religious life than Besant. Attracted to Theosophy in his youth, Gandhi is most famous for his nonviolent civil disobedience. Gandhi adapted this theory in part from JAINISM, an ascetic South Indian tradition whose ethics center around the practice of *ahimsa*, or nonviolence toward all living beings. Gandhi's influence on Martin Luther KING, Jr., and through him on the American CIVIL RIGHTS MOVEMENT is well known. But Gandhi's work was also closely followed by black newspapers and black intellectuals as early as the 1920s.

Hinduism's place in America changed dramatically when it began to arrive in person rather than on the page. A few Asian Indians came to the United States as early as 1820, but this immigrant flow was nothing more than a trickle until the last decade of the 19th century, when railroad work began to draw Indian laborers to western Canada and the United States. Still, by the time this first wave was cut off with the passage of restrictive immigration legislation in 1917, only about 6,000 Asian Indians had entered the United States, and the majority of those were Sikhs. Not until the repeal of the Asian Exclusion Act in 1965 did large numbers of Hindus emigrate to America.

The first Hindu missionaries to the United States came in 1893 in the wake of the WORLD'S PARLIAMENT OF RELIGIONS, a gathering of liberal religionists from around the world held in conjunction with the Chicago World's Fair. Like the Asian Indian immigrants who preceded them, these Hindu missionaries worked to transplant many of the diverse beliefs and practices that constitute Hinduism. They tended, however, to stress modernist elements of Hinduism—monotheism, caste reform, and the tradition's compatibility with science and with other religions—emphasized during the 19th century reform movement that historians have called the Hindu Renaissance.

One delegate to the parliament and the first great Hindu missionary to the United States was Swami VIVEKANANDA. A disciple of Ramakrishna, a Hindu mystic and devotee of the Hindu goddess Kali, Vivekananda had come to the United States in an effort to spread in the West the truths and practices of Advaita Vedanta, a nondualistic form of Hinduism that postulates the unity of the impersonal God, or Brahman, with the individual soul, or Atman. A smashing success at the parliament, Vivekananda stayed in America long enough to found the VEDANTA SOCIETY in 1894 as a branch of his India-based Ramakrishna Mission. The Vedanta Society, which now has centers in numerous American cities, aims to spread the doctrines and disciplines of Vedanta and to promote religious tolerance by preaching the fundamental unity of all religions.

The second important Hindu missionary to the United States also came as an invitee to an interreligious conference. Swami Paramahansa YOGANANDA arrived in Boston in 1920 as a delegate to the International Congress of Religious Liberals. Unlike Vivekananda, who eventually returned to India, Yogananda took up residence in the United States. His SELF-REALIZATION FELLOWSHIP, which is now based in Los Angeles, aims to teach the principles of Hinduism and the techniques of *kriya* yoga, a tantric discipline in which practitioners seek to achieve God-realization by manipulating their kundalini, or spiritual energy. Like the Vedanta Society, the SRF emphasizes commonalities rather than differences between Hinduism and Christianity. Its approach, however, is more practical and less philosophical, emphasizing the therapeutic and material benefits of Hindu yoga.

Although Vivekananda and Yogananda did more to arouse interest in Hinduism than to earn converts to it, a few Americans did formally convert to Hinduism early in the 20th century. Some went on to become teachers themselves. The Chicago attorney and NEW THOUGHT advocate William Walker Atkinson, for example, published numerous books on

Hinduism, including *Fourteen Lessons in Yoga Philosophy and Oriental Occultism* (1903), under the name of Swami Ramacharacka. A more controversial convert was Pierre Bernard, the founder of the Tantrik Order in America, who referred to himself as "Oom the Omnipotent."

Thanks to the efforts of Vivekananda, Yogananda, Atkinson, and Bernard, some Americans became Hindus in the early 20th century, but Hinduism did not become a popular religious alternative in America until the 1960s. Three factors conspired to create a favorable climate for American Hinduism. The first was the achievement of Indian independence in 1947. Independence fostered a proliferation of new religious movements in India, and many of those movements made their way to the United States. A second factor that spurred this Hindu turn was the COUNTERCULTURE, which gave a boost to alternative religions of all stripes. The final and decisive factor was the lifting in 1965 of the Asian Exclusion Act, which had restricted the flow of Chinese, Japanese, and Asian Indian immigrants to the United States since 1924.

Following this legislative watershed, a panoply of Asian Indian gurus moved to America and established followings here. Yogi Bhajan arrived in the United States in 1969 and gathered devotees into a collection of Sikh-influenced communes (see SIKHISM) called the Happy/Healthy/Holy Organization. The "boy guru" Maharaj-ji came to America in 1970 and brought his "lovers of God" into the Divine Light Mission (later, Elan Vital). Swami Muktananda Paramahansa toured the United States on three occasions between 1970 and 1981, and his followers founded the Siddha Yoga Dham Associates (SYDA) in 1974. The most controversial of these new gurus was Bhagwan Rajneesh, who arrived in 1981 and established a short-lived commune in eastern Oregon called Rajneeshpuram. This group was criticized by anticult groups and investigated by the U.S. government for a host of irregularities, including authoritarianism, drug use, and

weapons stockpiling. Rajneesh himself was arrested in 1985 for violating immigration laws and deported.

Other Asian Indian gurus who did not actually visit also earned substantial American followings. The International Sathya Sai Baba Organisation promotes the teachings of the faith healer Sathya Sai Baba, while centers associated with the Indian-based Sri Aurobindo Society spread the yogic techniques of the poet/philosopher Sri Aurobindo Ghose. Even a 19th-century Hindu guru has merited an American audience. Brought to Flushing, New York, from the Indian state of Gujarat in 1972, the Swaminarayan Mission and Fellowship promotes the worship of the Indian saint Sri Swaminarayan not only as an exemplary devotee of the Hindu deity Vishnu but also as an incarnation of God on earth.

Finally, a third class of gurus, American-born converts to Hinduism, achieved acclaim in the United States in the 1960s and 1970s. Franklin Jones (later known as Da Free John and Avatar Adi Da Samraj) split off from Swami Muktananda Paramahansa's SYDA to organize the Dawn Horse Fellowship (subsequently renamed The Free Daist Avataric Communion). Richard Alpert, a Harvard professor of psychology and friend of the former LSD investigator Timothy Leary, took the name of Baba Ram Dass after embracing Hinduism and earned American followers. Not surprisingly, these non-Indian gurus tend as a rule to Americanize Hinduism more freely than their Asian Indian counterparts. Many of them borrow generously not only from Hinduism but also from other Asian traditions. Among the most highly Americanized Hindu societies in America is the Hanuman Foundation of Baba Ram Dass. *Be Here Now* (1971), a cartooned text that functions as an unofficial scripture for the organization, draws on ideas derived from psychoanalysis, Tibetan Buddhism, Sikhism, Hinduism, Taoism, Christianity, and Judaism.

Of all the Hindu movements that emerged in America after 1965, two stand out most prominently: the TRANSCENDENTAL MEDITATION (TM) movement of MAHARISHI MAHESH YOGI and the INTERNATIONAL SOCIETY FOR KRISHNA CONSCIOUSNESS (ISKCON) of A. C. Bhaktivedanta Swami PRABHUPADA.

Maharishi Mahesh Yogi came to America in 1959 to lecture on an ostensibly scientific technique for spiritual liberation called Transcendental Meditation. Soon he had gathered hundreds of younger Americans into his Spiritual Regeneration Movement (SRM). TM provides classes in a simplified version of the teachings of nondualistic Hinduism, or Advaita Vedanta, and the practices of yoga. TM practice consists primarily of chanting and meditating on a mantra personally selected for the student by his or her guru. Maharishi Mahesh Yogi and his movement benefitted greatly from the Beatles' well-publicized but short-lived flirtation with TM in the 1960s.

A second important form of Hinduism transplanted to the United States in the 1960s was the devotional Hinduism of the International Society for Krishna Consciousness. Like the TM movement, the "Hare Krishnas" organized themselves around a charismatic guru, in this case founder A. C. Bhaktivedanta Swami Prabhupada. Prabhupada was a devotee of Lord Krishna, who is seen by most Hindus as one divine descent of Vishnu among many, but by Hare Krishna followers as the one Supreme Lord. Prabhupada arrived in the United States in 1965 and settled in Los Angeles.

Unlike most other Hindu missionaries to America who stressed Hindu philosophy, he emphasized a simple ritual: chanting a mantra to Krishna. ISKCON initially attracted an almost exclusively European-American membership, but more recently it has appealed to Indian immigrants as well. Members of ISKCON distinguish themselves from other Americans by adopting Indian names, wearing saffron robes, and shaving their heads after the manner of Hindu holy people.

Although both TM and the Hare Krishna movement can be seen as modern Western inventions, they can also be viewed as continuations of more long-standing reform movements within Hinduism. ISKCON members trace their tradition back to the 16th-century Indian reformer Caitanya, while Maharishi Mahesh Yogi acknowledges his primary debt to the 8th-century Hindu philosopher Shankara.

An important sidelight to all of these recent Hindu imports is the ANTICULT MOVEMENT. Asian Indians have been persecuted in America at least as early as the anti-Indian riot in Bellingham, Washington, in 1907. And Hinduism came under fierce attack in books such as Katherine Mayo's *Mother India* (1927) and Mersene Sloan's *The Indian Menace* (1929). But opposition to American Hinduism did not become organized until the 1970s, when relatives of some converts began the controversial practice of deprogramming in an attempt to deconvert their loved ones from "heathen" faiths. The widely publicized attempts by parents to save their children from the Indian gurus in the 1960s and 1970s points to the fact that these Hindu-based movements, like the earlier Zen movement within American Buddhism, tended to attract non-Asian individuals rather than families. Hindu families who came to America after the repeal of the Asian Exclusion Act built less controversial and more stable groups centered on a venerable Indian institution: the Hindu temple.

In the wake of the new immigration legislation of 1965, immigration from Asia in general and from India in particular skyrocketed. The 1990 census found 815,447 Asian Indians living in the United States, many of them Hindus. These new immigrants differed significantly from the cohort of the first quarter of the century. While earlier Indian immigrants had come from rural areas to work on American farms, the post-1965 immigrants came to a much greater extent from cities and worked in professional occupations. And while almost all of the earlier immigrants were men, the new immigrants came far more frequently as families. As a result, the more recent immigrants had both the means and the motive to build new temples.

Hindu temples arose in San Francisco and Los Angeles before World War II, but not until the 1970s did Hindu temples begin to spring up in many major American cities. In 1977 Asian Indians consecrated America's first Indian-style Hindu temples: the Sri Ganesha Temple (now the Maha Vallabha Gnapati Devasthanam) in Flushing, New York; and the Sri Venkateswara Temple in Pittsburgh, Pennsylvania. Since that time, Asian Indian immigrants and their children have built roughly 150 Hindu temples. According to Harvard University's Pluralism Project, in 2001 there were more than 800 Hindu centers in the United States. Estimates regarding the number of American Hindus vary widely, though the best estimates seem to center around 1 million adherents.

The construction of Hindu sacred spaces in America testifies to the fact that Hinduism has gone beyond influencing sympathetic American intellectuals to establishing itself on American soil. In the process of being transplanted here, Hinduism is also taking on new and decidedly American forms. Although this process is more rapid among European- and African-American students of Indian gurus, it is also evident among Indian-American devotees at Hindu temples.

One of the most obvious and important Americanizations of temple-based Hinduism is the tendency toward ecumenism. Two facts of Hindu life in America support this tendency: the relatively small size of the Indian-American population in any given U.S. city and its astonishing diversity. In India there are typically numerous temples in a city. Many are dedicated to either Vishnu or Shiva, two deities who along with the impersonal (and therefore almost entirely unworshipped) Brahma constitute what some have described as the Hindu "trinity." In American cities, however, there is often no more than one Hindu temple. Hindu temples in the United States attempt to appeal to all Hindus in their area by making room for a variety of gods and a wide array of devotional practices. Many American temples, including those in Flushing, New York, and Calabasas, California, have shrines dedicated to both Shiva and Vishnu.

Hindu temples in the United States often look on the outside like temples in India. On the inside, however, they appear like American megachurch complexes. There are often sanctuaries for congregational worship (rare in India) and kitchens, meeting rooms, and schoolrooms in the basement for social, cultural, and educational activities. One scholar has referred to this development as "split-level Hinduism."

Thus, even as Hinduism is serving to make American religion more pluralistic, America is furthering the already considerable pluralism within Hinduism. ISKCON members, for example, have taken their movement back to India, and some American-born Hindu gurus are beginning to attract followers in India. In this way, the most multifarious of the world's religions is becoming even more diverse.

SRP

Bibliography: John Y. Fenton, *Transplanting Religious Traditions: Asian Indians in America* (New York: Praeger, 1988); Carl T. Jackson, *The Oriental Religions and American Thought: Nineteenth-Century Explorations* (Westport, Conn.: Greenwood Press, 1981); ———, *Vedanta for the West: The Ramakrishna Movement in the United States* (Bloomington: Indiana University Press, 1994); Joan M. Jensen, *Passage from India: Asian Indian Immigrants in North America* (New Haven: Yale University Press, 1988); Raymond Brady Williams, ed., *A Sacred Thread: Modern Transmission of Hindu Traditions in India and Abroad* (Chambersburg, Penn.: Anima, 1992); www.hinduismtoday.com (*Hinduism Today* magazine).

Hobart, John Henry (1775–1830)

John Henry Hobart was the first Episcopal bishop of New York and leader of the traditionalist, or "high church," party in the early 19th century. Hobart stressed the importance of the EPISCOPACY and a general dislike for non-

Anglican Protestantism. He looked with suspicion upon ANGLICANISM's Reformation heritage and carefully traced the historic roots of the EPISCOPAL CHURCH back to the first-century Christian community.

Hobart was born in Philadelphia on September 14, 1775. After graduating from what is now Princeton University in 1793, he studied with William White, bishop of Pennsylvania. Ordained in 1798, Hobart served for brief periods in churches in New Brunswick, New Jersey, and in Hempstead, New York. After being called as an assistant minister at Trinity Church in New York City in 1801, he quickly rose to prominence and was consecrated bishop of New York in 1811. Extremely active in missionary work, he preached as far west as Michigan and did much to increase the size of the Episcopal Church.

Throughout his career and in numerous tracts and books, Hobart championed high-church Episcopalianism. The high-church tradition he inherited from the Church of England claimed two essential bases of authority: a theological one, grounded in Anglicanism's historical continuity with early Christianity, and a political one, secured by the ecclesiastical establishment in England. Although the outcome of the War for Independence forced American Anglicans to abandon their establishmentarian position, they continued to emphasize that membership in the church, the visible society of the redeemed, was essential to the Christian faith. Hobart's most famous work, *An Apology for Apostolic Order and Its Advocates* (1807), offered a vision of the primitive church, surrounded by a hostile population, as the most desirable model for the Episcopal Church to follow. When called upon to define the true nature of Christianity, Hobart stressed the formal and external over the experiential and internal. Although he did not live to see its arrival in America, many of his theological emphases matched the concerns of the later Anglo-Catholic movement (see ANGLO-CATHOLICISM).

Hobart died on September 12, 1830, in Auburn, New York, while undertaking a visitation of his diocese.

GHS, Jr.

Bibliography: Robert Bruce Mullin, *Episcopal Vision/American Reality: High Church Theology and Social Thought in Evangelical America* (New Haven: Yale University Press, 1986).

Hodge, Charles (1797–1878)

Charles Hodge was a Presbyterian minister and his denomination's most prominent theologian in 19th-century America. He was noted as a staunch supporter of CALVINISM and of a highly conservative, rationalistic method of BIBLICAL INTERPRETATION known as SCOTTISH COMMON SENSE REALISM.

Hodge was born in Philadelphia on December 28, 1797. He graduated from what is now Princeton University in 1815 and from Princeton Seminary in 1819. He then taught biblical literature at the seminary between 1820 and 1826. In 1826, he left the United States for three years of European study at Paris and at Halle and Berlin in Germany. In that period, he encountered the doctrinal indifference of both German PIETISM and the liberal theology of Friedrich Schleiermacher. As a result of his experience in Europe, Hodge returned to Princeton in 1828 with a determination to repel all threats to Protestant orthodoxy.

Patterning himself after Archibald Alexander, his mentor at Princeton, Hodge was guided by two principles. First, he was thoroughly opposed to intellectual innovation of any kind. He was content simply to defend beliefs contained in the Westminster Confession, the 17th-century theological document that is the Presbyterian standard of faith. Hodge's statement that "a new idea never originated in this Seminary" reflects his straightforward adherence to Protestant traditionalism at Princeton. Second, Hodge considered the formulation of theology to be merely a process of inductive reasoning. A Christian, he believed, could construct an objective system of truth by studying the "facts" contained in the Bible, which he saw as an infallible source of religious truth. This belief, the essence of the Scottish Common Sense philosophy, reflects the concern for scientific method that was a hallmark of 19th-century intellectual life.

For many years Hodge was the leader of the ultraconservative forces within Presbyterianism. As an Old School (see NEW SCHOOL/OLD SCHOOL) Presbyterian, he resisted efforts to cooperate with other denominations or to alter the theological standards of his denomination in any way. Thus, he opposed the modifications of Calvinist teaching on human sin and free will that Nathaniel W. TAYLOR advanced, and he fought REVIVALISM and the revivalistic "new measures" that Charles G. FINNEY popularized. Hodge was not troubled when the Old and New School factions split into two separate denominations in 1837, and he tried to prevent the eventual reunification of Presbyterianism in the North in 1869.

Hodge's publications were numerous. He served as editor of the *Biblical Repertory* (later renamed the *Princeton Review*) from 1825 to 1872. His wrote several commentaries on books in the New Testament, and his *What Is Darwinism?*, published in 1873, contains one of the earliest attacks on Charles Darwin's theory of evolution. Probably Hodge's most enduring work is his three-volume *Systematic Theology*, which appeared in the early 1870s. He trained more than 2,000 students during the years he taught at Princeton. His son A. A. Hodge and his student Benjamin B. WARFIELD both maintained the conservative tradition within Presbyterianism and made important contributions to debates on biblical authority during the fundamentalist (see FUNDAMENTALISM) controversy in the late 19th and early 20th century.

Hodge served for nearly six decades as a professor at Princeton. He died there on June 19, 1878.

GHS, Jr.

Bibliography: Peter Hicks, *The Philosophy of Charles Hodge: A 19th Century Evangelical Approach to Rea-son, Knowledge, and Truth* (Lewiston, N.Y.: Edwin Mellen Press, 1977); W. Andrew Hoffecker, *Piety and the Princeton Theologians: Archibald Alexander, Charles Hodge, and Benjamin Warfield* (Grand Rapids, Mich.: Baker Book House, 1981).

Holiness movement   An American Protestant movement that began in the mid-19th century, Holiness focused on the possibility of a Christian believer's gaining complete freedom from sin in the present life. This conviction first found expression among two major groups of Americans: METHODISTS seeking a return to the simplicity of the early history of their denomination, and participants in the revivals and reform activities inspired by the SECOND GREAT AWAKENING. By the end of the 19th century, large numbers of Holiness advocates had become alienated from the mainline denominations and began forming new congregations and churches, notably, the CHURCH OF THE NAZARENE and the SALVATION ARMY. Holiness denominations today emphasize the gifts of the Holy Spirit, including divine healing, and lively, enthusiastic forms of worship.

According to traditional Protestant teaching, Christians pass through two main stages on the way to salvation. At the first stage (JUSTIFICATION), one's sins are forgiven by God; at the second stage (SANCTIFICATION), believers are enabled to live godly lives. The Holiness movement has always had its greatest institutional impact upon American Methodist denominations, for, while Calvinists such as the Presbyterians have generally accentuated the importance of justification, Methodists have stressed sanctification. As Methodist founder John Wesley taught, serious Christians might even attain release from all conscious sin and achieve moral PERFECTIONISM. Holiness leaders now speak of "entire sanctification" or the "second blessing" of the Holy Spirit as the experience that perfects the believer's will.

Charles G. FINNEY, the famed revivalist of the Second Great Awakening, helped popularize Wesley's perfectionist ideals in mid-19th-century America. Finney believed that human beings could and should strive to seek God's blessing. Despite the persistent Calvinist belief that men and women were predestined for either heaven or hell, Finney taught that God had given Christians power to help decide their eternal fate. After the founding of Oberlin College in Ohio in 1833, Finney, the school's first professor of theology, and Asa MAHAN, Oberlin's president, explored together the doctrines of sanctification and perfection in Wesley's writings. In 1839 in *Scripture Doctrine of Christian Perfection,* Mahan described how believers might attain victory over sin through the presence of Jesus Christ within their hearts.

Phoebe PALMER, a lay Methodist evangelist, was another prominent figure in the early Holiness movement. She led a series of weekly prayer meetings for "the Promotion of Holiness," gatherings that featured prayer and personal religious testimonies. In Palmer's view, holiness was immediately available to the believer through faith in Jesus Christ. Conversion was the first blessing of God's grace. Entire sanctification occurred next, when a believer surrendered everything to God. The simplicity of this message won many disciples to Palmer's cause.

The urban revivals of 1857 and 1858, with their noontime prayer meetings and interdenominational lay leadership, further spread Christian perfectionist beliefs. In the sanguine religious climate of mid 19th century America, the expectation that a person could overcome sin seemed incontrovertible to many Christians, even members of Calvinist denominations. In 1858 Presbyterian minister William E. Boardman, a frequent participant in Palmer's prayer meetings, published *The Higher Christian Life* (see HIGHER CHRISTIAN LIFE MOVEMENT). This book furnished a classic statement of how a Christian might win victory over sin. Boardman was instrumental in attracting his fellow Presbyterians, as well as Quakers, Congregationalists, and Baptists, to the growing Holiness revival.

The same spiritual impulses that helped build up Christian denominations sometimes divided them as well. For example, the political implications of Holiness doctrines—the belief that personal and social sanctity were related—occasioned a major exodus from the ranks of the Methodist Episcopal Church in the 1840s. Although Methodists had once considered slaveholding to be sinful and forbade those who owned slaves to be church members, they moderated their views in the early 19th century. But rising abolitionist sentiment in the North brought the issue to the center of the church's life. When his denomination failed to condemn slavery unequivocally, New England clergyman Orange Scott convinced several thousand Methodists to withdraw and join him in organizing the Wesleyan Methodist Church. This denomination later became one of the principal Holiness churches in the United States.

The CIVIL WAR (1861–1865) brought the initial phase of the Holiness movement to an end, and religious attention centered instead on men in the armies. Not long after the war's conclusion, however, Methodist pastors John Inskip and William B. Osborn issued a call for a camp meeting to promote Christian sanctification. This event, held in Vineland, New Jersey, in July 1867, marked the beginning of a new stage in the Holiness movement. After the Vineland camp meeting, many involved in it formed what became known as the National Holiness Association and chose Inskip as their president. Although the National Holiness Association (now the Christian Holiness Association) was founded as an interdenominational organization, its focus quickly changed and became almost exclusively Methodist. Led by a close-knit group of Methodist revivalists, the association sponsored 52 CAMP MEETINGS between 1867 and 1883.

In the early 1870s, the husband-and-wife team of Robert Pearsall and Hannah Whitall Smith, who had each experienced an emotional "baptism of the Holy Spirit" a few years before, joined William Boardman in promoting Holiness teaching in Great Britain. At Oxford, England, in the summer of 1874, a convention was held in which the Smiths, Boardman, and Asa Mahan all participated. Anglican clergyman T. D. Harford Battersby, who had been inspired by the Oxford convention, organized an open-air conference at his parish in Keswick in July 1875. This Keswick conference soon became an annual event and one of the principal institutions of the Holiness movement.

By the mid-1870s, a growing spirit of "comeoutism" emerged in American Methodism. Despite its official commitment to keeping Methodists loyal to their denomination, the National Holiness Association tended to encourage, first, division and, eventually, the formation of new churches. Methodist denominational leaders also grew concerned about the emotionalism displayed at Holiness gatherings. When John P. Brooks, editor of *The Banner of Holiness*, left the Methodist Episcopal Church in 1885, he advocated the renunciation of denominations that suppressed Holiness and the creation of independent fellowships. "*In* the world but not *of* the world" became a popular Holiness aphorism, and participants in the movement began to condemn the worldliness they perceived among church members who had not experienced sanctification.

Daniel Sidney Warner's Church of God in Anderson, Indiana, was the first new church body spawned by the Holiness movement. Warner had been a member of a small German Pietist sect from which he had been expelled in 1878 after his experience of entire sanctification. Believing that all existing denominations were antithetical to genuine Christianity, Warner and five others announced in 1881 that they had entirely freed themselves from ecclesiastical organizations. Only God, they claimed, could know who were true Christians. Despite these initial anti-institutional beliefs, Church of God leaders later decided that, while the church itself could not be organized, the church's work should be. The Church of God is now headquartered at Anderson, Indiana. Emphasizing the restoration of primitive Christianity and faith healing, it has slightly more than 230,000 members.

Two of the largest Holiness bodies, the CHURCH OF THE NAZARENE and the Pilgrim Holiness Church, developed in a fashion similar to Warner's Church of God. Individuals first withdrew from the Methodist Episcopal Church, then formed independent Holiness fellowships, and finally organized separate denominations.

Phineas Bresee was pastor of the First Methodist Church in Los Angeles when members of his congregation requested him to call evangelists from the National Holiness Association to lead a revival. Bresee himself soon underwent an experience of sanctification that led him to renounce the Methodist ministry in 1895. Increasingly disturbed by the worldliness he alleged was corrupting American Methodism, Bresee founded a congregation known as the Church of the Nazarene that would welcome, rather than reject, the poor. The Church of the Nazarene quickly grew, and other Holiness bodies merged with it. The denomination reported an American membership of approximately 600,000 members in 2000.

Martin Wells Knapp, a Methodist pastor and founder of the Pilgrim Holiness Church, experienced sanctification in 1889 while reading the Bible. Although he organized an aggressive Holiness revival in Cincinnati, Ohio, he remained loyal to the Methodist Episcopal Church for a time. In 1897, however, Knapp and a handful of followers formed the International Holiness Union and Prayer League, and in 1901 he withdrew from Methodism altogether. Mergers with several other Holiness organizations eventually led to the formation of the Pilgrim Holiness Church in 1922. In 1968, the Wesleyan Methodist Church and the Pilgrim Holiness Church united and became the Wesleyan Church, a denomination that now contains about 110,000 members.

A number of other Protestant groups, not strictly Holiness denominations, were also influenced by the movement in the late 19th century. The SALVATION ARMY, for example, was founded by British Methodist William Booth in London in 1865 and brought to the United States in 1880. Booth and his wife, Catherine, intended the charitable system they developed to speed the work of saving the souls of the downtrodden. Acts of social relief were thought both to symbolize God's love for sinful, fallen humanity and demonstrate that the Salvationists took the social as well as the spiritual aspects of Christianity seriously. Booth's famous *In Darkest England and the Way Out* (1890) boldly proclaimed his goal: to save souls among a class of people often ignored by the more traditional Christian churches.

A. B. Simpson left the Presbyterian Church in 1881 in order to serve those neglected by traditional church structures. He had experienced the baptism of the Holy Spirit after reading William Boardman's *The Higher Christian Life* in 1874. Seven years later, after feeling that his weakened heart had been miraculously healed, Simpson was rebaptized by immersion. He organized a number of independent evangelistic and missionary ministries over the next few years, culminating in the formation of the Christian and Missionary Alliance in 1897. Simpson coined a phrase that expressed his version of the essential truths of the Christian gospel: "Christ our Saviour, Sanctifier, Healer, and Coming King." Although the Christian and Missionary Alliance was not intended to be a new denomination, but simply a movement bringing people from many churches together, by the 1960s its leadership acknowledged that it, too, had become a separate denomination.

In the early 20th century, a crisis occurred that further disrupted the already disparate Holiness movement and marked the birth of another new religious phenomenon. Holiness advocates for many years had used the term "baptism of the Holy Spirit" to describe the "second blessing" or "deeper work of grace" that accompanied entire sanctification. Some preachers began to identify speaking in tongues, the miraculous gift that Jesus' disciples received on the day of Pentecost (Acts 2), as the definitive sign that one had received Spirit baptism. The AZUSA STREET REVIVAL, which began in Los Angeles in April 1906, is generally regarded as the genesis of American PENTECOSTALISM. At that time, Holiness leader William J. SEYMOUR gathered thousands of people into the three-year revival he led. Inspired by speaking in tongues and extraordinary healings, Seymour's followers organized new churches based upon Pentecostal teachings.

Because Holiness groups stress the Holy Spirit's power, worship in this tradition is enthusiastic and often accompanied by shouts of praise. In some churches, worshipers lift their arms into the air to show that they have been moved by the Spirit. Unlike Pentecostals, however, Holiness Christians disapprove of speaking in tongues. Prayers for healing also are routinely offered and participants report experiences of being healed. Life on earth, Holiness doctrine teaches, is a continual struggle to renounce the world, root out sin, and attain eternal salvation.

GHS, Jr.

Bibliography: Melvin E. Dieter, *The Holiness Revival of the Nineteenth Century* (Metuchen, N.J.: Scarecrow Press, 1980); Charles Edwin Jones, *Perfectionist Persuasion: The Holiness Movement and American Methodism, 1867–1936* (Metuchen, N.J.: Scarecrow Press, 1974); Timothy L. Smith, *Revivalism and Social Reform in Mid-Nineteenth Century America* (1957; Baltimore: Johns Hopkins University Press, 1980).

homosexuality   See METROPOLITAN COMMUNITY CHURCH; SEXUALITY.

Hooker, Thomas (1586–1647)   As a leading Puritan divine, a founder of Connecticut, and driving force behind the CAMBRIDGE PLATFORM—the first official statement of the religious and political views of New England PURITANISM—Thomas Hooker played a major role in the development of CONGREGATIONALISM and colonial New England generally.

Like many of his Puritan contemporaries, Hooker, born July 7, 1586, was educated at Cambridge University. After receiving his B.A. degree in 1608, he remained at Cambridge as a fellow until 1618. As minister of the Anglican church in Esher, Surrey (1620–1626), and at St. Mary's in Chelmsford (1626–1630), Hooker developed a reputation as a brilliant and powerful preacher. His preaching drew large crowds and the attention of church authorities, who summoned him before a court of inquiry to question him about his Puritan tendencies.

Realizing that such a summons bode ill, Hooker jumped bond and escaped to Holland. In Holland he served as the minister of several English churches, but his views on church government brought him into conflicts with religious authorities there as well, and in 1633 he sailed to New England. Arriving in the MASSACHUSETTS BAY COLONY in September of that year, Hooker received a call from the church at Newtown (now Cambridge), outside Boston.

A scarcity of land and the awareness that Massachusetts was not big enough to contain the theological differences between him and John COTTON led Hooker and his congregation to the Connecticut River valley. There they founded the settlement of Hartford.

Hooker led in the drafting of the "Fundamental Orders," the basic law for the new colony of Connecticut. To a much greater extent than in Massachusetts Bay, political and religious government in Connecticut were grounded on popular consent. Church membership was not a requirement for voting, and limits on civil authorities were much greater.

There were religious changes as well. Under Hooker's leadership restrictions on church membership were eased. Hooker's theology also allowed for a greater role for human action in conversion, and with it a more active position for the ministry in bringing about acceptance of God's saving grace.

This greater freedom, however, did not include a separation between church and state. Hooker's view of society was no different from that of his fellow Puritans. The civil law, while forbidden to compel church membership, ought to guarantee conformity of religious behavior. Those who threatened religious unity and social cohesion deserved civil punishment. Given these views, it is not surprising that Hooker was repeatedly asked to publicly defend Puritan orthodoxy. In 1635, while still at Newtown, Hooker was chosen by colonial authorities to refute Roger WILLIAMS's views on the freedom of conscience. He served as a moderator of the 1637 synod called to condemn Anne HUTCHINSON and her followers (see ANTINOMIAN CONTROVERSY). At this synod Hooker first broached to Governor John WINTHROP the idea for a general meeting to forge a document detailing the Puritans' statement of faith and church governance.

Nothing came of this idea until September 1646, when the first of a series of ministerial assemblies met to debate those issues. Hooker was a leading voice in the deliberations but did not live to see the adoption of the final document incorporating most of his views on church government, the Cambridge Platform of August 1648. He had died on July 7, 1647, a victim of an epidemic that swept the region.

EQ

Bibliography: John H. Ball, *Chronicling the World's Windings: Thomas Hooker and his Morphology of Conversion* (Lanham, Md.: University Press of America, 1992); Sargent Bush, *The Writings of Thomas Hooker: Spiritual Adventure in Two Worlds* (Madison: University of Wisconsin Press, 1980); Frank C. Shuffelton, *Thomas Hooker, 1586–1647* (Princeton: Princeton University Press, 1977).

Hopkins, Emma Curtis (1853–1925)

One of the founders of the NEW THOUGHT movement, Emma Curtis Hopkins was not the first woman to inspire a new religious movement in the United States, but she was the first who unabashedly celebrated her womanhood and called upon the name of a decidedly female God.

Hopkins was born in Killingly, Connecticut, in 1853 and attended Woodstock Academy. She married in 1874, but the marriage was short-lived. Hopkins's career as one of the most famous apostates from the Church of Christ (Scientist) began when she moved to Boston in 1883 and enrolled in a class taught by Mary Baker EDDY, the charismatic founder of CHRISTIAN SCIENCE. Three months later Hopkins emerged as a Christian Science practitioner. She served as the editor of the *Christian Science Journal* from 1884 until 1885.

Hopkins broke with Eddy in the mid-1880s. One major source of tension between the two women was Hopkins's eclecticism. Whereas Eddy utilized her interpretive skills almost exclusively on Christian scriptures, Hopkins looked to mystics and philosophers from diverse religious traditions, including the religions of Asia, for spiritual insight. Hopkins's comparative bent is especially evident in her 12-volume lifework, *High Mysticism: A Series of Twelve Studies in the Wisdom of the Sages of the Ages* (1920–1922). In it she argues that both Jesus and Gautama Buddha were practitioners of the "spiritual science" of mental health.

Hopkins moved in 1886 to Chicago, outside the immediate sphere of Eddy's influence, and began her own ministry as an independent Christian Science teacher and practitioner. She founded the Hopkins Metaphysical Association and the Emma Hopkins College of Christian Science (later renamed the Christian Science Theological Seminary) as alternatives to Eddy's church and her Massachusetts Metaphysical College. Hopkins also published her own periodical, the *Christian Metaphysician* (1887–1897). Despite denunciations by Eddy, Hopkins's initiatives were surprisingly successful. One year after her move to Chicago she had organized followers in 17 cities across the United States.

There was from the beginning an incipient feminism in mainstream Christian Science, but Eddy, like Theosophical Society founder Helena Petrovna BLAVATSKY, downplayed both her status as a woman and the protofeminist elements in her theology. Hopkins did just the opposite. Her version of the Christian Trinity postulated three aspects of God, each manifested in a given historical epoch. God the Father lorded over the time of the Old Testament patriarchs. God the Son served both Jews and Gentiles during New Testament times. And God the Mother-Spirit was incarnating even as women were emerging from domesticity and moving into the public square in the late-19th century. In 1889 Hopkins translated this theology into practice by becoming a New Thought bishop and beginning to ordain women to the ministry. She thus became the first woman in America to ascend to the episcopacy.

Many of Hopkins's students went on to start metaphysical movements of their own. Charles and Myrtle Fillmore cofounded the Unity School of Christianity; Malinda Cramer taught Divine Science; and one of Hopkins's last students, Ernest Holmes, established the Church of Religious Science. Together with her students, Hopkins developed the spiritual alternative to Christian Science now known as New Thought.

SRP

Bibliography: Emma Curtis Hopkins, *High Mysticism: A Series of Twelve Studies in the Wisdom of the Sages of the Ages* (Santa Monica, Calif.: DeVorss, 1974); Beryl Satter, *Each Mind a Kingdom: American Women, Sexual Purity, and the New Thought Movement, 1875–1920* (Berkeley: University of California Press, 1999).

Hopkins, Samuel (1721–1803)

Samuel Hopkins was a Congregational minister, a theologian, and the most important disciple of Jonathan EDWARDS. Hopkins helped formulate a theology known as the NEW DIVINITY, which reconciled traditional Calvinist doctrines about human depravity and divine sovereignty to the

A student of Jonathan Edwards, Samuel Hopkins inspired the temperance, antislavery, and missionary movements that flourished in 19th-century Protestant churches.

egalitarian moral framework of early 19th-century American EVANGELICALISM. Hopkins believed that God could turn the hearts of sinners to righteousness, infuse Christians with "disinterested benevolence," and lead them into activities of social and moral reform.

Hopkins was born in Waterbury, Connecticut, on September 17, 1721. He graduated from Yale College in 1741. Profoundly affected by the commencement sermon Edwards delivered to the Yale students that year, Hopkins elected to study for the ministry under Edwards's tutelage at Northampton, Massachusetts. Between 1743 and 1769, Hopkins was minister of a frontier church in what is now Great Barrington, Massachusetts. Although his strict views on church membership forced him to leave Great Barrington, he was called in 1769 to the First Church in Newport, Rhode Island. He served in Newport for the remainder of his life.

Hopkins's most significant contribution to American theology was his teaching on sin. Sin, he believed, was embodied primarily in human selfishness and in acts of self-love, while true Christian virtue consisted of selflessness, or "disinterested benevolence." Thus, the genuinely converted led moral lives not because they thought good deeds improved their standing before God, but because they knew human goodness manifested God's grace and mercy. This position led Hopkins to conclude that believers should even be willing to be damned for the glory of God. Although his critics charged that these teachings would lead Americans to abandon earthly concerns altogether, the opposite in fact occurred. Hopkins stressed that the soul's regeneration depended upon an active exercise of the human will, and as a result of his dual emphasis on conversion and benevolence, he inspired a passion for social reform that later found expression in the TEMPERANCE, ABOLITIONISM and missionary campaigns.

Hopkins was himself located in an important port city where he could observe the slave trade firsthand. He was among the first Americans to condemn the institution of slavery. Believing it made a mockery of Christian efforts to evangelize the African peoples, he insisted that slaves were moral beings, equal in God's eyes to whites and in all ways deserving of humane treatment. In 1776 he sent a pamphlet to the members of the Continental Congress. How could Americans complain about the injustices they suffered at the hands of the British, Hopkins asked, when they also enslaved thousands of their fellow human beings in the colonies?

Hopkins's chief theological writings are contained in his two-volume *System of Doctrines,* published in 1793. He died at Newport on December 20, 1803.

GHS, Jr.

Bibliography: Joseph A. Conforti, *Samuel Hopkins and the New Divinity Movement: Calvinism, the Congregational Ministry, and Reform in New England Between the Great Awakenings* (Grand Rapids, Mich.: Eerdmans, 1981).

Howe, Julia Ward (1819–1910)

Julia Ward Howe was a social reformer, champion of ABOLITIONISM, and author. Her poem "Battle Hymn of the Republic" formed the lyrics for a popular song that inspired northerners dedicated to the destruction of slavery during the CIVIL WAR.

Daughter of a wealthy Episcopal banker, Julia Ward was born on May 27, 1819, in New York City. She married Samuel Gridley Howe, a doctor, reformer, and head of the Perkins Institute for the Blind in Boston, in 1843. After her marriage, Howe became increasingly attracted to Unitarianism and began attending James Freeman CLARKE's Church of the Disciples, which was noted for both its theological and its social radicalism. Howe also grew into an ardent supporter of the antislavery movement. She entertained the abolitionist crusader John Brown in her home and believed that his execution for inciting insurrection among Virginia slaves in 1859 was "holy and glorious."

After the Civil War broke out in 1861, Howe visited a Union army camp in Washington, D.C. She was so inspired by the military scenes she witnessed that, on her return to Boston, she composed a poem to accompany the popular song, "John Brown's Body," she had heard the troops singing. The "Battle Hymn of the Republic" was published in the February 1862 issue of *The Atlantic Monthly*. It rang with the rhetoric of POSTMILLENNIALISM and envisioned the Union cause as part of the eternal conflict of the forces of God against the powers of evil: "Mine eyes have seen the glory of the coming of the Lord:/ He is trampling out the vintage where the grapes of wrath are stored;/ He hath loosed the fateful lightning of His terrible swift sword:/ His truth is marching on." Although Howe's lyrics were not as

Both sides claimed God's blessing during the Civil War. Abolitionist Julia Ward Howe wrote the Union's crusading anthem, "Battle Hymn of the Republic."

popular with the soldiers as the simpler "John Brown's Body" version, they increased in popularity over the years and eventually brought her lasting fame.

After her husband's death in 1876, Howe actively espoused the cause of women's rights and served in the American Woman Suffrage Association and the Women's International Peace Association. An advocate of the ordination of women, she herself often preached in Unitarian pulpits. Although she published two books of poetry, as well as essays and drama, Howe's prominence as a writer rested principally upon the "Battle Hymn." In 1907 she became the first woman elected to the American Academy of Arts and Letters.

Howe died on October 17, 1910. She was so beloved that 4,000 people attended her funeral at Boston's Symphony Hall, and the president of the American Unitarian Association delivered the eulogy.

GHS, Jr.

Bibliography: Deborah Pickman Clifford, *Mine Eyes Have Seen the Glory: A Biography of Julia Ward Howe* (Boston: Little, Brown, 1979); Gary Williams, *Hungry Heart: The Literary Emergence of Julia Ward Howe* (Amherst: University of Massachusetts Press, 1999).

Hsi Lai Temple   Hsi Lai Temple is the largest Buddhist monastic complex in the Western Hemisphere and the most impressive architectural expression of Chinese BUDDHISM in the United States. Located in Hacienda Heights, California, in the vicinity of Los Angeles, Hsi Lai was built at a cost of $30 million and consecrated in 1988. The 20-acre temple complex includes not only a main shrine but also a meditation hall, lecture hall, library, international conference center, living quarters for monks and nuns, and lodging for visitors. A Buddhist college called Hsi Lai University is located nearby.

Hsi Lai, which means "Coming to the West," is an outreach project of the Fo Kuang Shan ("Buddha's Light Mountain") monastery in Taiwan, founded in 1967 by the Buddhist reformer Master Hsing Yun. Hsi Lai is also affiliated with the Buddha's Light International Association (BLIA), a lay society established by Hsing Yun in 1992. At the end of the 1990s, the United States had 19 Fo Kuang Shan–affiliated temples and centers and 18 BLIA chapters. The vast majority of BLIA members and Hsi Lai monks and nuns are ethnically Chinese, but some African Americans and Caucasians also participate, and many of the temple's activities are conducted in English as well as Chinese languages.

Fo Kuang Buddhism teaches "humanistic Buddhism." Scholars have described this socially engaged form of Buddhism as an effort to translate hopes for a better existence in the afterlife (the "Pure Land" in Buddhist parlance) into action for a better life here and now on earth. In an effort to create a this worldly utopia, Hsi Lai offers a wide variety of activities, including prayer services, meditation sessions, classes in Chinese languages and martial arts, summer camps, arts exhibitions, charitable events, and radio and television programs. The temple also promotes Buddhist ecumenism by sponsoring events that bring together American Buddhists of different nationalities and sects.

In the many countries in which his organizations operate, Master Hsing Yun has worked hard to cultivate ties with political leaders. In 1996 in Hacienda Heights, that strategy backfired when Hsi Lai was drawn into a national political scandal. At an April 29, 1996, visit by Vice President Al Gore, nuns raised more than $100,000 for the Democratic Party. Soon the media were portraying Hsi Lai monastics as secret agents for Taiwan while the United States Congress and Justice Department were investigating Hsi Lai leaders for violations of campaign finance laws. Defenders of the temple denounced the controversy as a tempest in a teapot that represented a return to the anti-Asian "yellow peril" rhetoric directed against Chinese and Japanese Americans in the 19th century.

Vice President Albert Gore's alleged fund-raising at this wealthy Chinese temple was used against him in his campaign for president of the United States in 2000. *(Cartoon by Mike Getetoz)*

Both the Hsi Lai temple and the BLIA have endured the controversy. The temple complex, which now houses roughly a hundred monks and nuns, remains a major tourist attraction for Buddhists and non-Buddhists alike. Hsi Lai University is beginning to attract a wide variety of American Buddhists. And Hsi Lai Temple's long list of activities keeps laypeople returning regularly to Hacienda Heights for a taste of the fruits of Buddhist monasticism.

SRP

Bibliography: Stuart Chandler, "Placing Palms Together: Religious Cultural Dimensions of the Hsi Lai Temple Political Donations Controversy," in Duncan Ryūken Williams and Christopher S. Queen, eds., *American Buddhism: Methods and Findings in Recent Scholarship* (Surrey, U.K.: Curzon Press, 1998), 36–56; www.hsilai.org (Hsi Lai Temple).

Hubbard, L. Ron   See SCIENTOLOGY.

Huguenots
The Huguenots, as they were popularly known (their name has no clear origin), were adherents of the REFORMED TRADITION in France. Although Huguenots arrived in the New World as early as the mid 16th century, a number of factors militated against the continuation of a separate French Reformed Church in America. Because the principal identity of the Huguenots had been religious rather than ethnic or national, most abandoned their French roots and joined other denominations, notably, the Dutch Reformed Church and the Church of England, by the mid-18th century.

French reformer John Calvin, who had been converted to Protestantism in 1534, settled permanently in Geneva, Switzerland, in 1541. Sending missionaries back to France to advance the Protestant cause in his native land, Calvin helped the Huguenot movement grow rapidly between 1540 and 1560. After a series of brutal religious wars that began in 1562 (including the infamous St. Bartholomew's Day Massacre of August 1572), the Huguenot leader Henry of Navarre succeeded to the

French throne as Henry IV. Although he renounced his Protestant allegiance in 1593, Henry eventually issued the Edict of Nantes (1598) and granted toleration to Protestants. Still, the edict offered only civil rights to the Huguenots, not approval of their religious faith, and harassment soon increased again. During the reign of Louis XIV, all forms of Protestant public worship were banned, and in October 1685 an order was issued to destroy church buildings and arrest ministers.

For many years prior to the revocation of the Edict of Nantes, Huguenots had been seeking refuge in other European countries. Of more than 2 million French Protestants, 400,000 emigrated from France in that period. Some made their way to America, most settling in the vicinity of what is now Charleston, South Carolina (as early as 1562), and near present-day New York City. Since Huguenot immigration to America came mainly through the Netherlands and England, close connections had been formed with the Reformed churches in those countries. Some of the first settlers at Plymouth (1620) and New Amsterdam (1626) were Huguenots with Anglicized or Dutch names. Indeed, several ministers of the Dutch Reformed Church in New York made a habit of preaching in French. By 1683 the New York Huguenots had secured a pastor of their own and formed churches in New Rochelle and New Paltz. By the end of the 17th century, French Reformed churches were established in New York City, Boston, Virginia, and South Carolina.

The Huguenots usually arrived in America in small groups, often without pastors to establish French-speaking congregations. Eager to forget France and its unhappy past, many chose to adopt the culture of the English and Dutch Protestants who had given them refuge. As a result, the French Reformed in New York generally became members of the Dutch Reformed churches (even the "French" church at New Paltz started to keep its records in Dutch about 50 years after its founding), while

Huguenots in the South tended to become Anglicans. In all, approximately 20,000 Huguenots came to America before the Revolution, the last migration of any consequence occurring in 1712 with the settlement of a group of French Protestants in Lancaster County, Pennsylvania.

Although individual Huguenots and their descendants were influential as members of the legal, medical, and commercial elite of the colonies, by 1750 a distinct Huguenot *religious* presence had virtually disappeared. The French Reformed community was almost effortlessly absorbed into the prevailing Anglo-American Protestant culture. Solely in the area around Charleston were the Huguenots numerous enough to have a major impact on a region, yet the memory of their presence even in the South Carolina low country today continues only in the surnames of prominent families such as the Legares, the Ravenels, and the Manigaults. And while in the North the names of prominent citizens like Paul Revere, Henry David Thoreau, and John Greenleaf Whittier suggest a common Huguenot past, little else "French" remains about these important figures.

GHS, Jr.

Bibliography: Jon Butler, *The Huguenots in America: A Refugee People in New World Society* (Cambridge, Mass.: Harvard University Press, 1983).

humanism   See SECULAR HUMANISM.

Humanist Manifesto   This proclamation of humanist values, signed in 1933 by a group of Unitarian ministers and several notable philosophers, articulated a religious acceptance of modernity (see MODERNISM, PROTESTANT). Its optimistic assessment of the future failed to attract wide support.

In the early 20th century the battle between religious liberals and conservatives in America intensified with the acceptance of SECULARISM among a broad number of intellectuals. For Unitarians (see UNITARIAN UNIVERSALIST ASSOCIATION) humanism became an increasingly attrac-

tive alternative to what many saw as an outmoded Christian liberalism (see LIBERALISM, THEOLOGICAL) that was still trying to reconcile the forms and symbols of the faith with modern science and values. Humanists, often representatives of what philosopher George Santyana called the "genteel tradition" in America, saw themselves as eagerly embracing the modern institutions and values, providing an important naturalistic framework for the discussion of pressing moral and social questions.

By the early 1930s humanists feared that American culture was returning to the religious infancy of its past. Under the press of social and economic crisis, NEO-ORTHODOXY was gaining the upper hand among serious intellectuals. Unitarians found in humanism the greatest rallying force since TRANSCENDENTALISM had swept through the denomination in the 19th century. In general, humanists favored naturalism over supernaturalism, science and reason over faith, democracy over tyranny, and human experience over revelation.

Eager to bring a clear perspective to bear in times characterized by both the hope of the New Deal and alarm over the rise of fascism in Germany, in 1933 a group of midwestern Unitarian humanists commissioned philosopher Roy Wood Sellars to draft a public statement of humanist goals and values. The document, a set of theses for debate, circulated among intellectuals. Some ignored or disparaged it, others amended it. In the end the "Humanist Manifesto" appeared in a spring 1933 issue of *The New Humanist*, bearing the signatures of 34 individuals, including John DEWEY. Half the signers were Unitarian clergy.

The manifesto issued 15 assertions, denying the divine creation of the universe and supernatural intervention in the order of things and urging that religion focus on satisfying the human search for self-fulfillment. While consistently using the word *religious* to indicate the new point of view advocated by humanists, the manifesto added that "there will be no uniquely religious emotions and attitudes of the kind hitherto associated with belief in the supernatural."

The manifesto is probably most significant for the fact that it failed to gather much support, though it aroused the suspicions of conservatives. A few months after publication, one humanist concluded it "fell like a dud in the battle-scarred career of American theological thought." Some of the original signers sought to revive and update it with a "Humanist Manifesto II" in 1973 and a "Secular Humanist Declaration in 1980." In its most recent form, *Humanist Manifesto 2000*, signers call for global institutions such as a world parliament to secure human rights and overcome poverty, war, and environmental degradation.

MG

Bibliography: Paul Kurtz, *Humanist Manifesto 2000: A Call for a New Planetary Humanism* (Amherst, N.Y.: Prometheus Books, 1999); David B. Parke, *The Epic of Unitarianism: Original Writings from the History of Liberal Religion* (Boston: Unitarian Universalist Association, 1980); http://www.iheu.org (International Humanist and Ethical Union).

Hunt, Ernest Shinkaku (1878–1967)

One of the earliest and most energetic westernizers of BUDDHISM, Ernest Shinkaku Hunt served as the director of the English department of the Honpa Hongwanji Buddhist Mission of Hawaii, an outgrowth of the Jodo Shinshu ("True Pure Land") sect of Mahayana Buddhism loosely affiliated with the BUDDHIST CHURCHES OF AMERICA. Hunt also founded the Western Buddhist Order and brought the International Buddhist Institute to Hawaii.

Born in England in 1878, Hunt graduated from Eastbourne College in Sussex. He encountered Buddhism while traveling through India during a stint with the British merchant marine. Intent on becoming a priest in the Church of England, he enrolled in an Anglican seminary but converted to Buddhism before being ordained.

In 1915 he moved to Hawaii with his wife, Dorothy Hunt, who was also a Buddhist.

Together the Hunts established Buddhist Sunday schools, where they instilled in the English-speaking Buddhist youth of Hawaii a love of all forms of Buddhism. In 1924 the Hunts were ordained in a joint ceremony by Yemyo Imamura, bishop of the Honpa Hongwanji Buddhist Mission of Hawaii. During this first Buddhist ordination ceremony in Hawaii, Ernest Hunt was given the name Shinkaku ("true-light bearer"). In 1926 Hunt ascended to the head of the English department, an arm of the Honpa Hongwanji Buddhist Mission of Hawaii that specialized in ministering to English-speaking Buddhists.

The Hunts focused their efforts on two groups: European Americans and Nisei, or second-generation Japanese Americans (especially Japanese-American youths). To these constituencies they preached an Americanized version of Buddhism. For use in Buddhist services, Ernest Hunt compiled a Buddhist catechism and a widely used English-language liturgical manual called the *Vade Mecum* (1932). Dorothy Hunt composed English-language Buddhist hymns that would soon be sung not only in Hawaii but also on the United States mainland.

In 1928 the Hunts gathered approximately 60 of their students into an English-speaking branch of the Honpa Hongwanji called the Western Buddhist Order. What drew students to this organization was its ecumenical stance. Although officially a part of the Jodo Shinshu sect, the Western Buddhist Order opened its arms to all Buddhists.

The Hunts collaborated with Bishop Imamura in 1929 to bring to Hawaii a chapter of the International Buddhist Institute (IBI), an ecumenical organization based in Japan that aimed to bring together all the world's Buddhists. Imamura became president of the institute, while Ernest Hunt was elected its vice president.

In all their endeavors, the Hunts promoted a Buddhism that was both nonsectarian and socially activistic. Champions of a Buddhist version of the SOCIAL GOSPEL, they inculcated in their Sunday school students not only Buddhist teachings but also Buddhist practices rooted in an ethic of active good will. Members of the Hunts' organizations visited prisons and hospitals and taught the blind and the deaf.

The ecumenical work of the Hunts ground to a halt when Bishop Imamura was replaced after his death in 1932 by bishops hostile to the ecumenical and internationalist agenda shared by Imamura and the Hunts. During World War II and the period of persecution of Japanese Americans, Hunt ministered to Buddhists in Hawaii privately and at his Island Paradise School. Eventually he made his way into the Soto Zen tradition. Ordained in that tradition in 1953, he became 10 years later the first non-Asian priest in the West to achieve the lofty rank of Osho. He died in Honolulu in 1967 at the age of 90.

SRP

Bibliography: Ernest Hunt, *The Vade Mecum, a Book Containing an Order of Ceremonies for Use in Buddhist Temples* (Honolulu: Honpa Hongwanji Buddhist Mission, 1927); Louise H. Hunter, *Buddhism in Hawaii: Its Impact on a Yankee Community* (Honolulu: University of Hawaii Press, 1971).

Hurley, George Willie (1884–1943)

A relatively unknown contemporary of Father DIVINE, Marcus GARVEY, and "Sweet Daddy" GRACE, George Willie Hurley founded the Universal Hagar's Spiritual Church (UHSC) in Detroit in 1923. Revered by some of his followers as divine, Hurley was one of the most important figures in African-American SPIRITUALISM.

Born in rural Georgia in 1884, Father Hurley was raised a Baptist. After studying for the Baptist ministry at Tuskegee Institute, he converted to Methodism. In 1919 he and his wife, Cassie Bell Martin Hurley, moved to Detroit, where they attended a black storefront church in the Holiness (see HOLINESS MOVEMENT) tradition. In the early 1920s Hurley became a member of the International Spiritual Church and began a preaching ministry. Prompted by a

vision, he established the UHSC in 1923. By the time of his death in 1943, Hurley's association boasted 37 churches in eight states. He was succeeded in his post as the spiritual head of the UHSC by his widow, "Mother" C. B. Hurley. Since Mother Hurley's death in 1960, the church has been run by a group called the Wiseman Board.

Hurleyites are educated in the ways of the UHSC through a number of means, including a School of Mediumship and Psychology, which according to Hurley is a modern resurfacing of the Great School of the Prophets, an ancient esoteric institute attended by, among others, Jesus. In this school, students learn how to communicate with spirits of the dead. As they are initiated into higher and higher mysteries they become "uncrowned mediums," "crowned mediums" and finally "spiritual advisers." The church also runs a secret order for men and women called The Knights of the All Seeing Eye. This order has its own rituals and titles.

Hurley's eclectic gospel mixes elements from spiritualism, ROMAN CATHOLICISM, black Protestantism (see AFRICAN-AMERICAN RELIGION), VODOU, FREEMASONRY, astrology, and black nationalism. Perhaps the most shocking element in that gospel is the affirmation that Hurley was himself divine. Hurley taught a dispensational theology in which Adam, the God of the Taurian Age, yielded to Abraham, the God of the Arian Age, who yielded to Jesus, the God of the Piscean Age. Jesus was then superseded by Hurley, the "black God of this Age." Hurley will rule earth in this capacity for seven millennia.

Hurley distinguished himself from other leaders in the black Spiritualist tradition by eagerly mixing religion and politics. His message contained a biting critique of segregation and other forms of racial oppression. A pioneering Afrocentrist, Hurley argued that civilization originated in Africa and that Ethiopians were God's chosen people. He also developed a festival called "Hurley's Feast" to supplant Christmas, which he believed was a white celebration. During this sacred week, which ends each year on Father Hurley's birthday, February 17, Hurleyites exchange gifts and cards and decorate trees at home.

The UHSC maintains a small membership today in New York, Detroit, and other major cities in the East and Midwest.

SRP

Bibliography: Hans A. Baer, *The Black Spiritual Movement: A Religious Response to Racism* (Knoxville: University of Tennessee Press, 1984).

Hutchinson, Anne (1591–1643)

A "woman of ready wit and bold spirit," as an opponent described her, Anne Hutchinson was at the heart of the ANTINOMIAN CONTROVERSY, one of the greatest religious and political controversies in colonial Massachusetts (see MASSACHUSETTS BAY COLONY). Her abilities were such that banishment was seen as the only way to remove her from influence in the colony.

Born in Alford, England, in 1591 (christened July 20), Anne was the daughter of Francis and Elizabeth Marbury. Her father, an Anglican minister, had been removed from office by the time of Anne's birth. By 1605, however, Francis was again in favor and received a series of prestigious appointments in London, where the young Anne was exposed to life in the capital and to new ideas, especially PURITANISM.

On August 9, 1612, Anne married William Hutchinson, a wealthy farmer and merchant from Alford. William shared Anne's religious concerns, and the couple attended, when possible, the sermons of John COTTON in Boston, England, 24 miles (a day-and-a-half journey) from Alford. The couple were committed Puritans and, as the religious situation deteriorated during the 1620s, decided to join the Puritan migration to America, arriving in Boston in September 1634.

Although Anne's admission to the church was delayed due to comments she had made aboard ship, the Hutchinsons were welcome additions to the colony. Anne had a gifted the-

Anne Hutchinson's unorthodox views prompted the Antinomian Controversy and led to her banishment from the Massachusetts Bay colony. *(Library of Congress)*

ological mind and soon began to hold religious meetings in her home. Originally these were small groups of five to six women. The quality of Anne's thought was soon recognized, and the numbers increased to "threescore or fourscore persons," according to John WINTHROP.

Hutchinson was most concerned with the covenant of grace. Like all Puritans, she believed human activity was useless in bringing about salvation. Unlike many of her contemporaries, Hutchinson rejected the claim that personal behavior was a clue to the presence of this grace within a person. "Sanctification," the purity of one's behavior, was no proof of "justification," the status of one's soul.

Hutchinson combined this with an insistence that grace was implanted in the soul by the Holy Spirit. The Spirit then took control of the person's life. For orthodox Puritans this came dangerously close to a claim for direct revelation that superseded Scripture.

These ideas struck at the heart of the Puritan experiment in New England. If true, what purpose did moral striving serve? If the church were unable to instruct the justified, what was the meaning and purpose of Scripture? The possible answers endangered the ordered society the Puritans were trying to create.

While Hutchinson's views immersed her in a much wider crisis—the Antinomian Controversy—there was another problem: her position as a woman in a society that limited positions of authority to men. By 1637 many authorities viewed her meetings as violations of Scripture and the cause of dissension and conflict in the colony.

Hutchinson was called before the General Court in November 1637. The charges against her were vague at best: holding meetings not "fitting" for her sex, promoting divisive opinions, and dishonoring the ministers. During questioning Hutchinson deftly parried every thrust. As a theologian she was superior to Winthrop—her main interlocutor—and in debate, his equal. Her responses finally drove Winthrop to the point where he attempted to cut off argument by telling her that "We do not mean to discourse with those of your sex."

By the end of the second day, the hearing was a draw, and it looked as though Hutchinson would be released with a censure and an admonition. At this time Hutchinson moved beyond the carefully worded and scripturally supported answers of her previous testimony. She told of direct revelations given her by God, revelations foretelling her persecution in New England, her deliverance from such a calamity, and possible judgment on the colony. This provided the court with an opportunity to condemn her. It declared her revelations devil-sent delusions. The session ended with the court placing her under house arrest until the spring, when she was to be banished from the colony.

Following her banishment, Hutchinson and her family took the path of many dissidents from Massachusetts and moved to Rhode Island (see WILLIAMS, ROGER). The following year she had a stillbirth, a "monster" in the language of the time, which proved to many the error of her views. In 1642 her husband died, and she moved to Long Island, where, in late August or early September 1643, she and 10 of her children were slain during an Indian war. For the rulers of Massachusetts this was final proof of her errors, for they could discern God's hand in picking "out this woeful woman, to make her . . . an unheard of heavy example."

(See also DYER, MARY.)

EQ

Bibliography: Emery J. Battis, *Saints and Sectaries: Anne Hutchinson and the Antinomian Controversy in the Massachusetts Bay Colony* (Chapel Hill: Institute of Early American History and Culture, University of North Carolina Press, 1962); Jean Cameron, *Anne Hutchinson, Guilty or Not?: A Closer Look at Her Trials* (New York: P. Lang, 1994); David D. Hall, *The Antinomian Controversy, 1636–1638: A Documentary History*, 2nd ed. (Durham, N.C.: Duke University Press, 1990); Winnifred Rugg, *Unafraid: A Life of Anne Hutchinson* (Boston: Houghton Mifflin Co., 1930); Selma R. Williams, *Divine Rebel: The Life of Anne Marbury Hutchinson* (New York: Holt, Rinehart and Winston, 1981).

Hutterites   The Hutterites are religious sectarians who emerged out of the Anabaptist movement of the Radical Reformation in 16th-century Europe. They distinguish themselves from the MENNONITES and the AMISH by their rejection of private property and their insistence on following the primitive Christian practice of communal ownership of goods. Like the Mennonites and the Amish, Hutterites manifest their withdrawal from the corrupt world into their biblically-based Christian communities by wearing plain clothing, living in rural areas, supporting themselves through the hard work of farming, and refusing to swear oaths or bear arms. They distinguish themselves from the Amish, however, by their willingness to make use of tractors and other modern conveniences.

The tradition of the Hutterian Brethren, as the Hutterites prefer to be called, began among Swiss Anabaptists in Moravia in 1528 under the influence of Jacob Hutter. A Tyrolean reformer who fled to Moravia to escape religious persecution, Hutter was burned at the stake in Austria in 1536 for his heretical insistence that Christians follow the apostolic model of holding "all things in common." Under the leadership of Hutter and successors (who used his martyrdom as a rallying cry for Hutterite vigilance in the face of the corruptions of the world), Hutterite colonies sprang up in Moravia in the 1530s and 1540s. They then spread to Austria, Germany, and Switzerland. During the Counter-Reformation, Hutterites fled to Hungary and subsequently made their way to Romania and the Ukraine.

Virtually all of Europe's Hutterites migrated en masse from Russia to the United States between 1874 and 1877. What prompted this migration was the same nativist "Russification" campaign that drove Mennonites and other German Russians to America during the 1870s. The first group of Hutterite immigrants, consisting of no more than 500 people, settled in South Dakota. There Hutterites organized themselves into three self-sustaining colonies, or *Bruderhofs*.

The Hutterites' refusal to proselytize clearly went against the grain in voluntaristic America. But thanks to the highest birthrate of any group in modern America and an extraordinary ability to contain defections, the Hutterites prospered. At the outbreak of World War I, there were an estimated 1,700 American Hutterites in 17 colonies. Because of their pacifist stance and the reluctance of the U.S. government to recognize its legitimacy, almost all of America's Hutterites fled to Canada during the war. By World War II, however, the Hutterites were officially recognized as conscientious objectors and returned in great numbers to the United States.

Because of their prosperity and longevity, many scholars see the Hutterites as the most successful example of Christian communism in the United States. While most experiments in COMMUNITARIANISM lasted only a few years, the Hutterites have survived for more than a century. In 2000 they reported 111 colonies with 6,100 members in the United States.

SRP

Bibliography: John A. Hostetler, *Hutterite Society* (Baltimore: Johns Hopkins University Press, 1997).

hymns, Gospel   See SANKEY, IRA DAVID.

I

Identity movement   The virulently racist and anti-Semitic religious movement known as Christian Identity (or Identity) began as a quirky theological movement within Victorian Protestantism. Originally known as Anglo (or British)-Israelitism, this group believed the 10 lost tribes of the Jews from the Northern Kingdom had migrated from Israel to the Caucasus (becoming Caucasians) and eventually settled in Britain and northern Europe, where they became the Anglo-Saxons. Jews, they believed, were descendants of the two tribes of the Southern Kingdom who, although captured by the Babylonians and exiled, were eventually allowed to return to Israel. In this view, the Anglo-Saxons and the Jews were related and together shared the right to be called the "chosen people."

Strangely, this vaguely philo-Semitic movement would be transformed in the early 20th century into a virulent anti-Semitic and racist ideology. This hatred reached such extremes that some groups would renounce all links to Christianity with its Jewish roots and its message of love and forgiveness. For these groups, the essence of life lay in struggle, especially racial struggle, and anything hindering this struggle violated the laws of nature.

This transformation began in the United States during the 1920s and 1930s with the writings of William Cameron, editor in the 1920s of the *Dearborn Independent*, the Michigan newspaper owned by Henry Ford. Cameron published the first major American version of the anti-Semitic forgery *The Protocols of the Elders of Zion*. Gerald L. K. Smith, one of the United States' leading right-wing demagogues, also was a believer in the Christian Identity ideology. Perhaps the most visible and organized Identity movement in the United States for years was the Worldwide Church of God, founded by the science fiction writer Garner Ted Armstrong. The church taught that Jews were evil and that Anglo-Saxons were the chosen people of God. Since Armstrong's death, however, the church has struggled to bring itself in line with the teachings of mainstream EVANGELICALISM and has renounced this doctrine. This turnabout paved the way for the group's entry into the NATIONAL ASSOCIATION OF EVANGELICALS in 1997.

In the 1940s–1960s, the anti-Semitic components of Identity were articulated by California lawyer Bertrand Comparet, Wesley Swift, the founder of the Church of Jesus Christ, Christian, which for decades made Identity central to its beliefs, and William Potter Gale, a former aide to Douglas MacArthur and director of guerrilla operations in the Philippines during World War II, who founded the Christian Defense League.

In this new version, the Jews were stripped of their Biblical roots and their connection with God. At first, the two southern tribes (the "House of Judah") were accused of intermarrying with heathens, thus defiling themselves and God's law. Later versions separated them completely from the Jews of the Bible, claiming they were merely the descendants of the Khazars, a tribal people from southern Russia who converted en masse to Judaism in 740 C.E.

In the most prevalent versions of Identity the white Anglo-Saxon-Celtic (brought in undoubtedly to incorporate the Scots) peoples are viewed as God's real "chosen people," who descend in an unbroken line from Adam and Eve. By nature and divine design they are the superior race. The modern Jews descend from Cain, who was born of a sexual liaison between Eve and the Serpent (the real original sin) in Eden. They are biologically evil, the "synagogue of Satan."

Nonwhites are "pre-Adamic" beings. They have no souls and are the biblical "beasts of the field." Cain mated with these peoples to produce today's Jews. As the spawn of Satan, the Jews are involved in a plot to unite the world under a single government, which will then be handed over to the rule of the Devil himself.

In order to prevent this catastrophe, whites in America, who constitute the true "House of Israel," must prepare for the bloody battle with the forces of evil, the people of color manipulated and led by the Jews, in a racial holy war. God's law on earth can only be established through victory in this battle, Armageddon. There the forces of good—the white "Israelites"—will be pitted against the armies of Satan, represented by the Jewish-controlled federal government. Identity followers believe they must wage an all-out war against the ZOG (the Zionist Occupied Government), all those of color, white "race traitors," and anyone else who stands in their way.

Identity followers also believe that America is the New Jerusalem and that the U.S. Constitution was given to their ancestors, the white Christian Founding Fathers, by God. They claim that the authentic Constitution consisted of just the first 10 amendments of the Constitution (the Bill of Rights) and the Articles of Confederation. Only white Christian men are "true sovereign citizens" of the republic.

Other Americans are merely "state citizens," illegally created through the FOURTEENTH AMENDMENT by an illegitimate "de facto" government. Since the modern American government is illegitimate, Identity followers believe the Internal Revenue Service, civil rights legislation, and abortion rights are also unlawful.

For nearly 50 years, the virulent racist theology of Identity has made inroads into racist and antigovernment groups such as the KU KLUX KLAN, neo-Nazis, Posse Comitatus, and racist skinheads. Currently it commands a large following beyond traditional white supremacists, including inside the patriot movement.

Explicit Identity groups such as The Covenant, Sword and Arm of The Lord (CSA), the White Patriot Party, Posse Comitatus, Aryan Nations, and the Order have been responsible for the racist right's most violent incidents since the 1970s. Murder, robbery, and savage attacks on individuals have characterized their methods. Timothy McVeigh, who bombed the federal building in Oklahoma City, placed two calls to Elohim City, a 22-year-old armed Identity enclave in Oklahoma headed by Robert Millar, just days before the attack.

Millar had close ties to some of the most violent Identity adherents. In April 1995, Millar personally supervised the transfer of the body of Richard Wayne Snell from Arkansas to Elohim City. Snell, an Identity adherent and CSA member, had been executed in Arkansas for the 1983 murder of a pawnshop owner he mistakenly thought to be Jewish. Previously, Snell had been convicted of murdering a black Arkansas state trooper in 1984.

Millar, who had brought both Snell and CSA founder James Ellison into the movement, believes that someone will soon be resurrected from the dead to lead the white Israelites in battle against the satanic federal government. After Snell's body arrived at Elohim City, the casket was left open for several days in anticipation of the possibility that Snell might be this "savior."

Although probably numbering no more than 20,000 committed members, the Identity Movement promotes anti-Semitic paranoia and hatred through numerous methods, including books, newsletters, audio cassettes, videos, shortwave and AM radio, satellite and cable television, camp meetings, far Right Patriot rallies, and church meetings. The Internet has been a particularly successful medium for promulgating the movement's views.

The growth of the computer industry also has supplied Identity with two large funders, Carl Story and Vincent Bertollini, who after retiring from the industry moved from California to Idaho, where they finance Identity propaganda. In one of their largest endeavors, they paid for the "11th Hour Remnant Messenger" to mail to 9,000 Idaho addresses a packet of Identity materials, including an introductory letter, an anti-Semitic booklet, and a poster explaining the group's Identity beliefs. This single mailing cost more than $100,000.

For some on the farthest right, the Christian Identity Movement is insufficient. It is tainted by Christianity's Jewish roots and its false message of love, when the true law of nature is struggle, the struggle for the victory of the species, the race.

The most visible of these groups is the World Church of the Creator (WCOTC), based in East Peoria, Illinois, and headed since 1970 by Matt Hale. Hale became Pontifex Maximus of the church in 1996, following the suicide of its founder, Ben Klassen, in 1993. The goal of the group is to make "this [the United States] an all white nation and ultimately an all white world." Its slogan is "RaHoWa," an abbreviated form of "Racial Holy War."

The Church of the Creator (the original name of WCOTC) and "creativity," the church's theology, were created by Ben Klassen, a one-time Florida state legislator born in Ukraine and raised in Canada. Founded in 1973, the Church of the Creator completely rejected "the Judeo-democratic-Marxist values of today" and desired to supplant them "with new and basic values, of which race is the foundation." The WCOTC attacks Christianity as the "tremendous weapon in the worldwide Jewish drive of race-mixing." Creators assert that Jews "concocted" Christianity in order to mongrelize and destroy the white race. Much of WCOTC's hatred and energies are directed against Jews, whom it accuses of being "parasites" who "control and manipulate the finances, the propaganda, the media and the governments of the world."

WCOTC has become one of the most virulent, violent, and quickly growing hate groups in the United States. Members have been implicated in numerous racially motivated assaults and arsons and at least one murder. The murder led to the conviction of several members and a civil judgment against the church that awarded nearly all of its assets to the family of the victim, a black veteran of the Persian Gulf War. This event led to Klassen's suicide and to the church's decline until it was revived by Hale in 1996.

Not until 1999 did the existence of the WCOTC come to awareness of most Americans. That Fourth of July weekend, WCOTC activist Benjamin "August" Smith went on a shooting rampage throughout Illinois and Indiana, leaving two dead and nine wounded before he fatally shot himself. All Smith's victims were either black, Jewish, or Asian American. In January 1999, Hale had named Smith "Creator of the Year" because of his success in distributing the church's anti-Semitic and racist tract, *Facts That the Government and the Media Don't Want You To Know.*

Although the incident's national impact was not as great as that of the Oklahoma City bombing, Smith's rampage was a clear reminder that religion in the United States manifests itself in numerous ways, not all of them positive. Sadly, many of those shot on the first day of the rampage were Jews on their way to services, and the final victim was a Korean man on his way home from church.

(See also ANTI-SEMITISM; NATIVISM; RELIGIOUS VIOLENCE; WORLDWIDE CHURCH OF GOD.)

EQ

Bibliography: James Aho, *The Politics of Righteousness* (Seattle: University of Washington Press, 1990); Michael Barkun, *Religion and the Racist Right* (Chapel Hill: University of North Carolina Press, 1997); ———, "Millenarians and Violence: The Case of the Christian Identity Movement," in Thomas Robbins and Susan J. Palmer, eds., *Millennium, Messiahs, and Mayhem: Contemporary Apocalyptic Movements* (New York: Routledge, 1997).

immigration   The United States is a nation of immigrants, so it should not be surprising that immigration has played an important role in American religious history. Beginning with the Puritans, immigrants brought with them different religious traditions and, once in the New World, those traditions underwent a wide variety of transformations.

Immigration is a complex process, and many different factors determine the ways religions develop and change. The race and ETHNICITY of an immigrant group, which help to determine its initial reception in America, have an enduring impact on the shape of a religious tradition. The occupational skills, languages, and literacy levels of immigrants and the stage of economic development in the United States at the time of their arrival are secondary factors that help to determine the subsequent development of their religion. Later migrations into a community as well as external developments in world history often play important roles in the reshaping of a religious tradition and can alter the relations among different religions in unexpected ways. All these factors have helped to create the pluralistic (see PLURALISM) landscape of contemporary American religion.

The way these different factors can work to shape and reshape a religious tradition is well understood in the case of American JUDAISM. German Jews arriving in the antebellum period faced relatively few barriers due to their ethnicity. They were well placed in terms of occupational skills and literacy, which enabled them to engage in the burgeoning commercial life of the expanding republic. They also shared with many Americans a set of moderate and progressive religious ideals derived from the 18th-century ENLIGHTENMENT, which enabled them to mute religious traditionalism and to resemble the host culture dominated by Protestants. This first wave of Jewish immigrants soon achieved a high level of social and economic integration, which enabled them to aid a second wave that arrived from Russia and eastern Europe around the turn of the 20th century.

Immigrants in this second wave arrived at a time when jobs were plentiful in the rapidly expanding urban-industrial order, so many were able to move into the middle class in a generation. These immigrants, however, brought with them religious traditions and cultural ideals that were different from those in the first wave. Due to social conditions in eastern Europe and Russia, Jews in the second wave tended to be both more traditionally religious and more politically radical than the Germans, which created conflict within the community. Eventually, interaction between the two groups resulted in the differentiation of their religious life into REFORM, CONSERVATIVE, and ORTHODOX JUDAISM. The progressive ideals of the first wave and the more radical ideals of the second worked together to give the American Jewish community as a whole a liberal cast that endured in subsequent generations.

External developments in world history also played a major role in the shaping of American Judaism. Germans migrated after the failure of the Revolution of 1848; Russians migrated in response to pogroms after the assassination of Czar Alexander II in 1881; Jews also migrated in the wake of the Bolshevik revolution and more recently after the fall of the Berlin Wall and the breakup of the Soviet Union. The community has also been reshaped by ZIONISM, the Holocaust, and the founding of Israel, developments that contributed to the distinctiveness of American

The Great Hunger drove 1.5 million Irish to immigrate to the United States after 1830. *(Library of Congress)*

Judaism and to American political culture in the 21st century. The ongoing evolution of the community with Hasidic immigration and changing fortunes in the Middle East continue to raise new questions about both the shape of the Jewish community and its contribution to the complex forces at play in contemporary American society.

Catholic (see ROMAN CATHOLICISM) immigrants also participated in the commercial and industrial expansion of the nation, thereby making their own move toward the American mainstream. However, the ways they assimilated gave a unique shape to the Catholic community, one resulting in different contributions to the current American scene. Catholic history is usually discussed in terms of a first, antebellum wave composed primarily of Germans and Irish and a second wave made up of distinct

groups of southern and eastern Europeans. The dominant group became the Irish, in large part due to their proficiency in English. As a result, the historical antipathy between Irish and Anglo-Protestants shaped the Catholic community's move toward the mainstream. The Catholic Church played an important role in Irish Americanization strategies. A unified American church was created in order to mediate intra-Catholic ethnic differences and to Americanize the immigrants, while it also served as a fortress to protect against total assimilation and to perpetuate Christian devotional traditions that were distinctly Catholic. This defensive strategy also resulted in the creation of Catholic parochial schools as an alternative to the public school system. External developments played an important role in the creation of the Catholic ethos and community.

Developments overseas such as famine and revolution set in motion different waves of Catholic immigration. The defensive strategies of the leaders of the American church were influenced in many ways by the efforts of the papacy in Rome to defend traditional orthodoxy against the encroachments of modernity.

This strategy was successful until VATICAN COUNCIL II, when the Roman leadership of the Church undertook to modernize Catholicism. Liberal developments resulting from the council effectively destroyed the fortress Church mentality originally formulated to maintain American Catholic identity. Great numbers of Catholics still remain in a church that is alternatively described as chaotic and thriving, but are conspicuously diverse in their political, social, and religious convictions. At the same time, the idea of cultural Catholicism—a distinctly Catholic ethos and sensibility—is often discussed but remains a largely uncharted force on the American scene.

The Jewish and Catholic experiences, along with those of others like Scandinavian Lutherans (see LUTHERANISM) and the Greek Orthodox (see ORTHODOX CHRISTIANITY), can be described as the classic east-to-west "immigrant saga" of peoples moving up from an ethnic periphery toward an allegedly post-ethnic mainstream, a story long central to America's melting-pot myth and history. But in the past 40 years, these histories have been set in a new context as a result of the CIVIL RIGHTS MOVEMENT and new patterns of immigration. The civil rights movement introduced into the old melting-pot story of America both the dynamics of race and highly politicized ideas about ethnicity. At the same time, new patterns of immigration refocused attention on the experiences of older communities once relegated to the margins and on newer immigrant communities.

One result of the CIVIL RIGHTS MOVEMENT was an explosion in scholarship about African-American (see AFRICAN-AMERICAN RELIGION) history, which has opened enormous and varied vistas obscured for centuries. Despite the existence of a substantial black middle class, race has also been shown to be a structural impediment that belies the normativeness of the older model of free immigrants moving to the center from the periphery. Certain standard dynamics of the process of immigration have, however, been recast in order to understand African-American religious history. The concern with premigration backgrounds has led to an exploration of the West African religions and ethnicities that existed before the passage into slavery. Questions about the stages of development in the American economy also have been recast, but with attention to the way in which racism consistently blocked the path to full participation by African Americans in the nation's economy. Discussions about the development of black Christianity now tend to follow an Afro-oriented, race- and economy-based story. The antebellum period marked the formation of a distinct African-American Christianity; postbellum churches served as the locus for the development of black ethnicity and identity; mid-20th-century churches provided networks through which the questions about racism and rights were pressed into the mainstream.

Current discussions of black Christianity tend to emphasize its distinct contribution to the variegated texture of the contemporary scene. In its many forms, black Christianity is now seen as having a unique character, largely a product of African origins, slavery, and the inequities rooted in racism. The introduction of race into the story of immigration has begun to reshape the discussion about the nation's religious traditions in other important ways. The fact that British Protestants and African slaves occupied demographically dominant niches during the colonial, revolutionary, and early national periods has highlighted a fact partially obscured in the older immigrant saga myth and history. The Protestant community that defined the 19th-century American mainstream was itself not post-ethnic, but a complex ethnicity of its own: white, largely British-American in culture, and Protestant in religion. Anglo-American Protestantism is now beginning to be seen as an ethnic history among other ethnic histories.

The centrality of race in American history and the renewed, politicized interest in ethnicity have also refocused attention on the religious histories of older communities that were once dismissed as marginal and on the religious traditions of newer immigrant communities. Questions about race and ethnicity and the relations between old and new groups within a single immigrant community are joined in complex ways in the case of Hispanics or Latinos, further decentering the old "immigrant saga," both history and myth. Older Mexican groups in the Southwest were not immigrants, but conquered people; subsequent migrations have not been east to west, but south to north. Race and ethnicity issues have also been recast as a result of the Spanish and Indian contributions to Mexican identity. Additional migrations by different Caribbean and South and Central American peoples, all of whom have distinct ideas about how Spanish and Indian, as well as African, elements factor into their identities, have given the Latino community an unparalleled ethnic complexity. Class variables, America's shift to a postindustrial economy, and the proximity of many Latin nations to the United States make generalizations about how the ongoing migrations are reshaping the nation's religious life highly problematic. Historians have only recently begun to turn their attention to the new forms of religion that are entering the United States with Latino immigration, to questions about the relations between Latin and North American Catholicism, and to the study of Latino conversion to Protestantism.

Engagement with questions of race and ethnicity and attention to new patterns of immigration have also drawn attention to America's Asian communities. Japanese and Chinese Americans have recently received greater attention than in the past, a development rooted in the importance of east Asia in the global econ-omy and in the explosion of immigration from Asia to the United States after 1965. But both groups have had long American histories. They have over generations brought to America religious values rooted in their premigration backgrounds and have made distinct contributions to the American culture and economy. Both groups also have been subject to unique pressures due both to racism and to external factors in world history. Recent migrations by many other peoples have complicated immensely the idea of an "Asian-American" community. Indians, Tibetans, Laotian, Vietnamese, and Cambodians, together with Iraqis, Iranians, Lebanese, and other west Asians who have longer American histories are contributing demographically modest but highly unique religious, cultural, and racial elements to the contemporary scene. Immigrants bringing to America HINDUISM, BUDDHISM, and ISLAM are now beginning to play a prominent role in American religious history.

Immigration has always played a central and complex role in American religious history. British Puritan immigrants dominated America's colonial and early national religious history. Roman Catholics and Jews substantially altered the religious landscape of mainstream America as a result of their 19th- and early 20th-century migrations. African Americans have long been central to the story of American religious history, although only recently have their contributions been brought to light. Latinos and Asians are only the most recent contributors to a great American legacy. Their impact on the religious life of the nation as a whole will be hard to assess until well into the 21st century.

RHS

Bibliography: Earl Shorris, *Latinos: A Biography of the People* (New York: Norton and Co., 1992); Stephen Thernstrom, ed., *Harvard Encyclopedia of American Ethnic Groups* (Cambridge, Mass.: Belknap Press of Harvard University Press, 1980); R. Stephen Warner and Judith G. Wittner, eds., *Gatherings in Diaspora: Religious Communities and the*

New Immigration (Philadelphia: Temple University Press, 1998); David K. Yoo, *New Spiritual Homes: Religion and Asian Americans* (Honolulu: University of Hawaii Press, 1999).

inerrancy The term *inerrancy*, when applied to the Christian Scriptures, signifies the belief that the original words of the Bible were divinely inspired and true in every detail, in scientific and historical facts as well as in religious doctrines. Inerrancy has always been one of the central tenets of American FUNDAMENTALISM. It is also a view held by many evangelicals and other theologically conservative Protestants today.

The concept of biblical inerrancy first appeared among Protestant writers in the late 17th century to combat Roman Catholic appeals to tradition and the authority of the church. Spokesmen for the Protestant Reformation stressed both the self-sufficiency of the Scripture in interpreting itself and the essential accuracy of its text. Protestants argued that the Bible was a book that even the simplest Christian could read and comprehend. As Reformed theologian Francois Turretin wrote, "the Scriptures are so perspicuous in things pertaining to salvation that they can be understood by believers without the external help of . . . ecclesiastical authority."

A philosophical system called SCOTTISH COMMON SENSE REALISM, which arose within Protestant ranks in the 18th century, gave further credence to the idea of inerrancy. The Common Sense philosophy came out of controversies during the ENLIGHTENMENT over the basis of human knowledge. Scottish clergyman Thomas Reid and others tried to give a solid metaphysical foundation to the everyday observations people made. Following the inductive methods of 17th-century scientist Francis Bacon, Reid and his followers asserted that the external world was just as it appeared to be. Common Sense thus provided a rational, scientific justification for every statement that appeared in the Bible: A person could simply believe whatever he or she read there.

The reliability of the Bible did not come up for debate among American Protestants until the mid-19th century. The publication of Charles Darwin's *On the Origin of Species* in 1859, however, signaled an important shift in the relationship of religion and science. Prior to that date, believers had followed the reasoning of Common Sense Realism and simply assumed that Christian faith, human intellect, and science were all fundamentally compatible. But the dissemination of Darwin's theories on organic EVOLUTION forever destroyed such a facile intellectual synthesis. After the Civil War, informed readers of the Bible were forced to ask whether the new scientific discoveries, particularly in the areas of biology and geology, were undermining or authenticating scriptural statements. How, for instance, could the world have been created in six days as the Book of Genesis claimed?

Responding to the challenges they faced, conservative Protestants fell back upon the philosophical tenets that had nurtured them in the past. Thus, as Presbyterian professor Charles HODGE of Princeton Seminary asserted in the early 1870s, the Bible should be accepted as a "store-house of facts." Theologians like Hodge believed not only that people had found divine truth in the depository of Scripture throughout the ages, but that they could do so still. The 1881 article "Inspiration," coauthored by Hodge's son Archibald A. Hodge and by Benjamin B. WARFIELD, moreover, represented a classic expression of the "certainty" offered by Common Sense Realism and inerrancy. Hodge and Warfield argued for the absolute trustworthiness of the plain reading of Scripture. Pressing their view with mathematical preciseness, they asked Christian believers to stand upon the unshakable ground of a Bible that was literally true in every detail.

In the late 19th century, the Bible became a battleground over which American Protestants fought, the Presbyterians especially.

Despite the liberals' claim that they wanted to bolster rather than undermine Christianity by appealing to lofty religious ideas not necessarily found in the Bible, they were swamped by the general conservative reaction within their denomination against those new forms of thought. Presbyterian traditionalists insisted upon the objective truth of both the Scriptures and the traditional creeds, and they vehemently defended inerrancy against critics who indicated obvious errors and historical discrepancies in the Bible. In the last decade of the 19th century, modernist Presbyterian professors Charles Augustus BRIGGS, Henry Preserved Smith, and Arthur Cushman McGiffert were convicted of heresy, and each eventually left the denomination. In 1910 the Presbyterian General Assembly affirmed inerrancy as the first of five essential points of Christian orthodoxy.

The Presbyterian action, of course, hardly silenced those who questioned the accuracy of the Bible. By the 1920s, the acceptance of evolution, and the consequent rejection of biblical inerrancy, had become widespread in American culture. Against this trend, the emerging fundamentalist movement mobilized. Under the leadership of statesman and politician William Jennings BRYAN, fundamentalists articulated the manifold threats they thought Darwinism posed to traditional Christian civilization. Bryan feared that evolution undermined faith in the Bible as the source of truth and would inevitably lead Americans into immorality and atheism.

J. Gresham MACHEN, a professor of New Testament at Princeton Seminary, was another religious leader who espoused the doctrine of inerrancy in that period. In his 1923 book *Christianity and Liberalism*, Machen charged that Presbyterians and other American Protestants were drifting away from their theological and spiritual moorings. Following the tradition of the Hodges and Warfield, Machen affirmed that the Bible contained "documentary evidence" and was an "infallible" guide for the Christian. He also stated that those who held beliefs contrary to his own definition of biblical orthodoxy should not be allowed to remain members of his church. As it turned out, Machen and his followers, not their modernist adversaries, left the mainline Presbyterian denomination in 1936, after liberals gained control of the General Assembly.

Although Machen's withdrawal from his denomination represented the end of the dominance of inerrancy within mainline Protestantism, the idea remained strong in other parts of American Christianity. Clearly, most evangelicals, and even members of nonevangelical denominations, wanted to believe in the essential truthfulness of the Bible in matters both of history and science and of doctrine and ethics. The doctrine of inerrancy, however, produced one of the most vexing controversies within conservative Protestantism since World War II.

In the 1950s, some evangelical scholars began to question the value of a wooden, literal exegesis of the Bible, since the Bible clearly contains some material errors. In 1967 Fuller Theological Seminary, the most prominent of the evangelical divinity schools, removed the doctrine of inerrancy from its statement of faith. Critics of inerrancy maintained that the Bible's infallibility defined the ability of Scripture to lead people to salvation and moral living, not to information about history or science. In response to this trend, Harold Lindsell, then the editor of the evangelical magazine *Christianity Today*, published *The Battle for the Bible* in 1976. He questioned the wisdom of the defection from the doctrine of inerrancy.

Recent debates about biblical literalism have not been limited to evangelical institutions of higher education and seminaries. Conservatives within the LUTHERAN CHURCH—MISSOURI SYNOD, for example, gained control of their denomination in the 1970s and forced an affirmation of inerrancy on the church. "The Chicago Statement on Biblical Inerrancy," drawn up in 1978, was published the next year in a volume called *Inerrancy*. Several scholars in that volume argued that the doctrine, when carefully defined, was both what the Bible teaches about itself and the central tradition of the Christian churches. In the 1980s, the SOUTHERN BAPTIST CONVENTION also split over this issue. The fundamentalist faction in the denomination began what some considered a purge of Southern Baptist colleges and seminaries that did not teach inerrancy. Inerrancy continues to remain, as it has been since the late 1800s, an acrimonious topic among conservative Protestants in the United States.

GHS, Jr.

Bibliography: George M. Marsden, *Fundamentalism and American Culture: The Shaping of Twentieth-Century Evangelicalism, 1870 1925* (New York: Oxford University Press, 1980); Jack B. Rogers and Donald K. McKim, *The Authority an Interpretation of the Bible: An Historical Approach* (San Francisco: Harper & Row, 1979).

Ingersoll, Robert Green (1833–1897)   A leading proponent of SECULARISM, orator and author Robert Green Ingersoll made a career of attacking religion. In response to a speech by Ingersoll, Mark Twain once said, "It was the supreme combination of English words that was ever put together since the world began." Twain was not alone in his estimation of Ingersoll's abilities. Whether applauded or cursed for the agnosticism that fueled his saberlike wit, Ingersoll captured the ears of his contemporaries in late-Victorian America.

Ingersoll was born August 11, 1833, to John and Mary Ingersoll, in Dresden, New York. Living within the religiously fertile atmosphere of the "BURNED-OVER DISTRICT," Ingersoll grew up subject to a breadth of religious influences. His father was a staunch Calvinist and minister in the Congregationalist Church; his mother was a reader of Thomas PAINE on the sly. With only an intermittent formal education to serve him, Ingersoll read voraciously, digesting the works of Paine, Shakespeare, the French *philosophes* (see ENLIGHTENMENT), and popular scientists. From his parents he gained a passion for social reform. He began to practice law prior to the Civil War, and having been commissioned with the rank of colonel in the Union army, was captured and imprisoned by the Confederacy in 1862. Upon release he gained prominence through his legal practice. He was appointed attorney general of Illinois in 1867 and took an active role in the Republican Party over the next two decades.

During the 1870s Ingersoll began lecturing extensively in addition to practicing law, publishing essays to support his family in what became a lavish manner. He quickly gained notoriety as the foremost agnostic of his day. He frequently likened organized religion to the institution of slavery, calling for abolition of mental servitude. Science, the achievement of human reason, provided modern people with a surer form of faith than had the churches, and Ingersoll's oratory urged his contemporaries to embrace science, progress, and the potential for human moral perfection with the same sort of emotional faith stirred up by more orthodox preachers.

In terms similar to contemporary European critics of religion such as Ludwig Feuerbach (1804–1872) and Friedrich Nietzsche (1844–1900), Ingersoll attacked religious belief in divine beings as a projection of human aspirations. He began his essay "The Gods" (1872) by claiming: "Each nation has created a god, and the god has always resembled his creators." Ingersoll's rationalist critique of religion ignited extensive opposition from clergy and the press, even supplanting Charles Darwin as the focus of orthodox apologetics (see EVOLUTION). However, he gained the lasting admiration and friendship of liberal churchman Henry Ward BEECHER. In subsequent essays he extended and developed his attack. In "Ghosts" (1877) he portrayed the limitlessness of human achievement unshackled from religious superstition: "Humanity is the sky, and these religions and dogmas and theories are but mists and clouds changing continually, destined finally to melt away." In "Some Mistakes of Moses" (1880) he offered a detailed, scathing examination of the idea that the Bible was divinely inspired.

Ingersoll complemented his commitment to human intellectual freedom with a firm support for human political rights. In his time he championed the extension of rights to women, children, and blacks, and due process for those convicted after the Haymarket Riot of 1886. He influenced people such as socialist Eugene Debs and the civil liberties lawyer Clarence Darrow. Although his thinking was far from original, he offered the most sustained and emphatic plea for religious toleration and freedom of thought of his day.

MG

Bibliography: David R. Anderson, *Robert Ingersoll* (Boston: Twayne, 1972); Frank Smith, *Robert G. Ingersoll: A Life* (Buffalo, N.Y.: Prometheus Books, 1990)

Insight Meditation Society

The Insight Meditation Society (IMS) is one of the most successful American Buddhist organizations catering to European-American converts and sympathizers. Its roots are in Theravada BUDDHISM, one of the three major Buddhist schools and the most popular Buddhist form in Southeast Asia. IMS teachers stress *Vipassana*, or insight meditation, a spiritual practice rooted in Theravada monasticism but adapted in the United States for a lay audience.

IMS was established in 1975 on the site of a former Catholic seminary just outside Barre, Massachusetts. The founders were a group of European Americans informed by the COUNTERCULTURE who had studied insight meditation with Theravada Buddhist teachers in Asia. At IMS, however, they taught a meditative practice largely shorn of the beliefs and rituals of that tradition. In the 1980s, IMS teachers supplemented this initial emphasis on insight meditation with instruction in *Metta*, or loving kindness meditation.

In 1988 IMS moved west, opening the Spirit Rock Meditation Center in Marin County, California. IMS and Spirit Rock are also associated with the Cambridge Insight Meditation Center in Cambridge, Massachusetts, the Vipassana Metta Foundation on Maui in Hawaii, and the Barre Center for Buddhist Studies, located near IMS headquarters in Barre. The group also publishes a journal called *Inquiring Mind*.

Because many of IMS's founding members, including Joseph Goldstein, Jack Kornfield, Jacqueline Schwartz, and Sharon Salzberg, were raised Jewish, IMS has come to be associated with "Jewish Buddhism." Sylvia Boorstein, a well-known IMS teacher, is perhaps the most widely recognized Jewish Buddhist in America. In books such as *That's Funny, You Don't Look Buddhist: On Being a Faithful Jew and a Passionate Buddhist* (1997), Boorstein presents herself not as a former Jew who has become a Buddhist but as a Buddhist who remains a faithful Jew.

Like many American ZEN centers, IMS appeals mostly to European-American lay converts who are seeking a meditative practice without monasticism. As cofounder Jack Kornfield put it, the goal of IMS is "to offer the powerful practices of insight meditation . . . without the complications of rituals, robes, chanting and the whole religious tradition." Because IMS does not keep a membership list (in fact, it refuses to distinguish between members and nonmembers), it is difficult to determine its size, but it is clearly one of the most vital Buddhist organizations in the United States today.

SRP

Bibliography: Sylvia Boorstein, *That's Funny, You Don't Look Buddhist: On Being a Faithful Jew and a Passionate Buddhist* (San Francisco: HarperSanFrancisco, 1997); Jack Kornfield, *A Path with Heart: A Guide Through the Perils and Promises of Spiritual Life* (New York: Bantam Doubleday Dell, 1993); http://www.dharma.org/ims.htm (Insight Meditation Society); www.spiritrock.org (Spirit Rock Meditation Center).

Institutional Church　See SOCIAL GOSPEL.

International Church of the Foursquare Gospel　See PENTECOSTALISM.

International Society for Krishna Consciousness (ISKCON)
The International Society for Krishna Consciousness (ISKCON) is an American outgrowth of the *bhakti yoga* ("discipline of devotion") tradition within HINDUISM. Hare Krishnas, as members of ISKCON are called, trace their origins to the *Vaishnava* tradition of devotion to the Hindu God Vishnu begun by the 16th-century Bengali reformer Caitanya. The more proximate founder of ISKCON is Abhay Charanaravinda Bhaktivedanta Swami PRABHUPADA (1896–1977).

A devotee of the Hindu God Krishna (who is typically represented as one of the avatars, or human incarnations, of Vishnu), the Indian-born Prabhupada worked as a businessman before renouncing the world and becoming a *sannyasin*, or world renunciant, in 1959. He moved to New York City in 1965 at the behest of his guru who had urged him to introduce westerners to Krishna. One year later he founded ISKCON. Buoyed by the COUNTERCULTURE, the movement spread across America. A San Francisco temple opened in 1967, and by the late 1960s ISKCON was centered in Los Angeles. The movement subsequently spread to India, where ISKCON maintains a temple outside Bombay.

ISKCON peaked in numbers and influence sometime around the death of Prabhupada in 1977. Since that time the organization has endured the sorts of trials that typically follow the death of a NEW RELIGIOUS MOVEMENT founder. In 1987 the Governing Body Commission, which had run the organization since Prabhupada's death, expelled one of Prabhupada's first disciples, Kirtanananda Swami Bhaktipada, the founder of a Hare Krishna commune in West Virginia called New Vrindaban, for deviating from ISKCON orthodoxy. Kirtanananda subsequently organized his followers into the International Society for Krishna Consciousness of West Virginia. In 1996, he was convicted of racketeering, fined, and sentenced to prison.

The Hare Krishna movement initially recruited primarily middle-class European Americans, but recently it has attracted some Indian immigrants and their children. The organization has also abandoned some rigor of the early COMMUNITARIANISM. While most recruits in the 1960s and 1970s did not work outside the movement, during the 1990s more than half of ISKCON's members were either self-employed or worked for non-ISKCON concerns.

The ritual practice of ISKCON members consists first and foremost of chanting a mantra: "Hare Krishna Hare Krishna Krishna Krishna Hare Hare Hare Rama Hare Rama Rama Rama Hare Hare." This mantra, which is typically sung to the accompaniment of cymbals and drums, invokes not only Krishna but also Rama, the other major deity of Vaishnavites whose name ISKCON members equate with that of Krishna. Another important feature of Hare Krishna spiritual practice is regular worship at the temple. There are approximately 60 ISKCON temples in United States cities. Each temple typically includes images of Krishna, Radha (Krishna's consort), Caitanya, and Prabhupada.

Hare Krishna devotees distinguish themselves from other Americans not only by chanting but also by their appearance (male members sport saffron robes and shaved heads), their diet (they refuse to eat meat or to take intoxicants), and their eager recruiting tactics. The presence of Hare Krishna devotees at American airports has aroused hostility from some Americans who regard ISKCON as the paradigmatic "cult" in America. In an effort to address accusations of brainwashing, ISKCON members recently have downplayed aggressive recruiting in public places.

ISKCON members differ in some important respects from other Hindus in India and the United States. American converts to Hinduism tend toward Advaita Vedanta, or nondualistic, Hinduism, a more philosophical and less devotional tradition that represents God as impersonal. And while most Hindus in India share the Hare Krishnas' preference for devotion to a personal deity, they do not share the insistence of ISKCON members that Krishna is the one supreme Lord. Still, the movement bears more similarities to the devotional Vaishnava Hinduism of India than it does to the American "cults" with which it is frequently grouped.

ISKCON publishes and distributes a magazine, *Back to Godhead,* as well as numerous books and tracts by Prabhupada. The most widely read text within the movement is Prabhupada's commentary, *Bhagavad-Gita As It Is* (1972). There are now perhaps 3,000 active Hare Krishnas in the Untied States, down from 15,000 to 20,000 in the late 1970s and early 1980s.

SRP

Bibliography: J. Stillson Judah, *Hare Krishna and the Counterculture* (New York: John Wiley & Sons, 1974); Nori J. Muster, *Betrayal of the Spirit: My Life Behind the Headlines of the Hare Krishna Movement* (Urbana: University of Illinois Press, 1997); E. Burke Rochford, *Hare Krishna in America* (New Brunswick, N.J.: Rutgers University Press, 1985); Larry D. Shinn, *The Dark Lord: Cult Images and the Hare Krishnas in America* (Philadelphia: Westminster Press, 1987); http://www.iskcon.org (ISKCON).

Ireland, John (1838–1918) Longtime archbishop of St. Paul, Minnesota (1875–1918), John Ireland was one of the most influential and controversial Roman Catholic prelates in the United States (see ROMAN CATHOLICISM). TEMPERANCE, racial equality, rural colonies for Irish immigrants, and the Americanization of the Roman Church were among his most significant and most suspect policies.

Born in Burnchurch, Kilkenny, Ireland, on September 11, 1838, Ireland came to the United States with his family at the age of 11. The family eventually settled in St. Paul, Minnesota Territory.

Sent to St. Mary's College in Chicago, he was encouraged by priests to further his studies in Europe. After several years of seminary study in France, he returned to St. Paul for his ordination on December 21, 1861. By this time Ireland already had joined the Union army as a chaplain, and in that position he served the 5th Minnesota until April 1863, when ill health forced him to resign. Ireland's war experiences remained a significant part of his life. After the war he was active in the affairs of the Grand Army of the Republic and remained a lifelong Republican.

Returning to St. Paul, Ireland became increasingly prominent in the diocese. He was a favorite of the bishop, who, recognizing his talents, designated Ireland as his representative to VATICAN COUNCIL I. There, he made many contacts among ecclesiastical authorities, and when the position of vicar apostolic for Nebraska became available, Ireland was chosen. Bishop Grace of St. Paul, who was suffering from poor health, petitioned the pope to cancel the appointment and name Ireland as co-adjutor bishop of St. Paul with right to succession. The pope consented and Ireland was consecrated on December 21, 1875, succeeding Grace after the latter's resignation in 1884. Four years later, St. Paul was made an archdiocese, and Ireland became archbishop. The long hoped-for and widely rumored appointment of cardinal never came, however. Ireland's career had made him too controversial, and his views aroused suspicion in Rome.

Ireland's support for the temperance movement angered German Catholics, as did his conviction that immigrants to the United States should shed their foreign culture and become Americans. This meant adopting the English language and building a uniform American Church. This proposal infuriated many Catholics, especially the Germans and Italians, who desired churches where their languages were spoken and their traditions observed. Rome fielded many complaints alleging that millions of Catholics had left the

Church due to the insensitivity of the predominantly Irish hierarchy (see CAHENSLYISM). Although the intervention of Cardinal James GIBBONS prevented the establishment of national parishes, the complaints drew attention to Ireland's vocal support for American social and political forms.

This commitment to the United States and its culture was the greatest source of trouble for Ireland. In a widely reprinted speech delivered in 1884, Ireland declared that the principles of the American republic were harmonious with those of the Catholic Church. Catholics in America should devote themselves to those principles by becoming active in society, he argued, and immigrants should assimilate into American culture.

These views were not welcome in Rome at a time when the Vatican increasingly viewed the modern world as its enemy. Ireland's distaste for religious orders and his emphasis on the active virtues suggested that he was a man ready to turn the Church upside down. No less disconcerting was a speech he delivered on the silver anniversary of Gibbons's consecration as bishop of Baltimore. Entitled "The Church and the Age," that speech proclaimed that "the watchwords of the age are reason, education, liberty and the amelioration of the masses." These were not comforting words to a papacy attached to monarchy, hierarchy, and tradition.

There were rumors that a heretical movement in America believed the Church should accommodate itself to the demands of the world, and Ireland increasingly became identified as a proponent. This was enough to deny him a cardinal's hat, especially after Leo XIII's official condemnation of AMERICANISM in 1899.

Representative of Ireland's commitment to America was his involvement in politics. A staunch Republican, Ireland served as an unofficial adviser to Presidents William McKinley and Theodore Roosevelt. He participated in negotiations to avert a war with Spain in 1898, but when they collapsed he publicly endorsed the war effort. Following the hostilities, he

John Ireland, a leading 19th-century archbishop whose midwestern experience influenced his commitment to American democracy. *(Library of Congress)*

aided in negotiations over Church lands in the Philippines and urged that Spanish priests be replaced by Americans.

Despite his multiple involvements, Ireland did not neglect his diocese. Although an able administrator, his speculation in western lands to support churches and seminaries often threatened the diocese and Ireland personally with insolvency. He loved to preach and spoke comfortably in English, French, and Latin. His long and florid sermons, reflecting his training in classics, often were reprinted in Catholic newspapers and magazines. Originally opposed to parochial schools because of the cost, he soon realized that they were the only means of ensuring religious instruction. They became an integral part of his diocese, as did several colleges and seminaries.

Unlike many controversial figures, Ireland had the good fortune to outlive his enemies. During his last years he received near-universal approbation. At his death on September 25, 1918, even the Jesuit magazine *America* lauded him as a "godly man, keen of intellect, strong of will, . . . a great man among the greatest men."

EQ

Bibliography: John Ireland, *The Church and Modern Society: Lectures and Addresses* (Chicago: D. H. McBride, 1896); James M. Moynihan, *The Life of Archbishop John Ireland* (New York: Arno Press, 1976); Marvin Richard O'Connell, *John Ireland and the American Catholic Church* (St. Paul: Minnesota Historical Society Press, 1988); James P. Shannon, *Catholic Colonization on the Western Frontier* (New York: Arno Press, 1976).

Islam   Adherents of Islam, one of the world's three major monotheistic religions, distinguish themselves from others by their adherence to the "Five Pillars" of Islam. The first is the recitation of the *Shahadah*, the Muslim creed, affirming that "there is no God but God and Muhammad is the prophet of God." The remainder are praying five times daily, fasting during the festival of Ramadan, giving *zakat*, or mandatory alms, and making the hajj, or pilgrimage to Mecca, if possible.

Although Muslims view Islam as the natural religion of the world and the culmination of a series of prophetic revelations that included the ministries of Moses and Jesus, historical Islam dates from 610 C.E. In that year a Meccan trader by the name of Muhammad (570–632) received the first of the revelations from God through the angel Jibreel (Gabriel) that would ultimately become the Qur'an, Islam's sacred scripture.

The beginnings of Islam in America are not as readily dated. While there are claims that Muslim traders may have reached the Western Hemisphere before Columbus, it is probable that the first Muslims came as part of the massive slave trade. Some scholars have estimated that 15 to 20 percent of the hundreds of thousands of slaves forcibly removed from West Africa to America were Muslims. Although some of the slaves retained altered forms of their cultural and religious practices, mixing them with their slaveholders' customs and beliefs, little of their Islam survived in America.

Islam has not piqued the interest and fascination of American intellectuals the way Buddhism and Hinduism have done. However, it did attract a few converts as early as the 19th century. Muhammad Alexander Russell WEBB (1846–1916) generally is regarded as the first American convert to Islam. While serving in Manila as United States consul to the Philippines between 1887 and 1892, Webb was introduced to and eventually embraced Islam. In 1893 he traveled to Chicago to represent the Islamic tradition at the WORLD'S PARLIAMENT OF RELIGIONS. That same year Webb organized the American Islamic Propaganda Movement and published the first of his three books, *Islam in America*. Webb was unsuccessful in building a strong movement, and his organization died with him in 1916.

The first sustained Islamic presence in the United States took place in the early 20th century as Muslims from the Ottoman Empire began to immigrate in significant numbers. In 1915 Muslims from Albania settled in Maine and constructed what probably was the first mosque in the United States. Lebanese Muslims built mosques in Highland Park, Michigan, in 1919 and Ross, South Dakota, in the 1920s.

The Islamic population increased markedly in the years following World War II, and with the numeric growth came a need for organizational stability. The first group to fill this need was the Federation of Islamic Associations of the United States and Canada (FIA) founded in Chicago in 1954 by Abdullah Igram, a Muslim of Lebanese descent. An outgrowth of the International Muslim Society (founded in 1952), it attracted a primarily Lebanese membership.

By the 1960s, the FIA was overshadowed by the Muslim Student Association (MSA), a more diverse Islamic organization established in 1952 to address the needs of Muslim students who came to study at American universities in increasing numbers. As the MSA grew it spawned numerous affiliated organizations, including the Islamic Teaching Center and such professional associations as the Islamic Medical Association, American Muslim Scientists and Engineers, and American Muslim Social Scientists.

In 1981 the MSA and its affiliates gathered to form the ISLAMIC SOCIETY OF NORTH AMERICA (ISNA). ISNA functions as the major unifying organization for mainstream Islam in the United States. Comprised primarily of Sunni Muslim immigrants and their children, the organization historically had its greatest strength among Muslims from the Indian subcontinent but has expanded to nearly all segments of American Muslims.

Shi'ite Muslims, members of the smaller of the two main divisions within Islam and a marked minority among American Muslims, have also formed their own institutions. Two of the largest are the Islamic Society of Georgia (established 1973) and the Islamic Society of Virginia (1982).

The organization among indigenous Muslims that most closely parallels immigrant organizations is the Muslim American Society (formerly the American Muslim Mission). The Muslim American Society, composed primarily of African Americans, is an outgrowth of three occidental Muslim movements: the NATION OF ISLAM (NOI), the MOORISH SCIENCE TEMPLE, and the Universal Negro Improvement Association (see GARVEY, MARCUS).

Noble Drew Ali (see DREW, TIMOTHY) founded the Moorish Science Temple in Newark, New Jersey, in 1913. Dismissing Christianity as a religion for whites, he promoted Islam (albeit in an idiosyncratic form) as the appropriate religion for blacks, whom he called "Moors" or "Asiatics." Jamaican-born Marcus Garvey established his quasi-religious Universal Negro Improvement Association in Jamaica before coming to the United States in 1916. Preaching black nationalism, black messianism, and invoking the "God of Africa," he was one of the most radical and popular proponents of black nationalism.

Both of these men influenced Elijah Poole (1897–1975), better known as Elijah MUHAMMAD, who developed the Nation of Islam into a major voice of black separatism and Islam, although in a heterodox form. The Nation of Islam had been founded in Detroit by Master Wali FARD Muhammad in 1930. After his mysterious disappearance in 1934, Elijah Muhammad elevated Fard to quasi-divine status and represented himself as Fard's messenger and prophet on earth.

Elijah Muhammad worked mightily to build up the Nation of Islam throughout the 1930s and 1940s. Hindered by NOI members' refusal to fight in World War II and the group's radical critique of American culture, the movement grew slowly until the late 1950s. Increasing resistance to segregation and racism made the black separatist message more appealing to many, and when delivered by MALCOLM X (1925–1963), it found a messenger with a broad appeal. The conversion of heavyweight boxing champion Muhammad Ali to the Nation of Islam also increased its visibility.

After Elijah Muhammad died in 1975, he was succeeded by his son Warith Deen MUHAMMAD. Trained in Islamic schools both in the United States and abroad, Warith Muhammad labored to bring the NOI into line with Orthodox Sunni Islam. He opened its doors to whites and immigrants and removed the emphasis on racial separatism that had been a distinctive mark of the NOI. He also eliminated heterodox doctrines including the cult that had grown up around his father and his status as "Prophet." In addition, the NOI changed its name several times, becoming in 1980 the American Muslim Mission and in 1994 the Muslim American Society.

The rejection of black separatism and white demonism as well as the alignment with Islamic orthodoxy alienated many members, including Louis FARRAKHAN, who led a group of followers out of Warith Muhammad's movement and reconstituted the old Nation of Islam. By the late 1990s even Farrakhan had begun to move closer to orthodox Islam, and in 2000 he publicly acknowledged his commitment to Islam.

While orthodox Islam gained converts slowly among Americans, several Islamic-influenced religious movements also have made their mark. Some of these, such as those mentioned, had a major following among African Americans, and others have had a broader appeal. Many have been organized around an individual, a guru, espousing some version of Sufism, a mystical tradition within Islam. In the United States these gurus have tended to blend Sufism freely with the teachings and practices of other religious traditions. Among the Sufi gurus who developed followings within the United States are George Ivanovitch Gurdjieff, Muhammad Subuh, and Meher Baba.

The most syncretic and well-known Islamic-based religious movement in America is the BAHÁ'Í FAITH. Cofounded in 19th-century Persia by a man known as the "Bab" ("Gate") and his most prominent disciple, Bahá'u'lláh, the Bahá'í tradition embraces an eclectic line of prophets that stretch from Krishna to Bahá'u'lláh himself and includes Buddha, Zoroaster, Moses, Jesus, and Muhammad. Although considered an apostasy by Muslims, the Bahá'í faith has appealed to some in the United States because of its apparent inclusiveness and emphasis on peace.

The immigrant Muslim community in the United States is generally quite prosperous financially but has experienced some insecurity given geopolitical realities. Attacks on the United States and its interests by Muslims abroad have created a negative picture of Islam among large segments of the U.S. population. Additionally, the conflict between the Arab countries and Israel has left most American Muslims in a minority on that issue.

Moreover, there have been problems caused by social adjustment and adaptation by American Muslims to the United States and by American culture to Islam. Issues involving the time and place to pray, the wearing of the head scarf, or *hejab*, in public by Muslim women, and the adjustment to Islamic holidays all have precipitated shifts in American Islam. Additionally, the freedom and openness of American society often created conflicts between immigrant parents and their American-born children, as had been the case with most other immigrant groups.

Still, Muslims have become increasingly integrated into American society. While exact figures are widely disputed, the number of Muslims in the United States is clearly increasing rapidly. By the start of the 21st century there were probably between 2 and 4 million U.S. Muslims, many of them American born. Muslim chaplains served in the U.S. military, and in January 2000 President Bill Clinton hosted the first celebration of Eid al Fitr (the closing of Ramadan) in the White House. Both President Clinton and President George W. Bush referred regularly to America's churches, synagogues, and mosques as key religious sites, prompting some to observe a shift of the American religious mainstream from the Judeo-Christian tradition of the 20th century to an "Abrahamic" or "Judeo-Christian-Islamic" tradition in the 21st. At the very least, Islam was coming to be viewed less as an alien religion and more as a distinctive thread in the fabric of American religion.

EQ/SRP

Bibliography: Yvonne Yazbeck Haddad, ed., *The Muslims of America* (New York: Oxford University Press, 1991); Michael A. Koszegi and J. Gordon Melton, eds., *Islam in North America: A Sourcebook* (New York: Garland Pub., 1992); Phyllis Lan Lin, *Islam in America: Images and Challenges* (Indianapolis, Ind.: University of Indianapolis Press, 1998); Clifton E. Marsh, *From Black Muslims to Muslims:*

The Islamic Society of Orange County, Los Angeles. Muslims have organized mosques for worship throughout the United States. *(Pluralism Project of Harvard University)*

The Resurrection, Transformation, and Change of the Lost-found Nation of Islam in America, 1930 1995 (Lanham, Md.: Scarecrow Press, 1996); Jane I. Smith, *Islam in America* (New York: Columbia University Press, 1999); www.islamworld.net (an exposition of Islam and Islamic links); www. isna.net (Islamic Society of North America).

Islamic Society of North America   Organized in 1981 by a merger of the Muslim Students Association in the United States and Canada and its various constituent organizations, including the Islamic Medical Association and the American Muslim Scientists and Engineers, the Islamic Society of North America (ISNA) is the largest Muslim organization in North America (see ISLAM). Located in Plainfield, Indiana, ISNA is an umbrella organiza-

tion comprised of individual members and affiliate organizations including the Muslim Students Association and the Muslim Youth of North America.

The main emphases of ISNA are the creation and maintenance of a strong American-based Islam comfortable with the realities of American culture and secure in its Islamic identity and practice. In order to accomplish these goals ISNA began in the 1990s a concerted effort to help strengthen local Islamic institutions, especially *masjids* ("mosques") and Islamic schools. Additionally, the society has overseen conversions, issued Islamic marriage certificates, and validated the Muslim status of Americans seeking to participate in the hajj, or pilgrimage to Mecca. ISNA also provides services for American Muslims to help them meet their religious obligations regarding banking (Islam prohibits charging interest) and the payment of the *zakat*, or annual charity tax.

In 2000, ISNA had about 14,000 individual members and 129 affiliated organizations representing nearly 1 million Muslims in the United States. Its annual convention, tradition-ally held over Labor Day weekend, is the largest gathering of Muslims in the United States, averaging more than 30,000 attendees.

EQ

Bibliography: Phyllis Lan Lin, *Islam in America: Images and Challenges* (Indianapolis, Ind.: University of Indianapolis Press, 1998); www.isna.net (ISNA).

J

Jackson, Jesse (1941–) Following the assassination in 1968 of the Reverend Martin Luther KING, Jr., no one exactly inherited his mantle as the voice of blacks and the conscience of whites. But the Reverend Jesse Jackson came close.

Born Jesse Louis Burns in 1941 in segregated Greenville, South Carolina, he took his stepfather's name while a teenager. A high school football star, Jesse Jackson enrolled at the University of Illinois but later transferred to North Carolina Agricultural and Technical College. In 1963 he joined the CIVIL RIGHTS MOVEMENT in Greensboro, North Carolina, and was promptly arrested for nonviolent civil disobedience. The following year he graduated from North Carolina A & T and enrolled in Chicago Theological Seminary. In 1965, he met King and joined the civil rights movement full time. King tapped him to run the Chicago operations of Operation Breadbasket, the economic arm of the SOUTHERN CHRISTIAN LEADERSHIP CONFERENCE (SCLC), a civil rights organization, and in 1966 he launched a boycott in Chicago. The following year he became Operation Breadbasket's national director and was widely recognized as one of the movement's rising stars.

Jackson was present when King was assassinated in Memphis, Tennessee, in 1968. Later that year he was ordained a Baptist minister. Resigning from SCLC in 1971, he started his own organization, Operation PUSH (People United to Save Humanity), a group dedicated to expanding economic and educational opportunities and promoting self-esteem among African Americans. In 1984 he left PUSH and established the National Rainbow Coalition, which focused more than his prior organization had on politics and social policy. This new group got its name from Jackson's desire to expand beyond his black base and incorporate into one grand progressive organization other minorities, the poor, and peace and environmental activists. In 1996 these two organizations would merge into the Rainbow/PUSH Coalition.

Jackson burst onto the national stage in 1983, when he declared his candidacy for the Democratic presidential nomination, a post he would seek again in 1988. In 1990 he was elected a nonvoting member of the Senate, where he represented the District of Columbia and pushed for D.C. statehood. At least since 1979, when he stirred a controversy by meeting Palestine Liberation Organization leader Yasir Arafat in Lebanon, Jackson also has had an international role as a freelance diplomat. In 1984 he went to Syria and won the freedom of a U.S. Navy pilot shot down over Lebanon. In 1990 he secured the release of hostages held by Iraqi president Saddam Hussein. In 1999 he met with Serbia's Radovan Milosevic to gain freedom for three U.S. soldiers captured during NATO air raids over Yugoslavia.

Jackson's real role in public life, however, is neither winning votes nor freeing captives, but stirring the conscience of the American people. An orator of unusual power and creativity, Jackson has carried the idioms of the African-American sermon into the public square. He has also carried the SOCIAL GOSPEL into the 21st century, arguing for a place at America's table not only for blacks but also for the poor and the oppressed. He remains a living example of the black church's commitment to liberating people from social as well as individual sin.

Jackson is not without detractors. He lost support among American Jews when he referred to New York City as "Hymietown." Some African Americans claim he has put his own ambition ahead of the advancement of the black community, and some more radical blacks prefer to call Louis FARRAKHAN of the NATION OF ISLAM their leader. Some in the media deride him as an opportunist, and by and large Democratic Party officials have never figured out precisely what to make of him. But Jackson's roots in the civil rights movement and his undeniable powers as a preacher have kept him in the public eye for decades.

In the late 1990s, Jackson served as an unofficial spiritual adviser to President Bill Clinton following Clinton's affair with White House intern Monica Lewinsky. Not long after, in 2001, Jackson admitted to sexual improprieties himself. His admission that he had fathered a daughter out of wedlock was particularly poignant given the fact that Jackson was himself an illegitimate child. Jackson initially pledged to take time off from his public work to attend to his personal problems, but he was quickly back on the stump, advancing the work of his Rainbow/PUSH Coalition. Jackson and his wife, Jackie Brown, have five children. Their oldest son, Jesse Jackson, Jr., was elected to the U.S. Congress in Illinois's Second Congressional District in 1995.

SRP

Bibliography: Elizabeth O. Coulton, *The Jackson Phenomenon: The Man, the Power, the Message* (New York: Doubleday, 1989); Marshall Frady, *Jesse: The Life and Pilgrimage of Jesse Jackson* (New York: Random House, 1996); Jesse L. Jackson, *Straight from the Heart* (Philadelphia: Fortress Press, 1987).

Jainism   Jainism is a religious tradition typically traced to sixth-century-B.C.E. India and founder Vardhamana Mahavira. There are two main Jain schools, which originally separated over whether the ascetic life required nudity. These are the Digambara (literally, "clad only in the four directions," in other words, nude) and the Svetambara ("white clad"). Jain monks and nuns take Five Vows (to abstain from violence, lying, stealing, attachment to material things, and sex) and practice Three Jewels (right belief, right knowledge, and right conduct). Because they believe that both humans and animals have *Jiva*, or soul, Jains practice *ahimsa*, or nonviolence, a teaching popularized in India by the Indian reformer Mohandas Gandhi and in the United States by the Reverend Martin Luther KING, Jr.

Jainism remains a relatively small religious tradition in the United States because Jain monks traditionally are prohibited from traveling abroad. In fact, they typically travel only on foot. So Jain beliefs and practices were initially brought to the United States by laypeople. Virchand Raghavji Gandhi may have been the first Jain to visit the United States. An attorney, he traveled to Chicago in 1893 to represent Jainism at the WORLD'S PARLIAMENT OF RELIGIONS. Jains did not arrive in significant numbers, however, until after 1965, when new legislation opened up immigration from Asia. In 1966 Jain immigrants organized the country's first Jain center in New York City.

Jain monks began coming to the United States in the 1970s. The first was Muni Sri Chitrabhanu, who delivered lectures on Jainism at Harvard University in 1971. Four years later he established the Jain Meditation International Center in New York City. The second pioneering Jain monk was Acharya Sushil Kumarji, who came in 1975. He established the International Mahavir Jain Mission in 1978 and opened Siddhachalam, an ashram in

Blairstown, New Jersey, in 1983. Both of these pioneering monks reached out to European-American sympathizers and converts as well as to Asian Indian immigrants and their children.

Today there are roughly two dozen Jain temples in the United States, most of them in major metropolitan areas. Roughly half are incorporated into larger Hindu temple complexes; the others are freestanding Jain temples. In Norwood, Massachusetts, Jains worship in the Jain Center of Greater Boston, a temple that was once a Swedish Lutheran church.

American Jains are knit together in the Federation of Jain Associations in North America (JAINA), an umbrella organization founded in the early 1980s. JAINA publishes a quarterly called the *Jain Digest*. The World Jain Congress estimates that there are roughly 25,000 Jains in the United States today, although others have placed that figure as high as 100,000.

SRP

Bibliography: Bhuvanedra Kumar, *Jainism in America* (Mississauga, Ont.: Jain Humanities Press, 1996); http://www.bharatonline.com/Jaina (JAINA); http://www.imjm.org (International Mahavir Jain Mission).

James, William (1842–1910)

The author of *The Varieties of Religious Experience* (1902), perhaps the most influential American book on religion ever written, James belonged to that generation of intellectuals who grappled with the enormous changes to American culture brought about by the rise of modern science and industry after the Civil War.

James was born in New York City to Henry, Sr., and Mary Walsh James on January 11, 1842. His family inherited wealth from his grandfather, staunch Presbyterian (see PRESBYTERIANISM) William James of Albany. James's father, Henry, Sr., lived a life of leisure. Though he graduated from both Union and Princeton Seminaries, Henry, Sr., was a free thinker, influenced by Europeans such as Emmanuel Swedenborg. Throughout James's youth he shuttled the family back and forth across the Atlantic in order to provide the children with a cosmopolitan education. James's own formal education culminated in an M.D. from Harvard in 1869.

After a serious bout with ill health, James was appointed instructor of physiology at Harvard in 1872. Trained in the sciences, he accompanied Harvard's Louis Agassiz on a research trip to Brazil in 1865. Over the next few years James's interests shifted from physiology and anatomy to psychology, and finally to philosophy. He became assistant professor of philosophy in 1880 and full professor in 1885, a post he held until retirement in 1907.

James's work ran along several lines. His first major contribution, *Principles of Psychology* (1890), became the basic text in that field for many years. He was particularly interested in telepathy, clairvoyance, and other forms of parapsychology. His scientific training led him to approach traditional philosophical questions about the nature of knowledge (epistemology) and the nature of reality (metaphysics) in a unique manner. James argued that the world was a "blooming, buzzing confusion," and that human consciousness, or experience, was always at best only partially able to order this confusion. Thus, for James there was always something "more" to reality than could appear in our efforts to make sense of it. In fact, James thought, such attempts inevitably yield concepts that gain their clarity at the risk of distorting what they seek to clarify. Thus, James spoke of the "pragmatic" view of truth, in which concepts were judged by their effectiveness at diminishing this risk.

These ideas were especially important for his study of religion. James, unlike many of his contemporaries, thought that the "more" to reality was what the great mystics as well as religious enthusiasts of all stripes claimed to experience. In *Varieties*, based on the prestigious Gifford Lectures that he delivered at Scotland's University of Edinburgh in 1901 and 1902, he drew upon an enormous collection of personal accounts of mystical experience and religious

William James, Harvard philosopher and psychologist. His *Varieties of Religious Experience* (1902) is probably the most influential book on religion ever written by an American.

conversion from classical authors such as Saint Augustine up to the revivalists of his own day. Attempting to analyze these experiences without reducing them to various physiological or psychological causes (the route taken by other scientifically minded contemporaries such as Sigmund Freud), he argued that they contained two basic perceptions of life. The first, which he called "the religion of healthy-mindedness," saw the world in positive terms. The second, the religion of "the sick soul," was more inclined to see the world as marred by death, sin, evil, and suffering. James contended that these two forms of experience were perpetual parts of human history. Since the experiential cores that gave rise to historic religions were

constant for James, he doubted that religion would pass away in modern times, as many of his scientific contemporaries predicted. In his own life, James was attracted to movements such as mind-cure and NEW THOUGHT, which promised a therapeutic cure to harried Victorian Americans. He died on August 26, 1910.

MG

Bibliography: Hunter Brown, *William James on Radical Empiricism and Religion* (Toronto: University of Toronto Press, 1999); William James, *The Varieties of Religious Experience: A Study in Human Nature.* (1902; New York: Penguin Books, 1982); Henry Samuel Levinson, *The Religious Investigations of William James* (Chapel Hill: University of North Carolina Press, 1981); Linda Simon: *Genuine Reality: A Life of William James* (New York: Harcourt Brace, 1998).

Jarratt, Devereux (1733–1801)   Devereux Jarratt was an Anglican clergyman and leader of the religious revivals in Virginia during the GREAT AWAKENING of the mid-18th century. Jarratt joined forces with Methodist preachers during the Awakening in the hopes of ending spiritual indifference and strengthening church life in pre-Revolutionary America. Although he remained sympathetic to Methodism for many years, he withdrew his active support after METHODISTS organized a new denomination separate from Anglicanism in late 1784.

Jarratt was born in New Kent County, Virginia, on January 17, 1733. Raised a lukewarm Anglican, he experienced a religious conversion and call to the ordained ministry as a young man under the influence of Presbyterian evangelists. Jarratt chose to remain a member of the Church of England, however, because he believed the established church offered him the widest opportunities for Christian service. He sailed to London and was ordained in 1762. Upon his return to Virginia, he served as rector of Bath Parish in Dinwiddie County for the next 38 years.

Desiring to counteract what he considered the generally irreligious state of colonial ANGLI-

CANISM, Jarratt traveled as an itinerant through-out Virginia and North Carolina during the southern phase of the Great Awakening from 1764 to 1772. While his preaching was unques-tionably evangelical and stressed the need for spiritual rebirth, he remained faithful to his Anglican heritage. Thus, he strenuously resis-ted the efforts of Presbyterians and Baptists who sought to coax Anglicans to withdraw from their church. Since the Methodists in Vir-ginia still represented a loyal contingent with-in Anglicanism, Jarratt worked closely with them in raising revivals. He became a close friend of Francis Asbury, who later would be chosen as one of the first superintendents of the Methodist Episcopal Church.

Jarratt's career in many ways embodied the institutional tensions that divided American Anglicanism after the War for Independence. By the end of his life, Jarratt found himself iso-lated from both Anglicanism and Methodism, the two ecclesiastical traditions that once nur-tured him. On the one hand, he was often regarded by his staid fellow Anglicans as a dan-gerous visionary and religious fanatic. His emphasis on the need for a personal, heartfelt religion seemed out of place amid the world-liness of Virginia Anglicanism in the period of the Revolution. On the other hand, despite his early cooperation with the Methodists, Jarratt attacked their official separation from historic Anglican traditions. He had hoped the Metho-dists would remain within the Anglican fold as agents of its continuing spiritual renewal, and he was bitterly disappointed when they abandoned his church.

Jarratt continued to serve as rector of Bath Parish after the organization of the new Episcopal Church in 1785. Although he still cooperated with Methodists on occasion, his autobiography reveals the resentment he har-bored in his later years. Continuing true to his evangelical convictions until the end, Jarratt died in Dinwiddie County on January 29, 1801.

GHS, Jr.

Bibliography: Devereux Jarratt, *The Life of the Rev-erend Devereux Jarratt* (1806; New York: Arno Press, 1969); Harry G. Rabe, "The Reverend Devereux Jar-ratt and the Virginia Social Order," *Historical Mag-azine of the Protestant Episcopal Church* 33 (1964), 299–336.

Jefferson, Thomas (1743–1826)

Before his death on the Fourth of July, 1826, the 50th anniversary of the colonies' independence from Britain, Jefferson penned the epitaph for his tombstone: "Here was buried Thomas Jef-ferson, author of the Declaration of American Independence, of the statute of Virginia for religious freedom, and father of the University of Virginia." By means of such achievements, Jefferson, third president of the United States, contributed not only to the political develop-ment of the country but also to securing its intellectual and religious freedom. While Jef-ferson's epitaph is an accurate estimate of his influence on later generations, it is perhaps ironic that his role as an architect of American religious liberty is often linked to his phrase "the wall of separation" between church and state. Though the phrase sums up Jefferson's own view, it is taken from personal correspon-dence, and not from any public document.

Born to Peter and Jane Randolph Jefferson on April 13, 1743, Jefferson grew up among both the gentry and the wilderness of VIRGINIA. Tutored privately from the age of five in Greek, Latin, and other languages, Jefferson began for-mal schooling at the age of 14, after the death of his father. He was enrolled for two years in private school, where he developed a deep love of scholarship. In 1706 he entered the Angli-can (see ANGLICANISM) College of William and Mary, where he was exposed to the worldview of the ENLIGHTENMENT. After two years of gener-al study he went on to read law for five more, until age 21, when he inherited a portion of his father's estate. Having grown familiar with Williamsburg's political elite during his studies, Jefferson was well connected for both a career as a lawyer and for public life. After

Thomas Jefferson, United States president and major architect of the Bill of Rights's separation of church and state. *(Painting by Rembrandt Peale. Princeton University)*

mitment to freedom and equality in the Declaration of Independence (1776), a document that has achieved a kind of scriptural status in American life (see CIVIL RELIGION). While other members of the Congress amended his writing, in particular deleting the portion condemning the institution of SLAVERY, Jefferson gave voice to widely shared views that human rights, such as "life, liberty and the pursuit of happiness" were not the products of historical custom, but the gifts of a divine creator, a law of human nature. Further, he argued that legitimate government authority, one which respects the rights of its citizens, stems from the people themselves. Because human beings are given rights and reason within the order of nature itself, they have a duty to resist the efforts of tyrants who might seek to remove them; such actions by tyrants are themselves contrary to nature. Consequently, the Declaration makes a powerful argument for the right of revolution.

If in political life authority was constrained by "the consent of the governed," then the same held true for religion as well. In Jefferson's own Virginia, the Anglican church had been the established religion since the colony's origin. While Virginia had seen the growth of other churches since the early days and the passage of a Declaration of Rights in 1776 affirming religious liberty, Anglican powers resisted the movement for disestablishment, with its curtailment of tax monies. Jefferson's own Statute on Religious Liberty, which he wrote in 1779, was not passed by the legislature until 1786, after lengthy efforts by his friend James MADISON. The statute, which guaranteed free expression of religion and prohibited the use of taxes to support religious institutions, became the model for the FIRST AMENDMENT of the United States Constitution.

Jefferson's own deistic religious views rested firmly upon the faith in reason he learned from his Enlightenment mentors at the College of William and Mary. A firm rationalist, a believer in the adequacy of human reason to

being elected to the Virginia House of Burgesses in 1769, Jefferson went on to serve as a delegate at the Second Continental Congress in 1775 (at which he wrote the Declaration of Independence), as governor of Virginia, 1779–1781, as secretary of state during George Washington's presidency, and as vice president under John Adams. His own election to the presidency in 1800 came after crucial philosophical divisions had emerged between the Federalists, who supported a strong presidency, and those associated with Jefferson, who remained committed to limited federal power and greater individual freedom.

Appointed by the Continental Congress to draft a rationale for separation from Britain, the 33-year-old Jefferson articulated his com-

discover the truth, Jefferson remained nominally Anglican but had little sympathy for Christianity's supernatural claims. He became quite anticlerical later in life. After his retirement he wrote, though did not distribute, a rationalist's version of the New Testament, popularly known as the Jefferson Bible, in which miracles of all sorts were removed from the biblical text, leaving behind a set of moral teachings that Jefferson thought all could assent to as an expression of the rational core of religion. While most of his fellow citizens were unwilling to abandon the Christianity being spread through widespread revivals, Jefferson's articulation of the need for religious freedom has been supported by generations of Americans.

Jefferson's stature in American life has always been contested. In the 1990s his views on race and his slaveholding practices received widespread scrutiny. DNA evidence indicated that he likely fathered children through his slave Sally Hemings. That revelation led many to reevaluate just how revolutionary Jefferson was in his understanding of key concepts such as equality and liberty.

MG

Bibliography: Noble E. Cunningham, Jr., *In Pursuit of Reason: The Life of Thomas Jefferson* (Baton Rouge: Louisiana State University Press, 1987); Jan E. Lewis and Peter S. Onuf, eds., *Sally Hemings & Thomas Jefferson: History, Memory, and Civic Culture* (Charlottesville: University Press of Virginia, 1999); Dumas Malone, *Jefferson and His Time*, 6 vols. (Boston: Little, Brown, 1948–81); Charles B. Sanford, *The Religious Life of Thomas Jefferson* (Charlottesville: University of Virginia Press, 1984).

Jehovah's Witnesses

Jehovah's Witnesses is a religious organization that grew out of the work of lay evangelist Charles Taze RUSSELL and his teachings about the imminent return of Jesus Christ. Members believe they are the elect of God and prophets of the coming millennium (see PREMILLENNIALISM), the thousand-year reign of Christ on earth. They often are seen as they walk from door to door, preaching their message of salvation. Over the years, the Witnesses have been called by a variety of names, including the Watchtower Bible and Tract Society, Millennial Dawnists, and Russellites. In 1931, however, they assumed their present title, which is derived from a passage in the Old Testament Book of Isaiah ("'You are my witnesses,' says the Lord, 'and my servant whom I have chosen'") and from their distinctive use of the biblical term "Jehovah" as the proper name of God.

"Pastor" Russell, the founder of the Jehovah's Witnesses, was raised a Presbyterian, but he became increasingly troubled about orthodox Protestant doctrines on eternal damnation and the reliability of the Bible. This crisis of faith led him into a program of private Bible study, and by 1872 he had gathered other like-minded people into an association of Christians examining biblical teachings about the approaching kingdom of God. Russell soon formulated his own elaborate scheme about the time of Jesus' return, the second chance the dead would be given to accept Christ, and the final, absolute (though painless) annihilation of the wicked. He asserted that in 1874 the "Millennial Dawn" had begun with the coming of Christ in the "upper air," and that 1914 was the year when the world would end and God's kingdom would be fully established on earth. Russell formed his adherents into the Zion's Watch Tower Society in 1884 in order to disseminate these views.

The cosmic cataclysm Russell predicted, of course, did not occur in 1914, but his death in 1916 prevented him from fully revising his prophecies. It was left to Joseph Franklin ("Judge") Rutherford, his successor as leader of the Watchtower Society, to vindicate Russell's position. Rutherford gave new life to the movement and helped popularize its slogan, "millions now living will never die." He was responsible for organizing the Witnesses into "Kingdom Halls," local groups similar to traditional churches, and he gave structure to the program of neighborhood evangelism. He was also far more cautious than Russell about fixing a precise date for affairs in heaven. Rutherford taught that Christ had only returned "in spirit" in 1914 and emphasized that his visible return was still a few years away.

When Rutherford died in 1942, Nathan H. Knorr and a group of directors assumed control of the Jehovah's Witnesses. During and immediately after this period, the movement experienced its most dramatic growth, nearly quadrupling in size in the 1940s until its worldwide membership stood at 456,000 in 1952. The Witnesses, however, have never adopted a formal organization. They purposely avoid any possible resemblance to conventional church bodies and clergy, which they believe are agents of Satan. Instead, the Witnesses regard each individual member as an adequate messenger of God's truth. The Watchtower Bible and Tract Society, headquartered in Brooklyn, New York, is—as its name implies—merely a publishing operation. It prepares materials for evangelistic activities, prints Russell's voluminous works of biblical interpretation, and publishes *The Watchtower*, the Witnesses' well-known and widely circulated magazine.

The Jehovah's Witnesses have had an important impact on American culture, not because of any intended desire to be involved in social or political issues, but because of their militant refusal to interest themselves in worldly concerns. The message elaborated by Russell and Rutherford has tended to appeal to a group of Americans often called the "culturally deprived," that is, men and women of the middle and lower-middle classes who feel they have little stake in society. The Witnesses have consistently condemned political, commercial, and religious establishments, in which they play no role. The government of the world, both civil and ecclesiastical, they say, are ruled by Satan and oppress the righteous. It is the duty of the followers of Jehovah, therefore, to remain aloof from them.

These antiestablishment views have had tremendous social consequences, for they have frequently brought the Witnesses into conflict with the law. Members have refused to salute the American flag; to serve in the military; to register for the draft; to allow their children to have blood transfusions (believed to represent the "imbibing" of blood); and even to obey local ordinances about trespassing and peddling without a permit. Accusations of disloyalty to their government have continually hounded the group. During World War II, at least 2,000 Witnesses were jailed in the United States for failing either to enter the military or to accept alternative service as conscientious objectors. Yet despite the hostility repeatedly directed against them both as individuals and as a group, opposition has usually strengthened the Witnesses' conviction that they, rather than the alien world surrounding them, are the elect of God.

In the last quarter of the 20th century, the Jehovah's Witnesses were one of the fastest-growing American religious bodies. In 1991 the organization reported approximately 860,000 members in more than 9,300 "Kingdom Halls" throughout the United States.

GHS, Jr.

Bibliography: M. James Penton, *Apocalypse Delayed: The Story of Jehovah's Witnesses* (Toronto: University of Toronto Press, 1985); Shawn Francis Peters, *Judging Jehovah's Witnesses: Religious Persecution and the Dawn of the Rights Revolution* (Lawrence: University Press of Kansas, 2000); Timothy White, *A People for His Name: A History of Jehovah's Witnesses and an Evaluation* (New York: Vantage Press, 1968); http://www.watchtower.org (The Watchtower Bible and Tract Society).

Jesuits   The Society of Jesus, or Jesuits, began on August 15, 1534, when Ignatius of Loyola, a Spanish nobleman and soldier, and six companions pledged themselves to poverty, chastity, and missionary work in the Holy Land or anywhere else the pope might send them. Officially established as a religious order inside ROMAN CATHOLICISM six years later on September 27, 1540, the Jesuits dedicated themselves to strengthening the Church and evangelizing among the "heathen."

Driven by religious fervor, intellectual strength, and self-discipline instilled by the *Spiritual Exercises* established by Ignatius, the Jesuits soon became powerful and successful. With their centralized authority and their emphasis on education the Jesuits fiercely fought the spread of the REFORMATION, leading one historian to dub them the "shock troops of the Counter-Reformation."

As missionaries and educators the Jesuits made their mark on the Western Hemisphere. Between 1566, the founding of the first Jesuit mission in the present day United States, and the order's suppression in 1773 by Pope Clement XIV, more than 3,500 Jesuit missionaries served in North America. They were the dominant Catholic religious force in NEW FRANCE and even NEW SPAIN, where they controlled higher education. In British North America they constituted nearly the whole of organized Catholicism. Only one priest in those colonies was not a Jesuit at the time of the suppression (see COLONIAL PERIOD: MARYLAND, COLONY).

Restored by Pius VII in 1814, the Jesuits experienced tremendous growth in the United States. From a mere two dozen members in 1815 they peaked at more than 8,000 in the mid-1960s, nearly one-quarter of the order's worldwide membership. Although declining to slightly fewer than 4,500 members by 1992, the Jesuits still had more priests in the United States than in any other country. The order has played a significant role in American history; notable American Jesuits include the early missionaries Jacques MARQUETTE and Eusebio KINO, the theologian John Courtney MURRAY, the former U.S. representative Father Robert Drinan, and antiwar activist Daniel Berrigan.

Education remains central to the Jesuit mission. In the United States they run 28 colleges and universities, as well as numerous secondary and preparatory schools. Committed from its inception to Roman Catholic intellectual life, the Jesuits in the United States continue

this tradition by publishing several of the most influential Catholic journals and magazines, including *Theology Digest* and *America*.

EQ

Bibliography: J.C.H. Aveling, *The Jesuits* (New York: Stein & Day, 1981); William V. Bangert, *A History of the Society of Jesus* (St. Louis, Mo.: Institute of Jesuit Sources, 1986); Thomas Aloysius Hughes, *History of the Society of Jesus in North America, Colonial and Federal* (London: Longmans, Green, and Co., 1910); Allan Greer, *The Jesuit Relations: Natives and Missionaries in Seventeenth-Century North America* (Boston: Bedford/St. Martin's, 2000); John J. Killoren, *"Come Blackrobe": De Smet and the Indian Tragedy* (Norman: University of Oklahoma Press, 1994); http://www.jesuit.org (Society of Jesus).

Jesus movement   The Jesus movement of the 1960s and 1970s emerged out of the student movement, EVANGELICALISM, and the COUNTERCULTURE. "Jesus People," as participants in the movement were called, wore their hair long, listened to "Gospel rock," and tuned in to Jesus rather than LSD. They were the praying wing of the Woodstock Nation.

Like the CHARISMATIC MOVEMENT, the Jesus movement originated among laypeople in California in the 1960s. One important figure in the movement was Ted Wise, who in 1967 founded a coffeehouse called the Living Room in the Haight-Ashbury district of San Francisco. This gathering place later developed into a Christian commune called the House of Acts. Among the groups that emerged from this beginning was the Berkeley-centered Christian World Liberation Front.

Members of the mass media embraced the Jesus movement as a good source for news and drama. The Jesus People made it onto the cover of *Time* magazine in 1971. They also inspired two Broadway hits: the rock opera *Jesus Christ Superstar* and the more sedate but equally countercultural pop musical *Godspell*.

The Jesus movement, again like the charismatic movement, rejected unambiguously the "DEATH OF GOD' THEOLOGY of seminary-based theologians in favor of a simple faith that centered on the life and teachings of Jesus Christ. They portrayed Jesus as a countercultural hero—a long-haired dropout who rebelled against both religious and political establishments on behalf of criminals, prostitutes, street people, and the poor. Despite their countercultural inclinations, the Jesus People were theologically conservative. Born-again Christians, they stressed both the authority of the Bible and the importance of conversion. Some borrowed from PENTECOSTALISM and the charismatic movement practices such as faith healing and speaking in tongues. Ethically, the Jesus People were decidedly square, shunning both drugs and premarital sex.

Some Jesus People mingled an apocalyptic message with this largely evangelical gospel. The world was coming to a quick end, they argued, and Jesus was to return immediately. Others devoted their energies to improving the world, preaching a SOCIAL GOSPEL that emphasized justice, peace, and brotherhood and sisterhood.

Despite their divergent positions, Jesus People agreed on the importance of fashioning their theologies not out of the proclamations of middle-aged clerics but out of their own experiences. Theirs was, therefore, a lay as well as a youth gospel. While secular student leaders were warning young people not to trust anyone over 30, the Jesus People were warning Christians not to trust anyone in a clerical collar.

The Jesus movement proved to be as evanescent as psychedelic art, fading away shortly after it peaked at "Godstock"—the Campus Crusade for Christ Expo '72 held in Dallas. It did survive, however, in Jesus People USA (JPUSA). Founded in 1971, that Chicago-based group is one of the longest-running experiments in American Christian COMMUNITARIANISM. JPUSA claims about 500 members and publishes an online magazine called *Cornerstone*.

SRP

Bibliography: David Di Sabatino, *The Jesus People Movement: An Annotated Bibliography and General Resource* (Westport, Conn.: Greenwood Press, 1999); Robert S. Ellwood, Jr., *One Way: The Jesus Movement and Its Meaning* (Englewood Cliffs, N.J.: Prentice-Hall, 1973); http://www.jpusa.org (Jesus People USA); http://www.cornerstonemag.com (*Cornerstone*).

Jones, Absalom   The first black Episcopal priest in the United States started life in SLAVERY. Born in 1746 in Sussex, Delaware, Absalom Jones was brought to Philadelphia by his master in 1760. A clerk in his master's store during the day, he attended Anthony Benezet's school for blacks in the evening, already having taught himself to read. He managed to purchase his freedom in 1786.

Committed to METHODISM, Jones attended St. George's Methodist Church until 1787, when he was among a group of three blacks accosted by a church usher during prayers and told to go to the rear of the church. Angered by this affront, Jones and his fellow victim Richard ALLEN led an exodus of St. George's black members and founded the Free African Society. Distressed by the society's Quaker orientation (see FRIENDS, THE RELIGIOUS SOCIETY OF [QUAKERS]), Jones and Allen left and organized the first African church in Philadelphia. In 1792 they began building, but construction was interrupted by a yellow fever epidemic. The following year, as construction resumed, they debated the affiliation of the new church. Although Jones and Allen favored affiliating with the Methodists, the majority of members, still smarting from their ill-treatment at St. George's, favored the EPISCOPAL CHURCH. Jones, whose commitment to the community of blacks was greater than his commitment to Methodism, accepted the call to be the church's pastor after Allen refused.

The new building for St. Thomas Episcopal Church was completed the following year and formally dedicated in July 1794. Jones was ordained as a deacon one month later. In

October the church was admitted to the Episcopal diocese of Pennsylvania, and the "Negroes" of St. Thomas were "given control over their local affairs forever." In 1804 Jones was ordained a full priest in the Protestant Episcopal Church.

Jones was a conscientious pastor and attentively ministered to the needs of his flock until his death on April 11, 1816. As a leader in the black community he spoke out against slavery and racism, joining with Richard Allen in the formation of several societies for black uplift and protection. Along with Allen and parishioner James Forten, Jones founded Philadelphia's African Masonic Lodge in 1798 and served as its first Worshipful Master.

(See also AFRICAN-AMERICAN RELIGION.)

EQ

Bibliography: William Douglass, *Annals of the First African Church, in the United States of America, Now Styled the African Episcopal Church of St. Thomas* (Philadelphia: King & Baird, 1862); Civet Chakwal Kristof, *Who Was the Reverend Absalom Jones* (New York: St. Moses the Black Anglican Catholic Church, 1987); C. Eric Lincoln and Lawrence Mamiya, *The Black Church in the African-American Experience* (Durham, N.C.: Duke University Press, 1990).

Jones, Bob, Sr. (1883–1968)

One of the major markers of 20th-century Protestantism has been FUNDAMENTALISM's conflict with all other theological views. Few were as consistent and unbending in their strident commitment to fundamentalism as Bob Jones, Sr., and his son and grandson. For more than 100 years they have fought against everything they viewed as deviating from the true word of God.

Bob Jones, Sr., was born in Skipperville, Alabama, on October 30, 1883, the 11th child of William Alexander Jones and Georgia Creal Jones. Although sickly as a child, he soon demonstrated gifts as a public speaker. Following his conversion at the age of 11, he began preaching the Gospel. He directed his first revival (see REVIVALISM) at 12 and by the age of

13 had his own church with 54 members. A devout Methodist, he was licensed to preach by the Alabama Conference of the Methodist Episcopal Church, South, in 1898 and was made a circuit rider the following year.

His talents and abilities led his parents to struggle to give Jones a more complete education than normally possible for a child of small-scale farmers, especially since most of the local schools had only a three-month school year. A family friend who was principal of a nine-month school offered to let Jones move in with his family to receive a full education. During this time both of Jones's parents died, leaving him an orphan at the age of 17.

After attending Southern University in Greensboro, Alabama (now Birmingham-Southern College), for two years, he embarked on a full-time evangelistic career. His success as an evangelist was soon cut short by tuberculosis of the throat. Sent out west to recover, Jones began to visit a medium who appeared to channel the spirit of his mother. When he asked this "spirit" why it never spoke of heaven or Jesus, it replied that Jesus was simply a great medium, just like the one he was visiting. This would be a turning point in his life, convincing Jones that the devil was actively at work in the world trying to ensnare the naive and innocent. From then on his charge would be to combat the devil and to defend true Christianity.

Recovering from his illness, much to the surprise of his physicians, Jones returned to evangelistic work. Preaching throughout most of the eastern and southern United States, he was popularly rated as second only to Billy SUNDAY as an evangelist. He was active in the leading fundamentalist organizations of his day, including the World's Christian Fundamentals Association, the Winona Lake Bible Conference, and Moody Bible Institute.

In 1926 he founded the school that now bears his name: Bob Jones University in College Park, Florida. Although bankrupted by the Great Depression, the school was revived and moved to its present location in Greenville, South Carolina, in 1947.

Under the leadership of Bob Jones, his son Bob Jones, Jr. (1911–1997), and grandson Bob Jones III (1939–   ), the university has been the visible monument to inflexible, separatist, and aggressive fundamentalism. The school is committed to "Christian religion and the ethics revealed in the Holy Scriptures; combating all atheistic, agnostic, pagan and so-called scientific adulteration of the gospel." It affirms the tenets of fundamentalism, including biblical inerrancy, a literal virgin birth, the Resurrection, and the biblical story of creation. Staunchly anti-Catholic, the Joneses identify the Roman Catholic Church with the whore of Babylon and do not recognize Catholics as true Christians. This stance caused a serious problem for presidential candidate George W. Bush in 2000, when he spoke at the university. Many wondered whether his uncritical appearance implied support for these positions. While Bush issued an apology a few days later, the event brought Bob Jones University back into the spotlight, a position it had commanded in the 1970s when school policy mandating racial separation and forbidding interracial dating led to the revocation of its tax-exempt status. (Although the school is now racially integrated, Bob Jones, Sr., had maintained that segregation was scripturally mandated, and he had been vocal in his opposition to the CIVIL RIGHTS MOVEMENT.)

One of the most distinctive elements of the Joneses' fundamentalism has been their tenacious commitment to separatism and their refusal to work or associate with any person or any organization that did not completely share their beliefs, even theologically conservative Christians. This led Bob Jones, Sr., to publicly criticize Billy GRAHAM (who attended Bob Jones University for a semester) for including nonfundamentalists in his crusades and for encouraging converts to attend whatever church they chose. In 1966 Jones declared with characteristic bravado that Graham was "doing more harm to the cause of Jesus Christ than any living man."

EQ

Bibliography: Mark Taylor Dalhouse, *An Island in the Lake of Fire: Bob Jones University, Fundamentalism, and the Separatist Movement* (Athens: University of Georgia Press, 1996); George Dollar, *A History of Fundamentalism in America* (Greenville, S.C.: Bob Jones University Press, 1973); R. K. Johnson, *Builder of Bridges* (Murfreesboro, Tenn.: Sword of the Lord, 1969); Edward L. Queen II, "Bob Jones, Sr., Jr, and III." In Charles H. Lippy, editor, *Twentieth-Century Shapers of American Popular Religion* (New York: Greenwood Press, 1989); Daniel Turner, *The History of Bob Jones University* (Greenville, S.C.: Bob Jones University Press, 1997); www.bju.edu (Bob Jones University).

Jones, Charles Colcock (1804–1863)

Charles C. Jones was a southern Presbyterian minister and the most famed white evangelist of African-American slaves in the mid-19th century. A major plantation owner and slaveholder who was popularly called the "Apostle to the Blacks," Jones made important contributions to the development of PROSLAVERY THOUGHT in the South prior to the CIVIL WAR.

Jones was born in Liberty County, Georgia, on December 20, 1804. Although he prepared himself for a mercantile career as a teenager, a religious conversion in 1822 led Jones into ministerial studies. Educated at Phillips Academy and Andover Theological Seminary in Massachusetts and at Princeton Theological Seminary in New Jersey, he was ordained to the ministry in 1830. He served in several capacities over the course of his professional career: as minister at the First Presbyterian Church of Savannah, Georgia (his only pastoral charge), between 1831 and 1832; as professor at Columbia Theological Seminary in South Carolina from 1837 to 1838, and from 1848 to 1850; and as corresponding secretary of the Presbyterian Board of Domestic Missions in Philadelphia between 1850 and 1853.

Jones is best known for his efforts in evangelizing slaves in the area around his native

Savannah. His most significant work, *A Catechism of Scripture, Doctrine and Practice,* first published in 1837, was designed for "the oral instruction of colored persons." This book was used extensively both in schools and in homes throughout the South. He also published a second volume, *The Religious Instruction of the Negroes in the United States* (1842), which was intended to augment the usefulness of the first. In 1850 *The Southern Presbyterian* summarized Jones's importance in countering the abolitionist challenge to the slave system of the South. No clergyman other than Jones, the journal noted, possessed the skill and intelligence necessary "to check the rabid zeal of Northern fanatics and secure the confidence and hearty cooperation of the South in sustaining missions among our own people."

Poor health forced Jones to retire in 1853 and live as a semi-invalid at his Georgia plantation. He died at home in Liberty County on March 16, 1863.

GHS, Jr.

Bibliography: Robert Manson Myers, ed., *The Children of Pride: A True Story of Georgia and the Civil War* (New Haven: Yale University Press, 1972).

Jones, James Warren (Jim) (1931–1978)

By leading his followers in a mass murder/suicide, Jim Jones, founder of the Peoples Temple, achieved worldwide attention in 1978. His movement reflected the continuing deep-seated appeal of millennial religion in American culture.

Born to James Thurmond and Lynetta Jones in Lynn, Indiana, on May 13, 1931, Jones later recalled conflicting influences: his father's support for the Ku Klux Klan and his mother's passion for helping the underprivileged. Finding a powerful emotional warmth and acceptance in PENTECOSTALISM, Jones became actively involved in ministry while still young, gaining recognition as a faith healer at Pentecostal conventions and conferences.

In the racially oppressive setting of Indianapolis after World War II, Jones was an active worker for desegregation and civil rights. He drew upon his Pentecostal background to create a spiritual climate in which he could speak of civil equality as the direct outgrowth of the healing power of Christian faith. Jones disturbed many of the white proponents of segregated churches in Indianapolis, however, and in 1954 he was forced to resign as associate pastor of the Laurel Street Tabernacle, Assembly of God (see ASSEMBLIES OF GOD), and form his own racially integrated church, named the Peoples Temple Full Gospel Church, in 1955. For the next decade Jones continued working in Indianapolis, his rapidly expanding church affiliating with the DISCIPLES OF CHRIST in 1960. He found a powerful example of the yoking of racial equality and religious enthusiasm in the work of Father DIVINE's Peace Mission in Philadelphia, which he visited several times. He later claimed to have inherited Father Divine's mantle of godhood.

In 1965 Jones and more than 100 members of his congregation relocated the temple to Ukiah, California, in order to avoid what he saw as the growing risk of nuclear war. Jones began speaking of what he called "Apostolic Socialism" as the coming kingdom of God, a utopia in which his followers would find both racial harmony and economic equality. Expanding his operations to San Francisco in 1970 after receiving official recognition by the Northern California-Nevada region of the Disciples of Christ, Jones gained a strong reputation as a socially concerned minister among liberal politicians and social activists in California, where he received many humanitarian awards. In 1976 San Francisco mayor George Moscone appointed him chair of the city's Housing Authority.

Membership in the Peoples Temple continued to expand, reaching between 3,000 and 5,000, or even higher according to the temple's own estimates. While Jones's message of racial and social equality attracted people of various backgrounds, approximately 75 percent of the membership at Peoples Temple were poor, urban African Americans. In spite of his dramatic success, Jones doubted that his vision of a socialist heaven on earth could coexist with the dominant forms of power shaping American society. Increasingly wary of persecution by government, the media, and organized religion, in 1977 he again moved the temple, this time to the jungles of Guyana. Like the Puritans before him, he hoped to create a perfect society in the wilderness, far removed from the corrupt influences of the dominant society. For more than a year the colony of Jonestown cleared land, planted crops, and sought to discipline themselves to serve the cause of what Jones's preaching now called "God Almighty Socialism." But as damaging reports from ex-members circulated in Congress and in the press back home, alleging sexual abuse, mind control, and restraints on individual freedoms, Jones and his utopian community prepared themselves for a supreme sacrifice as a testimony to their socialist commitments. A visit to Jonestown led by Rep. Leo Ryan, a California Democrat, in November 1978, during which Ryan sought to bring an ex-member's child back to the United States, triggered Jones's deepest fears. Following an attack on the delegation as it began the return flight to the United States, Jones and 913 followers imbibed cyanide-laced fruit drink. Their mass death, which Jones portrayed as an act of revolution against a corrupt society, set off extensive debates in America about the assumed dangers of new religious movements and "cults."

(See ANTI-CULT MOVEMENT.)

MG

Bibliography: David Chidester, *Salvation and Suicide: An Interpretation of Jim Jones, the Peoples Temple, and Jonestown* (Bloomington: Indiana University Press, 1988); Laurie Efrein Kahalas, *Snake Dance: Unravelling the Mysteries of Jonestown* (Victoria, B.C.: Trafford, 1998).

Jones, John William (1836–1909) J.
William Jones was a Southern Baptist minister and the most prominent champion of the LOST CAUSE MYTH. Jones preached an irenic but insistent message throughout the post–Civil War period: The Confederacy's political and spiritual ideals had been high ones, and despite being overwhelmed in battle, the South was righteous in the eyes of God.

Jones was born at Louisa Court House, Virginia, on September 25, 1836. Converted at a camp meeting revival as a young man, he enrolled at the University of Virginia, where he was active in religious activities and treasurer of one of the first college Young Men's Christian Associations (YMCA). After graduation, Jones traveled to Greenville, South Carolina, and became a member of the original class at the Southern Baptist Theological Seminary. He was ordained in June 1860 and commissioned by his denomination's Foreign Mission Board for work in China, but the outbreak of the CIVIL WAR permanently delayed his departure for the missionary field.

When Virginia seceded from the Union, Jones enlisted as a private in the Confederate army. After a year's service in the ranks, he assumed the role of regimental chaplain and, later, of missionary chaplain in General A.P. Hill's corps. In close cooperation with both General Robert E. Lee (an Episcopalian) and General Stonewall Jackson (a Presbyterian), he was instrumental in organizing what was known as "the Great Revival," a period of intense religious enthusiasm that gripped the Confederate army in Virginia during the winter of 1862–1863. Known thereafter as "the fighting parson," Jones made the Civil War and its memory the focus for his life's work.

After 1865, Jones served in a number of different capacities that placed him at the center of the religious, intellectual, and popular cultures of the postbellum South. His roles included the college chaplaincy, first, at Washington College (later Washington and Lee), then at the University of Virginia, and, finally, at the University of North Carolina; the secretary-treasurer's post in the Southern Historical Society; editorship of the *Southern Historical*

Society Papers; and the chaplain-general's position in the United Confederate Veterans. He wrote numerous books and articles about his wartime experiences and the virtues of the soldiers of the defeated Confederacy. His best-known published works were *Personal Reminiscences, Anecdotes, and Letters of Gen. Robert E. Lee* (1875) and *Christ in the Camp* (1887). The latter book contained a collection of upbeat stories about the significance of religious revivals in the Confederate armies. He also wrote an article on "The Morale of the Confederate Army" that appeared in General Clement Evans's influential 12-volume *Confederate Military History* (1899).

Afflicted by ill health toward the end of his life, Jones died at Columbus, Georgia, on March 17, 1909. He was buried at Hollywood Cemetery, the resting place of many prominent ex-Confederates in Richmond, Virginia. As one southern writer noted at his passing, Jones worshiped "Lee and Jackson next to his God" and "died not only in the 'faith once delivered to the saints,' but in the good old Confederate faith."

GHS, Jr.

Bibliography: J. William Jones, *Christ in the Camp; or, Religion in the Confederate Army* (1887/1904; Harrisonburg, Va.: Sprinkle Publications, 1986); Charles Reagan Wilson, *Baptized in Blood: The Religion of the Lost Cause, 1865–1920* (Athens: University of Georgia Press, 1980).

Jones, Samuel Porter (Sam) (1847–1906)

Sam Jones was a Methodist minister and popular evangelist in the post–Civil War South. One of the most recognized religious figures of his day, he was dubbed "the Moody of the South," thus equating him with the internationally celebrated revivalist Dwight L. MOODY. Jones used blunt, homespun language to convince the crowds who gathered to hear his sermons to resist the evils of profanity, gambling, and liquor.

Jones was born in Chambers County, Alabama, on October 16, 1847. Growing up in rural Georgia, he was educated by private tutors and in boarding schools. After serving in the Confederate army during the Civil War, he worked as a lawyer in Georgia between 1868 and 1872. Although his addiction to alcohol soon ruined his law career, Jones experienced a religious conversion and, honoring the deathbed request of his father, stopped drinking in 1872. That same year he was ordained to the ministry of the Methodist Episcopal Church, South, and began preaching in northern Georgia. He held several pastorates from 1872 to 1880, and in 1880 he became agent of the Methodists' North Georgia Conference Orphan's Home in Decatur, Georgia, a position he retained until 1892.

In raising funds for the orphans, Jones fashioned a message that stressed the moral sins of the city and the need for affluent Christians to give attention to the urban poor. He believed that true conversion brought a change in conduct and that deeds were just as important as confessions of faith. Jones's emphasis on the practical implications of Christianity helped bring the idea of a SOCIAL GOSPEL to the southern urban environment. When Jones came to Nashville, Tennessee, in the spring of 1885 and led a 20-day revival, he left the city "buzzing" with religious enthusiasm. Bringing together Methodists, Presbyterians, and Baptists, he launched a stinging attack on the moral apathy of the city's churchgoers. He accused prosperous businessmen of bringing damnation upon themselves, because they cared more about their money than about their souls. Jones so moved Nashville steamboat captain Tom Ryman that he discontinued the thriving liquor concession on his riverboats and (legend has it) dumped the bottles into the Cumberland River.

Jones's skills as an urban evangelist brought him an invitation from T. DeWitt Talmage, a popular preacher and Presbyterian minister in Brooklyn, New York, to conduct a revival in Brooklyn. Jones's success eventually led him to become a traveling preacher who drew capacity crowds in all the major American cities of the time. He tried to break down barriers between sacred and secular life and poured contempt on clergy who failed to deal with real-life situations. "We have been clamoring for . . . a learned ministry and we have got it today and the church is deader than it ever has been in history," he told a group in Memphis, Tennessee. "Half of the literary preachers in this town are A.B.'s, PhD.'s, L.L.D.'s, D.D.'s, and A.S.S.'s."

Jones reached the peak of his popularity in the 1890s. Several volumes of his sermons were published, some posthumously. Aboard a train bringing him home from a revival in Oklahoma City, Jones died near Perry, Arkansas, on October 15, 1906.

GHS, Jr.

Bibliography: Kathleen Minnix, *Laughter in the Amen Corner: The Life of Evangelist Sam Jones* (Athens: University of Georgia Press, 1993).

Jordan, Clarence   See KOINONIA FARM.

Judaism   Judaism in the United States has developed from a tiny minority to the point where, along with PROTESTANTISM and ROMAN CATHOLICISM, it has become one of the country's three major faiths. Like Protestantism and Catholicism, Judaism experienced tremendous transformations while responding to the distinctive social and cultural milieu of America.

Judaism as a religion is fundamentally tied to the idea of peoplehood. From the time that God promised Abraham that he would be the father of a great nation, the religion of the Jews has been inseparable from the people of Israel. In the land of Israel the Jews developed a complex and vibrant culture that persevered throughout several periods of foreign occupation and captivity. For nearly 3,000 years, until 70 C.E., within the holy city of Jerusalem stood the Temple where the priest performed the priestly duties of animal sacrifice and prayer.

During the period of Roman occupation this ritual reached its height. Under the Roman puppet king Herod—a convert to Judaism—

the temple was enlarged. Jewish communities spread throughout the Mediterranean world and Roman soldiers guarded the caravans of money these communities annually sent to the Temple. The Jews, although a conquered people, had a special status in the empire as a *religio legitas* ("recognized religion") and generally shared in the prosperity of the *pax romana*.

The period of Roman rule, however, contained the seeds of its own destruction. The Romans' behavior often offended Jewish religious sensibilities, and many Jews looked upon those who collaborated with the Romans as traitors to both their people and religion. Different Jewish groups competed for religious control and dominance; many of these groups are familiar to Christians from their reading of the New Testament, among them the Sadducees, Pharisees, and Zealots.

In 67 C.E. a revolt against Roman rule broke out. Initially successful, this rebellion was not suppressed completely until 73 C.E. Jerusalem, however, was taken in 70 C.E. and the Temple destroyed. Successive revolts in 115 and 132 led to the complete destruction of Jerusalem. When it was rebuilt as a Roman city, Aelio Capitolina, Jews were barred from entering it. These events led to a major transformation within Judaism. Unable to continue the Temple rites, Judaism was forced to adapt or die.

The process of adaptation undertaken by the Jews in the diaspora (the dispersal from their homeland) led to the creation of the Talmud, a compilation of the commentaries on the religious laws, both written and oral, given by God to Moses in the Torah. Judaism became a religion based upon a scrupulous observance of these religious laws while awaiting the arrival of the Messiah, who would restore the people of Israel to their homeland and rebuild the Temple.

In the period from the second century C.E. through the 15th century the Jews developed two major centers of religious life and thought—eastern and central Europe and

Spain. The Jews of eastern and central Europe, the Ashkenazim, led a difficult existence, suffering persecution from their Christian neighbors. They developed an inward-looking religious and social structure that emphasized the community and strict religious practice. The Jewish community in Spain, the Sephardim, lived in a less oppressive and more cosmopolitan society. This came to a crashing halt in 1492. In that year the 400-year war between Christian Spain and Muslim Spain ended with the fall of the Muslim city of Grenada to the armies of King Ferdinand of Aragon and Isabella of Castile. With the political unity of the Iberian peninsula secured, the monarchs proceeded to enforce religious unity. They decreed that all Jews must either convert to Christianity or leave. This event marks the beginning of the history of Jews in America.

While two Jews were among Columbus's crew and several accompanied other Spanish explorers, the year 1654 was the start of organized Jewish life in what became the United States. Descendants of expelled Spanish Jews who had been living in Holland went to Recife, Brazil, following its capture from Portugal by the Dutch. When the Portuguese recaptured the city in 1654, these Jews fled. Twenty-three of them traveled to the Dutch colony of New Amsterdam (modern-day New York). When the governor wrote to the colony's directors in Amsterdam complaining of the influx of Jewish refugees into the colony, fearful that they would next let in Lutherans, he was admonished and reminded that the Dutch Jewish community had invested heavily in the colony.

Receiving the right of public worship, these Jews formed the first Jewish congregation in America, Congregation Shearith Israel. In 1658 they were joined by 15 Jewish families from Holland, who established the first Jewish congregation in a British colony in Newport, Rhode Island. This community would build the Touro Synagogue (completed in 1763), the oldest synagogue in America. Jewish immigration increased after 1740,

The United States boasts the most vibrant Jewish community outside of Israel. Exterior of Temple Beth Shalom, Cambridge, Massachusetts. *(Pluralism Project of Harvard University)*

when the British Parliament granted Jews naturalization rights in the colonies. By the time of the AMERICAN REVOLUTION the Jewish community in the American colonies numbered about 2,000, with the community in Charleston, South Carolina, at 500, the largest. New York at that time had 30 Jewish families.

America's Jewish population was largely Sephardic and maintained a religious tradition described by many scholars as "dignified orthodoxy." They blended in with the rest of the colonists, and many had prominent places in colonial life. Although there was no rabbi in the colonies, the cantor—an individual who leads the recitation of prayers—took on the role of minister, and the laity passed on the religious traditions.

What had been the least oppressive society for Jews in the Western world became even less oppressive following the American Revolution and the framing of the CONSTITUTION. The national government's neutrality in religious affairs placed every religious community on a footing of independence and self-organization. This differed from the European and Islamic worlds, where even an oppressed community like the Jews had a governmentally accredited organization to oversee community affairs. The absence of such an organization had major implications for the way Judaism developed in the United States.

Following the end of the Napoleonic wars in 1815 and the failure of the liberal revolutions in Europe in the 1830s and 1840s, the United States experienced its first wave of massive immigration. In this wave came the first substantial numbers of Ashkenazic Jews, primarily from Germany. While there had been Ashkenazic Jews in America before this time, their numbers had been small and most had acquiesced to the Sephardic majority. There were some conflicts, however. In 1802 Jews of Ashkenazic background in Philadelphia withdrew to found their own synagogue. A similar occurrence took place in Congregation Shearith Israel in New York in 1825. Where no governmental authority oversaw the organization of the community, differences were resolved by separation.

These conflicts increased throughout the 19th century as Jewish immigration continued. Between 1800 and 1850 the Jewish population in the United States grew from 2,000 to 50,000. By 1860 it had reached 150,000. Nearly all these immigrants were central European Jews who followed the Ashkenazic ritual and came primarily from the regions of Europe influenced by German language and culture. This proved transformative for the American Jewish community and for Judaism as well, for

these German immigrants brought REFORM JUDAISM to America.

Reform Judaism has its intellectual origins in the ENLIGHTENMENT and its political roots in the period of Jewish emancipation (removal of restrictions placed on the Jews) during the French Revolution and Napoleonic period. These events challenged many of the traditional practices of Judaism. With the removal of legal proscriptions some felt that the insularity previously needed for communal protection was unnecessary. The new scholarship undertaken by many Jews educated in German universities demonstrated that many of the changes emerging in Judaism—preaching in the vernacular, for example—were not new at all. Most importantly, however, Reform had a social dimension. There was a growing dissatisfaction with those elements of Judaism that separated the Jews from their fellow citizens—modes of dress, forms of worship, dietary restrictions. In response to these new circumstances, certain congregations in Germany had changed the traditional structure of worship services. They translated prayers from Hebrew to German and dispensed with some prayers altogether. They introduced organ music, and the cantor or the rabbi delivered a weekly sermon. As German-speaking Jews arrived in the United States they brought these practices with them.

Although the Jewish congregation in Charleston had produced its own indigenous reform movement—the Reformed Society of Israelites—as early as 1824, Reform in the United States was primarily the work of these German immigrants. The first explicitly Reform congregation in America was Temple Har Sinai in Baltimore in 1842, but 1853 is probably the most significant year for Reform Judaism in the United States. In that year Isaac Mayer WISE, a rabbi from Bohemia, left his congregation in Albany, New York, and took over Congregation Bene Yeshurun in Cincinnati. By then Wise had become completely committed to the transformation of Judaism. Both a modernizer and an Americanizer, Wise looked upon America as Israel and Washington as Jerusalem. He used the term Hebrew instead of Jew and spoke of the Jewish religion, not the Jewish people.

A tireless propagandist and organizer, Wise published two weekly papers, *The American Israelite* in English and *Die Deborah* in German. In 1856 he published a major revision of the Hebrew prayer book, significantly titled *Minhag America* ("American Ritual"). He also was responsible for the formation of the Union of American Hebrew Congregations in 1873 and the establishment of Hebrew Union College, the first permanent school for the training of rabbis in the United States, in Cincinnati in 1875.

Although Wise's view of religion was quite radical, his work was directed primarily toward organizational goals, and he stressed unity with the Orthodox. As a result, Wise often was attacked by the more radical and intellectual proponents of Reform, primarily in the person of David EINHORN.

Einhorn had had a distinguished career as a rabbi in Europe before coming to the United States as rabbi of Temple Har Sinai in Baltimore. In seeking an intellectual basis for Reform, Einhorn looked with disfavor on Wise's Americanizing activities. He was committed to maintaining the German language and German thought for the Reform movement. "German research and science," wrote Einhorn, "are the heart of the Jewish Reform idea, and German Jewry has the mission to bring life and recognition to this thought on American soil." Einhorn and others brought to America a series of themes that made sense within the German context but basically were irrelevant in America.

They were concerned with such questions as: How can a Jew maintain that he is in exile from his homeland (Israel) and a citizen of a country? What is the nature of the hope for a personal messiah and the restoration of Israel and the temple rite? These radicals attempted to answer these questions at a conference held in Philadelphia in 1869, where they issued a statement (in German) outlining their views of Judaism. They rejected the messianic aim of the restoration of the Jewish state, claiming instead that the messianic aim of Israel was the "union of all the children of God." The exile of the Jewish people was not punishment for sin but part of the divine plan of dispersing the "Jews to all parts of the world for the realization of their high priestly mission, to lead the nations to the true knowledge and worship of God."

Wise, who was active in bringing American Jews together in various projects, viewed Einhorn's radicalism as destructive to the unity of the American Jewish community. By 1885, however, Wise presided over another conference of Reform rabbis in Pittsburgh that issued a declaration of principles known as the PITTSBURGH PLATFORM. This platform set out the principles of Reform. It rejected all parts of Jewish law not in keeping with "the views and habits of modern civilization" and proclaimed Judaism "a progressive religion, ever striving to be in accord with the postulates of reason." Such a radical statement was possible in 1885 because the possibility of union between the reformers and those who desired to retain the traditional elements of Judaism had been derailed two years earlier.

By 1880 the majority of the nation's 270 congregations and most of the 250,000 members of the Jewish community were Reform. There were opponents, however, centered primarily in the older Sephardic and Ashkenazic synagogues of the eastern seaboard and led by Isaac LEESER, cantor of Congregation Mikveh Israel in Philadelphia and editor of the *Occident*. While the traditionalists worked with the reformers in founding the Union of American Hebrew Congregations and Hebrew Union College, the issues that divided them were great. How much English (or German) should be allowed in the service? To what extent and degree should the dietary laws be followed?

Not until 1883 would different answers appear to these troubling questions.

The year 1883 seemed a high point for a unified American Judaism. The Union of American Hebrew Congregations was on its way to representing the entire faith, and Hebrew Union College was graduating its first class of rabbinical students. The school, knowing that many of its directors strictly observed Jewish dietary laws, engaged a Jewish catering firm to prepare the closing banquet. As the first course came, two rabbis rose from their seats and left the room. Shrimp, one of the forbidden foods (*trefa*), had been served them. The more orthodox were appalled. The event amply demonstrated the chasm that separated them from the Reform.

Sabato MORAIS, rabbi of Mikveh Israel, Morris Jastrow (1829–1903), rabbi of the Ashkenazic synagogue in Philadelphia, and Henry Pereira MENDES, rabbi of Shearith Israel were among those who joined together to create a traditionalist united front against Reform. This front found expression in the formation of the Jewish Theological Seminary (1887) in New York City and what is now known as CONSERVATIVE JUDAISM.

Conservative Judaism articulated a "positive historical" view of the religion, maintaining a reverence for the Jewish traditions that were not to be altered for mere convenience or utility's sake. These men accepted that Judaism was the result of historical processes and could be formed and reformed through those processes. They adopted certain innovations such as removing the curtain (*mehitzah*) that separated women from men in a synagogue. But they retained most of the traditional liturgy, dietary laws, and distinctively Jewish elements of the religion—especially the Hebrew language.

Though a minority among American Jews, the traditionalists persevered. The Jewish Theological Seminary held on, but barely. After the death of Morais, its first president, the seminary's future was in doubt. At this time, however, the United States was experiencing a new wave of Jewish immigration. The immigrants came from eastern Europe and were rigidly orthodox in practice. The older traditionalists felt that this group would provide them with an opportunity for growth. They would need rabbis that Jewish Theological Seminary could supply. But some trouble lay ahead. The Jews from Poland, Romania, Russia, Galicia, and Lithuania had centuries of tradition and practice separating them not only from Reform but also from the Orthodoxy of Mendes.

Between 1880 and 1920 the Jewish population in the United States grew from 250,000 to nearly 3.5 million; nearly all came from eastern Europe. These immigrants brought a history radically different from that of Sephardic or German Jews, upon whom they looked with suspicion. In eastern Europe, the Jews lived under laws and persecution more repressive and violent than elsewhere. Partially by requirement and partially by necessity they created close-knit communities where one lived nearly all one's life surrounded by other Jews and by the traditions and laws of Judaism. Their arrival in America produced a crisis that once again altered the face of the Jewish-American community.

This crisis was caused by several factors. The first was mutual hostility between the newcomers and the "older," more Americanized Jews. The older community viewed the newer immigrants as superstitious, vulgar, and ignorant. The immigrants looked upon this older community as heretics and traitors. Recognizing their differences from the dominant patterns of American Judaism, the new immigrants quickly began to develop their own institutions.

In 1887 several Orthodox synagogues formed the Association of American Hebrew Congregations and organized a search for a chief rabbi to oversee religious affairs. They chose Rabbi Jacob Joseph of Vilna (Vilnius), but factional conflicts caused the enterprise to fail. The absence of any power, whether state authority or communal pressure, to coerce obedience made it obvious that religion in the United States could not be reorganized on the European pattern. By 1888 it was equally obvious that Judaism had experienced the process of "denominationalism" that marked American Protestantism and that it was divided into the branches of Orthodox, Conservative, and Reform that exist today.

Virtually all eastern European Jews came to the United States with Orthodox religion; a large minority also brought a background in radical politics. Increasing political and economic pressures on the eastern European Jewish community had transformed many into urban industrial workers. This weakened religious practice and pushed many into the various socialist movements of eastern Europe. Simultaneously, increasing anti-Semitism drove many toward nationalistic expressions, preeminently to ZIONISM—the movement to establish a Jewish national homeland in Palestine.

Both of these strains were viewed with suspicion by older members of the American Jewish community. They feared that the radicalism of these immigrants would reflect poorly on the community, especially at a time when America was experiencing an upsurge in anti-Semitism. The immigrants' Zionist inclinations also flew directly in the face of what the American Reform movement stood for. In 1897 the Central Conference of American Rabbis, the organization of Reform rabbis, adopted a resolution officially condemning Zionism.

These eastern European Jews transformed American Judaism and were themselves transformed by it. Orthodoxy itself, one might argue, is an American phenomenon. Previously there was only Judaism. Orthodoxy as a self-conscious position becomes necessary only when there are other options, and in America there were. Religiously, the result of this second immigration wave was not only an expansion in the number of Orthodox congregations in the United States, but also growth in the numbers of Conservative and Reform as the

immigrants, or their children, moved into these less restrictive environments.

There was also a massive increase in the numbers of religiously unaffiliated Jews. The breakdown of traditional community structures caused by immigration and the absence of a legally defined status for the Jews in the United States disrupted many immigrants. The maintenance of Jewish dietary laws and avoidance of work on the Sabbath (Saturday) slid away as they tried to fit in to American society. For example, a 1935 survey of New York City youths between the ages of 15 and 25 discovered that 72 percent of Jewish males and 78 percent of Jewish females had not attended a religious service in the past year.

A small number of Jews arrived at this position via Reform. For them, a Judaism stripped of nearly all of its tradition was an empty shell, and they wandered off in other directions. Felix ADLER founded the ETHICAL CULTURE Society on just such a basis.

A larger number came to be unaffiliated through radical politics and secular Zionism. These people did not, however, leave their Jewishness behind. In fact, secular Zionism was deeply connected to Jewish culture and identity. Zionism revived Hebrew as a spoken language, revitalized the study of Jewish history (albeit with an ideological intent), and emphasized pride in Jewish cultural identity.

Socialism was also fused with a sense of Jewish identity, as the number of Yiddish workers' circles and the *Jewish Daily Forward* (a Yiddish-language socialist paper) attest. Both Zionism and socialism informed movements such as *Ha Shomer Hatzair*, which, while committed to a militantly secular version of Zionism, strongly affirmed connections with Jewish history and identity.

Most immigrants, or their children, who drifted into irreligion did so for none of these reasons. Nathan Glazer in *American Judaism* has suggested that they drifted into unbelief because they had nothing in which to believe. He argues that eastern European Orthodoxy failed to provide people with the doctrine and dogma necessary to deflect doubt and argument. There was no way to answer the question, "Why?" In America, where no one imposed anything and where other options existed for affirming one's Jewish identity, religion seemed much less relevant, especially when following the religious laws seemed to limit social advancement.

In 1927 Congress passed the last of a series of bills that effectively ended immigration. The end of immigration allowed the American Jewish community an opportunity to concentrate its attention on the processes of Americanization and acculturation as well as the strengthening of community institutions before the deluge of the Great Depression and the rise of Nazism in Germany.

Although the depression had no major impact upon Jewish-American identity, it did slow the rise in social status that had been typical of the community. Hitler's coming to power in Germany, World War II, and the murder of nearly 6 million European Jews by the Nazis did have a major impact upon the community, although the magnitude of this impact would not be fully apparent for nearly two decades. Most immediately, these events ended Reform hostility toward Zionism. In 1937 the Reform movement officially voiced its support for the creation of a Jewish homeland in Palestine as a place of refuge for European Jews threatened by Nazism. A commitment to Zionism, especially after the creation of the state of Israel in 1948, became normative for most American Jews.

With the end of the war, the soldiers who returned home rode the wave of economic prosperity, the GI Bill, and VA loans into the suburbs. This was as true for Jews as it was for gentiles. In the suburbs Jews built synagogues, sent their children to Hebrew school on Sundays and in the afternoons, and lived out the American dream. The synagogue became as much a place for the expression of Jewish identity as for religion. Most of these synagogues

were Reform or Conservative, although there were Orthodox synagogues as well. In this period of Jewish revival, the institutional forms of religion played a major role in maintaining Jewish identity.

Once again the requirement of choice played a role. As Jews moved from city neighborhoods, where 70 to 90 percent of the population might be Jewish and where one could feel Jewish without belonging to a single Jewish organization, to the suburbs where the percentage of Jews was lower, one had to create institutions that made affirming one's Jewishness possible. Between 1937 and 1956 the number of Conservative and Reform synagogues doubled, and the number of affiliated families increased from 75,000 to 200,000 and from 50,000 to 255,000, respectively.

The impact of the 1960s on the Jewish-American community was great. Beyond the CIVIL RIGHTS MOVEMENT, the student rebellion, and the VIETNAM WAR were two events that changed the directions taken by American Judaism. The first was what some have called the re-ethnicization of American society. This movement had its start in the demand for "Black Power" but found an audience among many younger American Jews, who found in a vocal Jewish identity another source of rebellion against the conformity of suburban society. This movement fused with the memory of the Holocaust and the creation of the state of Israel in the cauldron of the 1967 war between Israel and its Arab enemies.

The expressed Arab goal of driving the Jews into the sea presented Jewish Americans with a frightening prospect. Once again Jewish existence was threatened while the world looked on. This threat and the resultant Israeli victory awakened in Jewish Americans new and profound feelings about both their Jewish heritage and Judaism. As Richard Rubinstein (see "DEATH OF GOD" THEOLOGY) wrote in 1968, "I can report that many Jews who had imagined themselves to be totally devoid of any inner connection with Jewish life were overwhelmed by their involvement in Israel's trial . . . I must confess surprise over the depth of my own feelings." The 1967 war engendered a period of reflection that came up with this answer: the Jewish people must survive. Although few Americans viewed themselves as potential emigrants to Israel, the country became a symbol of Jewish survival, as did the Jewish faith and the heritage of the Jews as a people.

The result was a growing militancy among certain segments of Jewish-American society, seen in the formation of the Jewish Defense League. More representative was the growth in support for Israel. Contributions for Israel quadrupled between 1966 and 1967; immigration to Israel increased from 1,700 in 1967 to 9,200 in 1970. Although insignificant compared to the size of the Jewish community in America, this was a sizable growth. The increased interest in Israel it reflected was also demonstrated by the growing number of American Jews who visited the country. The continued existence of the state of Israel became part of the affirmation of Jewish-American identity and life.

The affirmation of Jewish identity intensified in the resurgence of traditional norms that emerged in the Reform movement and in a renewed interest in Orthodoxy itself, especially among Reform and Conservative youths. Some of this interest took the form of the *havurah*, or community. A *havurah* was a group of individuals joined together to affirm both their religious and cultural identity as Jews and to replicate the close-knit community that had marked earlier periods of Jewish life.

The renewed interest in religion also caused problems. As many younger Jews affirmed a more Orthodox life than their parents, new questions emerged. Preeminent among them was the role of women within the tradition. College-age American women desiring to affirm their commitment to the religious tradition were confronted with secondary status. Some rejected that role and attempted to maintain the tradition while changing aspects

of it. Others, unable to face the conflicts, affirmed the most stringent form of eastern European Judaism—HASIDISM.

Hasidism, a mystical strain of Judaism that emerged from the teachings of the Baal Shem Tov (1700–1760), added a new element to American Judaism. Centered on a spiritual teacher, or *rebbe*, Hasidism was insignificant in the United States until the Nazi period, when representatives of various Hasidic dynasties arrived here. Of the various Hasidic movements the most visible has been that of the Lubavitcher Hasidim. Under the leadership of Menachem Mendel SCHNEERSON, the movement took an aggressive proselytizing stance among American Jews and established centers in major university towns in the United States, resulting in a significant number of Jewish youth turning to Orthodoxy.

While the unity of American Jewry as a community seems secure, that of American Judaism is not. Conflicts among the various branches erupt continuously. The ordination of women as rabbis, accepted by the Reform movement in 1972, and the Conservative movement in 1985, is vigorously rejected by the Orthodox. Conflict over the validity of Reform and Conservative conversions and the refusal of Israel to recognize Reform and Conservative rabbis causes tensions as well. Additionally, Reform's increasing acceptance of gays and lesbians has intensified hostility among the three denominations.

This has been a common pattern in American religion. The absence of an overarching authority creates a situation in which conflict and dissension become the norm. It also has created the distinctly American forms of Judaism and given the United States the most vibrant and active Jewish community in the world outside of Israel.

EQ

Bibliography: Hasia R. Diner, *Jews in America* (New York: Oxford University Press, 1999); Arnold Eisen, *The Chosen People in America: A Study in Jewish Religious Ideology* (Bloomington: Indiana University

Press, 1983); Nathan Glazer, *American Judaism,* 2nd ed., rev. (Chicago: University of Chicago Press, 1972); Arthur Hertzberg, *The Jews in America, Four Centuries of an Uneasy Encounter: A History* (New York: Simon & Schuster, 1989): Irving Howe, *The World of Our Fathers* (New York: Harcourt, Brace & Jovanovich, 1976); David Kaufman, *Shul with a Pool: The "Synagogue-Center" in American Jewish History* (Hanover, N.H.: University Press of New England, 1999); Jacob Rader Marcus, *Early American Jewry.* 2 vols. (Philadelphia: Jewish Publication Society of America, 1961); Pamela Susan Nadell, *Women Who Would be Rabbis: A History of Women's Ordination, 1889–1985* (Boston: Beacon Press, 1998); Howard M. Sachar, *A History of the Jews In America* (New York: Knopf, 1992).

Judson, Adoniram (1788–1850)

One of the earliest American missionaries to labor among Buddhists in Burma, Adoniram Judson was a founding figure in the Protestant foreign mission movement (see MISSIONS, FOREIGN). Born the eldest son of a Congregational minister in Malden, Massachusetts, in 1788, Judson graduated as class valedictorian from Rhode Island College (now Brown University) in 1807, and upon graduating entered Andover Seminary. There he met a number of students, including Luther Rice and Samuel Mills, Jr., who had dedicated themselves to foreign mission service. After undergoing a profound religious experience, Judson also determined to seek a mission field abroad. Finding no immediate outlet for their aspirations, the group submitted their case to the General Association of Congregational Churches in Massachusetts, an action that resulted in the founding of the American Board of Commissioners for Foreign Missions, or ABCFM, in 1810. Within a two-week period in early 1812, Judson was ordained, married Ann Haseltine (1789–1826), and sailed with her for Calcutta among the first contingent of overseas missionaries.

During the long voyage to India, political and theological circumstances conspired to alter Judson's intentions. En route he and his wife, along with companion Luther Rice, embraced

Adoniram Judson. This Baptist missionary to Burma and his wives were models for several generations of young Protestant men and women. *(Billy Graham Center Museum)*

the doctrine of adult BAPTISM, and shortly after their arrival in Calcutta they were baptized by a British Baptist missionary. This denominational shift rendered untenable Judson's commission from the Congregational ABCFM. At the same time, the outbreak of war between the United States and Great Britain forced the couple to flee from the British colony to Mauritius and eventually to Rangoon, Burma, where they organized an American Baptist mission and where Judson labored for the rest of his life.

At the small missionary outpost, Judson sought to instruct the natives in the basic elements of evangelical Christianity. Committed to the importance of teaching in the language of his pupils, he worked diligently to master Burmese. Eventually he preached in the local tongue, translated and distributed missionary tracts, and began work on a Burmese edition of the entire Bible, which he finished 17 years later. Judson and his band of converts lived in constant fear of persecution from the Burmese government, and when war broke out between England and Burma in 1824, Judson was imprisoned along with other foreigners living in the country. He was incarcerated for 21 months, while his wife remained at the mission outpost, giving birth to their child in 1825.

Not long after Judson's release, both his wife and his daughter died of illness. In 1834 he married Sarah H. Boardman, the widow of another missionary, who worked with Judson and assisted in the completion of his biblical translation as well as tending to their four children. After Sarah Judson's death in 1845, Judson returned to the United States for the first time in more than 30 years and was greeted with acclaim as a pioneer Baptist missionary. During his visit he met Emily Chubbuck, a young writer whom he hired to write a biography of his second wife. The two married and returned to the mission in Burma later that year, where Judson labored until his death a few years later.

In his 1883 biography of his father, Edward Judson asserted that the missionary had baptized more than 7,000 Burmese and other tribal peoples, established 63 churches, and directed 163 missionaries and native pastors during his lifetime. He served as an important source of inspiration for several generations of young missionaries. In addition, all three of his wives, dedicated missionaries in their own right, inspired American women to take up the cause of foreign work. These examples of collaborative self-sacrifice and dedication served as models for evangelical foreign mission efforts into the 20th century.

LMK

Bibliography: Courtney Anderson, *To the Golden Shore: The Life of Adoniram Judson* (Boston: Little, Brown, 1956); William R. Hutchison, *Errand to the World: American Protestant Thought and Foreign Missions* (Chicago: University of Chicago Press, 1987); Francis Wayland, *A Memoir of the Life and Labors of the Rev. Adoniram Judson*, 2 vols. (Boston: Phillips, Sampson, 1853).

justification   The word *justification*, derived from the Latin *justificatio*, means "to make just" or, as it usually is understood in Christian circles, "to make righteous." The concept appears in the New Testament in the writings of St. Paul, who wrote in the Epistle to the Romans that "a person is justified by faith" (3:28). Justification is traditionally associated with the concept of divine grace and the belief that Jesus Christ acquits men and women of the eternal punishment due them on account of their sins.

The theology of the great 16th-century reformer Martin Luther is the starting point for understanding teaching on justification. Luther was deeply troubled by the medieval religious system and obsessed with the question of how a person could ever earn God's love or find salvation. After meditating on Romans, Luther decided that human beings could do nothing to save themselves. He concluded that only God justifies, that is, redeems, human beings from sin. Through the death and resurrection of Jesus Christ, sinners were made righteous in God's eyes, and the merits of Christ were credited to them. Faith, Luther said, was the act by which God reveals his gracious character and leads a person to depend upon him for salvation.

John Calvin, even more than Luther, emphasized God's sovereignty and the divine initiative in justifying sinners and granting them eternal salvation. Without divine grace, Calvin wrote, no one could ever repent and become a Christian. Calvin stressed divine grace so strongly that he denied that human beings had any free will at all in the process of justification. God had simply predestined from eternity the fate of humankind, arbitrarily choosing some souls for salvation and others for damnation. Although Calvin believed that the elect (see ELECTION) would inevitably lead pious, Christian lives, he also contended that no amount of human faithfulness could ever alter God's eternal decrees. The merits of Christ, not human merits, justified the sinner.

In the early 17th century, the followers of Dutch theologian Jacobus Arminius disputed Calvin's fatalistic logic about justification. Advocates of ARMINIANISM argued that God foreknew, but had not foreordained, who would be saved and who would be damned. Since God gave all people the opportunity to accept eternal salvation, the Arminians stressed the need for moral effort. While orthodox Calvinists believed that human beings received justification passively, Arminians argued that justification, though ultimately God's prerogative, demanded an active, human choice.

With the rise of PURITANISM in England in the early 17th century, justification became regarded as a stage in the process by which the believer attained salvation. Following the text of Romans 8:30 ("Those whom [God] predestined he also called; and those whom he called he also justified; and those whom he justified he also glorified"), Puritan theologians identified four stages in the order of salvation. At the first stage (effectual calling), men and women were brought to repentance and faith by the proclamation of the Christian gospel. At the second stage (justification), God accounted believers as righteous and forgave them their sins. At the third stage (SANCTIFICATION), God released Christians from the power of sin, thus enabling them to live godly lives. Puritans believed that the good works believers performed when they reached sanctification gave them assurance that God had justified them. And at the final stage (glorification), begun only when dying and completed at the last judgment, Christians were remade in the likeness of Christ.

Despite the stress that Luther, Calvin, and the Puritans placed upon justification, Methodist founder John Wesley dramatically altered the Protestant understanding of salvation and God's grace in the mid-18th century. Wesley transformed Arminian themes and adapted them to the new religious movement he formed. While earlier Protestant reformers had emphasized God's role in justifying recalcitrant humankind, Wesley underscored the responsibility of human beings in appropriating the salvation that God held out to them.

Wesley's heirs, the METHODISTS, grew rapidly in the early 19th century and became the largest Protestant denomination in the United States after about 1820. Democratic Arminian emphases on free will dominated the revivals of the SECOND GREAT AWAKENING, in which evangelists exhorted sinners to abandon evil and come to God. Consistent with the optimistic, self-reliant spirit of the early American republic, revival leaders assumed that individuals had the innate ability to reform themselves. Anyone could be converted, find salvation, and even achieve moral perfection in the present life.

Although Luther had once declared that Christians, while justified, remain sinners incapable of saving themselves, most American Protestants by the middle of the 19th century assumed that the power of accepting or rejecting God's offer of salvation lay entirely in their own hands. Thus, while the doctrine of justification still occupies an honored place in Protestantism, it no longer possesses the decisive theological significance it had at the beginning of the Reformation.

GHS, Jr.

Bibliography: George H. Tavard, *Justification: An Ecumenical Study* (Mahwah, N.J.: Paulist Press, 1983).

K

Kallen, Horace Meyer (1882–1974)

Through numerous books, public advocacy, teaching, and service to various Jewish organizations, Horace Meyer Kallen contributed to the ability of American Jews in the early 20th century to preserve their distinctiveness within American society. In a time characterized by Anglo-Saxon, Protestant NATIVISM, Kallen argued that "cultural pluralism" was actually the higher democratic ideal. For Kallen, a secularist at heart, Jews needed to retain their cultural as well as religious identity while refiguring their own self-understanding in light of modern science and modern democratic institutions.

Kallen, born in Berenstadt, Germany, on August 11, 1882, was the son of a German rabbi. He emigrated to America with his family while young. Intent on becoming a novelist, Kallen attended Harvard College, became interested in philosophy, and eventually completed a Ph.D. under William JAMES in 1908. After filling a few temporary teaching positions and an instructor's post in philosophy and psychology at the University of Wisconsin from 1911 to 1918, he moved to New York City and took an active role in founding the New School for Social Research, an institution that provided an intellectual home to American Jews struggling against traditionalism. He remained at the New School from 1919 in various roles until his retirement in 1969, and even then wrote actively until his death, February 16, 1974.

Kallen wrote extensively: on practical topics, such as *Culture and Democracy in the Unit-* *ed States* (1924) and *Individualism: An American Way of Life* (1933); and on issues of Jewish identity, as in *Judaism at Bay: Essays Toward the Adjustment of Judaism to Modernity* (1932). His underlying philosophy, influenced heavily by James's pragmatism, focused on finding a natural, empirical basis for human values. Following James, he emphasized the variety of immediate experience and viewed the human tendency to create dogmas, or systems of thought, as a denial of the reality of varied experience.

Such a radically pluralist view of the world, in which no particular system of belief would be capable of accounting for or defining all experience, enabled Kallen to make an important intellectual contribution to Jewish identity in American life. He saw democracy as the social system most capable of respecting the plurality of individual experiences. This was especially the case in terms of ethnic or cultural groups (see ETHNICITY).

In a truly democratic society ethnic groups, each encouraged to preserve its unique heritage, would contribute to the "symphony of civilization." In a 1915 article for the progressive journal *The Nation*, Kallen attacked nativism head on. He argued against the idea of America as a "melting pot" where ethnic and religious differences were abolished. In America Jewish cultural identity, or what he came to call "Hebraism," would preserve those elements of tradition that spoke to the conditions of modern life, such as the traditional concern for justice, and enable Jews to serve as a model for other ethnic groups in America.

Ultimately Kallen's philosophical efforts to find common ground between Jewish cultural identity and the growing secularism of American culture proved unpersuasive to large numbers of American Jews. Kallen's Hebraism entailed giving up the religious conviction that the Jews were a "chosen people." This became increasingly difficult for many Jews to do as the increasing ANTI-SEMITISM of the 1920s and 1930s made clear to them the extent to which they remained on the margins of American society.

MG

Bibliography: Horace Kallen, *Judaism at Bay: Essays on the Adjustment of Judaism to Modernity* (Salem, N.H.: Ayer, 1953).

Kaplan, Mordecai M. (1881–1983)

One of the most creative and significant American Jewish theologians of the 20th century, Mordecai Kaplan addressed the challenges modernity posed to JUDAISM and in the process led in the formation of the fourth denomination of American Judaism, RECONSTRUCTIONIST JUDAISM. While many abhorred his views, Kaplan articulated a coherent and consistent vision of Judaism and the Jewish people in the modern world.

Born in 1881 in Russia, Kaplan grew up in a pious Jewish family. In 1888 his father, Israel, a distinguished Talmudist, was invited to America as part of the cabinet of the newly appointed chief rabbi of New York, Jacob Joseph. The rest of the family moved to Paris for a year before joining him. While there Kaplan first experienced the tensions of being an observant Jew in the modern world. These tensions were exacerbated in New York, where Kaplan attended both religious and public schools. His introduction to secular learning and visitors at his home, especially the biblical critic Arnold Ehrlich, made Kaplan doubt the reality of miracles and Moses' authorship of the Torah.

Despite these doubts Kaplan remained a devoutly observant Jew, and after graduation

from the Jewish Theological Seminary (JTS) in 1902, the same year he received an M.A. degree from Columbia University, he became assistant rabbi at Kehillat Yeshurun in New York. In this Orthodox synagogue many members refused to recognize Kaplan's American rabbinical ordination and would not call him rabbi. During a honeymoon in Europe in 1908, however, he obtained an Orthodox rabbinical certificate, making Kaplan the first English-speaking Orthodox rabbi in the United States.

Unhappy at Kehillat Yeshurun and increasingly troubled by religious doubts, Kaplan considered leaving the rabbinate. Solomon SCHECHTER, president of Jewish Theological Seminary, convinced him to remain. Impressed with Kaplan's abilities, Schechter appointed him dean of the newly created Teachers Institute at the seminary and, shortly afterward, named him a professor of homiletics. In these positions Kaplan influenced hundreds of young rabbis and teachers for half a century.

Kaplan's activities extended beyond the classroom. His vision of the synagogue as something more than a religious institution was realized in the building of the first Synagogue Center in 1917. Here Kaplan was a rabbi of a congregation whose activities were social and cultural as well as religious. His increasingly unorthodox views created dissension within the congregation, and Kaplan resigned in 1922. He was joined by 22 families who with Kaplan founded the Society for the Advancement of Judaism (SAJ) in New York City.

The SAJ became a laboratory for Kaplan's ideas and the nucleus of the Reconstructionist movement. There Kaplan defended his concept of Judaism as a civilization, the need to reconstruct Judaism in light of the modern world, and his increasingly naturalistic view of God. Feeling isolated at JTS, he resigned in 1927 but was convinced to remain.

Despite his increasingly heterodox ideas, Kaplan was highly regarded within CONSERVATIVE JUDAISM and in 1932 was chosen president of the Rabbinical Assembly. Always searching to make Judaism more meaningful, Kaplan published several new prayer books based on the experiments with ritual undertaken at SAJ. One of these, a prayer book for the Sabbath services, so enraged the Orthodox rabbis (see ORTHODOX JUDAISM) that they issued a ban of excommunication against Kaplan and publicly burned the book. In a jointly authored article several of Kaplan's colleagues at JTS called him "unlearned in the law" and urged him to stick to homiletics.

As his views became increasingly radical and his view of God more naturalistic, Kaplan's influence within Conservative Judaism decreased. Many of his disciples urged him to separate from the Conservative movement. This he was loath to do.

After he finally did so, following his retirement from JTS in 1963, Kaplan focused all of his energy on developing Reconstructionist Judaism as a vital, independent branch of Judaism. Although becoming a separate entity violated his view that Reconstructionism should integrate all of Jewish culture and civilization, Reconstructionist Judaism remained a model for attempts to incorporate all aspects of Judaic life, culture, and religion. As such it was a success, and when Kaplan died at the age of 102 in November 1983 he could rest secure in the knowledge that many who had initially viewed his ideas with abhorrence had adopted much of his thought.

EQ

Bibliography: Ira Eisenstein and Eugene Kohn, *Mordecai Kaplan: An Evaluation* (New York: Jewish Reconstructionist Foundation, 1952); Emanuel S. Goldsmith, Mel Scult, and Robert M. Seltzer, eds., *The American Judaism of Mordecai M. Kaplan* (New York: New York University Press, 1990); Jeffrey S. Gurock and Jacob J. Schachter, *A Modern Heretic and a Traditional Community: Mordecai M. Kaplan, Orthodoxy, and American Judaism* (New York: Columbia University Press, 1996); Mordecai Kaplan, *Judaism as a Civilization* (New York: Schocken, 1967); Richard Libowitz, *Mordecai M. Kaplan and the Development of Reconstructionism* (New York: Edwin Mellen Press, 1983); Mel Scult, *Judaism Faces the Twentieth Century: A Biography of Mordecai M. Kaplan* (Detroit: Wayne State University Press, 1993).

Keithian controversy   The Keithian controversy, a split within the Religious Society of Friends (Quakers) (see FRIENDS, RELIGIOUS SOCIETY OF [QUAKERS]), was precipitated in 1691 by the teachings of George Keith (1638–1716). An educated Scotsman holding degrees in philosophy, theology, and mathematics from the University of Aberdeen, Keith became a Quaker during the 1660s and was close to the movement's founder, George Fox, and to William PENN, both of whom he traveled with on preaching tours.

Often imprisoned in England for his religious beliefs, Keith came to America in 1684 at the invitation of William Penn. While serving as a schoolmaster in Philadelphia (see PENNSYLVANIA COLONY), Keith was accused by local Quakers of claiming that salvation was the result of the crucifixion of the historical Christ rather than of the workings of the spiritual Christ within. Keith wrote numerous pamphlets defending his views and organized his followers into a group known as "Christian Quakers." This schismatic move led the Philadelphia Yearly Meeting to disown him and his followers.

Returning to England in 1693, Keith continued to propagate his views on the historical Christ and the importance of the Bible. Attempts by the London Yearly Meeting to mediate the dispute and constant warnings to Keith to exercise patience were to no avail. As a result, he and his followers were disfellowshipped by the London Meeting.

Keith's growing concern for the doctrines of traditional Christianity at the expense of the distinctive Quaker doctrines of the inner Christ and continuing and immediate revelation—a defense of which he had once written—led him to return to the Church of England, where he was ordained a priest in 1702. In that year he returned to America as an Anglican missionary to the Quakers. Although he met with little success, later Anglican priests working among the remnants of Keith's Quaker followers managed to bring several hundred of them into the Church of England.

EQ

Bibliography: J. William Frost, ed., *The Keithian Controversy in Early Pennsylvania* (Norwood, Pa.: Norwood Editions, 1980).

Kennett, Jiyu (1924–1996)

Born Peggy Teresa Nancy Kennett in Sussex, England, in 1924, the Reverend Roshi Jiyu Kennett was one of the most important westernizers and feminizers of ZEN in America.

Kennett was baptized in the Church of England and initially felt called to the Anglican priesthood, but at the age of 16 she joined a community practicing Theravada BUDDHISM, a form popularized in Southeast Asia but spread via refugees and immigrants to England. After studying Mahayana Buddhism, a form widespread in East Asia, under a series of Chinese and Japanese instructors, including D.T. SUZUKI, at the London Buddhist Society, Kennett turned to Zen. Shortly after receiving her bachelor's degree in music from the University of Durham in 1961—she was an accomplished professional organist—Kennett left Great Britain in order to study Zen more formally under Asian masters.

In Asia, Kennett studied both Rinzai and Soto Zen, the two most important forms of Zen Buddhism. She was ordained in the Chinese Rinzai Zen tradition in Malaysia in 1962. Later that same year she was ordained in the Soto Zen tradition in Japan and was given the name of Jiyu ("Compassionate Friend"). She also became the first woman in approximately 500 years to receive training at the prestigious Sojiji Temple in Yokohama. After being licensed as a full teacher of Zen in 1968, she served for a time as an abbess, or spiritual leader, of her own Japanese temple.

Kennett moved to the United States in 1969 and shortly thereafter established the Zen Mission Society, now the Order of Buddhist Contemplatives. She also founded Shasta Abbey, a monastery in northern California devoted to training and ordaining Buddhist priests and nuns.

In keeping with the injunction of her Zen master in Japan, Kennett worked to adapt Zen creatively to foreign circumstances. Approximately half the trainees and half the priests at Shasta Abbey have been women. Her first book, *Selling Water by the River* (1972), contains a call for Zen priests to westernize and feminize Zen through the use of *upaya*, or "skillful means." Through her Shasta Abbey Press, Kennett also published *How to Grow a Lotus Blossom, or, How a Zen Priest Prepares for Death* (1993) a few years before her own death in 1996.

Although students at Shasta Abbey shave their heads and make a practice of bowing, they eat at tables instead of on the floor, take their tea English style, wear cassock-like robes and clerical collars, and address priests as "Reverend." Moreover, in keeping with Kennett's love of Christian music, they sing Zen texts to organ accompaniment in tones that sound strikingly like Gregorian chants. Kennett seems to have Anglicized Zen as much as she Americanized it, leading one Buddhologist to remark that Shasta Abbey presents us with "the curious state of affairs in which Japanese Zen, in trying to become American Zen, ultimately turns out to be British Zen."

SRP

Bibliography: Sandy Boucher, *Turning the Wheel: American Women Creating the New Buddhism* (Boston: Beacon Press, 1993); Jiyu Kennett, *How to Grow a Lotus Blossom, or, How a Zen Buddhist Prepares for Death* (Mt. Shasta, Calif.: Shasta Abbey Press, 1993); ———, *Selling Water by the River* (New York: Vintage Books, 1972); http://www.obcon.org (Order of Buddhist Contemplatives).

Keswick movement

See HIGHER CHRISTIAN LIFE MOVEMENT.

King, Martin Luther, Jr. (1929–1968)

The man who would come to symbolize the

struggle for black political equality in the United States (see CIVIL RIGHTS MOVEMENT), Martin Luther King, Jr., was born Michael Luther King, Jr., on January 15, 1929. He adopted the name Martin in the mid-1930s to match his father's name change—although he remained "Mike" to his closest friends. The oldest son of a powerful and influential black minister, Martin was raised within a comfortable environment—albeit one limited by the constraints of the segregated South (see SEGREGATION).

A precocious and sensitive child, he was groomed to succeed his father at Ebenezer Baptist Church. He entered Morehouse College in Atlanta in 1944. Although interested in studying law or medicine, the influence of Benjamin Mays, president of Morehouse, and relentless family pressure turned him toward the ministry.

Following his graduation in 1948, King went north to Crozer Theological Seminary, where he graduated at the top of his class in 1951. Encouraged by his professors at Crozer and unsure about entering the pulpit, King went on to graduate school at Boston University, where he began to formulate his own theological views. Marked by a combination of personalism, moral action, and a deep awareness of sin, these views helped King overcome his religious doubts by making moral action rather than belief the root of Christianity.

During his graduate work King encountered the work and writings of Mahatma Gandhi. Although he rarely quoted Gandhi in his writings, King was deeply affected by Gandhi's use of nonviolent action to transform unjust social and political systems. King was especially moved by the hints of transformative suffering within Gandhi's ideas—that the suffering of innocents could be used to transform social evil. For Gandhi, as for King, evil could be redeemed by love if one were willing to take the viciousness of that evil upon oneself.

While completing his dissertation, King accepted a call from Dexter Avenue Baptist Church in Montgomery, Alabama, delivering his first sermon as pastor designate in May 1954, two weeks before the Supreme Court handed down its decision in *Brown v. Board of Education*, declaring segregated public schools to be illegal. During that summer, King commuted between Montgomery and Boston in order to finish the research on his dissertation. When King became the full-time pastor at Dexter he immediately moved to assume control. In his first sermon, he discussed his view of the rights of a minister and followed it immediately with a plan for revitalizing the church. King's first year at Dexter was enormously successful. He brought the church and its finances under his control, received his Ph.D., and was constantly in demand as a speaker and guest minister. His success was so great that his father felt compelled to warn him against pride, reminding him that the devil always struck persons when they were highest.

King's second year at Dexter was radically different from the first. On December 1, 1955, Rosa Parks, a black maid returning home from work, was arrested for refusing to give up her seat to a white man. Mrs. Parks's personality and stature were such that she was the perfect test case of Alabama's segregation law. The decision to carry the case to court made by Mrs. Parks in consultation with E. D. Nixon, the acknowledged leader of Montgomery's black community, and Clifford Durr, the renegade white Southern patrician lawyer—would be a historic turning point.

In response to Mrs. Parks's arrest the Woman's Political Council—a black woman's organization composed primarily of professors at Alabama State University—planned a boycott of the city's buses. A ministers' meeting held on December 2 to plan a mass meeting on the boycott chose King to lead the organization, which they named the Montgomery Improvement Association. For nearly a year the Montgomery bus boycott remained in effect, until November 13, 1956, when the U.S. Supreme Court affirmed an appeals court decision that Alabama's state and local laws requiring segregation were unconstitutional.

The Reverend Martin Luther King, Jr., and associates leave the White House after meeting with President Lyndon B. Johnson. (*Library of Congress*)

This victory was followed by the formation in January 1957 of the organization that eventually became known as the SOUTHERN CHRISTIAN LEADERSHIP CONFERENCE (SCLC). The success of the Montgomery bus boycott pushed King into the public eye. He appeared on the cover of *Time* magazine and received even more invitations to speak both in the United States and abroad. In 1958 he traveled to Ghana at the invitation of Kwame Nkrumah, its president. This was followed the next year by a trip to India, where King met Prime Minister Jawaharlal Nehru and deepened his interest in Gandhian nonviolence.

Increasing public and family demands led King to resign from the pastorate at Dexter effective January 1960, ostensibly to join his father at Ebenezer Baptist Church in Atlanta. In reality King would be leading "a broad, bold advance of the southern campaign for equality," as he said in the sermon announcing his resignation. The events and results of this campaign lay beyond anyone's imaginings.

From the time he arrived in Atlanta until his assassination in 1968 King's name would become linked with three events—the Birmingham protest of 1963, the March on Washington in the same year, and the Selma-to-Montgomery march of 1965. Other campaigns led by King in Albany, Georgia (1962) and Chicago (1966), and even the Memphis garbage workers' strike that resulted in his murder are overshadowed by these three.

The reasons are quite significant. In both Birmingham and Selma the stark contrast between peaceful black protesters and the vicious savagery of law enforcement officers broadcast nationwide through the new medium of television moved the nation. The discipline of the protesters, the undeservedness of their suffering, and the eloquence of their actions spoke accusingly as they were blasted across streets by fire hoses, set upon by police dogs, and clubbed down by mounted police.

The eloquence of these acts was matched by King's oratory at the March on Washington. Before a crowd of 250,000 (organizers had hoped for 100,000), King gave one of his most memorable speeches. He told his audience about his dream, a dream, he said, that was rooted in the American dream.

> I have a dream that one day every valley will be exalted. . . . And when this happens . . . we will be able to speed up the day when all God's children, black men and white men, Jews and Gentiles, Protestants and Catholics will be able to join hands and sing in the words of the old Negro spiritual, 'Free at last! Free at last! Thank God Almighty we are free at last!'

The march galvanized American public opinion and aided in the passage of the Civil Rights Act of 1964, the year that King's commitment to nonviolent social change resulted in his receipt of the Nobel Peace Prize.

In the last years of his life King expanded his views in several directions. Concerned about the inability of civil rights legislation to deal with urban poverty, he turned his attention northward. A 1966 campaign in Chicago met with little success and much hostility, increasing King's concern that solving the problems in the South might prove easier than solving those in the North.

The VIETNAM WAR also drew King's attention. In 1967 he delivered his "Beyond Vietnam" speech, in which he claimed that the evils of poverty, racism, militarism, and imperialism were inextricably linked. This speech alienated many of King's early supporters and led to an increasing disinformation campaign against

King directed by J. Edgar Hoover and the FBI, a campaign that had begun much earlier.

In the midst of planning a second March on Washington, a racially integrated "poor people's campaign" on behalf of economic justice for all Americans, King traveled to Memphis to aid the city's black garbage collectors, who were striking for the right to unionize. Stepping out onto the balcony of the Lorraine Motel on April 4, 1968, King was felled by an assassin's bullet fired by James Earl Ray.

King's moral power was not killed, however. Although many rejected his emphasis on moral suasion and redemptive suffering as a means of transforming society, his message permeated American society. Above all, King called America to its best self, to realize that in which it claimed to believe. For this reason King became one of the great religious figures in American history.

(See also AFRICAN-AMERICAN RELIGION.)

EQ

Bibliography: Taylor Branch, *Parting the Waters: America in the King Years, 1954–1963* (New York: Simon & Schuster, 1988); Michael Eric Dyson, *I May Not Get There With You: The True Martin Luther King, Jr.* (New York: Free Press, 2000); David Garrow, *Bearing the Cross: Martin Luther King, Jr. and the Southern Christian Leadership Conference, 1955–1968* (New York: William Morrow, 1986); Martin Luther King, Jr., *The Autobiography of Martin Luther King, Jr.* (Boston: Little Brown, 1999); ———, *Stride Toward Freedom: A Leader of His People Tells the Montgomery Story* (New York: Harper & Row, 1958); ———, *Why We Can't Wait* (New York: Harper & Row, 1964); David L. Lewis, *King: A Critical Biography* (New York: Praeger, 1971); Stephen B. Oates, *Let the Trumpet Sound: The Life of Martin Luther King, Jr.* (New York: New American Library, 1982).

Kino, Eusebio Francisco

One of the most important Spanish Catholic missionaries to the Americas, Eusebio Kino is known as the apostle to Sonora and Arizona for his work along the modern United States–Mexico border. Although much of this work met with Indian hostility, governmental animosity, and the suppression of the Spanish JESUITS in 1783, his lifelong struggle remains as an example of the relentless determination and faith shown by the Spanish missionaries.

He was born Eusebio Chino in Segno, Italy, on August 10, 1645. He was always a religious child, and a serious illness led him to promise to enter the Jesuit order if he were spared. After his recovery he joined the Society of Jesus (1665) and took the name Francisco (after Francis Xavier, the Jesuit missionary who died of a fever in 1552 while trying to enter China as a missionary) as a sign of his desire to undertake a mission to China.

After 13 years of study in Innsbruck and Ingolstadt, where he developed a strong interest in mathematics and cartography, he was assigned to his first mission post, NEW SPAIN. An inability to obtain transportation left him stranded in Spain for two years, but he finally arrived in Vera Cruz in 1681. Joining the Atondo expedition to Baja California in 1683 as cartographer, he remained there as a missionary until a massive drought forced him to return to Mexico City in 1685. During this time he adopted a Spanish form of his name, spelling it either Kino or Qino.

Venturing to the border regions in 1687, he began his missionary and exploring work in modern-day Sonora, Mexico, and Arizona, establishing missions as far north as what is now Tucson, at San Xavier del Bac. In Arizona alone he claimed to have personally baptized more than 4,500 Pima Indians. Kino also introduced cattle into the region, using them as a means of financing his work.

The maps he drew of his travels aided colonial authorities as they struggled to establish their authority in the region. Among other discoveries, his explorations proved that Baja, California, was not an island but a peninsula (1701). He died at Mission Magdalina in Sonora on March 15, 1711.

(See also ROMAN CATHOLICISM.)

EQ

Bibliography: Herbert E. Bolton, ed. and trans., *Kino's Historical Memoir of Pimeria Alta* (Cleveland: A.H. Clark, 1919); ———, *Rim of Christendom: A Biography of Eusebio Francisco Kino, Pacific Coast Pioneer* (New York: Macmillan, 1936); Ernest J. Burrus, *Kino and Manje: Explorers of Sonora and Arizona* (St. Louis, Mo.: Jesuit Historical Institute, 1971); Charles Polzer, *A Kino Guide: A Life of Eusebio Francisco Kino, Arizona's First Pioneer and a Guide to His Missions and Monuments* (Tucson, Ariz.: Southwestern Mission Research Center, 1968).

Kohler, Kaufmann (1843–1926)

One of several German rabbis who came to the United States because their views were too radical for their homeland, Kaufmann Kohler helped to create American REFORM JUDAISM and to sustain it. Committed to harmonizing JUDAISM with modern science, he pushed for a progressive view of that religion as destined to take to the whole world the message of the unity and righteousness of God and of justice for all humanity.

Born May 10, 1843, to a devout Jewish family in Fuerth, Germany, Kohler began religious study at age five, entering the rabbinical seminary of Mayence at 14 and the yeshiva at Altona five years later. He followed this with several years of study with Samson Raphael Hirsch, founder of Jewish neo-Orthodoxy, an attempt to harmonize modern society and Orthodox Judaism.

Studies at the universities of Munich and Berlin undermined the young man's Orthodox beliefs, causing him much anguish. Kohler became increasingly attracted to the Reform movement, and the publication in 1867 of his doctoral dissertation, a plea for adaptation of religious forms to changed historical circumstances, was hailed by Reform leaders. But the Orthodox were appalled, and he was soundly criticized in the Orthodox press. This reaction made a rabbinical career in Germany impossible, and Kohler was urged to go to America.

Welcomed in New York by Rabbi David EINHORN, whose son-in-law he later became, Kohler found a spiritual father for his religious mission. Shortly after assuming rabbinical duties at Temple Beth-El in Detroit, he attended the Philadelphia Conference of Reformers in 1869 and ardently supported the statement of principles drafted by Einhorn. After two years at Beth-El, Kohler became rabbi at Sinai in Chicago. In 1879 he was called to be Einhorn's successor at Temple Beth-El in New York, where he became the chief spokesman for Reform Judaism, a position he maintained until his death on January 26, 1926.

While at Beth-El he became embroiled in a pulpit debate with the Conservative rabbi (see CONSERVATIVE JUDAISM) Alexander Kohut—a debate that drew in nearly all the Jewish press and the various rabbis who weighed in on the side of their respective heroes. In an 1885 sermon Kohut had challenged the very validity of Reform as a legitimate expression of Judaism.

Rabbi Kaufmann Kohler, a founder of Reform Judaism and president of Hebrew Union College in the early 20th century.

Kohler responded intemperately, describing Orthodoxy as "fanatical; offensive and anachronistical," and calling for "a Bible purified from all its offensive and obnoxious elements." Kohler declared that he distinguished in the Bible "the kernel from the husk, the grain from the chaff, the spirit from the form."

In order to bolster the position of Reform in the aftermath of this debate, Kohler invited the leading Reform rabbis to a conference "for the purpose of discussing the present state of American Judaism. . . ." This meeting, held in Pittsburgh in November 1885, produced a document that determined the direction of Reform Judaism for a half-century. Known as the PITTSBURGH PLATFORM, it is a mirror of Kohler's thinking. Perhaps in no section is this more true than in section 6, which declares Judaism to be a "progressive religion, ever striving to be in accord with the postulates of reason."

In 1903 Kaufmann was asked to become president of Hebrew Union College, the center for the training of Reform rabbis. Accepting the position only after the school explicitly stated its commitment to reform, Kohler served for 19 years, strengthening both its academic and its pastoral content. He added courses—many of which he taught—in biblical criticism, apocryphal and Hellenistic literature, and the Christian scriptures.

Kohler was deeply concerned with the maintenance of Judaism and the Jewish people. His desire to save what was valuable, what he called the positive side of Reform, often is missed in the alterations Reform made in traditional Judaism. Although the destruction of old forms was necessary in his view to save the religion, the significant task was, as Kohler wrote, "building up Judaism, render[ing] it the object of love, of pride and joy for all, the source of comfort and peace for every thirsting soul, a fount of life and inspiration to Jew and Gentile alike."

EQ

Bibliography: Kaufmann Kohler, *Dr. Kaufmann Kohler, Personal Reminiscences of My Early Life* (Cincinnati: n.p., 1918); ———, *Jewish Theology Systematically* and *Historically Considered* (New York: Macmillan, 1918); Murray Polner, *American Jewish Biographies* (New York: Facts On File, 1982).

Koinonia Farm   Koinonia (Greek for "fellowship") Farm was founded by Baptist minister Clarence Jordan near Americus, Georgia, in November 1942. Koinonia drew its name and operating principles from the earliest Christian churches described in the New Testament Book of Acts. Koinonia was intended to be an example of an interracial community in which members pooled their material resources and shared all property.

Jordan, a native of Georgia, earned a doctorate in New Testament studies from Southern Baptist Theological Seminary in 1939 and served as a minister to inner-city African Americans in Louisville, Kentucky. During his graduate studies, he became committed to pacifism, racial justice, and the ideals of communal living. After Jordan meet Mabel and Martin England, who had been American Baptist missionaries in Burma, the three decided to place all their money into a rundown 400-acre farm in south Georgia. The farm was established as a racially integrated community that practiced Christian brotherhood and peace.

Although both Jordan and the Englands had some agricultural training, none had much practical experience. Jordan used to joke that, every morning, he would climb his roof to see what the neighboring farmer was doing that day. The greatest obstacle to Koinonia's survival, however, was not the founders' lack of agricultural expertise, but racist opponents who objected to their integrated living arrangement. The community endured an economic boycott for many years. Members of the Ku Klux Klan also periodically threatened violence to warn of their hostility to the mixing of races. Eventually, as the CIVIL RIGHTS MOVEMENT blossomed in the late 1950s, Koinonia received national support, developing a mail-order constituency that helped it survive without local support. Jordan responded as well by writing a "Cotton Patch Version" of the New Testament—the Bible translated into the southern rural vernacular.

The Englands left Koinonia soon after World War II, but Jordan continued with his social experiment. By 1956, 60 people, of whom 25 percent were black, lived on the farm. Although Jordan died in 1969, he reorganized Koinonia with Linda and Millard Fuller shortly before his death. They transformed Koinonia Farm into Koinonia Partners and established the Fund for Humanity to provide capital for low-cost housing. The Fullers withdrew from Koinonia in 1976 in order to found HABITAT FOR HUMANITY. Habitat has built more than 95,000 houses worldwide using the funding plan initiated at Koinonia.

The decision Jordan and the Fullers made revived the community, and many new members flocked to it throughout the 1970s and 1980s. Koinonia's relationship with the local community also began to change. Most of Koinonia's neighbors now do business with it; the one local merchant who still refuses its trade claims to base his objection not on Koinonia's racial position but on its peace protests. The community celebrated its 50th anniversary in 1992 and continues to function actively today through the efforts of adult residents and a group of volunteers.

GHS, Jr.

Bibliography: Andrew S. Chancey, "'A Demonstration Plot for the Kingdom of God': The Establishment and Early Years of Koinonia Farm," *Georgia Historical Quarterly* 75 (1991), 321–53; Tracy Elaine Meyer, *Interracialism and Christian Community in the Postwar South: The Story of Koinonia Farm* (Charlottesville: University Press of Virginia, 1997).

Krauth, Charles Porterfield (1823–1883)
Charles Porterfield Krauth was a Lutheran (see LUTHERANISM) minister and theologian. During the theological crisis that developed in the mid-19th century between liberal American-born and conservative European-born Lutherans, Krauth became the chief spokesman for the traditionalists. He urged unswerving loyal-

ty to the historical beliefs and practices of Lutheran orthodoxy.

Krauth was born in Martinsburg, Virginia (now West Virginia), on March 17, 1823. His father, Charles Philip Krauth, was himself a prominent Lutheran minister. The elder Krauth served as president, first, of what is now Gettysburg College in Pennsylvania and, later, of the General Synod, his denomination's central organizational body. Charles the younger received his undergraduate degree from Gettysburg College in 1839, and two years later he graduated from Gettysburg Seminary. He was ordained to the ministry in 1842. Over the next 20 years, Krauth served pastorates in several locations: Baltimore; Martinsburg; Winchester, Virginia; Pittsburgh; and Philadelphia. He resigned his position at St. Mark's Church, Philadelphia, to become editor of the *Lutheran and Missionary* in 1861.

During his years in the parish ministry, Krauth undertook a thorough study of the classic theological texts of German Lutheranism. He discovered in those writings standards of orthodoxy from which Lutherans in the United States were clearly falling away. Krauth resisted the efforts of Lutheran leader Samuel SCHMUCKER to create a new "American Lutheranism" that was lax in doctrine and open to fellowship with other Protestant churches. While Schmucker wanted his denomination to become more like other mainstream American Protestant churches, Krauth believed Lutherans possessed a theology, polity, and liturgy that were and ought to remain unique. He fostered a sense of denominational exclusiveness based on historical documents such as the Augsburg Confession, the 16th-century statement of essential Lutheran beliefs.

Since Krauth's views coincided with those held by large numbers of German immigrants entering the United States in the 1840s and 1850s, his opinions received a wide hearing. Meanwhile, the entire Lutheran General Synod seemed headed toward schism over the questions Krauth and others raised. First, Lutheran conservatives formed a new seminary at Philadelphia to teach a more traditional theological curriculum than what was available at the denomination's seminary at Gettysburg. Krauth was chosen as the first professor of systematic theology at Lutheran Seminary, Philadelphia, in 1864. Next, conservatives seceded from the General Synod and formed the General Council of the Evangelical Lutheran Church in 1867. Krauth composed a creedal document, the "Fundamental Principles of Faith and Church Polity," around which representatives of the General Council could unite.

Beginning in 1868 Krauth functioned both as professor of theology at Lutheran Seminary and as professor of philosophy at the University of Pennsylvania. Well known for his biblical scholarship, he served on the American Revision Committee of the Old Testament from 1871 until his death. In 1882 Krauth became editor of the newly established *Lutheran Theological Review,* a journal founded to express the orthodox ideas he championed. His most important publication was *The Conservative Reformation and Its Theology* (1871), a book that influenced the thinking of many Lutheran ministers about the nature of their church.

Krauth intended his final scholarly task to be the composition of a biography of the great Protestant reformer Martin Luther. Krauth died at Philadelphia on January 2, 1883, before bringing that project to completion.

GHS, Jr.

Bibliography: Adolph Spaeth, *Charles Porterfield Krauth,* 2 vols. (New York: Christian Literature Co., 1898–1909).

Krishnamurti, Jiddu (1895–1986)

A native of India, Jiddu Krishnamurti was raised to be a Theosophical leader (see THEOSOPHY), but he left behind both his homeland and the Theosophical Society and went on to become an independent guru in the United States.

Krishnamurti was born in 1895 in Madanapalle, India. While Krishnamurti was still a boy, his father went to work at the Theosophical Society and moved his family to its head-

As a child in India, Krishnamurti was recognized by Annie Besant as a Theosophical leader, but Krishnamurti split from the Theosophical Society in 1929 and went on to become an independent spiritual teacher. *(Photograph by Johnson Studios, Ojai. Courtesy of the Krishnamurti Foundation of America Archives)*

quarters outside Madras. When Krishnamurti was 14, Annie Besant, then the president of the Theosophical Society, prophesied the coming of a messianic figure called the World Teacher. In 1911 Besant founded the Order of the Star of the East and tapped Krishnamurti to lead it. To educate him for that mission, she brought him to England. That education, which included extensive travel, seemed to be going well when Krishnamurti achieved a spiritual awakening while meditating under a pepper tree in 1922 at his U.S. base of Ojai, California. However, in 1929 Krishnamurti renounced the messianic role assigned to him, separated from the Theosophical Society, and began a long career as an independent spiritual teacher.

Krishnamurti's teachings are hard to categorize, in part because he taught his listeners to reject all authority, including his own. But his message was clearly a call to spiritual self-reliance. "Truth is a pathless land," Krishnamurti wrote. "Man cannot come to it through any organization, through any creed, through any dogma, priest or ritual, not through any philosophic knowledge or psychological technique." Truth, he insisted, could only be experienced immediately and intuitively in the here and now. This message of freedom proved tremendously appealing to Americans tuned in to the COUNTERCULTURE. They eagerly embraced him in the 1960s and 1970s as a world teacher of a different sort.

Toward the end of his life Krishnamurti emerged as an important figure in the ongoing dialogue between modern science and Asian religions. In 1999 his book *Think on These Things* was named one of the 100 Best Spiritual Books of the Century. Krishnamurti died at age 90 in 1986 at his American headquarters in Ojai, California. Although Krishnamurti was as averse to organization as he was to doctrine, his legacy lives on in the Ojai-based Krishnamurti Foundation of America, established in 1969.

SRP

Bibliography: Jiddu Krishnamurti, *Think on These Things* (New York: HarperCollins, 1989); Mary Lutyens, *Krishnamurti, His Life and Death* (New York: St. Martin's Press, 1991); Roland Vernon, *Star in the East: The Story of Jiddu Krishnamurti* (London: Constable, 2000); www.kfa.org (Krishnamurti Foundation of America).

Krishna Consciousness See INTERNATIONAL SOCIETY FOR KRISHNA CONSCIOUSNESS.

Ku Klux Klan A nativist (see NATIVISM) and racist organization, the Ku Klux Klan has experienced several declines and resurgences in its long history. The Klan has had three distinct manifestations which, although linked by basic beliefs, are chronologically and organizationally separate.

The original Ku Klux Klan was formed in Pulaski, Tennessee, in 1866 in the wake of the Confederate defeat in the CIVIL WAR. Originally a social fraternity, it was soon taken over by Confederate veterans under the leadership of Nathan Bedford Forrest (1821–1877) and became a local vigilante group. It soon moved into political terrorism designed to prevent the establishment of Republican government and black political equality. For half a decade various Klans, for they were all local in form and organization, terrorized much of the South until local militias or the federal government managed to crush them.

The original Klan seems to have had little religious motivation. The same cannot be said for the rejuvenated Klan of the 1920s. The 1920s Klan drew its inspiration from the 1915 movie *The Birth of a Nation* by D. W. Griffith, which was based on Thomas Dixon's novel *The Clansman*. This Klan directed its animosity not only against blacks but also against Jews, Catholics, and immigrants. An extreme version of the reaction to urbanization, industrialization, and immigration that emerged after World War I, the Klan preached a return to small town Protestant values and Anglo-Saxon superiority. Primarily a political movement, this Klan was less violent than its earlier incarnation. It also developed the Klan signature of cross burning. While this Klan provided many people an opportunity to express their fears and hatreds, it was politically quite unsuccessful despite a membership that numbered nearly 2 million. Although in many areas political candidates needed Klan endorsement to ensure election, only two Klan-endorsed laws seem to have been passed during this period: an Alabama statute requiring state inspection of convents, and an Oregon law requiring all children to attend public school. Both were later overturned by the courts. This Klan collapsed when it was discovered that in many states, especially Indiana, its leaders were criminals and con men who used the organization for personal gain.

The period after World War II saw another resurgence of the Klan, driven by fear of Communism and the CIVIL RIGHTS MOVEMENT. Although marked by divisions and numerically small in this period, probably peaking at 25,000, this version of the Klan was quite violent, and its various groups accumulated large caches of weapons and explosives. Following a decline in the early 1970s the Klan reemerged in the 1980s, this time affiliated with neo-Nazi and other white supremacist groups. This Klan continued its attacks on Jews and blacks, although many groups softened their anti-Catholicism and spoke of saving white, Christian America. The Klan also became increasingly a part of the IDENTITY MOVEMENT, which viewed the Anglo-Saxons as the true biblical Israelites and Jesus as a white Anglo-Saxon.

Damaged by its violent reputation and financially weakened by several successful civil lawsuits, the various Klans had dwindled to about 10,000 members by the 1990s. Since it lacked a distinctive identity, hangers-on drifted between the Klan and the numerous other racist groups that dotted the American political fringe. All of these groups continued to appeal to a vision of Christian America brought on by violence and excluding everyone different from themselves.

(See also ANTI-CATHOLICISM; ANTI-SEMITISM; SEGREGATION.)

EQ

Bibliography: David M. Chalmers, *Hooded Americanism: The First Century of the Ku Klux Klan, 1865–1965* (Garden City, N.Y.: Doubleday, 1965); William Harvey Fischer, *The Invisible Empire: A Bibliography of the Ku Klux Klan* (Metuchen, N.J.: Scarecrow Press, 1980); Nancy MacLean, *Behind the Mask of Chivalry: The Making of the Second Ku Klux Klan* (New York: Oxford University Press, 1995); Jack Nelson, *Terror in the Night: The Klan's Campaign Against the Jews* (Jackson: University Press of Mississippi, 1996); Patsy Sims, *The Klan* (Lexington: University Press of Kentucky, 1996); Wyn Craig Wade, *The Fiery Cross: The Ku Klux Klan in America* (New York: Oxford University Press, 1998).

L

Landmark movement   See BAPTISTS; GRAVES, JAMES ROBINSON.

Lavey, Anton Szandor   See SATANISM.

Lee, Ann (1736–1784)   Born the daughter of a blacksmith in Manchester, England, Ann Lee became known in America as the founder of the SHAKERS, a utopian religious movement that advocated communitarian living, celibacy, and the strict separation of the sexes. From a small group of eight immigrants in 1774, Lee's movement grew to encompass communities from Maine to Indiana by the 1840s, and her spiritual vision of sexual relations as the root of all human sinfulness became the basis for a prominent religious organization that prospered into the 20th century.

Ann Lee had already demonstrated her deep religious piety well before leaving England. In the 1760s she came under the influence of James and Jane Wardley, members of an enthusiastic group known as the "Shaking Quakers" for their spiritual outbursts. She apparently experienced religious visions during this period, but it was not until after her marriage, and the subsequent deaths of four children during infancy, that Lee had the vision that changed her path. In 1770 she received a revelation that the original sin of Adam and Eve was sexual intercourse, and that once human beings abstained from sin they would recognize that the millennium had, in fact, already arrived along with this newly revealed truth.

Impelled by poverty and persecution, Lee, her husband, and a small group of followers fled to America in 1774 and settled in Watervliet, New York. There they established a way of life based on the dictates of a celibate life and a socialist millennial community, consecrating all of their worldly work to God. "Mother Ann," as head of this association, soon came to be regarded as the second coming of Christ, a female incarnation that corresponded to the first, male incarnation. For believers, her leadership demonstrated that the godhead was both male and female, and this bipartite notion of divinity in turn reinforced the importance of the separation of sexes in their communities. For members of the United Society of Believers in Christ's Second Appearing, Ann Lee's life and leadership had ushered in the kingdom on earth.

Although her leadership and religious experience proved integral to the growth of Shakerism, Ann Lee died before the movement began to expand. In 1785, one year after her death, the first Shaker community was founded in New Lebanon, New York. In death, however, Mother Ann was deified and extolled as the new messiah, and her legacy has provided spiritual inspiration for Shakers to the present day.

LMK

Bibliography: Jean M. Humez, ed., *Mother's First-Born Daughters: Early Shaker Writings on Women and Religion* (Bloomington: Indiana University Press, 1993); Stephen J. Stein, *The Shaker Experi-*

ence in America (New Haven: Yale University Press, 1992); John McKelvie Whitworth, *God's Blueprint* (Boston: Routledge, Kegan, and Paul, 1975).

Lee, Bruce (1940–1973)

Bruce Lee was a movie star and America's best-known martial artist. Though he is not typically regarded as a religious figure, through his influence the martial arts made their way into American culture. Those arts, in turn, have been a key vehicle for the popular transmission across America of the beliefs and values of ZEN and TAOISM.

Though born in San Francisco's Chinese Hospital, Lee was raised in Hong Kong. Legend has it that he was sickly child who was bullied at school, so in 1954 Lee began to study the Wing Chun style of kung fu. After he was expelled from school in Hong Kong, Lee went to San Francisco and then Seattle, where he attended high school and studied philosophy at the University of Washington. In 1964 Lee was married. He and his wife moved to Oakland and opened a kung fu school. Two years later he began to star as Kato, a valet and chauffeur, on the TV series *The Green Hornet*. Soon he was starring in movies, most notably *Enter the Dragon* (1973), and training actors such as Steve McQueen and athletes including former basketball star Kareem Abdul-Jabbar.

Lee's early and mysterious death at the age of 32, reportedly from an allergic reaction, secured his status as an American icon. Today in martial arts dojos across the United States, countless young Americans pay homage to Lee and to successors such as Jackie Chan. Although some instructors downplay the philosophical and religious roots of the various martial arts, students typically learn something about key Taoist notions such as chi and yin/yang and Zen concepts such as emptiness and egolessness.

As for Lee, he explicitly rooted his fighting in religion in *Tao of Jeet Kune Do*, an enduringly popular book published posthumously in 1975. That book, which has sold more than a quarter million copies, included an application of Buddhism's Eightfold Path to Lee's distinctive martial arts style, called Jeet Kune Do. It also included hints on how to transcend karma and achieve spiritual liberation. "Jeet Kune Do," Lee concluded, "is the enlightenment."

SRP

Bibliography: Stephen B. Cox, *Western Martial Arts: Ethos, Tradition and Spirituality* (Reading, Mass.: Coxland, 1999); Bruce Lee, *Tao of Jeet Kune Do* (Santa Clarita, Calif.: Ohara Publications, 1975); http://www.bruceleefoundation.com (Bruce Lee Educational Foundation).

Lee, Jarena (1783–?)

A pioneer in American religion and literature, Jarena Lee was the first African-American woman to write her spiritual autobiography in America. She was also one of the first women of any race to break through the Victorian "cult of true womanhood" to become a preacher.

Born female and black in 1783 in southern New Jersey, Lee began life as an outsider times two. She had a conversion experience in 1804 at the age of 21 and was "born again." Shortly after joining Bethel African Methodist Episcopal Church in Philadelphia, Lee inaugurated her career as a preacher by standing up, interrupting the congregation's male minister, and proclaiming her glorious salvation. Four years after her experience of JUSTIFICATION, Lee was blessed with SANCTIFICATION, the second experience of grace described by the pioneering Methodist John Wesley.

In 1811 Lee approached the minister of Bethel A.M.E. Church, the Reverend Richard ALLEN (1760–1831) and reported that she had been called by God to preach. Allen responded by informing her that she must have been mistaken, and Lee for a time repressed her call to a Christian ministry. Taking up a life as a wife and mother, she married Joseph Lee, a minister of a black church outside Philadelphia, in 1811 and moved out of the city. After her husband died unexpectedly and Lee found herself alone with two children, she moved back to Philadelphia.

In 1819 Lee once again dramatically interrupted a service at Bethel Church. This time, however, she stood up to offer her own interpretation of the Gospel reading of the day. To Lee's surprise, Allen, who had since become bishop of the newly independent AFRICAN METHODIST EPISCOPAL CHURCH, responded to this second incident by sanctioning Lee's now-evident call to preach.

Although Lee was never ordained, she spent her remaining years as an itinerant revivalist. Her work took her to states up and down the eastern seaboard and west into the frontier as far as Dayton, Ohio. In one year, she traveled an estimated 2,325 miles and preached 178 sermons. Although Lee confined herself largely to calling her listeners to Christ, she did join the American Antislavery Society in 1840.

Lee is remembered primarily for her remarkable memoir, which first appeared in Philadelphia in 1836 under the title *The Life and Religious Experience of Jarena Lee, A Coloured Lady, Giving An Account of Her Call to Preach the Gospel.* In this book, Lee shares with her readers the despair that preceded her justification, the doubts that nagged at her until her sanctification, and the triumphs and difficulties associated with living a life as an African American, a woman, and an itinerant evangelist.

SRP

Bibliography: William L. Andrews, ed., *Sisters of the Spirit: Three Black Women's Autobiographies of the Nineteenth Century* (Bloomington: Indiana University Press, 1986); Frances Smith Foster, *Written by Herself: Literary Production by African American Women, 1746–1892* (Bloomington: Indiana University Press, 1993).

Leeser, Isaac (1806–1868)   A religious traditionalist who struggled against the radical changes of REFORM JUDAISM, Isaac Leeser recognized the need for JUDAISM to make adjustments simultaneously to American society and modernity. His 44-year career in the United States was spent trying to maintain traditional Jewish practice without creating an isolated and insular community. For this reason Isaac Leeser deserves to be called the unofficial founder of CONSERVATIVE JUDAISM in the United States.

Born in Neuenkirchen, Prussia, on December 12, 1806, Isaac Leeser was tutored privately until he entered the *Gymnasium* of Münster. At the age of 18 his formal education ended when he immigrated to the United States. He spent five years working at an uncle's store in Richmond, Virginia. During this time he taught Hebrew and other subjects in Richmond's Jewish community and achieved a degree of fame by rebutting a series of anti-Semitic articles that appeared in a local paper. His erudition so impressed the congregation of Mikveh Israel Synagogue in Philadelphia that he was invited to be its *hazzan,* or cantor.

During his 21 years there Leeser devoted himself to the welfare of American Judaism. He published a monthly newspaper, *The Occident and American Jewish Advocate,* in which he voiced his opposition to Reformers such as Isaac WISE and promoted his version of a traditional yet Americanized Judaism. For despite his opposition to the Reformers, Leeser did not reject all changes. He translated both the Sephardic (1837) and Ashkenazic (1848) rites into English and preached in English, taking on a role traditionally reserved for the rabbi and leading to his resignation from Mikveh Israel in 1850.

Leeser's major concern, however, was the continuation and stability of Jewish life in the United States. To this, more than anything else, he devoted himself. Convinced that the maintenance of Jewish life lay in religious education, he wrote or translated several textbooks for Jewish schools, including the first Hebrew primer (1838). Committed to the idea that all Jews should know Hebrew (and aware that large numbers did not), he translated the Hebrew Bible into English (1845).

Following his resignation from Mikveh Israel, Leeser traveled around the United States and was disturbed to find that families in small towns were greatly in need of religious leaders. To provide those leaders, in 1867 he founded the first rabbinical school in the United States, Maimonides College.

In the pages of *The Occident* Leeser repeatedly issued calls for the creation of an organization that could provide the educational and religious institutions necessary to insure Judaism's survival in the United States. He even joined forces with Isaac Wise in 1849 to effect its creation, with no success.

Like Isaac Wise, whom he resembled in so many ways, Leeser was convinced that America was the promised land for the Jews. While, unlike Wise, he supported Jewish colonization efforts in Palestine (see ZIONISM), Leeser viewed the United States as a nation where Jews and Judaism could flourish. As he wrote, "This country is emphatically the one where Israel is to prepare itself for its glorious mission of regenerating mankind." Leeser devoted his efforts to this vision until his death on February 1, 1868.

EQ

Bibliography: Moshe Davis, *The Emergence of Conservative Judaism: The Historical School in Nineteenth-Century America* (Westport, Conn.: Greenwood Press, 1977); Milton Feierstein, *Isaac Leeser: Founder of Jewish Education in the United States* (Buffalo: State University of New York at Buffalo Press, 1971); Henry S. Morais, *Eminent Israelites of the Nineteenth Century* (Philadelphia: E. Stern & Co., 1880); Lance Jonathan Sussman, *Isaac Leeser and the Making of American Judaism* (Detroit: Wayne State University Press, 1995).

Leland, John (1754–1841)

John Leland was a Baptist minister and opponent of the Anglican religious establishment in Virginia during the era of the American Revolution. Leland's writings and public speaking made him a key figure in securing the passage of Thomas JEFFERSON's Bill for Establishing Religious Freedom in the Virginia House of Burgesses in 1786. This bill was an important first step toward the eventual separation of church and state in the United States.

Leland, born in Grafton, Massachusetts, on May 14, 1754, was brought up as a member of the Congregational Church. After undergoing a conversion experience when he was 18 years old, he was rebaptized by immersion and later licensed as a Baptist preacher. He moved southward in 1776 and began service as an itinerant evangelist in Orange County, Virginia. In traveling throughout Virginia, Leland founded many new churches and immeasurably aided the development of the Baptist denomination. After his ministerial credentials were challenged by some of his fellow BAPTISTS, he was ordained again in 1786. Leland eventually became one of the most effective leaders of the Separate, or revival-oriented, Baptists in Virginia.

Because of their refusal to comply with the church establishment in colonial Virginia, Baptist preachers were repeatedly imprisoned and their worship services disrupted. The Baptist General Committee, to which Leland belonged, repeatedly circulated petitions to the Virginia legislature in an attempt to have their grievances redressed. Joining with the Presbyterians, who similarly dissented from Anglicanism, Baptists sought freedom to worship without legal constraints.

Leland believed that the most effective thing a government could do for Christianity was leave it alone. To make his argument, he drew an analogy to the deaths of Christian martyrs in the early church. Leland observed that state establishments of religion had done more to harm the cause of Jesus Christ than all the persecutions of Christianity combined. He remarked that while the official support of religion warmly "hugs the saints," it also corrupts the faith. Persecution, on the other hand, "tears the saints to death, but leaves Christianity pure." In alliance with rationalist exponents of religious freedom such as Thomas Jefferson and James MADISON, Leland and the Baptists eventually saw their position vindicated. They witnessed, first, the disestablishment of

Anglicanism in Virginia in 1786 and, later, the passage of the FIRST AMENDMENT to the United States Constitution in 1791.

Leland proved to be outspoken on behalf of freedom in another sphere as well. African Americans in the South had been turning to the Baptists in great numbers. Baptist polity gave black Christians leeway in creating their own fellowships, improvising their own forms of worship, and ordaining their own clergy. Leland welcomed the conversion of slaves to Christianity, but he worried about the physical conditions of their bondage. In 1790 he presented to Virginia Baptists an antislavery resolution condemning the institution not only as a violent deprivation of God-given rights, but also as inconsistent with the republican political ideals for which all Americans had struggled in the Revolution.

Leland returned to Massachusetts in 1792 and devoted himself for nearly 50 more years to Christian evangelistic activity. He never settled into a single home but crisscrossed New England during that period. He became renowned as a preacher who promoted both spiritual piety and religious liberty. Having championed the separation of church and state in debates over the continuing religious establishments in the New England states, Leland lived to see Congregationalism disestablished in Connecticut in 1818 and in Massachusetts in 1833. He died at Cheshire, Massachusetts, on January 14, 1841.

GHS, Jr.

Bibliography: Lyman H. Butterfield, "Elder John Leland, Jeffersonian Itinerant," *Proceedings of the American Antiquarian Society* 62 (1952), 155–242.

liberal Protestantism   See MAINLINE PROTESTANTISM.

liberalism, theological   The term theological liberalism when applied to Christianity covers a wide area of Protestant theology, and what many might consider "liberal" others would consider normative. As it developed in its classical form in the United States during the late 19th and early 20th century, liberal theology began with the premise that theology must integrate the findings of science and history into its work. As a result, liberal theologians attempted to reconstruct theology in light of biblical criticism (see BIBLICAL INTERPRETATION), evolutionary theory (see EVOLUTION; SCIENCE AND RELIGION), archaeology, and geology.

Related to this premise was liberalism's view that theology had to speak to the conditions and realities of its particular historical period, that is, that theology is historically conditioned. For this reason it should not be surprising if religious language reflected the level of scientific knowledge available at the time it emerged. In the Bible creation was condensed into days. Miracles were readily accepted, and social views matched those of the surrounding culture. Theology's goal was to get behind these relative truths and discover what was pure, true, and eternal.

For liberal theologians the primary elements in the Christian message centered on the following: that God is love, that in the person of Jesus Christ God had affirmed the importance of humanity and had shown what humanity should and could become, and that as Lord of time God was in control of the world. As a result of these claims liberal theology dispensed with many traditional understandings of Christianity.

The first of these was the belief in eternal damnation. Such a concept was inconsistent with the liberals' understanding of God's love. Following a theological development that had a long history in Christian thought and in the United States since the late 17th century, liberal theologians were often universalists, believing that all eventually would be redeemed or saved (see UNIVERSALISM).

In making Jesus the model of what humanity could and should become, liberal theology minimized, but did not reject, his divinity. Jesus' significance lay less in his redemptive sacrifice for human beings as an atonement for their sins than in his life. Jesus remained the son of God, but liberal theology emphasized his moral teachings and his life as a moral exemplar. For liberal theology the true message of Christianity was its morality.

Given their understanding of divine providence—God's control over history—the liberal theologians were strong believers in progress. Progress was the norm as human beings used the divine gift of reason to uncover error and to discover natural laws that enabled them to create a better world. Human beings had a role in creating the kingdom of God; they had both the ability and the obligation to build a good society on this earth (see SOCIAL GOSPEL). Given this belief in progress and in human ability, liberal theology had a relatively weak doctrine of sin. Sin was to them error or ignorance, not an inherent element of fallen existence that perverted everything. Sin could be overcome by removing the things that led to it—ignorance, drunkenness, poverty, and so forth.

Liberal theology prompted several reactions that soon displaced its dominance in American Protestant theology. Fundamentalists (see FUNDAMENTALISM) reacted to liberal theology's blunting of traditional Christian doctrines and its accommodation to modern science, especially evolution. MODERNISM took liberal theology to the extreme, removing all supernaturalism from theological reflection. NEO-ORTHODOXY, while accepting liberal theology's accommodation to science and the modern world, rejected its views on progress and sin.

Despite the fact that it was superseded in the second half of the 20th century, theological liberalism had a major impact on American religion. Nearly all theology done in the 20th century either built upon the groundwork set by liberal theology or was articulated in opposition to it. For this reason, despite its seeming naiveté, it remains a serious theological force.

(See also AMES, EDWARD SCRIBNER; FOSDICK, HARRY EMERSON; MATHEWS, SHAILER)

EQ

Bibliography: Sydney Ahlstrom, *Theology in America: The Major Protestant Voices from Puritanism to Neoorthodoxy* (Indianapolis, Ind.: Bobbs-Merrill, 1967); William R. Hutchison, ed., *American Protestant Thought in the Liberal Era* (Lanham, Md.: University Press of America, 1981).

liberation theology *Liberation theology* is a term used to describe a group of theologies that perceive the centrality of the Christian message as the actualizing of social justice. Liberation theology developed in Latin America during the 1960s as the "Third World Priests Movement." This movement, initially restricted to ROMAN CATHOLICISM, emerged among priests who were concerned with the political and economic oppression of their parishioners and convinced that the Gospel commanded feeding the hungry, freeing the captives, and healing the sick. This view was affirmed by the Roman Catholic bishops of Latin America at their 1968 meeting in Medellín, Colombia. There the bishops proclaimed that the existing situation in their countries was oppressive and that Christians needed to work to radically transform society in the spirit of the Gospel. They encouraged the formation of "base Christian communities," where groups of Christians would meet for Bible study and prayer and to formulate a Christian response to their lives. The base communities spread quickly. By 1980 there were more than 100,000 such groups, despite the hostility of political and social elites as well as many bishops.

The significance of the movement was undeniable, and it soon entered into Latin American Protestantism, primarily through the work of José Miguez Bonino, an Argentinean Methodist theologian. The movement met with even greater hostility in Protestant circles, since many Protestant leaders felt that it undermined the spiritual message of the Gospel and deflected attention from evangelism and individual conversion.

In its Latin American form, liberation theology entered into American consciousness in

1973 with the translation of Gustavo Gutiér-rez's *A Theology of Liberation*. At this time it merged with a more indigenous form of liberation theology developing in the United States, primarily among African Americans (see AFRICAN-AMERICAN RELIGION).

The significance of liberation theology grew steadily throughout the 1970s and the 1980s. There were, however, countervailing forces. Pope John Paul II and Cardinal Josef Ratzinger, head of the *Congregation fide*, the papal office responsible for ensuring religious orthodoxy, led the counteroffensive. The pope, having lived under Communist domination for much of his life, was disturbed by the key role that marxism played in liberation theology, particularly in its sanctioning of class conflict.

In the United States liberation theology also met with much hostility and resistance, especially during the presidency of Ronald Reagan, when conflicts over U.S. foreign policy in Central and South America were hotly debated. Critics complained that, like Protestant liberalism, it aligned itself too closely with secular ideologies and political platforms.

Liberation theology has two major methodological assumptions: the preferential option for the poor and contextualization. The preferential option for the poor means that those who are weak, despised, sick, and imprisoned are those to whom the Gospel is first given and those whose cries Christians have a primary obligation to hear. This involves attending to their material as well as their spiritual needs. In the Gospels the first manifestations of Jesus' messiahship were acts responding to people's physical needs. He healed the sick, fed the hungry, and raised the dead. Liberation theologians argue that Christians must act in a similar fashion, but through political means to make their work most effective.

The second point, contextualization, speaks to the fact that liberation theology is a theology done in response to the needs of a particular sociopolitical location and is done from the bottom up. The base communities played a fundamental role in enabling this theology. They were places where people read Scripture and interpreted it in light of their own experiences. In the process, they learned that social and economic deprivation was not what God had intended for anyone.

In the United States liberation theology took on numerous forms dictated by a radically different context. African Americans and Hispanics have developed the most traditional liberation theologies by responding to their own forms of political and social oppression. Other socially marginal groups also applied liberation theology to their situations. This trend has been most fully developed by feminist theologians (see FEMINIST THEOLOGY) who have argued that social conditions have blinded people to the liberating religious message proclaimed to women by Jesus.

The power and influence of liberation theology on U.S. theology and religious practice have been quite significant. As a result theology in the late 20th century was much more open and responsive to concerns beyond those of white males, who had previously dominated the field. Equally important, liberation theology altered the basic perceptions of the role of theology, and even those who were not supportive of the movement were forced to articulate their understanding of theology in response to the questions asked by liberation theologians.

Nonetheless, the long-term impact of liberation theology was uncertain at the beginning of the 21st century. With the collapse of Communism in the 1980s, liberation theology lost a great deal of its rhetorical force. While few liberation theologians viewed the Communist model as a viable alternative, the existence of a countervailing form of social organization that appeared to be relatively functional and able to meet the minimum economic needs of its people gave liberation theology's economic and social claims some power. The absolute and utter discrediting of Communism and the growing openness of most European social democratic parties toward market economics also signified the increasing intellectual isolation of liberation theology. Finally, the slow collapse of authoritarian governments in South and Central America in the face of growing democratization also undercut a great deal of the impetus behind the movement.

EQ

Bibliography: David B. Batstone, *Liberation Theologies, Postmodernity, and the Americas* (New York: Routledge, 1997); James Cone, *A Black Theology of Liberation: 20th Anniversary Edition with Critical Responses* (Maryknoll, N.Y.: Orbis, 1990); Gustavo Gutiérrez, *A Theology of Liberation: History, Politics, and Salvation* (Maryknoll, N.Y.: Orbis, 1973); George C. L. Cummings, *A Common Journey: Black Theology (USA) and Latin American Liberation Theology* (Maryknoll, N.Y.: Orbis Books, 1993); José Miguez-Bonino, *Doing Theology in a Revolutionary Situation* (Philadelphia: Fortress Press, 1974); Rosemary Radford Ruether, *Liberation Theology: Human Hope Confronts Christian History and American Power* (New York: Paulist Press, 1972).

Lincoln, Abraham (1809–1865)   More than any other public figure in American history, Abraham Lincoln, the 16th president of the United States, profoundly shaped the expression of American CIVIL RELIGION. During the CIVIL WAR, Lincoln delineated the moral dilemmas his nation faced in the struggle with slavery and transformed the idea of the Union into a mystical, religious cause.

Lincoln was born near Hodgenville, Kentucky, on February 12, 1809. He spent his youth on the edges of poverty as his family moved from Kentucky to Indiana and then to Illinois. He was postmaster of New Salem, Illinois, from 1833 to 1836 and studied law during that period. After moving to Springfield, Illinois, in 1837 and opening a law office, his reputation grew rapidly. Lincoln represented the Whig party in the Illinois legislature from 1835 to 1843 and in the United States House of Representatives from 1847 to 1849. He joined the newly formed Republican Party in

1856. Despite losing to Democrat Stephen Douglas in the race for the United States Senate in 1858, Lincoln received the Republican nomination for president two years later and was elected after a bitter four-sided campaign. Following his election, seven southern states seceded from the Union, prelude to the beginning of the Civil War in 1861.

There has always been considerable controversy about Lincoln's religious beliefs. As a young man, he turned against the Baptist faith of his parents and demonstrated little use for Christian creeds and formal theology. Still, he never explicitly rejected the teachings of the Bible, and biblical references appeared frequently in his speeches and political writings. After the death of his four-year-old son in 1850, Lincoln regularly attended Presbyterian churches in Springfield and Washington, but never officially became a member of any denomination. As he stated in 1846, when challenged about his religious beliefs, "That I am not a member of any Christian Church, is true; but I have never denied the truth of the Scriptures; and I have never spoken with intentional disrespect of religion in general, or of any denomination of Christians in particular."

Lincoln's piety remained genuine but unconventional throughout his lifetime. While he was certainly casual about external religious observances, the vicissitudes of his public career and the unhappiness he experienced in his family life continually drove him into contemplation of the divine will. His mother died when he was a boy, and two of his sons died as children. Above all, the tragedy of the Civil War forced him to ponder how the providence of God related not only to him as an individual, but also to the nation as a whole. In the Gettysburg Address of 1863, he expounded a public religious faith, explaining the meaning of American nationalism in theological terms. Lincoln thought that the United States was called by God to be a proving ground for democracy. He believed that only the victory of the Union in the Civil War could preserve the United States's God-given mission of championing human freedom, a cause he once called "the last best hope of earth."

Lincoln's second inaugural address of March 1865 contains the most enduring ethical statement ever articulated by an American political leader. Lincoln noted the irony that northerners and southerners read the same Bible and trusted the same God for aid in their fratricidal war. Yet Lincoln also saw a religious meaning that could transcend the narrow interpretations the Union and the Confederacy assigned to the conflict. He envisioned the Civil War as the punishment of a righteous God against *both* sections, and he called upon *all* Americans to repent of their public sins. Slavery had placed the nation under God's judgment, he said, and every ounce of blood drawn by a slaveholder's lash promised to be requited by the blood shed by soldiers in the war.

Lincoln's assassination in Washington, D.C., on Good Friday (April 15) in 1865 made him a martyr and symbolic figure of forgiveness in the public eye. Having suffered immense psychological agony during a struggle in which he sent thousands of young men off to die, he demonstrated his faith in the national cause by laying down his own life at its end. Lincoln had destroyed slavery, preserved the Union, and embodied the nation's wartime sacrifice

GHS, Jr.

Bibliography: Allen C. Guelzo, *Abraham Lincoln: Redeemer President* (Grand Rapids, Mich.: Eerdmans, 1999); Glen E. Thurow, *Abraham Lincoln and American Political Religion* (Albany: State University of New York Press, 1976); William J. Wolf, *Lincoln's Religion* (1959; Philadelphia: Pilgrim Press, 1970).

Lipscomb, David (1831–1917)

David Lipscomb was the most influential leader of the CHURCHES OF CHRIST between the Civil War and World War I. Editor of the *Gospel Advocate*, the principal paper of the RESTORATION MOVEMENT in the United States, Lipscomb wished to see the primitive simplicity of apostolic times reestablished within American Christianity.

Lipscomb was born in Franklin County, Tennessee, on January 21, 1831. He graduated from Franklin College in Nashville in 1849. He made his living as a farmer for a while, but in the mid-1850s he began to serve as a lay preacher for the Disciples of Christ, the denomination Alexander Campbell and Barton STONE had organized in 1831. When the the Civil War ended and order was restored in his state, Lipscomb assumed control of the *Gospel Advocate* with the support of Tolbert Fanning, its former editor. In 1891 he founded the Nashville Bible Institute, which after his death was renamed David Lipscomb College in his honor.

Lipscomb believed that the Bible was the all-sufficient rule for Christian life, and he advocated absolute trust in its teachings. He thought loyalty to the plain teachings of Scripture required that believers take no active role in earthly affairs. During the Civil War, he was adamant that Christians should not participate in the fighting, and the last election in which he cast a vote was in 1860. In his book *Civil Government* (1889), Lipscomb argued that God had originally intended to be the world's sovereign. Although Satan gained dominion when humankind transferred allegiance from God to earthly rulers, Jesus would one day return from heaven, destroy all governments, and inaugurate the reign of God on earth.

Applying these arguments about the dangers of worldliness to the life of the church, Lipscomb attacked the use of instrumental music in worship and opposed missionary societies and other ecclesiastical agencies. None of these, he argued, had warrant either in the Bible or in primitive Christian history. Lipscomb's extreme positions revealed how severe the division in the ranks of the Disciples of Christ had become. In 1906, after prodding by Lipscomb, the United States Census Bureau first recognized the existence of two separate denominations: Lipscomb's militantly antimodern group, now called the Churches of Christ (Noninstrumental), and the more mainstream Christian Church (Disciples of Christ).

Lipscomb wrote constantly on religious topics in the *Gospel Advocate* from 1866 until 1913. In 1913 he retired from his work as a writer, preacher, and teacher at the Bible Institute. Lipscomb died at Nashville on November 11, 1917.

GHS, Jr.

Bibliography: Robert E. Hooper, *Crying in the Wilderness: A Biography of David Lipscomb* (Nashville: David Lipscomb College, 1979).

literalism, biblical   See INERRANCY.

literature and Christianity   The relationship between religion and American literature has been both fruitful and complex. Some of the most significant works of the American literary canon have dealt with religious themes or employed religious imagery. Indeed, American literature cannot be fully understood without an appreciation of how authors have made use of religious ideas. While organized institutional expressions of religion and formal theology have had little place in American writing, religious concepts have been consistently vital. Even in writing that implicitly rejects traditional beliefs, questions about life's ultimate meaning and the spiritual struggles in which individuals engage have often played critical roles.

The complicated relationship between religion and literature in America begins with the Puritans who settled New England in the 17th century. Unlike their more worldly fellow church members who remained in the Church of England, the Puritans were suspicious of the arts. The most important book for them was the Bible, and they rejected all that was not contained within its pages. Yet as human beings struggling to understand the workings of divine providence, Puritans were naturally forced to provide interpretations of the Bible understood in the light of their own personal and communal histories. Sermons were the key form of Puritan literature, but poetry and biographies, too, described the reflections of men and women on God's place in their lives.

The earliest example of American literature is Pilgrim governor William BRADFORD's *History of Plymouth Plantation,* a work begun in 1630 but not finished until 1650. His description of the arrival of the Pilgrims at Cape Cod in 1620 is matchless: "Being thus arrived in a good harbor and brought safe to land, they fell upon their knees and blessed the God of heaven." Bradford goes on at length to compare his people with the people of Israel at the time of the biblical exodus. In Bradford's mind, the Pilgrims were God's new chosen people. They, like the Israelites of old, had escaped from the bondage of the past and, in the wilderness, were seeking a promised land to which God had called them.

Puritan poet Anne Bradstreet arrived with the first group of Massachusetts Bay settlers in 1630. Mother of eight children, Bradstreet wrote in the midst of domestic duties about her religious experiences and the pleasures of family life. In 1647 her brother-in-law took a copy of her poetry to London, where it appeared in 1650 as *The Tenth Muse, Lately Sprung up in America*—the first published poetry written in the New World. Most of Bradstreet's work is based upon the interaction between the natural world and God who created it, between the realities of earthly life and the hope of heaven. This dichotomy is skillfully evoked in the poem she penned "Upon the Burning of Our House" in 1666: "Thou hast a house on high erect / Fram'd by that mighty Architect, / With glory richly furnished. . . . / A Prize so vast as is unknown, / Yet, by his Gift, is made thine own. / There's wealth enough, I need no more; / Farewell my Pelf [Riches], farewell my Store. / The world no longer let me Love,/ My hope and Treasure lies Above."

Congregational minister Jonathan EDWARDS, credited with initiating the New England phase of the GREAT AWAKENING, is generally recognized as the last great writer of the Puritan tradition. Edwards recorded an account of the revivals in his church in *A Faithful Narrative of the Surprising Work of God*. That work, published in London in 1737, had a tremendous influence on the later efforts of evangelists and revivalists. His 1740 sermon "Sinners in the Hands of an Angry God," moreover, is probably the most famous sermon in American history. It contains a memorable description of the sinner held by God like a spider over the pit of hell: "You hang by a slender thread, with the flames of divine wrath flashing about it, and ready every moment to singe it, and burn it asunder." As this graphic image suggests, Edwards sought to evoke emotions that would reinvigorate the spiritual fervor of those who heard or read him.

When the great age of American literature dawned in the early 19th century, PURITANISM as a religious phenomenon had disappeared from the churches of the United States. Its legacy remained, however, in many of the writings of the period, especially in the work of Nathaniel Hawthorne, who sensitively explored the Puritan heritage. His story "Young Goodman Brown" (1835) and the novel *The Scarlet Letter* (1850) describe characters who are wrestling with questions of sin and evil. Although he disdained Puritan theology, Hawthorne clearly believed Puritan notions about depravity and the deviousness of the human heart. He dissected personalities and the society in which his characters lived to bring to light the psychological darkness that lurks within even the most upright circumstances.

Herman Melville was another mid-19th-century writer who explored religious themes. His two greatest works, *Moby Dick* (1851) and *Billy Budd* (1891), ostensibly tales about life at sea, examine the nature of evil. Captain Ahab of *Moby Dick* feels wronged by nature and attempts to conquer it, but his quest proves demonic and destructive. The character Billy Budd, on the other hand, is all innocence, yet the reality of evil still dooms him. Before he

is hanged for a murder he had committed inadvertently, Budd forgives the man who condemned him and displays unmistakably Christ-like qualities. At the moment of Budd's death, Melville wrote, "it chanced that the vapory fleece hanging low in the East, was shot thro with a soft glory as of the fleece of the Lamb of God seen in mystical vision, and simultaneously . . . Billy ascended; and, ascending, took the full rose of dawn."

Although still heir of Puritanism's stress on the human experience of God, mid-19th-century TRANSCENDENTALISM diverged from past theological systems through its emphasis on the fundamental perfectibility of humankind. Ralph Waldo EMERSON, renegade Unitarian minister and leading figure of the transcendentalist movement, believed that truth was found within concrete experiences, not within the "corpse-cold" rationalism of theological systems. He also believed that God was discoverable in the natural world, as his meditations in the 1836 essay "Nature" reveal. This emphasis appears as well in the writings of Emerson's friend Henry David THOREAU. In his masterpiece, *Walden*, published in 1854, Thoreau described an extended stay in a rustic cabin where he went to escape the increasing materialism of American society. "I went to the woods because I wished to live deliberately," he wrote.

Another figure in the American Renaissance, Emily Dickinson, also understood the spiritual advantages of seclusion. One of the greatest American poets, Dickinson lived reclusively in Amherst, Massachusetts, where she composed more than 1,500 poems, all discovered after her death in 1886. While she spurned the institutional church, her poetry (as in "I Never Saw a Moor") described her search for God's presence: "I never spoke with God, / Nor visited in heaven; / Yet certain am I of the spot / As if the chart were given." Dickinson was also obsessed with death, which she often depicted in personal terms. The poignant "Because I Could Not Stop for Death" begins with the stanza: "Because I could not stop for Death, /

He kindly stopped for me; / The carriage held but just ourselves / And Immortality."

Some pieces of American literature, while not renowned for their artistic genius, have still expressed ideas that profoundly shaped religion and culture in the United States. No popular writer has been more influential in her lifetime than Harriet Beecher STOWE. Stowe's most famous and enduring work, *Uncle Tom's Cabin* (1852), was written to arouse northern opinion against the evils of slavery. Stowe portrayed her hero, the slave Uncle Tom, as a sacrificial figure who symbolically redeemed America from the sin of slavery. *Uncle Tom's Cabin* sold more than 300,000 copies in its first year of publication. Despite Stowe's prayer that the United States would repent, abolish slavery, and be spared God's wrath, she was (as Abraham LINCOLN quipped when he first met her) "the little woman who wrote the book that made" the Civil War.

The Civil War had a tremendous effect on all aspects of American life, including both Christianity and literature. Elizabeth Stuart PHELPS, for instance, was a best-selling novelist in the post–Civil War era who was obsessed with questions about the Christian afterlife. Her most famous work, *The Gates Ajar* (1868), challenged traditional, dour concepts about heaven and hell. The novel told the story of Mary Cabot, who learns that the soul of her brother Royal, who had been killed in battle, was safe in heaven. Americans whose loved ones had died in the Civil War found *The Gates Ajar* so comforting that the book was reprinted more than 50 times between 1869 and 1884. Phelps also composed a sequel, *Beyond the Gates*, that described how heaven resembled some of the most pleasant and important aspects of earthly life.

A perspective far different from Phelps's appears in the work of popular short-story writer Ambrose Bierce. Although Bierce's fiction, like Phelps's novels, exemplifies the disillusionment with traditional religious beliefs often expressed in post–Civil War America,

Bierce was a pessimist and an agnostic. Yet despite his rejection of the strict Protestant upbringing of his youth, his stories are still laced with religious terminology and themes. Bierce served in the army for three years and wrote prolifically about the experiences of men caught up in the madness of battle. He evokes the idea of divine purpose, but as a distant and malign, not gracious, force that thwarts the stories' protagonists. Men suffer and die, Bierce wrote, and fate inexorably crushes even the best and brightest among them.

As Bierce's religiously tinged fiction contains meditations upon the shortcomings of God, no modern American writer better captured the depravity of the human heart than Mississippi novelist William Faulkner. In the fictional Yoknapatawpha County, Faulkner created a gothic world in which flesh and spirit were constantly at war. Faulkner's vision was essentially a tragic one, reflecting his upbringing in a region still nursing sad memories from the war. Yet in the tragedy of Confederate defeat, which the LOST CAUSE MYTH embodied, religious hope had emerged. As Faulkner's character Brother Fortinbride declares in *The Unvanquished* (1938), the southern people had turned their attention to religion, where they found the spiritual strength they needed to survive.

Flannnery O'Connor was another 20th-century writer who explored religious themes within the lives of fictional southerners. "While the South is hardly Christ-centered," she stated in a 1960 lecture, "it is most certainly Christ-haunted." Although O'Connor was a Roman Catholic, her characters were usually fundamentalist Protestants, outlandish people who discover the Christian God whom sophisticated, rational men and women ignore. As an apologist for Christianity, she sought the traces of divine grace even in the most depressing situations. O'Connor's novels and short stories contain moments when the expectations of their characters are dramatically overturned. At those times they are enabled to confront the mysteries of God's universe and turn toward faith.

Modern African-American authors are exploring religion in the South from the perspective of those who have experienced degradation and oppression. Toni Morrison's novels *Tar Baby* (1981) and *Beloved* (1987) grapple with the problem of human sinfulness and the power of myth. Morrison envisions that one of the tasks of her fiction is to recover the deepest meanings in myths and use them to strengthen contemporary African-American culture. Black writers also recognize the central, though not always beneficial, role of the church in the lives of African Americans. Zora Neale Hurston's *Their Eyes Were Watching God* (1937) and Alice Walker's *The Color Purple* (1982), for instance, examine this important topic.

Although American society in the early 21st century might appear to be heading toward increasing secularity, serious fiction writers continue to wrestle with questions of faith. Although these authors do not write to affirm traditional religious tenets, they still take seriously questions of religious identity. The wry satire of Walker Percy's novels, for example, communicates a sense of human fallibility and of the precarious nature of existence. Despite the overt sexuality in many of his stories, the prolific John Updike writes with notable sensitivity toward theological matters. In *Roger's Version* (1986), a seminary professor, trained in the skepticism of neo-orthodox theology, matches wits with a young computer wizard intent on proving the existence of God, and the farcical novel *The Witches of Eastwick* (1984) contemplates the nature of evil. Finally, John Irving's best-seller *A Prayer for Owen Meany* (1989) is a lengthy meditation on divine predestination. Religious ideas appear consistently throughout the novel, beginning with its opening sentence, when the narrator says of his friend Owen Meany: "I am doomed to remember a boy with a wrecked voice . . . because he is the reason I believe in God."

Of course, not all of America's religiously inspired writers have grappled first and foremost with the Bible, or even with Christian themes. Jack Kerouac of the BEAT MOVEMENT integrated Buddhist ideas into novels such as *Dharma Bums* (1958), while Christopher Isherwood's work was influenced strongly by Hinduism. The contributions of Jewish writers, both secular and religious, to American letters is long, stretching from Saul Bellow and Allen Ginsberg to Norman Mailer and Philip Roth.

GHS, Jr.

Bibliography: Sacvan Bercovitch, *The Puritan Origins of the American Self* (New Haven: Yale University Press, 1975); David W. Noble, *The Eternal Adam and the New World Garden: The Central Myth in the American Novel Since 1830* (New York: Braziller, 1968); David S. Reynolds, *Faith in Fiction: The Emergence of Religious Literature in America* (Cambridge, Mass.: Harvard University Press, 1981).

Little, Malcolm   See MALCOLM X (MALCOLM LITTLE).

Log College   See GREAT AWAKENING.

Longinqua Oceani   A papal encyclical, or doctrinal letter, addressed to the Roman Catholic Church in the United States (see ROMAN CATHOLICISM) by Pope Leo XIII on January 6, 1895, *Longinqua Oceani* represented a turning point in papal involvement with the American Church. The encyclical signified greater papal attention to American culture and contained explicit warnings to Catholics against aggressive Americanization.

Most of the letter involves internal church matters. It lauds the American Church on the formation of Catholic University and defends the pope's recent appointment of an apostolic delegate as a sign of the high regard in which he holds the American Church. The pope also commends the American hierarchy on its work to regularize and stabilize Church life. The remainder of the letter, however, addresses tensions between the values of American culture and Catholic doctrine.

Although warmly praising the young nation and its "latent forces for the advancement alike of civilization and of Christianity," the pope warns against many of the ideals of the American republic. Recognizing that the Church "unopposed by the Constitution and government of [the] nation . . . is free to live and act without hindrance," the pope gave thanks for the well-ordered society created by that republic. He pointedly noted, however, that despite the successes and growth of the Roman Church under this system, "it would be erroneous to draw the conclusion that in America is to be sought the most desirable status of the Church. . . ." This implicit rejection of church and state separation would cause much suspicion of Catholicism and Catholics for decades (see ANTI-CATHOLICISM).

Several paragraphs caution against the dangers inherent in an unfettered press and direct Catholics to increase the number of journalists committed to improving virtue and strengthening religious observance. The pope also warns Catholics to be circumspect in their readings and to join only Catholic organizations "unless forced to do otherwise by necessity."

Longinqua Oceani signified a growing concern within the Roman Catholic Church that segments of the Church in the United States were becoming too enamored of American political and cultural values. It was a reminder that Rome remained committed to its traditional view of the relationship between church and state and to an authoritarian and hierarchical view of the world.

EQ

Bibliography: Jay P. Dolan, *The American Catholic Experience: A History from Colonial Times to the Present* (Notre Dame: University of Notre Dame Press, 1992); John Tracy Ellis, *Documents of American Catholic History* (Milwaukee, Wisc.: Bruce Publishing Co., 1956); James Hennesey, *American Catholics: A History of the Roman Catholic Community in the United States* (New York: Oxford University Press, 1981).

Lost Cause Myth The term *Lost Cause Myth* refers to political, social, and religious ideas advanced by southern whites in defense of the culture of the SOUTH in the period after the CIVIL WAR. Edward A. Pollard, editor of the *Daily Examiner* in Richmond, Virginia, coined the phrase through the publication of his book *The Lost Cause: A New Southern History of the War of the Confederates* (1866). Soldiers, politicians, novelists, poets, journalists, and clergymen rallied to a continuing ideological battle with the North and expressed their region's frustrations at the cultural upheavals of the Reconstruction and New South periods. The Lost Cause writers argued that the South, though defeated in battle, had emerged a moral victor after 1865.

Religious ideology proved to be one of the most crucial elements in the myth-making about the meaning of the Civil War. White clergy and others eager to vindicate their people saw in the Confederate defeat universal spiritual lessons about redemption in the midst of suffering. Worldly debasement, as the crucifixion of Jesus Christ demonstrated, could be transformed by faith into a symbol of God's enduring love. Roman Catholic priest and poet Abram Joseph Ryan of Mobile, Alabama, expressed this idea well. While "crowns of roses" worn by conquerors always fade, he said, "crowns of thorns" inflicted upon the conquered are enduring.

Northern Christians, of course, had their own interpretation of southern defeat, one first enunciated in antebellum ABOLITIONISM: God had punished the South for the sins of slavery and rebellion. Although few white southerners dared admit that slavery was the principal cause of divine displeasure or that the institution per se was sinful, some conceded that abuses and deficiencies in a generally beneficent system (coupled with other sins like Sabbath-breaking and intemperance) had caused God's wrath to be turned against them. By admitting that they had strayed from divine laws, pious southerners transformed their wartime suffering into a providential means of chastening and conversion. Even defeat became a testament of ultimate vindication by God.

Throughout the rest of the 19th century, white spokesmen in the South moralized against the evils of northern society and pointed with pride to their own provincial culture, untouched by the spirit of the modern age. Only in the churches of the defeated South, they said, did men and women still practice true piety. Central to the myth of the Lost Cause, moreover, was the belief that the Confederate army had been a special bearer of Christian spirituality and virtue. Many Confederate generals were extolled as paragons of heroism and religious faithfulness by clergy like Robert Lewis DABNEY and John William JONES, who had served in the army during the war. Jones, a former chaplain in the Army of Northern Virginia, also published a popular history of the revivals that had occurred among the Confederate troops. His *Christ in the Camp* (1887) extolled the soldiers' religious faith as the factor that enabled them to endure defeat, build up their churches and ruined homeland, and seek reconciliation with the North.

Many other former Confederate soldiers discussed REVIVALISM in the southern armies and the religious faith of the men with whom they served. D. H. Hill (Presbyterian lay theologian and general), Clement A. Evans (a general ordained to the Methodist ministry in 1866), John Brown Gordon (a general converted during the war and first commander of the United Confederate Veterans), Robert Stiles (son of a Presbyterian minister), and Carlton McCarthy (an officer in the Richmond Howitzers) all linked the supposed moral superiority of southern soldiers with their piety. Most outstanding of all, not as a writer but as an ethical exemplar, was Robert E. Lee, once commander of the Confederacy's chief army. The figure of Lee provided an answer to the most troubling theological question with which southern whites grappled: why did God allow the righteous South to be conquered by a godless enemy? Lee was portrayed in Christlike terms: morally spotless, betrayed by lesser men, yet forgiving of all. His Confederate career shone like a beacon of rectitude in the midst of degradation and ruin.

Religion stood at the heart of the southern mythology about the Civil War. Romantic images of gallant outnumbered soldiers praying with their generals around the campfire gave the Lost Cause a quality that inspired many white Americans in the late 19th century. Religious apologists for postbellum southern society imagined that spiritual, not temporal, goals were the only ones worth pursuing. Religious victory in the midst of worldly defeat furnished a seductively powerful image in an otherwise demoralized time. As a result, the Lost Cause and the memory of defeat, rather than forcing the collapse of the South's religious tradition, actually helped rejuvenate it.

GHS, Jr.

Bibliography: Charles Reagan Wilson, *Baptized in Blood: The Religion of the Lost Cause, 1865–1920* (Athens: University of Georgia Press, 1980).

Lutheran Church—Missouri Synod The Lutheran Church—Missouri Synod is the largest Lutheran denomination of German background and the second-largest denomination of Lutheranism in the United States today. The Missouri Synod was founded by emigrants from Germany in the 1830s who were critical of the cold rationalism, doctrinal laxity, and state-imposed worship of the established churches in their native land. The denomination has always remained loyal to this heritage. It has remained conservative in its theology, emphasizing strict adherence to 16th-century Reformation creeds and the infallibility of the Bible, as well as the autonomy of local congregations.

Hundreds of thousands of Germans arrived in the United States between 1830 and 1920. Approximately 2 million German Protestants had come to America by 1880, and the majority were Lutherans. The Midwest held a special appeal for these Germans, who tended to move into a triangular area outlined by the cities of St. Louis, Cincinnati, and Milwaukee. The Missouri Synod acquired its name because its headquarters were located in St. Louis, where the Lutheran immigrants most responsible for the denomination's formation had first settled.

About 700 Saxon Germans under the leadership of Martin Stephan came to Perry County, Missouri, in 1839 to establish a Lutheran "Zion on the Mississippi." Influenced by PIETISM with its stress on godly living, this group had left Saxony to escape the spiritual indifference that marked German Lutheranism at the time. Stephan himself, accused of sexual misconduct and mismanagement of funds, was deposed from his position. Leadership fell instead on Carl F. W. WALTHER, who served a congregation in St. Louis and edited a popular periodical, *Der Lutheraner*. Walther's Saxons allied themselves with other German immigrant groups, including missionaries sent to the American Midwest by Bavarian pastor Wilhelm Loehe, and organized the German Evangelical Lutheran Synod of Missouri, Ohio, and Other States in April 1847.

Walther served as the synod's first president (1847–1850), and the denomination soon took on his distinctive theological cast. Upholding an objective rule of faith, Walther believed that the Bible and the traditional Lutheran doctrinal system contained all the essentials of salvation. He looked, therefore, to the scriptures and to the confessional statements of Martin Luther both to foster personal piety and to combat heretical teachings. Distrustful, moreover, of a centralized bureaucracy and of clerical authority generally, Walther's Lutherans developed a democratic polity for their church and stressed the need for laity to have an equal voice with clergy in church affairs. They also rejected praying and worshiping with other Protestants, even other Lutherans, who were not in complete doctrinal accord with them.

Under the leadership of the first two presidents, Walther and F. C. D. Wyneken, who together served from 1847 to 1878, the church steadily expanded. Missouri Synod

Lutheranism became a distinctive subculture for German immigrants in the Midwest, meeting not only religious, but also social, educational, and even medical needs. The church's combination of doctrinal orthodoxy and pragmatic organization also was highly effective in swelling its membership. Acculturation to American society came slowly, and the Missouri Synod retained an ethnic identity longer than any other major Lutheran denomination. Only the persecution of German Americans during World War I eventually hastened the process of assimilation. The word "German" was finally dropped from the denomination's title in the wartime period, and in 1947 Lutheran Church—Missouri Synod was adopted as its official name.

In the first half of the 20th century, some leaders in the synod attempted to reach out into the American religious mainstream. Through publishing and radio ventures, and through auxiliary organizations such as the Lutheran Laymen's League and the Lutheran Woman's Missionary League the denomination began to emulate many features of American evangelical Protestantism. The Missouri Synod was also strengthened by mergers with two churches that had long been related to it: the Finnish-descended National Evangelical Lutheran Church and the Slovak Evangelical Lutheran Church. These churches were absorbed in 1964 and 1971, respectively.

The Missouri Synod, like a number of other denominations, enjoyed its greatest growth from the 1930s to the 1960s. However, the uneasy alliance that existed between theological moderates and conservatives in the denomination was severely tested at the end of that period. Tensions over the proper authority of the Bible and over the value of ecumenical relations with both Lutheran and non-Lutheran bodies split the church in the early 1970s. What occurred in the Missouri Synod in many ways paralleled the split between fundamentalists and modernists in mainline Protestantism early in the 20th century. Conservatives feared that modern biblical scholarship and openness to theologically liberal denominations would undermine the synod's historic traditionalism.

The schism took place during the militantly conservative presidency of J. A. O. Preus. In 1974 the majority of students and faculty at the synod's principal seminary, Concordia in St. Louis, withdrew and formed a new school, Christ Seminary-Seminex (Seminary in Exile). Liberal pastors and congregations left the denomination at the same time and created an independent Association of Evangelical Lutheran Churches in 1976. That schismatic body comprised roughly four percent of the denomination's membership, about 110,000 people in 272 churches. The association later merged with the mainline Evangelical Lutheran Church in America in 1988.

The Missouri Synod's doctrinal positions remain as rigid today as they did when the denomination was founded more than a century and a half ago. The church is committed to biblical literalism, opposed to the ordination of women to the ministry, and bound to a thoroughly conservative political and social worldview. Nevertheless, some Missouri Synod Lutherans believe their church ought to practice greater toleration of opposing theological opinions. They fear that members of the denomination fight far too much, focusing more on each other's faults than on their strengths.

In 2000, the Lutheran Church—Missouri Synod reported slightly more than 2.6 million members and nearly 5,300 congregations within the United States.

GHS, Jr.

Bibliography: Walter O. Forster, *Zion on the Mississippi: The Settlement of the Saxon Lutherans in Missouri, 1839–1841* (St. Louis, Mo.: Concordia Publishing House, 1953); Alan Graebner, *Uncertain Saints: The Laity in the Lutheran Church—Missouri Synod, 1900–1970* (Westport, Conn.: Greenwood Press, 1975); Milton L. Rudnick, *Fundamentalism and the Missouri Synod* (St. Louis, Mo.: Concordia Publishing House, 1966); http://www.lcms.org (Lutheran Church—Missouri Synod).

Lutheran Church in America   See EVANGELICAL LUTHERAN CHURCH IN AMERICA.

Lutheranism   Lutheranism is a Protestant church tradition derived from the teachings of the 16th-century German reformer Martin Luther (1483–1546). Although the history of American Lutheranism extends back to colonial times, the forebears of most 20th-century Lutherans arrived as immigrants to the United States from Germany and Scandinavia in the 19th century. Up until World War II, Lutherans generally held themselves separate from the dominant evangelical Protestant culture of the United States. Their continuing foreign-language use, structured liturgical worship, and commitment to traditional Lutheran creeds made American Lutherans distinctive. The majority of Lutherans today, however, especially those belonging to the large EVANGELICAL LUTHERAN CHURCH IN AMERICA (ELCA), are part of the theologically liberal Protestant mainstream.

Martin Luther's theology provides the intellectual basis for Lutheranism. Luther's principal contribution to Christian thought is contained in his teaching on JUSTIFICATION by grace through faith. Luther was deeply troubled by the medieval religious system in which he had been raised. He was obsessed with the question of how a person could ever earn God's love or find eternal salvation. After meditating on the New Testament Epistle to the Romans, Luther decided that human beings could do nothing to save their souls. He concluded that God alone "justifies," that is, redeems human beings from sin. Faith, he said, was the divine gift by which God reveals his gracious character and leads a person to depend upon him for salvation.

Luther, like all the original Protestant reformers, believed that the Bible contained all that Christians needed to know about their faith. He rejected many of the religious customs and traditions of medieval Roman Catholicism because he thought they obscured, rather than illuminated, the true nature of God. The creedal statements that Lutherans developed, especially the Augsburg Confession (1530), composed by Luther's disciple Philip Melanchthon, condensed biblical teachings and set forth the central themes of Christian belief.

Over the years, however, Lutherans have often disagreed about the interpretation of the Bible and their denominational creeds. Some Lutheran bodies, the LUTHERAN CHURCH—MISSOURI SYNOD and the Wisconsin Evangelical Lutheran Synod, for example, have insisted that the words of the Bible are literally correct in every detail. They teach that the Lutheran confessions must also be accepted literally, since they are in fundamental agreement with the biblical text. But the ELCA, now the largest American Lutheran denomination, takes a far broader approach to these documents. Most ELCA leaders, while by no means rejecting past statements about the faith, tend to emphasize God's continuing revelation to present-day Christians.

Luther and his contemporaries intended to maintain the traditional threefold Catholic order of ordained ministers—bishops, priests, and deacons. As time passed, however, many Lutherans abandoned that polity because they did not consider it of primary importance to the Christian faith. Lutheran experience in the New World, moreover, encouraged the growth of a different church order. It was especially cumbersome to have to rely on the centralized ministry of a bishop in the fluid society of the American frontier. As a result, most Lutheran churches in the United States adopted a polity in which clergy and laity shared leadership in local congregations. Synods, that is, federations of congregations with the power to ordain clergy, were administered by executive officers, not bishops.

The earliest Lutherans in America came from Sweden and the Netherlands to the New York area in the 1620s. Forced to worship at the established Dutch Reformed Church, Lutherans tended to accept many of the practices of that tradition. However, after the English took over the colony in 1664, Lutherans were free to organize on their own. By 1669 the two oldest Lutheran congregations in America, at Albany and at Manhattan, had been founded. When Finns and Swedes settled along the Delaware River in the 1630s, the colony's governor was required by the Swedish crown to provide for Lutheran worship. When the English assumed control over that area, they implemented the same policy of toleration as was present in New York.

With the opening of Pennsylvania in the 1680s, Lutheran emigrants from the German Rhineland began to arrive in large numbers in America. Since they shared the same language and German ethnic culture with fellow settlers of the German Reformed tradition, Lutherans and German Reformed generally organized joint churches and worshiped together. Further complicating Lutheran church life was the arrival in 1741 of Moravian leader Count Nicholas von Zinzendorf, who hoped to bring all Christian groups together in a single fellowship. Zinzendorf was particularly anxious to include Lutherans in his united Christian body, and while not formally ordained as a Lutheran minister, he posed as one in America.

Church authorities back in Germany determined to take action against these deviations from proper Lutheran church order in America. They dispatched Henry Melchior MUHLENBERG, now considered the patriarch of American Lutheranism, from Germany to America in 1742. Muhlenberg wished his church to remain loyal to Luther's teachings. The most effective step he took toward attaining that ideal was the formation of the Pennsylvania Ministerium in 1748, the denomination's first permanent governing body. Muhlenberg had always complained of a number of institutional deficiencies fostered by the American religious environment: adults woefully lacking in religious training; no established procedure for calling clergy when parishes were vacant; and laity possessing too much power in church life. With the formation of the Ministerium, Muhlenberg addressed all these concerns, thereby helping to regularize Lutheran church life.

In the late 18th century, German Lutherans in the mid-Atlantic states began to move southward along the Shenandoah Valley and westward across the Appalachians. Since the Pennsylvania Ministerium was incapable of providing for those distant settlements, new synods had to be formed. By the early 19th century, leaders in these synods sought a national body to unite them and make corporate decisions about worship and doctrine. Despite some resistance to the principle of a centralized hierarchy, the formation of the General Synod of the Evangelical Lutheran Church in 1820 gave a new common direction to Lutheranism in the eastern United States.

In the period that followed, Samuel Simon SCHMUCKER, president of the General Synod's new seminary at Gettysburg, Pennsylvania, helped integrate his denomination into the Protestant evangelical movement that dominated the religious landscape of the United States. Schmucker especially opposed the narrow doctrinal conservatism of the "Old," or "Historic," Lutherans, who insisted upon strict adherence to classic Lutheran confessions. He believed that Americans should not have to be bound to antiquated ecclesiastical documents and argued that the genius of the new "American Lutheranism" would lie in its ability to adapt to changing cultural and religious circumstances. Under Schmucker's direction the General Synod, which was centered in the East, eventually gathered together two-thirds of the Lutherans in the United States.

Meanwhile, thousands of other Lutherans from Scandinavia and Germany flooded into the Midwest each year between 1830 and World War I. Some 60 new Lutheran church bodies were started by Swedes, Norwegians, Danes, Finns, Germans, and others between 1840 and 1875. Among those new denominations were two highly conservative churches that remain independent today: the Lutheran Church—Missouri Synod, founded in 1847, and the Wisconsin Evangelical Lutheran Synod, founded in 1850.

The Missouri Synod is still the largest Lutheran organization in the Midwest. It was organized by German immigrants who settled in Perry County, Missouri, in 1839. Influenced by PIETISM, with its stress on godly living, this group had left Germany to escape the spiritual indifference that then marked Continental Lutheranism. Under the leadership of Carl F. W. WALTHER, Lutherans in Missouri allied themselves with other German immigrant groups and became a distinctive subculture that met many diverse needs. Acculturation to American society came slowly, and only the persecution of German Americans during World War I completed the process of assimilation.

World War I proved to be a critical point for all American Lutherans. The conflict not only suspended the flow of immigrants to the United States but also heightened a self-conscious "Americanism" among many recently arrived ethnic groups. Most Lutherans also recognized the value of an agency that would represent their common interests. As a result, the National Lutheran Council, which represented eight Lutheran church bodies, formed in 1918. Such semiformal cooperation eventually led to the amalgamation of a number of independent Lutheran synods into two large denominations by the 1960s: the eastern-oriented Lutheran Church in America and the midwestern, heavily Scandinavian American Lutheran Church. Concern about the authority of the Bible and allegiance to the historic Lutheran confessions, however, helped the Wisconsin Synod and the Missouri Synod resist the trend toward merger.

By the mid-1960s, many believed that the Lutheran divisions in the United States were about to end, as the Lutheran Church in America and the American Lutheran Church began to discuss the possibility of one final merger.

After a radically conservative theological movement took control of the Missouri Synod in 1969, about 110,000 moderates left the denomination and founded the Association of Evangelical Lutheran Churches. This group also joined the talks about unification. An accord was reached at a meeting in Columbus, Ohio, in 1987, and the next year the Lutheran Church in America, the American Lutheran Church, and the Association of Evangelical Lutheran Churches officially became the ELCA.

There are about 9 million Lutherans in the United States today. The ELCA is one of the largest American Protestant denominations with its more than 5.2 million members. The Lutheran Church—Missouri Synod, itself a major denomination, contains about 2.6 million members. Finally, the Wisconsin Synod, still an independent body, has a membership of about 420,000 people.

(See also KRAUTH, CHARLES PORTERFIELD.)

GHS, Jr.

Bibliography: E. Clifford Nelson, ed., *The Lutherans in North America* (Philadelphia: Fortress Press, 1975); Eric W. Gritsch, *Fortress Introduction to Lutheranism* (Minneapolis: Fortress Press, 1994); Theodore G. Tappert, ed., *Lutheran Confessional Theology in America, 1840–1880* (New York: Oxford University Press, 1972).